MIDDLE EAST CRUCIBLE

AAUG Monograph Series: No. 6

MIDDLE EAST CRUCIBLE

Studies on the Arab-Israeli War of October 1973

edited by
Naseer H. Aruri

THE MEDINA UNIVERSITY PRESS INTERNATIONAL
WILMETTE, ILLINOIS
1975

First published in the United States of America in 1975 by
The Medina University Press International
P.O. Box 125
Wilmette, Illinois 60091

A joint publication of the Association of Arab-American University Graduates,
Inc., and Kuwait University

Naseer Aruri is Professor and Chairman of the Department of Political Science,
Southeastern Massachusetts University. He is the author of *Jordan: A Study
in Political Development* (1972), editor of *The Palestine Resistance to Israeli
Occupation* (1970), and co-editor of *Enemy of The Sun: Poems of Palestinian
Resistance* (1970).

CONTENTS

PREFACE

As a result of the fourth Arab-Israeli war certain realities have been brought home, with the Arabs demonstrating a hitherto unknown capacity to fight in a tougher, more coordinated, and more effective way. Although the Israelis achieved successes that matched their gains in the 1967 war, the price in 1973 was much greater—not only in the proportion of soldiers lost to population, but in the reduction of Israeli diplomatic influence. Israel found herself with fewer international allies as the Arabs simultaneously imposed an oil embargo and revealed an ability to influence world opinion. As for the superpowers, the war imposed a new strain on relations between Washington and Moscow.

On the Arab side, the principals were Egypt and Syria with other Arab countries and Palestinian commandos supplying volunteers and war materiel. Israel received logistical support from the United States; and included in her army and air force were a significant number of Jewish volunteers from the Americas, Western Europe, and the Union of South Africa.

There was bitter fighting for over two and one-half weeks with tank battles on a formidable scale and heavy losses of material, aircraft, and men. The Arab forces endeavored to inflict maximum losses on their enemy and, despite serious reverses, achieved a partial stalemate in a struggle lasting three times longer than that of 1967. For the Israelis there was no repetition of the swift triple victory of 1967. On October 22 there was an initial cease-fire on the Egyptian front in response to a resolution of the United Nations Security Council. This broke down in less than twenty-four hours and fighting again resumed for two days. Then on October 24, in response to a second Security Council resolution, a more or less effective cease-fire came into operation on both the Syrian and Egyptian fronts. By the end of October the military results were in and appropriate conclusion could be drawn. The Egyptians had retained a long strip of territory east of the Canal, running southwards from Port Said to the area of Ismailia, and another strip from a point east of the Great Bitter Lake to the Gulf of Suez—in all, some 400–450 square miles of Sinai. Having eventually crossed the Canal in force against stubborn Egyptian resistance, the Israelis gradually expanded their bridgehead on the west bank around the city of Suez. But the October 24 Security Council resolution required Israel to withdraw back across the Canal to the line that her forces had reached by October 22.

The military situation remained ambiguous despite the Arab military improvement since the 1967 campaign. But the political repercussions had been somewhat more decisive in the Arab favor. Israel had made special efforts to gain friends in Africa by aid programmes, technical training, and political subversion in coordination with Caetano's Portugal, the Union of South Africa, and other NATO countries. One highly significant consequence of the October war, therefore, was the complete diplomatic abandonment of Israel by all the African countries with the exception of the Bantustan nations under the control of white-ruled South Africa. Added to this diplomatic pressure, the Organization of African Unity supported the Arab economic embargo of Israel and called on Israel to give up her conquests of 1967.

On the initiative of Egypt and Syria a summit meeting of Arab heads of state was held at Algiers, November 26–28. The summit conference issued declarations on a total economic embargo of South Africa, Portugal, and Rhodesia. In return for Africa's support, the Algiers conferees announced an ambitious program of Arab aid to Organization of African Unity countries. It was at Algiers, too, that oil was endorsed as a political weapon to neutralize Israel's allies (principally the United States and Holland) and to win international support for the Arab side. Finally, the summit meeting recognized the Palestine Liberation Organization as the sole legal representative of the Palestinian people.

Even before October, 1973, most developed nations faced the prospect of an overall oil shortage, particularly with worldwide inflation increasing and rising fuel consumption. The fuel crisis was only accelerated by the decision of the Arab leaders, formally announced at Algiers, to use oil as a political weapon. For years Western nations had assumed that the Middle Eastern oil-producing states had virtually no choice but to sell their oil at prices generally acceptable to their Western customers. And it was true that the Arab oil-producing states were dependent on their Western clients for aid and technology as well as for the manufactures and capital goods needed for development. The cutbacks in oil production, followed by steep price increases, had a profound political and economic impact on the industrially advanced nations of the West. The Oil Embargo, as the cutbacks in oil production came to be known, had the effect of making the October war more than just a local conflict. By coordinating their political and economic policies, the Arab members of the Organization of Petroleum Exporting Countries (OPEC) suggested the possibility of a future powerful and united Arab nation emerging from the October conflict—an Arab superpower.

And because of the 1973 October War the stature of the Palestinian people increased to the extent that the United Nations General Assembly gave formal international recognition of the legitimacy of their struggle for national self-determination as well as their right to sovereignty and national independence. Yasir Arafat (chairman of the PLO) was invited by the U.N. secretary general, Dr. Kurt Waldheim, on majority vote of the U.N. member states, to address the 1974 General Assembly.

But what seemed to be the yield of the war, whether in the area of closer Arab coordination, worldwide recognition of Palestinian rights, the use of oil as a political weapon, or the growing isolation of Israel, has in fact deteriorated into the cooperation of conservative Arab regimes with the objectives of American policy in the region. The ascendancy of American influence in the Middle East was highlighted by the frequent visits which Secretary of State Henry Kissinger made to the area, the cease-fire, and the disengagement agreements which he was instrumental in bringing about. Indeed Middle East diplomacy at this time became synonymous with the American Secretary.

He secured a disengagement agreement between Egypt and Israel and Syria and Israel, but the momentum of his mission came to a halt with the collapse of the step-by-step diplomacy in March of 1975. Israel refused to return the strategic Mitla and Giddi passes and the Abu Rhudeis oil fields in Sinai to Egyptian sovereignty without an Egyptian pledge of nonbelligerency. Apparently angered by Israeli inflexibility, the United States announced its intent to reassess its Middle Eastern policy, thus serving notice to Israel that a continuation of their special relationship is contingent on Israeli understanding of America's *own* interests in the Middle East. In the meantime, the chief protagonists moved on their own to insure the survival of the diplomatic momentum. The unilateral reopening of the Suez Canal by the Sadat government, the symbolic reduction by Israel of her forces near the Canal, and the mutual praise by Israeli and Egyptian leaders of each others "steps towards peace" are symptomatic of the cordial atmosphere which has been created on the Sinai front under American auspices. Egypt and the United States share at least two common interests in the Middle East: avoiding a breakout of hostilities for the time being; and preventing a reassertion of Soviet influence in the region.

These two points constituted the bases for the cordiality which prevailed at the Salzburg talks between Presidents Ford and Sadat on June 1 and 2, 1975. Sadat's desire to avoid war seems to reflect the conclusion reached by conservative Arab regimes that further gains are best achieved by diplomatic means, and that the key to a negotiated settlement lies in the hands of the United States. Similarly Sadat's anti-Soviet policy reflects the ascendancy of Arab conservatism and the erosion of radicalism, a trend which followed the massacres of September, 1970 in Jordan.

The Ford-Sadat consensus on the need to avoid war and to check Soviet influence in the region illustrates the extent of reorientation in Egyptian policy since Sadat's rise to power and particularly in the aftermath of the October war. For the United States, both points have been permanent features of its foreign policy since World War II; but for Egypt they are a recent phenomenon, and must necessarily belong in the category of concessions which Egypt had to make as a price for settlement. For the Sadat-Ford agreement in Salzburg did not include an American commitment to an Israeli-Syrian interim settlement or to the pre-June, 1967 boundaries or even to setting up a miniscule Palestinian State in the West Bank and Gaza.

The extent of Egyptian concessions was further revealed in the Egyptian-Israeli interim agreement which was negotiated by Kissinger in September, 1975. Not only did Egypt abandon her earlier insistence on regaining the Mitla and Giddi passes, but it also agreed that the interim settlement would stand by itself and not be tied to arrangements with Syria, Jordan, or the Palestinians; or to a timetable of Israeli withdrawal. In fact, Egypt has agreed to another three years of Israeli occupation of the bulk of Sinai. Its deployment along a narrow strip between the Gulf of Suez and the Israeli emplacements is a purely civilian deployment. And the Abu–Rhudeis oil fields will remain as hostages for Israel inasmuch as the road connecting these fields with the Gulf of Suez—which is the same road to Sharm Al-Shaykh—will only be open to Egyptian civilian traffic. Moreover Egypt has agreed to a deployment in Mitla and Giddi based on an American presence, independent of the United Nations. Egypt has in fact relinquished its right to determine the mandate of the United Nations Truce Supervisory Organization by pledging to renew such mandate annually and to "concert actively" with the United States to get the General Assembly to renew it in the event a "third force," i.e. the U.S.S.R. or China vetoed renewal in the Security Council. Additionally Egypt permitted the passage of all Israeli cargo through the Suez Canal and accepted the principle that free navigation includes the right of Israeli ships to use the Straits of Bab Al-Mandab. The United States has received from Egypt "an expression of its intention to reduce hostile propaganda" including the halt of diplomatic efforts to discourage Third World nations from resuming ties with Israel and to press for Israel's ouster from the United Nations.

As for Israel, it has agreed to return the Abu-Rhudeis oil fields in exchange for an American commitment to provide Israel with some $350 million annually for the cost of buying oil on the world market. It handed over the Mitla and Giddi passes to the United Nations and it settled for an Egyptian renunciation of the use of force. In return for these modest concessions Israel gained what amounted to an American security guarantee: The United States agreed to hold "consultations" with Israel in case a third party—meaning the Soviet Union—intervened militarily. Additionally, the United States agreed to be "fully responsive . . . on an ongoing and long-term basis" to Israel's military requirements. The first installment on this military aid pledge, which is expected to be in the range of $1.8–$2.5 billion in grant aid, will enable Israel to acquire the latest equipment in the American arsenal. This may include the Pershing missile, a ground-to-ground ballistic missile with a range of at least 450 miles. Other equipment include the F-15 and F-16A fighter planes, the sixty-mile range Lance missile, and the laser-guided "smart bombs."

Parenthetically, this massive introduction of American military might, which must be seen in the context of the Egyptian-Israeli interim settlement, represents a devastating escalation of U.S. strategy in the region. Just as the decision by the Lyndon Johnson Administration to supply Israel with the F-4 Phantom enabled Israel to strike deep inside Arab territory, the Ford-Kissinger strategy aims at putting every major Arab city in the Middle East at the mercy of its potent surrogate. The Ford-Kissinger strategy can be defined in terms of control of and access to the region's most strategic resource—Arab oil. But gone are the days when American forces had to intervene militarily on behalf of real or alleged American interests. Today, the United States restricts its role to supplying the military muscle which enables surrogates in key regions of the world to maintain the balance in her favor.

The interim settlement of September, 1975, in addition to making

Israel the supreme military power of the region, makes the United States the *only* superpower in the Middle East. The Soviet presence in Egypt of the past two decades is rapidly vanishing in favor of an American presence which is becoming manifest in economic, political, and military dimensions. The expulsion of the Soviet Union from Egypt, which is but a prelude for an overall Soviet eclipse in the entire region, has been a long-standing objective of U.S. foreign policy. It has been defined as the price for an American initiative to pressure Israel into making territorial concessions. By the same token, it has also been the price for investments of oil money in Egypt by conservative Arab regimes.

The Ford-Kissinger strategy seems to be aimed at creating a transformation in the very nature of the Arab-Israeli conflict. Conservative Arab regimes have been anxious to cooperate with American policy in the region but were frustrated by the ascendancy of radical Arab nationalism in the fifties and sixties. These regimes are now emerging as secondary surrogates who would eventually work within the framework of the American design unhindered by the confines of the Arab-Israeli conflict. Once this conflict is settled territorially, a viable constellation of American surrogates would embark on an attempt to pacify the region in order to mark it safe for the multi-national corporations and their local partners. Surely the inclusion of Sadat's Egypt in this constellation alongside Saudi Arabia, Iran, and Israel would represent a triumph of American foreign policy and a region-wide shift toward *pax Americana.*

It may be recalled that the October war was launched in order to move the superpowers toward a settlement on the basis of U.N. resolution 242. After two years of negotiations and "shuttle diplomacy" the Arab world is no more closer to resolution 242 than it had been in November, 1967. In fact if Kissinger's diplomacy succeeds in bringing about an Egyptian-Israeli settlement then Egypt would be effectively neutralized. Israel, equipped with American weapons and technology, could then have a free hand in dealing with Syria and the Palestinians. The Arab world would be dismembered and any resurgence of Arab radicalism would have been checked for some time to come. Such were the objectives of American policy in the Middle East on the eve of the 1967 June conflict. That they are about to be realized in the aftermath of the 1973 October War is a sad commentary on the political acumen of contemporary Arab leadership. It hardly dignifies the memory of Arab soldiers who fell in the line of duty and in what they have innocently considered a "War of Liberation."

The apparent success of American foreign policy in the Middle East in the aftermath of the October war is likely to be a short-term triumph. Recent years have witnessed the collapse of Kissinger's "framework of international order." The American vision of a "generation of peace" has been dealt a severe blow in Vietnam, Cambodia, Pakistan, Ethiopia, Greece, and Portugal. It would be surprising indeed if the Kissinger design endured in the Middle East.

The essays which follow are original contributions prepared specifically for this volume. The idea itself was conceived shortly after the October war while I was spending a sabbatical year at Kuwait University. Special thanks are due to Anwar al-Nouri, secretary-general of Kuwait University, who made available a generous grant which enabled the Association of Arab-American University Graduates to commission the essays in this volume in co-sponsorship with Kuwait University. Thanks are also due to Professor Ibrahim Abu-Lughod whose helpful comments on individual chapters as well as general assistance in identifying contributors were well beyond the call of duty. My colleagues at Kuwait University, Professors Aziz Shukri, Hani Faris, and Walid Khadduri gave freely of their time and energy at the initial phase of preparing this volume. I also acknowledge with thanks the support of Carl Senna who offered much editorial assistance. A debt of gratitude is also owed to my research assistant John Moran and to my secretary Mrs. Elizabeth Tucker as well as Ms. Ruth Szala. Their efficiency and loyalty expedited this entire task in many ways.

NASEER H. ARURI

Southeastern Massachusetts University
North Dartmouth, Massachusetts
September 1975

MIDDLE EAST CRUCIBLE

Ibrahim Abu-Lughod

THE OCTOBER WAR AND THE PROSPECTS FOR SETTLEMENT OF THE ARAB-ISRAELI CONFLICT

MUCH OF THE WRITINGS in the post-October, 1973, period have tended to emphasize that regional and international factors are converging to produce a negotiated settlement of a conflict that has bedeviled the world for over a generation. It has been argued somewhat persuasively that the direct protagonists in the Arab-Israeli conflict now view a military solution to their conflict as untenable; that prolongation of the conflict as a result of overconfidence, arrogance, or misapprehension on the part of one or more of the protagonists will lead to the direct involvement of the two superpowers with disastrous consequences; that prolongation of the conflict will in fact mean, on the basis of the October performance, that war in the Middle East will become *total* war for the protagonists, which would entail the destruction of civilian centers in the area and the use (and misuse from the United States standpoint) of the oil resource to bring about a cessation of Western, particularly American, support for Israel; and that the use of this economic power by the Arabs, which has already produced havoc in the industrial systems of the West, will be disastrous for the structure of world economy.

Additionally, Western observers of the Middle East scene have asserted that the Arab world has undergone important changes over the past few years, changes that have helped produce a climate more conducive to political settlement. These observers have argued that the Arab world, despite certain appearances to the contrary, has moderated its revolutionary thrust. They note that the assumption to power by President Sadat in Egypt in the wake of the more militant Nasser has already produced important changes in direction in Egypt's internal and external policies; and they point out that the new wealth in the Arab world in areas where there is a commitment to orderly change in conjunction with the West, and the increasing influence of regimes committed to such procedures of change, have contributed enormously to the earnest search for a settlement that would restore Arab honor, strengthen the regimes committed to a stable Arab order, and remove from the arena of internal political struggle one of the more disruptive issues of modern times—namely, the Arab-Israeli conflict. Equally significantly, observers are apt to note a fundamental shift in Arab attitudes toward Israel as an entity. Previously muted voices calling for some acceptance of an altered Israel—one surely more moderate in territorial aspirations, more regionally oriented in attitude and affiliations, and more content with equality with the adjacent powers—have found a more receptive audience in the altered world of the post-October period.

These important shifts in the realities of the Middle East or in the perceptions of the Middle East have the October war as a decisive backdrop. That war revealed conclusively that the Arab military performance is not to be treated with the disdain exhibited during the 1967 June War and after. It also made clear the capacity of the Arab states to use their oil resource, exaggerated though the claims of that use may have been, in the pursuit of military-political ends. And the fact of Arab political solidarity for limited ends gave credence to the Arab assertion of greater solidarity in the future for larger national goals, a circumstance that may place in serious jeopardy all existing or potential limitations on Arab sovereignty in all endeavors of national life.

For Israel, the October war was a telling event. It revealed not only that Israel cannot dominate all the Arab states all the time but that its dominance over a limited portion of the Arab world will be challenged successfully; the longer Israel maintains its position on the premise of absolute dominance, the more it assures the challenge to that dominance. While Israelis may debate the significance of the Arab military performance and its ultimate meaning for the viability of Israel, they have concluded that their interaction with the Arab states on the old premises has significant penalties for them. They cannot with impunity assert their stated dominance.

More important perhaps are two developments which became apparent shortly after the October war. First, the increasing political and diplomatic support which the Arabs obtained from the world community signaled to Israel its growing isolation in the world. The fundamentally altered structure of relations with the African states—which Israel had carefully built with American support over two decades— was one important casualty of the October war, although this was perhaps more symbolic than real. More significant in terms of Israel's orientation were the altered relations with the European world. Israelis could not escape the conclusion that to continue relations with the Palestinians and the Arabs on the basis of premises inherited from the period of absolute Euro-American dominance would increasingly alienate Israel from Europe. Second, the voices of dissent within Israel, voices insisting on some degree of accommodation with the Palestinians and the Arab states, became much more vociferous. Thus, pressures were exerted on the Israeli establishment to come to terms with the Arabs, not on the basis of the total denial of the Palestinian presence and the absolute military dominance of the Arab states, but on the basis of meeting some of the national aspirations of the Palestinians and restoring Arab sovereignty to some areas occupied in June, 1967. The question for the Israelis increasingly became one of insuring Israel's legitimacy and some degree of security and, at the same time, assuring the national survival of the Palestinians and the restoration of Arab sovereignty over Israel-occupied territories.

The regional transformations in power relations and in the attitudes of the adversaries seem to be convergent, then, and are thought to be moving inexorably toward producing an accommodation based on negotiation rather than conflict. It has become equally evident that the superpowers themselves, for different reasons, have developed a similar convergence of interests in the direction of promoting a settlement of the Arab-Israeli conflict. The Soviets have become more forthright in advocating a political solution to the conflict and in insisting that such a settlement include appropriate provisions for the national rights of the Palestinian people. The Americans, on the other hand, have been much more inflexible. Only with the release of the forces of the October war and its aftermath, did the United States seem to develop a more flexible approach to the conflict. It was this new flexibility that enabled the United States—despite its previous handicaps—to exert a greater initiative acceptable to most parties involved in the conflict, an initiative which resulted in the disengagement agreements between Israel and Egypt, and Israel and Syria. Its resumption of diplomatic relations with the Arab states excepting Iraq and Yemen and its promises to provide some degree of economic and technical assistance to Egypt and Syria epitomized the changing nature of relations between the United States and the Arab states. From chief adversary of Arab aspirations—in large measure owing to its total commitment to Israel—the United States was transformed into an active mediator between Arab and Israeli, in search of an equitable settlement that would meet at least the minimum aspirations of each protagonist.

There is no doubt that the Palestine and Arab-Israeli conflicts continue to be dominant in the thinking of Arabs and Israelis. Yet the realities of the situation in the post-October period have tended to reduce the regional conflicts to incidentals of a much larger problem. It increasingly became clear that the concern of American policymakers was more with the global importance of issues highlighted by the Arab-Israeli confrontation than with the conflicts themselves; and it was the imperatives of dealing with these larger issues, be they economic or political, that prompted the evidently serious American efforts toward an acceptable political settlement. Such a settlement is thought to be conducive to a possible growing collaboration between the Arab states and the United States which might assure the latter's global hegemony, a reasonable solution to the energy question, the smooth flow of Arab financial resources to the United States, and the increased flow of American manufactures to all Arab countries, while at the same time preserving the territorial integrity, honor, and internal development of the Arab states.

My intention in this essay is to identify the components of such a settlement that presumably would be acceptable to all the participants in the Arab-Israeli conflict. Arabs and their supporters in the world take for granted that the principal participants include not only the Arab states and Israel, but, equally importantly, the Palestinians. That this is denied by Israel and to a lesser extent by the United States is part of the historical record. Yet, since the termination of the October war, there has grown a recognition that any settlement that would endure in the Middle East must accommodate the Palestinians as a national community. The support which the Arab position has commanded in the world was demonstrated conclusively when, in October, 1974, the United Nations not only invited the Palestine Liberation Organization to present its view of the aspirations of the Palestinians but, additionally, conferred on the PLO the legitimacy which it had acquired regionally. The fact that in November, 1974, the United Nations reaffirmed the right of the Palestinians to determine their destiny and to national independence and sovereignty signaled to all concerned that accommodating the Palestinians is a necessary prerequisite to an enduring settlement of the Arab-Israeli conflict.

NEGOTIATING POSITIONS

The demands of the protagonists in the Arab-Israeli conflict are stated in absolute terms. The Arab states have insisted on total withdrawal of Israeli troops from all occupied areas as a necessary condition of an ultimate settlement. (From time to time some Arab states suggest additional conditions, but it is presumed that the more expansive of these demands are not taken too seriously by those who make them.) The Palestinians have insisted on a reconstitution of the entire state of Israel and have from the onset of their struggle against European Zionists conceived of Palestine as one state to be governed democratically. The radical alteration of Palestine in the meantime and the decisive alteration in the political, demographic, and economic nature of Palestinian society have not altered materially the basic vision of a Palestine that would comprehend Palestinian Arab and Israeli Jew. While the Palestinians continue to hold on to their vision of a transformed Israel, considerable pressures have been exerted on them by some Arab states, by the Soviet Union, and by a number of Afro-Asian and European supporters to modify their program. The assumption of these supporters and sympathizers is that what the Palestinians are really striving for is a national *patrie* and a national identity that would deal constructively with the reality of a dispersed people. Hence the generated pressures are intended to lead to the abandonment of the Palestinian vision of a democratic nonsectarian Palestine in favor of a Palestinian state in portions of Palestine yet to be evacuated by Israeli troops.

While Israel's map remains to be revealed, it is generally understood that some adjustments in the 1949 armistice lines to remedy Israel's perennial feelings of insecurity are necessary. Former Secretary of State Rogers in his two proposals of December, 1969, and August, 1970, gave an indication of the kind of adjustments that are thought to be necessary. Discussions of modalities of existence involving demilitarization of certain areas and conceding sovereignty abound. But whatever territorial adjustments are made will have to be undertaken with a view toward normalizing relations between the Arab states and Israel. In one form or another this would entail recognition and acceptance of Israel. The history of interaction among the protagonists suggests that this is a matter of contention. Certain Arab states have reiterated unambiguously that recognition of Israel is possible within the context of a total settlement. Israel has so far cast aspersions on the stated position of these states on the basis of their past behavior. The Israelis' absolute denial of the Palestinian presence and correspondingly the Palestinians' absolute demand for a total transformation of the Israeli presence makes it imperative for these two protagonists to resort to armed conflict. No dialogue is possible on the basis of such absolute assumptions. The long history of the Arab-Israeli conflict has generated the mutual distrust and misgiving normal among protagonists. Therefore Israeli protestations of peaceful intentions are treated with the same degree of suspicion and distrust that Israel reserves for Arab protestations of peace. The absence of meaningful dialogue in the past in part stems from this mutual reading of the intents of the protagonists.

Efforts at conciliation have not been lacking in the past. A United Nations Palestine Conciliation Commission was established in 1949. Individual initiatives by the United States and Britain were launched in the fifties. Following the 1967 June conflict other efforts were made by the United Nations mediator Gunnar Jarring, and, in 1972, by the Mission of Heads of African States. None of these efforts succeeded in producing the desired accommodation. The October war has brought about the most recent effort by the United States, acting through its secretary of state. Thus far this initiative has generated hopes that at long last the conflict might be more amenable to a solution. Whether this will be the case remains to be seen. For the moment it is critical to understand the assumptions and perhaps the intent of the mediator in order to comprehend the nature of the settlement that might be arrived at.

It should be emphasized at this point that the foreign policy of a superpower does not necessarily represent the reflections and efforts of one man. For the basic interests of a superpower within a changing world reality are much more compelling and enduring than the predilections of a secretary of state. Yet secretaries of state in the past have left an indelible mark on the process of policy formation and implementation and frequently have determined the type of policy pursued by the superpower. It is not necessary to point out that Secretary of State Dulles' vision of the world contributed to the rigid polarization of the world community, led the U.S. to look with disfavor upon the efforts of the nonaligned, and to adopt the policy of "pactomania" and the threat of "massive retaliation." While Secretary of State Kissinger is even more given to individualistic performances than Secretary of State Dulles was, it should not be assumed that his approach is totally unchallenged; nor should it be assumed that his premises are the determining ones. For it is quite clear that pressures for a negotiated settlement acceptable to the Arabs have come from different domestic groups and groups influential within American society. It is evident that the multinational corporations and the banking community have exerted enormous pressures in that direction. Yet Kissinger's position over the past few years and the singular role that he has played in dealing with the Middle East justify our concern with the type of settlement he is envisioning and the assumptions which guide him in carrying out his efforts toward that settlement.

RECENT U.S. POLICIES

The present efforts of Mr. Kissinger and the policy they exemplify should be viewed against the background of two related policies pursued with mixed results by the United States in the past. The first policy was essentially one of confrontation. Underlying it was the premise that Arab nationalism as it expressed itself in the activist policy of the late President Nasser—a policy that sought a modest transformation of the internal structure of the Arab world from one basically dependent, agriculture-based, feudalist-capitalist in mode of production, and politically fragmented to one independent, industrialized, socialist in structure, and with some degree of political cohesion—presented a serious threat to Western, and specifically American, economic and strategic interests in the Middle East. The continued importance of Nasser in the Arab world, his drive and the pursuit of his goals, entailed serious Egyptian and Arab commitment to the Palestinian struggle against Zionism and Israel. Furthermore, both the vision of Arab nationalists and internal commitments necessitated an activist international policy, one that sought collaboration with the socialist system of power and favored active support to liberation movements throughout the world. Such policies entailed opposition to the Western system of power.

Although American policy over the last two decades zigzagged, the confrontational nature of that policy remained constant. The active concern of American policymakers with the search for allies within the Arab world, which involved setting up an abortive alliance system, supporting and relying upon Israel as a possible bulwark against an active Arab nationalist thrust, and imposing penalties and difficulties on ideologically activist regimes, demonstrates this quite clearly. The confrontational approach made it necessary for the United States to support Israel in its attacks on the Arab states and to support regimes that were threatened by the Arab nationalists' regimes. The 1967 June War and the inflexibly hostile policy pursued by the United States after the war dramatized the policy of confrontation. Its overall purpose was to undermine and ultimately destroy all regimes in the Arab world that assumed a national-reformist character.

A second premise underlying the confrontational policy of the United States comprised two contradictory elements. On the one hand it was assumed that Arab commitments to the Palestinians or to the support of regimes in conflict with Israel were absolute. On the other hand it was assumed during and after the 1967 June War that such Arab commitments were in fact compromised by those regimes that felt threatened by the nationalists; and it was assumed that those regimes would acquiesce in a *fait accompli* that would diminish the strength and significance of the nationalists led by Nasser. The fact that those regimes failed to exercise any pressure on the United States in the few years after the 1967 June War was viewed as dramatic evidence that the Arab-Israeli conflict, while serious, paralleled an inter-Arab conflict of equal seriousness. Thus the United States was able to pursue a policy of direct confrontation with the nationalists and at the same time was able to extend military and economic assistance to Israel without having to risk penalties from those Arab states wherein American economic interests lay.

The second subsidiary policy which the United States pursued during the same years was one of selective alliances with regimes thought to be threatened by the Arab nationalists. The strengthening of Jordan against the rising threat of the Palestinian resistance, the careful cultivation of the Saudi state, the building up of Iran, and the support of Oman against the National Front for the Liberation of Oman reflect the U.S. assessment that the Arab world is in fact fragmented and each Arab state has its own interests, fears, and problems. In this view these regimes, although to some extent concerned with a resolution of the Arab-Israeli struggle on terms acceptable to the Arab adversaries of Israel, are nevertheless prepared to collaborate with the United States, despite its total support of Israel, in return for the assistance they stand to receive in their inter-Arab struggle.

Over the years these policies failed in their primary objective, namely, the crippling of Egypt's Nasser. They likewise failed in the secondary objective of obtaining a cessation of the Arab-Israeli conflict on terms favorable to Israel. Though Egyptian power and influence in the Arab world waned dramatically after the June war, Egypt was able to win support for the Palestinians and their struggle and for a policy of defense against the entrenchment of Israeli occupation of Arab lands. The increased participation of the Soviet Union in the defense system of Egypt enabled it to withstand the constant combined American-Israeli pressure.

These two policies failed to keep the Arab-Israeli conflict from erupting in 1973; and, what is worse, hostility to the United States increased in areas where it had been somewhat muted. The oil embargo imposed in October, 1973, augured ill for subsequent relations between all Arab states and the United States and confirmed quite clearly the centrality of the Arab-Israeli conflict to the total political ambience of the Arab world. Hence there was need for a new policy which would have a total settlement and a transformed relation with all Arab states as an immediate objective.

KISSINGER'S POLICY

The revised American policy aims at stabilizing the region by obtaining legitimacy for the entire system of states. That stability, if obtained, "makes it possible for all powers to adjust their differences within the framework of the system rather than its overthrow."[1] It seems that Mr. Kissinger's reading of the Arab-Israeli conflict as evidenced by the steps he has taken to bring about its resolution, attributes Israeli hostility and disruption in large measure to Israel's lack of legitimacy within the Arab world; hence the principal task of American policy is to obtain for Israel the legitimacy it has sought but failed to obtain. American policy since the October war has been premised on the assumption that legitimacy for Israel is essentially attainable. If it is attained, then it will be possible for Israel to negotiate its territorial disputes with the Arab states.

Thus far, however, Israel has followed a disruptive foreign policy in the region because it has felt threatened. To use the terminology Mr. Kissinger applied to Napoleonic France, Israel has followed a "revolutionary foreign policy; its motivation. . . . may well be defensive; it may well be sincere in its protestations of feeling threatened. But the distinguishing feature of a revolutionary power is not that it feels threatened . . . but that nothing can reassure it. Only absolute security—the neutralization of the opponent—is considered a sufficient guarantee, and thus the desire of one power for absolute security means absolute insecurity for all the others."[2] The history of relations between the Arab states and Israel is essentially the history of interaction between powers obsessed with feelings of insecurity. Israel's policy of absolute dominance based on its security considerations has prevented the protagonists from reaching any kind of settlement. The task therefore at present is to negotiate a settlement

1. Henry Kissinger, *A World Restored* (Houghton Mifflin: Boston), 1957, p. 5.
2. *Ibid.*, p. 2.

which would produce the needed feeling of security for Israel but would not be based on dominance. The fact that Mr. Kissinger has sought to obtain a settlement between the protagonists for whom the conflict is relative suggests quite clearly that his interpretation of Egyptian, and to some extent Syrian, needs and requirements is similarly based.

For a number of years now, observers have noted that Egypt's primary interests have shifted considerably; it has been suggested that after the 1967 June War Egypt's technocratic class and policymaking elite began to press for a policy of internal development hindered in the past by Egypt's direct entanglement with the Arab world and its hostile relations with the West. The gradual relaxation of the activist policy of Nasser in the Arab world, and his coming to terms with previous rivals and opponents—although in part dictated by his desire to obtain their political and financial support for Egypt's defense against Israel—and the intensification of that policy under President Sadat, suggested that Egypt is prepared, under certain conditions, to disengage itself from the Arab-Israeli conflict. The problem for the mediator therefore is to produce a settlement that would aim at restoring the honor as well as assuring the security of Egypt.

While Syria's evolution and commitments differ from those of Egypt, nevertheless a similar diagnosis has been arrived at. It has been contended that Syria's absolute commitment to the Palestinian struggle was a function of its rejection of the political fragmentation of the Arab world, a fragmentation effected by European colonialism. In part therefore Syria's opposition to Israel represented its defense of the Arab national *patrie.* Yet the evolution of Syria's politics over the past decade suggests strongly that Syria has come to terms with the new realities of the Arab world, realities that legitimate the existing states.[3] In that sense therefore Syria's conflict with Israel is relative, territorial, and a matter of security, rather than a conflict over the Arab national homeland.

It is now quite clear that Kissinger's approach to the conflict is premised on the serious possibility that Egypt's and Syria's national— as differentiated from their Arab—aspirations can be reasonably met by a twofold approach: on the one hand by restoring their honor with the retrieval of their occupied territory from Israel, and on the other hand by responding favorably to their needs for economic development through direct American and American-Arab economic

3. This assessment of Syria's politics was advanced by Itamar Rabinovich in *Syria under the Ba'th, 1963-1966, The Army-Party Symbiosis* (Jerusalem, 1972).

assistance. The disengagement agreements and the pursuit of other interim agreements which are intended to produce further Israeli withdrawals represent efforts to separate the protagonists and place them sufficiently distant to remove the fear of military attack. Whatever final shape the agreements might assume, it is reasonably clear that some form of demilitarization and neutral supervision of the Sinai and the Golan Heights will be effected. In this way several objectives will be accomplished: first, security for Israel and Egypt and Syria; second, retrieval of Egypt's and Syria's national honor by the evacuation of the occupation forces; and, third, some form of political legitimation for Israel. Egypt and to some extent Syria will be further rewarded with the economic assistance and combined foreign capital desperately needed for internal economic and social development. The fact that Egypt has moderated its activist policy toward the Arab states of the peninsula and toward the United States makes it much easier for it to obtain that economic assistance which Nasser was able to obtain from the Soviet Union. A fundamental reorientation of Egypt's national direction and perhaps Syria's is thus one of the chief benefits to be obtained by an American policy which might succeed in inducing Israel to modify its previous Arab policy based on dominance.

PALESTINIAN GOALS

While an agreement that might produce the legitimation that Israel seeks is not difficult to attain in the abstract, Egypt's Arab orientation places serious obstacles before any such settlement. Egypt's commitment to the Palestinians is historic, and it was clearly understood that that commitment entailed the acceptance of what national goals the Palestinians had formulated for themselves. Over the past few years, however, certain shifts in Egypt's policy have been noted. For one thing, the Egyptian media began to raise doubts about the feasibility of realizing the Palestinian national goals as stated by the Palestine National Council; for another, it was thought that the international environment is not tolerant of the attainment of these national goals and thus places important constraints on the ability of the Arabs to help attain them. When Egypt declared its readiness to accept the state of Israel as an entity, it became impossible for it to uphold mutually contradictory stands: one that would accept the state of Israel and the other that would adhere to the support of the Palestinian national goal of the liberation of Palestine. Hence,

Egypt advanced the thesis of legitimacy of two states in the former mandated Palestine. Increasingly it has become clear that Egypt's readiness to come to terms with Israel—whatever the shape of an Israeli-Egyptian accommodation might be—is premised on the realization of the Palestinian aspiration for statehood in portions of Palestine. The pressure that has been exerted since June, 1973, for an independent Palestinian state in portions of Palestine thus is linked directly to the efforts to promote an Egyptian-Israeli accommodation. Viewed in this way, then, Egypt is the key to settlement. Whatever Syria's doubts may be, it is assumed that it would not risk being isolated in the struggle against Israel. Thus some accommodation between Israel and Syria is dependent on the new arrangements of power relations that will emerge as a consequence of an Egypt-Israeli accord.

The legitimation of the Palestinian aspiration has thus become an important question for American policy; for while some have argued that is is possible for Egypt to reach a separate accord with Israel, the obvious fact is that any accord failing to meet some Palestinian aspiration will not be honored. The combined public Arab pressure will not allow such an agreement to be carried out. Further, the strong commitment of some Arab states to Palestinian aspirations and the commitment of others to a reasonable settlement of the Jerusalem question prevent a bilateral settlement between Egypt and Israel from reaching the final stage. While some have insisted that accommodation between Israel and Jordan might solve a particular difficulty, such an accord would prolong the Palestinian struggle and would have unpredictable consequences for the stability of the region. It is therefore thought that the legitimation of the Palestinian aspiration which could be effected through some kind of territorial statehood in portions of Palestine would produce a committed Palestinian entity, one that would develop the necessary norms appropriate for a stable political system. The transformation of the Palestinian resistance movement into a Palestinian state thus becomes an important objective of a final settlement that would legitimate the entire political order.

Just as legitimation of Israel within the Arab world would have an important effect on Israel's previously disruptive policy, the legitimation of the Palestinians would produce a more accommodating Palestinian community. It is thought that the Palestinian state would not follow the revolutionary path which the Palestinian resistance has pursued, thus assuring Israel's security on the one hand and contributing to the demise of revolutionary movements in the Arab world on the other. It will be recalled that the containment of the revolutionary thrust of the Arab world was a significant objective of American foreign policy. Accordingly, that policy over the past few years has aimed at either the defeat or the transformation of the Palestinian revolution. The military support to Israel in its effort to destroy the Palestinian resistance, the support to Jordan, and the subtle efforts exerted in Lebanon were intended to bring the Palestinian revolution to an end. Yet the gradual change in American attitude evident in the past two years, to one of meeting some of the Palestinian aspirations, suggests strongly that a different approach to the Palestinian question has in fact emerged and will be pressed upon Israel and Jordan simultaneously. While the change in the U.S. attitude is not publicly acknowledged, it is quite clear from official statements supporting "the interests" of the Palestinians, interests that should be "woven into the fabric of settlement," that the American promoters of the idea of a Palestinian state in portions of the West Bank and the Gaza Strip have succeeded in persuading policymakers that it is necessary to obtain legitimacy for some Palestinian aspirations in order to bring stability to the region. Hence the considerable pressures on Israel to "deal" with the Palestinians.

It was suggested earlier that certain rewards await each of the protagonists so that each has developed an interest in a negotiated settlement. What would the Palestinians gain from a policy that would legitimate some but not all of their aspirations? Pragmatists have argued the advantages of a state as a solution to the national identity question and to the human problems of dispersion. Equally important is what might await the Palestinians if no Palestinian state emerges; for it is quite clear that at best they can expect a policy of "benign neglect" that would leave them in a position not very different from the one that prevailed in 1948-67. Perhaps the Palestinians may come to the realization that a state in portions of Palestine represents the only hope of salvaging their national identity. And here Mr. Kissinger's diagnosis of a similar dilemma faced by a defeated state is perhaps applicable to the dilemma facing the Palestinians. Speaking of an option which a defeated state may exercise, Mr. Kissinger observes, "it may become convinced of its physical impotence and strive to save its national substance by adaptation to the victor. This is not necessarily a heroic policy although in certain circumstances it may be the most heroic of all. To cooperate without losing one's soul, to assist without sacrificing one's identity, to work for deliverance in the guise of bondage and under enforced silence, what harder test of moral toughness exists?"[4] Can we assume that American policy toward the Palestinians today is guided by this moral assessment? Are the Palestinian leaders more heroic for accepting the alienation of portions of their *patrie* but at the same time existing in a state of their own within the shadow of a dominant Israel?

CONCLUSION

Thus the provisions and objectives of a final settlement become apparent. First, such an agreement would confer legitimacy on Israel and the Palestinians, and both would become units of the Middle East state system. Second, the Arab territories to be evacuated by Israel would constitute a buffer for some time to come, thereby insuring a state of mutual security for all protagonists. Third, and finally, the settlement would include a general agreement and guarantee for the mutual protection and security of the different powers in the region. While such a settlement is eventually to be concluded among the regional powers themselves, its guarantee would come essentially from the United States and perhaps from the Soviet Union. The question that remains to be answered is: Would an agreement based on these assumptions and modalities work in the contemporary Arab world?

An American policy based on successful co-opting of many but not all Arab states is bound to face serious difficulties. For one thing, the states that have opted for an ultimate settlement based on conflict have the capacity within the Arab state system to cause serious disruption. The fact that some of these states cannot at the moment bring their full weight to bear on the course of events because of internal difficulties and even external threats to their territorial integrity does not detract from their ability to marshal considerable public support for a more conflictual approach; further, they may translate their commitments and resources more effectively when the extent of political concessions demanded of the "confrontation" states becomes more appreciated in the Arab world.

In conjunction with the presence of states committed to a different approach, the revolutionary impact of the previous nationalist effort and the Palestinian assertion is not a spent force. American policy may continue to assume that the new wealth in the Arab world and

4. Kissinger, *op. cit.*, p. 19.

the strategy of development adopted by the new technocratic elites
will lead to the acceptance of a bourgeois path for development;
but what is evident is that the new wealth, unevenly distributed as
it is among the Arab states and unevenly distributed and utilized
within each of them, is bound to create more fundamental contradictions within each Arab society. The fact that the political regimes
in the Arab world have accepted a strategy of development essentially
inspired by the European–American model at a time when bold and
radical alteration in the basic structure of Arab society is required,
will in due course give new directions to an Arab revolutionary
movement that seeks total independence. That it is those regimes
which are willing to accede to an alienation of a significant part
of the Arab national *patrie* and to the legitimation of the state that
has arisen in that part will simply add to the flames of discontent.

The American vision of a legitimate political system in the region,
one composed of sovereign states committed to its preservation, each
eager to pursue what has been defined as its "national" interests
in tandem with American interests, sounds logical enough; but the
world is not a mechanical world with various pieces that fit neatly
together. Other American visions of a stable political order have gone
up in smoke: in Vietnam, Greece, Portugal, Ethiopia, Cyprus. Why
should the Arab world today, a world which has undergone significant
ideological and structural experiences over the past two decades, be
an exception? A settlement of the type portrayed above, although
in the very short run it may appear enduring, is certain in the end
to produce its own dialectic.

PART I: THE CONFLICTING SOCIETIES

Ahmed S. Khalidi

THE MILITARY BALANCE, 1967–73.

ONE OF THE MOST TRYING military subjects to write about or discuss is that amorphous and ill-defined topic known as the "military balance." This is not merely due to its extensive ramifications but also to the very necessary task of approaching it in the most wary and meticulous manner. Far too often judgements about the supposed military balance between a set of conflicting parties (and it is understood that nobody discusses the military balance between non-conflicting parties, eg., France and England) are disproven almost as soon as they are pronounced. Although the dynamic that is inherent in the "military balance" leaves a narrow margin for prognostication, military balance can be reduced to a certain number of essential factors. In this study we shall examine the quantitative and qualitative factors of the Middle East military balance that are common to the military balance between any set of conflicting parties. In addition we shall study those factors that are unique to the region, including the role of the superpowers.

A QUANTITATIVE ASSESSMENT

The increase of the quantitative strength of the main protagonists of the Middle East conflict is indicated in Tables 1-7. These figures, although derived from various authoritative sources, remain highly tentative, pointing to general increases in the numbers and types of equipment in service with the various protagonists. Information about major arms deals or transfers can usually be compiled from specialized military journals or publications or occasionally the daily press. A certain undefinable percentage of arms transactions remain secret, only to be revealed whenever the sponsor, recipient, or manufacturer deems it necessary.[1]

Tables 1, 2, and 3 trace as accurately as possible the increase (between 1968-73 inclusive) in the number and kind of weapons available to the Egyptian, Syrian, and Israeli land forces during the October war. The number and kind of weapons available to the air forces and navies of the three major protagonists are shown in Tables 4 and 5. The process of reconstruction and reorganization undertaken by Egypt, Syria, and Israel during the latter half of 1967 renders it difficult to make any meaningful comparison of their land forces prior to the end of 1968.[2] However as an indicator of the extent of reorganization and reconstruction necessitated by the 1967 war, especially with regard to Egypt, it may be of interest to give an idea of the extent of Egyptian losses. During the 1967 June War Egypt lost: 550 out of 930 tanks; 350 out of 570 heavy artillery pieces; 450 out of 1,000 light artillery pieces; 250 out of 370 fighter aircraft; and 55 out of 70 bomber aircraft.[3]

Weapon Maintenance and Training

A thorough examination of military strength must go beyond the sum total of weapon strength and consider the availability of the weapons for battle. The question of maintenance is clearly vital. For if a country has 100 aircraft but only 10 are servicable at any one moment, it becomes meaningless to point to the total number of aircraft in its possession. Furthermore the fact that our hypothetical country can only field 10 per cent of its air force does not mean that it can only field a similar percentage of its army or navy. It is a totally

1. Usually it is not too difficult for the outside observer to collect reliable information about the types of various weapons in possession of a country (if not their actual quantities) especially if these types are imported and not locally manufactured. However, a recent reminder of how tenuous such an assumption can be was a public display by the Israelis of two major American weapons systems, the transfer of which to Israel had not been previously announced. See *An-Nahar*, July 9, 1974.

2. In all tables the figures for any given year relate to quantity and type of material available at the end of that year. All tables have 1968 as their starting date.

3. See A. S. Khalidi, "The Arab Israeli War of 1967," *United Services Institute of India Journal*, April-June, 1970. Losses for other Arab countries and Israel in the 1967 war are very hard to come by. Total losses of material by Jordan and Syria have not been given by any authoritative source, and Israel has only very recently released figures for its total losses in aircraft (46). See *Armed Forces Journal*, October, 1973.

different problem to maintain a tank, than to maintain an advanced missile system. Moreover even within a certain branch of the armed forces the standard of maintenance need not be constant; for example, it is easier to maintain a type of tank that has been in service for a couple of years, than to maintain a type of tank that has just been received.

With regard to the Middle East it is possible however to form a tentative judgement on the level of servicability in various branches of the different armed forces. Every year the Israeli state comptroller publishes a report on the level of serviceability in the Israeli armed forces. In April, 1973 this report revealed that much equipment was either lost, damaged, or misplaced by the Israeli army each year.[4] In the year 1970-71 for instance equipment valued at 18.9 million (Israeli) pounds was lost or unaccounted for. Only 4 million pounds worth of this equipment was lost due to enemy action. In the following year Israeli military equipment valued at 17.4 million pounds was lost excluding that lost due to enemy action. In one vehicle maintenance unit twenty officers out of a total of eighty-nine in the workshops had undergone no special training course. In the air force it was found in 1971 that only 8,500 out of a total of 670,000 items were carried on the list of stockpiled material. There is no equivalent publically available report on the serviceability of the various branches of the Arab armed forces. However in 1971, a leading Western military journal reported that the Egyptian air force rate of loss of aircraft due to training accidents was about ten aircraft per month, "four times the accident rate of most Western air forces."[5] In 1973 the Institute of Strategic Studies estimated that 200 out of a total of 540 Egyptian aircraft were "in storage."[6]

The level of serviceability is also related to the number and the quality of personnel. These in turn reflect several factors, including the type of training programs available, the ability to adapt to technological change, and the complexity of equipment received. In 1970 President Nasser indicated that whereas the Israelis had two pilots per plane, the Egyptian air force had more planes than it did pilots.[7] In an effort to close this "technological gap" Egypt embarked on a policy of conscripting large numbers of university graduates during

4. *The Jerusalem Post*, April 26, 1973.

5. *International Defence Review*, No. 4, 1971.

6. *The Military Balance 1973-74* (London: Institute for Strategic Studies, 1973).

7. *Arab-Palestinian Documents 1970* (Beirut: Institute for Palestine Studies, 1972) [in Arabic], p. 60.

the early seventies. In 1973 this gap, though considerably foreshort-ened, had still not been totally closed. In the summer of 1973 a Western military commentator estimated that, compared with an Israeli air force average of 30 to 35 hours flying time per month, the Egyptian air force average was no more than 10 hours.[8] On the whole it appears that with regard to the air force, which may be considered a test case for the necessary high standards of training and maintenance, the Israelis maintained a higher level of overall efficiency than their Arab protagonists from 1967-73.

Military Deployment

The question of deployment is as vital as that of serviceability. It is not sufficient to have high standards of maintenance and training if the country is unable to commit the requisite number of forces to battle.

In 1967 when the June war began, the Egyptian army totalled approximately 150,000 men of whom 80,000 were deployed in Sinai and 40,000 in the Yemen.[9] The armed strength of some of the "second-line" Arab states is given in Tables 6 and 7. It will be seen that if the Iraqi armed forces had been deployed in strength in either Syria or Jordan prior to the outbreak of the 1973 October War, they might have made a greater impact on the conduct of operations. The question of the proper deployment of Arab strength is not however merely an operational one. At the basis of the problem and compound-ing its technical intricacies lies the question of political coordination. Thus, whereas in 1967 the Israelis were able to deploy 120,000 men against the Egyptian front alone and later rapidly switch these forces to the other fronts,[10] the degree of political and operational coordination achieved by Egypt and Syria in October, 1973 made it much more difficult for the Israelis to concentrate against any one front.

It follows that a simple addition of figures for both sides and subsequent comparison is highly misleading. The sheer numerical figures for the military strength of each party must be progressively reduced taking into account the constraints of maintenance, personnel training, and operational deployment.

8. D. Nicolle, "The Imbalance of Power," *Middle East International,* June, 1973.

9. Khalidi, *op. cit.*

10. C. Douglas-Home, "The Balance of Power," *Middle East International,* January, 1972.

EFFECTIVENESS OF AVAILABLE AIR AND ANTI-AIRCRAFT
WEAPONRY

The problems relating to a mere numerical assessment of the military balance have been mentioned. However even sheer quantity of weaponry is not a sufficient indicator of military strength, for example, a plane that can deliver say 5,000 kg. of ordnance is clearly not equivalent to a plane that can deliver half as much.[11] Differences between individual weapons can therefore be translated into differences in tactical firepower. Two factors must be considered. The first relates to the raw performance characteristics of each individual weapon, and the second is the process of interaction between the various individual weapons, i.e. their performance as a system. A highly effective attack aircraft cannot operate at the optimum level unless it is fully integrated into a system which comprises radar installations, anti-aircraft missiles, and electronic jamming equipment.

Aircraft Characteristics[12]

TYPE	MAX SPEED AT ALTITUDE	COMBAT RADIUS	PAYLOAD
Mig 21J Fighter interceptor (Soviet)	Mach 2.1	500 km	Cannon and 2 Atoll AAM's and Light bombload
Mig 17 Fighter (Soviet)	Mach 0.96	575 km	Cannon and 2 Atoll AAM's or 500 kg bombload
SU-7 Fighter bomber (Soviet)	Mach 1.96	460 km	Cannon and 1000 kg bombload
F104A Fighter interceptor (American)	Mach 2	490 km	2 Sidewinder AAM's and Light bombload

11. Although this problem relates to quality of weaponry, it has been included in the section dealing with the quantitative balance, as firepower can be quantitatively measured.

12. Information for this section was compiled from *Jane's All the World's Aircraft 1973-1974* (London, 1973); E. Luttwak, *Dictionary of Modern War* (London, 1971); and H. Ayoubi and H. Abdullah, *The Arab-Israeli Military Balance 1973-74* (Beirut, 1974) [in Arabic]. Mach One equals the speed of sound which varies from 1156 km/h at sea level to 1072 km/h at 10,000m. altitude. Combat radius refers to effective radius of action at optimum payload/speed capacity. Payload will differ according to mission. In the above typical payload is given.

Aircraft Characteristics (continued)

TYPE	MAX SPEED AT ALTITUDE	COMBAT RADIUS	PAYLOAD
F4E Phantom Fighter bomber (American)	Mach 2.2	800 km	Cannon and 2 AIM4D and 4 Sidewinder AAM's or 7500 kg bombload
A4E/H Skyhawk Attack aircraft (American)	Mach 0.9	800 km	Cannon and 4500 kg bombload
Mirage 3C Fighter bomber (French)	Mach 2.1	640 km	Cannon and 2 Sidewinder AAM's and 900 kg bombload
Super Mystere Fighter interceptor (French)	Mach 1.1	435 km	Cannon and 2 Matra AAM's or 900 kg bombload
BAC Lightning Fighter interceptor (British)	Mach 2	–	Cannon and 2 Firestreak AAM's and Light bombload
BAC Hunter Fighter bomber (British)	Mach 0.9	400 km	Cannon and 900 kg bombload
AN-12 Transport (Soviet)	–[13]	Range 3400 km [14]	100 troops or 20 ton payload
C-130 Transport (American)	-	Range 4000 km	92 troops
Mi-6 Helicopter (Soviet)	-	Range 620 km	65 troops 12 ton payload
CH-53 Helicopter (American)	-	Range 415 km	64 troops
AB–205 Helicopter (American)	-	Range 550 km	15 troops can be armed with cannon and ATGW's
Super Frelon Helicopter (French)	-	Range 650 km	30 troops or 4 ton payload

13. Speed of transport aircraft and helicopters is not a highly relevant characteristic.

14. Maximum Range is a more useful characteristic of transport planes and helicopters than combat radius.

Anti-Aircraft Weapons Characteristics[15]

TYPE	RANGE/KM	COMMENT
SAM 2 Surface-to-Air missile (Soviet)	30	Operates in static bases of 6 missiles (1 per launcher)
SAM 3 Surface-to-Air missile (Soviet)	20	Operates in static bases of 8 missiles (2 per launcher)
SAM 6 Surface-to-Air missile (Soviet)	30	Operates on mobile tracked vehicle carrying two missiles.
SAM 7 Surface-to-Air missile (Soviet)	Approx 3	Operated by infantry. Fired from shoulder-held tubes. Also mounted on light vehicles.
ZSU-4-23 mm Anti-Aircraft Self-Propelled gun (Soviet)	2	Four-barrelled mobile tracked vehicle firing at 4,000 rounds per minute. Radar controlled.
HAWK Surface-to-Air missile (American)	30	Operates on semi-mobile launcher carrying 3 missiles.

Analysis

Soviet fighter and fighter-bomber aircraft (Mig 21, Mig 17, SU-7) in service with Egypt, Syria, and Iraq tend to have both restricted range and payload as compared to U.S. and French aircraft (F4, A4, Mirage) in service with Israel (see Tables 4 and 6). The mainstay of the front line Arab states air forces[16] is the Mig 21, which has only a 500 km. combat radius and a light bombload compared to the F4 Phantom's 800 km. combat radius and 7500 kg. bombload. This difference while reflecting conflicting design requirements of the Soviet and U.S. air forces nevertheless allows ostensibly for a distinct advantage for the Phantom over the Mig 21. This may be mitigated by the specific circumstances of such a confrontation. A Phantom loaded down with 7500 kg. would be less maneuverable than a lightly armed Mig 21. However, a Phantom on an interception mission is both marginally faster than the Mig 21 (by 0.1 Mach) and carries 6 AAM's as opposed to 2 AAM's. In addition a Phantom cannon with 6,000 rounds per minute rate of fire clearly surpasses the 600

15. Information for this section was compiled from R. Arndt, *Weapons and Equipment of the Soviet Land Forces* (Regensburg, 1971); *Jane's Weapon's Systems 1973-74* (London, 1973); and R. Ashkar and A. S. Khalidi, *Weapons and Equipment of the Israeli Armed Forces* (Beirut: Institute for Palestine Studies, 1971).

16. Excluding Jordan—see Table 6.

rounds per minute rate of fire for the Mig 21's cannon. The performance characteristics of Israel's U.S.-made fighter and attack aircraft are on the whole superior to any Soviet types possessed by the Arabs including American, British, and French aircraft in the Jordanian, Saudi, Iraqi, and Libyan inventories (see Tables 6 and 7).

In other types of aircraft the performance characteristics of Soviet and U.S. aircraft are more equally balanced. Both the Arabs and Israelis possess transport planes of generally the same performance. The Soviet AN-12 in service with Egypt and Syria compares favorably with the U.S. C-130 in service with Israel. Egypt, Syria, and Israel greatly increased their complement of helicopters between 1968 and 1973. Although Soviet helicopters such as the Mi-6 are very similar to the American CH-53 or French Super Frelon in service with Israel, Soviet helicopters do not have the capacity to carry any armament. Israeli armed helicopters such as the AB-205 were designed to deal with the problem of counterinsurgency posed by the Palestinian resistance, the Arab states generally not having to deal with any such problems.

Because modern aerial warfare can no longer be examined as merely a confrontation between individual aircraft, the traditional dogfight although still of vital significance is not the only measure of aerial superiority. In the Middle East the essential exchange has come to be that of aircraft vs. ground defence, rather than aircraft vs. aircraft.[17] In terms of numbers and quality, Arab anti-aircraft weaponry far outclassed Israeli weaponry between 1967 and 1973. The buildup of the Egyptian and Syrian air-defence systems and their possession of such weapons as the SAM 6, SAM 7, and ZSU-23 has no equivalent on the Israeli side (see Tables 1, 2, and 3). These extensive anti-aircraft systems were offset to some extent as the United States supplied Israel with Electronic Counter Measures (ECM) to jam the SAMs guidance systems. The importance of ECM's was recognized by all parties prior to the 1973 war, and the experience of the war bore out their significance.[18]

With regard to air warfare in the Middle East the following observations can be made:

1. In 1967 the air war in the Middle East was essentially a conflict

17. For a discussion of the exchange between aerial offence and land-based defence see E. Luttwak, "(Mig 21 + Mig 23 + SAM 2 + SAM 3) − (F-4 + A4 + AGM) = ?," New Middle East, December, 1971.

18. In 1972 Israel was said to have " 'ECM talent' second only to the U.S. and the U.S.S.R." (Aviation Week and Space Technology, February 21, 1972).

between aircraft in the traditional dogfight or ground attack role. To a lesser extent it featured offensive Israeli air action against primitive ground defences. In point of fact the course of the air war was determined by the early destruction of the Arab air forces on the ground.

2. By 1973 the air war in the Middle East had changed radically. The relatively primitive engagement of aircraft vs. aircraft or aircraft vs. anti-aircraft guns of 1967 became a highly complicated confrontation between two integrated systems in 1973. The first system comprised the SAM-ZSU-23 defence of Syria and Egypt and the second comprised the Phantom-ECM-ASM offense of Israel in the event the latter after initial devastating setbacks was able to reassert itself.[19] This was due as much to Israeli ability to negate the SAM's by the use of ECM and ASM's and evasive maneuver, as it was to Egyptian negligence in allowing the SAM system to be destroyed on the ground by the Israeli force that penetrated the west bank of the Canal.[20]

3. It should be noted that while the SAM systems in Egypt and Syria were (by definition) designed for air-defence, the mobility of the SAM 6 and SAM 7 allowed for offensive ground action against Israel. This emphasizes the danger of too narrow a definition of 'offensive' and 'defensive' weapons. In practice the definition applies essentially to the tactical use of such weapons rather than their ostensible designation.

4. The 1973 war saw for the first time the extensive use by the Arabs of air mobile heliborne commandos. It is noteworthy that the Israelis apparently refrained from the use of their heliborne troops (except in isolated incidents) possibly because of the less than total air superiority enjoyed by the Israeli air force.

---

19. It was estimated that the Israelis lost 30 aircraft in one day to Syrian missile defences at the outset of the war (*Aviation Week*, October 22, 1973).

20. *The Sunday Times Insight on the Middle East War*, (London, 1974). The operational problems of such complicated systems as the SAM network in Syria can be pointed to: the Syrians apparently shot down a large number of their own aircraft with their missiles (*Flight Magazine*, June 27, 1974). The Israelis also apparently shot down a number of their own aircraft (*Aviation Week*, December 16, 1973).

TANKS, ARMORED VEHICLES, AND ANTI-TANK WEAPONS

Tanks and Armored Vehicles[21]

TYPE	WEIGHT	ARMAMENT	RANGE	ARMORED PLATE
T54/55 tank (Soviet)	36 tons	100mm gun	600 km	85mm
T62 tank (Soviet)	36 tons	115mm gun	600 km	80mm
M48 Patton tank (American)	48 tons	90mm or 105mm gun*	500 km	100mm
M60 tank (American)	48 tons	105mm gun	500 km	–
M4 Super Sherman tank (American)	30 tons	105mm gun*	240 km	50mm
Centurion tank (British)	52 tons	105mm gun*	200 km	–
BTR40 APC (Russian)	6.5 tons	12.7mm and 7.62mm machine guns	500 km	13.5mm
M3 Half-Track (American)	8.4 tons	12.7mm and 7.62mm machine guns	320 km	6mm
M113 APC (American)	10 tons	12.7mm and 7.62mm machine guns	640 km	Aluminum
AML 60/90 AC (French)	5.5 tons	60mm mortar or 90mm gun	600 km	–
Saladin AC (British)	11.6 tons	76mm gun	160 km	–

21. Information for this section was compiled from *Jane's Weapon Systems 1973–74,* R. Ashkar and A. S. Khalidi, *Weapons and Equipment of the Israeli Armed Forces,* and R. Arndt, *Weapons and Equipment of the Soviet Land Forces.*

*The Israelis have fitted 105mm guns on virtually all tanks in their possession; the M48 in service with Jordan (see Table 6) has a 90mm gun and the older types of Centurion and Sherman in service outside Israel have 85 and 76mm guns respectively.

Anti-Tank Weapons

TYPE	WEIGHT	RANGE	COMMENT
Snapper wire-guided anti-tank missile (Soviet)	21 kg	500-2000m	Oldest of Soviet anti-tank missiles. Can be fired from BTR 40 APC's and Jeeps. Can penetrate 500mm of armor plate. Has an explosive head of 7 kg.
Swatter ATGW (Soviet)	20 kg	400-2500m	Can be fired from BTR40 APC's and other vehicles. Can penetrate 500mm of armor plate. Has an explosive head of 7 kg.
Sagger ATGW (Soviet)	11 kg	200-2500m	Newest Soviet anti-tank missile. Can be fired from vehicles or from hand-carried one man firing mounts. Can penetrate 350mm of armor plate. Has an explosive head of 3.2 kg.
RPG-7 (Soviet)	5.9 kg	300-500m	Shoulder-fired anti-tank Rocket Projectile Gun. Can penetrate 320mm of armor plate.
106mm recoiless rifle (American)	(3)	1500m	Jeep-mounted anti-tank gun. Effective against concrete emplacements.
SS11 ATGW (French)	36.5 kg	550-3300m	Jeep-mounted or heliborne anti-tank missile. Can penetrate 650mm of armor plate. Has an explosive head of 8 kg.

Analysis

Israeli M48, M60, and Centurion tanks are on the whole superior to the T54/55, the mainstay of the Syrian and Egyptian armies (see Tables 1 and 2). The British-made 105mm. tank gun fitted on virtually all Israeli main battle tanks enjoys greater range than the 100mm. gun of the T54/55 (5,000m. vs. 3,000m.). As most tank battles in the Middle East occur at about 800-1200m. range, the more telling advantage of the 105mm. gun over the 100mm., is its greater muzzle velocity, (1700mm/sec vs. 1000mm/sec). This allows the 105mm. gun to get the vital first shot off before the 100mm. gun. Furthermore the 105mm. gun fires highly effective Armor Piercing Discarding Sabot

(APDS) ammunition whereas the T54/55 only fires conventional and less effective Armor Piercing (AP) ammunition.[22] Although the T55 is fitted with infrared night fighting equipment, the fire control and optics on the Israeli M48, M60, and Centurions is considered to be superior to that of the T54/55.[23] One distinct advantage of the T54/55 series is that its silhouette is considerably smaller than that of Western tanks and thus offers a smaller target. The Soviet T62 tank is superior to the T54/55 series in that its 115mm. gun has a muzzle velocity of approx 1700m/sec and its capacity to fire APDS ammunition. However it appears that not enough of these tanks were available to the Arab forces in 1973 to make sufficient impact on the battlefield.

The characteristics of Soviet-made anti-tank weapons indicate their general superiority to Western equipment in Israel hands (see Table 3). The most outstanding Soviet anti-tank weapons and the most effective in the 1973 war were the Sagger ATGW and the RPG-7. Together these weapons accounted for a high percentage of Israeli tank losses. The effectiveness of the one man (carried in a portable suitcase) Sagger apparently came as a complete surprise to the Israelis.[24]

With regard to tank warfare in the Middle East the following observations can be made:

1. In 1967 the Israelis depended on massive, mobile 'mailed-fist' tank operations against static Arab defences. The classic blitzkrieg combination of tank penetrations and air superiority allowed for great armored mobility given total air control.

2. In 1973 tank warfare had little of the mobility that characterized the 1967 war. Neither side achieved any great armored penetration with the exception of the Israeli invasion of the west bank of the Canal in the later stages of the war.

3. In 1973 the innovative use of Egyptian, and to a lesser extent Syrian, infantry armed with ATGW's blunted to a large extent the traditional Israeli reliance on armored attacks.

4. The offsetting of Israeli superiority in the quality of tanks by the extensive use of ATGW's on the Arab side once again indicates that 'defensive' weapons can be tactically employed offensively. The

---

22. See appendix to Insight on the Middle East War.

23. It is of interest to note that in the 1965 Indo-Pakistan war, the superior and more complicated fire control system of the Pakistani M48 over the Indian Centurions was apparently more of a hindrance than an advantage as it entailed more complicated computations. Such problems are not likely to be faced by Israel (London Times, November 5, 1965).

24. See Al-Taqsir [The Shortcoming] (Beirut: Institute for Palestine Studies, 1974) [Translated from Hebrew].

initial Egyptian offensive which crossed the Suez Canal was composed
almost exclusively of infantry with Sagger's and RPG-7's.[25]

5. Israeli doctrine apparently failed to account for the effectiveness
of modern anti-tank weapons which can penetrate any known tank
armored plate. This appears to be all the more surprising given that
the Israelis were the first to use ATGW's in combat in 1956 (SS10's).[26]

ARTILLERY AND MISSILE WEAPONRY

Artillery Weapons[27]

TYPE	WEIGHT	RANGE	COMMENT
122mm gun° (Soviet)	5 tons	15.3 km	Fires at a rate of 7–8 rounds per minute.
130mm gun° (Soviet)	8.6 tons	27 km	Fires at a rate of 6 r/m
203mm gun (Soviet)	20 tons	29 km	Fires at a rate of 1 r/m.
240mm rocket launcher° (Soviet)	9.6 tons	11 km	Lorry mounted with 12 tubes. Fires two salvos per hour.
M107 175mm Self-Propelled Gun (American)	28 tons	32 km	Mounted on tracked vehicle with a range of 640 km. Crew of 13 men.
M109 155mm SPG (American)	23 tons	14 km	Mounted on tracked vehicle with a range of 360 km. Crew of 7 men.
M110 203mm SPG (American)	26 tons	16 km	Mounted on tracked vehicle with a range of 640 km. Crew of 13 men. Rate of fire 1–2 r/m.
L-33 Sultam 155mm SPG (Israeli)	41 tons	21 km	Mounted on Sherman chassis. Range 260 km. Crew of 8 men.
25 Pounder (88mm) gun (British)	1.7 tons	12 km	Towed by special trailer. Crew of 6–7 men.

25. General Shazli, Egyptian chief of staff (*Al Akhbar*, November 21, 1973).

26. *Jane's All the World's Aircraft 1962–1963* (London, 1962).

27. Information compiled from R. Arndt, *Weapons and Equipment of the Soviet Land Forces;* and H. Abdullah, *Weapons of the Israeli Army* (Beirut, 1974) [In Arabic].

°The Israeli army uses captured Soviet artillery of the indicated types.

Analysis of Artillery Weapons

The most outstanding difference between Israeli and Arab artillery is that Israeli artillery is virtually all self-propelled whereas Arab artillery is almost wholly of the towed variety (see Tables 1, 2, and 3). This reflects Soviet-Western differences in doctrine, the Russians preferring massive set-piece artillery barrage actions, and the Israelis tending to follow Western doctrine with regard to mobile artillery action. The very effective Soviet 130mm. gun can penetrate 250mm. of armor at 2,000m. in the anti-tank role and is outgunned only by the American M107. The latter, though mobile, has the disadvantage of being very heavy and lacks the capacity to carry its own ammunition. The Soviet 203mm. gun, while firing 155kg. shells as opposed to the 90kg. shell of the M110 203mm. American SPG is much too ponderous a weapon for mobile warfare. The Israeli prediliction for mobile artillery extends to all types of heavy weaponry including 160 and 120mm. mortars and 90mm. guns which have been fitted onto M3 Half-Tracks and Sherman tank chassis. Greater reliance on mobility rather than numbers in artillery allows for more extensive battlefield support but less intensive concentration of fire power.

The following observations may be made on the role of artillery in the Middle East:

1. In 1967 artillery played a secondary role to tank warfare in the offense but was the main Arab ground defensive weapon.

2. In 1973 Arab artillery support was a vital adjunct to the Arab offensive especially where it was used to reduce Israeli fortifications along the Bar-Lev line. In effect Arab artillery played the offensive role of fire support assigned to the Israeli air force and a great deal of the latter's capacity was taken up in suppressing Arab artillery fire.

3. Soviet-made 122 and 240mm. RL's made up for mobile artillery support which was otherwise generally lacking on the Arab side. Israeli mobile artillery does not seem to have played a large role during the 1973 October War.

Missile Characteristics[28]

TYPE	RANGE	WARHEAD	COMMENT
Atoll Air-to-Air Missile (Soviet)	–	–	Infrared homing device.

28. Information compiled from R. Arndt, *Weapons and Equipment of the Soviet Land Forces;* Ashkar and Khalidi, *Weapons and Equipment of the Israeli Armed Forces;* H. Abdullah; *Weapons of the Israeli Army;* and *Jane's Weapons Systems 1973-74.*

Missile Characteristics (continued)

TYPE	RANGE	WARHEAD	COMMENT
Frog 3 and 7 Surface-to-Surface Missile (Soviet)	Frog 3: 35 km Frog 7: 65 km	450 kg 545 kg	Unguided bombardment missile.
Styx Surface-to-Surface Missile (Soviet)	40 km	400 kg	Guided ship-launched missile.
Sidewinder AAM (American)	3.6 km	4.4 kg	Infrared homing device.
Sparrow AIM-7 AAM (American)	15-26 km	27 kg	Semi-active radar homing.
Shrike Air-to-Surface Missile (American)	12-16 km	–	Anti-radar missile. Homes on enemy radar signals.
Walleye ASM (American)	12 km	385 kg	T.V. guided missile for use against enemy emplacements.
Shafrir AAM (Israeli)	5 km	11 kg	Infrared or semi-active radar homing.
Gabriel SSM (Israeli)	21 km	150 kg	Combination of visual, radar, and T.V. guidance. Ship-launched missile.

Analysis of Missiles

Israeli American-made missiles (see Table 3) are of a greater variety and sophistication than Soviet-supplied Arab missiles. The Israeli buildup in sophisticated Air-to-Surface missiles was initiated after the cease-fire of August, 1970 in response to the buildup of Egyptian SAM defences. Both Shrike and Walleye were supplied with a view to countering the SAMs and to form (along with other missiles) part of the Israeli Phantom and Skyhawk plus ECM response to the SAM threat.

Both the Sparrow and the Sidewinder, along with the Israeli-made Shafrir, gave Israel the edge in AAM's in the 1973 war. The Russian-built Frog missiles, although operational for some time in Egypt, were not used in the 1973 war, but Syrian Frog missiles were reportedly fired at Israeli air bases in northern Israel. The Frog missiles suffer from lack of a guidance system and were originally designed for tactical nuclear bombs where great accuracy is not required. Only very large quantities of such missiles would have any impact on the Middle East conflict.

The Gabriel ship-launched missile appears to have acquitted itself honorably in the 1973 war and is reportedly responsible for the sinking of 13 Egyptian and Syrian missile boats for a loss of only 3 Israeli Saar-class missile boats.[29]

An analysis of missile warfare in the Middle East conflict points to the following:

1. In 1967, missile warfare was limited essentially to the use of AAM's in aerial dog fights. However the Israelis made full use of an anti-runway missile (the concrete-dibber) against Arab airfields.[30]

2. In 1973, missile warfare played a much more extensive role with regard to air-to-air missiles, air-to-surface missiles, and ship-launched missiles. It is not known how many planes were lost to air-to-air missiles, nor has there been any concrete information with regard to the performance of American air-to-surface missiles.[31]

3. In spite of Israeli possession of pilotless Drones (see Table 3) little or no use of them in the offensive role has come to light.[32] Their role seems to have been restricted to battlefield surveillance and reconaissance.

A QUALITATIVE ASSESSMENT

The Morale of the Protagonists
Morale by definition is not quantifiable nor subject to precise definition. Furthermore the problem of indicating high or low morale is primarily a problem of representation: what number of people,

29. *Aviation Week,* October 15, 1973. It is important to note that while the Osa and Komar class missile boats in service with Egypt carry 2 and 4 Styx missiles respectively, Israeli Saar-class boats carry 8 Gabriel missiles. Thus although Israel was outnumbered in missile boats in 1973, it was superior in the total number of ship-launched missiles it could deliver at any one time (see Table 5).

30. *Flight Magazine,* June 24, 1967.

31. During the course of the 1973 war Israel reportedly received a number of additional types of ASM's from America such as the T.V. guided Maverick, the anti-radar Standard Arm Missile, the Hobo 'smart' bomb, and the Rockeye Missile (*Aviation Week,* November 5 and December 3, 1973). The performance of these missiles is said to have been very accurate.

32. In 1971, it was reported that Israel had acquired these Drones for "suppression of Egyptian/Soviet AA defenses along the Suez Canal," *International Defence Review,* October, 1971.

and in what positions have to make what nature of statements (or actions) to indicate the level of morale? And yet the morale level is an essential factor in the assessment of military strength or capability. A soldier who is both highly trained and highly motivated will presumably fight better with a given weapon than one who is neither trained nor motivated and yet armed with an identical weapon. Furthermore morale is not a constant and may vary depending on the course of the conflict. An army fighting with high morale may rapidly collapse if it suffers certain setbacks. Thus, compounding the problem of ascertaining morale in general, is the problem of ascertaining morale at any given moment.

Given all these problems one may point to certain indicators regarding the morale of the opposing parties in the Middle East. In 1967 the Egyptian rank and file must have been unsure of the purpose for its deployment in Sinai. Was it to fight a defensive war? To liberate Palestine? To defeat the Israeli armed forces? In 1973 it must have been clear to the Egyptian rank and file that they were waging an offensive war to liberate Egyptian soil.[33] Conversely, whereas in 1967 the Israeli rank and file was certain as to the purpose of the war, ie, to 'defend the existence of Israel' (regardless of whether this belief was justified or not), in 1973 the ordinary Israeli soldier could not have been totally convinced of the necessity of dying on the Suez Canal.[34] Furthermore during the course of the 1973 war the gap between the supposed capability of the Israeli Army and its performance must have had no little impact on morale.[35]

It is important to note that morale will depend on: (1) the degree of motivation in any given war (knowledge of the war's purpose); and (2) the difference between expected and actual performance in that particular war and previous wars. It may be safely conjectured that whereas in 1967 the Israelis could derive satisfaction from both factors, in 1973 they could derive satisfaction from neither. Conversely the Arabs in 1967 could derive little satisfaction from motivation or performance, but in 1973 Arab morale was high.

33. See General Ahmad Ismail, supreme commander of the Egyptian armed forces, in an interview with Hassanain Haikal (*Al-Ahram*, November 18, 1973).

34. For a good impression of Israeli morale during and after the 1973 war see *Al-Taqsir*.

35. "In the recent war the (Israeli) soldiers had experience of isolation in battle . . . the terrors of encirclement, the shame of being taken prisoner, and the fear of having an empty magazine" (*Ha 'aretz*, November 2, 1973). The writer of the article indicates that all these symptoms were unfamiliar to the Israeli army before.

Tactical Doctrines

Tactical doctrine relates to the ability to use firepower in the most suitable manner to achieve strategic ends. A party that has sufficient quantities of advanced weaponry, a high standard of training and maintenance, suitable strategic deployment, sufficiently concentrated firepower, and high morale and motivation must strive to utilize this conglomeration of factors in the most effective operational manner. To have a potentially effective air force is not sufficient, to be able to use it at the right time and place in conjunction with the other operational elements of the armed forces is the crux of the matter.

In the 1967 war Egyptian doctrine was based on the ability of concentrated land forces in defensive positions to absorb an enemy attack and defeat it on its own terms. The Egyptian air force was prepared to receive the enemy's first strike and then turn to the counterattack. A similar doctrine was adopted in Jordan and Syria. In principle this doctrine was sound, but in practice it was catastrophic. None of the Arab countries had taken sufficient precautions to protect their air forces; all Arab operational plans collapsed within hours of the outbreak of war.[36] In 1973 Arab operational plans were much more meticulous and coordinated.[37] The crossing of the Bar-Lev line, in itself a major operational problem, was ingenuously solved by the use of water hoses to break down Israeli sand barriers and the use of infantry with anti-tank missiles to confront Israeli armored counterattacks. The plan was coordinated with the existence of an integrated air-defence system based primarily on anti-aircraft missiles to neutralize the effectiveness of the Israeli air force. However the initial success of Arab operational planning broke down after the intrusion of unexpected factors such as the Israeli breakthrough to the west bank of the Suez Canal.

In 1967 Israeli operational planning displayed a high degree of awareness of the effectiveness of air superiority. This was manifested in the meticulously planned air strike on June 5, 1967.[38] In 1973 Israeli operational planning appeared initially incapable of adapting itself to the unexpected effectiveness of anti-tank and anti-aircraft missiles. Israeli accounts of the 1973 war suggest that its armored forces were totally unprepared for the Egyptian and Syrian use of large quantities of anti-tank missiles.[39]

36. See Khalidi, op. cit.
37. See General Ismail and General Shazli.
38. See Winston and Randolph Churchill, The Six Day War (London, 1968).
39. See Al-Taqsir.

In comparing the tactical doctrines of the protagonists in 1967 and 1973 these observations can be made:

1. In 1967 Egyptian, Syrian, and Jordanian doctrine based on the primacy of defensive positions was unable to forsee or cope with the combination of rapid moving armored penetrations and enemy air supremacy. Israeli doctrine used and totally exploited the ability of rapid moving armor and air attack to cut off and destroy immobile Arab forces.

2. In 1973 Egyptian and Syrian operational planning, while initially exploiting to great advantage the combination of infantry borne anti-tank and anti-aircraft missiles, was unable to cope with the fluidity of the battle and remained to a large extent transfixed by the very meticulous planning which contributed to initial successes. Arab tactical deployment remained basically inflexible and incapable of fully exploiting its own hard won success. Israeli operational planning while initially totally upset by the rapidity and determination of the Arab attack, was in the last analysis capable of the requisite minimum of flexibility to prevent complete disaster.

3. Arab tactical doctrine in both 1967 and 1973 relied a great deal on the Russian example: attack across a broad front with massive artillery support, within a slow moving but meticulous operational plan. Israeli tactical doctrine in both wars depended largely on the combination of air and tank assault along a narrow front to achieve deep rather than broad penetration. It may be argued that what Arab tactical doctrine demands is further flexibility whereas what Israeli doctrine demands is less flexibility.[40]

Self-Image of the Protagonists

In determining the military balance the subjective assessment of each side of its own and its opponents' military strength must be taken into account. In the last analysis it may be argued that the 'military balance' is very much a state of mind (both in the minds of the parties to the balance and the outside observers). It may be sufficient for one side to believe in the 'balance' for it to be maintained or to believe in the 'imbalance' for it to be disrupted. There is thus

40. See *Al-Taqsir*. According to the Israelis many losses were suffered due to the excessive initiative taken by Israeli commanders who would attack with little or no preparation or coordination with the other branches of the Israeli armed forces. Even General Sharon's attack across the Canal was undertaken against the advice of the Israeli high command and at one stage was in dire danger of collapse. Too much flexibility can yield chaos.

a continuous process of interaction between the subjective and objective balances.

The Israeli victory of 1967 grossly inflated the Israelis' impression of their own power while at the same time it allowed for a sense of security against Arab attack. By 1969–70 during the Egyptian-Israeli War of Attrition and increasing Soviet involvement in Egypt, Israeli fears centered mainly around the danger of an Israeli-Soviet military clash. Arab military strength was to a large extent discounted. By June, 1970 American sources were reporting that a message had been sent by the Israelis to Moscow warning the latter that in case of a full-scale confrontation between Israel and the Soviet Union, the first 50,000 Russian troops involved in battle would die.[41] At the same time Israel estimated that Egyptian strength had been so reduced in the War of Attrition that it would take five years for the Egyptians to recover.[42]

The military balance in 1970 as viewed by Western observers was:

> . . . narrowed to constitute very largely that ('balance') existing in the relative strength of aircraft on both sides even though in this area of measurement the 'balance' has obviously favoured the Israelis . . . the rough ratio worked out by the (U.S.) government but never politically acknowledged is that if Israel has one modern jet for every four possessed by her neighbors, she will be able to defend herself . . .[43]

By 1971 the Israeli image was further reinforced. Based on the strategic doctrines of secure borders and deterrence, the Israelis now saw themselves in the following light:

> The last four years since the Six Day War have been years of great achievements for the Israeli Army. Today (our) army is large, well-equipped and of international stature. It is an army with a pool of the finest and most experienced fighters in the world. The Israeli Army is infinitely more powerful than before and there is little room for comparison between its strength today and that already powerful force that defeated the Arab armies in 1967.[44]

41. *Aviation Week*, June 1, 1970.

42. *Ibid.*, May 11, 1970.

43. A. J. Cottrell, "The Role of Air Power in Military Balance in the Middle East," *New Middle East*, April, 1970.

44. *Yediot Aharonot*, June 7, 1971.

The Bar-Lev line along the Canal was considered not only a deterrent to the Egyptians but also a trap for their destruction.[45] In early 1972 in the opinion of one qualified Western observer:

> . . . even if one assumes that the efforts of Syrian, Jordanian, and Palestinian organizations were to be coordinated (a wild if not unprecendeted assumption) . . . the idea of a resumption of general hostilities in Sinai is almost inconceivable unless the Egyptians intended to suffer another severe mauling. . .[46]

During this period General Dayan reported that the state of Israel was the "most powerful force in the area," and that it was "the second most powerful state in the Mediterranean basin after France."[47] Not long before the 1973 October War, General Sharon then commander of the Israeli southern command voiced the remarkable view that:

> Israel is now a military superpower. . . . All the forces of the European countries are weaker than we are. . . . Israel can in one week conquer the area from Khartoum to Baghdad and Algeria.[48]

It must be admitted that most educated Arab opinion between 1967-73 was of the view that Arab success in a new regular war between the Arab states and Israel was unlikely. To the Arab observer it was not so much a matter of whether Israel could be defeated militarily. They questioned whether the Arabs could act militarily against Israel at all. In an attempt to be pragmatic Arab unofficial estimates on the whole tended to downgrade Arab capabilities while exaggerrating Israeli strength. However it is apparent that the Arab military was not quite so susceptible. General Ismail has outlined his own estimation of Israeli strengths and weaknesses with admirable clearheadedness. Israel's "four basic advantages" were seen as: "Its air superiority, its technological ability, its rigorous training, (and) the fact that it could rely on rapid aid from the United States which

45. While depending on their ability to defend the canal the Israelis had formulated the doctrine that "Israel would rather win West of the Canal than lose East of it." (General Dayan, *Davar*, July 11, 1971.

46. C. Douglas-Home, *op. cit.*

47. *Bulletin of the Hebrew Press* (Beirut: Institute of Palestine Studies, April 16, 1972) [In Arabic].

48. *Yediot Aharonot*, July 26, 1973.

would ensure it constant reinforcements." Israel's weaknesses were seen as long lines of communications, its inability to absorb heavy losses, its limited economic capacity for long wars, and its "overbearing arrogance."[49]

With regard to the subjective balance of power in the Middle East one may reach the following conclusions:

1. In 1967 the Arabs grossly overestimated the balance in their favor and underestimated Israeli strength and capabilities. The Israelis had a realistic assessment of the balance and the best manner to exploit it in their favor.

2. In 1973 general Arab opinion succumbed to the view that regular Arab military action against Israel was not only unlikely to occur but would in any case lead to total disaster. Arab high-ranking military and political opinion was apparently less deceived. The Israeli leadership as well as general opinion was lulled into a false sense of security and well being by past achievements and ostensible military strength.

3. Western 'expert' opinion played a large part in adding to the illusion of Israeli effortless superiority.

ROLE OF THE SUPERPOWERS

We have dealt with the quantitative and qualitative factors in the Middle East balance in terms that are relevant not only to the Middle East but to any balance between any conflicting parties. In considering those aspects that are unique to the Middle East, one of the most outstanding is the degree to which the superpowers as well as Europe and Japan have a direct interest in the conflict. The extent of external power involvement differs from that of any other area of the Third World due to the geopolitical importance of the Middle East and its oil reserves.

More directly relevant to the balance of power is the fact that both local parties to the conflict derive their sources of arms from the outside (see Tables 8 and 9). Iran and Israel accounted for over four times the value of American arms shipped to the Arab states. The general attitude of the U.S. government to the balance in the area has been summed up as follows:

. . . the term was conceived as a balance in which the superior number of Arab people would be offset by technology, particularly aircraft. I

49. *Al-Ahram*, November 18, 1973.

think aircraft was the central element in this balance as far as U.S. policy was concerned. What actually happened is that it created an imbalance in terms of air power which enabled the Israelis to have superiority. In other words it created an imbalance in favor of Israel. . . . The concept of military balance (in the Middle East) is that Israel will be able to defend itself against a coordinated Arab attack. If Israel should find itself vulnerable to Arab attack, then there is an imbalance. . . . The U.S. is committed to an Israeli edge which will permit it to win under such an attack. It is a commitment to an imbalance, I think the Nixon Administration would concede that.[50]

It may be safely stated that American arms policy in the area after 1967 was based on the premise that only a militarily superior Israel could deter the Arabs from launching an all-out war against Israel.

The 1973 war upset the notion that the imbalance in Israel's favor was sufficient to deter large-scale military action by the Arabs aimed at restoring the pre-1967 status quo. The undermining of the credibility of the Israeli deterrent vis-à-vis the maintenance of the post-1967 status quo, casts a new light as to the effect of the massive American arms aid to Israel since the war.[51] The determination of the Arab states to regain their lost territories suggests that the Israeli deterrent will increase in proportion to the territorial concessions Israel is willing to make.

Soviet arms policy in the Middle East since 1967 has generally served to offset the advantages gained by Israel by the acquisition of qualitatively superior weaponry. The challenge posed to the Arab strategic depth by Israeli air predominence centered on the Phantom was not met until the Egyptians and later the Syrians received sophisticated missile defences from the Soviet Union.[52] In terms of political objectives, the Soviet Union has consistently affirmed its support for Arab attempts to restore the pre-1967 status quo. In effect while American arms policy prior to 1973 served to maintain the post-1967 status quo, Soviet arms policy allowed for Arab attempts to reverse it.[53]

50. Interviews with American defence analysts, *Journal of Palestine Studies*, Spring, 1972.

51. See D. Tahtinen, *The Arab-Israeli Military Balance since October 1973* (Washington, D.C.: American Enterprise Institute for Public Research, 1974).

52. See Tables 1-4.

53. For a full discussion of Soviet and American arms policy in the Middle East see H. Sirriyah, *Arms Race Strategies in the Middle East Conflict* (American University of Beirut, 1974) (Unpublished M.A. Thesis).

The local powers in the Middle East continue to rely heavily on external supplies of advanced weaponry from the United States and the U.S.S.R. Although Israel attempted from 1970–73 to attain a certain level of self-sufficiency with regard to weapons supplies, the 1973 war showed all too clearly the extent of Israeli reliance on the United States.[54] The principal Arab parties to the conflict were similarly dependent on supplies and reequipment from the Soviet Union. The role of the superpowers in the 1973 war differed in one respect from the 1967 war: Whereas in the latter it was relegated to replenishing the local powers' inventories after the war was over, in 1973 both the United States and the U.S.S.R. delivered large quantities of arms during the course of the fighting. In the 1973 war the conduct of military operations and the duration of the fighting were to a large extent subject to the availability of weapons and equipment from the superpowers.

GEOGRAPHICAL FACTORS

The Israeli concept of 'secure borders' was evolved and refined after the 1967 war. Previously it was an integral part of Israeli military doctrine that the borders of the state were not defensible and therefore any Israeli military initiative must aim at carrying the war into enemy territory. The 'natural borders' attained by Israel after 1967—the Suez Canal, the Jordan River, and the Golan Heights—not only served to provide strategic depth, but also allowed for some relaxation of the doctrine of 'the best defence is offence'. The fortification of the Bar-Lev line was intended to deter an Egyptian attack but also indicated Israeli willingness to adopt a defensive posture.

The new lines gained by Israel after 1967 were also seen as ideally suited to Israel's limited manpower resources and, furthermore, Arab strategic depth was reduced in proportion to the Israeli gains thus exposing Arab civilian and industrial centers to Israeli air and ground attack.[55] On the Arab side the advantages inherent in the Arab

---

54. The United States airlifted 22,300 tons of military equipment to Israel between October 13 and November 14, 1973, in 18,500 flying hours and 366 missions. This equipment included M48 and M60 tanks as well as heavy artillery and helicopters (*Armed Forces Journal*, December, 1973). This does not include sea shipments or direct Israeli shipments.

55. *Jerusalem Post Magazine*, June 2, 1973.

geographic position prior to 1967 were to a large extent reduced. The 10 km. waist of Israel in 1967 had now expanded to an Israeli presence threatening the Arab heartland. The predominant geographic problem facing a concerted Arab attack against Israel—the problem of distance—remained essentially unchanged. For example, the considerable military potential of Iraq and Algeria could not be fully brought to bear against Israel without tremendous logistical problems.

In 1967 the Israelis, while suffering from a lack of strategic depth, had the advantage of operating on interior lines. This allowed for rapid movement of troops and equipment from one front to the other (Sinai to the West Bank). In 1973 this advantage was to some degree lost due to the much longer lines of communications that separated the Suez Canal from the Golan Heights. On the other hand the Suez Canal and the Sinai Desert presented both a formidable natural obstacle and a buffer zone against Arab attack.[56] In 1967 the Arabs were hampered by politico-military constraints and failed to take advantage of the lack of Israeli strategic depth. In 1973 although the Israeli deterrent based on natural borders failed to prevent an Arab attack, it made it much more difficult for the Arabs to attain large-scale territorial gains.

MILITARY POTENTIAL

Actual military strength must be combined with potential military strength[57] in order to have a comprehensive understanding of a country's military power. Three main factors underlie a country's capacity for waging war: (1) its economic and technological capacity; (2) its administrative capabilities; and (3) the political foundations of its military power.[58] Economic and technical capacity will depend on the size and structure of the population, the extent of that nation's territory and its natural resources, the productivity of its labor force,

56. Dayan, while obviously concerned about the political implications of the fall of the Bar-Lev line, was reportedly willing to concede the Suez Canal to Egypt after the first few days of the 1973 war on the grounds that the Egyptians would make little headway in the rest of Sinai (*Ha 'artez,* May 5, 1973).

57. Military potential is a more inclusive term than 'war potential' which is sometimes used in the same context. Military potential covers such activity as export of arms which is not directly related to war.

58. K. Knorr, *Military Power and Potential* (Lexington, Mass: Heath Lexington Books, 1970), p. 25.

and the stage of its economic and technical development. Its administrative skills reflect these factors and determine the efficiency with which they are transformed into actual effective military force. In turn the proportion of economic, technological, and administrative resources allocated to creating and expanding military capabilities and a country's ability to use this strength will depend on the motivation of that country's leadership and its political base. The extent of public support for its military policies and the degree to which these policies conflict with the need to expend resources for other purposes is an important consideration.[59]

The main indicator of a country's economic capacity is its Gross National Product (GNP) which reflects the size of the country in terms of population. Its stage of development is expressed in terms of GNP per capita.[60] It may be taken as a general rule that high GNP per capita indicates an economy with abundant capital, advanced technology, and high labor productivity. These characteristics define the basic resources available for the production and/or deployment of technologically advanced weaponry.[61]

From 1967-72 Israel almost doubled its GNP and registered the highest rate of growth among the countries directly involved in the Middle East conflict. (For the GNP of selected Arab countries from 1967-72, see Table 10.) Egypt, Jordan, and Israel lead all other countries in the percentage of GNP spent on defence (see Table 11).[62] In 1971 Israel spent almost twice as high a percentage of its GNP on defence as it had in 1967 although this dropped in 1972. By 1972 Egypt was spending a higher percentage of its GNP on defence than any other country in the world. In a comparison of defence expenditure per capita for Middle Eastern and other countries, it will be seen that Israel spent over three times as much per capita on defence by 1969 as it did in 1967, and continued to spend more than any other country in the world through 1972 (see Table 12). Whereas Egypt spent 1/8 of its GNP per capita on defence in 1967, it allotted

59. *Ibid.*, pp 26-27. Knorr has rightly pointed out that there are in fact few characteristics which do not directly or indirectly affect a country's ability to generate and employ military power.

60. This generalization is misleading with regard to the oil states whose GNP and GNP per capita are not directly related to the stage of economic growth.

61. Knorr, *op cit.*, p. 54. High GNP per capita for the oil-producing countries is not an accurate indication of the stage of their economic development.

62. The countries chosen for comparison with the Middle East in Tables 11 and 12 are the four countries with the largest defence expenditures in the world.

1/5 in 1973; Israel similarly increased its expenditure from 1/10 in 1967 to 1/5 in 1973 (see Tables 12 and 13).

The Technological Gap

It is important to examine the implications of the stage of economic growth attained by the local parties to the Middle East conflict in terms of their ability to develop indigenous defense industries. Israel is the only country in the Middle East with a wide enough scientific and technological base to allow for the development of advanced weapons locally. One measure of the technological gap between the Arabs and the Israelis is the number of publishing scientists (see Table 15). Between 1967 and 1971 the Israeli scientific output remained over double the scientific output of the whole Arab world. In terms of output per capita the differences are tremendous. The Israeli output is four times the Egyptian output while Egypt's population is twelve times that of Israel (see Table 14). A comparison of per capita output reveals that one Israeli produces as much science as one hundred Arabs—the gap for Jordan is 250:1; for Egypt it is 50:1.[63]

The results of this technological gap become immediately apparent with regard to the Israeli defense industries. Locally Israel produces the Galili automatic rifle, mortars of various calibers up to 160mm., the British 105mm. tank gun under license, the Shafrir air-to-air infrared missile, the Gabriel ship-to-ship missile, the Arava light transport plane, the Magister Jet trainer under license from France, the Reshef class missile boat, the Barak Mach 2.2 jet aircraft (an upengined and redesigned version of the Mirage fighter aircraft), and a very wide variety of light and heavy ammunition and communication and electronic equipment. Similarly the Israelis have upgunned and reengined virtually their whole tank force with the 105mm. British gun and a 750 hp. diesel engine. Artillery and mortars of virtually every caliber have been fitted onto mobile chassis and used as self-propelled guns.[64] In addition to this large array of conventional weaponry, Israel is the only serious local contender for the nuclear club in the Middle East. It has been estimated that since 1971 at the latest, the Israelis have had the option of producing a nuclear device within six months to one year.[65]

63. See A. Zahlan, *Science and Higher Education in Israel* (Beirut: Institute for Palestine Studies, 1970) and "The Science and Technology Gap in the Arab-Israeli Conflict," *Journal of Palestine Studies,* Spring, 1972.

64. See R. Ashqar, *Israeli Military Industry* (Institute for Palestine Studies, 1973) [Unpublished paper—in Arabic].

65. See F. Jabber, *Israel and Nuclear Weapons* (Institute for Strategic Studies, 1971).

In comparison no major item of modern weaponry has of yet been produced and put into operational use by any of the Arab states. Although Egypt, Syria, and Iraq have military industries, these are primarily concerned with the production of ammunition and light ordnance. Egypt is the only Arab state to have attempted the production of an indigenous jet fighter aircraft; the project (HA300) was cancelled in 1969.[66] The Egyptian–built surface-to-surface missiles first displayed in 1963 and whose present status is uncertain, appear to be of little military significance.

One element in the technological gap between Israel and the Arab countries is the apparent lack of concern of the latter towards funding scientific research and development (R and D), a key factor in the production of indigenous weaponry. The total spent on R and D in the whole 'Arab world is negligible whereas Israeli R and D expenditure rose from approximately $100 million in 1967 to slightly less than $250 million in 1973.[67] Israeli R and D efforts are reflected not only in its ability to produce advanced weapons locally but also in its ability to export them. Thus Israeli military exports rose from $19.3 million in 1967 (7.6 per cent of all exports excluding diamonds) to $102 million (17.3 per cent) in 1973.[68] No Arab country has attained anything like this degree of self-sufficiency.[69] Despite Israeli attempts to attain self-sufficiency, the 1973 October War revealed the degree to which Israel was dependent on the United States. The Israelis apparently suffered from a lack of ammunition by the fourth day of the war and needed a vast infusion of U.S. weaponry to be able to withstand the initial Arab attacks.[70]

Arab potential, although misdirected in the past, may have a decisive impact on the conduct of any future war. The revenues from the oil resources of the major oil-producing Arab states afford a considerable capacity for setting up local defence industries and acquiring new and costly weapons systems from abroad (see Tables 16 and 17). The cost of the 1973 war and of any future conflict is thus

66. *Flying Review International,* July, 1970.
67. *Armed Forces Journal,* October, 1973.
68. *Ibid.*
69. In July, 1973 Israeli Defence Minister Dayan stated that 48 per cent of all Israeli weapons were locally produced. (*Ma'ariv,* July 16, 1973).
70. See *Insight on the Middle East War.*

likely to have a much greater impact on Israel than on the Arab states given some degree of political coordination between the latter.[71]

Administration and Popular Support

The administrative capabilities of the opposing sides have already been touched upon. However one main measure of these capabilities is the efficiency of the call-up system in the different opposing armed forces. In this context there is an essential difference between Israel and the Arab states. Whereas the latter depend largely on the standing regular forces, the former's main striking force is the reserves. The Israeli system depends on the ability to deploy its highly trained body of reserves numbering approximately 200,000 men within 48 to 72 hours (see Table 3). This calls for a highly developed administrative and logistical branch in the Israeli armed forces. Although this system appears to have malfunctioned rather badly in 1973 when compared with 1967,[72] the degree of Israeli mobilization of manpower remains great relative to the size of its population. Out of an estimated 600,000 men of military age (18-45)[73] Israel can field in time of war almost one-half (300,000 men).[74] Egypt with the largest standing army (285,000 men) in the Arab world (see Table 1) has a total of 7 million men of military age.[75] Thus even if one took into account the 500,000 men of the Egyptian reserves the total mobilized manpower in time of war would still be less than one-seventh the men of mobilizable age.

71. Whereas the 1967 war cost Israel approximately $100 million a day, the 1973 war cost $250 million—a total of $6 billion. Total Israeli defence expenditure as of November, 1973 was eleven times that of 1966. It is estimated that 40 per cent of the Israeli GNP will be spent on defence in 1973-74. The total dollar debts in Israel amounted to $1,500 per capita as of the end of 1973 (*Armed Forces Journal*, January, 1974). The Israelis have estimated that whereas they had 400 aircraft and 2,000 tanks in 1973, they will need a total of 1000 aircraft and 4,000 tanks in the next five years (*Ma'ariv*, October 30, 1973). Total Israeli defence expenditure has been uprated from $10 billion for the coming ten years in 1972 (*Jerusalem Post*, October 8, 1972) to $8 billion for next five years (*International Herald Tribune*, July 18, 1974).

72. See "The Preliminary Findings of Agranat Commision on the War," *Davar*, April 3, 1974.

73. *The Military Balance 1972-1973*.

74. Even in peacetime it is estimated that 1/4 of all civilian wage earners in Israel work on defence-related projects of one nature or another (*Yediot Aharonot*, January 29, 1971).

75. *The Military Balance 1972-1973*.

These differences do not only relate to administrative ability but also reflect the different military needs of the opposing parties. Israel depends on its highly trained reserves primarily because the cost of maintaining a large standing army would be prohibitive. Israel's scarcity in manpower also indicates the degree of economic strain imposed by total mobilization and explains to a large extent the Israeli military doctrine of short and rapid wars of decision.

It remains difficult to formulate a precise definition of the extent of popular support for military action on both sides in the 1967 and 1973 wars. It may be of interest to note that the notion that Israel was 'faced with annihilation' in 1967, a view put forward at the time by the Israeli government and widely accepted both inside and outside Israel, was later debunked by some of the highest ranking officers in the Israeli army.[76] On the other hand the determination of the Arab leadership to take military action toward restoring the pre-1967 status quo was consistently underrated both inside and outside the Arab world.[77] One measure of the interaction between popular feeling and the political will of the leadership is the extent to which the actual conduct of the war is subject to criticism. In the case of Israel there is a clear cut difference between popular reaction to the 1967 and 1973 wars, culminating in the fall of the Meir-Dayan government after the latter. On the Arab side, although the repercussions of the 1967 war were widely felt, the changes in political leadership and the interaction between this leadership and the popular base cannot be ascertained in such a definitive manner. There is little doubt however that the position of President Nasser was very badly shaken by the events of 1967. The 1973 war has not yet become the subject of overt criticism in either Egypt or Syria. The full extent of public support for the October war, still seen as an Arab victory, will in the last analysis be clarified with the crystalization of its political consequences.

76. Several members of the Israeli general staff in 1967 suggested in 1972 that the June war in no way threatened the existence of Israel. General Peled wrote that "the idea that the danger of genocide menaced us all in June, 1967 . . . is nothing but a bluff conceived and developed after the war." This was later supported by General Weizman who declared: "There was never any danger of our extermination and this hypothesis was never held in any serious assembly" (*Ma'ariv*, April 4, 1972). General Bar-Lev commented, "We were not threatened with genocide . . . and we never thought or said that such an eventuality was possible" (*Ma'ariv*, April 18, 1972).

77. In June, 1972, General Dayan reportedly saw no danger of war for 10-15 years (*Jerusalem Post Magazine*, June 2, 1972).

TABLE I
Egyptian Land Forces, 1968-73

	1968	1969	1970	1971	1972	1973
Regulars	180,000	180,000	250,000	275,000	285,000	285,000
Reserves	100,000	100,000	150,000	200,000	300,000	500,000
Active	15 Inf, 6 Arm, 1 Para Brig, 8 Art Reg, 10 Comm Batt	15 Inf, 6 Arm, 2 Para Brig, 8 Art Reg, 10 Comm Batt	4 Inf, 3 Arm, 4 Mech Inf Div, 2 Arm Brig, 15 Art Reg, 18 Comm Batt	5 Inf, 3 Arm, 4 Mech Div, 2 Para Brig, 16 Art Reg, 20 Comm Batt	5 Inf, 3 Arm, 4 Mech Div, 2 Para Brig, 16 Art Reg, 28 Comm Batt	5 Inf, 2 Arm, 3 Mech Div; 2nd Arm, 2nd Inf Brig, 1 Airborne, 1 Para, 6 Art Brig, 26 Comm Batt
Tanks and Carriers	20 JS-3, 500 T54/55, 100 T34, 50 PT-76, 150 SU-100, 1100 BTR40,50,152 (APC)	20 JS-3,T-10, 650 T54/55, 150 T34, 50 PT-76, 150 SU-100, 1200 BTR40,50,152 (APC)	30 JS-3,T-10, 1000 T54/55, 250 T34, 150 PT-76, 150 SU-100, 1500 BTR40,50,152 (APC)	50 JS-3,T-10, 1300 T54/55, 250 T34, 150 PT-76, 150 SU-100, 1800 BTR40,50,152, OT-64(APC)	50 JS-3,T-10, 1500 T54/55, 400 T34, 150 PT-76, 150 SU-100, 2000 BTR40,50,152, OT-64(APC)	50 JS-3,T-10, 1800 T54/55, 100 T34; 150 T62, 150 PT-76, 150 SU-100, 2500 BTR40,50,152, OT-64(APC)
Artillery	JSU-152, ZSU-57SPG, 700 122,130,152mm How, 120 160mm Mortar, 122,240mm RL, 37,57,85mm, AA Gun	JSU-152, ZSU-57SPG, 800 122,130,152mm How, 120 160mm Mortar, 40 122,240mm RL, 37,57,85,100mm, AA Gun	JSU-152, ZSU-57SPG, 1500 122,130,152, 203mm How, 120 160mm Mortar, 40 122,240mm RL, 37,57,85,100mm, AA Gun, ZSU-4-23mm AA, SPG	JSU-152, ZSU-57SPG, 1800 122,130,152mm How, 40 203mm How, 40 122,240mm RL, 37,57,85,100mm, AA Gun, ZSU-4-23mm,AA,SPG	JSU-152, ZSU-57SPG, 1800 122,130,152mm How, 40 203mm How, 40 122,240mm RL, 1000 37,57,85,100mm, AA Gun, ZSU-4-23mm AA,SPG	JSU-152, ZSU-57SPG, 2000 122,130,152mm How, 40 203mm How, 60 122,240mm RL, 1000 37,57,85,100mm, AA Gun, ZSU-4-23mm AA,SPG
Missiles	Snapper, Swatter ATGW, 180 SAM,Atoll AAM, Kennel ASM, 15 Frog,Samlet, Styx SSM	Snapper, Swatter ATGW, 300 SAM2,Atoll AAM, Kennel ASM, 25 Frog, 25 Samlet, Styx SSM	Snapper, Swatter ATGW, 350 SAM2,Atoll AAM, Kennel ASM, 25 Frog, 25 Samlet, Styx SSM*	Snapper, Swatter, Sagger ATGW, 420 SAM2,Atoll AAM, Kennel ASM, 25 Frog, 25 Samlet, Styx SSM+	Snapper, Swatter, Sagger ATGW, 420 SAM2, 800 SAM3,6,7,Atoll AAM,Kennel ASM, 25 Frog, 25 Samlet, Styx SSM	Snapper, Swatter, Sagger ATGW, 1500 SAM2,3,6,7,Atoll AAM, Kennel ASM, 25 Frog, 160 Samlet, Styx SSM

Source: Tables 1-4, 6, and 7 were compiled from The Military Balance 1968-1973, Aviation Studies International 1968-73, DMS Market Intelligence Reports 1971-1973, The Almanac of World Power 1971, and other sources compiled by the Institute for Palestine Studies, Beirut.
*Plus 600 SAM3's under Soviet supervision.
+Plus 700 SAM3's, SAM4's, and SAM6's under Soviet supervision.

TABLE 2
Syrian Land Forces, 1968-73

	1968	1969	1970	1971	1972	1973
Regulars	50,000	60,000	75,000	100,000	100,000	125,000
Reserves	40,000	40,000	90,000	150,000	160,000	200,000
Active	5 Inf, 2 Arm, 2 Mech 2 Mech Brig 6 Art Reg 1 Para Batt	6 Inf, 2 Arm, 3 Mech Brig 6 Art Reg 1 Para Batt	6 Inf, 4 Arm, 4 Mech Brig 7 Art Reg 1 Para Batt 3 Comm Batt	2 Inf, 1 Arm, 2 Mech Div 7 Art Reg 1 Para Batt 5 Comm Batt	2 Inf, 2 Arm, 2 Mech Div 8 Art Reg 1 Para Batt 7 Comm Batt	3 Inf, 2 Arm, 2 Mech Div 10 Art Reg 3 Para Batt 12 Comm Batt
Tanks and Carriers	200 T54/55 200 T34 80 SU-100 500 BTR40,152(APC)	300 T54/55 200 T34 80 SU-100 700 BTR40,50,152 (APC)	35 JS-3 700 T54/55 150 T34 100 SU-100 OT-64(APC)	35 JS-3 800 T54/55 150 T34 100 SU-100 1000 BTR40,50,152, OT-64 (APC)	35 JS-3 900 T54/55 140 T34 100 SU-100 1200 BTR40,50,152, OT-64(APC)	35 JS-3 1300 T54/55 150 T62 100 T34 100 SU-100 100 PT-76 1500 BTR40,50,152, OT-64 (APC)
Artillery	350 122,130,152mm How 122,240mm RL 120 160mm Mortar 37,57,85mm AA Guns	500 122,130,152mm How 122,240mm RL 120 160mm Mortar 37,57,85mm AA Guns	700 122,130,152mm How 122,240mm RL 120 160mm Mortar 37,57,85,100mm AA Guns	800 122,130,152mm How 122,240mm RL 120 160mm Mortar 37,57,85,100mm AA Guns	1000 122,130,152mm How 122,240mm RL 120 160mm Mortar 37,57,85,100mm AA Guns	1200 122,130,152, 203mm How 122,240mm RL 120 160mm Mortar 37,57,85,100mm AA Gun ZSU-4-23mm AA,SPG
Missiles	60 SAM2,Atoll AAM, Styx SSM	60 SAM2,Atoll AAM, Styx SSM	90 SAM2,Atoll AAM, Styx SSM	90 SAM2,Atoll AAM, Styx SSM	Sagger ATGW 90 SAM2,3,Atoll AAM, Frog, Styx,SSM	Sagger ATGW 500 SAM2,3,6,7,Atoll AAM,Frog, Styx,SSM

TABLE 3
Israeli Land Forces, 1968-73

	1968	1969	1970	1971	1972	1973
Regulars	60,000	60,000	65,000	65,000	65,000	80,000
Reserves	200,000	210,000	210,000	210,000	210,000	205,000
Active	5 Inf, 3 Arm 1 Para Brig	2 Inf, 2 Arm, 1 Mech, 1 Para Brig	2 Inf, 4 Arm, 1 Mech, 1 Para Brig	4 Inf, 4 Arm, 1 Para Brig	8 Inf, 4 Arm, 5 Mech, 1 Para, 3 Art Brig	3 Inf, 4 Arm, 4 Mech, 2 Para, 3 Art Brig
Reserves	16 Inf, 8 Arm Brig	19 Inf, 9 Arm Brig	19 Inf, 9 Arm Brig	14 Inf, 11 Arm, 3 Para Brig	5 Inf, 12 Arm, 4 Para Brig	5 Inf, 12 Arm, 3 Mech, 3 Para Brig
Tanks and Carriers	150 M48 225 Centurion 200 Sherman 150 AMX-13 100 T54/55 30 AML60/90 AC 1000 M3 HT BTR40,50,152(APC)	300 M48 400 Centurion 200 Sherman 120 T54/55 30 AML60/90 AC 1300 M3 HT BTR40,50,152(APC)	300 M48 450 Centurion 200 Sherman 120 T54/55 30 AML60/90 AC 1500 M3 HT BTR40,50,152(APC)	400 M48 100 M60 600 Centurion 200 Sherman 120 T54/55 30 AML60/90 AC 1500 M3 HT BTR40,50,152(APC) M113(APC)	450 M48 150 M60 600 Centurion 200 Sherman 120 T54/55 30 AML60/90 APC 1500 M3 HT BTR40,50,152(APC) M113(APC)	450 M48 150 M60 750 Centurion 200 Sherman 120 T54/55 30 AML60/90 APC 1500 M3 HT BTR40,50,152(APC) 450 M113(APC)
Artillery	250 155,105mm SPG 81,120mm Mortar 106mm Recoiless Rifle 20,30,40,90mm AA Gun	300 155,105mm SPG 122,130mm How 81,120,160mm Mortar 106mm Recoiless Rifles 90mm AT SPG 20,30,40mm AA Gun	300 155,105mm SPG 24 M109 155mm SPG M107 175mm SPG 122,130mm How 81,120,160mm Mortar 106mm Recoiless Rifles 90mm AT SPG 20,30,40mm Gun	300 155,105mm SPG 50 M109 155mm SPG M107 175mm SPG 122,130mm How 81,120,160mm Mortar 106mm Recoiless Rifles 90mm AT SPG 20,30,40mm AA Gun	300 155,105mm SPG 50 M109 155mm SPG M107 175mm SPG M110 203mm SPG 122,133mm How 81,120,160mm Mortar 106mm Recoiless Rifles 90mm AT SPG 20,30,40mm AA GUN	300 155,105mm SPG 50 M109 155mm SPG M107 175mm SPG M110 203mm SPG L-33 155mm SPG 81mm Mortar 900` 120,160mm Mortar 240mm RL 106mm Recoiless Rifles 50 90mm AT SPG 300 20,30,40mm AA Gun
Missiles	SS10, SS11, Cobra ATGW HAWK SAM MATRA R-530, Side- winder AAM Nord AS-30 ASM	SS10, SS11, Cobra ATGW HAWK SAM MATRA R-530, Side- winder, AIM-4D AAM Nord AS-30 ASM Gabriel SSM	SS10, SS11, Cobra ATGW HAWK SAM MATRA R-530, Side- winder, AIM-4D AAM Nord AS-30, Walleye, Shrike ASM Gabriel SSM MD-660 SSM Northrop MOM-74, Ryan BOM-34 Pilotless Drone	SS10, SS11, Cobra ATGW HAWK SAM MATRA R-530, Side- winder, AIM-4D, Shafrir AAM Nord AS-30, Walleye, Shrike ASM Gabriel SSM MD-660 SSM Northrop MOM-74, Ryan BOM-34 Pilotless Drone	SS10, SS11, Cobra ATGW HAWK SAM MATRA R-530, Side- winder, AIM-4D, Shafrir AAM Nord AS-30, Walleye, Shrike ASM Gabriel SSM MD-660 SSM Northrop MOM-74, Ryan BOM-34 Pilotless Drone	SS10, SS11, Cobra HAWK SAM MATRA R-530, Side- winder, AIM-4D, Shafrir AAM Nord AS-30, Walleye, Shrike ASM Gabriel SSM MD-660 SSM Northrop MOM-74, Ryan BOM-34 Pilotless Drone

TABLE 4
Egyptian, Syrian, and Israeli Air Forces, 1968-73

	1968	1969	1970	1971	1972	1973
Egypt	105 Mig 21 20 Mig 19 60 Mig 17 45 Su-7 30 Il-28 10 Tu-16 60 Transports 50 Helicopters	120 Mig 21 20 Mig 19 120 Mig 17 90 Su-7 30 Il-28 12 Tu-16 60 Transports 60 Helicopters	150 Mig 21 165 Mig 17 105 Su-7 30 Il-28 15 Tu-16 60 Transports 70 Helicopters*	200 Mig 21 210 Mig 17 110 Su-7 25 Il-28 20 Tu-16 75 Transports 150 Helicopters+	220 Mig 21 200 Mig 17 120 Su-7 10 Il-28 20 Tu-16 75 Transports 180 Helicopters	220 Mig 21 200 Mig 17 130 Su-7 25 Il-28 20 Tu-16 75 Transports 190 Helicopters
Syria	60 Mig 21 30 Mig 17 20 Su-7 20 Transports 15 Helicopters	60 Mig 21 50 Mig 17 20 Su-7 20 Transports 15 Helicopters	90 Mig 21 80 Mig 17 40 Su-7 25 Transports 20 Helicopters	100 Mig 21 80 Mig 17 45 Su-7 30 Transports 35 Helicopters	100 Mig 21 100 Mig 17 45 Su-7 35 Transports 40 Helicopters	120 Mig 21 100 Mig 17 50 Su-7 35 Transports 50 Helicopters
Israel	70 Mirage 3 20 Super Mystere 35 Mystere 35 Ouragan 10 Vautour 2N 17 Vautour 2A 48 A-4 Skyhawk 35 Transports 40 Helicopters	16 F-4 Phantom 70 Mirage 3 20 Super Mystere 35 Mystere 30 Ouragan 10 Vautour 2N 17 Vautour 2A 70 A-4 Skyhawk 50 Transports 60 Helicopters	76 F-4 Phantom 65 Mirage 3 15 Super Mystere 30 Mystere 30 Ouragan 10 Vautour 2N 15 Vautour 2A 90 A-4 Skyhawk 60 Transports 70 Helicopters	110 F-4 Phantom 65 Mirage 3 15 Super Mystere 30 Mystere 30 Ouragan 10 Vautour 2N 15 Vautour 2A 120 A-4 Skyhawk 60 Transports 80 Helicopters	120 F-4 Phantom 65 Mirage 3 15 Super Mystere 25 Mystere 25 Ouragan 10 Vautour 2N 15 Vautour 2A 130 A-4 Skyhawk 65 Transports 85 Helicopters	150 F-4 Phantom 24 Barak 60 Mirage 3 15 Super Mystere 25 Mystere 25 Ouragan 10 Vautour 2N 15 Vautour 2A 225 A-4 Skyhawk 70 Transports 85 Helicopters

*Plus 100 Soviet-manned Mig 21s.
+Plus 150 Soviet-manned Mig 21s.

TABLE 5
Egyptian, Syrian, and Israeli Navies, 1968-73

	1968	1969	1970	1971	1972	1973
Egypt	6 Destroyers 8 Minesweepers 12 Submarines 18 Missile Boats 4 Escorts 2 Corvettes 40 Light Craft 20 Landing Craft	6 Destroyers 8 Minesweepers 12 Submarines 20 Missile Boats 3 Escorts 2 Corvettes 50 Light Craft 20 Landing Craft	5 Destroyers 8 Minesweepers 12 Submarines 20 Missile Boats 2 Escorts 2 Corvettes 50 Light Craft 20 Landing Craft	5 Destroyers 12 Minesweepers 12 Submarines 20 Missile Boats 2 Escorts 2 Corvettes 50 Light Craft 20 Landing Craft	5 Destroyers 12 Minesweepers 12 Submarines 20 Missile Boats 2 Escorts 2 Corvettes 50 Light Craft 20 Landing Craft	5 Destroyers 12 Minesweepers 12 Submarines 20 Missile Boats 2 Escorts 2 Corvettes 50 Light Craft 20 Landing Craft
Syria	2 Minesweepers 6 Missile Boats 20 Light Craft	2 Minesweepers 6 Missile Boats 20 Light Craft	2 Minesweepers 8 Missile Boats 20 Light Craft	2 Minesweepers 8 Missile Boats 20 Light Craft	2 Minesweepers 8 Missile Boats 20 Light Craft	3 Minesweepers 8 Missile Boats 30 Light Craft
Israel	1 Destroyer 1 Frigate 3 Submarines 15 Light Craft 5 Landing Craft	1 Destroyer 1 Frigate 4 Submarines 7 Missile Boats 15 Light Craft 5 Landing Craft	1 Destroyer 1 Frigate 4 Submarines 12 Missile Boats 15 Light Craft 7 Landing Craft	1 Destroyer* 4 Submarines 12 Missile Boats 20 Light Craft 10 Landing Craft	1 Destroyer* 4 Submarines 12 Missile Boats 20 Light Craft 10 Landing Craft	1 Destroyer* 3 Submarines 13 Missile Boats 30 Light Craft 10 Landing Craft

Source: The Military Balance, 1968-1973, with author's own modifications.
* Used for training.

TABLE 6
Jordanian and Iraqi Armed Strength, 1968-73

	1968	1969	1970	1971	1972	1973
JORDAN						
Air Force	12 Hunter 4 F-86 6 F-104 8 Transports 4 Helicopters	15 Hunter 4 F-86 12 F-104 8 Transports 8 Helicopters	20 Hunter 4 F-86 18 F-104 12 Transports 10 Helicopters	30 Hunter 18 F-104 12 Transports 10 Helicopters	35 Hunter 18 F-104 15 Transports 10 Helicopters	35 Hunter 20 F-104 4 F-5 15 Transports 10 Helicopters
Army	50,000 Men: 110 M47/48 105 Centurion 150 Saladin, Ferret(APC) 200 M113, Saracen(APC) 30 105,155mm How 25 Pdr Gun	50,000 men: 160 M47/48 140 Centurion 150 Saladin, Ferret(APC) 200 M113, Saracen(APC) 30 105,155mm How 25 Pdr Gun	60,000 men: 160 M47/48 150 Centurion 250 Saladin, Ferret(APC) 300 M113, Saracen(APC) 30 105,155mm How 25 Pdr Gun Tigercat SAM	60,000 men: 160 M47/48 150 Centurion 300 Saladin, Ferret(APC) 350 M113, Saracen(APC) 30 105,155mm How, 203mm How 25 Pdr Gun Tigercat SAM	65,000 men: 200 M47/48 15 M60 150 Centurion 300 Saladin, Ferret(APC) 400 M113, Saracen(APC) 50 105,155mm How, 203mm How 25 Pdr Gun Tigercat SAM	70,000 men: 200 M47/48 30 M60 200 Centurion 300 Saladin, Ferret(APC) 400 M113, Saracen(APC) 50 105,155mm How, 203mm How 110 25 Pdr Gun Tigercat SAM
IRAQ						
Air Force	60 Mig 21 45 Mig 17, 19 20 Su-7 40 Hunter 8 Tu-16 40 Transports 20 Helicopters	60 Mig 21 45 Mig 17, 19 40 Su-7 35 Hunter 8 Tu-16 45 Transports 30 Helicopters	60 Mig 21 50 Mig 17, 19 50 Su-7 35 Hunter 10 Il-28 8 Tu-16 50 Transports 40 Helicopters	60 Mig 21 50 Mig 17, 19 50 Su-7 30 Hunter 10 IL-28 8 Tu-16 70 Transports 55 Helicopters	60 Mig 21 20 Mig 17 50 Su-7 30 Hunter 10 IL-28 8 Tu-16 70 Transports 55 Helicopters	90 Mig 21 30 Mig 17 60 Su-7 30 Hunter 10 IL-28 8 Tu-16 12 Tu-22 70 Transports 60 Helicopters
Army	70:000 men: 300 T54/55 180 T34 55 Centurion 40 Chafee AML/60, Ferret (APC) 122, 130mm How	75,000 men: 350 T54/55 140 T34 55 Centurion 40 Chafee AML/60, Ferret (APC) 122,130mm How	85,000 men: 450 T54/55 140 T34 55 Centurion 40 Chafee 70 AML/60,Ferret (APC) BTR 40, 152(APC) 122,130,152mm How	85,000 men: 800 T54/55 60 T34 55 Centurion 40 Chafee 70 AML/60,Ferret (APC) BTR 40, 152(APC) 300 122,130,152mm How	90,000 men: 900 T54/55 40 T34 50 Centurion 40 Chafee 45 PT-76 110 AML/60,Ferret (APC) BTR 40, 152(APC) 400 122,130,152mm How 30 SAM2	90,000 men: 900 T54/55 40 T34 50 Centurion 30 Chafee 45 PT-76 110 AML/60,Ferret (APC) 1300 BTR 40,50,152, OT-64(APC) 700 85,100,122,130, 152mm Gun 37,57,85mm AA Gun 60 SAM2,3

TABLE 7
Armed Strength of Selected Arab Countries in 1973

Country	Army	Air Force	Navy
Algeria	55,000 men: 300 T54/55, 100 T34, 50 AMX-13, 85 SU-100 15 JSU-152 SPG 122,152mm How 240mm RL 57,85,100mm AA Gun	35 Mig 21 70 Mig 17 20 Su-7 30 IL-28 15 Transports 50 Helicopters	9 Missile Boats 3 Minesweepers 18 Light Craft
Libya	20,000 men: 200 T54/55, 30 Centurion, T34 40 Saladin, 200 M113(APC) Ferret, BTR 40,50,152 Saracen(APC) 175 105,122,155mm How 300 Vigilant ATGW	35 Mirage 3 17 Transports 30 Helicopters	1 Frigate 1 Corvette 3 Missile Boats 10 Light Craft
Saudi Arabia	36,000 men: 85 M41,M47, 30 AMX-30, 200 AML 60/90(APC) HAWK SAM Thunderbird SAM Vigilant ATGW	35 Lightning 15 Hunter 15 F-86 12 Transports 30 Helicopters	8 Hovercraft
Kuwait	8,000 men: 100 Vickers, Centurion 250 Saladin, Saracen, Ferret(APC) 20 155mm How 10 25 Pdr Gun Vigilant ATGW	12 Lightning 8 Hunter 5 Transports 5 Helicopters	Light Craft
Lebanon	15,000 men: 60 Charioteer, 40 AMX-13, 40 M41,M42 AML 60/90, Panhard, M113, M59(APC) 122,155mm How 106mm Recoiless Rifle Entac ATGW	5 Hunter 5 Mirage 2 Transports 10 Helicopters	Light Craft

TABLE 8
Middle East Sources of Major Weapons
(In $ U.S. Millions at Constant 1968 Prices)

| Country | 1965 - 1969 | | 1950 - 1969 | |
	Average Amount (annually)	Average % (annually)	Total	% of Total
United States	139	31.2	1010	23.5
Britain	57	12.8	535	12.4
France	20	4.5	498	11.6
U.S.S.R.	213	47.9	1971	45.8
Other	16	3.6	290	6.7
TOTAL	445	100.0	4304	100.0

Source: The Arms Trade with the Third World, S.I.P.R.1, Stockholm, 1971.

TABLE 9
U.S. Arms Sold or Given to Middle Eastern Countries, 1967-72
(In $ U.S. Millions)

Country	Amount	% Cash
Egypt	-	-
Libya	35.3	84
Jordan	214.1	48
Lebanon	1.4	-
Syria	-	-
Iraq	0.5*	80
Saudi Arabia	519.0	74
TOTAL ARAB STATES	770.3	67
Israel	1581.6	37
Iran	1762.2	70

Source: Armed Forces Journal, October 1973.
*1967-68.

TABLE 10
GNP of Selected Middle Eastern Nations, 1967-72
(In $ U.S. Billions)

Country	1967	1968	1969	1970	1971	1972
Iraq	2.20	2.25	2.80	3.12	3.66	3.50
Israel	3.60	3.90	4.50	5.40	6.20	6.85
Jordan	0.50	0.50	0.70	0.64	0.81	0.68
Syria	1.05	1.09	1.35	1.46	1.80	1.93
Egypt	5.10	5.50	6.30	6.43	6.91	7.50

Source: The Military Balance 1968-1974.

TABLE 11
Per Cent of GNP Spent on Defence, 1967-72

Country	1967	1968	1969	1970	1971	1972
United States	9.5	9.3	8.4	7.4	7.5	7.2
U.S.S.R.	9.0	11.1	8.4	7.9	7.6	7.5
France	5.0	4.8	3.5	3.3	3.2	3.1
Sweden	3.9	3.9	3.8	3.4	3.4	3.6
Algeria	3.9	4.7	4.4	4.0	2.3	2.0
Egypt	12.7	12.5	13.2	18.9	21.4	20.2
Iran	4.9	5.6	5.4	7.4	8.0	6.2
Iraq	9.1	9.1	10.4	8.3	9.4	8.8
Israel	11.5	15.4	18.0	19.9	22.3	18.2
Jordan	11.1	14.7	19.4	18.6	13.6	17.4
Libya	1.5	1.6	1.5	2.1	2.3	2.6
Saudi Arabia	11.9	8.9	8.8	9.4	8.9	*
Syria	10.7	12.1	12.3	10.4	9.8	11.5

Source: The Military Balance 1968-1974.
*Not available.

TABLE 12
Defence Expenditure Per Capita, 1967-72
(In $ U.S. Dollars)

Country	1967	1968	1969	1970	1971	1972
United States	368	396	393	373	378	399
U.S.S.R.	147	169	164	222	*	132
France	106	121	123	118	101	121
Sweden	125	125	128	143	145	184
Israel	124	224	400	483	470	404
Iraq	27	30	32	30	24	31
Jordan	53	39	59	47	37	49
Saudi Arabia	71	64	54	53	53	*
Syria	22	25	33	29	27	38
Egypt	21	22	25	38	43	43
Algeria	*	*	13	13	7	15
Iran	*	*	21	27	34	30
Libya	*	*	25	43	40	59

Source: The Military Balance 1968-1974.
*Not available.

TABLE 13
Per Capita GNP, 1967 and 1973
(In $ U.S. Dollars)

Country	1967	1973
Egypt	160	210
Syria	180	290
Jordan	280	280
Iraq	260	350
Israel	1280	2200

Source: The Military Balance 1968-1974.

TABLE 14
Population of Selected Middle Eastern Countries,
1967 and 1973
(In Millions)

Country	1967	1973
Egypt	31.50	35.70
Syria	5.60	6.70
Jordan	2.10	2.56
Iraq	8.50	10.10
Israel	2.80*	3.10*

Source: The Military Balance 1968-1974.
*Jewish population only.

TABLE 15
Number of Scientific Authors
(First Authors Only)

Country	1967	1971
Egypt	293	443
Lebanon	58	89
Total Arab World*	465	750
Israel	1125	1739

Source: A. Zahlan, "The Science and Technology Gap in the Arab-Israeli Conflict," Journal of Palestine Studies, Spring 1972.
*Above mentioned Arab countries plus Algeria, Kuwait, Libya, Iraq, Jordan, Morocco, Syria, Saudi Arabia, Tunisia, Sudan, and Yemen.

TABLE 16
Crude Oil Revenues for Major Arab Oil Producers, 1960-80
(In $ U.S. Millions)

Country	1960	1965	1970	1974	1980+
Abu-Dhabi	-	30.0	240.7	7,040*	11,600-18,400*
Saudi Arabia	333.7	662.6	1,210.0	23,240	38,500-57,900
Kuwait	444.8	605.1	833.6	8,280	10,700-13,900
Iraq	239.6	331.1	538.3	5,500	9,100-13,700
Algeria	-	-	325.0	3,700	#
Libya	-	351.1	1,351.0	7,900	#

Source: The Significance of Arab Oil, Arab Information Center, New York, and other private sources.
*1974 and 1980 figures for United Arab Emirates.
+Maximum and minimum figures for 1980 given on the basis of a four per cent per annum increase in price with dollar price as of December 1973. Fluctuation in projected revenue based on different possible growth rates of output.
#Not available.

TABLE 17
Unit Cost of Weapons System, 1973-74
(In $ U.S. Millions)

Weapons System	Country	Unit Cost	Description
F-14	United States	25.80	Advanced interceptor aircraft
Mirage F.1.	France	4-5.00	Advanced interceptor aircraft
Jaguar	Britain-France	3-4.80	Advanced attack aircraft
F-4E (Phantom)	United States	4.10	Fighter-bomber
Mirage III	France	2.5-2.80	Fighter-bomber
Mig 21	U.S.S.R.	1-1.50	Interceptor
Centurion	Britain	0.20	Main battle tank
M60	United States	0.35	Main battle tank
Chieftan	Britain	0.45	Main battle tank
122mm Howitzer	U.S.S.R.	0.14	Heavy artillery

Source: D.M.S. Market Intelligence Reports, The Military Balance, 1973-1974, and other sources.

A Glossary of Terms used in Tables 1–3 and 6–7

AA: Anti-Aircraft.
AAM: Air-to-Air Missile.
AC: Armored Car.
APC: Armored Personnel Carrier.
Arm: Armored.
ASM: Air-to-Surface Missile.
ATGW: Anti-Tank Guided Weapon.
Batt: Battalion.
Brig: Brigade.
Comm: Commando.
HT: Half-Tracked vehicle.
How: Howitzer.
Inf: Infantry.
Para: Paratroop.
RL: Rocket Launcher.
Reg: Regiment.
SAM: Surface-to-Air Missile.
SSM: Surface-to-Surface Missile (or Ship-to-Ship Missile).
SPG: Self-Propelled Gun.

Al-Haytham al-Ayoubi

THE STRATEGIES OF THE FOURTH CAMPAIGN*

ORIGINS OF THE STRATEGIES

ISRAEL EMERGED FROM THE 1967 WAR as a stunning military conqueror, organized and disciplined, capable of waging modern war with all of its logistical and technological complexities, and with its demands for planning, coordination, movement, speed, and initiative in making decisions. Israel's greatest achievements in the 1967 war were the destruction of the Arab armed forces, the consecration of the myth of its superior and unbeatable army, and the takeover of large areas of Arab land outside the Green line. The military occupation of new Arab land gave Israel a wide-ranging political freedom of action and put it in a position to benefit from a new geographic-strategic depth in any future confrontation with the neighboring Arab countries.

Immediately after the cease-fire and after the end of the war of attrition at Suez, Israel could have used its new advantages to bargain over the hostage Arab population and occupied lands for political gains. The Israeli leadership, however, saw the situation in a completely different light. The 1967 victory became an historic opportunity to realize the Zionist dream of expansion. Accordingly, Israel's new political line advocated the necessity of keeping the occupied territories; simultaneously she called for peace in such a provocative manner so as to guarantee Arab rejection of the negotiation route to peace. This secured Israeli expansion while providing the Israeli position with sympathy from world public opinion. In contrast to the Israeli

*Translated from Arabic by Edmund Ghareeb.

attitude the Arabs were shown as possessed of an uncompromising position and in opposition to any peace initiatives.[1]

The Israelis based their new concept on the following assumptions:

1. The two great powers prefer to see tranquillity and stability in the sensitive Middle East. The Soviet Union seeks to keep any confrontation between the little partners from leading to one between the two great powers. Peace and stability can be only guaranteed by continued United States military presence in the area; that presence serves to protect the American vital interest (oil). Western Europe seeks stability to insure a continued flow of oil to continental ports.[2]

2. The United States believes that a "strong Israel" is the ideal means for achieving stability in this unstable region. Israel will either contain the neighboring Arab countries and deter them from war, or quickly defeat them if the Arabs attack. A preemptive attack would be necessary if internal pressures reach an unacceptable level; Israel would also mobilize her forces if the level of her deterrent force capability fell to such a degree as to encourage Arab leaders to attack. Zionist forces in the United States have the strength to pressure the United States government to supply Israeli military and economic needs; and the Zionists in the United States can insure that America will support Israel in her refusal to comply with United Nations resolution 242 (which was backed by the United States.)

3. The United States knows that it needs a "strong Israel" to prevent the spread of Soviet influence in the region.[3] It also knows that the Israelis are its partners in the Middle East and that Israel needs the

1. In criticizing the new Israeli line, R. Yonkin described the viewpoint of Israeli policy which became salient after the war: "It is not political development that will preserve our positions, but the opposite. It is the position in the region as it emerged after the Six Day War, and as we made it ourselves—that will determine the new political development" (*Al Hamishmar*, November 2, 1973).

2. Schweitzer, the political columnist for the Israeli paper *Ha'aretz*, pointed to this issue before the October war when he said that: "Israel as a big regional power . . . is one of the major guarantees for stability, and it is the first condition for insuring the continued supply of oil" (*Ha'aretz*, August 24, 1973).

3. In 1971, Menachem Begin, the leader of the rightist Likud bloc, declared: "The Israeli people have helped to save American lives. The closing of the Suez Canal has meant and continues to mean that less Soviet ammunition and weapons reach the enemies of the United States in Southeast Asia, and consequently has saved American lives in Vietnam. The Americans must know what we have done for them. The weapons that were given to us were not because of our (beautiful) eyes, but because of the common interests between a small nation and a large nation" (*Ma'ariv*, March 18, 1971).

United States as much as the United States needs Israel.[4]

4. Egypt, like the other Arab nations, faces internal difficulties and regional conflicts and is trapped in the contradiction between liberationist aspirations and limited material resources. The Israeli military gave her a powerful inferiority complex as a result of the 1967 war. Egypt did not recognize the status quo but did not, at the same time, have the instruments to change it. It was risky moreover to talk of war without being able to wage it. And it was especially difficult to prepare for war after the ouster of Soviet technicians and the tension in Soviet and Egyptian relations in 1972; that allowed the Israelis a political justification for maintaining the status quo.

5. The Palestinian revolution had witnessed wide expansion in 1969 and 1970 but clashed with regional strategies of the Arab confrontation states (Egypt, Syria, and Jordan.) Still, the Palestinians called for continuation of the armed struggle until "the liberation of all the homeland" or the creation of a democratic Palestinian state.[5] In contrast, the confrontation states saw it in their interest to accept the peace proposals and initiatives either publicly or privately—so long as these initiatives guaranteed a return of the territory which had been occupied in 1967 without adventuring into a war with unknown consequences. Furthermore, the forces of the Palestinian revolution had continued to decline in morale and materiel since the end of the fighting on the Suez Canal (August, 1970). This decline was hastened by the elimination of the revolution's material and political bases in Jordan by the Hashemite authority, in the campaigns of September, 1970 and July, 1971. The forces were weakened still further as Israel erected barriers on the Jordanian and Lebanese borders.[6] All this was to isolate the secret cells of the revolution

4. And in 1972 Yitzhak Rabin, then Israeli ambassador to Washington, discussed his country's opposing the Soviet Union when he said, "Israel and what it symbolizes in its way of life appear, in American eyes, to be standing in the face of the Soviet Union and communism" (*Ma'ariv*, January 14, 1972).

5. The goals of the revolution moved between these two slogans in accord with the different positions of the Palestinian revolution and its strategic concept.

6. Along the Israeli-Jordanian and Israeli-Lebanese borders Israel has built a line of barriers (barbed wire, electric lines, mines, observation posts, patrols, etc.) similar to the Maurice line built by France on the Algerian-Tunisian border and the McNamara Line which the Americans tried to build along the 17th parallel between North and South Vietnam, in order to prevent the fighting and support patrols which originate in the revolution's bases in Arab countries from infiltrating into the occupied territories.

inside the country. The Palestinian revolutionary forces were struck a heavy blow in the Gaza Strip in 1971 and 1972; the Israeli border guards used extremely cruel oppressive measures against the people of the Strip.[7]

6. Israel believed that she could absorb the people of the occupied territories, root out nationalist tendencies, and weaken the state of animosity by making the conquered people give up hope in the Arab governments. Israel's strategy was to improve Arab economic conditions and lead them to a consumer society—the Arabs would be tied to the Israeli economy through "Hebrew Work" and the policy of "open bridges."

7. Israel believed that the Arab mind was extremely hostile to Israel and the Jewish people; the only way to deal with the Arabs was through force. Israel felt that the Arab people were a non-fighting people; Arabs ignored reality, were subjected to illusory images, were divided politically and incapable of agreement. Israel's psychologists and Arab affairs experts exaggerated this view by advocating that Arabs had to be treated in accordance with the following three principles:

a) force must be constantly used;
b) concessions must never be made that encouraged more concessions;
c) it is useless to negotiate with the Arabs except to improve Israel's image before the world.[8]

7. Revolutionary activity increased in the Gaza Strip in 1970 as did its military operations, especially the hurling of grenades at Israeli patrols. This led Israeli journalist Amnon Kapeliouk to call Gaza "the city of grenades" in *Al-Hamishmar*, November 12, 1970. It also led British journalist Robert Graham to compare the situation in this struggling city with conditions resembling those in a city "under siege" (*Financial Times*, March 3, 1971). The Israeli government, in order to arrest the deteriorating situation in the Strip, voted on January 3, 1971 to follow tough security measures and ordered into Gaza a unit of Israel's border guards better known as the "Green Berets." The deployment of this unit was made necessary by the disciplinary situation of the Israeli armed forces which refused to fire on civilians. In an angry debate at the Knesset (January 20, 1971 session) Meir Felner, a member of the Rakah bloc, condemned the methods used by the border guards to preserve order, saying "They have brought the Border Guards into the Strip to do the things that the Army refused to do" (*Ma'ariv*, January 21, 1971). Uri Avineri, a member of the Knesset, discussed the same matter when he said, "What the soldiers of Israel's defence forces refuse to execute they send the border guards to do" (*Ma'ariv*, January 21, 1971).

8. Aharon Jiveh criticized all of these views and proved their uselessness when he said, "It appears to me that the era of the experts on Arab psychology, who influenced us with their views and analyses before the war, in all their varieties, has ended. They had better find themselves another source of income. . . . There was no better

8. The Arab oil states were incapable of using the oil weapon against Israel, nor could they put pressure on states supporting Israel; the oil states would be the first losers of an oil boycott.[9]

Based on these eight assumptions Israel's policymakers decided to preserve the situation of "no peace–no war" which existed in the region under the umbrella of Israeli deterrence and America's total support of Israel. In this way Israel would create new facts which the world would be accustomed to and the Arabs would accept as a *fait accompli*. That de facto position would eventually become a de jure position. This would realize some of Zionism's dreams to create the map of a new Israel.[10]

Israeli Conceptual Errors

When Israel's friends directed her attention to the dangerous situation in the region, the Israelis would shrug their shoulders, answering "The Arabs know our address," or, "There is nothing that can burn in this region except the oil wells on the west bank of the Gulf of Suez." Thus the Israelis lost the greatest chance for peace since the beginning of the Arab-Israeli confrontation,[11] because the Israeli security idea emerged from a mistaken political concept.[12] It was

---

demonstration of strength than the Seven Days War—and what was the result? Submission? Sadat has prepared for a new war" (*Davar*, December 10, 1973).

9. In 1972 Hagay Eshed wrote, "The West European states and the Arab states themselves realize that one must not exaggerate the value of using the oil weapon against Israel because Israel is capable of blocking the flow of oil from the Middle East to Europe." In May, 1972, Israel's Foreign Minister Abba Eban declared that "The threats of the Arab nations are unrealistic and ought to be ignored." He went on to add, "The Arab states have made many threats in the past but they have failed to carry them through" (Israel Monotominy Broadcast, May 17, 1973).

10. The logic behind Israel's ideological view was: The Arabs lost some of their lands in the 1948 war, and they refused to accept defeat; then they lost new lands in 1967 and they refused to accept defeat; but in time they will learn to live with it.

11. Ephraim Auerbach, Professor of Jewish Studies at the Hebrew University, criticized the hard line position of the Israeli government which wasted the chance for peace. "Until 1967, at least, we truthfully declared . . . an interest in peace; but our actions and all our initiatives were not consistent with the statements. Therefore the gap widened between the announcements on the one hand and the daily actions on the other. We did not make use of all the possibilities and opportunities" (*Ma'ariv*, November 23, 1973).

12. Professor Jacob Talmon also criticized Israel's policy of escaping peace probabilities in an article titled "Self-Account," (*Ha'aretz*, November 30, 1973), saying Israeli leaders wanted the world to give it a period of time, to leave it alone and allow

to embody the military lines necessary to hold the occupied territories by force while keeping Israeli military action to a minimum and relying instead on deterrence. Israel's security concept drew its significance from the political concept and placed itself in its service. The political concept offered the rationale for the arrangements based on security assumptions which, in turn, were founded on the idea that the Arab armies were incapable of going to war and would be exposed to certain defeat if they initiated such actions.

Israeli leaders, journalists, military and political spokesmen, and the media bureaucracy asserted these two ideas until they became absolute dogmas.[13]

How did the Israelis adopt an erroneous security concept which led to disaster? The first error came with the attempt to modify the security concept and to make it fit a politically erroneous concept. Other errors in psychological military evaluations of the basic facts of the struggle compounded the first error.[14]

Israeli theorists began with the idea that the Arab soldier is a non-fighter who is unable to hold out under heavy fire and strong armored and aerial attacks. They also believed that Arab leaders were unprepared to wage a modern war.[15] Added to this error in evaluation, the Israelis failed to comprehend the powerful psychological factor

---

it to create facts, and to put new facts before the Arabs, the United States, and the world. Whenever the desire to annex increased, Israel had to believe more than once that there was no threat of Arab retaliation. Whenever a truce occurred, the possibility of annexation emerged. Also, settlements and annexation were portrayed as tools to fortify security. This specific concept was a substitute for war and a guarantee against it.

13. Israel Sweitser placed the responsibility for the brainwashing of the Israeli public for years on the Israeli government: "The error of the public stems from the error of the leaders. They are the experts on these issues who have the information and the responsibility and were the source of the error. The others merely followed blindly" (Ma'ariv, October 26, 1973).

14. Professor Jacob Talmon backed this view by saying, "It is possible to say that the assurance of security became part of a dogma and the basis of a political program, and it became in the end a rooted interest. This feeling of security was strengthened by arrogance, by the prophecy of uniting all the homeland, by the theory of absolute superiority of the Israeli army and the eternal backwardness of the Arabs, and by the accepted beliefs about the ideally secure borders which resulted from the war. The feeling of security resulting from all these factors increased our belief in them" (Ha'aretz, November 30, 1973).

15. "One beat on a can is all that is necessary to scare the birds into flight. . . . War is not for them (the Arabs)." Teddy Proyce criticized this erroneous view and wondered how the Israelis forgot that "the Arab, through the past 20 years, was not

brought on by the shame of the 1967 June defeat and the desire
of the Arab to surpass himself. He had to destroy the humiliating
image the world held of him after the war; at the same time the
Arab had not had the chance to fight the war as it ought to have
been fought. The Arabs had to reverse a defeat that they did not
deserve and did not participate in shaping.

From the cultural level, the Israelis depended on the Arabs' long-
standing technical and scientific backwardness. They exaggerated the
scientific and technological gulf which separated Arab societies from
Israeli society.[16] The Israelis thus believed that the Arab armies would
remain weak despite the number and quality of the weapons supplied
by the Soviets, and that there was a gap between the level of the
Arab fighter and the level of the modern fighting machine at his
disposal.

But the Israelis did not understand the reality of how the Egyptian
and Syrian armed forces developed; nor did they understand the
significance of the quantitative and qualitative transformation brought
about with Soviet aid. They imagined that the exit of Soviet experts
from Egypt in July, 1972, had weakened Egypt's fighting force. They
entertained the military concept that secure borders meant the Suez
Canal, the Jordan River, and the Golan Heights. What was most
dangerous was the belief in the ability of a "legendary" Israeli
intelligence system to forewarn Israel of Arab military preparations

---

a bad fighter. . . . He fought in many positions with courage and dedication. But
the advocates of the 'war isn't for them' have covered and distorted that. The best
example of this is the war of attrition where, despite the heavy blows, especially
those of the air force, inflicted on the Egyptian soldier, he showed an unbelievable
capacity to hold out. This characteristic emerged clearly through some of the previous
wars and battles, but these were forgotten because of the arrogant statement and claims
of superiority which were expressed by some of the military leaders and politicians"
(*Davar*, October 25, 1973).

16. Professor Ernest Bergman, chairman of Israel's Committee for Atomic Energy,
estimated that "the gulf in educational levels and in technological achievements between
Israel and Arab states is widening . . . and the Arabs are 100 years behind Israel
in the sciences and technology" (*Davar*, April 11, 1971). In an interview with the
British *Jewish Observer* (October 22, 1971), Bergman declared, "Israel's survival is
based to a great extent on the technological gulf between Israel and its neighbors.
And in order to insure our survival we must not allow this gulf to become narrower."
Professor Yuval Nihman, chairman of the Physics Department at Tel Aviv University,
said on this issue that "Israel enjoys a relative superiority over Egypt of 7 to 1 in
technological fields. This ratio was 4 to 1 in 1967. And if the Israeli development
continues at its present rate, the gulf between the two countries will continue to
widen in the near future" (Jewish Telegraph Agency, April 14, 1971).

for attack. Finally, the Israelis believed that the Sinai, which they intended to keep, sufficiently increased Israel's strategic depth. With the Sinai under Israeli control, Israel's military command could easily mobilize her reserves, throw them quickly into battle, and have a wide margin to maneuver in place.

To put the new security plan into effect, the Israelis constructed a new strategy of setting up fortified positions on the borders which they reached during the 1967 war. There they built military settlements in the occupied areas to create "new facts" to deter the Arabs from waging war. By creating a strong working military force (air force, armor, self-propelled artillery, mechanized and airborne infantry) Israel would achieve non-nuclear deterrence. This strategy permitted the initiation of limited retaliatory operations during the "no-peace–no-war situation." If the circumstances became favorable, the armed forces could deliver deterring blows; or, if circumstances were not propitious and the Arabs attacked, the Israelis could repel the advance until the strategic reserve was mobilized and thrown into battle. This would set the stage for the Israeli "response" operations and carry the battle beyond the borders of the state.

This strategy basically has not changed from the strategy initiated by Ben Gurion since the creation of the state. It was based on putting a quick end to the fighting by using qualitatively superior forces to balance the quantitative Arab superiority, initiating the attack, transferring the battle deep into the enemy's territory, and confronting the enemy separately while avoiding battle on two simultaneous fronts. It differs from Ben Gurion's strategy with some modifications made with the passing of time. Yigal Yadin, for example, made the modification of creating a reserve army to solve the problem of quantitative deficit, where the soldier became a "citizen on leave 11 months a year." Moshe Dayan expanded what he described as the "military operations in peace time," which were not more than "retaliatory operations" used as tools of foreign policy. Yigal Allon added to it the concept of the "preemptive counter-strike" to abort the plans of the enemy, for Arab intentions form a security problem and represent "a motive and rationale for war." In addition, Shimon Peres and Ben Gurion added the concept of "non-nuclear deterrence" to secure stability during the time periods between the total military confrontations. The last modification was made after the 1967 war by adding the "secure borders" concept; these were described by Abba Eban as "borders that can be defended without having to resort to preemptive strikes." [17]

17. *Davar*, January 3, 1974.

Arab Defensive Strategy

If we look at the other side of the trenches, we find that the Arab countries neighboring Israel (with the exception of Lebanon) [18] adopted a purely defensive strategy to counter Israel's interference strategy. Consequently they established permanent and stable fronts composed of a long string of forward posts guarded by mine fields with defensive strong points behind it. The Arab armies surrounding Israel were inevitably forced to live a period of negative defense, with no positive responses except mobilizations lasting a few weeks during the crises. [19] Furthermore, these armies did not retaliate against Israel's revenge operations except by "repelling" or "returning the fire." [20] They did not respond by movement or dashes within the enemy's borders for fear of escalation and involvement in total war.

The roots of the defensive Arab strategy from 1949 to 1973 stemmed from the Arab policy of quieting the borders with their "strong neighbor" until local and international circumstances created hostilities on the borders. This policy was based on the following assumptions:

1. Israel is an existing internationally-recognized state which cannot be interfered with or penetrated so long as the international community will rush to her aid militarily and politically.

2. Imperialism protects Israel as a base-state and a beachhead that secures imperialistic interests. This view was supported by the Tripar-

18. After the 1948 war, Lebanon withdrew from the circle of struggle, adopting a defensive policy based on respecting the 1949 truce agreement and on international guarantees, basically America's, which guaranteed Lebanon's security and borders. Lebanon did not participate in the 1956, 1967, or 1973 wars and was not exposed, prior to the emergence of commando bases in its territory, to any vengeful Israeli operations.

19. A. Deri, Lt. Colonel H. Ayoubi, *Toward a new Arab Strategy*, Dar Al-Yakaza, (2nd ed.; Beirut, 1973), p. 188.

20. Israel initiated retaliatory actions before 1973 under the following situations:
1. After operations by irregular infiltrators into occupied territories.
2. After accidental clashes with border patrols.
3. After Arab border posts prevented Israeli farmers from crossing the borders and taking control of no-man's lands by creating a fait accompli.
4. When Arab forces shelled Israeli forces diverting the waters of the Jordan River.
5. As a means of indirectly deterring the forces of the Palestinian revolution, by forcing the host country to keep the lid on the revolution (this became especially evident after the 1967 war).
6. When the internal situation deteriorated and Israel wanted to divert attention to the border, to keep its citizens occupied with security issues.
7. When the Israeli leadership realized that the level of deterrence had dipped to an unacceptable level and that it was necessary to stage operations to raise public morale and bring deterrence back to its desired level.

tite Declaration (signed by the United States, Britain, and France) of 1950 which guaranteed the borders of Israel and its territorial integrity. The presence of the U.S. Sixth Fleet, the British and American air and naval bases around and within the Arab world, as well as U.S. military bases in Western Europe, serve to embody the material force capable of intervening quickly and effectively to protect Israel.[21]

3. The radical Arab states are incapable of opposing imperialism and its military bases head-on and they cannot rely on active Soviet military support if they attack Israel. Although opposed to Israeli aggression, Moscow cannot, at the same time, support aggression against the Israeli territories that were defined in the Rhodes agreement (1949). Moreover, the training, armament, and sometimes even the leadership of the Arab armed forces are controlled by the imperialistic states which protect Israel.

4. Preserving the status quo and preventing Israel from expanding are the most that Arab nations can achieve within the framework of the international and local balance of power—which imperialism tilts in Israel's favor. The establishment of an Israel "militarily superior" to her neighbors was an easy task in the period 1949-1955 because the European powers were the sole source of arms for the Arab states and Israel. NATO countries had a monopoly over arms in the Middle East; they were able to guarantee Israel's military superiority and control the arms level on both sides. In 1955, Syria and Israel broke the arms monopoly and began to arm themselves with weapons from the Eastern bloc and particularly the Soviet Union. From then on the keys to arming the area were out of the hands of imperialism and NATO countries. To balance the Soviet arms and guarantee Israeli superiority, the western countries redoubled their supply efforts making both the Arab countries and Israel into huge depositories of arms. It also set the technological direction along lines which, as a function of the rising level of arms, were in conflict with the economic potential of the region and its cultural and technical needs.

5. Confronting an advanced industrialized, imperialist base such as Israel cannot be achieved so long as the Arab countries remain divided and technologically undeveloped. Two problems emerged:

21. The Sixth Fleet and the bases of the military belt surrounding the Arab world in Iran, Turkey, Greece, Cyprus, Ethiopia, and the Indian Ocean is part of the belt surrounding the southern flank of the Soviet Union. At the same time, it is also a belt surrounding the Arab world and guarding southern Europe. The forces of NATO both perform their European duties and pose a threat to the Middle East and North Africa, a matter which made the security of NATO and the Arab lands dialectically interconnected.

One blocking development, the other blocking unity. The economic, social, and cultural development of the Arab countries required large amounts of capital for investment. Yet the countries most seriously concerned with the conflict (Egypt, Syria, Jordan, and Iraq) had only a small amount of capital and the biggest part of their budgets went for defense.[22]

The goal of Arab unity made it necessary to struggle against Arab class and national divisions. The old imperialism had tied regionalism to the interests of the ruling classes and regionalism became part of the Arab ruling class and a cause of its prosperity. Inasmuch as the classes which benefited from regionalism were the first obstacle to the struggle for Arab unity, so the first goal of the unification movement was to remove artificial entities and the Balkanization ever present in Arab societies. This effort worked to foil imperialist and Zionist plots which fought unity and institutionalized Arab Balkanization. Thus social and political fragmentation were the major conditions for continued economic exploitation and were factors in Arab military weakness.

These assumptions led to the Arab policy of preserving the status quo. To carry out this policy, a defensive Arab strategy developed but it was a regional mentality and was blind to the relationship between regional and national security. If regional security came before national security, it followed that there was no need to create an active Arab defense system. So in spite of attempts to develop bilateral or multilateral Arab military pacts, Arab alliances turned out to be indecisive military tools.[23]

In addition to regionalism, the reasons for the failure of Arab defense measures were: (1) the policy of axes (the Baghdad axis and the Cairo axis); (2) the failure to conceptualize "the goal of the wager" or awareness of the danger to all Arab countries; (3) the pressure on the Arab countries tied to imperialism; and (4) the fear of the traditional Arab governments of the growing power and influence of the radical Arab states among the masses and the rise of the Nasserist tide after 1956.

Because of the failure to develop a pan-Arab defense system, those

22. Defense expenditures ranged between 10 and 23 per cent of a GNP which was already too low to develop the countries. From this it can be said that the presence of Israel in the Arab area and its expansionist designs not only created an economic threat, but were also a barrier to the countries' development and modernization.

23. Such as the Syrian-Egyptian agreement (1955), the Syrian-Jordanian (1956), the Common Defense Agreement between Egypt and Saudi Arabia (1956), the Unified Arab Command (1964), etc.

Arab nations that surround Israel were forced to bear the whole burden. They were all basically poor but had to strengthen their armies at the expense of economic development.[24] The Arab countries distant from the direct conflict and wealthier than the confrontation countries were able to concentrate more on internal development (Algeria, Tunisia, Morocco) or on investing surplus capital in the imperialist countries themselves. Wealthy oil–producing states, namely, Saudi Arabia, Kuwait, and the sheikhdoms of the Persian Gulf, thus ignored the need to build the required Arab defense force.[25]

So emerged a "war by proxy" with the poor confrontation countries waging the struggle on behalf of the whole Arab nation. The rich Arab countries limited their support mainly to moral and political support and occasional economic aid. Iraq and Lebanon were exceptions to this general Arab response. Iraq strengthened her military forces even though she was distant from the center of conflict and not a confrontation country. Lebanon, by contrast, was entirely passive even though she borders Israel and has lost some inland waterways and land to Israel's expansion plan. In short, the Arab financial capacities were not being used in the fateful struggle. The confrontation countries would not allocate the necessary funds to transform and modernize the Arab armies; nor could they exploit Arab manpower

24. The per-capita incomes of the countries which took care to strengthen their defense forces were: Egypt, $197; Syria, $279; Jordan, $268; Iraq, $345. The incomes in the countries which, in the past, did not concern themselves greatly with strengthening their forces, were: Libya, $2,111; Tunisia, $378; Algeria, $350; Saudi Arabia, $2,119; Kuwait, $3,829; and Lebanon, $624. U.N. Statistical Yearbook, 1972 (New York, 1973).

25. American experts estimated the currency wealth of the Arab oil countries in 1973 at about $500 million and estimated that in 1974 alone it would increase to $40-60 billion; by 1980 it will reach about $750 billion (New York Times, March 12, 1974). Defense expenditures in Egypt were 23.2% of its 1971 GNP; Syria, 11.18% in 1971; Iraq, 9.6% in 1972; Jordan, 17.4% in 1971; Algeria, 1.8% in 1972; Libya, 3.17% in 1973; Morocco, 2.7% in 1972; Saudi Arabia, 21% in 1973; Tunisia, 1.3% in 1972; Lebanon, 3.9% in 1972; and Kuwait, 3.14% in 1971. (Military Balance, 1973-74 [London: Institute for Strategic Studies, 1973]). One notes from these figures that the richer Arab countries spend less on defence. It must also be noted that the expense of the Jordanian forces does not mean that these forces are being strengthened for any confrontations with Israel, despite the fact that Jordan is one of the confrontation countries. Instead, imperialism has assigned a special mission to the Hashemite regime against the radical Arab countries and against the Palestinian revolution. After all, it is impossible to understand how imperialism would arm Jordan to confront Isreal, while it arms Israel to be stronger than all the Arab countries combined. The increase in defense spending by Saudi Arabia, which is not a confrontation country, stems from the growing need to face the Iranian threat from the east.

in actual battle.[26] Economic, social, and cultural development in the confrontation countries, moreover, had declined, and with that fell the level of logistical technology. The most apparent consequence of Arab miserliness was that the Arab soldier lagged behind the Israeli soldier in the ability to use modern weapons imported from the advanced industrial nations.

In a word, the Arab military strategy was "war by proxy." Not only did that strategy create obstacles for the coordination of a unified all-Arab force, but it had two other major deficiencies as well. The first problem was that the Arab countries failed to choose an appropriate strategy. An industrially advanced Israel, using the most modern Western arms, could follow a strategy of annihilation expressed in the traditional blitzkrieg. This suited Israel's limited human resources and large material ones, as well as the narrow geographic depth of her land. The Arabs chose the same strategy without taking into account the technological realities, the Arab balance of national resources, Arab population, and Arab geographic depth. The Arabs could not use the strategy of exhausting the enemy because the petit bourgeois and bourgeois of Arab regimes were incapable of mobilizing the masses or resources. Without a unified massive effort, there could be no protracted war on large territories, no large-scale maneuvers, no heavy attacks, and no organized strategic retreats. The failure to use the entire geographic and human resources at their command deprived the Arabs of a chance to fight a war suited to meet Israel's technical superiority.

The second Arab deficiency stemmed from the failure to comprehend the position of the Arab-Israeli struggle in the larger international competition between the Western and Eastern blocs. The Arabs were unable to put this understanding in a proper perspective even when the international relationship was acknowledged. From its inception the Arab-Israeli conflict was an integral part of the international struggle. Prior to the creation of Israel in 1948, international sympathies were different from the present ones. In 1948 Israel received most of her land and air forces from the Eastern bloc, especially Czechoslovakia.[27] The Eastern bloc, at the time, believed that establishing a modern socialist state in the region would create an advanced revolutionary socialist base in the midst of political and economic

26. Egyptian armed forces consist of 298,000 men in the air force, navy, and army. These forces represent 5 per cent of the men eligible for military duty.

27. J. Lartegmy, *The Walls of Israel* (New York: M. Evans *et al.*, 1969); R. Jackson *The Israeli Air Force Story* (London: Tom Stacey Ltd., 1970).

feudalism. The newly independent Arab states, some still nomadic societies, were tied to the two mandate powers (Britain and France) which wanted to preserve former Western positions and links to the Arab countries.

In the early fifties Israel was tied to imperialism despite her proclaimed "nationalist socialism." And during that decade the Eastern bloc stopped supplying her with arms. The Arab-Israeli struggle was transformed into a struggle between forces of the Eastern and Western blocs. This occurred when the Western monopoly over arms shipments was broken in 1955. Since then Israel and the radical Arab countries (Syria, Egypt, and Iraq)[28] concerned with the struggle have played the role of partisans in the international conflict. The pre-1948 relationship was reversed. A Western–supported Israel came to play the role of the imperialist "policeman" who suppresses Arab unity and protects imperialism's oil interests in the Arab world.[29] On the other side, the Eastern bloc supported the Arab radical countries in opposition to Israel and imperialism.[30] The continued Western military support of the Arab countries opposed to Israel was an exceptional manifestation of this equation and cannot be explained, unless such Arab armies were being prepared to play another role in the internal Arab struggle between the Arab liberation movement and its opponents.

In spite of the simplicity of this strategic equation it contained two flaws which kept it from being a clear and firm basis for the struggle. The first one was the difference in size between Soviet and American interests in the region—a difference which led Washington to be willing to give more support to the third parties than Moscow. Israel, therefore, received unlimited political, economic, and military aid, including direct military intervention. The Arabs received unlimited political and economic aid, as well as large amounts of military aid; but the latter amount was always less than the imperialist military aid to Israel.

The other flaw was that the petit bourgeois regimes in the radical

28. Iraq did not join the radical Arab camp until after the overthrow of the Hashemite monarchy in 1958.

29. Western support to Israel originally came from Britain and France. The Federal Republic of Germany joined the countries supplying arms to Israel after 1956. These three countries backed Israel until the 1967 war when General de Gaulle embargoed French arms to the countries involved in the conflict. After this, Western support resumed again from Britain and the United States with the latter as the leading supplier.

30. Eastern bloc military aid began with Czechoslovakia supplying the radical Arab states. Afterwards the Soviet Union became the main supplier of these states.

Arab states, and the feudal, bourgeois, and clannish regimes in the traditional Arab states, have viewed the Soviet Union with a caution that in some cases bordered on animosity. At best they could only work with the Soviets in half-way measures and with the greatest reluctance. Under the cultural imperialism of the West, conservative Arab leaders wanted to imitate the West even in Western lifestyles.

The rich Arab countries have dealt with imperialism in terms of financial investments and economic influence. But in doing so these Arabs allowed a subtle American counter-strategy: Arab investment in the United States was always partially taxed and so transformed into U.S. economic and military aid to Israel. Notwithstanding her nationalist socialism, Israel has been totally tied to the U.S. economy. Through the Zionist influences in the United States, Israel has attempted to put political and economic pressure upon the U.S.S.R. to force the Soviets to stop aiding the Arabs. The Arab side has shown a consistent animosity to its Soviet ally in public and in private, and, furthermore, the Arabs have long befriended the imperialist bloc which sustains Israel and exploits Arab wealth.

THE ARAB SIDE

Locked in by local and international limitations, the Arab countries were yet able to preserve a defensive strategy until the 1967 war. But the strategic occupation of new Arab territories during that war dramatically changed their position. A new situation emerged. Israel had doubled her size and subjugated an Arab population almost equal to her own.

At the same time the picture of Israel as a weak, beseiged nation in need of world help to save it from a massive enemy (the well-known picture of David and Goliath) was changed to the image of an aggressor state. Clearly Israel's external maneuvers had moved her toward a dead end: She could not convince the world of her desire for peace while she occupied Arab land by force.

By responding positively to all peace initiatives, the Arab states benefited from the strategic and political corner in which Israel put herself. At the same time they rejected the Israeli logic which asked them to negotiate under duress.[31] The Arabs thus won the political

31. Reserve Colonel Meir Bail discussed the reasons for the failure of the Israeli international political maneuver. He said the question required independent research, but it would be a tragic mistake to believe that the political crisis was sent from heaven and by higher forces (*Yediot Aharonot*, November 4, 1973).

contest. Arab success was based on a number of factors:

1. The Arabs were assisted in winning the international diplomatic struggle by the Soviet bloc, particularly Soviet support for Arab demands of total Israeli withdrawal from occupied territory. Soviet support was based on an important ideological principle: the illegitimacy of occupying the territory of others and the right of every people to self-determination; and a practical position: the Eastern bloc could not agree to the occupation of territories in the Middle East, lest this be understood as a sign of weakness and encouragement to the imperialist camp to occupy territories and create facts in other parts of the world.

2. The United States guaranteed the security of Israel, but not her expansion. Total U.S. support for Israel, despite Israeli aggression, would have weakened U.S. influence in the Arab world. U.S. support further strengthened the bond between the radical Arab states and the Soviet Union and increased the Soviet influence in the region. It also led the masses in the more conservative Arab states to urge their governments to take more radical stands—stands which certainly endangered America's national interest.

3. Western Europe rejected Israel's position in spite of guarantees to Israel's security and territorial inviolability. National security interests and the need for vital Arab energy required Europe not to make enemies of the Arabs. In addition, ancient economic and cultural links with the Arab world and geographic proximity made Europe more qualified than the Soviet Union to fill the economic-political vacuum which would result from the Arab move away from a pro-Israel United States.

4. The failure of the mediation efforts of the African leaders, the arrogant behavior of Israeli assistance delegations in some of the African states, newly-independent African anger against white racial imperialism, and the yet fresh and painful memories of European occupation also contributed to the brilliant success of the Arab foreign policy.

The Third World had already supported the Arab position. In addition, Spain and Greece had supported the Arab position, both as a matter of principle and for cultural and economic reasons. The governments of the Islamic countries (particularly Iran, Turkey, and Pakistan) were under pressure from their populations, who were sympathetic to the need to liberate the Holy Lands and free Jerusalem from Israeli domination.

Successful Arab diplomatic efforts secured the first condition required to move from defense to offense—favorable world opinion.

In the present world where international interests are often interlinked, world opinion has a great deal of influence on regional conflicts.[32]

The second condition for taking the offensive was military preparation. The Arab armies had been trained, armed, and fully prepared for a battle of national liberation. They saw that the balance of power in the region could be changed but that success depended on military surprise. It was also necessary for war to be resumed quickly before new American weapons shipments to Israel tipped the balance of power in her favor—such as the Lance missiles, Phantoms, skyhawks, and armed helicopters.

The third condition necessary for the Arab offensive was a state of military relaxation in Israel. This occurred after Sadat's constant threats of war, which never materialized, and because the Israeli leaders believed the Egyptian armed forces (especially the air force and air defense systems) were in a much weaker position after the ouster of the Soviet advisors from Egypt.[33]

The fourth condition was that Arab diplomatic measures had only led to Israeli obstinacy. Furthermore, there was growing internal pressure in the Arab countries to find an end to the "no-war–no-peace" situation. The Arabs benefited from this state of international detente. The Israelis mistakenly saw this as a factor contributing to the "no war–no-peace" situation. In Israel's view the Arabs were indecisive and unsure about starting a war for two reasons. First, the Soviet Union might not support the Arabs; and, second, an Arab offensive might jeopardize improving relations with the United States.

The Arabs hid neither their desire to liberate the occupied territories, nor their preparation for hostilities. After the 1967 war President Nasser of Egypt announced Arab policy as the reversal of Israeli gains by military force. But this policy did not necessarily prevent the Arab states from using all other means to achieve the same goal. Coordination between military and political means during and after the war were complete after President Sadat's speech on October 16 in which he announced his willingness to stop fighting and resume negotiations to secure withdrawal. That coordination was an excellent Arab military-political operation; for Nasser's policy goals were then united

32. *Le Monde*, October 10, 1973.

33. *Ma'ariv*, October 26, 1973. The Israelis considered the ouster of Soviet advisors a strategic victory for them and a guarantee of the no-war-no-peace situation, for it lessened the growing Soviet influence in the area. The number of Soviet advisors was only 17,000. This figure is taken from the statements of President Sadat after the war.

with the restoration of Palestinian interests. The Arabs thus demonstrated a clear grasp of the Clausewitzian dictum that "war is an extension of politics by other means." In this respect they successfully emulated the Israelis in 1967.

While the success of the international efforts made it possible to move from the defense to the offense, it defined the size, nature, and degree of violence of the offensive military action at the same time. This action was limited to the territories occupied in the 1967 war, and remained within the framework of activity against military targets, without taking the form of a total victory as defined by Ludendorf. Because of this limit the Arabs had to carry out military operations under the following conditions:

1. Armored and mechanized Egyptian forces failed to move deep into the Sinai for fear that the United States might interpret such action as moving close to Israel's international borders. This interpretation might then become a rationale for direct United States intervention. Beachheads were established on the first day by forces crossing onto the east bank of the Canal (which were expanded by the second line forces to between 10 and 16 miles along the axis of the passes—those of Rummana, al-Khabiyya, Giddi, and Mitla). But stopping there meant that the Arabs lost the chance to reach the passes during the first days of the war when the Israeli forces, especially the air force, were busy giving cover to the mobilization and calling up the reserve army in the fighting on the Syrian front.[34]

Had the Egyptians occupied the passes they would have gained the benefit of strong defensive positions and a narrow front (concentration of forces). They could have taken the tanks, equipment, artillery, and ammunition the operational Israel Reserve Brigades had stored near these passes. This would have deprived Israel of the chance to fully prepare her reserves before throwing them into battle. The Egyptians also would have gained for themselves a new springboard for a future attack to the east, if opportunity had permitted such an attack. It would also have given better cover to the Egyptian Strategic

---

34. There is a mistaken belief that the Egyptians delayed because they were afraid to move away from the network of ground-to-air missiles on the west bank of the Canal, and because they applied Soviet military tactics. The Soviet tactics, however, assert the opposite policy: the need to move quickly and in depth into many formations and to take advantage of victory whenever the real balance of power allows it. Similarly, the presence of surface-to-air missiles carried on half-tracks would have allowed armored cars and mechanized units to advance under the cover of these missiles, which could move at the same speed as the fighting forces. Consequently we conclude that the main reason for the Egyptian slowdown on the east bank was political.

Armored Reserve Forces crossing the Suez Canal, and would have made penetration of the Deversoir very difficult for the Israelis.

The Egyptians violated two basic principles: they failed to concentrate forces and to take advantage of initial victory. They also violated the concept of coordinating one's attack on two fronts; this is a basic condition for the success of a maneuver on external lines against a centralized enemy. By the time they sought to counteract this mistake by pushing forces east to relieve pressure on the Syrian front and by moving the Armored Strategic Reserve across the Canal to support the beachheads moving to the passes, it was too late. The Israeli operational and strategic reserves were in position. The forces of General Sharon across the West Bank were ready to do their task. The movement of the Egyptian strategic reserve ought to have supported the offensive and relieved pressure on the Syrian front; instead, Egyptian actions deprived the West Bank of armored forces and made it easier for the Israelis to penetrate the Deversoir.

2. The Arabs failed to strike deep into enemy territory despite the Israeli's in-depth attacks on civilian targets in Syria and Egypt. Egypt had conventional ground-to-ground missiles (SCUDS) and a superior navy that would have permitted such offensive tactics. This behavior was a clear violation of the nature of war, which, to quote Clausewitz, is "violence pushed to its maximum limit." One cannot say that this limitation rose out of an implicit agreement between the two fighting sides to limit action and not to follow the dangerous road of escalation—a likely matter in any war—because the Israelis did not refrain from escalating the fighting at every opportunity. The Arabs limited themselves to targets outside the recognized borders of Israel, in order not to provoke the United States, which guaranteed the security of Israel. It was sufficient to strike at Israeli armed forces on Egyptian territory, since the Israeli presence there is an embodiment of aggression that Washington may keep silent about but is not in any position to defend.

3. The Egyptians failed to apply the principles of indirect approach as defined by Liddel Hart. Without naval or air diversionary landings on the Israeli beaches, the strangling strategy employed by two Egyptian destroyers (in cooperation with South and North Yemeni forces at Bab-al-Mandab) was incomplete and limited. This prevented the Egyptian navy and air force from blockading Mediterranean harbors to keep Israeli ships from unloading strategic materials and arms. Undoubtedly, an Arab strategic strangling in the southern area of the Red Sea would have been more effective than a naval blockade in the eastern Mediterranean. It would have denied Israel oil supplies

84 / CONFLICTING SOCIETIES

from Iran, fuel being vital to modern mechanized warfare. Egyptian commandos might have attempted to blow up the oil wells on the eastern side of the Gulf of Suez, since that is where Israel gets 70 per cent of her oil. Blockading the eastern Mediterranean, on the other hand, did not deny Israel important strategic materials since much of these materials were carried on foreign ships, particularly American ships.[35]

The Arabs entered the war for limited political purposes. Consequently the war was a limited one for them, and a strategy of direct attack was applied within locally and internationally defined limits of action.

THE ISRAELI SIDE

The war surprised Israel because her leadership held a one-dimensional understanding of the Clausewitzian concepts that: (1) the destruction of any nation's armed forces deprives it of its shield of defense and forces it to submit to the will of an opponent; and (2) holding the territory and population of any nation gives its opponent a mortal blow and forces concessions. We do not deny that these Clausewitzian ideas were correct in the second half of the 19th century and remained an excellent guide into the first part of the 20th century. However there are two important new factors which the Israeli leadership did not take into consideration:

1. Two major socialist powers emerged in the second half of this century: Soviet Union and China. Since World War II, the industrial, military, and political capabilities of the socialist camp have vastly increased. Thus national liberation movements and countries in contradiction to imperialism, regardless of the degree and sharpness of contradiction, have resources which deprive the Clausewitzian theory of its former validity. Imperialism will use any means available to it in defense of its interests. But such desperation permits the national liberation forces more rational and controlled response. As the recent history of liberation struggles in Korea (1950), Vietnam (1960, 1968, and 1975) and Israel (1973) have shown, desperate measures too often miss their aim. With the socialist powers behind them, modern liberation forces can sustain initial losses to an extraordinary degree and quickly recover.

35. The attempts of Soviet ships to penetrate the American blockade at Haiphong, the British blockade of Ireland, and the inability of the Egyptian navy to block foreign ships in the 1973 war show that a sea blockade cannot achieve its aims in limited wars where the superpowers support warring third factions.

2. In the past, occupation of territories, important cities, or vital areas signified an opponent's defeat. But in the 20th century, war is no longer a struggle between two armed forces; it is a struggle between peoples moved by strong ideological currents and rooted beliefs. These conflicts do not end when a number of villages, cities, or territories are occupied. Fighting does not stop unless the will of the opponent is shattered or bled to death, or unless intervention by other states puts an end to the fighting. This new type of war has new characteristics. Revolutionary forces may ignore the value of the land and strengthen popular resistance and morale. Given the will to fight they may prolong the war until the enemy is tired of fighting and is convinced of the futility of settling the conflict by force of arms.

The Israelis have added to their misfortune by misunderstanding the transformations that have occurred in the Arab world. The true balance of power in the region has not been what they thought it was. In the end the Israelis were too confident in their military abilities.[36] Bitterly disappointed by the outcome of the 1973 war, they became angry at neutral countries as well as the United States. Where did the Israelis go wrong?

Israeli strategy relied on its intelligence system to gather information on the Arab armies, but the Israeli general staff placed too much confidence in the Israeli intelligence apparatus alone. The military command had received definite assurance from their intelligence chief, Eliahu Zaira, that he would inform the chief of staff of any Arab military movements.[37] The alert was planned early enough to activate the Israeli army and to mobilize the reserves. On the basis of this assurance, the Israeli leadership lowered the active forces (regular and reserve) to the lowest possible limit (120,000), keeping only a

---

36. One can expand in this area and understand the mentality prevalent among leaders after the 1967 war, which spread to the Israeli masses, by referring to the "Israeli Boasting Dossier" to be found in the Palestine Liberation Organization Research Center in Beirut.

37. There is no room here to mention all the statements by Israeli officials, which were monitored by Arab scientific research institutes concerned with the study of the Palestinian issue and the Arab-Israeli conflict. It is sufficient to give here some respresentative remarks. Hayim Tsadok, chairman of the Security and Foreign Affairs Committee in the Knesset, declared: "If war was launched we have the ability to respond and inflict a shattering blow on the enemy" (Hebrew Israel Broadcast, October 22, 1971). Former Israeli Defense Minister Moshe Dayan said: "I don't know what will happen on the 7th of this month if the Egyptians open fire, but I know what will happen on the 8th" (J.T.A., March 2, 1971).

thin defensive curtain in the front line, while 298,000 Egyptian and 132,000 Syrian soldiers were under arms. The aim was to lighten the burden on the Israeli economy since an early warning intelligence system permitted a smaller standing army.

Today it is well known that Israeli intelligence received information from more than one local and international source to the effect that Syrian and Egyptian forces were mobilizing for an attack. These reports, however, were constantly ignored. The information was simply analyzed and evaluated along the previously mentioned idea of Israeli superiority. The mobilizations were interpreted as maneuvers and demonstrations of strength; the chance of an Arab attack was thought to be zero. When these views were finally changed and Israel was sure that an attack was coming on the evening of October 6, they warned the active forces and began mobilization. But it was too late. The intelligence system had failed to give the promised time margin. The security margin was further shortened because the Arabs attacked at 2:00 P.M. instead of 6:00 P.M. The attack came like a whirlwind.[38]

The war came as a surprise for many reasons, but the inability of the Israeli intelligence to evaluate information correctly and to give an early warning were the most important factors.[39] In fact the warning was so short that the active forces were not prepared to hold on. It was so difficult for the Israelis to believe that the Arabs would attack that preparations for a successful mobilization were never executed. The Israeli armed forces were not able to carry out the repelling operation successfully in accordance with defence plans; and because of the lack of warning time, the strategic reserves could not assemble and retalitate. Consequently the Bar-Lev line collapsed and the Syrians were able to penetrate the Golan with remarkable ease and speed. The Israeli leadership was forced to throw the operational reserves and as much of the strategic reserves as could be gathered into the battle piecemeal during the first few days. It was not until later that it could make up a strong strike force to

38. It led Raphael Pinker to say on the fourth day of the war: "They surprised us. They caught us in our underwear. They caught us while we were at the height of our confidence and happiness, when we were more sure of ourselves than we should have been, and when we believed that we could beat any enemy in six days" (Al-Hamishmar, October 9, 1973).

39. David Eleazar, the Israeli chief of staff, criticized the intelligence in an interview: "This time the warning was very brief and insufficient" (Ha'aretz, November 2, 1973). Haim Bar-Lev supported this view when he said: "All the achievements of the Egyptians and the Syrians at the first stage were caused by insufficient warning and surprise" (Ma'ariv, November 2, 1973).

use effectively. Because of this early limitation in forces, the Israelis had to violate the most basic rules of concentration and mobilization of forces in the appropriate time and place.

The second failure in the Israeli strategy emerged when the secure border concept, adopted by the Israeli military for political purposes, collapsed. After 1967, these leaders announced that Israel was holding defensible borders which would deter the Arabs from thinking about attacking the Golan Heights, Suez Canal, and the Jordan River. Lengthy argument took place within the Israeli leadership concerning the military significance of secure borders and the inability of any borders, regardless of how secure, to repel an attack in modern warfare. There could be no security in an era of sophisticated long range weapons.

The secure border theory, however, was not a military view—it was instead an attempt to justify the occupied territories and to bargain over them. This is the reason why its advocates won the argument and embodied it in the Bar-Lev line on the Suez Canal and the Allon line along the cease-fire line in the Golan. They also developed a special operational concept of how to benefit, at the same time, from both building the fortifications and striking a counterblow with an armored fist.

The construction of these two lines and their attendant false security lowered Israeli vigilance. Yitzhak Rabin, the Israeli ambassador in Washington, was led to say: "Israel is capable of defending itself against the unified Arab forces for any period of time—five, twenty, or fifty years—as long as we are not denied the equipment necessary for our defense."[40] The heavy dependence on the Bar Lev line was based on its strong fortifications, the armored fist concentrated behind it, an Israeli air force capable of eliminating any Egyptian beachhead within hours and, above all, the Suez Canal, described by former Air Force Commander Ezer Wizeman as "the best anti-tank barrier ever built in history."[41]

The Egyptian attack, however, was not a tank attack. It was initiated by commandos in rubber boats and by heliborne troops. This attack did not need the support of the Egyptian air force, because the Egyptians found it sufficient to use heavy artillery and missile barrages against the fortifications, the armored Israeli tactical reserves, and the transportation routes toward the passes. The Israeli tank force was not sufficient to sweep away the bridgeheads. In fact the opposite

40. *Near East Report*, May 7, 1972.
41. *Ma'ariv*, April 15, 1971.

occurred, as the Israeli tanks fell into the trap of Egyptian infantry men armed in an unprecedented manner with anti-tank missiles.[42] The Israeli air force intervened to destroy the bridgeheads before they could be strengthened and to destroy the pontoon bridges set up by the Engineering Corps on the night of October 6, but it was met by a wall of surface-to-air missiles and prevented from accomplishing its mission. Its losses in attacking planes were seventy per cent; and at that level of loss, the air force had to discontinue its mission. The easy Egyptian crossing of the Suez and the Israeli failure to eliminate the beachheads demonstrated the inaccuracy of one of the foundations of Israeli strategy, and led to a new idea: that it is possible to cross waterways in spite of the enemy's air superiority, if the attacker can limit the action of the air force with a net of effective (well-aimed, heavy, and mobile) surface-to-air missiles.

POSITIONAL SECURITY MARGIN

One of the factors in the Israeli strategy after 1967 was the reliance on the positional security margin following the widening of the state's strategic depth as a result of the territories occupied in the 1967 war. The Israeli leaders asserted that the existence of these territories provided them with wide maneuverability, and that they could thus fight away from population centers and important industrial installations. As General Ezer Wizeman stated in 1971: "I prefer to have Sinai under Israeli control with fewer planes than to have our stockades full of Phantom planes and Sinai under Egyptian control."[43]

The large territories, however, do not fight by themselves. Forces are needed to fight upon them. But the presence of these forces away from the supply centers puts the defender in a difficult logistic position, making him an easy target—especially if the geographic limitations for his actions had been previously defined and there was satisfaction with a limited achievement. This is all the more true if the defender is a state with a small population and is consequently sensitive to human losses. In fact Israel's retention of the occupied territories did help keep its vital and populated areas away from the danger of war, but this would not have been true had the Egyptians used their long-range weapons to strike at targets deep inside it.

42. The 190th Armored Israeli Brigade fell into a similar trap in which most of its tanks were lost and its commander, Brigadier Assaf Yagouri, was taken prisoner.

43. *Ibid.*

In addition to this positive aspect to the retention of territory, there was a negative aspect. The strategy of fighting on internal lines is used by a central state surrounded by enemies. But the continued occupation made that strategy inappropriate. In previous wars Israel had succeeded in applying this strategy successfully. She would settle the fight with one of her enemies before the other enemy was mobilized. After Israel had neutralized the first front, she then moved her forces to the second front. What allowed Israel to achieve this goal was her small size, the good condition of her roads, and the mobility of her armed forces (air force, paratroopers, armored infantry, and self-propelled artillery). The 1967 war was the best example in recent years of executing a strategy of systematic action on one front at a time.

In the 1973 war, however, the distance between the Egyptian and Syrian fronts was an obstacle in the deployment of land forces from one front to another and prevented, in large measure, the execution of this strategy. Arab fighting on the two fronts was coordinated in the very first days of the war. But the logistical problems would have been much greater had the Egyptians continued their advance to the east and not stopped at the bridgeheads. Or had the Jordanians entered the war and created strategic difficulties for the Israelis on the Egyptian front. The distance between the two fronts created obstacles for the air force as well. The number of sorties that each squadron could carry out in one day was reduced because of the long distance it would have to have crossed from its base to the theater of operations, or from one theater to another.

Furthermore, the Israeli military did not apply the "fighting on internal lines" as effectively as it had in the 1967 war; it was not able to conclusively settle with one front in order to move to the other. In 1967 Israel concluded the battle with Egypt by effectively using the "back-breaking" method and then turned to the Jordanian and Syrian fronts. In 1973 she applied the tactic of "striking at the soft underbelly."[44] This was because of the narrow margin for maneuver at the Golan (12–16 miles); the great threat of Syrian forces

44. The army fighting on internal lines applies the method of backbreaking or striking the stronger opponent and ending the battle with him in a manner which would make the weaker adversaries automatically fall through the second blow. He does this when he is sure of his ability to bring about this conclusion without leaving himself open to serious blows by the weaker opponents. The army uses the method of striking the "soft underbelly" or striking the weaker opponent if this enemy is in a position to threaten vital sectors and the stronger adversary is slow-moving and distant from these vital positions. This direct blow to the weaker opponent usually is also an indirect blow to the stronger ally.

reaching the areas overlooking the Hula and Tiberias plains; the wide margin for maneuver provided by the Sinai Desert (124 by 124 miles); and the possibility of making a stand at the line of passes 19-22 miles from the Suez Canal for a sufficient period of time and with limited forces. The most the Israelis could do was to retake the Golan and advance beyond the "violet line"[45] to form a pocket of 12 by 12 miles on the Damascus-Kuneitra road. In fact they were stopped at the outskirts of Sasa. Despite large Israeli concentrations on the Syrian front they could not break through to threaten the rear and overturn the strategic balance.

The reasons for the perseverance of the Syrian army lines were the difficulty of the volcanic rock terrain and the scarcity of roads and paths. These prevented the Israelis from waging the mobile war to which they were accustomed. The entry of the Iraqi forces (an armored brigade and a mechanized brigade) into the battle and their participation in the counterattacks repelled the Israeli advance. Additionally, there were heavy nightly counterattacks against the forward Israeli tanks by Syrian commandos armed with unexpectedly large numbers of anti-tank weapons. The Israeli air force was unable to create panic among the Syrian land forces. Finally, the Israelis failed to use airborne forces to create "strategic dams" behind the Syrian forces. All of these factors led to the stability of the front and the transformation of the battle from the stage of the "mobile war" to the stage of the "stable fronts," in which operations are limited to air sorties, exchange of artillery fire, missiles, and tanks, while making limited offensives and local counterattacks.

During this period and on October 14, prior to the achievement of a decisive victory in the north, the Israelis moved their real aerial effort and some of their land forces to the south to confront the Egyptians; the latter had advanced to the east to take some of the pressure off the Syrian-Iraqi forces. However, the tenacity of the Syrian line, the increase in its power as a result of the arrival of new Soviet equipment, fresh Iraqi forces, and a Jordanian armoured brigade (the 40th Brigade), and the sensitivity of the Israeli pocket—all of these factors forced the Israelis to keep large land forces in the north. Thus they could not concentrate completely against the Egyptians. This was a violation of the principle of "gathering one's forces." It weakened the Israeli forces operating in the Sinai, and delayed their supporting the Deversoir opening. If the Israelis had been able to take advantage

45. The violet line was the cease-fire line after the 1967 war.

of the early victory there, they could have ended the fighting on the Egyptian front before the intervention of the big powers and the cease-fire.

The Israeli evaluation in the beginning of the maneuver was correct. They moved towards the smaller and more dangerous enemy to remove him from the battle. They practiced the "soft underbelly" strike. But the belly was not as soft as they imagined; they were never able to conclude the battle. When they moved towards the bigger opponent who was beginning to concentrate for attack, the smaller adversary was able to wage a counteroffensive, eliminate the Israeli pocket, and advance into the Golan after the absence of the air force from the theater of operations. The Syrians applied the strategy of "lure and strike" even though they did not offer the lure willingly or in accordance with a plan. Still, they were ready to exploit the new situation.

Syrian President Asad declared after Egypt's acceptance of the cease-fire resolution (Security Council resolution 338) that Syria was surprised by this action and intended to wage a long war.[46] It appears that the Syrians, the Iraqis, and the Jordanian brigade were planning before the cease-fire to launch a counterattack on both sides of the pocket to eliminate it, and that this attack was delayed several times and put off completely after the cease-fire resolution.

The Israeli strategy prior to 1973 depended on the interchange of action and deterrence. The creation of the superior Israeli force was originally aimed at deterring the Arabs, preventing them from thinking about war and the removal of Israeli occupation.[47] But this deterrence was not complete in any stage of the conflict because the Arab forces were formidable. The intensity of the emotions behind the conflict, and the size of the human, military, and economic force which the Arabs could gather were simply too much for the Israelis to neutralize. The 1973 Arab military operations were an extension of the 1967 Sinai campaign and the operations of the Palestinian revolutionaries. Consequently the Israeli deterrence was always tied to action against

46. *Al-Thawra*, (Damascus), October 30, 1973.

47. Yigal Allon defined the goal as "arriving at a result: that Israel is an accomplished fact in the region that cannot be eliminated and that the outcome of any attempt to attack it is certain failure." Israeli deterrence was based on the "superior force," "raising the level of (misdaqiyya)," "insuring the active escalating deterrence," and "relying on the enemy's ideology." cf. Yigal Allon, *A Curtain of Sand* (Beirut: Planning Center, 1969 [Arabic language edition]), p. 37.

the Palestinians and the Arab armies. By limiting her military posture to retaliatory strikes, Israel expected to achieve "direct deterrence" against the Palestinians and to force the Arab armies to suppress the Palestinian resistance.

But limited Israeli action during intermediate periods of peace occurred when "deterrence" declined to an unacceptable level. It was characterized by "offensive initiative," "flexible response," "the more violent response," and "the continuous response." Whenever the Israeli deterrence declined too far and Arab preparedness became a threat to Israel, the Israeli army would move from limited action aimed at strengthening the deterrence, to total action: war. And war meant the "preemptory abortive strike"—to move the battle with all its cost to the opponent's land so as to deprive him of the military initiative and surprise.[48]

In order to launch a preemptive strike the Israelis had to achieve three conditions: internal political support, external political support, and the appropriate tool of execution. The first was secured before the 1967 war as a result of the dynamism of the Zionist idea and exaggeration of the danger of extermination.[49] The second requirement was achieved by the success of their foreign policy which was based on the legitimacy of an internationally recognized Israel and the failure of the Arabs to present their case. The third condition was to be achieved by cooperating with the superpowers (as in the 1956 war)[50]

48. Yigal Allon was the theoretician of the "preemptory abortive strike" in Israel. In his words: "Israel has taken for itself a basic right in the development of a fighting force capable of a preemptive counterattack, in order to avoid allowing Israel to come under a surprise total Arab attack. This will be initiated when it becomes apparent that the enemy is preparing to attack or to penetrate any vital defensive position" (*Ibid.*, p. 3). Allon defined the conditions under which Israel must launch its preemptive abortive strike in *Ibid.* and *The Creation and Development of the Israeli Army* (Beirut: Dar Al Awda, 1971 [Arabic Edition]).

In the latter he mentions that there was a consensus in Israel that under the following conditions it would be Israel's right, if not its duty, to enter into a war: (1) If attacking forces concentrate in a manner that would form a threat to Israel; (2) If it becomes apparent that the enemy plans a surprise air attack on Israel's air bases; (3) If an air attack occurs, regardless of how local, on our atomic plants and scientific institutions; (4) If the guerilla war—planting mines and throwing of bombs—reaches a stage where the operations of positive defense and retaliation are unable to repel it; (5) If Jordan enters into a military pact with another Arab country and allows foreign military forces to concentrate on its territory, especially in the West Bank of the Jordan River; (6) If Egypt closes the Tiran Straits.

49. The hysterical Arab statements and threats about the extermination of Israel's people, eg., throwing the Israelis into the sea.

50. Britain and France.

or by creating a strike force dependent basically on air power, armor, and mechanized and airborne troops (as in the 1967 war).[51] Thus they were able to attack successfully in 1956 and 1967.

In September, 1973, the Syrian and Egyptian armies concentrated an attack force on the Israeli borders. The Israeli leadership had to apply an announced strategy and to execute a preemptive strike. However, the general situation had changed. The conditions for attack were no longer there. The internal mobilization had lost its strength after Israeli leaders declared that the security situation was excellent. The Arab armies, in that view, were not a threat to Israel after Arab "extermination threats" had fallen to the boasts of Israeli political and military leaders and after this concept was criticized by respected Israeli theoreticians.[52]

Foreign political support had declined badly because of the failure of Israeli foreign policy. Israeli Premier Golda Meir spoke of this situation before the *Ma'arakh* leadership on October 25, saying that: "(The present) called for courage . . . we no longer have in the civilized world but one friend—the United States."[53] This decline greatly affected Israeli freedom of action. It prevented the Israelis from launching a preemptive strike.[54] More significantly, the Israelis failed to achieve air deterrence. The Egyptians and the Syrians had ground-

---

51. The *Jerusalem Post* of September 20, 1968 reported that the forces which have the first priority are the air force, armored force, and airborne troops. The other armed forces are to a great extent supporting elements.

52. Reserve Brigadier General Mattityahu Peled, head of provisioning and supply in the General Command of the Israeli army in 1967, researcher at Shiloh University and professor of Middle East history at Tel Aviv University, wrote in an article in *Ha'aretz* (March 19, 1972), that the idea that Israel was threatened with extermination in June, 1967 and that it fought to save its existence was "a ruse which arose and was developed only after the war." He also said that the Israelis, either as a group or as individuals, were not threatened with extermination. He asked, "When was the last time Israel was open to an Arab attack? It was in 1948, as I read history." And although Yigal Allon does not agree with all of Gen. Peled's views, he asserted in *Davar* (June 15, 1972): "We were not threatened with extermination at that time." In an interview with Rov Goldstein which appeared in *Ma'ariv* (April 4, 1972), Gen. Ezer Weizman, head of operations in the Israeli army and head of the Herut Movement, said: "There was no threat of extermination. Yet in spite of that there was no choice but to attack the Egyptians. We had no choice." Weizman repeated his views in *Yediot Aharonot* (June 6, 1972) when he wrote that Israel was not really threatened with annihilation, even if it hadn't launched the war in June, 1967, even if it hadn't defeated the Egyptians, Syrians, and Jordanians: "But its existence would not have continued in the same manner it was then, or as it is today."

53. *Al Hamishmar*, November 25, 1973.

54. Reserve Colonel Meir Peil explained why Israel did not launch this preemptive

to-ground missiles capable of striking targets up to 50 miles inside Israel; Egypt alone had SCUD missiles, with a range of 186 miles, which balanced the Israeli air deterrent with an Arab missile deterrent.[55]

There remains the other condition that the Israelis needed: the military force. In spite of the Israeli army size, the erroneous intelligence interpretation led to the failure to mobilize. The Israeli forces had been mobilized several times previously and the warnings had proved false. Each time, however, the treasury had paid a heavy price. When it became clear that an attack was imminent on the morning of October 6th, the opportunity for a preemptive war had been lost. The Israeli command called up only the air force and active land forces to repel the invaders because it had relied on a preemptive attack to give it time to mobilize the reserves. The Israeli army was forced during the first days of the war to move to a defensive strategy which had not been used since 1948 (excluding the war of attrition, 1969-70). The facts of the 1973 war prove that Israel's failure to launch a preemptive war on the eve of the 1973 war did not stem from a nonaggressive moral position but from the absence of military and political requirements for such an attack.

GENERAL EVALUATION

The 1973 war was a limited one, fought by third sides as proxies for the Big Powers; it was fought under the shadow of the policy of "detente and competition." This fact gave the strategy of fighting a special imprint; it led each side to try the strategy that was suitable

---

strike: "On the eve of the Yom Kippur war, when the Syrian and Egyptian forces were preparing to attack, the state of Israel was . . . in a critical position in the extent of our political freedom of action. . . . The only state which continued to support Israel was the U.S. This would not have permitted us in any way to launch a preventive war on the eve of Yom Kippur in 1973. And if we had launched a preventive attack, they would have stopped us in one or two days and would have pushed us back and forced us to surrender, with U.S. pressure, most of our political and regional gains achieved in the Six Days War" (*Yediot Aharonot*, November 4, 1973).

55. Zeev Shiff mentions that the introduction of these weapons into the Mid-East upset the deterrent strategic balance and "one of the results was that Israel lost the deterrent that it had gained through its superior air force, or that the Israeli deterrent met an equal weight in the counter Arab deterrent. . . . In other words, Israel's strategic arm was limited in its operations against its main enemy. This strategic fact is what returns us to the pre-1956 war period" (*Ha'aretz*, February 4, 1974).

to its political ends and to apply that strategy within the framework of "freedom of action" given to it by the Big Powers. The Israelis sought to conclude the battle, destroy the Arab armies, and reestablish the status quo before any Big Power intervention and escalation of the conflict. On the other hand, the Arab armies were doing whatever they could to prolong the war so that this intervention would be possible and the Arab-Israeli conflict could be brought back into discussion.

The Arab side achieved an incomplete victory with its strategy. Its victory would have been greater had the Syrians been able to hold on to the positions that they occupied in the Golan and Mt. Hermon; or had the Egyptians penetrated into the passes, regained the oil wells on the eastern bank of the Gulf of Suez, or at least prevented the Israelis from pentrating the Deversoir.

Along with the limited strategic Arab success, there was an incomplete Israeli strategic failure which was symbolized by the collapse of the "no-war–no-peace" condition and of the policy of "not one inch of the territories without peace and full Arab recognition." This failure would have been greater had the Israelis not regained what they had lost on the northern front and had they not occupied more ground on the two fronts.

The overall view of the strategies employed in this war bore the influence of Foch and Clausewitz, rather than Fabius Maximus, Napoleon, Liddel Hart, and Guderian. The Clausewitzian imprint was very clear since both sides used direct strategy to achieve a conclusion through violent battle between conventional forces armed with the most modern weapons. The battles on both fronts took the form of direct clashes and violent tests of strength on the open ground. They did not use wide–scale strategic maneuvers in spite of the mobility of the forces on both sides. Moreover, they did not reach for larger ends in spite of their similar ability to upset the strategic balance of one another by indirect operations; they did not do so in spite of the existence of a wide area for maneuvers in the Sinai and on the southern axis of the Syrian front (the Hauran sector and the south of Damascus from the "violet line" to the Ghouta of Damascus).

The only important strategic movements in this war were the quick movement of Iraqi and Algerian forces to the theater of operations (from the distant strategic depth to the center of the battles) and the movement of Israeli reserves from concentration points to the breach in the Deversoir area and a semicircle to surround the Third Army and the city of Suez.

The strategy in this war (on both sides) did not take on a "revolutionary" characteristic in the material sense (ideological or psychological fragmentation) nor in the Guderian or Napoleonic sense. Were it not for some revolutionary manifestations in choosing the time to begin the attack in a previously unknown manner (1400 hours) and in blocking Israeli air superiority by surface-to-air missiles, using the infantry heavily against tanks, and clearing the air from the ground in the Deversoir—if it were not for all that—this war would have remained closer to a great duel. Except for glimpses of brilliant military initiatives, it could then have been carried on by armies from the Middle Ages, or WW I armies equipped with modern weapons.

Liddel Hart completely disappeared from the Syrian front. But his indirect tactics appeared in the strategic strangulation of Bab-al-Mandab and in the Israeli threat to the rear of the Third Army on the west bank of the Canal. It was then that General Sharon's forces exploited the cease-fire on October 22nd by continuing their advance south to the Adabiyya port of the Gulf of Suez and encircling Suez and the Third Army on October 24.

The consumption of equipment and ammunition occurred on an unprecedented scale and pace. On both sides, it was higher than the estimated rate based on experience in WW II and the Korean War. This consumption did not match the economic or productive capacities of the warring sides. The material base for those sides would not have permitted a continuation of the fighting at the high scale on which it occurred for more than a few days. Were it not for the American and Soviet airlifts, the Arab and Israeli war machines would have ground to a halt after one week of fighting and would have been forced to use more primitive methods with less violent and heavy air power. They would have returned to a war of stable trenches which depended on limited fire power, human resources, and the potential hidden in the fighting individual.

The intervention of the Big Powers, however, allowed the continuation of heavy fighting at a rapid pace. The Big Powers, then, intervened when the crisis reached a stage that threatened the escalation to fighting between the Big Powers themselves. They put an end to the fighting before the fighters achieved their goals and before their fighting will was destroyed.

In short, the war ended as it began, with each side holding firm to the political goals for which it entered the war. The search for peace began between two forces that used violent means (war) and the war ended with a twilight in which neither victor nor vanquished could be distinguished.

Hani A. Faris and As'ad Abdul Rahman

ARAB UNITY

NATIONS EXPERIENCE an extensive amount of soul-searching in the wake
of major crises. Leaders, values, and institutions are subjected to severe
scrutiny and are judged harshly by what are often newly evolved
criteria. The behavior of the Arab world in the period 1967–73 presents
no exception to this general rule. One is struck by the volume of
self-doubt and self-criticism that took place. Few aspects of Arab
life, if any, escaped unscathed. The gap between leaders and followers,
the ruler and the ruled, widened to such an extent that it was difficult
to envision how it could be bridged. The trend in Arab politics was
that Arab regimes lost popular confidence. Rarely could the Arab
intellectuals in good conscience afford any longer to defend or even
to justify the status-quo. Liberals and conservatives became outmoded
political categories and their ideologists were being rapidly replaced
by radicals of the revolutionary and fundamentalist type.

Repeated setbacks and failures to effect desired national objectives,
above all the humiliating defeat of 1967, led to the reexamination
of basic national issues. In the process, the principal casualty was
unity. A threefold attitude emerged within this context; namely,
disillusionment, dissociation, and displacement. Several diehard Arab
nationalist movements lost faith in the feasibility of their plans and
many formerly valued and active nationalist elements withdrew to
an apolitical life. The more significant development in the 1967–73
inter-war period was, however, the general shift in the assignment

of national priorities that occurred. Disillusionment and dissociation forced displacement. Schemes, impulses, and hopes in the objective of uniting the Arab world under one political organization were deferred to secondary and local objectives. Provincialism gained the upper hand in the inter-war period. In an attempt to explain this phenomenon, Mohamed Amin al-'Alim, a leading Egyptian Marxist theoretician, wrote:

> Retreatism surfaced among many writers of the various Arab countries in a feeling of provincialism that was antagonistic to former feelings of unity. This was a natural outcome of the belief that the true participation demanded by unity presupposes radical solutions to the problems, especially the political ones, that the Arab world found itself experiencing. The repeated let-downs in arriving at this true participation resulted in provincialist political movements that were satisfied with half-solutions and with partial victories or gains. . . .[1]

The 1973 October War seems to have checked, if not reversed, the above process. Among the most serious repercussions to the Arab world of the war was the question that the war raised as to the prospects of unity. The war heralded a new era of unity of ranks and purpose.[2] Inter-Arab relations have been radically transformed; the potential for common Arab action seems unlimited. Given the bleak picture of unity that prevailed prior to the war, how and why did the war effect the now dominant optimism?

The observer of Middle East politics is perplexed to explain the solidarity of Arab regimes that was demonstrated in October and the post-October, 1973 days. For the first time in two and a half decades of strife with Israel, and despite seemingly helpless disunity and constant bickering, the initiative was seized by the Arab side. A two front, well-planned, and well-coordinated effort to engage Israel militarily and wrest the 1967 occupied territories was launched. Immediately, military and financial assistance poured to the two combatant Arab armies from neighboring Arab countries. Without the previously

---

1. *Al-Nahar* (Beirut), June 30, 1974.

2. "Unity of ranks" and "unity of purpose" were two slogans coined and popularized by President Nasser in his speech of February 22, 1962. While the first slogan stressed the need for solidarity among Arab regimes irrespective of their diverse socio-political philosophies, the second slogan called for cooperation among regimes with shared outlooks only. The present amalgamation of the two slogans is meant to indicate that all Arab regimes are pursuing the same goals.

well-known verbose threats that never materialized and the promises of an assistance that was not forthcoming, Arab regimes dispatched troops to front line duties. Iraq, Kuwait, Jordan, Saudi Arabia, Algeria, and Morocco partook in the war effort. Arab delegates also speedily met to consider common policies. Their decision to use the most powerful weapon in their arsenal, i.e., oil, was the most striking.[3] For once in modern history, the Arabs were able to confront Israel and her allies as a unified force.

Cooperation among Arab regimes has given rise to a major question: Did October's solidarity signal a new pathway to Arab unity? Was it a manifestation of a unity, informal and undeclared, prevailing in the post-October Arab world? Or, was it a mere passing phase? Did the October war enhance the chances for Arab unity and introduce new aspects into the relations among Arab regimes?

PATHWAYS TO ARAB UNITY

The political heritage of the past quarter-century offered various pathways to Arab unity.[4] Four different pathways to unity are manifest in the modern history of the Arabs: Contractual, progressive, revolutionary, and functionalist. Each of these pathways commands a school of thought, has its own heroes, advocates, and followers, and invokes specific political experiments to demonstrate its efficacy. Though they fit into a chronological order and have enjoyed their zeniths at different times, these pathways do not fall into exclusive stages. They continue to affect unitarian schemes even when overshadowed by more powerful ideas.

The Contractual Pathway: The Experiment of the Arab League
The first attempt at Arab unity was formal and contractual in outlook and found its chief expression in the institution of the Arab League.

3. In an attempt to pressure Western Europe, Japan, and the United States into a neutral if not friendly position, oil production was sharply cut and an oil boycott of the United States and Holland was instituted. A common Arab policy in the field of oil had been ruled out by many, especially Western circles, and the success of the Arab oil ministers in agreeing on means and objectives in their Kuwait meeting boosted their image abroad and fortified the morale of their people. Finally, the huge financial transfer with which oil-rich countries assisted Syria and Egypt was one other sphere in which Arab solidarity effectively expressed itself.

4. These are first delineated and assessed and the contribution of October to these pathways is considered. The Arab milieu at the time of the war is then discussed in terms of both setting and issues. Finally, the study concludes on an attempt to determine whether or not the war advanced the prospects for unity, and if so, why and on what terms.

The experiment relates to the period of infancy of the nationalist movement and reflects the traumas, contradictions, and weaknesses of the national idea itself. Unlike later attempts at unity which were always partial, this first attempt was intended to be all-inclusive. In so doing, it had to override the jealousies, rivalries, and diversities then existing among the seven original contracting Arab states by allowing for a loose association. The principle of state sovereignty could not be weakened or altered. Nevertheless, the resultant League of Arab States was a far cry from the demands of the nationalists, many of whom felt that the newborn creation was a betrayal of national hopes and a move aimed at circumventing demands for a national supra-state polity. True enough, members of the League did not envision their association as a step toward complete or even partial political unification and were disinclined to relinquish any of the authority they inherited from the retreating colonial powers. Provincial concerns, however, were countered by other trends. Popular sentiment, threatening developments in Palestine, common interests, and the encouragement of some of the Big Powers necessitated the working out of some level of cooperation. The League, then, was the product of the conflicting forces of Arabism and provincialism operating in an international setting that favored the former.

As the first embodiment of unitarian feelings, the League has not in any direct manner furthered actual political mergers among Arab countries. Its effect and contribution have been strictly indirect. Two such indirect effects may be cited. First, the collection of all Arab countries within one organizational framework deterred the potential for the growth of greater provincialism at a critical period of political development. It thus helped preserve Arab national identity from dissipation. Second, an equally important and indirect contribution of the League to the prospects of unity has been in the functional field.[5] The various conferences, specialized agencies, treaties for regional cooperation, and other social, cultural, and economic activities have helped sensitize Arab countries to the benefits of mutual coopera- tion and coordination of policies; this has decreased the level of their individual dependence on the outside world and increased Arab inter-dependence. Abdul Khaleq Hassouna, the former secretary gen- eral of the League, in his address on the occasion of the Tenth Anniversary of the League said:

5. For a detailed account of the League's functional activities and programs, see Robert Macdonald, *The League of Arab States: A Study in the Dynamics of Regional Organization* (Princeton: Princeton University Press, 1965), pp. 169–220.

The fact is that the League has paved the way for the political, military, economic, and social unity of the Arabs. The pact of the League, the Convention of Arab Collective Security, the Arab Cultural Treaty, the many economic and financial agreements which culminated in the conclusion of the Economic Convention between Arab states and in the project of the Arab Development Bank, and the continuous series of conferences and seminars which were held during the last thirteen years, all these are the supports on which the foundation of our unity has been built.[6]

The league remains the most enduring of a series of attempts aimed at uniting the Arab world. The fact that it was unable to check political disunity did not make the nationalist faction oblivious to the benefits accruing from the provision of a forum for the exchange and coordination of official views and policies.[7]

The Progressive Pathway: The Experiment of the United Arab Republic

The second pathway to unity was underlined in the ideological struggle that split the Arab world into "progressives" and "conservatives" and led to the political merger of Egypt and Syria in a United Arab Republic between the years 1958–61. Unlike the League experiment which was premised on a harmony of interests and aspirations among Arab countries, this new phase in the nationalist movement pitted one ideological camp of Arab countries against another. It also caused a corresponding division among the populace which crisscrossed national boundaries. New elements were injected into Arab political life in this phase. Among these elements were the rise of mass movements, the introduction and spread of ideologies, and the addition of a socioeconomic dimension to nationalism. One Arab scholar described the ideological strife which raged as the "great debate between dynamic and static nationalists."[8]

Beginning with the mid-1950's, Arab regimes gravitated towards

6. Quoted in Fayez Sayegh, *Arab Unity: Hope and Fulfillment* (New York: The Devin-Adair Company, 1958), p. 137.

7. The League as one pathway to unity has three distinctive features which explain its longevity and at the same time incapacitate it as a vehicle for political union. These are comprehensiveness in membership, absolute dependence on officialdom, and the contribution to political objectives through indirect means of functional activities.

8. Fayez Sayegh, "Arab Nationalism: The Latest Phase," *Middle East Forum al-Kulliyah* (Beirut), November, 1957.

either of two camps: "progressive" or "conservative." The former was typified by a general animosity toward the West, a movement toward closer cooperation with the East, a desire for rapid socio-economic development, the repudiation of age-long traditions and institutions, and the enthroning of new social classes, especially elements belonging to the middle classes. The latter were less amenable to change, maintained close cooperation with Western countries, especially the United States and Britain, were dominated by traditionally powerful social classes (aristocrats and landowners), and based their legitimacy on tradition. Membership in the two ideological camps has been fluid. Egypt, Syria, Iraq, and Algeria, on the one hand, and Saudi Arabia, Jordan, and Morocco, on the other, are, respectively, the leading countries in the progressive and conservative camps.

The progressive-conservative split originated with the 1952 Egyptian coup and the rise of a patriotic, socially-minded, and aggressive group of army officers to leadership positions. Immediately this group undertook a series of measures that undermined the old system and challenged the remaining authority of colonial England. At first the new leadership had no specific ideological orientation to guide its actions and it adopted something of a trial and error approach. Gradually, however, a system of beliefs began to crystallize. The person who was to give that system concrete expression was Gamal Abdal Nasser. Accounts of Nasser's rise to power and his philosophy abound and there is no need to repeat them. What needs to be asserted, however, is Nasser's domination of the Arab scene throughout his stay in power. Early in his career, Nasser scored a number of feats that gained him praise and followers throughout the Arab world. He was able by his actions and sayings to sway the masses in most Arab capitals and remained unequalled by any other Arab leader in political talents and charisma. His activities carried considerable weight by virtue of his leadership of the strongest and most populous Arab country. Things seemed to happen in the Arab world in the late fifties and early sixties only through the initiative of Nasser or as a reaction to his initiatives.

Nasser's significance as a historical figure did not derive from personal qualities alone. Rather, his influence emanated from an ability to articulate the hopes and aspirations of a large spectrum of Arab society. Essentially, Nasser personified to the Arab masses a dynamic and innovative leadership, willing to challenge and transform the hated status quo. His domestic reforms were outclassed only by his foreign policies, which greatly raised his esteem among non-Egyptian Arabs. The nationalization of foreign financial and commercial institutions, the nationalization of the Suez Canal, the assistance given to the Algerians in the struggle against French colonialism, the rejection of Western-sponsored military alliances, the arms deal with the Eastern bloc that ended the Western embargo of arms shipments to Egypt, and the championing of the Palestinian cause were the measures responsible for Nasser's meteoric rise to popularity. He came to be viewed as the leader who restored Arab dignity and reasserted Arab national identity. Nationalists of all colors looked upon him as the one man capable of effecting the objectives of Pan-Arabism.

The first political union in modern Arab history materialized on February 1, 1958 when Egypt and Syria proclaimed the founding of the United Arab Republic. A unitarian form of government with one president and one national assembly was adopted. Sovereignties of the member units was wholly submerged by the new Republic. It was felt that the union normalized what was an abnormal state of disunity. There not only was the common identity of the population, but a shared political outlook. The joint Egyptian-Syrian proclamation of February 1 announced: "They (the Egyptian and Syrian delegates) came out of this with the convictions that the elements conducive to the success of the union of the two Republics were abundant, particularly coming so recently as they did after the two countries' joint struggle—which had brought them even closer to one another— made the meaning of nationalism considerably clearer, stressed the fact that it was a movement for liberation and rehabilitation."[9] The new pathway to unity which the 1958 merger of Egypt and Syria underlined, then, called for common ideological orientations among participants.

The Egyptian-Syrian union was overwhelmingly popular at the mass level, but vehemently opposed by the privileged class and conservative elements.

The first effect on Arab politics that the union had was to alarm and alert conservative regimes to the dangers posed by the upsurge in nationalist sentiment. Iraq and Jordan, the two pillars of the conservative bloc in the Arab world, felt threatened by its development and hurriedly announced the formation of an Arab union between them. In spite of the countermove, the Egyptian-Syrian union continued to reverberate throughout the Arab world. The first impact was the civil war in Lebanon and widespread unrest in Jordan, which were followed by a dramatic coup in Iraq. By the summer of 1958,

9. For the text of the Proclamation, see *Basic Documents of the Arab Unifications* (Documents Collections, No. 2 [New York: Arab Information Center, 1958]), pp. 5–6.

the tide of Arab unity appeared to be irreversible.[10]

In conclusion, the second pathway to political unity was charted by the dynamic and change-oriented Arab regimes. Unity represented one policy available to these regimes in the offensive against static and status quo-oriented Arab regimes. As such, unity assumed in this phase an ideological garb with progressive socioeconomic connotations. Hence, the all comprehensive unity of the former phase was replaced by unions or attempts at union limited to systems with shared ideologies. Also, while prospects for unity were formerly at the complete mercy of officialdom, mass involvement in politics forced Arab political leaders of all shades to become more responsive to the popular ideal of unity.[11]

The Revolutionary Pathway: A Consequence of 1967

The third pathway to unity has yet to be embodied in an actual political experiment; it is the product of the split within the progressive camp that crystallized after 1967. It is proposed by regimes and movements that seek the radical transformation of their societies and includes forces of the 'old' and the 'new' Arab left. Syria under Jadid and Zayyan, South Yemen, the Ba'th, the Arab Socialist Action party, the various communist parties, several organizations within the Palestinian resistance (especially the PFLP and PDFLP*), and a growing number of Arab intellectuals uphold this motion of unity.

Proponents of this kind of unity divide Arab regimes into bourgeois and petit bourgeois. The former, they argue, are archaic regimes that have to be destroyed before any meaningful change within their societies can take place. They are hostile to any unitarian measures

10. Malcolm Kerr, in his study on the role of ideology in Arab politics, described the situation at the time as one in which Pan-Arabism assumed the month of predestination. See *The Arab Cold War 1958-1964: A Study of Ideology in Politics* (London: Oxford University Press, 1965), pp. 21-22. Several attempts at Arab political unity have taken place since 1961. In 1963, two Ba'thist-led delegations from Syria and Iraq opened negotiations with Nasser in Cairo with the intention of forming a tripartite union. The agreement arrived at was never implemented. Unity talks were also held between Syria and Iraq in August, 1963 but the fall of the Ba'th in Iraq later that year ended the attempt. An agreement in principle to unite Egypt and Iraq ended with the ouster of President 'Arif. The last of these unsuccessful attempts was made on September 2, 1971 when Egypt, Syria, and Libya established the Federation of Arab Republics. Post-October developments and the present state of Egyptian-Libyan relations do not augur well to the future of the Federation.

11. "No Arab leader is strong enough to ignore its appeal . . . each leader justifies himself in terms of his devotion to this ideal."

*Popular Front for the Liberation of Palestine and Popular Democratic Front for the Liberation of Palestine.

and incapable themselves of initiating unions. The latter, it is maintained, are anti-imperialist and patriotic but lack clear ideological commitments. They oscillate between socialism and liberalism as their interests demand. Political unity among countries that are under the 'opportunistic' and 'unstable' leadership of the petite bourgeoisie fail to withstand the test of time unless they transform society into a socialist order. Socialism, then, is the necessary condition for the success of unity.[12]

Advocates of the post-1967 socialist road to unity do not discount the possibility of petit bourgeois initiated and led unions, but they are divided as to whether or not such unions are worthy of support. Some maintain that nationalists must construct socialist systems in their individual countries prior to their merger. Others accept a partial transformation toward public ownership of the means of production, popular democracy, increased productivity, and redirection of Arab trade relations as sufficient cause for progressive forces to support attempted unions. The ongoing debate is reminiscent of the conflict between the two theories of 'socialism in one country' and 'permanent revolution.'

The point at which socialism became inextricably linked to all calls for unity was 1967. The Arab-Israeli war of that year fully estranged the nationalist movement from the United States and led to the 'Marxization' of the nationalist and the 'nationalization' of the Marxist. The penetration into nationalist thought and the domination of leftist ideology was perhaps one of the most striking developments in the Arab world after the war. The process began with the increased conviction that the Arab-Israeli conflict was not only between two nationalities, but also a struggle between two modes of life. Accordingly, the Arab-Israeli conflict went beyond regional causes and became closely tied to the international competition between capitalism and socialism. Arab society, therefore, had to undergo radical change before it could hope to militarily defeat Israel. To Arabs with knowledge of the hostile attitudes of the U.S. government, Marxism offered an ideology which could be utilized to transform Arab life, counter Israel's growing menace, and challenge Western encroachments in the Middle East.

But exponents of the revolutionary pathway to unity were handicapped by serious shortcomings, not the least of which was their

12. A most revealing publication containing the views of most Arab leftist groups on the question of unity during the 1967-1973 inter-war period is the special issue entitled "Unity and the Arab Revolution" of *Al-Thaqafa Al-Arabiyya* [The Arab Culture] (Beirut), No. 6, November, 1971.

own narrow and doctrinaire outlook. The rigid orthodoxy of both the old as well as the new Arab left contributed to the relegation of unity to a position of secondary status.[13] Class struggle and the dictatorship of the proletariat were emphasized at the expense of national solidarity. A more serious consequence, however, was the inability of the left to adapt the Marxist model of social conflict to Arab realities. Preaching the rule of workers in predominantly agricultural and even tribal societies caused them to be inattentive to the existing complex of archaic loyalties. The eventual outcome of the spread of the new ideologies was not the desired revolt of the masses, but their increased alienation from their political systems. This condition was demonstrated in the 1973 October War. Compared to the three former military engagements with Israel, the 1973 war witnessed the least amount of mass involvement and participation.[14]

The Functionalist Pathway: An Outgrowth of the October War

A new outlook to Arab unity was introduced in the wake of the October war. It has since become the gospel of the official leadership and dominates the political literature. This outlook proposed the functional integration of Arab societies as a prelude to political merger and aimed to replace former ideologies with what has been called "the development ideology."[15]

Two factors have led to the rise of the above outlook: the ability of Arab regimes to coordinate policies in the October war and the wealth acquired by Arab countries as a consequence of the recent rises in oil prices. Both factors explain the optimism that now characterizes the mood of Arab public opinion and its vision of the future.

This new direction to Arab unity originated with the inter-war period. It reflected a deeply transformed milieu which resulted from a constellation of multidimensional changes and complex interactions that took place during the past few years. The sequential changes exhibited themselves in two distinct phases: the period between June, 1967 and August, 1971 and the period thereafter.

13. The two Arab leftist writers who represent an exception to this general trend and who continuously caution other leftists to the trappings of their dogmatic position are Ilyas Murqos and Yaseen al-Hafiz. See their articles in *Ibid.*, pp. 14–19 and 20–23.

14. For insight into the manner in which the reactions of the Arab masses were affected by leftist ideologies, see "The Fourth Arab-Israeli War," *Palestine Affairs*, No. 27, (November, 1973), p. 32.

15. See the call made by Mohamad Jaber al-Ansari entitled "Economic Integration is a Historic Condition for Any Unity," *Al-Anwar* (Beirut), May 4, 1974.

THE NEW OUTLOOK, PHASE⁴ I: FLUX AND CRYSTALLIZATION

The changes that took place from June, 1967 to August, 1971 could be discussed under three major categories: local, regional, and international.

Local Developments

Most Arab states had experienced basic socioeconomic and political changes since 1967; these were a result of the crystallization of earlier undercurrents and completely new developments.

On the socioeconomic level,[16] several Arab countries intensified their modernization efforts, though in each case there was a different motive. In both Egypt and Syria military considerations necessitated a comprehensive restructuring of the armed forces. The outcome in the two states resulted in huge and sophisticated military establishments populated by better educated officers and soldiers. In Saudi Arabia, a major drive for modernization gathered momentum as of the mid-1960's. By the beginning of the seventies, Faisal's "White Revolution" had left its imprint on Saudi society. Some features of the new Saudi state, such as modern military and civil bureaucracies, took definite shape and made themselves felt socially. Similar but more modest processes were taking place in Libya and the two Yemens. Finally, the class of Arab intellectuals increased its number in geometric progression.

These rapid and far-reaching socioeconomic changes would not have been possible without the abundance of oil revenues that followed the sharp rise in Arab oil production, especially in the early seventies. Saudi production in 1973, moreover, increased by thirty per cent.

Concomitant with, or perhaps because of, these socioeconomic developments, the area experienced major political changes. These included the emergence of new political forces, leaderships, ideologies, organizations, and problems. Indeed, the political scene was characterized by turmoil, violent upheavals, and sudden unexpected drastic shifts.

For one thing, official leaderships in most Arab states were supplanted by means of military coups, new political arrangements, and elections, as well as natural death. New governing elites came to power in Iraq, Yemen, Sudan, Libya, and Syria through the intervention of the armed forces. The two abortive, though very serious, military

16. For a detailed review of socioeconomic developments, see Charles Issawi, "Economic Development in the Middle East," *International Journal*, XXVII, No. 4 (Autumn, 1973), 729-747.

coups in Morocco resulted in the elimination of several powerful political figures. The leadership of the post-1967 independent republic of South Yemen suffered from deep ideological and organizational conflict which culminated in extensive political purges. In the Gulf area new political formations, namely the union of Arab Emirates and the states of Qatar and Bahrain, emerged. The Lebanese parliament, after a serious crisis of presidential succession, managed to elect a new head of state in 1970. Finally, Nasser's death in September, 1970 presaged far-reaching consequences that affected the entire Arab world.

The changes in political leadership ostensibly enhanced the translation of the concept of Arab unity into concrete deeds. One of these deeds was the formation of the Federation of Arab Republics (FAR) which was carried out on the basis outlined in the 1969 Tripoli Charter.[17] Libyan President Múammar Qaddafi, who conceives of himself as a zealous Nasserite, was the driving force behind the Federation. Unfortunately, however, the unitarian arrangement proved to have little practical significance. By mid-1973 relations between Egypt and Libya, on the one hand, and Libya and Sudan, on the other, deteriorated to an unprecedented low.

Meanwhile, the post-1967 Palestine liberation movement gathered momentum very quickly. It became an important and active factor in Middle Eastern politics, following the deposition of the official leadership of the Palestine Liberation Organization (PLO) and the ascendance to power of a new revolutionary elite.[18] The latter comprised a wide ideological and organizational spectrum. Ideologically, it ranged between an extremely rightist wing in Fatah and ultra-leftist splinters of the Popular Front for the Liberation of Palestine (PFLP), while, organizationally, it consisted of eleven officially recognized groups. From late 1967 until mid-1971 the Palestine liberation movement attracted and inspired wide sectors of the Arab masses. Other Arab forces modelled themselves on the movement and spread the ideas of revolutionary politics.

A further by-product of the new revolutionary environment was the emergence of the "new left" which rallied around forces of the Palestinian resistance and regarded it as the spearhead of an Arab revolution. Consequently, the strategies and tactics of the Palestinian

17. Signed by Egypt, Libya, and the Sudan on December 27, 1969.

18. For a thorough and up-to-date analysis of the subject, see Ibrahim Abu Lughod, "Altered Realities: The Palestinians Since 1967," *International Journal*, XXVII, No. 4 (Autumn, 1973), 648-669.

commandos became those of the new left. In this connection, it is ironic to note that the new left followed in the footsteps of the old by emphasizing provincialism instead of Pan-Arab concerns.

Regional Hostilities

The volatile nature of Middle Eastern politics was due to a myriad of economic, social, ethnic, and religious cleavages inherent in the nature of the transitional societies of the region. The principal concern here is of two kinds: primary and secondary regional hostilities or the Arab-Israeli enmity and intra-Arab contradictions.

Despite the seeming intensification of enmities in the aftermath of the 1967 debacle,[19] the Arab-Israeli conflict was undergoing a process of disentanglement. The two major landmarks of this process were U.N. resolution 242 (November 22, 1967) and the Rogers Plan of 1970. Both proposals were accepted by the Arab states as an indication of official Arab readiness to end the state of war with Israel. That meant that the Arabs would recognize Israel's pre-1967 borders and would reduce the Palestinian cause from a movement aimed at national liberation to a humanitarian problem of refugees. In addition to the strategic shift in the Arab position, the Palestinian leadership changed its view of the Israelis as well. Under the new theory, the Israelis were to stay with the repatriated Palestinian Arabs and share with them equal rights and obligations in a de-zionized, secular, and democratic state.[20] This stand became the official program of the movement at the Fourth PLO Congress in 1968 and was reaffirmed by successive congresses, including the twelfth which was held June 1-9, 1974. In spite of the radical concessions made by the Palestinians and other Arabs, Israel continued to act arrogantly and to flout U.N. resolutions and world public opinion. Endorsed by Western support, Israel in the 1967-73 period held to an unyielding position regarding the occupied territories and the fate of the Palestinians.

Israeli militancy did not issue from a vacuum, but had several sources: the highly mobilized and organized resources of Israeli society

19. This includes the Palestinians' acts of resistance, the war of attrition, and the almost continuous raids and reprisal raids along all cease-fire and armistice lines.

20. It should be noted in this context that a small number of Palestinian personalities living under Israeli occupation, of whom Sheikh Mohamad Al-Ja'bari, Aziz Shihadeh, and Rashad Al-Shawwa were the most eminent, advocated a variety of highly compromising proposals to resolve the Arab-Israeli conflict. Their plans were outrightly repudiated by the PLO leaders who branded these personalities with treason.

and world Zionism, the direct and indirect assistance of Western countries in general and that of the U.S. Government in particular, and inter-Arab and intra-Arab disputes and disunity.

Post-June, 1967 Arab intra-state relations with reference to unity and disunity were not, until President Nasser's death, dissimilar from those that characterized the Arab scene prior to the third Arab-Israeli war. They oscillated between overall summit meetings and sectional bloc politics. The one postulated cooperation and coordination of policies, the other generated disruptive tendencies and heightened distrust between leaders. For instance, the 1967 Khartoum and 1969 Rabat conferences were a continuation of the policy of summit meetings initiated by President Nasser in late 1963, a policy that had suffered from almost total paralysis by 1966. Whereas the mini-summit meetings of Egypt, Iraq, and Syria in 1963 and the 1969 Tripoli Conference attended by the leaders of Egypt, Libya, and the Sudan illustrated the opposite tendency.

The battlefield of intra-Arab conflicts was not, however, restricted to the halls in which Arab kings and presidents convened. Their differences were generally accompanied by severance of diplomatic relations and vehement mass media vilification campaigns against each other. More serious were the instances in which the Arab "cold war" erupted into fierce and costly fighting, for example, the various Syrian-Lebanese and Syrian-Jordanian skirmishes in 1969 and 1971. Further examples of this point include the unfortunate bloody confrontations between the Jordanian and Lebanese armed forces and the clash between Jordanian and Palestinian commandos. The Jordanian-Palestinian hostilities reached their peak in September, 1970, and terminated in July, 1971. The incidents between the Lebanese and the Palestinian forces occurred in October, 1969 and May, 1973.

A major outcome of the intra-Arab political and military confrontations was the revival of old schisms along provincialist lines which punctured the long hoped for solidarity of the Arab masses. Inasmuch as rifts among Arab regimes have been recurring phenomena, so divisions in the ranks of Arab peoples have been contrary to the traditions of at least a half-century of intensive nationalist education and Arab nationalist sentiment. Two significant examples are worth mentioning. The first relates to countries of the Arab Maghrib and the second to the countries of the Mashriq.

Each of the signatories of the Tripoli Charter was subjected to severe criticism by provincialist anti-Pan-Arab forces within their countries. The non-Arab southerners, the pro-Mahdi northerners, and the communists united in Sudan against the charter and the proposed

FAR.[21] In Egypt, the 'Ali Sabri abortive coup of May, 1971, capitalized on "Egyptian disappointment" with its "Arab experience" in order to oppose unity measures and exploit residues of Egyptian provincialism. Finally, while it is difficult to cite concrete examples that indicate Libyan provincialism, it is nevertheless known that there exists fear among large sectors of the population regarding the possibility of being "swallowed" by the Egyptians.

The second example illustrating provincialism stems from Palestinian relations with Lebanon and Jordan. Entrenched Lebanese provincialism was bolstered as a result of the various clashes that took place between the Palestinian commandos and the Lebanese army. Centripetal tribal forces surfaced among East Jordanians as a consequence of the growth of Palestinian consciousness and precipitated a civil war between the two.

In brief, anti-Pan-Arab forces dominated after 1967. None seemed able to challenge the prevailing hegemony, so the tide of Arab nationalism appeared as if it were completely subdued.

International Rivalry

The Middle East has always been an arena for great power rivalry. Religious, political, economic, and military factors have induced foreign interventions in the affairs of the region. However, the advent of Arab nationalism, the escalation in the Arab-Zionist confrontation, and the polarization that gripped Arab society and divided it into progressives and conservatives fomented further international rivalry and added an external factor to the Middle East cauldron. British and French colonialism sought to reestablish itself via Israel in the 1956 Suez War. Failure was directly attributable to superpower interventions and pressures and their displacement by the United States and the U.S.S.R. as the principal Middle East powers. In this instance, the Soviet-Arab relations were cemented and Israel transferred her allegiance from Europe to the United States.

The United States attempted to domesticate and contain Nasser and the Pan-Arab nationalist movement in the aftermath of Suez by replacing confrontation with accommodation as official U.S. policy. Financial loans, foodstuffs, cultural programs, recognition of the legitimacy of nonalignment, and others were the tools of the new policy. In spite of recurring strains and temporary discontinuities, the policy of accommodation continued until 1965. The reversal of the policy in that year was in line with U.S. global strategy of indirect

21. See Peter Bechtold, *op. cit.*, pp. 159–160.

intervention and the nurturing of client states. Consequently, Saudi Arabia, Iran, and Israel became the pivotal American axis in the region. Simultaneously, the United States sought to whittle down Nasser's power and influence until his eventual deposition, which in fact was a primary objective of the 1967 June War.

But, contrary to U.S. and Israeli expectations, Nasser was not toppled after the June debacle. Indeed Arab sentimental solidarity in defeat proved so effective that President Nasser had to return to office and rebuild the nation's armed forces and reestablish its morale. With Nasser's determination to carry on and with the hostility of the United States to Arab objectives, the Soviet Union was able to seize the opportunity and enter the area unopposed in force. Relations between Egypt and the Soviet Union were consolidated. Syria, Iraq, and Algeria followed suit. The Arab-Soviet policy of collaboration continued unimpeded until the death of Nasser on September 28, 1970, and the succession of Sadat.

PHASE II: DISENCHANTMENT AND ENTENTE

With Nasser out of the scene, there was no unifying Arab personality. Nasser's successor, Anwar Sadat, did not enjoy the prestige and influence that Nasser had. He lacked the charisma required to surmount crises and outlive the state of stalemate which characterized Arab-Israeli relations. Dissension reached new peaks and Sadat was under pressure to extricate Egypt from the dilemma of "no war–no peace." This situation had intensified disenchantment with his regime and was being replicated elsewhere in the Arab world.

The sources of dissatisfaction were numerous:

1. The dissatisfaction of the Arab masses with the regimes' inability to end Israeli occupation. The "no war–no peace" formula which supplanted the attrition war in early 1970 contributed to popular discontents.

2. The impotence of the leaders of Egypt, Syria, and Jordan to liberate their national territory caused a steady decline of their power positions and, consequently, the questioning of their legitimacy. Their inability to score striking achievements on the home front cast more doubt as to their eligibility to rule. On the national level, the leadership was also in a state of paralysis, as demonstrated by their inability to develop FAR into a credible political arrangement that would restore Arab unity. The weakness of these regimes was evident during the fighting between the Palestinian commandos and the Jordanian regime

when both Egypt and Syria expressed solidarity with the Palestinians without being able to translate their words into deeds.

3. Other Arab leaders such as King Faisal were similarly exposed to a barrage of attacks from foreign and domestic forces which relentlessly urged him to "erase the consequences of the 1967 aggression." Because the occupation of the Sinai Peninsula brought Israeli forces to the northern flank of Saudi Arabia, public fears pressured the regime to form an entente with Egypt which came into fruition in the October war. In addition, Israel's unchallenged control of religious sites in the Holy Land was the source of personal embarrassment to Faisal, the most eminent Arab Islamic leader. Furthermore, the very close Saudi-U.S. relations presented the monarchy with two options: either to sever relations or to utilize its good offices with the United States so that Israel would be forced to withdraw. Finally, the "leadership vacuum" created by Nasser's death tempted the King to strive for the leadership of the Arab world; and that presupposed his readiness to assume the leading role in the confrontation with Israel.

Faisal's opportunity to start his assumption of Arab leadership came after the ascendance of Syrian President Hafez Asad to power. The Syrian coup eliminated Salah Jadid's leftist regime in November, 1970. Sadat purged his leftist vice-president, Ali Sabri, in May, 1971. From Faisal's point of view, these two events paved the way for cooperation with the new elite.

Cooperation between Saudi Arabia, Egypt, and Syria developed into an implicit alliance whose aim was to win the confidence of the Arab masses through the achievement of an Israeli withdrawal. Steps were taken to reach an understanding with the United States. Prince Sultan Ibn Abdul-Aziz, the Saudi king's special envoy, conducted several rounds of negotiations with top U.S. officials. The two parties seem to have reached an accord which stipulated that the United States would use its influence with Israel in return for the dismissal of Soviet advisors from Egypt. The Egyptian president wasted no time in executing his part of the agreement. He terminated the mission of Soviet supporting personnel on July 18, 1972, under the pretext of Soviet failure to fulfill earlier promises of "offensive weapons." Egypt's gesture, however, was not reciprocated by the Americans. Subsequent Saudi threats to use the "oil weapon" failed to move the United States.

The United States' total disregard of Arab wishes, together with continued Israeli obstinacy and arrogance, became unbearable. The embarrassment of Arab leaders, especially those of Egypt, Syria, and

Saudi Arabia, was unprecedented. These leaders became convinced that the only way out of the stalemate was through fighting. Hence Egypt and Syria began to seriously prepare for a joint attack and they set out to achieve solidarity with all Arab regimes. With Saudi backing, Egypt and Syria normalized relations with Jordan in September, 1973 with a view to completing the ring around Israel.

The fourth Arab-Israeli war broke out with a coordinated Egyptian-Syrian surprise attack on October 6, 1973. The war signified an historic turning point and established new military and political facts.[22] In that conflict Arab unity was to depend on the level of Arab solidarity, the nature of Arab leadership, the ideological content, and the degree of mass involvement and participation.

The October War and Arab Solidarity

Arab solidarity in the four Arab-Israeli wars exhibited a wide variety of expressions.[23] In the first Arab-Israeli war of 1948, Arab military and political coordination was minimal. In fact, latent rivalries and distrust among Arab leaders accelerated once the fighting erupted. These leaders, especially those of Egypt and Jordan, had different political and territorial ambitions. Militarily, units from five Arab countries participated in some of the battles of that war.[24]

In the 1956 war, Arab solidarity was not as strong as in the preceding war. When Britain, France, and Israel attacked Egypt in concert, the Middle East was torn asunder by warring independent and pro-Western camps led by Egypt and Iraq respectively. Their political and propaganda war had commenced with the introduction of the Baghdad Pact proposal in late 1953. During the war itself, Iraqi airports were placed at the disposal of the British and used in their campaign against Egypt. Egypt fought alone. Of the other Arab states, only Syria offered troops and blew up the oil pipeline. The remainder restricted themselves to verbal support. The emergency meeting held in Beirut and attended by some Arab leaders was no more than a case of demonstrative diplomacy. Arab disunity was at its apogee.

At the time of the third Arab-Israeli war of 1967, Arab inability

22. A study prepared by a team of researchers at the Palestine Research Center in Beirut offers a comprehensive documentary of the war. See Asad Abdul-Rahman (ed.), *al-Harb al-Arabiyyah al-Israiliyyah al-Rabi'ah* [The Fourth Arab Israeli War] (Beirut: Palestine Research Center, 1974).

23. The expression "Arab solidarity" refers here to solidarity among regimes.

24. Excluding the volunteers' "Army of Rescue," these units were from Egypt, Jordan, Iraq, Syria, and Lebanon.

to cooperate became evident six months prior to the conflict when the Rabat summit conference of 1966 was indefinitely postponed. Arab official declarations of "unlimited support" to the fighting countries did not materialize.

Whereas Arab solidarity was lacking in previous confrontations with Israel, it was astonishingly present in 1973. This time it was not confined to verbal and moral support. It included material assistance given to Egypt and Syria by most Arab states. This action contrasted sharply with past wars especially since it was not accompanied with the usual fanfare. Indeed, nothing less would have satisfied skeptical masses and restored their confidence in the leadership.

Arab solidarity expressed itself in three areas: military, political, and economic. Militarily, cooperation between Egypt and Syria reached the point of almost full coordination and harmony manifested in the Egyptian-Syrian High Command, the jointly drawn plans of the surprise offensive, and the day-to-day management of battles. Military participation on the part of other Arab countries was similarly impressive on both fronts. In spite of the suddenness of the attack, several Arab states managed to quickly dispatch their best units to the battlefields. More importantly, these units were immediately placed under the Syrian and/or Egyptian field commands and were effectively incorporated into the fighting armies. This was in sharp contrast with past Arab military behavior when each of the participants fought its battles alone.

Politically, the Arab states utilized a whole array of diplomatic means to mobilize world opinion in their favor. In addition to their coordinated efforts at the U.N., each of the Arab countries made its own contacts with other states. The most significant diplomatic initiatives were those from Saudi Arabia between four Arab foreign ministers and the American president; the Algerian president's trip to Moscow and his meetings with Soviet leaders; the Libyan and Algerian diplomatic campaigns in Africa and Asia; and, finally, the Egyptian moves in Western Europe as well as the Syrian contacts with the leaders of Eastern Europe and other communist countries. Indeed, the Arabs have never been so successful in mobilizing world opinion behind their cause as they were during the October war.

Economically, Arab solidarity took two forms: financial contributions to Syria and Egypt and the use of oil as a political weapon against the enemy and its supporters. Though no exact figures are available as to the volume of the contributions, it is safe to assume that such contributions surpassed all previous records.

On "the oil front" Arab oil-producing countries established three major precedents: (1) For the first time they utilized oil as a political weapon and decided to lower production by at least five per cent monthly as of October, 1973; (2) The decision was an act of defiance against foreign oil corporations and their mother countries. Iraq went further than others by nationalizing the Dutch and U.S. oil companies; (3) The imposition of an oil embargo against the United States and Holland which revealed the determination to reward and punish friend and foe.

Shift in Leadership

A notable difference between the 1973 war and the 1956 and 1967 Arab-Israeli military confrontations is that the latter two were led by President Nasser who symbolized the progressive leadership, while the former was led and directed by the traditionalists, as was the 1948 war. The special role of King Faisal in the October war can be seen in the following:

1. King Faisal was privy to the secret timing of the Egyptian-Syrian surprise offensive. It is known that he was the only Arab leader besides Presidents Asad and Sadat to have prior knowledge of the date. Indeed, some speculate that he was in on the planning and preparations from the outset.

2. The proceedings of the Kuwait Conference of October, 1973 revealed the leading role played by Saudi Arabia in setting the tone and pace of the conference. While conferees vacillated between the option of nationalizing their oil industries or cutting off the oil, they had to settle for a scaled five per cent monthly reduction in compliance with Saudi Arabia's will. Shortly after the Kuwait Conference, Saudi Arabia imposed an oil embargo on the United States and Holland. The importance of this move lies in the fact that sixty per cent of U.S.-Arabian oil imports come from Saudi Arabia. By embarking on such a policy, Saudi Arabia secured and guaranteed her continued leadership of the economic war against Israel's supporters.

3. The leadership of the Saudis was not only asserted before and accepted by the Arabs, but it was also acknowledged and deferred to by foreign powers, including the United States whose secretary of state, Dr. Henry Kissinger, became a frequent pleader at Saudi gates. Similarly when the Arabs delegated the Saudi Arabian and Algerian oil ministers to explain and justify the Arab position in foreign capitals, officials hurried to win the favor of al-Yamani, Saudi Arabia's oil minister.

4. Saudi leadership of the 'oil front' also proved itself in making the Arab oil-producing countries reverse earlier decisions and resume

the pre-September, 1973 oil supplies. Evidence of Saudi leadership was patent at the second Kuwait Conference of December 8th, 1973 when decisions were adopted in spite of strong opposition from radical Arab countries.

Ideological Content
Arab solidarity was maintained during the war partly because the ideological debate was highly muted, if not consigned to oblivion. A sense of pragmatism sustained the Arab alliance and mobilized the Arabs en masse. This policy was expressed in the following manner.

Within the Arab context, Syrian and Egyptian relations were normalized with Saudi Arabia and Jordan, two former ideological rivals, and propaganda campaigns against Iraq ceased. Syria, the staunch radical of the area, especially sought out the friendship of the conservative states of the Gulf as well as Morocco. This change of position was most striking in the case of Syria's approaches to Lebanon's right-wing elements—traditionally Syria's foes.

The erosion of ideology was reflected in the destruction of relations between Egypt and the Soviet Union and the crisis of relations between Saudi Arabia and the United States. Progressive and conservative classifications lost their meaning and the national cause became paramount.

The policy of pragmatism also meant renewal of relations with states regarded unfriendly in the past. For instance, the resumption of relations with the United States after a complete cutoff of seven years attests to this policy. Hyperbolic language was abandoned during and after the war. Statements and public speeches were noted for their moderation, if not understatement. A case in point is the omission of critical references to the United States by President Asad and praise for the Americans from President Sadat.

Mass Involvement and Participation
The 1973 October war marks the lowest point in Arab mass involvement and participation: Not a single demonstration in any Arab capital occurred. There was no rush of volunteers and no general call to arms. From beginning to end the war was fought on the battlefield between conventional armies. The only exception was the Palestinian guerrilla warfare.

The October war represented the unity of regimes, the 1967 war represented the unity of tears, the war of 1956 represented the unity of aspirations, and the war of 1948 represented the unity of faith. The 1948 war demonstrated mass involvement and commitment to the preservation of the Arab identity of Palestine. The Army of Rescue (Jaysh al-'Inqath), a melange of volunteers from Egypt, Sudan, Syria, Lebanon, Iraq, and other Arab countries, made that involvement into a concrete form and forced the regimes to assume their obligation to Palestine. The unified offensive of seven Arab armies into Palestine on May 15, 1948, and their eventual defeat highlighted the incompetence of the Arab regimes. Because of the intense rivalries among the political systems, the armies were not allowed to act in unison and the national cause was jeopardized. Afterwards the legitimacy of the regimes eroded; and political upheavals and assassinations swept the countries surrounding Palestine.

In the second war, President Nasser had made strong attempts to reinvolve the Arab masses in national affairs. Bypassing their governments, he appealed to the people directly. The war saw a great identity of interests between Nasser the leader and the Arab peoples. President Nasser's rapport with the masses forced the Arab regimes to pay lip service to solidarity.

In 1967, the mass Arab reaction of support which erupted on June 9 and 10 when President Nasser relinquished office, persuaded him to resume his leadership. Since other Arab governments had abdicated their responsibility, no one was capable of channeling this reservoir of energy and putting it to the service of an Arab nation. Political energy was squandered and the masses were seriously alienated. By 1973 neither the Arab masses nor the Arab leaders had initiated the process of interaction. The masses became mere spectators; policy became mere official proclamation. Because of past experiences, the masses no longer trusted the general Arab leadership. Such trust had to be reestablished on the battlefield before it could hope to restore its political credibility.

CONCLUSION

What happened is not until now a union or a federation, but it is more than a mere solidarity necessitated by events that happened or are happening in the region.[25]

This statement depicts a condition that most students of Arab politics note in their studies. They are at a loss to satisfactorily explain why unity exercises such a powerful grip on the imagination and actions

25. Adel Abu Shanab, "Akthar min mugarad tadamun" [More than mere solidarity], Al-Ma'rifah (Damascus), No. 143 (January, 1974), p. 176.

of the Arabs yet they are well aware of its workings. Most studies corroborate this conclusion. The present course of events is not the product of recent developments; it is caused by widespread Arab feelings of a common identity and a wish to establish an Arab political union that cancels present boundaries.

In its modern history, the movement for Arab unity has passed through four stages. Each of these stages underlined a pathway to the achievement of Arab unity. The first called for the provision of a forum for cooperation and coordination of policies among Arab regimes; the second classified regimes into dynamic and static ones and confined unitarian moves to the former; the third demanded the radical transformation of Arab life and institutions and emphasized the role of public movements; the fourth pathway to unity will require the integration of the Arab world through the mobilization of resources and their use for common development projects.

In each of the above four stages, one notices the existence of a trend that opposed the dominant fourth trend but was eclipsed by it. The contractual outlook was, for instance, opposed by the aspirational, the progressive by the conservative, the revolutionary by the fundamentalist, and the functionalist by the fusionist.

As to the effect of the October war on Arab unity, the performance of the Arab side would not have been impressive had it not been for the Arab ability to forego differences for the sake of common goals. This policy proved the soundness of Nasser's strategic plan of action which favored the idea of "Unity is the road to Palestine" to "Palestine is the road to unity." Without the political and military coordination of policies that preceded and outlined October, the outcome of the war would not have been much different from the outcome of former Arab-Israeli wars.

As previously shown, the solidarity of Arab regimes reached an impressive level only after the suppression of ideological differences. To arrive at this condition, a price had to be paid which was in the form of a recognition by progressives of the leadership of Faisal and their readiness to coexist with conservative regimes. The whole affair took place in the absence of any popular involvement.

In addition to the desire to discuss national issues in common, the bridging of differences between the two warring ideological camps reflected the transformed socioeconomic realities of the region. The sharp increase in the income of Arab oil-producing countries, especially those of the peninsula, was accompanied by increased financial, military, and political power. By the late sixties, conservative regimes were no longer in a defensive position vis-à-vis progressives. They could afford to modernize their economies and civil bureaucracies without having to alter their political systems. Their affluence sufficed to moderate internal social unrest and neutralize outside critics. The yearly financial contributions made by Saudi Arabia, Kuwait, and Libya to Egypt and Syria served as early as the 1967 Khartoum Conference to compromise the position of Arab progressives.

The Arab world now stands at the crossroads. Three currents are urging for dominance: the wish to conserve tradition, the wish to liberalize, and the wish to revolutionize. All three currents share in a sense of historic mission for the Arab world. The first visualizes it in the founding of an Arab-Muslim society, the second in a secular democratic society, and the third in a Pan-Arab revolution that has a socialist content. Presently, the liberal and the conservative schools have coalesced in the interests of their self-preservation to propose a non-ideological, functional approach to Arab problems. Their endeavor could predominate. The vast inflow of oil revenues provides the Arabs with the material means to realize the Arab-Muslim vision. It is not certain, however, that they have the capacity and determination to undertake such a task. Deeply rooted suspicions, local peculiarities, personal idiosyncracies, and the flippancy of Arab officialdom present serious hurdles that need yet to be overcome.

In addition to the sense of historic mission and the instinct for self-preservation, the conservative-liberal alliance must take account of the popular will that continually exerts pressure on them to perform. Failure to do so might well leave the Arab world with only the third option of revolution.

Elaine Hagopian and Halim Barakat

THE NEW ARAB GENERATION

UNIVERSITY STUDENTS IN LEBANON coming from various parts of the Arab world have constituted a vanguard movement that may be viewed as leading the forces for change in the Arab world against the forces for maintaining the established order. Student movements have kept Arab issues alive and have passed them on to the new generations.

The present student movements may be traced back to the last quarter of the nineteenth century. They began to emerge during the second quarter of this century, at which time the struggle for independence was beginning to take shape. Increasing national awareness brought about some organized political action. Two political movements started to take root among students in the 1930's: the Arab Nationalist Movement, and the Syrian Social Nationalist party. Both were founded at the American University of Beirut by students and faculty members, and both concerned themselves with questions of national identity and the struggle for independence. For almost three decades the two movements dominated the political arena on the University campus and competed for control of student societies. Students argued about what factors constituted a nation, and to which nation they belonged, that is one Arab nation, or different Arab regions

The participants were students from various parts of the Arab world studying at the American University of Beirut. Three sessions were held and tape recorded in February, 1974. The transcription of the sessions was distributed to each participant for review and clarification in May, 1974. The final copy was edited in October, 1974.

or states. Although there were a few communists who allied themselves with Arab nationalists, they were not accepted. Marxian class analysis was almost totally foreign to Arab nationalist political thinking at that time.

The impact of the Palestine calamity from the 1940's to the present on the development of the student movement in Lebanon, where all orientations from the Arab world are expressed, is comparable to that of the Vietnam war on the development in the United States, but it has been more lasting. The 1948 Arab defeat aroused feelings for revolt; the 1967 defeat created a mood for revolution. Specifically, the Palestinian uprootedness or diaspora has contributed to the following developments in regard to the student movement: (1) Students have been more involved in ideological political parties and organizations. (2) Students have become increasingly disenchanted with the West and more aware of its imperialistic designs for the area. This awareness has been coupled with deep feelings of alienation from Western culture. (3) Students have grown increasingly disenchanted with their own traditional culture and institutions. (4) There has been an increasing shift from purely nationalistic interpretations to social class analysis. In other words, there has been an increasing awareness of the relevance of class analysis. The shift has been demonstrated much more clearly after the 1967 defeat. (5) Palestinian students have constituted the core of the student movement at least since 1967.[1]

The above developments are reflected in the following discussion. The participants are not representative of all student groups on university campuses in the Arab world. However, many of the discussants are known as student activists, and they do articulate the feelings and ideas of progressive student groups who constitute the vanguard movement in opposition to the dominant trends in the Arab society. They reject the dominant reconciliatory mood that is being promoted by Arab regimes presently. Other orientations are also expressed here by students who are not members of any political movement.

The present discussion was highly unstructured. The participants were presented with two sets of questions. First, they were asked to describe their perceptions of the October war, its causes and objectives, and the consequences. Second, they were asked to describe their visions of the future with particular reference to the solution of the Palestine problem.

HALIM BARAKAT

1. Details on the development of the student movement in Lebanon can be found in Halim Barakat, *Commitment to Change: A Sociological Study of the Student Movement in Lebanon*, forthcoming.

Drs. Barakat and Hagopian: How do you interpret the October war, the events leading up to it, its objectives, and its consequences?

Dikran: First of all, the 1967 June war, instead of resolving the so-called Arab-Israeli conflict, presented further complications, and elucidated once and for all the bankruptcy of the petit bourgeois Arab military regimes. All the active participants in the Middle East drama, that is the Arab states, Israel, and the world powers, remained ill at ease because the reasons that had led to the actual fighting in 1967 had not been eliminated. They simply were dormant; more precisely, they became latent.

Essentially there were two options for resolving the conflict: namely, (1) diplomacy, and (2) war. To say the obvious, diplomacy failed after 1967, giving way to war, the October war of 1973. Perhaps we can say that the June war impregnated the October war, and October, 1973 was the date of delivery. But was the October war really option 2, or only a technique to move the stalemated option 1?

The fact that Sadat proposed an international peace conference *early* in the October war, which has come to be known as the Geneva Conference, suggests that he had really opted for resolving the conflict through diplomacy. The question that has to be asked is, "What political changes took place in the Arab world between 1967 and October, 1973 that postulated the limited yields of early diplomacy over another round of full war to regain all or most Arab rights?"

The key changes within the Arab states and in inter-Arab state relations during this interwar period can be summarized as follows: (1) Egypt's posture was weakened and it came to rely on aid from fellow Arab states, namely Saudi Arabia, Kuwait, and Libya (the latter being less important). (2) Saudi Arabia's wealth became realized in practical terms, that is, it could be used as a pressure to resolve the conflict. The flood of dollars and Western European currencies into Saudi Arabia and other oil-producing countries is the number one problem of the world monetary system for the next decade. "In another decade, this desert nation of five million to eight million persons is likely to have reserves of about $30 billion in gold and foreign exchange. That would clearly be more than double the present American total, and it clearly would turn this developing country into a monetary giant."[2] (3) After Nasser's death in 1970, Sadat opened the door wide for a more intimate relationship between Egypt and Saudi Arabia. King Faisal could never forget Nasser's assault during

2. *Time*, February 18, 1974, pp. 14–15.

the 1950's and 1960's on Saudi Arabia's political conservatism and orientation to the United States. Hence, Nasser's death brought about the end of a political epoch and ushered in a new one whose ideological inclination took a fundamentally different course. (4) Additionally, Sadat opened Egypt to foreign capital, and in particular to U.S. capital. *Time* magazine summed up the matter:

> Sadat wants to attract not only Western capital but also the oil money flowing into the Arab world in rapidly increasing amounts. Foreign capital is being enticed by such moves as Sadat's recent decision to sign a World Bank agreement that protects foreign investors against losses from nationalization.[3]

And (5) these political and economic ideological shifts were coupled with the release of right-wing political prisoners in Egypt, most of whom were returned to high public office.

Thus, Egypt under Sadat, constantly moving to the right, finally made its "peace" with the United States and thus opened the door for the Saudi-Egyptian entente to solidify. Gone was the Nasser era accent on trying to effect an Arab nationalism that required the development of one Arab nation based on the political and economic transformations of all Arab countries leading to a form of Arab socialism which could confront all Arab problems from unity and economic strength. The transformations were to result from the Arab liberation movement of which the Palestinian Resistance Movement was a basic element. In the place of Nasser's concept of a United Arab Republic has come a concept of Arab nationalism which requires only coopera-tion between sovereign, brotherly Arab states, regardless of ideology, to achieve Arab goals.

The point I am stressing here is that because of all the factors named, Saudi Arabia could and did move to the center of the stage and began to play a dominant role in shaping Arab policies in conjunction with Egypt. Thus the period marked by Nasser's charisma ended, and closed-room politics emerged.[4]

---

3. *Wall Street Journal,* January 23, 1973, p. 1.

4. A major expressing of this new right wing approach to Arab problems was the December, 1972 conference of Arab ministers held in Kuwait. This conference was convened directly after the 1972 American presidential election. In the election campaign, Nixon stressed the Middle East as a high priority foreign policy issue. He thus "opened" the door to the new entente to consider how to move to engage the United States in resolving the conflict.

The new Egyptian-Saudi entente gave rise to a new axis of Arab power: Arab reaction, the strengthening of the right wing. Now after the October war, we notice that the new tune being played is one of diplomacy, one of detente with the United States. The resolution of the Arab-Israeli conflict in the terms of this detente means a partial and compromised settlement of the Palestinian problem and of the larger conflict, the elimination of anything referred to as the Palestinian Resistance Movement, and of the idea of resistance itself. What we are faced with at this point in time is the fact that the Arab right wing recognized that the only way to maintain its power is by strengthening its alliance with the United States. This alliance postulates the need for striking down the progressive forces in the region, which in turn requires a demonstration for the Arab people that the Arab-Israeli conflict is being resolved, compromised though it may be. This was the intent and basis of the October war.

Fuad: The consequences of the 1967 June war pushed the Arab progressive regimes, specifically Syria and Egypt, into a corner. They had to reexamine the reasons for this situation. The basic problem, of course, was related to the fact that these regimes had not really transformed their society, and thus the situation in which they found themselves is attached in a basic form to the class structure of the regimes.

I would like to distinguish two periods between 1967 and 1973. The first period, 1967-70, was characterized by the passing of U.N. resolution 242 and its acceptance by Nasser. As we know, that resolution calls for, among other things, the withdrawal of Israel from the occupied Arab lands resulting from the June war, a recognition of Israel, and a vague reference to the rights of Palestinian refugees.[5] For Nasser, resolution 242 provided a kind of exit given the balance of power after the June war. Nasser wanted to effect resolution 242 because it would allow a gain of at least the lands occupied in 1967 which Egypt could not regain by itself, given the limitations of Egyptian power at that time. But it was not possible to effect resolution 242 because Israel could not be forced to give back the lands; it had superior power. Israel wanted only to sign a treaty, keep the lands, and have what it called peace. For the Arab world, however, it would

5. Editors' Note: In the Spring, 1974 meeting of the Palestine National Council, the Palestinians rejected the definition of their situation as a refugee problem. They insisted that it be defined as a problem of national rights. The U.N. General Assembly has recognized this situation, and the matter will be debated Fall, 1974.

have been surrender. Therefore, the Arab regimes, and especially the Egyptian regime, had to look for another exit. This was the war of attrition.

Nasser initiated the war of attrition in March, 1970 as a tactical move, not as a strategic one. The greatest evidence of that is that when the war of attrition started, the American diplomatic moves started, that is from the visit of Sisco to the Rogers Plan in 1970. That Plan was intended to stop the war of attrition, to stop the new fighting spirit that had been growing in the region, and to strike at the consolidation of efforts between the Palestinian Resistance Movement and the Egyptian regime. The aim of the Rogers Plan was not to find a solution to the Arab-Israeli problem. Unfortunately, the Resistance Movement was tricked into believing that it was. The pressure on Nasser was accelerated, and the actual goals of the Rogers effort were achieved. Nasser was further weakened and the Arab world more divided. Thereafter, diplomatic efforts from the United States ceased.

Hani: The massacre of Palestinian Resistance fighters in Jordan in September, 1970 is a direct result of the real intent of the Rogers Plan.

Fuad: The second period, 1970–73, is marked by the death of Nasser and the emergence of Sadat. Sadat turned away from the progressive Arab nationalist line which Nasser had established, if not effected, and permitted the reemergence of the right wing elements in Egypt. This wing does not have abstract ideals floating about, so much as it has interests. To effect these interests, a solution to the Arab-Israeli conflict that would be approved by the United States had to be found. They could choose between the two options Dikran has already noted: (1) diplomacy or (2) war.

During this second period, then, a search was made by the new ruling class in Egypt, along with their new Saudi partners, to find the means to engage the United States to apply pressure on its client, Israel, to resolve the Middle East crisis. For the United States to do so, the Americans would have to determine that settlement would be in their own best interests, and that the terms of settlement would not limit the strength of Israel for the immediate future.

In the early part of the second period, diplomatic exits were sought. Moves were made which Egypt and Saudi Arabia hoped would initiate the diplomatic process towards settlement. Newspapers reported that King Faisal had been promised by Nixon that if Sadat removed the

Soviet advisers from Egypt, American policy would change. Sadat expelled the Soviet advisers. He also began a series of economic changes which Dikran has noted. He further changed the structure of the Arab Socialist Union (the major political body of representation and participation in Egypt) by expelling its progressive cadres and enabling the returned agricultural capitalists to dominate the Union's leadership. But after all of these changes in internal and external policy, there was no response from the American side. The Americans did not yet feel that Egypt was securely within the American imperialist sphere, and thus did not act after all these moves were made. Thus, the attempt to initiate a diplomatic solution during this early stage of the Saudi-Egyptian entente failed.

The failure of these efforts to net results increased pressure on Sadat to take some action to "erase the results of the June war." The Egyptian regime was faced with internal problems as a result of the student movement in 1972 and 1973. This movement created for the Egyptian regime a somewhat critical situation. The students represented popular forces whose interests started contradicting those of the ruling class in Egypt. This movement was one of rejection of the regime, as well as a new basic movement. The regime began to fear that the student movement would transfer its radicalism to other sectors within the Egyptian nation and that the Egyptian regime would then have no choice but to suppress these movements. This, in turn, would pose a danger to the regime and to the ruling class.

Thus, the October war was the exit. The war was not to liberate the lands by force so much as to strengthen the regime's position and bring about diplomatic efforts. The proof of this aim, as noted by Dikran, is Sadat's speech during the war and his early appeal for a peace conference in Geneva. After the war, there was a chain of retreats, the most distinctive of which were the limited disengagement on the Suez Canal and the codification of the new economic policy as developed by Abdul Aziz Hijazi. The latter policy would now allow Egypt to fall more completely within American imperialist interest, and thus encourage the United States to become engaged in bringing about a settlement.

Hani: I think that the real reason for the October war was the need to secure Saudi oil from Western threats. It is true that it was Egypt and Syria who fought, but it was really Saudi Arabia's war, or, in other words, the oil war. New factors emerged on the scene that were not seen at the time of the 1967 war, factors mainly related to the "energy crisis." The West needs Arab oil. Saudi Arabia has the biggest oil reservoir in the world. Consequently, it is in a position to control much of the destiny of the Western world for the immediate future. (References to Saudi Arabia here include also the collection of oil countries that exist in its sphere, such as Kuwait and the United Arab Emirates).

The Western-Israeli threats to Saudi Arabia started to accelerate in March, 1973, with talk of occupying the sources of energy (see Senator Fulbright's statement of that period).[6] Saudi Arabia is an open country and has no military ability of any significance. While essentially oriented toward the United States, it was viewed by the United States as too weak to suppress potential radical advances in the Gulf area by Iraq, Southern Yemen, Dhofar Province, Oman where presently there is revolutionary activity being carried out, and by the influence of the Palestinian Resistance Movement. Most of these forces are interested in a strong united Arab world able to command its destiny better, a goal seen as detrimental to Western interests, but particularly to U.S. interests.

The United States was interested in securing the oil and the pipelines. Thus, in May, 1973, the United States made a huge arms deal with Iran, America's proxy in the Gulf area. From that time on, Saudi Arabia started changing its stand with respect to oil. For the past twenty years, Saudi Arabia had said that it wanted to sell oil because the latter had nothing to do with politics. But beginning in early 1973, Sheikh Ahmad Zaki Yamani, the Saudi oil minister, and King Faisal started mentioning the possibility of using oil as a political weapon in the Arab-Israeli battle if U.N. resolution 242 was not executed. And, in fact, Saudi Arabia was interested in executing resolution 242 so that there would be a period of settlement in the Middle East and a checking of radical forces which have grown because of the inability of Arab regimes to resolve Arab problems. Radical forces worry U.S. interests. Control of them would enable Saudi Arabia to solidify its leadership over the region, the profit King Faisal gained from the Arab defeat in 1967, and prevent American intervention. Thus, Saudi needs and gains coincided with Egyptian needs and failures, and the October war was the "solution." The "oil weapon" was used to give substance to the military war and to pressure for diplomacy to effect resolution 242.

Sadat opted for surrender of the Arab national cause by means of war. The complete surrender could not be made openly. But I would maintain that the limited October war was Sadat's way of

6. Recently (October, 1974), President Ford has again raised the threat of American military intervention in the Gulf to secure U.S. interests.

actually surrendering the Arab national cause and allowing a strengthening of Arab reactionary forces in the Arab world which serve both the conservative elements of Arab society and the U.S. interests.

Ahmad: The leaders of the October war, coming as they do from a specific reactionary class, were carrying out the interests of their class and not those of the Arab masses. The first day the war was declared, I thought that it would be a limited war. This soon became quite evident, as the Egyptian Army stopped at a specific line after crossing the Suez Canal. This situation confused me and raised many questions that were answered later on after Egypt's declaration of the cease-fire. Sadat, then, started presenting his concessions. The conscious public, or that segment of the public that is distinguished by almost complete consciousness, was not convinced by Sadat's presentation of the problem. It was calling for continued fighting until all Arab lands had been liberated. Why had Sadat stopped the war? What would his next step be?

Now everything is clear. Sadat has started agreeing and cooperating with the Americans. The coming years will demonstrate the negative effects of this cooperation on the lives of the Arab masses.

First of all, the beginnings of this disaster date back to an earlier period, when the economic structure in Egypt failed to develop a viable socialism under Nasser. Thus Sadat could justify his rapid move to the right by the failure of socialism.

Second, the Egyptian bourgeoisie reached the stage of industrialization after it had moved into the stage of services and commercial trade with the Arab countries and with foreigners. It thus reached a stage where it did not have capital sufficient for commercial trade. Egypt was forced to seek capital in order to finance industry at home. Such capital is attached to the Western commercial countries. This is a very important point.

Third, imperialism is trying to grant a role to the Arab oil and reactionary countries in order to contain progressive movements in their spheres. The role of Israel will be to serve as the controlling country. In other words, these Arab reactionary countries will execute locally the imperialist plan. Should these countries fail to carry out the imperialist plan, Israel will emerge as the spearhead of American imperialism: it will emerge again as a military power that will smash any Arab national liberation movement working against imperialism.

Nadim: When the October war broke out, the Arab masses were not prepared to accept the "peaceful" solution, or rather the reactionary political line. They favored continuation of the battle and the progressive political line of thought. When the war began, many thought that things had changed and that it was possible to define Sadat's and Faisal's regimes, which were backed by other Arab nationalist regimes such as Algeria, as progressive or semiprogressive in their line of thought. Of course, after the war, all such thoughts vanished.

The war was fought for two reasons: first, the idea was to remove the Israelis from the 1967 occupied lands. With respect to Egypt, the battle became purely Egyptian nationalism. The same was true for Syria, though with some different shadings. This meant that both Egypt and Syria wanted to get back their land. The Arab nationalist outlook which had been declared since 1948, was deleted. Second, the war was fought because Syria, Egypt, and especially Saudi Arabia felt the presence of a thorn that had to be pulled out—the Palestinian Resistance. Before October the political initiative was in the hands of the Resistance. Now, the Palestinian Resistance is succumbing to the moves of the regimes and trying to salvage what it can under the circumstances.

Fuad: It is true that the forces of Arab nationalism became weaker after the October war, but the idea of Arab nationalism was not weakened. What was weakened was Egypt's role in the Arab liberation movements and the establishment of Arab unity. Egypt will not leave the "Arab university" and will not deny being an Arab country. The idea of Arab nationalism is basically attached to the idea of democratic liberation on the Arab level and to liberation from imperialism. Egypt may be "disengaged" for now, but Egypt, by virtue of its position within the Arab world, will not and cannot abandon Arab nationalist goals and the fight against imperialism.

Omar: The idea of Arab nationalism was strongly attached to the idea of regaining the occupied lands. After the October war, a new political tone was initiated by Sadat and supported by the rest of the leaders in order to have "peace" with Israel. This new tone presents a clear contradiction between the idea of nationalism and the idea of recovering the land.

In general, the outlook has clearly become an operation of escapism so that the masses will accept the reality created by Sadat—and they will not think of going back to Arab nationalism. Therefore, the force of Arab nationalism has reached a period of dissipation.

Hani: In the eyes of the people, that is, the average citizen, Sadat is a national hero. The mass political awareness in Egypt is almost completely absent; there is not even minimum political awareness. Since these regimes fought, regardless of their aims, they have become national regimes, and their leaders have become national heroes in the eyes of the masses. The Palestinian Resistance Movement could have played a role opposing that of the regimes if the Resistance had been strong enough. For Egypt and Syria in particular, if the Palestinian Resistance had been able to reach the Arab masses with an understanding of a popular war of liberation, it would have been a different struggle. But the Resistance was not able to reach the Arab masses effectively. It reached some groups of the Arab masses, but not in a manner capable of protecting the Revolution and protecting the Arab national line of thought.

Dr. Barakat: Would you like to comment on the energy crisis and its role in the October war?

Dikran: It is a mistake to believe everything one reads in the newspapers. The American press started reporting an energy crisis, and everyone started crying over it. But the question is not really one of an energy crisis. True, the Arab world possesses the ability to circumscribe to a certain extent the technological power of the West. The potential use of this ability was not fully exploited in the October war, and this means that we have a way to travel before we actualize that ability. During Fall and Winter of 1973, the United States did not have an energy crisis, but a profit crisis.

If we take the top American oil companies, and if we follow their profit reports for 1973, we find that in each quarter, absolute quantities and profit rates are higher than in the preceding one. This is a very important point. Oil supplies that were available in the United States were not being sold because monopoly capital set a certain price for selling the commodities in order to insure increased profits. Such a system requires that not all available supplies be sold so as to maintain a high price and, hence, high profits. In other words, American oil companies are increasing their profits to unheard of proportions. The last quarter reports (Fall-Winter 1973) indicate an increase even during the period of the October war.

So now we can come to talk about the "energy crisis" and relate it to the Middle East. One of the things that the United States and most of Europe did not anticipate was not the cutting off of oil—oil was not really cut off[7]—but the unexpected behavior of Arab and

---

7. If oil were cut off directly, secondary sources would have sold oil to the United States, and those secondary sources would have purchased Arab oil.

other oil-producing countries in greatly increasing the price of oil. As a result of this increase in producer prices, the oil companies urged an increase in selling prices. In other words, oil companies were interested in increasing the prices so as to maximize their profits in sales, and the "Arab boycott" permitted the companies the opportunity to withhold sales and raise prices.

The Arab countries do have a weapon, a potential weapon, in oil, but so long as that weapon is in the hands of the Arab bourgeoisie, in the hands of the Arab ruling classes, it can only serve the imperialist plan and program in the area. Perhaps this sounds simplistic, but I think it is important to consider this situation. Saudi Arabia is not about to support the revolutionary liberation movement in the region. By supporting the Egyptian and Syrian governments, it was/is in fact diluting the political radicalism that these regimes possessed in the past, diluting their radicalism so as to assure and insure the domination of the right wing in the region.

Now, I would like to talk about some other developments. As a direct result of the war, there is a new balance in the region. Though Israel proved that it still possesses military prowess, it was nevertheless caught by surprise, thereby losing its previous claim to invincibility. In short, Israel was dealt a psychological blow from which it is presently suffering—political instability, economic and social problems, etc.

In the 1950's and 1960's, Israel was viewed as a partner to imperialism. The context of this partnership was articulated in 1966 by Robert McNamara, at that time U.S. secretary of defense, when he was lecturing in Montreal to a group including some Israeli leaders. He said in effect that the United States could not go on fighting wars, that it would have to depend on regional powers—that is, Israel, Iran, Brazil to control areas and to effect its interests against the interests of local progressive movements. Israel was seen practically from its inception as a strong instrument of U.S. imperialism in the Middle East. Such a role not only served American interests, but served Israeli interests in the area which could be firmly supported by American resources. That is, in order to fulfill the design of political Zionism and to expand in the area, it had to have military superiority to defeat the indigenous Palestinian population and Arab neighbors, at whose expense, Israeli interests were being met. This superiority kept the Arab world in disarray and in an underdeveloped state. This served Western imperialist interests, and especially those of the United States.

The October war changed the status of Israel from a partner to a client. That is, the cracks in Israeli military strength were demonstrated. This suggested to the United States that it should broaden its alliances in the area to control progressive forces, and not simply rely on the present form of Israel. Hence, the growing detente with Egypt and other Arab regimes, previously more radical, is an attempt to develop and solidify such alliances. Thus, to do so, a settlement of the Arab-Israeli conflict must be found in a manner to rob the initiatives of the progressive forces and strengthen the right wing in the Arab world. This does not mean an abandoning of Israel as an important instrument in the area, but it does mean that American and Israeli interests are not one hundred per cent meshed as they were in the past. Therefore, compromised and mild though some of the suggested solutions to the Arab-Israeli conflict are, Israel is concerned about them. (In point of fact, however, if such solutions as are being discussed are ever effected, Israel may actually be in a stronger position economically in the area and be able to effect its own and U.S. interests better).

The point being made here, however, is that no longer can Israel select the means to effect imperialist interests, means it selected on the bases that they served its own interests best. The Israeli elector chose the right wing throughout the history of the state. The right wing has now shown itself as being incapable of effecting its program for Israeli interests. This fact will postulate social upheaval in Israel. In turn, this will make Israel more dependent on the United States. Thus, as a dependent state, rather than a partner in strategy, it will be like all client states. It will have to receive orders from the United States in the same way that reactionary forces in the past have received orders, e.g., the regime of South Vietnam.

On another level, and perhaps the most important, are the new international developments. Historically, each government (in the capitalist world) has been obliged to serve the interests of its state. But with various revolutions (socialist) succeeding and acquiring state power, certain countries (e.g., the Soviet Union and China) have claimed to stand for internationalism and the interests of all exploited peoples. However, by virtue of their being nation-states, they do put the interests of their state above their international obligations. We should not forget however that a great deal of economic and military aid has been presented to the various liberation movements by both the Soviet Union and China. Therefore, these socialist countries, objectively speaking, are perhaps the only friend that the Arabs have.

Within this nuclear age, the superpowers, primarily the United States, the Soviet Union, and the People's Republic of China, have developed a rapprochement, a so-called detente for pragmatic reasons. These superpowers, particularly the United States and the Soviet Union, are uninterested in supporting another war in the area. They want to calm down the region. The Soviet Union is still committed to helping some progressive movements, but only viable ones. The Vietnamese had proved themselves, and therefore deserved—and not only deserved but demanded—Soviet aid. The question is, then, "Can the Arab people's movement prove itself in the area to attract Soviet help?" If not, then the Soviet Union will cooperate in calming the region until such time as a viable progressive movement can develop.

Fuad: Do you mean that all the international powers, including China and the Soviet Union, want to quiet down the area?

Dikran: Yes, with minor exceptions for China, although I don't want to get into the subtleties of the matter. This situation is part of the major development of the 1970's, the ending of the cold war as such. This development must be taken into close consideration as we look at national liberation movements in the world. Such movements can no longer gain the automatic and outright support of any nation. They must prove themselves as a power, earn the right of support.

Fuad: With regard to what Dikran has said, it is a mistake to present one's analysis of the situation from the viewpoint of the strategy of international accord or strategy of balance of power. There is no doubt that there is a balance on the international level, a balance of nuclear powers, if you will. However, what is called the international accord does not mean what Dikran said it does, namely that the international powers want to "cool down" the area. This is incorrect. The proof is that the international balance was not able to stop the Vietnamese revolution from pursuing the full rights of the Vietnamese people. What keeps the Arab liberation movement from completion is not the international variables but the class factor, the social and political structure on which the movement had been built.

Dikran: If you will recall, I did point out that the international accord does not prevent the socialist countries from helping progressive movements. However, the accord does tend to make that support selective, i.e., it is given only to those movements that appear viable. The Vietnamese movement was viable; the Arab liberation movement so far is not.

Fuad: The point is that the accord does not mean quitting on progressive movements in the area as your idea that the big powers want to quiet down the area seems to imply. The reasons for the continual disasters of the Arab liberation movement can be related to mechanisms, or the machinery of the movement, which govern the acts, behavior, and programs, the entire political setup. The Arab liberation movement used to present duties larger than its mechanisms were capable of achieving; consequently there was a kind of demagogism and exaggeration, which was uncovered by the June war. However, this behavior continued after 1967 because it was embedded in the prevailing Arab ideology. What made the Arab liberation movement fail was not the international balance, and not the strategy of international relief, as much as it was its own mechanisms, the limitations of its class potential.

Another factor that contributed to the failure of the movement was the inability of the leadership to tie, in practice, the struggle against Israel and imperialism to the struggle against the ruling-class forces in each Arab country. It did this in theoretical terms, but not in practice.

Leila: There is a great gap between the causes of the war and its consequences. The reason for this is the gap between the Arab regimes and the Arab masses, a gap that is characteristic of underdeveloped countries like ours. True, the war was staged by the Arab regimes, and possibly even in collaboration with the big powers hoping to solidify reactionary forces in the Arab world. Nonetheless, soldiers fought and died, whole villages were destroyed, masses were deprived, both Arab and Israeli.

The most important consequences of the October war are on the mass level, both in Egypt and in Israel. In Egypt, the war restored the confidence of the Egyptians in themselves. Following the 1967 war, the image of the Egyptian soldier was that of an ignorant, undernourished Arab who left his boots all over the desert before running away from the Israeli army. Now the image of the Egyptian soldier is that of a young university graduate who has mastered the art of modern weapons and engineering.

Although the Egyptians realized that they had not won the war, the fact that they had not lost it was in itself a victory. It is a sad commentary on man that the skills demonstrated in arms and killing have gained more respect and admiration from the world than the thousands of years of Egyptian civilization.

With respect to Israel, after the October war, for the first time in Israeli history, the Israelis had some doubts about their military establishment and, as a result, about their political leadership. The civilian population demanded an investigation into the mistakes committed during the war. Most important of all, people who had hoped that the 1967 war would be the last big war Israel would fight, started doubting the expansionist policy of the government. A number of Israeli and Jewish intellectuals within and outside of Israel have frequently forecast the end of Israel if the government does not change its policy with regard to the Arab world. The October war enhanced these forecasts. Zionism has led Israel to its present situation as a racist, expansionist state. More and more people within Israel are realizing that the price of Zionism might be too high to pay. If Israel does not withdraw completely from Arab lands and recognize Palestinian national rights, then the October war will have been only one round in the series of battles of the Arab-Israeli conflict.

Drs. Barakat and Hagopian: How do you see the future of the Arab world and the resolution of the Palestinian question? What options do Arabs have?

Hani: U.N. resolution 242 aims to achieve a return to the borders of June 4, 1967; the recognition of the state of Israel as an established economic and political system; cooperation with Israel on the part of the Arab world, including granting Israel the right of passage in the Suez Canal and Sharm al Sheikh, and other rights as well. These aims represent a hidden end: Israel being a technologically advanced country, it would end up with complete economic control over the Arab world.

The October war was started on the basis of making the Israelis retreat to the borders of 1967 as specified in resolution 242. This means that it was not a war of liberation, but a war to break the political stalemate that diplomatic efforts had failed to do earlier. Even so, the operation of October 6 as a military demonstration to break this stalemate was not able to achieve even its limited aims one hundred per cent. By this I mean specifically that the Israeli infiltration of the west bank of the Suez Canal during the war posed a problem for Egypt, since the Canal represented the most important axis in the war. Egypt has had to renounce more and more; and the bargaining is no longer on the basis of resolution 242 vis-à-vis return of Arab lands occupied in the June war. If agreements are reached in Geneva, they will probably be on the basis of the disengagement agreements.

What I want to present now is what I imagine at the present stage Egypt and Saudi Arabia are thinking, for the Saudi-Egyptian axis is leading the Arab world. Saudi Arabia and Egypt are concerned with extracting the Soviet Union from the area, returning to the 1967 borders, and solving the Palestinian problem by establishing a weak, and economically unviable Palestinian entity or state on part of the land of Palestine.

One possible reason for suggesting a plan for the Palestinian entity is not to execute it but to promote dissension among the Resistance: some will agree to the idea while others will not. After some time members of the Resistance will turn against each other; and in the end there will be no group capable of refusing or accepting the plan.

On the other hand, Israel will not accept a peaceful settlement, even if the Arabs actually want permanent peace in the region, because Israel is established on the basis of expansion. The question was never, at any time, will Israel attack? But rather it was, when and how will Israel attack? Israel is interested, as part of the international Zionist strategy which Israel aims to achieve, in establishing the greater Israel—the big Israel. So Israel, primarily will not accept retreat from lands that it occupied. Israel may tactically retreat from a specific stand and hence retreat to an inconvenient position. But from there it will prepare the chance for a new blow and a new expansion in a way that will make such an operation more perfect.

I feel first, that a peaceful settlement in any form should be refused. No matter how you look at it, it cannot provide a logical result in this region. Second, if it is not possible for the revolutionary cadres in the Arab world, and the Palestinian Resistance in particular, to refuse such plans, they should at least not be part of them. If we cannot forbid the settlement, we should not recognize Israel and thus concede our historical right to liberate the land and to liberate Arab society.

The effects of such peace plans are dangerous not only for the Palestinian people but for the Arab world as a whole. What will happen if the peaceful solution is achieved? The peaceful settlement is coming from America, which means that America will be the power present in the Arab world for a long period of time—we don't know how long. But as long as this presence continues, exploitation and imperialist theft in the Arab world will be sustained, right wing forces in all the Arab world will be strengthened, and the Arab revolution as exemplified by the Palestinian revolution will be ended or at the least, rendered ineffective.

From this point on, therefore, the Arab revolutionary cadres should start working on a new basis of operation, a new style of work that has many features. The earlier stage of the Resistance has ended. The peaceful settlement may be coming. Thus, at this decisive moment, all these cadres should be building their strength so that even with the initiation of the peaceful solution, they can start again effectively. This is basic: to move toward transformation to an underground movement and a stronger form of confrontation.

Dikran: We are really talking about the potential of the revolution. What I want to talk about is how we perceive its actualization. I am quite convinced of the fact that the dynamic element of the revolution emanates from assessment of the historic conditions facing a particular people at a particular point and time in history.

The Arab revolutionary forces, and particularly the Palestinian revolutionary forces, must be careful to assess their situation carefully so as not to misinform their future strategy. The Palestinian national problem is at the heart of the Arab-Israeli problem. Therefore, to elucidate what I mean here, let us take a look at the proposed plans to solve the Palestinian question and how the revolutionary forces, given the particular conditions facing them, should assess these plans.

Let us recall here that one of the conditions we face is the rapprochement between the superpowers. Let me concentrate for a moment on events taking place (early 1974). First, Kissinger visited Jordan, the major area of the translation of the peace proposals. The major actors are Egypt and Saudi Arabia, but the major place to solve the core problem of Palestine is Jordan. Thus, Jordan had to be shaped up to accept whatever proposal the United States might come to favor: (1) an "independent" Palestinian state consisting of the present Israeli occupied West Bank of Jordan (an area which was originally part of historic Palestine), and the Gaza Strip, also presently occupied by Israel,[8] or (2) The Husayn plan (originally sponsored by the United States) which is to give the Palestinians "autonomy" on the West Bank and in Gaza, but in federation with Jordan on the East Bank. Husayn favors the latter, but the United States has not made up its mind as yet. Thus, the visit by Kissinger was to remind Husayn that he exists only by the grace of the United States.

Pressure on Husayn came in the form of a suggestion to Husayn by Kissinger that he cut the size of the Jordanian army. By doing so, Kissinger was reminding Husayn that he is expendable, that his army is expendable, and that there are many waiting on the periphery who are more than willing to assume the role that the United States wants at this point in time. Also, since the Jordanian army employs

---

8. This solution has not actually been proposed officially, only discussed as of October, 1974.

at least a quarter of the population, Kissinger's suggestion also was something of an economic threat. In other words, Kissinger was saying, "Husayn, if you want to remain in our favor, you will have to accept our peace plans whatever we decide they will be." If the United States cut back aid to the Jordanian army, economic crises would result in civil war in Jordan.

Ceausescu, the Rumanian president, "representing the Soviet Union" visited the area shortly thereafter. The purpose of his visit was to get the Palestine Liberation Organization to accept the idea of the Palestinian entity, whatever its final form, as a terminal point rather than as a point for departure for liberation since no viable Arab liberation movement exists.

These events, then, reflect the effect of the East-West rapprochement. They also reflect the Saudi-Egyptian entente. I am not here presenting a conspiracy thesis, for I am against the theory of conspiracy as a way to explain social phenomena. I am looking here at the present balance of power; I am looking at the historic stage we are in, the nuclear age we are in, the fact that social analyses have recognized that there must be coexistence in order to be able to live because there is something that can make both powers perish. It is in this context that the federation with Jordan plan and the "proposed" Palestinian state have been posited.

The real question is not whether we are for or against the Palestinian state. Rather, given the present balance of power internationally and locally, the real issue for us is to expose and stop the imperialist plan, a plan whose ultimate aim is not only the extermination of the Resistance but also the elimination of the idea of resistance and hence revolution.

Let us look at the ideas of the "proposed" state, since that is the most discussed solution. If the principal contradiction is between imperialism and the forces of its negation, the Arab masses, then in discussing this solution, we must first and foremost determine whose solution it is and under what specific historical conditions it is being "proposed." Simply put, I am not against the establishment of a Palestinian state, nor am I opposed to a Palestinian "national authority" to rule over this state. I do, however, have serious reservations as to the actualization of Palestinian and Arab liberation in the present historical context through this plan.

Some of the Palestinian and other proponents of the "proposed" state who have been mistakenly comparing our case to that of the Vietnamese believe that a mutilated Palestinian state would be the first step toward complete liberation of Palestine. But they fail to establish the proper basis on which such a comparison could actually be made. The Vietnamese, in following a step-by-step process to their liberation did so only as a result of political and military strength. They went to Paris because they had a mass armed movement at their disposal. In accepting a cease-fire, they did so because they maintained the right to oppose U.S. intervention in their internal affairs, plus they had the PRC, a well-organized revolutionary force in the southern part of Vietnam controlling a major part of that region.

But a step-by-step process for the liberation of Palestine and the Arab world proposed by some Palestinian leaders like Hawatmeh of the PDFLP, is not based on the same conditions. To accept a Palestinian state on part of Palestine, without having a mass base to continue the process of full liberation, is to assess the situation wrongly, and to misinform the future strategy of the Arab liberation movement, and especially the Palestinian revolution. Had the Resistance Movement enjoyed such conditions as the Vietnamese, the establishment of the "proposed" state would have been the direct result of armed struggle, and not of the "benevolence" or "altruism" of imperialism.

The answer to why the presently "proposed" state should be rejected is, simply, Look who is proposing it. This "proposed" solution is an attempt to eliminate the progressive Arab movements.

I think that in the future the Arab Gulf, because of its key location and its economic resources, will play a more important role than it has in terms of initiating progressive political developments in the Arab world. I would still maintain, however, that the axis of revolutionary politics, if it is to be a dynamic factor, has to come out of Egypt or Syria or both. This is largely because political ideas of the area have developed there and continue to do so. (They being the present core of reactionary politics, will also pose their negation eventually.) Thus, the Palestinian Resistance Movement, I imagine, will be cut down to size. It will be regarded as a subset of the Arab liberation movement, not as its spearhead. In short, the Palestinian Resistance Movement, though it occupied a central role in the development of the Arab liberation movement, did not make it as the historic agent of revolutionary change in the Arab world. It was a historical movement, but not the historic movement.

Further, the Arab struggle is one of national liberation, which of course included the liberation of Jews from Zionism. While the struggle should not wait for the consciousness of the ordinary Jew to negate the present imperialist position of Israel, it should not forget about this either. In other words, you cannot ask the Arab revolutionary to wait for the working class of Israel to develop a revolutionary consciousness. But within this strategy, the Arab must keep in mind the idea that unless the working class people in Israel free themselves from Zionist ideology, which views everybody as an enemy and which is based on racial discrimination and conflict, a full liberation will be more difficult. Thus the assessment of the Arab liberation movement as it develops its new strategy must include not only an analysis of Arab society, but an analysis of Israeli society—an understanding of the basic class contradictions in these societies.

Last, given the underdeveloped context of the Arab world, the question is which class, which element of Arab society, can actually lead this struggle? I think that the answer is quite obvious. The only sector that can lead it consists of a certain and small element of the educated petite bourgeoisie. However, the backbone of the struggle would be the working people of the Arab area. The educated petite bourgeoisie are the small percentage of the educated element of the population who can understand the contradictions between imperialism and the Arab people. At the same time, they must commit class suicide. By arming themselves with proletarian ideology, they recognize that their ideas are inseparable from the conditions of the masses. They know that if they isolate their ideas from the masses they cannot continue. If this revolutionary petite bourgeoisie are not armed with a solid political party deeply rooted among the working class and the peasantry, then their chances of success are nil.

There are, I think some major things that we as intellectuals (revolutionary) must take seriously. First of all we need a renaissance (intellectual-political-social) whereby we begin to challenge the reactionary elements of our society's thinking. Our task is to introduce new ideas, but not in the abstract form. As a Marxist, I find that we lack real, thorough studies of our society. We must have a precise class analysis. Reading Marx is not enough; we must translate Marx's methodology into the existing conditions of Arab society, and not into our textbook notion of what that reality might be.

Fuad: For the future, we don't need to change the type of our struggle, only to improve its mechanisms. How can we make the masses stand beside us, carry arms with us, demonstrate with us to achieve practical gains that can be seen by the masses as actual gains to them. We have neglected this point; or in other words, we have been ignorant of its meaning. The Palestinian liberation movement has to crystallize a program of stages in accordance with the developments achieved since 1965. This program might include the establishment of a "national authority" in the West Bank and Gaza. The condition of the West Bank and Gaza has not changed in its economic structure in the same manner that lands occupied by Israel since 1948 have changed. Therefore, the new Palestinian program to take these lands from the occupying authority will be organically different from the program to liberate the lands occupied in 1948.

However, I am not convinced that the liberation movement will get anything from Geneva. The Arab representatives at the Geneva Conference are either representatives of regimes running after the United States or representatives of groups no longer able to continue the struggle due to solidification of the bourgeois class structure possessing power. Egypt, the United States, and Saudi Arabia will not offer solutions or gains that may be of use to the armed Palestinian struggle. This does not forbid, however, the specification of a program of stages as a necessity of a strategy for the near future, a clear objective to get the masses to struggle for a tangible goal.

I do not approve of the Resistance going to Geneva because, given the prearranged agreements for the Geneva Conference, it will not achieve anything. The Resistance, however, has to be flexible and know how to play this international game being played in Geneva. The immediate task of the Resistance Movement is to disrupt the American-Israeli plan by not allowing the return of the West Bank and Gaza to King Husayn's sovereignty, by seeking the recognition of the participants at the Geneva Conference that the PLO is the legitimate representative, and the only one, of the Palestinian people. Such factors will disrupt Kissinger's plan because Israel will never accept the PLO.

I have never believed, even at the time that the Palestinian revolution was at its peak that this revolution could be called the spearhead. I have never conceived of a successful Palestinian revolution except within the context of a general Arab revolution. That is, I believe that the way to liberate Palestine is through the liberation of Cairo and through the liberation of Damascus. One cannot conceive of a real Palestinian revolution, or of a Palestinian movement, except through revolutionizing the Arab countries and the Arab states.

In so far as the leadership of the Palestinian movement has not changed, and its political orientations are basically within the same sectarian attitude of the past, I do not expect any change in the short run of the players operating on behalf of the interests of the Palestinian people. This leadership was needed; and I do not find it unnatural that this leadership is going to participate in the so-called peace agreement that will develop at the Geneva Conference.

As for the future, I think that the progressive forces will move underground and that there will be a kind of interaction between the Palestinian revolution and the general Arab revolution including movements in the Arab Gulf and North Africa. I think that Egypt cannot play an independent role unless the rest of the Arab world is liberated from the existing reactionary movements.

Nadim: There is one question that I would like to raise. If the proposed peace plans go through, will Israel continue to be an expansionist state, or will it become only a finely tuned spearhead of an economic and social Western imperialism in this area? Will the role of Israel become simply that of a regional power through which all imperialist plans will be carried out, or will it be that and still remain an expansionist state, racist, etc.? Whichever the case, I think the outcome will be the same: the Arab masses will become more aware, and this will force a certain form of struggle.

But the problem now, as we have all said, is how can this awakening be carried out with utmost efficiency; how can this change in the socioeconomic relationships in the Arab world be crystallized and actualized? As we all become more conscious, we start with a central recognition, which is that for any person who believes in a concept of justice—and here I don't want to become involved in an emotional or a romantic kind of discussion—but for anyone concerned with the concept of justice, the proposed formation of the Palestinian state on only part of the Palestinian land is not acceptable.

Souad: It is rather strange to me to hear you all talk about these issues—sincerely, yes, and passionately too, but also objectively. You seem to dissociate yourselves from what you are saying and talk as if those things existed outside yourselves, and yet I know that what you say means a lot to you. You all believe that these issues are important, critical, that they constitute one of your major concerns in this life, in this society we are living in. I suppose I have a different way of looking at things. I want to say that when I talk, I can't separate myself, my feelings, my way of thinking from the issues with which I am dealing. Yet you can challenge me because I *seem* totally indifferent to the situation in the Arab world, the struggle of the Palestinian people, the cruelty, the killings of many innocent people, and the war against Zionism.

It is difficult to explain this to you, for just as you believe that what you say and do is worthwhile and meaningful, I feel that the whole situation is, at the very least, a crazy power game and, at most, completely meaningless and futile. Look, we only have this one life, so what is the use of striving after high ideals. I suppose it is a question of what we intend to do, what we should do with our lives. I deeply believe that we should preserve them at any cost. I cannot accept the idea of violence.

You might confront me here with all of the suffering and misery going on and all of the bombings of the refugee camps and so on, and ask me whether the struggle is not then justified precisely in order to preserve human life. This would be difficult for me to answer. I admit that I have been a fortunate person and have not had to witness such human suffering firsthand, and thus it seems removed and distant from my life. So perhaps I cannot appreciate the situation.

Yet if both Israelis and Arabs are really interested in preserving human life and are sincere in their peace efforts, it should be possible to work something out. It would not be fair to the Arabs for Israelis to continue using those worn-out arguments that the Arabs should simply integrate the Palestinians into their own societies. The Palestinians would not accept this without some sort of a fight to regain their homeland, their dignity, their identity. I know that Arabs do not want to throw the Jews into the sea, as is commonly mentioned, but are in fact prepared to live in peace within the same land as in the past, but minus Zionism. So the Zionists have to accept the blame and consequences of their expansionist policies, their distortions of the whole issue, and especially their treatment of innocent Palestinians.

For me, the whole confrontation seems ridiculous: Zionists and their definition of reality based on a specific area of land, as if they are going to take land with them when they die; and Palestinians who strive after a dream. It all comes to nothing in the end, death makes everyone equally nothing—so what is all the fuss about? If only people could come to understand that this meaning we are projecting on the social world is exactly that, a projection—if people could come to realize that there is a great possiblity that there is nothing before or after this life, that we are born to die, perhaps they would reconsider their projections of meanings. I believe that somehow people must come to be aware of what is going on in the world, in their lives—not these petty problems of whether I should be an Israeli or a Palestinian, but the more important issue of continuing human life and guaranteeing it without a stack of illusions. I suppose I believe in the old idea of the rationalist, that if we are conscious of the absurdities we create, we will cease to participate in them and come to recognize our common humanity.

I suppose that even my way, which I have not really outlined, would involve even more time and sacrifices for how does one change people's values and projections resting on centuries of alleged traditions? How does one tell another that land, nations, religions are all meaningless, for they just divide people and give excuses and justifications for a lot of human misery, and that it all comes to nothing in the end, just death?

Dr. Barakat: Let's say you start with something real, a group suffering from injustice. What should it do about its conditions in the actual world of struggle? Should it surrender, or should it do something about its condition?

Souad: I really don't know. But I am still against violence.

Dr. Barakat: In order to develop a new consciousness, people need to liberate themselves from their illusions about their conditions. As Marx noted: "The call for men to abandon their illusions about their condition is a call for men to abandon a condition that requires illusions."

Dikran: We must free ourselves of wishful thinking, something that Marx implies in the quote noted by Dr. Barakat.

Souad's framework of discussion can be identified as a humanitarian liberal framework, which assumes that no other framework commands moral authority or possesses the capacity to seek specific ideals and goals.

Ideals must be posited in the existing material conditions of society and not as thoughts that one might entertain in the abstract. "Peace," "justice," "freedom" are all philosophical concepts that cannot be understood unless we test them in the realm of the real. Assuming we are all for peace, let us look at the following example: A Vietnamese working in his ricefields is suddenly confronted with a B-52 air raid. Should he throw flowers and flash the peace sign or should he run to his military post in order to shoot at the B-52? If he were to run to his Sam-6 base, would he be not peaceful? In other words, to be peaceful one must first look at the real world, diagnose it, and then suggest what ought to be. Upon so doing, one can plan programmatically how to bridge the gap between is and ought to be. In short, one cannot wish away falling bombs!

Souad: I can't see where that bridge is, so I can't talk about it. I can only talk about what ought to be, but I don't know how to get there.

Dikran: But at the same time you can't allow yourself to talk about what ought to be without considering what we have now. You can't talk about peace to a Vietnamese when you have a B-52 flying over him. You can't talk about peace, love, and brotherhood to a person in South Africa when he is subjected to the occupying regime. This is a luxury that we petit bourgeois scholars can afford ourselves. But you cannot ask that of a person who cannot allow himself the luxury of thinking of what ought to be.

Dr. Barakat: There is one reality for the South African black and the Palestinian and it negates attempting to be "human" in your sense, Souad. It is just like saying to him to surrender his humanity. When you preach to the Palestinian of love, peace, and so on, it means give up.

During the war, Sadat asserted that we Arabs do not love war for its own sake. This is not really the question. Such accusations are meant to confuse the issue: Palestinians and their fellow Arabs have suffered injustice. People suffering from injustice have to do something about it. Can they do anything about their conditions by following your idea of doing nothing?

Dikran: Does it help the Palestinian living in a refugee camp, who is dehumanized and terrorized by constant Israeli assault to follow your ideas? Palestinians have been pushed out of their homeland by Zionists, pushed into the camps, and pursued there constantly by Israeli bombs. Should they die by trying to follow your formula of passivity, as if the Israelis were going to disappear tomorrow, or should they struggle to restore themselves to a more human condition?

Dr. Barakat: The Palestinian must either assert himself or accept injustice.

Dikran: To be peaceful is a luxury Palestinians cannot afford. Their humanity is denied by accepting the status quo, by accepting the conditions that require illusions, as Marx says. Arab nationalism is a revolt against the colonial domination by the Western nations. It is also an expression of the rejection of the status quo. Arab nationalist groups refuse to accept the status quo. We are faced with two world outlooks: one says, "Peace is what is required," the other says, "Yes, peace is required, but only peace with equality for all."

A COMMENTARY

The new generation discussants have expressed themselves very articulately with regard to their perceptions of the October war and the future of the Arab world. I would like to address myself to problems that the discussants have covered, but by way of another dimension. Ultimately, the problem we are all concerned with is the right and capacity of each nation to determine its own destiny insofar as this is possible in a world of nation-states. In order to have this "control," two elements are required: (1) real economic development and (2) a viable polity to employ this economic base for the benefit of its citizens, and to assure the power of the state to negotiate its rights within the international community. To date, it is quite obvious that the Arab states as a whole have not succeeded in producing these necessities. The October war is seen by some Arabs as a turning point on the road to the successful accomplishment of these endeavors. It is seen by others as a regressive stage but one that will in the long run, produce those conditions which will allow the fulfillment of these endeavors.

Before assessing these two views, I would like to review the historical process by which various nation-states were able to effect these two conditions and to discuss the relevance of their experiences for the Arab world. In this historical exploration, we must begin with the industrial transformation of the economic bases of society, as well as the development of the nation-state as the basic unit of polity.

In the eighteenth and nineteenth centuries, the dominant concepts of economy in Europe shifted from a peasant- and guild-based system to an industrial and highly productive system embodying constant technological advance; and the concept of polity shifted from a system deriving legitimacy from theology to one based on secular concepts and laws. In Western Europe and its offshoot, the United States, the economic and political transformation occurred first, placing these areas in a more powerful position. For them, and especially England, the process was a natural outgrowth of the synthesis of their intellectual and technological advances. Once these nations became established, their economy required resources and markets; their polity was able to effect these, drawing on the strength of earlier economic gains.[9] Their expansion in the world was aimed at securing the highest standard of living as well as the most powerful position for themselves. In short, their liberal development brought about their vested interest in controlling other areas of the world in order to assure their own ascendancy and continued development. At the same time, it created conditions making it difficult for "competitors" to follow in their footsteps. It became quite clear that an industrial capacity gave strength to the polity and that the polity in turn felt a commitment to prevent "competitors." The imperialist-colonialist period followed.

For Russia the basic problems of economic development—capital (fluid and material), intelligentsia, labor supply, and adequate food for non-food-producing workers—were more difficult to resolve in a world that already consisted of developed Western nations with vested interests. Ultimately, however, the Russians succeeded, first by creative substitution for the Western processes, and then with a different ideological concept than that of the West.[10] Thus Soviet economic development has afforded the Russians the power they have today.

China was even more isolated by the developed world than the Soviet Union had been. China had to resolve the basic problems of economic development from within its own human and material resources, and had to do that within the context of a very advanced technology in the world, difficult with which to compete. China has not yet fully developed its capacity; but even so, by sheer weight of population and a highly sophisticated development in crucial areas, it is able to exert more of its political influence in the world.[11]

For the Third World nations, the problems of transformation of their economic bases, and hence their ability to exert political pressure in the international community on behalf of their nations, have been even more severe. These Third World nations, the former victims of the economic and political expansion of the West, start with less, have further to go, and often have less-developed human and material resources with which to work than the nations that were transformed earlier. They also have the additional problem of having had the

9. See E. H. Carr, *The New Society* (Boston: Beacon Press, 1957); and T. Ashton, *The Industrial Revolution: 1760-1830* (New York: Oxford University Press, 1964).

10. See Alexander Gerschenkron, "Russia: Patterns and Problems of Economic Development, 1861-1958," in *Economic Backwardness in Historical Perspective* (Cambridge: Harvard University Press, 1962), pp. 119-151.

11. See Helmut Callis, *China: Confucian and Communist* (New York: Holt, c.1959).

physical presence of Western nations on their soil.

While the West and the East have different ideological approaches, essentially they both compete to control the Third World: The West by controlling the economic resources of an area and thus limiting the area politically; the East by assisting economic development in expectation of an ideological conversion, or at the very least, the creation of walls to contain the West. (This differentiation, though quite oversimplified, is adequate for the basic discussion in this essay.) The East has also set criteria of personal gain in offering aid to the Third World. Now, with the East-West detente, things are even more confused. The United States, inheritor of the Western dominance in the world, is interested in supporting friendly regional countries that will control an area for it, and will assure American and Western interests; the Soviet Union and China are to some extent interested in strengthening Third World nations to confront Western control, thus making them indebted and dependent on the East.

Many Third World nations, dependent as they are on the industrial capacities of the West and the East, are not in a position to influence local and international issues of concern to them without such help. Their polities tend to vary in strength according to their ability to marshal the industrial productions of other nations to serve as a basis for negotiating their own interests. However, since the economic system from which they draw their resources is not their own, these polities, while rooted in the interests of their citizens, are rooted also in the interests of their benefactors. Thus they tend to be weak as individual nations. This is so even when local interests coincide with the interests of the benefactors, for at any time the relationship could change and the "client" state be left as an empty shell.

For the West, and now more specifically the United States, Israel was not simply a means to get rid of the Western Jewish problem at the expense of the Arabs. Israel was also a means to have a nation, indebted to the West and tied to it economically, play the role of proxy for the West (United States) in the strategic Middle East. For the Arabs this presented a double problem: one of injustice to the Palestinian Arabs who were excised from their homeland to "solve" the Jewish problem, and one of having in their midst an alien body plugged into the resources of the United States and designed to prevent the Arabs from developing economically and politically and securing their rights. There has been a third problem as well: the Israelis, beyond playing their role as proxy, have developed their own state interests, which have been effected up to October, 1973 at the continued expense of the Arabs. These interests have been made possible because

Israel has unobstructed material assistance from the United States and a social system that can absorb and use this aid. In this present period, however, Israeli state interests as defined by Zionism may overstep the interests of the benefactor. Even though the United States can pressure Israel to its will, there are some dangers in this for the United States. If it pressures Israel too much to compromise its Zionism, internal crises may result in Israel, making it a weak proxy. At the same time, the United States has not yet solidified its relations with the Arab regimes and thus needs Israel. Last, not to be underestimated, is the capacity of the Zionist structure in the United States to create internal problems should the United States pressure Israel too much. In one sense, then, Israel is a client state and thus weak; on the other hand, it still has some strength due to its role in the Middle East and its overseas structures.

Up to the 1973 October War, the Arabs as an Arab "nation" were unable to exercise sufficient economic and hence political power to influence decisions on issues of concern to them. This was true for the Palestine problem as well as the larger problem of which it is symbolic, namely, the Western policy to restrict the economic development and political power of the Arab world. Although Western and other foreign business enterprises thrive in the Arab world, and although in some areas there is a facade of growth and development, in reality much of the development is plugged into the systems and interests of other nations. Essentially, therefore, the Arab condition has continued to regress from the inception of the Zionist colonization in the area.

Now, however, three main factors combined for the October war which have contributed to what may be a change in the Arab situation in some views, while appearing as further regressions to others: (1) a greater commitment of assistance from the Soviet Union, following her ideological-political as well as economic interests; (2) Arab oil and accumulation of wealth from this vital resource; and (3) the welling of the subjective but real factor of restoration of Arab dignity.

The 1973 October War occurred. Indeed it was, and was intended to be a limited war, one that would initiate negotiations and progressive steps to "restoring" Arab rights. Those who see the war positively argue that it was enough to fight a limited war and then to see how much negotiating mileage could be clocked from this demonstration of Arab power constructed from the three factors named above. Thus, such individuals see the "opening" to the West as positive, and whatever economic and political gains it brings is all to the better—a step ahead of where the Arabs were before. Those who see the gains to be made from the war in this manner have no illusions about resolving the core Palestinian question as such with full or even minimum justice. Yet, they argue that a peace settlement will "contain" Israel and give the Arabs a chance to develop. Thus, they conclude, eventually the Palestinian problem will work itself out one way or another.

Others who criticize this view argue that the class that led and supported the efforts of the leadership were not interested in the full rights of the Arab "nation" but in their own class interests which are tied to establishing a relationship with the West. This essentially means to them that the former historic Arab combatants, especially Egypt and Syria, will begin to acquire the facade of development that will not be indigenous, but Western. As such, the Arabs will be in worse condition because of the distortion and commitment of indigenous capital, labor, and intelligentsia to Western interests. Further, the price for this facade of development will be the abandonment of the Palestinian cause. A number of the new generation discussants have argued these points well. They further stated that the reemergence of the Arab right wing will finally polarize the class contradictions and new upheavals will occur. These upheavals will finally remove this class along with the reactionary elements in Israel. Thus, and only then, will the full rights of the Arabs be restored. That is, the deprived classes, in their argument, will seize power and all of the Arab economic resources which will allow them power in the international circles. Therefore, they conclude, that while the Arab progressive forces are in retreat, they will gain in the long run.

I do not wish to argue one view over another here. Rather, I think it important to raise some questions and make some observations for assessing the "accuracy" of these views.

Given the actual condition of the Arab "nation," politically and economically, and given the rather vast and impressive array of Western power with its refined Israeli instrument hoisted in the face of the Arabs, it would not be realistic to think that anything other than the limited October war could take place as an Arab effort to restore Arab rights. To consider the possibility of a popular Arab armed struggle as an alternative to the October war would be unrealistic if only because of the disarray at the mass level in the Arab "nation," and especially the variety of ideological orientations within progressive circles. In this situation, Marxian thought is significant, but the conditions are not yet relevant. Thus, understanding these limitations, the questions that need to be asked now are: (1) Is the October war the final act of the present Arab regimes to resolve the Middle East problems? or (2) Is it one stage within a strategy based on the constant assessment and solidification of the improving economic and political abilities of the Arab "nation" to go to the next step toward full restoration of Arab rights in their area? Many believe the answer to the first question is yes, and the answer to the second, no.

Certainly, the signs to date (October, 1974) seem to indicate that the many have answered the questions correctly: Sadat's abrupt criticism of and "break" with the Soviet Union; the encouragement of foreign interests to invest in Egypt and Syria; the de-Nasserization campaign; the warm reception for Nixon in Egypt; and the rather homely advances made to Israel by Mrs. Sadat. On the other hand, it is difficult for some Arab veterans of the Arab scene to believe that Egypt will allow itself to be tempted by the baubles of the West, and to disengage from the "Arab battle of destiny" to restore full Arab rights. It is difficult for them to believe that Egypt really believes, after such bitter experience with the United States and Israel, that the result of the October war will contain Israel. This, to them, seems hardly true in the light of two facts: (1) an even greater U.S. commitment to Israel and (2) the continuing Israeli commitment to its Zionist ideology and all that it requires. It is difficult for them to believe that Egypt would allow the Palestinian question—the microcosm of the larger Arab problem with the West—to be "resolved" either by the continual and brutal Israeli bombings of the Palestinian refugee camps or by an American-sponsored and -controlled Palestinian ministate. It is equally difficult for these observers of the scene to believe these things of Syria as well. However, it seems to them somewhat plausible that Sadat is clever enough to exploit whatever Western and Arab resources become available to him as a step toward restoring Egypt physically and economically. This, they imagine, would be part of an Egyptian effort to strengthen the Arab world and to use diplomacy to get back as much of the Arab losses as possible.

On the other hand, it may well be that the class factor may limit the view of the present Arab leadership. However, as Dikran noted earlier, the working class of Israel does not behave politically as a working class, but is presently more engaged in the needs of Zionist ideology. We might ask, therefore, is it not intellectually open to question that Arabs, for reasons perceived as more just, have an equally strong commitment to restore their full rights and dignities, and that class may not be the operative explanatory concept for the near future, even if it becomes relevant domestically? If this proves to be true, then certainly all of the present signs supporting the view of the

October war as the terminal effort of the Arabs, will find a different writing in history. Even so, many note that these signs represent a rather large commitment by Egypt to a very different policy, and it is difficult to assess the consequences of withdrawal from such commitments. Thus, indeed, Egypt's policy may correspond to the discussants' analysis of it. After all, the Egyptians have suffered much and have tired of war. Perhaps they do want to disengage from the pre-October definition of the Middle East problem, and to restore some semblance of a developing and dynamic society to Egypt. Sadat, as well as others, know well that such "development" would be only an illusion of development, but he may be willing to settle for that.

In attempting to assess whether the October war represents a terminal point or a beginning for the Arab initiative to restore Arab rights, two observations should be made. First, we must recall that few believed Sadat when he said that he would go to war if the international community would not use its resources to resolve the Middle East problem with justice. He has said repeatedly in the months after the October war (as has Asad of Syria) that Egypt will not rest until the occupied lands are restored and the rights of the Palestinians are recognized (though what is meant by "the rights of the Palestinians" is not made clear). Few believe him now. Second, we must also recall that it was impossible for some Arab observers and intellectuals to believe initially that the Arabs, and especially the Egyptians, did not have some capacity to respond forcefully to the Israeli attack of 1967. A number of them engaged in wishful thinking that in fact Nasser had better equipment and organization and would counterattack. Today some of these same observers are expressing a belief— somewhat more cautious, but a belief—that Sadat's Egypt does have a strategy to restore all Arab rights, beyond what the October war will yield. Whether this is reality or illusion, dreams, will become exposed over the next two years.

Perhaps the most important new development in the Arab world is the beginning institutionalization of the intellectual process that will help to assess the various events. Thus, whether moving with the regimes, or with the class struggle, a greater fund of knowledge will be in the hands of the Arab leadership and people. Additionally, a greater base of economic resources and infrastructure will also be available to be employed more wisely in the area of political power and influence. The Arabs do have within the borders of their numerous states, the human and material resources to solve the basic problems of economic development. It is a question of organizing and utilizing them more effectively. In this sense they have a greater advantage than most Third World nations. But until they can acquire the organization and inter-Arab agreements necessary, they are dependent on foreign assistance and productions. That is, although various attempts have been made in the past to begin to develop political unity of Arab countries, the experiences have resulted in failure. These attempts were born under political pressure and were not built on a careful foundation of institutions. At the present there is not much discussion of Arab nationalism. However, it may be that the present relief from the pressure to actualize immediately the Arab "nation" will allow the development of inter-Arab institutional apparatuses growing out of mutual practical interests rather than ideology. These, while they may stem from the particular class in command today, may nonetheless be a basic infrastructure for further growth. Thus, if such developments occur, some of the present leadership may be a casualty of the result, unless they can transform themselves for the next stage.

Thus the strategy of stages, if it does exist, may be realistic; and if it does not, the coming convulsion expected from the contradictions of class interests will finally force the economic and political development of the Arab world. Of course, however, there are other equally possible developments. Not least among these is that Israeli aggression may force a new confrontation whether or not the Arab regimes want it and whether or not the class stage is ready. Another possibility is a Palestinian initiative resulting in the takeover of what presently constitutes Jordan,[12] eventually drawing in Syria, Iraq, and possibly Lebanon, into a new confrontation with Israel. The role of North Africa, and especially Algeria, is yet unknown. Thus there are many options, and some may happen simultaneously.

Whatever develops in the short or long run, one thing is quite clear: the October war marks a turning point in the basic political and economic restructuring of the Middle East in favor of the Arabs. It seems that in the view of American foreign policy makers, this restructuring should disengage Egypt and Syria from the Arab national line, relate to the pragmatism of Algeria to keep it aloof from Arab nationalism, and continue to recognize Saudi Arabia as a force against progressive movements in the Gulf. Further, Israel would be strengthened and "integrated" economically into the Arab world and would thus be the mainstay regional power for the United States. The Palestinian problem is yet being debated, but there will be some concept of limited recognition. Thus, in this scenario, the Arab "nation"

12. See Ibrahim Abu-Lughod, "Palestinian Options," (mimeographed, Spring, 1974).

would be sufficiently mutilated and ineffective. The actual forces of contradictions that exist in the Middle East, as has been noted in this discussion, are such that the U.S. plan for the area has little chance of success. Therefore, the Israelis would most probably be best advised to request membership in the larger renaissance of the Middle East and to abandon their Zionist ideology. Such foresight would indeed serve the peoples of the area well. It would avoid the prolonged conflict that finally will achieve the same results, namely, the reduction of Western imposition in the area to a more equitable relationship based on mutual interests and the disappearance of Zionist ideology and all of its manifestations. Simultaneously, as the Arabs develop and effect these ends, they will become less dependent on the Soviet Union; that relationship will also be one based on mutual interest. Only when these results are achieved will there be real security for all of the communities of the Middle East.

ELAINE HAGOPIAN

Khalil Nakhleh

THE POLITICAL EFFECTS OF THE OCTOBER WAR ON ISRAELI SOCIETY

When we returned from the war, we found ourselves part of a stunned and grief-stricken nation, perplexed and worried. We returned home to the routine of our work, bewildered at the sight of people who continued as though nothing had happened, as though there had been no war, as though it had not changed us at all. In shock, we watched the attempts to cover up the mishaps and mistakes that caused this war to take place as it did and to end as it had.

Israeli military correspondents [1]

In less than 24 hours, Israel was transformed from a military power, even in global concepts, from a state with an army the fame of which had become a model to the world; from a country which—six short years ago—had won the most brilliant victory in the history of modern warfare; from a state with, according to her leaders' declarations, 'an army that was never in a better state'—to a country fighting with clenched teeth for its very existence. A country living under the shadow of extermination.

The same correspondents [2]

AT FIRST ONE IS AT A LOSS to reconcile these apparently contradictory evaluations by respectable Israeli correspondents. Yet it has been

1. Ben-Porat et al., Ha-Mahdal (Tel Aviv: Special Editions Publishers, 1973), p. iii.

2. Ibid., p. 8.

difficult to discern radically significant changes in Israeli attitudes as a consequence of the 1973 war. Although it did not produce any social cataclysm, the war nevertheless brought about many expressions of lost confidence in Israel's leadership and military capability.

One could almost compile a lexicon of labels referring to the war as viewed by Israelis. The war has been expressed as a "shock," a "flood," a "thunderstorm," an "earthquake," a "ma-ha-dal" (a mishap bordering on corruption), a "binyan Klafim" (the collapse of a 'house of cards') and so on. Such labels immediately raise the questions: How much can sudden military reversals affect the psychological and social structure of a society? What will the effects be? How temporary will they be? How long?

The 1973 October War had the obvious effect of mobilizing Israelis and rallying them in support of the Zionist state. In all previous wars one might have used Israel as an example of the close relationship between military threat and political unity. After the October war the relationship was less apparent. The public seemed to care less for the issue of overwhelming military superiority and expansion. Apparently, though, only the politicians and military command had not really changed.

For many Israelis the change in public attitudes was not significant. But in observing little change in public spirit, there was still the admission of change. Furthermore, the war had tangible effects that were directly related to the loss of public confidence in Zionism.

The present shape of the Israeli economy, for instance, cannot be directly attributed to the war, but the war had a direct impact on economic production and overall economic health. In an article in *Ot* magazine, Ephraim Debert, the economic advisor to the minister of finance, wrote:

> We and our children will have to pay the economic cost of this war for years to come. . . . The cost of the Yom Kippur War is larger than anything familiar to us. It is too early to estimate the exact cost now, but it is fair to say that the cost will run into the tens of billions of Israeli pounds. Even without direct losses, the slowdown in the economic activity during the war led to a loss of 2 billion Israeli pounds, and 1974 is expected to register at least one billion Israeli pounds more.[3]

Addressing himself to the same concern, Minister of Commerce Haim Bar Lev admitted that, because of mobilization, 80,000 of a total

3. as quoted in *Al-Ittihad*, December 4, 1973.

of 295,000 employed in industry were unemployed during October, 1973.[4] Moreover, about sixty per cent of the industrial workers from the territories did not report to work during that same month. This led to a drop of thirty-five per cent in industrial production.

The construction industry, citrus production, and tourism were hit the hardest. The last two had a noticeable impact on the country's foreign reserves since they constitute the main sources of foreign currency. As a result of the war, Debert estimated that Israeli exports dropped by forty per cent which translates into a loss of $250 million.

POLITICAL COSTS

Israel's prewar ruling elite perhaps suffered the most direct impact of the war. The war provided a sudden, immediate, and convincing invalidation of prewar policies and assumptions. The basic premises of prewar policies, as espoused by the ruling Ma'arakh, were that: (1) a state of "no-war-no-peace" was beneficial to Israel's security; (2) the retention of occupied territories and the establishment of Jewish settlements on them was imperative for Israel's security; (3) the economic and political integration of Palestinian Arabs in the territories was the most effective way in depressing Palestinian autonomy; and (4) an overall and constant rejection of Arab demands, however moderate, was a necessary ingredient of a mighty Israel. The prewar ruling triumvirate of Golda Meir, Moshe Dayan, and Israel Galili embodied and acted upon these premises in one way or another. Characteristic of these premises, the Galili document of "creeping annexation" stood as the platform for Labor in the coming election.

There was pronounced public shock at the amount of spilled blood, the degree of cruel practices, the military reversals, and the fragile cease-fire. Many people, for the first time, came to feel that an active Israeli peace policy ought to be at least publicly discussed by Israel's leadership, since it would be far better to initiate a peace option from Israelis—in the event of a superpower intervention—than to have a settlement imposed on Israelis. Such feelings made it seem that Israel's civilian and military leadership, her national policies and ideologies, Zionism, and the electoral system itself were open questions.[5] It was clear then that the war had had the effect of a political earthquake that saw a decline in the popularity of prewar

4. *Al-Ittihad*, November 23, 1973.
5. cf. Eric Rouleau, *Los Angeles Times*, April 14, 1974.

political leadership and the sharpening of Israeli political differences.

The effects of the political challenge were related to three factors. One was the decline in the popularity of the prewar political leadership and consequent political polarization; the second was the returns for the election for the 8th Knesset, the Arab vote, and the position of Rakah; and the third was the mood of the Arab minority in pre-1967 Israel and Israeli-Arab relations.

Leadership, Popularity, and the Elections

The legendary figure Moshe Dayan had acquired almost divine proportions by the successes of the 1967 war and yet he was rendered very dispensable by the 1973 October War; for it made him fallible. Thus public opinion held him responsible for the failings and unpreparedness of the Israeli army. The decline in Dayan's popularity in Israeli public opinion can be traced by a poll taken in June, 1970. It showed that 91 per cent of the Israelis sampled considered Dayan as the most popular leader. Ninety-five per cent of those polled in January, 1972 said that Dayan was the best possible defense minister. Only four months before the war, Dayan was placed in second place after Golda Meir as popular choice for the premiership. In June, 1973, 58 per cent supported Dayan's policies of gradual integration in the occupied territories. But one month after the war, a poll indicated that only 36 per cent favored the continuation of Dayan as defense minister, and only a meager 2 per cent supported his candidacy for the premiership.[6]

Golda Meir's popularity followed a similar path, however, it was not as steep as Dayan's. A poll sponsored by *Ha'aretz* showed that in February, 1974 only 21.5 per cent thought Prime Minister Meir should keep her post. A similar poll taken before the October war showed 65.2 per cent as backing the premiership of Mrs. Meir.

Although stunned Israelis laid the responsibility for misinterpreting intelligence information and for the shocking human losses on the minister of defense, the ruling elite persisted in supporting him. The government did respond, however, to public criticism by appointing the Agranat commission to investigate the conduct of the war.

With the breakout of the war only twenty-six days before the election date for the 8th Knesset, a decision was made to postpone national elections to December 31, 1973. However, by October 6th all candidates lists were already submitted. There was spreading demand and public pressure to reopen those lists after the war so that additions, alterations,

6. Ben-Porat, *op. cit.*, p. 281.

or substitutions could be introduced. In spite of that pressure the Knesset decided against all such proposals. While it consented to delay elections until after the war, it maintained intact the prewar candidate lists. "This parliamentary decision," one writer observed, "was like providing summer uniforms on an icy winter day or like teaching someone to play Chopin in the style of a march-tune."[7]

In Labor Alignment (Ma'arakh) at this time there were strong and vehement internal gyrations by illustrious members such as Mati Peled for the reopening of electoral lists. These individuals felt that since voting would be on postwar issues, the candidates had to also be postwar. Moreover, this group protested against the embodiment of prewar policies, namely, the Galili document. To placate opposing factions and to prevent irreversible party cleavages, Labor worked out a substitute platform for the Galili document. The new fourteen point platform, which became known as the 'Sapir document,' was too vague to indicate any substantial departure from prewar policies. But it was formulated in a way which would allow different interpretations. While the platform demanded, for example, "defensible borders" and declared "no return to the borders of June 4, 1967," it still spoke in terms of "territorial compromises." This classic Kissingerian-type document led Naftali Feder, the political secretary of Mapam (one of the partners in the Ma'arakh) to express that "Mapam considers the Labor Party's fourteen point program, not as the 'Sapir Document' . . . but as a radical move toward the Mapam position. It is a truly dovish platform and marks a substantial shift by our Labor partner in our direction."[8]

The impact of the dissatisfaction within Labor was diffused, at least temporarily, thanks to the appearance of a new partisan threat—the Likud. While dethroning all familiar deities, the war created a new one—General Ariel Sharon, the self-acclaimed hero of the Canal crossing. Highly critical of the conduct of his superiors (who happened to be prominent Ma'arakh members) in the war, General Sharon was the moving force behind the formation of Likud. The appearance of the Likud gave the dissatisfied group of intellectuals and retired generals within Labor no viable political alternative. Consequently, these people decided to stay within and support the Ma'arakh, at least for the sake of elections, and they formed a group called "Nevertheless—Ma'arakh."

7. Nathan Yalin-Mor, "The Confusing Elections: Post Mortem," New Outlook, XVII, No. 2 (1974), 29–34.
8. Naftali Feder, "Mapam Views Labor Platform as Radical Shift in Its Direction," New Outlook, XVI/XVII (1973–74), 47–48.

The war, while serving as a focal campaign issue for all major parties, introduced no substantial changes in the range of available options for the Jewish electorate. Simplistically, the Likud was characterized as the "war ticket," while the Ma'arakh was the "peace ticket." In campaign advertisements, the Likud criticized "the government of the day, whose overlong rule has resulted in a deep social, moral, and economic crisis." They criticized the government for failing to preempt the Arab attack on October 6; they refused to accept U.N. cease-fire resolutions 338 and 339, and they were opposed to any territorial concessions. Furthermore they called for the "rejection of withdrawals which would endanger the peace and security of the nation," and "upholding our right to the Land of Israel. . . ."[9]

The Ma'arakh presented itself as the party of peace initiatives. It dwelt in its campaign advertisements on the constant opposition of Gahal (the major party in the Likud) and on the successes its approach had brought, namely, the achieved Israeli-Egyptian disengagement and the release of Israeli P.O.W.'s from Egypt. "We offer the road to peace," they claimed.[10]

Utilizing the impact of the war, the Independent Liberals hit hard at both blocs. They campaigned on the basic claim that "the Alignment failed indeed; the Likud is idea-bankrupt." Their campaign advertisement declared that: "The idea that the status quo is the most desired situation, and that it could continue for many years, has toppled. The occupied territories did not exclude the possibility of war; nor could they constitute a kind of substitute for peace. The right-wing Likud demands rigidity, and the consequence of that would be war. . . . The Alignment maintained a confused medley of ideas. . . . Only the Independent Liberals had always been . . . supporters of a policy of peace initiative, open to territorial compromise."[11]

Gahal called for a national coalition government similar to that which dominated the scene from 1967 to 1970. (Gahal withdrew in 1970 to magnify their opposition to the Rogers Plan.) But Gahal's tactic, in effect, provided no alternative to the electorate. Furthermore, Gahal's partnership in the ruling coalition for three years minimized, in the public view, the ideological differences between the two main blocs.

The net result of the election was a slight decline in support for Ma'arakh (by about 11,000 votes), which constituted a loss of five seats, and a gain of about 118,000 votes for the Likud, or an increase

9. *Ibid.*, pp. 52–54.
10. *Ibid.*, p. 53.
11. *Ibid.*, p. 54.

of seven seats. Had it not been for the Bader-Ofer Admendment which favored big parties and discriminated against small ones in the apportionment of seats, the Likud would have gained only four seats, and the Ma'arakh would have lost seven.[12]

Although the Likud's strength increased from 26 per cent of the total vote in 1969 to 30.6 per cent in 1972, no apparent substantial shift to the right resulted. It was then fair to conclude that the crossover Labor votes for the Likud were a sign of protest against Labor's policies and conduct of the war, rather than a significant shift in ideological stance. Actually, much of traditional Ma'arakh support went to Shulamit Aloni's "Citizen's Rights Movement" List which received over 35,000 votes, or three Knesset seats. Aloni had previously splintered from Labor.

Another beneficiary of traditional Labor votes was the Moked List (the combined Maki and T'chelet Adom movement.) Moked showed a gain of about 6.4 thousand votes over 1969. All this indicates, in effect, that one has to be careful before interpreting these results as manifesting significant ideological shifts in Israeli political opinion as a result of the war. Whereas Likud won seven additional seats, a similar ideological bloc (National Religious party—Mafdal) lost two. Furthermore, the increase in Likud's strength does not explain the increase of the Peace Movement's strength by two seats. The Peace Movement won twelve seats in the 1973 elections (Independent Liberals, four; Rakah, four; Shulamit Aloni, three; Moked, one) as compared to ten seats in the 1969 election.

Except for the appearance of a large number (thirty-three per cent) of new faces in the 8th Knesset which pointed towards a generational shift, and save for the internal gyrations within Labor which led to the formation of new political movements, the October war appears not to have introduced any radical change in Israel's internal political forces.

New Political Movements

It seems that the labels of "dove" and "hawk" are taken very seriously in Israel as characterizing one's thinking on the occupied territories, Palestinian Arabs, and the general attitude towards the Arab world. One is an extreme dove in Israel, for example, if one talks about returning the occupied territories, recognizing the right of Palestinian Arabs for self-determination, and trusting Arabs altogether. It is fair

12. *Le Matin An-Nahar*, March 4, 1974.

to say that there were various dovish elements who criticized the prewar policies of "creeping annexation" before the war but they were never effective because the assumptions motivating those policies were not challenged. But the October war did just that. Consequently, a heated debate erupted again between doves and hawks in an attempt to explain the "earthquake" which shook the country on October 6, 1973. Feeling the pressure to respond to the various accusations by the hawks, a dovish observer, Naftali Ben Moshe, wrote: "No, it was not our policy, and we doves need not beat our breasts (nor take the blame). . . . The ones who should do some deep soul-searching are the hawks and other extremists with their delusions and halluci- nations. . . . We doves did not suffer from the illusion that the state of neither-war-nor-peace was good for us and could go on indefinitely until the Arabs softened and agreed to far-reaching concessions."[13]

There were two discernible new political movements which were attributable to the October war and to the policies of the ruling Alignment prior to it. These were: (1) the Ideological Circle for the Clarification of Problems of State and Society; and (2) the Shinui Reform party. The Circle is a group of about seven hundred Jewish intellectual Laborites who became disenchanted enough with the policies of their own party to criticize it but were, at the same time, too worried about becoming a marginal group to leave it. Toward the end of November, 1974, they went to great lengths to indicate that they represented the "extreme dovish" part of the political continuum. While they represented marginal political views, they certainly were not marginal in political influence. They chose, however, to remain in the main stream of party politics.

At their July, 1974 convention in Tel Aviv, they adopted a platform which consisted of three sections: security and foreign policy, social policy, and a critique of the Labor Party.[14] Their views then deviated from the official position of the government regarding foreign policy in that they were: (1) willing to return to the June, 1967 boundaries; and (2) ready to recognize the Palestinian right of self-determination. But the group was not politically homogeneous regarding the realiza- tion of the two points.

In an interview with *New Outlook* editors the immediate concerns of the group were internal reform and the development of a framework through which their views could be heard. In response to the question: "Did the Yom Kippur War create an atmosphere that made the position

13. *Al-Hamishmar*, November 27, 1973.
14. *New Outlook*, XVII, No. 7 (1974), 53–68.

of the government more congenial to your point of view?", Yohanan Peres, one of the group's spokesmen answered: "The Yom Kippur War alone wouldn't have done the job—there was a popular revolt against the government which we didn't create, but in a way catalysed and provoked. We were also the main expression of this mood inside the party." [15] The position held by this circle was that Rabin's government represented a long-awaited change in direction. Accordingly, as they viewed it, their first task was "to prevent a premature overthrow of this government. The second was to reform the party and to create a new atmosphere and a new way of voting inside the party."

The group, furthermore, defined one of their main functions as educational in nature—educating both the Israeli and the Arab publics. "The importance of this education process," as one member commented, "is that we are a group which is still regarded, if you look at Israel's history, as a 'legitimate' group—we are not a marginal group, not a group from which any statement of this kind would immediately be disregarded, not a group which is not really part of Israel proper." This concern with avoiding marginality enticed the group against admitting members from marginal segments of Israeli society, especially Arabs.

Another group which clearly was galvanized into political action by the October war was the Shinui Reform Party. Unlike the "Ideological Circle" which was crystallized around effecting reforms in the Labor party by working from within, the Shinui ("change") saw the futility in that approach, and decided on forming a new political party. The initiator of Shinui was Professor Amnon Rubenstein, the dean of Law Faculty at Tel Aviv University. He voiced despair that the individual Israeli had no way of bringing any influence to bear on the political system. He complained that without a constituency electoral system, Knesset members were appointed by the party hierarchies and they did not depend on the voters. He had many friends who had a certain reluctance about entering politics, but decided to put personal feelings aside because they felt that Israel was facing a real emergency.

The rabid despair generated by the war was the moving force behind Professor Rubenstein's political activity. During the war for the first time he heard young men in the army talking of the possibility of emigrating. Rubenstein felt a deep-rooted and despairing scepticism about the prospects of change. Out of such despair Shinui sprung into being. On October 22, 1974 the *Jerusalem Post* reported that

15. *Ibid.*

the organization had fifteen hundred registered members with a mailing list of three thousand.

The Changing Mood of Arabs in Occupied Lands

Among other things the October war shattered the myths which have characterized the relationship between Israeli authorities and the Arab population both in pre-1967 Israel and in the occupied territories. The assumptions of the office of the advisor on Arab affairs, namely, that Arab national feelings would be submerged with time, material advancement, and stringent means of government controls, were rendered false by the 1973 war and the subsequent course of events. Starting with the war, the events of the last year gave the Arabs in Israel a new impetus for manifesting their national and cultural identity. One indicator of this was the Arab support given to Rakah ("New Communist List"—anti-Zionist and pro-Arab party) in the 1973 elections.[16]

Of the 145,000 Arab votes cast for the Knesset, Rakah received 43,000 votes, or about 30 per cent. About one-half of the Arab vote went to Ma'arakh and its Arab-affiliated Lists; 12,000 votes went to the Mafdal (NRP), and 6,000 went to Likud. Rakah increased its overall strength by 37.4 per cent from 38,827 votes in 1969 to 53,353 votes in 1973. This gave Rakah one additional seat in the Knesset, thus giving them two Arabs and two Jewish members. The shift in Arab votes to Rakah was more easily observed in election returns for municipalities and local councils in Arab localities. About 25 per cent of all Arab localities in Israel (including Nazareth) cast between 50 and 80 per cent of their votes for Rakah. This contrasted with only 10 per cent of those localities where between 50 and 80 per cent of the votes went for Rakah in the 1969 elections. In 1973, 60 per cent of Nazareth's vote went for Rakah.

There was almost immediate alarm in the Israeli government at the Arab support for Rakah. Samuel Toledano, the advisor to the prime minister on Arab affairs stated that "the extremists among the Arabs in Israel started 'raising their heads' now."[17] He expressed his displeasure with the nationalistic mood of the Arabs in Israel since the October war. He blamed Rakah for effectively helping these "extremists" in perpetuating the following points in the Arab milieu: (1) that the U.S.S.R. is the true friend of the Arabs, and that it was the U.S.S.R., who returned to them their worth and prevented their

16. *Al-Ittihad*, January 4-18, 1974.
17. *Yedioth Aharonot*, December 11, 1973.

humiliation; (2) that the Arabs are seeking peace and Israel is rejecting it; and (3) that keeping the territories is not a guarantee for peace and that the October war proved just that.

After the 1967 war Toledano further claimed that the Israeli Arabs emphasized the Israeli part of their national identity; the Arabs were ashamed and wished to dissociate themselves from their Arab identity. But after the October war the value of the Israeli part of their hyphenated identity plummeted while the Arab value increased. To remedy this asymmetrical development Toledano suggested "launching a massive attack in different directions, especially in information."

When, in December, 1974, I asked various Arab friends in Israel whether the October war had changed the Arab mood in Israel, they replied that the war revitalized the national identity of the Arabs; that, in stark contrast to 1967, the Arabs did not feel humiliated; they did not have to conceal that they were Arabs in buses or among Jewish co-workers. In contrast to the period after 1967 no public insult to the Arabs went unchallenged.

The reaction to Rabin's visit to Nazareth on November 26, 1974 was a good illustration of the new mood. A visit was arranged for the Prime Minister to come to Nazareth and give a speech to Arab and Jewish students. This was perhaps the first time that a speech by Rabin was interrupted and the first time in public that he was subjected to a barrage of hostile questions. In an answer to an Arab question: "Why do you refuse to negotiate with the PLO at a time when it is recognized by the U.N. as the representative of the Palestinian people?", Rabin responded: "We will not sit with those who have proved themselves for the last twenty-seven years to be terrorists. And you better keep in mind that were you in Syria and had you addressed the prime minister in this manner you would have been hanged." Because of those kinds of questions, Rabin had to cut his speech short.[18]

This incident received a wide range of inflammatory coverage in the Israeli press. Much commentary appealed to the government to use an "iron fist" in squashing this kind of spirit. Subsequently, it became clear to this writer that while the October war encouraged the reemergence of Arab national identity, it nonetheless changed nothing in the government's prewar policies toward the Arab minority.

There are various indications to show that the mood of Palestinians in the occupied territories, especially in the West Bank, has changed because of the impact of the October war and the events that followed it. It is fair to conclude, however, that the change in mood did not

18. *Al-Ittihad*, November 29, 1974.

lead to a simultaneous change in the perception of the West Bank Arabs toward Israel. One Jerusalem Arab lawyer, who was recently deported, commented: "Personally, I attach little importance to the tactical struggles or differences between the Center and Right, as both these blocs believe in the organic link with the United States and American aid. This situation has not changed even after the October war. . . . In the October war it was proved that Israel's sole support is America, and any attempt to suggest that it is in our power to make her our ally against Israel is misleading and erroneous, because America and Israel are one and the same in many respects."[19]

Another leading West Bank personality who was also recently deported by Israel admitted in the same interview quoted above that the October war did affect the views of those personalities who previously supported King Husayn. Various elements that had identified with King Husayn before the war now changed their minds. Others of the Palestinian bourgeois families declared their identification with the PLO. In other words, the dream of King Husayn of establishing the United Arab Kingdom was shattered by the war and subsequent events.

With the October war the West Bank Palestinians began to establish themselves as a recognizable political force. The Palestine National Front (PNF) was formally established in August, 1973 to coordinate activities and national forces within the occupied territories and to serve as a liason with the PLO. But since the end of the October war the PNF took the leadership in staging several demonstrations of civil disobedience. On June 8, 1974 the Palestine National Council "called for reinforcing the PNF as the fundamental base of the PLO inside the occupied territories."[20]

Both Israeli and foreign reporters have commented on the resurgence of passive and, at times, active resistance in the territories as a result of the October war. James Adams of the *Wall Street Journal* wrote: "Political ferment is once more at work in Nablus, long known to its inhabitants as the 'mountain of fire' of Arab patriotism. This surge of popular feeling is clearly the result of the October 6 attack on Israel and the subsequent diplomatic maneuvering."[21] In that same report Dr. Israel Stockmann, an Israeli specialist on the West Bank, admitted that there was a postwar change in the local atmosphere. As Stockmann reportedly saw it: "The (Palestinian) population no longer cooperated with a military government, no matter how liberal,

19. *New Outlook*, 1974, pp. 53–58.

20. *MERIP Reports* (Middle East Research and Information Project), No. 31, 1974.

21. *Wall Street Journal*, January 15, 1974.

unless such cooperation was imposed on them by force. They would not cooperate with Israelis, not so much because of the war and the chances of Israel's retreat but mainly because of Palestinian national feelings."[22] Further evidence for the resurgence of this mood abounds. *Ma'ariv* reported that in spite of the stiff warning by the military governor of the occupied territories against participation in the Palestinian Conference which was held in Cairo, or risking a charge of "working with terrorist organizations," many representatives of the occupied territories left the country for Cairo.[23]

Massive demonstrations pervaded the West Bank—demonstrations of young students expressing support for the PLO, women demanding the release of political prisoners, and others. The demonstrations, by and large, were nonviolent. But Israeli reaction was swift, violent, and at times savage. Available data does not allow me to present a precise comparison of the number of arrests in the prewar and postwar periods. But deportation of leading and respectable personalities became the most often used weapon by Israel. Dr. Hanna Nasser, president of Bir Zeit College, was recently (November 22, 1974) expelled from Israel on the charge that he incited riots and opposition to Israel. But Terence Smith of the *New York Times* on that same day reported that he saw "Dr. Nasser doing everything he could to avoid a confrontation between the marching students and Israeli soldiers. Not only were Nasser's efforts successful, but the soldiers kept their distance until the demonstration ended peacefully."

Reports seem to show, however, that various techniques of harassment, internment, and deportation have been used increasingly since the October war. After the October war hundreds of people were thrown into jail without trial or charge. Recent events in the West Bank have clearly shown that Palestinian nationalism in the occupied territories is on the rise. This development was commensurate with the October war and the subsequent Rabat Conference and pro-Palestinian U.N. resolutions.

SOCIOCULTURAL COSTS

> Before the war we were very happy (but) the war took us by surprise, it was a shock. Not that we lost—but a lot of our self-confidence is gone.
>
> A Jerusalem housewife[24]

22. *MERIP Reports*, No. 25, 1974.
23. *Ma'ariv*, January 13, 1974.
24. *Wall Street Journal*, April 1, 1974.

There is now a kind of apocalyptic climate in Israel. We lost the October war psychologically, and for the Israelis that is enough to shake all their beliefs. You hear it from everybody now, that the very existence of the Jewish state in the Middle East is at stake. People are talking about the failure of Zionism.

Amos Kenan, Israeli playwright[25]

Culturally the war took a heavy toll. The impact of the war, of course, has still to be determined in the sense that no one can predict how long its effects will last. Nonetheless the October war clearly generated many doubts among Israelis about basic normative, ideological, and psychological postulates of their existence. The war forced Israelis from various walks of life to raise hard and incessant questions about Zionism, the credibility gap of the country's leadership, the perpetual state of war, their place in the Middle East, and their relationship with the Arabs. Returning soldiers, high school students, housewives—all raised questions which hit at the core of Israeli culture. Their questions, as of this writing, remain unanswered.

The credibility of political and military leaders was seriously questioned for the first time in the life of Israel. Capitalizing on their successes in the 1967 war, when it was shown that their information was more accurate than that of the Arab side, military leaders in the October war continued to paint a rosy picture when the real situation was dismal. "From the beginning," wrote the authors of *Ha-Mahdal*, "this was a psychological mistake of major magnitude. In a country like Israel, every family is represented on the front line, complete neighborhoods know each other, and stories travel at lightning speed; the truth cannot be hidden. . . . As a soldier returning from the Hermon battle put it: 'We are allowed to die—but it's forbidden to know.' "[26]

This "crisis of faith" did not stop with the country's leadership; it was extended to the motivating ideology of the country—Zionism. Many high school students started posing skeptical questions of a quite unfamiliar kind: "How long will we fight for this country?" "Does it make sense to die for the Zionist idea?" and so on. These kinds of questions often left the teachers confused and flustered. The students often turned the classes into sessions of heated debate. The Ministry of Education appreciated the magnitude of these doubts since the students might be the very soldiers who would have to

25. *National Observer*, April 6, 1974.
26. Ben-Porat, *op. cit.*, p. 284.

fight a future war; they would have to be motivated by the very same issues which they presently questioned.

This storm of severe doubts did not subside. *Ma'ariv* reported on December 16, 1973 that the heated debate was continuing between students and teachers in an attempt to come to grips with these questions. In a panel of students, educators, and representatives of the Ministry of Education held at Tzevta Club in Tel Aviv, some students criticised Zionism as a movement without justice. Moreover, the war was beginning to force others to question the cause which renders dying for one's country a welcome end.

The October war was a major factor in the sharp decline of immigration. According to figures provided by the Jewish Agency in Jerusalem, 16,853 immigrated to Israel between January and June, 1974, as compared with 24,374 in the same period of 1973. This means that immigration to Israel dropped by 35 per cent in the first half of 1974. The immigration of Americans to Israel followed an even steeper pattern: 1,177 Americans immigrated to Israel in the first half of 1974 as compared with 1,908 American immigrants in the same period of 1973, or a drop of 38 per cent. In the period after the 1967 war, the annual rate of immigrating Americans to Israel was put at between 5,500-7,300. Twenty per cent of those, however, found living in Israel very difficult and returned.[27]

Another indicator of the strength or weakness of the ideology after the October war may be deduced from immigration figures for Russian Jews, and specifically, from what is termed as the "dropout rate"—the percentage of Jews who manage to get out of Russia but elect to settle in the United States, Canada, and other countries. According to available figures, the dropout rate jumped to 22 per cent in July, 1974, as compared with 4 per cent in July, 1973.

A more sensitive issue than immigration rates is the issue of emigration. Officials in the Agency shy away from providing any figures on the claim that existing figures are not reliable. But various reports attest that the talk about emigration has definitely increased after the October war. In a poll conducted by Israel's Public Opinion Research Institute at the end of March, 1974, it was found that more than 10 per cent of those polled were thinking of emigrating. The poll reported that 6.5 per cent of the adults have definite plans to leave and 20.2 per cent of the 18–29 age group are considering emigration.[28] Furthermore, the above quoted *New York Times* report

27. *New York Times*, August 15, 1974.
28. *National Observer*, April 6, 1974.

found that applications for nonimmigrant visas at the Canadian Embassy in Tel Aviv went up 60 per cent in the first half of 1974 as compared with the same period in 1973. The increase in the American Embassy for the same period was 25 per cent.

CONCLUSION

At least temporarily, the October war vehemently interrupted the accepted patterns of Israeli life—both on levels of ideology and action. A flood of serious questions appeared in the commentaries of those who set public opinion in Israel, and those, on the outside, who have been observing the Israeli scene since its inception. The perpetual impact of the preoccupation with such questions as: "Do we have the ability for self-examination?" and "Do we have the capacity to analyze the facts?" must be judged empirically and in a longitudinal manner. But the fact remains that the assumptions which held Israeli society together for twenty-seven years are being challenged.

A leading Israeli psychologist sees Israel's basic dilemma as a contradiction, on the highest ideological level, between "the Israeli creed" (the ideal of a democratic and enlightened society) and "theocratic, racist laws."[29] Rendering these contradictions bare was a powerful impact of the war.

Another leading Israeli intellectual viewed the situation in Israel after the October war as the "worst off" since 1948. Israel is back now to the "Jewish predicament."[30] So far, Israel has not shown any substantial shift in direction, at least as it is translated in leadership and public policies. Of course, a discernible change did take place in the ruling generation—from pioneers to sabras, but as Eric Silver rightly observed, this change has not been reflected in policy. "Mr. Rabin," wrote Silver, "will do nothing on impulse or by default. His administration is equally unlikely, however, to do anything out of imagination or flair. The danger for 1975 is that his very sobriety, his stubborn sense of fundamentals . . . will drag Israel into dogmatism, and from dogmatism into war."[31]

The October war, while it favored the reemergence of national identity among the Arabs, was to introduce no substantial change in Israel's policy towards the Arabs within its domain. Israel followed the all too familiar pattern which may be interpreted as: "let the

29. *Ibid.*
30. *Time,* December 2, 1974.
31. *The Guardian,* January 4, 1975.

world think whatever it may about the Palestinians, but those under our control cannot be allowed to manifest those feelings." Viewed in this light, then, the push-pull relationships between the Right and the Center in Israel represent sheer maneuvers in public relations. Furthermore, it is clear to Israeli and non-Israeli observers, that since the October war the manifestation of Arab Palestinian national identity in the occupied areas cannot be submerged again into oblivion; it has to be directly met.

Elias Shoufani

THE OCTOBER WAR AND THE ISRAELI PRESS

> After what happened, I ran into a leader of the 'Israeli New Left.'
> He turned to me and asked: 'Well, now, have you finally changed your
> views?' I answered: 'I am sorry to say, I have not changed anything.
> What took place here? It was an accident. It should not have happened.
> It could have not. But it is only an accident. It is not corruption. I
> am under no obligation to change my ideology, my beliefs, or the views
> I held before October 6th, because of what happened on October 6-7.
> I am under no obligation whatsoever. In my opinion, nobody is under
> the obligation to change his view of the Israeli Defense Forces.
>
> Dr. Herzl Rosenbloom,
> editor of *Yediot Aharonot*
> in *Ma'ariv*, January 6, 1974

IMMEDIATELY AFTER THE CESSATION of fighting in the October war seven
disgruntled military correspondents of different Hebrew newspapers
put together a book on the war from the Israeli viewpoint. They
called the book, *Ha-Mahdal*. The term can be roughly translated in
English as "the shortcoming"; it has become an unflattering attribute
of the October war in Israel.[1]

Ha-Mahdal was a severe indictment of the Israeli political leadership
and the military command; by Israeli standards it was a best seller.

Portions of this study were published in the *Journal of Palestine Studies*, Vol. III,
No. 2 (Winter, 1974).

1. *Ha-Mahdal* (Beirut: Institute for Palestine Studies, 1974), [Arabic translation].
Ha-Mahdal has been translated into French and Arabic.

Like the majority of Israeli journalists and commentators, the authors of *Ha-Mahdal* sought to explain Israel's failure in the war in terms of external factors. They viewed the crisis that Israel faced as resulting from a constellation of adverse circumstances, mostly accidental, and from a chain of mistakes which originated in negligence by the Israeli ruling establishment. As they evaluated it, what happened to Israel on the external level resulted chiefly from Russian planning, training, and arming of the Arabs; and so, on the internal level, a convergence of objective factors caused the *mahdal*. The subjective factors, however, remained the same. The balance of forces between Israel and the Arab world was not seen as having changed to the extent where the new status quo constituted a threat to the existence of Israel. Such problems as there were could be isolated and solved. The Israeli state and the Jewish people were deemed resourceful enough to withstand the crisis on their own terms. In short, no need was felt to reexamine the validity of the basic assumptions of the Israeli settler society.

DID THE ISRAELI PRESS HAVE ITS OWN 'MAHDAL'?

Between January 4th and 18th, 1974, the Israeli press council held a series of symposia in which the role of the local press during the war was discussed. The mass circulation daily *Ma'ariv* reported on the first session under the title, "The Confusion in the Israeli Society During the Emergency Period Also Jolted the Press."[2] According to the *Ma'ariv* report on the first session of the symposium, the speakers were critical of the media and were not satisfied with their own performance as journalists. But the bulk of the blame was directed at the censorship and the official spokesmen of the government and the army.

Yaakov Rabbi, of *Al-Hamishmar*, opened the first session and dealt with the impact of the "information game," in its positive and negative aspects. He maintained that suppression of information during the first days of the war helped raise the morale of the Israeli public. "But later on, information channels were opened slightly, giving an unbalanced and vague picture." According to Rabbi, censorship in the first few days of the war was vital and silence about the Israeli penetration to the west bank of the Suez Canal was in order. "Later on, however, the bewilderment of newspaper readers intensified, when

2. *Ma'ariv*, January 4-18, 1974.

reports on the situation at the front arrived through foreign press (via their correspondents in Israel), while the Israeli newspapers were not given the opportunity to function normally." Rabbi observed that frustration among local journalists mounted when foreign journals published interviews with some Israeli commanders while the local press was subjected to strict censorship. He compared the situation with that of an ostrich that, "buries its head in the sands of the native country, and raises it up in a foreign land."

The second speaker, Moshe Jaque, of *Ma'ariv,* emphasized that the Israeli press was thrown into confusion during the war. He accused it of delinquency for not exposing the defects of the Israeli army in the period between the two wars, 1967-1973. Jaque said: "Even when we knew of all sorts of defects, we always submitted to the will of the censor, who addressed us in the name of morale." He called for a free access to information instead of press briefings. According to Jaque, "the greatest distortion during the war was caused, in fact, by the inability of the Israeli newspapers to get a clear picture of what was taking place on the battlefields." He went on to say: "Even after the war, we received information on the war from Israeli sources through foreign newspapers and correspondents."

Daniel Bloch, of *Davar,* pointed out that the prime minister of Israel has no press secretary as is the practice in democratic countries. "The press," he said, "did not fulfill its duty before the war; it did not develop additional means of thinking in the field of reporting on security matters. As a result of this, news about enemy military concentrations on the eve of the war was played down."

Professor Shlomo Avineri, who participated in the symposium as a frequent contributor to *Ha'aretz,* stressed the necessity for public and press criticism of all institutions of the state, including the army. Another professor, Arieh Harel, expressed his suspicion that "just as in the past the press and the television nurtured the 'god of peace.' At the present we are in a state of emergency, and the press too has to examine what is allowed and what is prohibited, in accordance with the criteria of a state in siege."

A week later, January 11, 1974, the second session of the symposium was held. The session was opened by Noah Moses, the publisher of *Yediot Aharonot* which covered the session. According to Moses, the Israeli press "cannot publish the whole truth." He criticized the press for being "an easy partner to the establishment, by accepting all sorts of 'no's' with regard to publishing information." Moses pointed out the fact that news, whose publication in the Israeli press was forbidden by the censorship, reached foreign media from Israeli sources; and found its way back to local newspapers. Moses disclosed that on the eve of the war, his newspaper received a request from the military spokesman and a high official "not to cause consternation and to play down news about enemy concentrations on the borders." Moses concluded that "the press took part in creating the atmosphere of complacency, hence it was guilty."

Gershom Shoken, editor of *Ha'aretz*, called for an end to censorship on the Israeli press and urged that a lesson be learnt "from the freedom of the media in the United States." He pointed out that "had the Israeli press published news concerning security matters in the same way it did on economic and political affairs, it would have given a warning of the dangers inherent in the buildup of Arab forces, in advance, while expressing doubt in our secure victory." Shoken emphasized that "the Israeli press did not fulfill its duty in matters of security." According to him, the Israeli press, voluntarily or under duress, "accepted the limitations on publications in this field, and did not stand up for its views." As a result, he went on to say, "the press did not develop great military commentators, as it did in other fields."

In the third session of the symposium, Zeev Shiff, of *Ha'aretz*, complained about the hardening of relationships between military correspondents and the security apparatus. He called for terminating the present system of military information, whereby each newspaper delegates one correspondent to deal with military matters, pending army approval. He also urged a change in the policy of supplying military information "not for publication" to the Editor's Committee.[3]

Meir Ben-Gur, secretary-general of the press council, asked rhetorically: "Was not there a *mahdal* of the press? Did the press know how to read war signals in the Arab world before the war? Did the experts and commentators in the Israeli press know how to analyze the situation, as did those foreign correspondents who visited Arab countries and whose words sounded like prophecies after the war?" According to Ben-Gur, the press and public opinion mutually reinforced one another "in creating an atmosphere of gloom, as a result of which a vicious circle of deteriorating morale was formed." He blamed the press for exaggeration in reporting "deficiency in the supply of eggs," while ignoring "many heroic deeds of the war."[4]

Most participants in the discussions of the symposia were obviously not satisfied with the role that the Israeli press played during and immediately after the October war. But, like the Israeli ruling estab-

3. *Yediot Aharonot*, January 20, 1974.
4. *Ibid.*

lishment, the press has sought to explain its shortcomings in terms of external factors. The greater part of the blame has been borne by the military censors and spokesmen. But, while censorship could be held responsible for concealing information from the public, it could not be held accountable for what the newspapers printed, or did not bother to dig out from sources other than the army's spokesmen.

ISRAELI CENSORSHIP

The Israeli press has been subject to military censorship since the establishment of the state. In Israel military censorship has often been used as a political tool, employed in suppressing information that was deemed disadvantageous to the ruling party, or to the government. The "Lavon Affair" was a prime example of how Israeli leaders used press censorship for political ends. Even when the scandal was public knowledge abroad, and became a matter of personal conflict between Ben Gurion and Lavon—and so had nothing to do with the security of the state—censorship continued and the matter was publicly suppressed. On the eve of the October war, Israel was in the middle of a tough elections campaign for the eight Knesset. The ruling party, Ha-Maʿarakh, conducted a highly demagogic propaganda campaign using Israel's "achievements," particularly in the field of security, for its political ends. Ha-Maʿarakh wanted to give the Israeli voter the impression that all was quiet on the borders, and used military censorship to suppress any news to the contrary.[5]

The Bar-Lev line, for instance, was used in the election campaign to give credence to government claims about Israel's strength and security. An advertisement for the ruling party, carrying the headline: "The Bar-Lev Line," was printed on huge placards and was published in the press. In it was said: "Quiet on the banks of Suez. In Sinai, Gaza, the West Bank, Judea, Shomron, and the Golan, also. The Lines are Secure, The Bridges Open, Jerusalem United, Settlements Built, And Our Political Position Solid. This is the Result of A Balanced, Courageous, And Farseeing Policy . . . You Know That Only Ha-Maʿarakh Could do That."[6] Any news that hinted at disquiet on the borders, or at the possibility of war, was deemed harmful to the ruling party's propaganda line, and consequently deleted or toned down by the military censors.

5. *Ha-Mahdal*, p. 59.
6. *Ibid.*

On the morning of Friday, October 5, 1973, a news report was turned over to the censors giving details of Egyptian activities on the west bank of the Suez Canal. In the original text, it read:

> Egyptian fortification activities on the west bank of the Suez Canal were intensified in the last few days, and they now include a multitude of mechanical equipment. Large units of the Egyptian army are engaged in fortification works. Indeed, it is possible to observe on the Egyptian side of the Canal an intensified movement of Egyptian vehicles. Fortification works include building staging areas and earth ramps, which enable the Egyptians to see beyond the Israeli ramp. These ramps function as tank and anti-tank gun positions, and in some places along the Canal it is possible to observe tanks positioned on the edge of the ramp. Reliable sources said yesterday that in the past, there were such incidents when fortification works were intensified at the time when militant declarations were issued from Cairo. As remembered, this week, the Egyptian News Agency announced that a state of full alert was declared in the Canal area. From various portions of the Canal it is possible to observe intensified movement of Egyptian vehicles, and in recent days Egyptian airplanes have been seen circling a few miles west of the Suez Canal. The Israeli army is carefully watching what takes place on the Egyptian side, and all measures were taken to prevent any possible Egyptian surprise.

Out of this report, only the last sentence was published in *Ma'ariv* on the eve of the war. The military censorship deleted all the rest, for fear that such news might lead to a state of consternation in the Israeli public.[7]

As the October war broke out, Israel's leadership, aware of the early devastating successes of Arab armies, was not confident of the Israeli public's ability to absorb such painful news. Furthermore, conscious of how great was its responsibility for the mishaps afflicting Israel, the leadership had no interest in exposing itself. These considerations led to the adoption of a policy of concealing news from the public in order to maintain national morale and cover up failures. The tools for the execution of that policy were the censors and the military spokesman. "Until the present day," says an author of *Ha-Mahdal*, "the Israeli media has been permitted to report to the Israeli public on successes and achievements only; strict prohibition is imposed on the publication of failures, mistakes and defeats."[8]

7. *Ibid.*, p. 58.
8. *Ibid.*, p. 269.

A salient example of news concealment was the Israeli media's reporting on the Mount Hermon position. Only its recapture by the notorious Golani Brigade was reported in the last day of the war on the Syrian front. That it fell into Syrian hands in the first hours of the war, and that its commander had deserted his place without even telling his soldiers, was never brought to the Israeli public's attention.

Throughout the war the Israeli media were permitted to publish only censored news. Heavy losses, burned tanks, downed airplanes, broken lines, etc., were the exclusive lot of the enemy; the Israeli army was only "improving positions." The censors prevented the publication of any news that might blemish the rosy picture which the Israeli leadership tried to present to its people.[9] But Israel is a small country, and in time of war almost every family has one member in the army; so news circulates informally and easily. The discrepancies between the official bulletins as they were released and reported by the media, and the orally transmitted news from the front, created a credibility gap that could not be bridged during the war.

MILITARY SPOKESMEN

Since military censorship has been a permanent fixture of the Israeli media since the establishment of Israel itself, the failures of the press that relate to the October war cannot be explained away wholly through censorship. The military spokesmen bore much more responsibility for press failures than the censors. During the war, the official information apparatus of Israel was under almost total army control. The Ministry of Foreign Affairs has a section that deals with information, but this too was tied up with the military. Zeev Shiff described the situation:

> What happens today in the field of information on security matters borders on chaos. Army officers, with the rank of colonel, sit in on Israel's radio and television stations, guiding and directing the broadcasting authority, a situation that reminds me of South Vietnam in bad old days. I am convinced that in communist totalitarian countries where information is in party hands things are done in a more elegant way. The guides do not wear uniforms. . . . I am sure that the army officers

9. *Ibid.*, p. 270.

do not infiltrate the broadcasting authority. The latter has sought to be 'raped,' in order to obtain information, pictures, and interviews. The Israeli army trades with information whose publication the censors approve. It is surprising that directors of the broadcasting authority approve of such methods, which started before the war.[10]

Military information has always been taboo for Israelis. The pre-state heritage of underground terrorism was transmitted to the Israeli army through its officer corps, many of whom were commanders of terrorist units in the last years of the Mandate. After the establishment of the state, the army enjoyed a special treatment from the local Hebrew press and Zionist-controlled foreign media. No doubt this treatment by Jews in Israel and elsewhere tended to spoil it. At its inception the Israeli army was considered so much a 'sacred cow' that average citizens, who were ignorant in military affairs, were not permitted to publicly criticize any aspect of it.[11] Israeli newspapers which dared criticize the army had to pay dearly for their "audacity." The weekly *Ha'olam Hazeh* has been vilified by the Israeli army since the early fifties. A quarter of a century ago, the editor of the weekly questioned some of Israel's army practices regarding conscription of women and treatment of war invalids.[12] There is no law prohibiting soldiers from reading *Ha'olam Hazeh,* but the education officer does not buy it for soldiers to read.

The Correspondents Syndicate

The Israeli army decides who should be the military correspondent of each newspaper. It introduced the military correspondents syndicate, and using the ever available if often obscure excuse of state security, the army was able to select from among reporters those whom it approved for membership in the priviledged syndicate. Any reporter who trespassed those limits delineated by the army could find himself excluded from the syndicate for "security reasons." This power provided the Israeli army with a strong weapon against the media. Furthermore, there have been cases when the high command pressured some newspapers to dismiss their military correspondents from their jobs for voicing criticism of the army and its commanders.[13]

10. *Ha'aretz,* January 1, 1974 and January 3, 1974.
11. *Ha-Mahdal,* p. 270.
12. *Ibid.,* p. 271.
13. *Ibid.*

Military information in Israel has been under the control of the intelligence branch of the army. Thus, the military spokesman was an intelligence officer whose background often led him to conceal information rather than reveal it. [14] Using the excuse of state security, the military spokesman could exclude any unpleasant news on the army from publication, or any undesirable correspondent from receiving such information. He could always justify his actions by resorting to the excuse of precaution lest such information reach the enemy. "As far as I am concerned," Dayan has declared, "the Israeli army is a closed institution, unless we decide where and when to open it." [15]

In time, particularly after the victory of 1967, Israeli army officers became increasingly sensitive to criticism. An officer who felt hurt by a press report excommunicated the reporter from the area of his command. Criminal acts in the army were reason enough for a high ranking officer to call newspaper editors fror an emergency meeting to clarify the matter. The military spokesman and his staff even intervened in the layout of news concerning the army. "In the year preceding the Yom Kippur war, when news on embezzlement and other criminal acts in the army became more frequent, the military spokesman turned to newspaper editors personally and asked them not to place such news in a prominent place." A cashier in a bank, "caught in the act of embezzlement does not manage to get such a fat headline as a captain in the Israeli army caught embezzling," the military spokesman exclaimed. [16]

In addition to the syndicate of military correspondents, which has given the information apparatus of the Israeli army control over the flow of news relating to security, the army introduced another innovation—"The Committee of Daily Newspaper Editors." This committee was meant to secure further supervision on news about the army at the final stage before reaching the public. The editors were invited periodically for conferences with high ranking officers, or even the minister of defence himself. There they were briefed on matters that were considered of a secretive nature and not for publication. Through this privileged treatment, the army was able to ask in return that the newspapers abstain from publishing news that was uncomplimentary to it. [17] The editors thus became a tool of the army for

14. *Ibid.*
15. *Yediot Aharonot*, February 11, 1974.
16. *Ha-Mahdal*, p. 271.
17. *Ibid.*, p. 272.

self-imposed censorship by the media.

In Israel, all interviews with army personnel awaited the approval of the military spokesman. The latter, in order to tighten the grip on information from the army, used to authorize such interviews only if the reporter signed, in advance, a declaration permitting the spokesman to delete any portions that he deemed unfit for publication.[18] Deletions by the spokesman were not necessarily for security reasons—that was the function of the military censor; the censorship was designed to preserve the image of the army. Hence, the whole operation was given the euphoric name of "divrur"—wording. The media generally submitted to this regulation, and gave the military spokesman the right to edit all interviews with military personnel. Furthermore, the spokesman, by using this prerogative, could determine a priori the topics to be discussed in the interview, as well as select the "appropriate" person to treat the subject in question.

The Israeli military spokesman, however, has enjoyed a high degree of credibility, particularly since the June war of 1967. The Israeli media itself played a significant role in building up the credibility image of the spokesman, while foreign press and other media from abroad (especially in the United States) contributed a great deal to the building of that image as well. The Israeli military spokesman could easily capitalize on his assets and get away with things that others could not afford. This image, and the popular reverence of the army, led Israelis in general to place blind trust in the announcements of the spokesman. This public consensus around the army and its various institutions put the press in a disadvantageous position vis-à-vis the army. For the press, it was obviously futile to try to swim against the tide; it simply went along with the general mood of complacency.

Loss of Credibility

The 1973 October War, however, shattered the carefully contrived image of the Israeli military spokesman. His communiqués in the first few days of the war led the Israeli soldiers on the front to coin the saying: "The Egyptians learned from the Israeli army how to fight, and the Israelis learned from the Egyptians how to lie."[19] Even on the Yom Kippur eve, when the Israeli high command had obtained enough disturbing information about the situation on two fronts, the military spokesman went on issuing his soothing bulletins in conformity with the government line in the election campaign. Thus, the

18. *Ibid.*
19. *Ibid.*, p. 268.

evening newspapers of Friday, October 5th, came out with the headline: "No special state of preparedness on the border." The military spokesman issued the bulletin after consultation with the commander-in-chief of the army and the chief of intelligence.[20]

During the first day of the war, the communiqués of the military spokesman were cryptic and vague.[21] But the Israelis, who were bewildered by the outbreak of the war, remained optimistic; the brief, generalized, bulletins did not disturb them much. Being confident in the superiority of their army, and having been exposed to continuous denigration of Arab armies, the Israelis tended to interpret the scarcity of news from the front as a stratagem by their army to lead the enemy astray. The speeches of the prime minister and the minister of defence, which were televised during the evening hours of the first day in the war, gave further credence to the prevailing optimism.[22]

On the second and third days of the war, the Israeli military spokesman lost his credibility. Military correspondents joining army units on the front began to return home with different versions of the story. Rumors about falling Israeli lines and losses in life and material began to circulate. Also, Arab communiqués sounded more trustworthy and balanced than before, particularly as they were supported by evidence from the battlefield, while foreign media began to voice suspicions of the Israeli military spokesman. All this put the Israeli high command in an awkward position. The government decided to nominate General Aharon Yariv as a military spokesman, and Yariv blatantly debunked the communiqués of his predecessor in front of television cameras broadcasting live from his first press conference. Yariv's talk devastated whatever credibility the Israeli military spokesman's office had left and, when Yariv left his post a few days later, the office was unable to regain its credibility until the end of the war.[23]

PRESS REPORTS DURING THE WAR

Much criticism has been leveled against the Israeli press for its shortcomings during the October war. Many readers protested that newspapers were instrumental in depressing morale, while others

20. *Ibid.*, p. 273.
21. *Ibid.*
22. *Ibid.*
23. *Ibid.*, p. 279.

accused the press of blowing up minor irregularities out of proportion in time of emergency. In their view the brilliant side of Israel's conduct of the war under adverse circumstances was ignored.[24] Some critics asserted that the press in Israel was part of the establishment and, like other segments of it, the press had its own *mahdal*, though its shortcomings were not the worst in Israeli society.

In response to such criticism, Herzl Rosenbloom, editor of *Yediot Aharonot*, replied:

> Gentlemen, we are forgetting one thing. This state, during those twenty-five years, had many military victories, each one more fantastic than the last. How could we, in such a situation and under such circumstances, when the whole world stood stunned in front of small Israel's actions—how could we come out in criticism of Israel's army? We could not, and that was very natural.[25]

Yaakov Rabbi, from *Al-Hamishmar*, complained about the lack of trustworthy information and blamed the Israeli journalists for "not doing their homework." In his evaluation, they did not read correctly all the signals of the approaching war. They did not draw the right conclusions from the multitude of reports by foreign journalists who visited the Arab world during 1973. Rabbi continued:

> Military analysts and political columnists, as well as institutes for strategic research in the United States and Western Europe, foresaw the possibility of a large-scale war in the Middle East; they even published their forecasts, which in time proved to be real prophecies. The Israeli press either disregarded those forcasts totally, or did not ascribe enough importance to them. It was carried away on the wave of complacency and exaggerated self-confidence.[26]

Yona Cohen, from *Hatzofeh*, remarked on the shortcomings of Israeli journalists saying: "It is said that every state has the press it deserves. It seems, however, that in the emergency period after the Yom Kippur war, the people and the state of Israel deserve a much better press than they have." In Cohen's view, the Israeli press since the October war had fallen short of expectations on two levels: the material that

24. Barukh Ben Yehuda, *Yediot Aharonot*, January 13, 1974.
25. Meir Zayit, *Ma'ariv*, January 1, 1974.
26. *Al-Hamishmar*, January 24, 1974.

it published, and material that it did not. He accused the Israeli journalists of having contributed to the *mahdal* by not questioning the validity of what political or military leaders said. As an example, Cohen pointed out the reaction of journalists to the explanations of an army officer, while on a tour to the Bar-Lev line. The journalists were surprised by the small number of soldiers who manned the fortifications there. In response to their queries about the matter, they accepted without questioning the answer given to them: "Do not worry, everything will be O.K." According to Cohen, the Israeli press had very little influence on the ruling establishment since the latter is hardly concerned with public opinion.[27]

Initial Confidence and Optimism

From the first day of the war, the Israeli press reflected the state of fear and anxiety which prevailed among the surprised, angry, and frustrated Israelis: surprised, because they did not expect the Arabs to dare to challenge their army's superiority; angry, because of the loss of their state's deterrent power on the holy day of Yom Kippur; and frustrated, because the lightning victories which they expected from their armed forces did not occur. Newspapers described some of the scenes in Israel's streets as the mobilization started: people clustered around transistor radios in front of their houses; men who were called to service cried as they parted from their families; soldiers urging their wives to hurry packing their clothes; others rushing through the streets seeking a ride to their staging areas. Because of the blackout on news of the front, rumors were spreading very fast.[28] On the second day, shelters which had been used as warehouses were being cleared; despite appeals by the ministry of commerce and industry to the contrary, people were "hysterically" hoarding food supplies and other consumer goods; banks were crowded in the early hours of the morning with people who wanted to withdraw their savings; civil defence groups comprising youth organizations were activated.

But the press, while describing the consternation which affected the Israeli public, was itself much more confident and optimistic than the military analysts and spokesmen in the first few days. It exuded confidence in the Israeli army; it came out with broad headlines depicting victories on the ground, control of the air, the tide being turned, and an ultimate glorious end to the war. With such confidence

27. *Hatzofeh,* January 1, 1974.
28. A. Koren, *Al-Hamishmar,* October 8, 1973.

the war's ignominious start was to be effaced. Typical of that optimism was a caricature by Dosh in the mass circulation *Ma'ariv*. Dosh drew "little Israel" with a gun in hand, standing against Egyptian President Sadat on the east side of the Canal. Sadat was raising his hands and calling "Help!"[29] The leading daily *Ha'aretz* came out on October 7 with the broad headlines: "The Israeli Army has Checked The Enemy and Is Ready For Counterattack." Among other headlines were the following: "The Attacking Armies of Egypt and Syria Have Suffered Hundreds of Casualties"; "Several Airplanes were Shot Down, Ten Egyptian Helicopters loaded with Soldiers were Downed"; "Our Forces Have Suffered Tens of Casualties in Sinai, Some Israeli Tanks were Hit"; "The Reserve Is Being Mobilized and Dispatched to the Front"; "Washington is Sure That Israel Will Check The Attack, The Battle Is Expected to Last A Day or Two." Neither the fall of the Bar-Lev line, nor the capture by the Syrians of Fort Hermon were reported from Israeli sources. Such news was relayed in the form of "Arab sources claimed" and was toned down.

On October 7, Zeev Shiff, military correspondent of *Ha'aretz*, wrote in a front page article:

> Taking into consideration the fact that the enemy struck first, one should not look at the Egyptian and Syrian achievements as if they are of any significance, especially not from a geographical point of view. The Syrians were surprised by their meagre achievements. All their penetrations on the ground, except in one place, were stopped completely in the first stage . . . Syrian losses in armor and men were substantial. The number of destroyed Syrian tanks reached many scores.[30]

As for the Egyptian front, Shiff said:

> The Egyptians have achieved more than the Syrians, yet nothing of significance up to the present. Their concrete military achievement has been the establishment of two bridges over the Canal. The Egyptian superiority is only temporary. It is possible to suppose that, in the next stage, they will seek a cease-fire and defend their achievements through the Security Council. It is impossible to suppose, however, that Israel will accept a cease-fire before defeating the enemy or worse.[31]

29. *Ha-Mahdal*, p. 273.

30. From the story of *Ha-Mahdal* we know that the Syrian thrust was not blocked, rather they struck deeper in the direction of Tiberia. It was not until much later in the war that the Syrians were halted and driven back.

31. Zeev Shiff, *Ha'aretz*, October 7, 1973.

After two days of fighting, Shiff wrote:

The optimism of Mrs. Golda Meir, the prime minister, and Mr. Moshe Dayan, the minister of defence, has a foundation to stand on. There is no doubting the victory of the Israeli army in this new war which has been imposed on us. At the time of writing these lines, in the second day of coordinated Syrian-Egyptian attack, signs of victory, which will occur in the second and third stages, are becoming clear. And as always under such circumstances, the problem is the price of the Israeli victory. No less important is the price that the Egyptians and Syrians will have to pay for what they have done. For this is a fundamental matter, which will determine to a large extent whether it will be beneficial for them to try their luck in the future, and repeat such attacks.[32]

Loss of Optimism

After three days of fighting *Ha'aretz* sounded more restrained. Its headlines were not as provocative as the first day. The restraint could be attributed to the press conference of General Yariv, who had taken over the task of military spokesman in the meantime and made the first statement to the effect that "the war will not be of short duration."[33]

Yariv took over as military spokesman because his predecessor had lost all credibility. As result of the early communiqués by their military command, the Israelis operated on the assumption that the war would be limited and of short duration. Yariv disabused the Israelis of this early impression and brought them down from the world of dreams about glorious victories to the reality of a long and bitter war. Before the Yariv appearance on television, the Israeli public had been anxious to hear good news, the military spokesman and the Israeli media tried to satisfy that public's needs. The swing from one extreme to the other, however, jolted the Israeli public's morale and caused a credibility gap between that public and its media. Beginning with the first hours of mobilization, many did not take the matter with seriousness commensurate with the dimensions of the danger to the very existence of Israel.

The Israelis were stunned by the first successes of the Arab armies. After the early bulletins of the military spokesman and the "messages to the nation" by the prime minister and the minister of defence,

---

32. *Ibid.*, October 8-9, 1973. Shiff wrote this after the talks of the prime minister and minister of defence on Israeli television at the evening of the first day in the war.

33. *Ibid.*, October 10, 1973.

as well as the "vision of broken bones" by the chief of staff, the Israelis were carried away on a wave of high morale, as if the war were already won. Yariv shattered these illusions and put things in a more objective perspective. He said that Israel was paying a high price in trying to check the attacking Arab armies. He emphasized, however, that Israeli lines were being stabilized. He claimed that all lands lost to the Syrians in the Golan had been recovered, and that the Egyptians were held 3-5 miles east of the Suez Canal. He added that Egypt and Syria had lost more than 150 airplanes in three days of fighting.[34]

Among the headlines of *Ma'ariv*, on October 10, 1973, were the following: "The Airforce Has Begun An Intensified Strategic Bombardment of Syria"; "In The Golan: The Israeli Army Tries to Accomplish Another Penetration In Order To Defeat The Enemy"; "In Sinai: The Israeli Army Avoids Frontal Attack"; "Hundred Israeli Prisoners of War on Egyptian Television"; "The Political Editor of *Ha'aretz*: Achievements and Patience"; "The Military Editor of *Ha'aretz*: A New Situation"; "American Military Experts: The Israeli Army Is Capable of Beating Back The Egyptians and The Syrians, But At A Very High Cost."

Yoel Marcus, political editor of *Ha'aretz*, wrote: "At the end of eighty hours of fighting within the framework of a total war between the combatants, experts estimate that the Israeli army achieved two admirable feats: it is now in the process of getting Syria out of the war, and has achieved air superiority that will impede any significant operation by the Egyptian and Syrian airforces."[35] It is known that some Israeli positions in the Golan, particularly that of Mount Hermon, remained in Syrian hands till the last day of fighting. Also, Syrian fighting ability was not paralyzed; they were able to sustain a war of attrition, on a very high level, for eighty days after the cease-fire.

WHO WON THE WAR?

In general the consensus in the Israeli press was that Israel won the war. The debatable questions were: How big was the victory? What good would it do? At what cost was it achieved? Some journalists claimed the victory to be greater than that of 1967. In support of that claim the press pointed to the new territorial acquisitions, the

34. *Ibid.*
35. *Ibid.*

fact that the Arab side sought a cease-fire, the adverse circumstances under which Israel's army had fought and won, the magnitude of the surprise attack that the small regular army faced and blocked, and, finally, how the tide had turned when mobilization peaked. Yet the tone was apologetic. In comparison with the 1967 triumph and the clamour which ensued, the writing in 1973 was lackluster and rang hollow. There were no heroes to worship and an accusing finger was pointed at the leadership. There was not much talk about credit, but there was a great deal about investigative committees to determine the responsibility for mistakes.

General Mattetyahu Peled observed that Israel had been spoilt in past wars by not paying the price that such wars usually exact. In his view Israel was dragged into the war against her will. Yet the expectations accorded to it were as high as those of previous wars which had been initiated by Israel. The great disappointment occurred when those expectations failed to materialize: "People were called from their houses during a holiday, they were dispatched directly to the front, and they have remained there ever since . . . the preliminary list of casualties was published before we saw the end of the war. In addition, the enemy seemed different from what we were used to in the past. His way of fighting is different, and there is no comparison between the effort required from our fighters now and what we were used to in the past, even in the war of independence." [36]

Yo Edelstein blamed the Israeli government for not having struck first and preempted the Arab assault, thus reducing "the large number of casualties who fell in the first wave, which swept over the poorly manned positions on the Suez and the Golan Heights." Edelstein maintained that the October war brought back to Israel the feeling of fear for the very existence of the state, as was the situation during the war of 1948. He criticized the Israeli generals, who contributed to the atmosphere of complacency which had prevailed since the 1967 June War, by denying that Israel was threatened with destruction at that time. Edelstein went on to say: "Then came the war of Yom Kippur and brought back with it the feeling of fear; it washed out the statements of the generals, which were imbued with exaggerated self-confidence." He stressed that "Israel's back was still up against the wall." [37]

36. *Ma'ariv*, October 19, 1973.
37. *Hatzofeh*, October 19, 1973.

Eliahu Salpetter criticized the government for not directing the war effort towards political ends. He presumed that the Israeli army would inflict a devastating blow on its adversaries, but he doubted that such a blow would deter the Arabs from pursuing their aims by force of arms. He urged the Israeli government to gear the war towards a cease-fire, tied up with direct negotiations for the implementation of the U.N. resolution 242. Otherwise, he warned, the Arabs would "persist in preparation for the fifth and sixth rounds."[38]

In summing up the results of the war, Zeev Shiff wrote: "The cease-fire saved the Egyptian army and helped it keep some important achievements, while reducing to a large extent the military success of the Israeli army on the southern front. We caused heavy losses to the Egyptian army, but we did not succeed in reaching our aim of annihilating its forces and destroying its military base. The destruction of hundreds of Egyptian and Syrian tanks and planes will soon be compensated for by the Soviet Union." He saw no strategic significance in the new territorial acquisitions by Israel; on the contrary, he maintained that they constituted a burden on Israel's army. But he ascribed much importance to the fact that the Egyptian army held on to its gains on the Canal, where its forces were dug in with hundreds of tanks. In his view, this was an "achievement which will remain intact even if we occupied the cities of Suez, Isma'iliya or Port Fuad. This military achievement will give the Egyptians political advantages, and will guide the steps of the U.N. and the great powers in imposing a settlement. . . . And if no settlement is achieved, the Arabs will remain convinced that starting the war was useful, and would be worthwhile to try again in the future. . . . The minimum required of us, on that front, was to drive the Egyptians back from Sinai . . . That, we did not achieve."[39]

Shabtai Teveth, however, held the view that Israel's army should have aimed at the destruction of Arab morale during the war, either by demolishing the Russian equipment or by decimating the armed forces themselves. Neither aim was realized. Teveth went on to say: "In fact, even without the cease-fire, it is doubtful whether Israel's army could have succeeded in decimating the Egyptian army . . . to smash the Arab army in a short period, the Israeli army needed much larger forces than it had. On the other hand, to achieve the aim with available means, would have needed a protracted and exhausting war." Teveth thought that the new cease-fire lines were not as good for Israel as those of 1967, particularly since the Egyptian

38. *Ha'aretz*, October 23, 1973.
39. *Ibid.*

soldier had gained more confidence in himself and in his equipment. If this was so, he asked:

What then did we achieve? Our only important gain is the lesson we learnt from the Yom Kippur war. There will be no place for complacency and arrogance among us, nor shall there be talk about our readiness to absorb the first strike. In addition, we now recognize the necessity of developing organizational ability, and better methods of dealing with Soviet equipment, which will enable us to destroy the morale of the Arab army immediately after the renewal of fighting—for it will undoubtedly be renewed, as long as peace is not realized.[40]

ISRAELI ASSESSMENTS OF THE ARAB FORCES

For Israel the October war was full of surprises, but somehow the stress was shifted from the major elements of surprise to the minor and superficial ones. Timing the attack on Yom Kippur was singled out as the decisive element and hence it was given wide publicity. In fact the Israeli command knew of Arab military preparations some time before the start.[41] The real surprise seems to have been the magnitude of the thrust and the perseverance of an adversary that had been deemed incapable of mounting an offensive on such a scale. Above all, however, the shocking experience was the discovery that Israel's army was not as good as it thought itself to be. Its performance disappointed its supporters, its country, and chiefly itself. In Haim Hertzog's view, the major surprise was the shattering of the peace in which the Israelis were basking.[42]

Most Israelis, particularly since 1967, had developed a low opinion of Arab soldiers. Some writers reminded their countrymen of the fact that on many occasions in past wars the Arab soldier had stood his ground firmly when given a fighting chance. General Mattetyahu Peled, for instance, wrote a short time before the cease-fire on October 22nd: "It is obvious, up to this point, that the Egyptian soldier continues to show a strong fighting spirit and has not lost his will to carry on in the war, despite the heavy losses and the stunning developments to which he has been exposed on the battlefield. We know this phenomenon, and remember it well from the war of

40. *Al-Hamishmar*, October 24, 1973.

41. Edith Zartal, *Davar*, October 12, 1973. See also Y. Frez, *Ma'ariv*, October 5, 1973; and S. Ofer, *Davar*, October 7, 1973.

42. *Ha'aretz*, October 8, 1973.

independence. It is worth mentioning that during the Sinai campaign of 1956, instances where the Egyptian soldiers fought stubbornly and effectively were not infrequent."[43] Other journalists also dwelt on the harmful results of the Israeli attitude towards Arab soldiers. They pointed to instances where Egyptian soldiers displayed an "unbelievable ability" to persevere.[44] Partly through experience, but mainly through inculcation, the Israeli soldier acquired the notion that war was not a matter for Arabs to indulge in. Hence, the simple fact that Arab soldiers did not run away this time startled the Israeli soldier and man in the street alike.

Mark Gefen remarked on the prevalent attitude towards Arab armies: "The average Israeli, for one reason or another, believes that it is enough to press a button in order to defeat the Arab armies under any circumstances." Gefen observed that the Israelis were stunned by the early successes of the Arab armies, and for them, the first two days of the war, two days of fear and doubt before the Israeli army regained the initiative, seemed longer than two months.[45]

In the October war, Zeev Shiff observed a higher motivation to fight among Arab soldiers. He ascribed that to "the feeling of national humiliation . . . after the successive military debacles." He added:

> We noticed that the Arab fighter improved in several matters: his field tactics gave the impression of being good and coherent, despite the fact that they were doctrinal and inflexible; preparation of the forces was more profound, and the training they went through was apparent. These forces broke through into fields which they had not entered before, such as night combat and effective employment of armour in large numbers in the dark. . . . It was possible to notice improvements over the past in Arab technical command of the arms and weapon systems they possessed. . . . Their combative spirit was better, they even displayed a spirit of sacrifice in many instances.

Still Shiff maintained that all these improvements related to standstill warfare. In a mobile war, like the one that raged on the Golan, "the Arab soldier failed in most confrontations."[46] On the tactical level, Shiff admitted that the Arab soldier presented the Israelis with several

43. *Ma'ariv*, October 21, 1973.

44. T. Preuss, *Davar*, October 25, 1973.

45. *Al-Hamishmar*, October 10, 1973.

46. *Ha'aretz*, October 30, 1973.

surprises. Among other things was the deployment of infantry, armed
with a personal anti-tank gun, against heavy armor. "What surprised
us, in particular, was the quantity of such weapons, especially in
the hands of Egyptian infantry," he said. Shiff explained that the
Israeli army built its armored units on the principle of facing similar
forces, "but the enemy created a situation in which we were not
always successful." He deployed infantry against armor, and although
he "exposed many of his soldiers to death, he achieved a tactical
surprise." To explain this tactical surprise, Shiff said: "We believed
that tanks always overwhelm infantry that stands in their way, and
lo and behold, the Egyptians daringly leapt onto the tanks . . . Egyptian
infantry succeeded in exhausting Israeli armour in the first stages,
and built bridges all along the canal . . . It became clear to us, as
one Israeli leader put it, that the Egyptian fellahin had turned into
tank-hunters." [47]

Shabtai Teveth thought that Israeli overconfidence swayed the
government from a preemptive attack. Teveth discounted Israeli talk
about the deterrent power of their army, and argued that it was without
foundation, because Arab armies, whenever defeated, have always
become more determined to rebuild their forces and challenge the
Israeli army anew. [48]

The most disturbing surprise, however, was in Israel's discovery
of the limitations of its power. Before the October war, Israelis
developed the illusion of being a big power in the area, to the extent
of seeing themselves as policemen of the Arab world. They were
entrusted with the power and the task of standing up to the Soviet
Union in the Middle East. They were convinced of their deterrent
power against the Arabs, and they felt that they would soon be
self-sufficient in armament. They believed themselves secure in the
occupied territories without having to make peace with the Arabs.
These notions of the Israelis were nourished by their previous successes. When they looked back on their achievements during twenty-
five years of political independence, they saw only a success story.
Suddenly the October war destroyed this self-image. Israeli soldiers,
symbols of heroism in the society, surrendered to the one man they
despised most—the Arab soldier. Israelis recognized their vulnerability
and dependence on outside powers for their very existence and the
arrogant dismissal of world public opinion before the war turned
into a gloomy feeling of isolation. Moshe Dor wrote: "The war of

47. *Ibid.*, November 4, 1973.
48. *Al-Hamishmar*, October 10, 1973; *Davar*, October 8, 1973.

Yom Kippur smashed, like a giant fist, the fool's paradise in which we spoiled ourselves, until we were struck by lightning."[49]

THE CREDIBILITY GAP

On the home front in Israel, the October war left many marks. Civilian life was practically paralyzed during and after the fighting. Israel's economy suffered heavily; the routine of life and feeling of security in a self-confident community were shaken; and a whole range of relationships in a society veering towards capitalism was ruptured. But probably the most important development on the internal front was the loss of confidence by the Israeli public in its political leadership. Political commentators wrote extensively on this subject, and will, most likely, continue to do so for some time to come.

Concerning the impact of the war on Israel's internal front, one writer asked rhetorically: "Will our life really return to what it used to be before? Is it possible for it to do so? Are we going to forget? Could we do so?" Israel's political leadership was accused of bankruptcy and failure to measure up to its responsibility. The leadership was seen as so weakened by intra-party strife that there was considerable public doubt that it could perform its duties in such difficult days. The public was clearly passing through a crisis of confidence in the system and the media. Many people had the feeling that they had been deceived and were not told the truth.

Yoel Marcus commented on the state of affairs inside Israel during and after the war: "There is no doubt today that the public is passing through a crisis of confidence; it has no confidence in the existing constants, in the system, or in the media. Many have the feeling that they were deceived and were not told the truth, worse still—no body has told them the truth yet." According to Marcus, the credibility gap developed in stages when "the public discovered in each stage new things that it did not know in the earlier." He went on to say: "Everything began with the first day of the war, when a campaign of distortion, coverup, misinformation, and sheer lies was under way, seemingly, to raise morale. This reached the point where Hebrew programmes from Radio Cairo and Jordan television, during the first days of the war, became more reliable sources of information than those of Israel." Marcus pointed out that it was through Jordan's television that the Israelis learned of the fall of the Bar-Lev line,

49. *Ma'ariv*, October 30, 1973.

while their military spokesman was still talking of "counterattacks" and "destroying the enemy." Also, the Hebrew programme of Radio Cairo informed the Israelis of what happened to the armored brigade of Colonel Assaf Yagouri. Marcus added: "It was on the same day, when an official commentator in Tel Aviv boasted that our airforce had destroyed all the bridges which the Egyptians had built over the canal, that a correspondent of *Newsweek,* who accompanied the Egyptian force which crossed the Canal, reported that 70,000 Egyptians with 900 tanks had crossed over the bridges which were not in existence." Marcus concluded: "Through this campaign of misleading, boasting communiqués, contradictions, imprecision, and intentional cover-up, the faith of the public was dealt another blow."[50]

Ha'aretz (November 23, 1973), gave a summary of a poll that was conducted after the war which included all parts of the country. It was designed to test the popularity of the political leadership in Israel. "The Israeli public," the summary stated, "is engulfed in much confusion with regard to its stance vis-à-vis the political leadership." The poll found that the popularity of Golda Meir and Dayan had declined, but that the public was unable to choose replacements to lead Israel in this difficult time. About half the population did not approve of Meir's conduct of state affairs. Dayan was seen as less of a leader after the war, but the majority did not want him to resign. Yigal Allon took the lead in the poll as the most viable replacement for Meir, with 20.5 per cent of the vote. Second came Menachem Begin with 11.5 per cent; Dayan ran third with 10.5 per cent.[51] The paper pointed out that "the most striking phenomenon with regard to the question of the prime minister was that 39.9 per cent of the public were unable to select a candidate for the position."

The credibility gap was not limited to the political leadership: it also extended to the military command. This loss of confidence reached beyond particular personalities to the military as a whole. The most important reason given for this attitude was that the leadership was either incompetent or lacking proper intelligence. Describing the gap that separated the public from the ruling establishment, Levi Yitzhak Hayerushalemi wrote:

> He who mixes with people today . . . who visits military bases and posts, would clearly realize to what extent the public does not care

50. *Ma'ariv,* October 30, 1973; *Ha'aretz,* November 6, 1973.

51. Menachem Begin is leader of the Herut party, allied to the liberals in the Gahal and, more recently, Likud lists.

for the 'burning issues' which occupy politicians of all kinds. . . . What
infuriates one is the fact that this small and narrow group did not learn
anything from the awesome shock which affected us; they talk about
it as if it had spared them. They continue to talk and write in the same
arbitrary way which poisoned us in the period between the last two
wars as if nothing had happened. In the past they emphatically said:
'the deterrent power of Israel's army existed beyond any shadow of
a doubt.' Today they say: 'Israel's army lost its deterrent power.' Is
that not a bitter draft to swallow?[52]

ISRAEL, THE WAR AND THE WORLD

After 1967, Israel defied the world community by refusing to
implement U.N. resolutions on the conflict. It felt itself capable of
disregarding world public opinion, so long as it enjoyed the support
of the United States. As for the United States itself, Israel began
to see in it an ally that could not afford to be antagonistic. A general
attitude of contempt towards the world organization and international
public opinion spread in Israel. This was the parallel of a similar
and clearly noticeable tendency to break free of the custodianship
of the World Zionist Organization. During the war, however, a feeling
of isolation came to dominate Israel; her reaction to the general attitude
of most states in the world was one of anger. In view of her political
isolation, Israel felt that she was left with only one reliable ally—the
United States—and only one faithful friend—the Jewish people.

In the Israeli press there were complaints that Israel was unable
to use her most effective weapon—the army—because of international
intervention to impose a cease-fire. There were bitter protests against
the attitude of the world; and there was regret that Israel was ruled
by an old leadership, which had formed its ideas in a different era;
there were allusions to the Free World and the murder of six million
Jews during World War II.[53] It was clear that Israel's situation in
the world was viewed as deteriorating. It was also clear that there
were many reasons if that observation was true. Among other things,
there was the problem of the self-interest of states and ideological
differences between Zionism and communism. There was anti-Semi-
tism which had been dormant for some time but had flared up again
during the war.

Another problem was the informal alliance with the United States.
It seemed that the more the Israelis became isolated in the international

52. *Ma'ariv*, November 7, 1973 and November 14, 1973.

53. *Ha'aretz*, October 16, 1973 and November 13, 15, and 16, 1973; *Davar*, November
2, 1973.

arena, the more difficult it became for the United States to continue its support. Certainly the United States had not stood by Israel as the Soviet Union had stood by the Arabs. There was the feeling, expressed in several forms throughout the Israeli media, that although Israel had won all the wars that she fought against the Arabs, her victory created a vicious circle of continuous wars. For example, Egypt had favored the Jewish struggle against the British during the Mandate but had now become Israel's chief adversary. Israel was viewed in effect as a Rhodesia with the difference that Israel was surrounded by enemies. There was a call for installing a political leader at the head of the military establishment.

Venomous attacks were directed by the Israeli press against the Soviet Union, which was blamed for many Israeli troubles. The Soviet Union was accused of having succeeded in having the United States execute Russian policy in the Middle East; to top this off, Kissinger was seen as a Chamberlain. There was a call for an extensive propaganda campaign in the United States and elsewhere, over the heads of the local governments, in the conviction that public opinion in the world still supported Israel. The Israeli government was warned against making a fatal mistake in misreading Soviet intentions.[54]

Israel's reaction to the repeated severance of diplomatic relations in Africa was one of frustrated anger. In many cases there were irrational and highly emotional attacks on African states and leaders. *Yediot Aharonot* published an unsigned article about Ethiopian Emperor Haile Selassie which resorted to sheer name-calling. Others more cooly suggested cooperation with Christian missionaries to improve Israel's image in Africa.[55] Finally there was the matter of Jewish support for Israel; material aid was deemed not enough. World Jewry understood Israel's needs in terms of contributions, but the Jews in the diaspora did not seem to understand that Israel would never be really safe until her population was eight or ten million. World Jewry was blamed for not giving enough importance to the "fact" that the Jews had no existence without the state of Israel. As one commentator wrote: "It is forbidden for us to allow Jews to set their consciences at rest by financial contributions, irrespective of their generosity. We must push for immigration. Funds are necessary, but immigration is vital."[56] Thus the war had once again brought Israelis face to face with the inherent weakness of their situation: they were a small population attempting to impose its will upon the surrounding area.

54. *Ma'ariv*, November 9, 1973; *Ha'aretz*, November 9, 1973.
55. *Yediot Aharonot*, October 24, 1973.
56. *Davar*, November 2, 1973.

PART 2: INTERNATIONAL DIMENSIONS

Janice J. Terry

THE WESTERN PRESS AND THE OCTOBER WAR: A CONTENT ANALYSIS

DID THE 1973 OCTOBER WAR and the Arab oil boycott transform Western attitudes regarding the Middle East? Many observers are convinced that the Arab military successes, coupled with the message that the Arab nations, through their oil resources, had the power to bring Western industry and life-styles to a crashing halt, significantly altered U.S. and European opinions of Israel and the Arab nations. This study examines three U.S. and two European newspapers during a four-month period before the war, the month of the war itself, and a four-month period following the war in order to ascertain in quantitative terms whether or not the media did, in fact, significantly modify its Middle East coverage.

METHOD

The *New York Times,* the *Washington Post,* and the *Detroit Free Press* were selected as the U.S. newspapers to be analyzed; the *Times* (London) and the French *Le Monde* were selected as representative of leading European newspapers.

Articles pertaining to the Middle East, although not those containing speeches or government statements, were coded on IBM coding forms

This paper appears also in Arabs in America: Myths and Realities, ed. by Baha Abu-Laban and Faith T. Zeadey (Wilmette, Ill.: Medina University Press International, 1975).

on a scale from one to ten.[1] In each case, the title of the newspaper, the date, the type of article, and the attitudes revealed in it were coded. The general attitude toward the conflict and breakdowns on attitudes toward the United Nations, specific Arab nations, the Palestinians, and the Arab oil boycott were included on the coding form. Whether or not the coverage linked the conflict to the superpower rivalry between the United States and the U.S.S.R. was also noted. For the European press, attitudes toward Continental détente with the Arab nations and opinions regarding U.S. policies in the Middle East were coded.[2] Finally, articles were classified as news articles, editorials, features, or cartoons.[3] Only major articles were coded; when the coverage was massive, as during the war, news items grouped under one headline were coded as one article.

The attitudes were coded as being either for or against Israel or Arab nations. An article was considered to be for one side if its attitude toward the actions of that side was favorable or if it described that side in favorable terms. An article was coded as being against one side if it displayed hostility toward the actions of that side or described that nation or its leadership in unfavorable terms. In cartoons, caricatures with racially derogatory features or disparaging stereotypes were coded as negative. An article was coded as neutral if it lacked value-laden adjectives, presented both sides of the case, or merely provided information or news coverage of events.

Once all of the articles had been coded, the information was transferred to IBM punch cards. The computer was then fed the data and was programed to tally the number of articles and types of attitudes

1. For previous studies of the same U.S. newspapers from 1948 to 1973, see Janice Terry, "A Content Analysis of American Newspapers," in The Arab World: From Nationalism to Revolution, ed. Abdeen Jabara and Janice Terry (Wilmette, Ill.: Medina University Press, International, 1971); Janice Terry and G. Mendenhall, "1973 U.S. Press Coverage on the Middle East," Journal of Palestine Studies, vol. IV, no. 1 (Autumn, 1974). Data from earlier years cited in the present study are from these two earlier papers. Gordon Mendenhall assisted in the computer programing for the present study.

2. The statistical data for 1973 concerning the superpowers are somewhat blurred owing to the détente between the former cold war rivals, although to some extent the 1973 war exacerbated many of the old antagonisms. Support for the détente softened the formerly strident U.S. editorial stance against Soviet policies in the Middle East, but after the October war more negative articles again appeared. European coverage differed notably from U.S. coverage on this issue.

3. It is somewhat difficult to distinguish between editorials and features in Le Monde. For purposes of this study, items classified in Le Monde as "Viewpoints" ("Points de Vue") were coded as editorials.

revealed, and to provide statistics comparing the coverage in the five newspapers by type of article. Tabulations were obtained on the frequency of occurrence of those articles dealing with the Arab-Israeli conflict, the United Nations, the Palestinian refugees, and the commandos. Percentages of occurrence were also tabulated. Secondly, tabulations were obtained on those items dealing with attitudes as dependent variables, using the type of article and newspaper as the independent variables. Comparisons were then obtained for coverage prior to the war (June–September 1973), during the war (October 1973), and after the war (November 1973–February 1974). In this manner a statistical picture of any differences in coverage before and after the war could be quantitatively noted. Differences among the newspapers, and between the U.S. and the European media, are clearly evident.

The volume of material, with 2,616 articles coded, offers numerous possibilities for further grouping and analysis. The nuances of some articles and cartoons are necessarily lost because of the broad categories that are demanded by the volume of the material. This methodological problem can only be overcome by a complex and expensive word tabulation. This study does, however, clearly document the press coverage in terms of volume and general attitudes for these five newspapers—both in the United States and in Europe. In addition, it reveals some significant differences among Western newspapers.

GENERAL RESULTS

A total of 2,616 articles were coded (see Table 1). The data on the *New York Times* are somewhat deceptive, as news articles under one headline were coded as one article. As a consequence the number of news articles coded for the *New York Times* is not indicative of the number of column inches devoted to Middle East news; in terms of space allotted, the *New York Times* coverage was, in fact, more extensive than the statistics indicate.

The extensive coverage in *Le Monde* is notable because, unlike the other newspapers coded, it does not publish a massive Sunday edition, but rather a joint Sunday and Monday edition. Thus *Le Monde* has only six days of publication to the seven for the other newspapers. As with the *New York Times,* many articles under one headline were coded as one article, indicating that *Le Monde*'s Middle East coverage is the most extensive of any of the papers analyzed.

In the nine-month period of time covered, both *Le Monde* and the *Washington Post* each published over 600 articles on the Arab-Israeli conflict and the oil boycott as it pertained to the Middle East and the West. This is a massive increase in total coverage in comparison with that of previous years. For example, in 1968 the *Washington Post* published only 49 articles, while the *New York Times*, the *Washington Post*, and the *Detroit Free Press* collectively published only 275 articles—less than one-third what the *Post* singly published in the months before and after the 1973 war. In 1948, another peak year of coverage, articles in the same newspapers totaled 1,140; these figures, of course, more closely approximate the 1973 data. Unfortunately, no comparable statistics are available for the European press, but it seems likely that its volume of coverage has increased similarly.

In all of the newspapers most of the news coverage was neutral. As might be expected, opinions and attitudinal biases became more apparent in editorials and features. In its total coverage, the *New York Times* contained 7.1 percent pro-Israeli and 2.1 percent anti-Arab material for a total of 9.2 percent favoring Israel (see Table 2). This compares with 0.8 percent pro-Arab, 0.5 percent anti-Israeli, and 1.1 percent pro–Palestinian refugee coverage, which totals 2.4 percent pro-Arab material. Similarly, the *Washington Post* coverage was 5.8 percent pro-Israeli and 2.3 percent pro-Arab; the *Detroit Free Press*, 6.8 percent pro-Israeli and no pro-Arab material; the *Times*, 2.7 percent pro-Israeli and 2.3 percent pro-Arab; and *Le Monde*, 2.5 percent pro-Israeli and 2.5 percent pro-Arab. Thus the European newspapers were more nearly balanced in their total coverage than were the U.S. newspapers.

The figures also indicate a marked drop in pro-Israeli/anti-Arab editorial coverage (see Table 3). In 1948, 31 editorials in the *New York Times* (57.4 percent of total editorial coverage in that paper) favored Israel; in 1968, 6 editorials (37.5 percent) did so; and in the period of this study, 11 editorials (10.9 percent) favored Israel. Similar declines are found in the other U.S. newspapers.

In features, the pro-Israeli stance of the U.S. press becomes more pronounced. The *New York Times* issued 23 features favorable to Israel (23.7 percent of total feature coverage in that paper), the *Washington Post*, 17 (16.0 percent), and the *Detroit Free Press*, 8 (17.7 percent). At the same time, the *New York Times* published 6 pro-Arab features, (6.2 percent), the *Washington Post*, 9 (8.5 percent), and the *Detroit Free Press*, none. In other words, there were approximately twice as many pro-Israeli features as pro-Arab ones. In spite of this bias, the feature coverage has become more balanced, for pro-Arab features were almost totally absent in pre-1973 coverage.

Le Monde had 7 pro-Israeli features (4.6 percent) and 8 pro-Arab (5.2 percent), while the *Times* had 12 pro-Israeli (14.1 percent) and 7 pro-Arab (8.2 percent).

The data indicate that mention of the Palestinians as a separate entity in press coverage has become quite frequent. In the U.S. media this is not a *re*appearance of the Palestinian entity, but its first quantitative appearance. In 1948 the Palestinians were mentioned in the three U.S. newspapers in 12 articles, and in 1968 in only 23. In this study the Palestinians were mentioned specifically in 541 articles: 191 in the *New York Times*, 96 in the *Washington Post*, 42 in the *Detroit Free Press*, 91 in the *Times*, and 122 in *Le Monde* (see Table 17). For the U.S. press alone this is a startling increase of over 1000 percent! There was an indication that while there may be growing sympathy for or at least awareness of the Palestinian case, there is also growing hostility to most commando activities. There were 2 *New York Times*, 2 *Washington Post*, 4 *Times*, and 5 *Le Monde* features indicating sympathy for the Palestinians (see Table 3). In contrast there were 10 *New York Times*, 2 *Washington Post*, 3 *Detroit Free Press*, 4 *Le Monde*, and no *Times* features criticizing the commandos (see Table 4). Editorials in these newspapers also reflected this attitude.

The European attitudes with regard to the oil issue contrast considerably with those of the U.S. press. To a great extent this reveals the greater dependency of Europe on Arab oil, and the determination of European leaders not to alienate the Arab states (see Tables 5-8). Consequently, the *Times* published only 1 editorial criticizing the Arab embargo and *Le Monde* published 5, whereas there were 12 anti-Arab editorials in the *New York Times* and 15 in the *Washington Post*. The U.S. editorials, as well as features, tended to stress the "blackmail" aspects of the boycott, a theme completely absent from the European press coverage.

Finally, the two European newspapers occasionally criticized U.S. policies in the Middle East (1 news article, 1 feature, and 1 editorial in the *Times*, and 1 editorial in *Le Monde*; see Table 9). *Le Monde* reflected the independent French policy in international affairs and stressed the best interests of Europe in 1 news article, 7 editorials, and 4 features. However, both newspapers were unanimous in praising the efforts of Henry Kissinger in the Middle East. The *Times* printed 5 editorials and 2 features lauding Kissinger. Even the generally less pro-U.S. French press picked up the trend; *Le Monde* issued 3 editorials, 4 features, and 3 cartoons commending Kissinger's diplomacy.

THE OCTOBER WAR: BEFORE AND AFTER

Not surprisingly, press coverage was at its peak during the October war, and at times equaled or surpassed the total coverage in the four months preceding the outbreak of hostilities. In the four months following the war, the extent of coverage remained at least 10 to 20 percent higher than in the period prior to October. This indicates a continuing interest in Middle East news, in the possibility of a resolution of the Arab-Israeli conflict, and in the Arab oil embargo. The total coverage in the five newspapers after the war was more than twice that of the months prior to it (see tables 10-13). The distribution among news articles, features, editorials, and cartoons remained fairly consistent, indicating an increase in coverage in all types of articles (see Table 14). Interestingly, the European newspapers had a somewhat higher level of coverage prior to the war than the U.S. newspapers. The European media, therefore, evidence a continuing interest in Middle Eastern affairs, while the U.S. press tends to be more "crisis oriented."

Editorial coverage of the war and its aftermath tended to favor the Israeli position; however, there were some pro-Arab editorials, whereas there had been few if any in the years before 1973 (see tables 15-16). There were also some anti-Israeli editorials, although these were outnumbered by pro-Israeli editorials four to one. The war also strained the U.S.-U.S.S.R. détente. Although there were no editorials criticizing Soviet policies in the Middle East before the war, during the war U.S.S.R. actions in the Middle East were criticized several times. Editorials also stressed a certain sympathy for the Palestinian refugees, who were generally depicted as victims.

Mention of the Palestinians as a separate entity did not increase during the war or afterward, but remained fairly constant (see Table 17). This seems to support the hypothesis that notice of the Palestinian entity emerged after the 1967 war when the Palestinian commandos forced world attention to face the reality of Palestinian grievances. During the war, mention of the Palestinians actually dropped slightly; this was probably owing to the focus on institutionalized polities and the military confrontations among internationally recognized governments. Articles continued to reflect opposition to commando activities (see Table 18).

Certainly the most notable change in coverage concerned the issue of the oil embargo, which became a major news item during and after the October war (see tables 19-23). Only 78 articles were published on oil and the Middle East prior to the war; after the war 368 such articles were published. Editorial coverage more than tripled, with a number of editorials merely discussing the problems and complexities posed by the Arab embargo. There were very few pro-Arab articles, most of them appearing in the European press.

Tables 24 and 25 primarily indicate an increase, following the October war, in the volume of coverage of the Arab-Israeli conflict, but do not reveal any important changes in attitudes toward the Arabs or the Israelis. However, neutral coverage did increase slightly, and this may be indicative of the beginning of changing attitudes. On the other hand, it may also merely represent an attempt by the press to include more balanced material from both Israeli and Arab sources. The European newspapers had fewer pro-Israeli articles both before and after October 1973 than did the U.S. press. They also issued fewer anti-Arab articles. Thus the European press had begun to alter its coverage, or to reach a greater balance in its coverage, prior to the war.

Table 1

Number of Articles on the Middle East, June 1973 - Feb. 1974

Newspaper	No.	%
New York Times	462	17.7
Washington Post	662	25.3
Detroit Free Press	292	11.2
Times	508	19.4
Le Monde	692	26.4
TOTAL	2,616	100.0

Table 2

Attitude toward the Arab-Israeli Conflict

Attitude	New York Times		Washington Post		Detroit Free Press		Times		Le Monde		Total	
	No.	%	No.	%	No.	%	No.	%	No.	%	No.	%
Neutral	329	86.6	498	88.8	236	90.1	451	94.0	607	94.4	2,121	91.1
Against both	2	0.5	13	2.3	7	2.7	5	1.0	4	0.6	31	1.3
Pro-Israeli	27	7.1	30	5.3	15	5.7	12	2.5	16	2.5	100	4.3
Pro-Arab	3	0.8	6	1.1	-	-	1	0.2	4	0.6	14	0.6
Anti-Israeli	2	0.5	3	0.5	1	0.4	4	0.8	3	0.5	12	0.5
Anti-U.S.S.R.	5	1.3	4	0.7	-	-	-	-	-	-	10	0.1
Anti-U.S.	-	-	-	-	-	-	-	-	-	-	-	-
Anti-Arab	8	2.1	3	0.5	3	1.1	1	0.2	-	-	15	0.6
Sym. for refugees	4	1.1	4	0.7	-	-	6	1.3	9	1.4	23	1.0
TOTAL	380		561		262		480		643		2,326*	

*Total here is less than total on Table 1 because not all articles mention the Arab-Israeli conflict.

Table 3

Pro-Israeli/Anti-Arab and Pro-Arab/Anti-Israeli Coverage *

Type of coverage and attitude	New York Times No.	%	Washington Post No.	%	Detroit Free Press No.	%	Times No.	%	Le Monde No.	%
Total editorials	101		61		30		52		65	
Pro-Israeli	6	5.9	11	18.0	5	16.7	1	1.9	9	13.8
Anti-Arab	5	4.9	1	1.6	-	-	-	-	-	-
TOTAL	11	10.9	12	19.7	5	16.7	1	1.9	9	13.8
Pro-Arab	-	-	-	-	-	-	-	-	4	6.1
Anti-Israeli	1	.9	2	3.3	-	-	2	3.8	3	4.6
Sym. to refugees	-	-	2	3.3	-	-	2	3.8	4	6.1
TOTAL	1	.9	4	6.6	-	-	4	7.6	11	16.9
Total features	97		106		45		85		152	
Pro-Israeli	21	21.6	15	14.1	7	15.5	11	12.9	7	4.6
Anti-Arab	2	2.0	2	1.9	1	2.2	1	1.2	-	-
TOTAL	23	23.7	17	16.0	8	17.7	12	14.1	7	4.6
Pro-Arab	3	3.1	5	4.7	-	-	1	1.2	-	-
Anti-Israeli	1	1.0	2	1.9	-	-	2	2.3	3	1.9
Sym. to refugees	2	2.1	2	1.9	-	-	4	4.7	5	3.3
TOTAL	6	6.2	9	8.5	-	-	7	8.2	8	5.2
Total cartoons	2		19		21		-		15	
Pro-Israeli	-	-	4	21.0	2	9.5	-	-	-	-
Anti-Arab	-	-	-	-	-	-	-	-	-	-
TOTAL	-	-	4	21.0	2	9.5	-	-	-	-
Pro-Arab	-	-	1	5.3	-	-	-	-	-	-
Anti-Israeli	-	-	-	-	-	-	-	-	-	-
Sym. to refugees	-	-	-	-	-	-	-	-	-	-
TOTAL	-	-	1	5.3	-	-	-	-	-	-

*Details may not add to total owing to rounding.

Table 4

Attitude toward the Commandos

	Pro No.	%	Anti No.	%	Neutral No.	%	Total No.
New York Times							
News articles	1	0.8	1	0.8	124	98.4	126
Editorials	-	-	15	88.2	2	11.8	17
Features	-	-	10	62.5	6	37.5	16
Cartoons	-	-	-	-	-	-	-
TOTAL	1		26		132		159
Washington Post							
News articles	-	-	-	-	65	100.0	65
Editorials	-	-	10	90.9	1	9.0	11
Features	-	-	2	16.7	10	83.3	12
Cartoons	-	-	-	-	-	-	-
TOTAL	-		12		76		88
Detroit Free Press							
News articles	-	-	1	3.1	31	96.8	32
Editorials	-	-	3	75.0	1	25.0	4
Features	-	-	3	60.0	2	40.0	5
Cartoons	-	-	-	-	-	-	-
TOTAL	-		7		34		41
Times							
News articles	-	-	4	6.1	61	93.8	65
Editorials	3	27.3	9	69.2	4	30.8	13
Features	-	-	-	-	8	72.7	11
Cartoons	-	-	-	-	-	-	-
TOTAL	3		13		73		89
Le Monde							
News articles	-	-	-	-	68	100.0	68
Editorials	2	15.4	9	69.2	2	15.4	13
Features	1	6.2	4	25.0	11	68.7	16
Cartoons	-	-	1	100.0	-	-	1
TOTAL	3		14		81		98

Table 5

Attitude on Oil Embargo in News Articles

Attitude	New York Times	Washington Post	Detroit Free Press	Times	Le Monde
			No. of news articles		
Neutral	181	126	44	66	99
Pro-Arab	-	-	-	-	-
Anti-Arab	-	-	1	-	-
Russia benefit	-	-	1	-	-
Pro-U.S.	-	-	2	-	-
Oil as good for U.S./Arabs	-	-	-	-	-
Oil as good for Europe	-	-	-	-	1
Oil as good for Europe/Arabs	-	-	-	-	-
Anti-oil companies	-	-	-	-	-

Table 6

Attitude on Oil Embargo in Editorials

Attitude	New York Times	Washington Post	Detroit Free Press	Times	Le Monde
			No. of editorials		
Neutral	37	2	4	15	4
Pro-Arab	-	-	-	-	3
Anti-Arab	12	15	2	1	5
Russia benefit	-	-	-	-	-
Pro-U.S.	1	6	-	-	-
Oil as good for U.S./Arabs	3	1	1	1	-
Oil as good for Europe	-	-	-	-	3
Oil as good for Europe/Arabs	1	-	-	-	3
Anti-oil companies	-	-	-	-	1

Table 7

Attitude on Oil Embargo in Features

Attitude	No. of features				
	New York Times	Washington Post	Detroit Free Press	Times	Le Monde
Neutral	33	10	7	14	14
Pro-Arab	2	2	1	2	—
Anti-Arab	22	13	12	1	—
Russia benefit	1	—	1	1	—
Pro-U.S.	1	6	3	—	—
Oil as good for U.S./Arabs	4	2	1	1	—
Oil as good for Europe	—	—	—	—	9
Oil as good for Europe/Arabs	—	1	—	—	—
Anti-oil companies	—	—	2	—	—

Table 8

Attitude on Oil Embargo in Cartoons

Attitude	No. of cartoons				
	New York Times	Washington Post	Detroit Free Press	Times	Le Monde
Neutral	1	—	2	—	2
Pro-Arab	—	—	—	—	—
Anti-Arab	—	5	7	—	—
Russia benefit	—	—	—	—	—
Pro-U.S.	—	—	1	—	—
Oil as good for U.S./Arabs	—	—	—	—	—
Oil as good for Europe	—	—	—	—	1
Oil as good for Europe/Arabs	—	—	—	—	—
Anti-oil companies	—	—	—	—	—

Table 9

European Attitude toward U.S. Policies in the Middle East

Newspaper and attitude	News articles	Editorials	Features	Cartoons
Times				
Pro-U.S. support for Israel	1	1	1	—
Anti-U.S. support for Israel	1	—	1	—
Neutral	—	—	—	—
Pro-U.S., anti-Arab	—	—	—	—
Pro-U.S., pro-Arab	—	5	—	—
Pro-Kissinger	—	—	2	—
Pro-Europe	—	—	—	—
Le Monde				
Pro-U.S. support for Israel	—	1	—	—
Anti-U.S. support for Israel	—	1	—	—
Neutral	—	1	—	—
Pro-U.S., anti-Arab	—	—	—	—
Pro-U.S., pro-Arab	—	—	—	3
Pro-Kissinger	—	3	4	—
Pro-Europe	1	7	4	—

Table 10

Number of News Articles on the Arab-Israeli Conflict before and after the October war

Newspaper	June-Sept. 1973		Oct. 1973		Nov. 1973-Feb. 1974		Total
	No.	%	No.	%	No.	%	No.
New York Times	86	33.3	30	11.6	112	55.0	258
Washington Post	83	17.5	122	25.7	269	56.7	474
Detroit Free Press	22	11.2	57	29.0	117	59.7	196
Times	95	25.4	94	25.1	185	49.5	374
Le Monde	147	32.0	99	21.6	213	46.4	459
TOTAL	433		402		926		1,761

Table 11

Number of Editorials on the Arab-Israeli Conflict before and after the October war

Newspaper	June-Sept. 1973		Oct. 1973		Nov. 1973-Feb. 1974		Total
	No.	%	No.	%	No.	%	No.
New York Times	19	18.8	25	24.7	57	56.4	101
Washington Post	11	18.0	14	22.9	36	59.0	61
Detroit Free Press	1	3.3	8	26.7	21	70.0	30
Times	12	23.1	15	28.8	25	48.1	52
Le Monde	12	18.5	20	30.8	33	50.8	65
TOTAL	55		82		172		309

Table 12

Number of Features on the Arab-Israeli Conflict before and after the October War

Newspaper	June-Sept. 1973		Oct. 1973		Nov. 1973-Feb. 1974		Total
	No.	%	No.	%	No.	%	No.
New York Times	19	19.6	14	14.4	64	65.9	97
Washington Post	9	8.5	30	28.3	67	63.2	106
Detroit Free Press	7	15.5	12	26.7	26	57.8	45
Times	12	14.6	35	42.7	35	42.7	82
Le Monde	31	20.4	28	18.4	93	61.2	152
TOTAL	78		119		285		482

Table 13

Number of Cartoons on the Arab-Israeli Conflict before and after the October War

Newspaper	June-Sept. 1973		Oct. 1973		Nov. 1973-Feb. 1974		Total
	No.	%	No.	%	No.	%	No.
New York Times	2	66.7	-	-	1	33.3	3
Washington Post	1	5.3	5	26.3	13	68.4	19
Detroit Free Press	1	4.8	4	19.0	16	76.2	21
Times	-	-	-	-	-	-	-
Le Monde	-	-	5	33.3	10	66.6	15
TOTAL	4		14		40		58

Table 14

Percentage Distribution of Articles on Middle East Conflict before and after the October War

	June-Sept. 1973	Oct. 1973	Nov. 1973-Feb. 1974
New York Times			
News articles	68.3%	43.5%	53.8%
Editorials	15.1	36.2	21.6
Features	15.1	20.3	24.2
Cartoons	1.6	-	0.4
Washington Post			
News articles	79.8	71.3	69.9
Editorials	10.6	8.2	9.4
Features	8.7	17.5	17.4
Cartoons	1.0	2.9	3.4
Detroit Free Press			
News articles	71.0	70.4	64.8
Editorials	3.2	9.9	11.5
Features	22.6	14.8	14.8
Cartoons	3.2	4.9	8.8
Times			
News articles	79.8	65.3	75.5
Editorials	10.1	10.4	10.2
Features	10.1	24.3	14.3
Cartoons	-	-	-
Le Monde			
News articles	77.4	65.1	61.1
Editorials	6.3	13.2	9.4
Features	16.3	18.4	26.6
Cartoons	-	3.3	2.9

Table 15

Editorial Coverage of Arab-Israeli Conflict before and after the October War

Attitude	June-Sept. 1973	Oct. 1973	Nov. 1973-Feb. 1974	Total
		No. of editorials		
Neutral	24	41	87	152
Against both	3	6	4	13
Pro-Israeli	3	11	18	32
Pro-Arab	1	2	1	4
Anti-Israeli	5	2	1	8
Anti-U.S.S.R.	-	3	1	4
Anti-U.S.	-	-	-	-
Anti-Arab	-	1	5	6
Sym. to refugees	1	2	5	8

Table 16

Feature Coverage of Arab-Israeli Conflict before and after the October War

Attitude	June-Sept. 1973	Oct. 1973	Nov. 1973-Feb. 1974	Total
		No. of features		
Neutral	45	70	175	290
Against both	-	5	1	6
Pro-Israeli	10	15	36	61
Pro-Arab	-	2	7	9
Anti-Israeli	3	1	-	4
Anti-U.S.S.R.	-	3	3	6
Anti-U.S.	-	1	-	1
Anti-Arab	2	-	4	6
Sym. to refugees	3	2	8	13

Table 17

Mention of the Palestinians

	No. of articles		
	June-Sept. 1973	Oct. 1973	Nov. 1973-Feb. 1974
News articles			
New York Times	56	13	84
Washington Post	29	10	30
Detroit Free Press	6	4	24
Times	24	5	25
Le Monde	40	11	21
Editorials			
New York Times	7	3	4
Washington Post	2	1	9
Detroit Free Press	-	-	3
Times	6	5	9
Le Monde	4	10	14
Features			
New York Times	6	4	14
Washington Post	2	2	11
Detroit Free Press	2	1	2
Times	4	5	8
Le Monde	5	6	11

Table 18

Attitude toward Commandos before and after the October War

Newspaper, type of coverage, and attitude	No. of articles		
	June-Sept. 1973	Oct. 1973	Nov. 1973-Feb. 1974
New York Times			
Editorials			
Anti-commando	8	2	5
Pro-commando	–	–	1
Neutral	1	–	–
Features			
Anti-commando	4	1	5
Pro-commando	–	–	–
Neutral	2	1	3
Washington Post			
Editorials			
Anti-commando	2	1	7
Pro-commando	–	–	1
Neutral	–	–	–
Features			
Anti-commando	1	–	1
Pro-commando	–	–	–
Neutral	1	1	8

Table 19

Editorial Attitudes on Oil Embargo before and after the October War

Attitude	No. of editorials			
	June-Sept. 1973	Oct. 1973	Nov. 1973-Feb. 1974	Total
Neutral	6	11	45	62
Pro-Arab	1	1	1	3
Anti-Arab	7	7	21	35
Russia benefit	–	–	1	1
Pro-U.S.	–	1	6	7
Oil as good for U.S./Arabs	1	–	5	6
Oil as good for Europe	–	–	3	3
Oil as good for Europe/Arabs	–	–	3	3
Anti-oil companies	–	–	1	1

Table 20

Feature Attitudes on Oil Embargo before and after the October War

Attitude	No. of features			
	June-Sept. 1973	Oct. 1973	Nov. 1973-Feb. 1974	Total
Neutral	11	15	53	79
Pro-Arab	–	–	7	7
Anti-Arab	4	4	40	48
Russia benefit	–	–	1	1
Pro-U.S.	2	3	5	10
Oil as good for U.S./Arabs	6	–	2	8
Oil as good for Europe	–	–	9	9
Oil as good for Europe/Arabs	–	–	1	1
Anti-oil companies	–	–	2	2

Table 21

Cartoon Attitudes on Oil Embargo before and after the October War

Attitude	No. of cartoons			
	June-Sept. 1973	Oct. 1973	Nov. 1973-Feb. 1974	Total
Neutral	-	3	2	5
Pro-Arab	1	-	-	-
Anti-Arab	1	-	11	12
Russia benefit	1	-	-	-
Pro-U.S.	1	-	-	1
Oil as good for U.S./Arabs	-	-	1	1
Oil as good for Europe	-	-	1	1
Oil as good for Europe/Arabs	-	-	-	-
Anti-oil companies	-	-	-	-

Table 22

Attitude on Oil Embargo in U.S. Press before and after the October War in features

Newspaper and attitude	No. of features		
	June-Sept. 1973	Oct. 1973	Nov. 1973-Feb. 1974
New York Times			
Neutral	3	6	24
Pro-Arab	-	1	2
Anti-Arab	3	1	18
Russia benefit	-	-	1
Pro-U.S.	-	-	1
Oil as good for U.S./Arabs	3	-	1
Oil as good for Europe	-	-	-
Oil as good for Europe/Arabs	-	-	-
Anti-oil companies	-	-	-
Washington Post			
Neutral	1	1	8
Pro-Arab	1	-	2
Anti-Arab	1	-	12
Russia benefit	1	-	-
Pro-U.S.	1	3	2
Oil as good for U.S./Arabs	-	-	-
Oil as good for Europe	1	-	-
Oil as good for Europe/Arabs	-	-	-
Anti-oil companies	-	-	-
Detroit Free Press			
Neutral	-	1	7
Pro-Arab	-	-	1
Anti-Arab	-	3	9
Russia benefit	1	-	2
Pro-U.S.	1	-	-
Oil as good for U.S./Arabs	-	-	-
Oil as good for Europe	-	-	-
Oil as good for Europe/Arabs	-	-	-
Anti-oil companies	-	2	2

Table 23

Attitude on Oil Embargo in European Press before and after the October War in Features

Newspaper and attitude	No. of features		
	June-Sept. 1973	Oct. 1973	Nov. 1973-Feb. 1974
Times			
Neutral	5	4	5
Pro-Arab	–	–	2
Anti-Arab	–	–	1
Russia benefit	–	–	1
Pro-U.S.	–	–	–
Oil as good for U.S./Arabs	1	–	–
Oil as good for Europe	–	–	–
Oil as good for Europe/Arabs	–	–	–
Anti-oil companies	–	–	–
Le Monde			
Neutral	2	3	9
Pro-Arab	–	–	1
Anti-Arab	–	–	–
Russia benefit	–	–	–
Pro-U.S.	–	–	–
Oil as good for U.S./Arabs	–	–	–
Oil as good for Europe	–	–	9
Oil as good for Europe/Arabs	–	–	–
Anti-oil companies	–	–	–

Table 24

Editorial and Feature Coverage of Arab-Israeli Conflict, Not Inclusive
of Oil Issue or Other Items, before and after the October War

Newspaper, type of coverage, and attitude	No. of articles		
	June-Sept. 1973	Oct. 1973	Nov. 1973-Feb. 1974
New York Times			
Editorials			
Neutral	13	14	27
Against both	1	1	-
Pro-Israeli	-	2	4
Pro-Arab	-	-	-
Anti-Israeli	1	-	-
Anti-U.S.S.R.	-	3	-
Anti-U.S.	-	-	-
Anti-Arab	-	1	4
Sym. to refugees	-	-	-
Features			
Neutral	9	7	33
Against both	-	-	-
Pro-Israeli	4	1	16
Pro-Arab	-	1	2
Anti-Israeli	-	1	-
Anti-U.S.S.R.	-	2	-
Anti-U.S.	-	-	-
Anti-Arab	2	-	-
Sym. to refugees	-	1	1
Washington Post			
Editorials			
Neutral	-	1	21
Against both	-	1	1
Pro-Israeli	-	6	5
Pro-Arab	-	-	-
Anti-Israeli	2	-	-
Anti-U.S.S.R.	-	-	1
Anti-U.S.	-	-	-
Anti-Arab	-	-	1
Sym. to refugees	1	-	1
Features			
Neutral	2	10	38
Against both	-	3	1
Pro-Israeli	2	4	9
Pro-Arab	-	1	4
Anti-Israeli	1	-	-
Anti-U.S.S.R.	-	-	3
Anti-U.S.	-	-	-
Anti-Arab	-	-	2
Sym. to refugees	1	-	1

Table 25

Editorial and Feature Coverage of Arab-Israeli Conflict, Not Inclusive
of Oil Issue or Other Items, before and after the October War

Newspaper, type of coverage, and attitude	No. of articles		
	June-Sept. 1973	Oct. 1973	Nov. 1973-Feb. 1974
Times			
Editorials			
Neutral	7	10	15
Against both	1	2	1
Pro-Israeli	1	-	-
Pro-Arab	-	-	-
Anti-Israeli	2	-	-
Anti-U.S.S.R.	-	-	-
Anti-U.S.	-	-	-
Anti-Arab	-	-	-
Sym. to refugees	-	-	2
Features			
Neutral	5	26	19
Against both	-	1	-
Pro-Israeli	-	6	5
Pro-Arab	-	-	1
Anti-Israeli	2	-	-
Anti-U.S.S.R.	-	-	-
Anti-U.S.	-	-	-
Anti-Arab	-	-	1
Sym. to refugees	1	-	3
Le Monde			
Editorials			
Neutral	4	11	11
Against both	-	-	2
Pro-Israeli	2	2	5
Pro-Arab	1	2	1
Anti-Israeli	-	2	1
Anti-U.S.S.R.	-	-	-
Anti-U.S.	-	-	-
Anti-Arab	-	-	-
Sym. to refugees	-	2	2
Features			
Neutral	27	20	72
Against both	-	-	-
Pro-Israeli	-	3	4
Pro-Arab	-	-	-
Anti-Israeli	-	-	-
Anti-U.S.S.R.	-	-	-
Anti-U.S.	-	-	-
Anti-Arab	-	-	-
Sym. to refugees	1	1	3

Eqbal Ahmad

WHAT WASHINGTON WANTS

The Arabs believe in persons, not in institutions. They saw in me a free agent of the British government, and demanded from me an endorsement of its written promises. So I had to join the conspiracy, and, for what my word was worth, assured the men of their reward. In our two years' partnership under fire they grew accustomed to believing me and to think my government, like myself, sincere.

T. E. Lawrence, *Seven Pillars of Wisdom*

Kissinger is a man of his word. I trust him completely. He is the first U.S. official who has dealt with our problems who has proved himself to be a man of integrity—direct, frank and far-sighted. . . . Kissinger, under the guidance of President Nixon—and you cannot separate the two—has revolutionized the thrust of U.S. policy in our area and before that in the rest of the world. . . . They are now doing the unthinkable in the Mideast. Kissinger is a man of vision, imagination, and perhaps most important of all, trust.

Anwar Sadat, interview with de Borchgrave
in *Newsweek*, March 25, 1974

We are trying to get a [Middle East] settlement in such a way that the moderate regimes are strengthened, and not the radical regimes. We are trying to expel the Soviet military presence. . . .

Henry Kissinger, background briefing
at San Clemente, June 26, 1970

A QUARTER OF PEACE IN VIETNAM for which he received half a Nobel Prize is another matter. But with respect to the Middle East it is hard to deny Golda Meir's description of Henry Kissinger as a "miracle worker."One may use a phrase less divine, but the accomplishment certainly establishes Dr. Kissinger as the confidence man of modern diplomacy.

It is difficult to imagine a more unlikely mediator between Israel and the Arabs. As a special assistant at the White House, and later as secretary of state, he was a party to the conflict. On Israel's side. To say this is not to accuse Kissinger of inventing either American imperialism or its support for Israel. The two have been linked since before the Zionist state became a reality. Yet Kissinger has made unique contributions to that relationship. The promotion of Israel from a secondary surrogate to becoming the best armed primate of pax americana in the eastern Mediterranean is due entirely to Kissinger's strategy. Understandably, he helped sabotage the Rogers Plan after it had gained, through the promulgation of the cease-fire, the tactical objectives of achieving a stalemate along the Suez Canal and of isolating the Palestinians from the support of Egypt in the battle with King Husayn.

During the October war, he played the decisive role in the massive resupply of Israel[1] without which Israel could not have launched the offensive to cross the Suez Canal and reconquer the Golan Heights. Thanks also to Kissinger's manipulations and Arab ineptitude the cease-fire was achieved only after the Israelis had crossed the Canal, secured a bridgehead, and created an enclave on the western side. Then it was violated until Israel had isolated Egypt's Third Army. These violations had the cover of a global nuclear alert initiated by Dr. Kissinger—the first since the Cuban missile crisis of 1962. A few weeks later he appeared before the world in the arms of Anwar Sadat who proclaimed him a "friend" and a "brother." Stunned, people spoke of him as the miracle man, the magician, the untier of knots.

DIPLOMACY OF DECEPTION

Nor was Dr. Kissinger's or President Nixon's general record in the conduct of diplomacy such as to inspire confidence. A measure of manipulation and duplicity is part of diplomatic tradition. All govern-

1. To date history's biggest operation of this kind involving an estimated $2.5 billion of military supplies in less than 2 weeks.

ments do on occasion manipulate allies, mislead enemies, and misinform the public. But only rarely have they considered systematic deception, cynical manipulation, and calculated betrayal as the primary instruments of policy. The Nixon-Kissinger government belonged in that category. Examples are too many to be enumerated here. In foreign affairs, the deceptions associated with the bombings and invasion of Cambodia are the best known. That 3,360 B-52 raids against neutralist Cambodia (between March, 1969 and May, 1970) could have been secretly carried out, under Kissinger's supervision, without the knowledge of even the air force secretary, taxes credulity. Yet it was not an atypical occurrence. In a well-researched article, Tad Szulc, former diplomatic correspondent for the *New York Times*, has shown that the essential parts of Kissinger's negotiating strategy in Vietnam were violence and manipulation including concealments, deception, and deliberate false promises to the Vietnamese.[2]

Dr. Kissinger considers manipulation to be a primary weapon of effective diplomacy. He tells us that Metternich "excelled at manipulation not construction." And this has an asset. For, "when the unity of Europe came to pass, it was . . . not through Castlereagh's good faith but through Metternich's manipulation."[3] Otto von Bismarck, the only other statesman to have invoked the admiring interest of Henry Kissinger, also had a predilection for a diplomacy of deception. Dr. Kissinger describes him as being "unencumbered by moral scruples," a "statesman" who put the "principle of utility above that of legitimacy."[4]

We do not suggest that Kissinger regards Metternich and Bismarck as heroes and is impelled by the need to imitate them. He is an intelligent functionary and critical enough scholar not to do that. Rather, we suggest deeper reasons for his preference, ones which promise for his foreign policy a bipartisan life beyond the present government. Kissinger's global strategy for maintaining the primacy of the United States through a new equilibrium of power enjoys ideological and structural symmetry with Metternich's model. Ideologically, it holds conservative aims in a revolutionary moral setting. Hence, it is driven to dissemble its intent. "It is the dilemma of

2. Tad Szulc, "Behind the Vietnamese Cease-Fire Agreement," *Foreign Policy*, No. 15 (Summer, 1974).

3. Henry A. Kissinger, *A World Restored* (N.Y.: The Universal Library, 1964), p. 318.

4. Henry A. Kissinger, "The White Revolutionary: Reflections on Bismarck," *Daedalus*, pp. 888, 914.

conservatism," Kissinger writes, "that it must fight revolution anonymously, by what it is, not by what it says."[5]

Structurally, his global strategy seeks to promote antagonistic collaboration between competing states, a policy which Kissinger recognizes "can never be legitimized by its real motives." "Its success depends," he believes, "on its appearance of sincerity, on the ability, as Metternich once said, of seeming the dupe without being it. To show one's purpose is to quote disaster; to succeed too completely is to invite disintegration."[6] The games approach to world politics, so popular in Washington, reinforces the tendency toward secrecy and deception; especially when your games are poker and chess. As Kissinger put it: "You can't tell your chess opponent your game-plan."[7] At the very least, making the game-plan public cannot be part of the game-plan.

TIME BOMB: THE JANUARY DISENGAGEMENT

The disengagement accord with Egypt satisfied Kissinger's requirements of a stable agreement: it had the appearance of being a compromise by both sides and of rendering satisfaction to both. Egypt gained the Third Army, the withdrawal of Israeli forces from both sides of the Canal, and the possibility of augmenting state revenues by reopening it. Israel obtained an arrangement which permitted military demobilization, granted it a cease-fire line along the most favorable strategic formation in the Sinai, left the lucrative Egyptian oil fields of Abu-Rhudeis under its occupation, and interposed a U.N. buffer zone between the contending armies. Since each side is viewed as having gained equally from the accord, their interest in respecting its terms in letter and spirit is presumed. The January disengagement agreement is believed to have created a negotiating momentum and improved the chances of a peace settlement. However, a critical look suggests the opposite conclusion—notwithstanding Syria's necessary and tactically wise acceptance of its reality.

Far from being equitable, the January disengagement yielded Israel primary gains and conceded Egypt benefits of secondary importance. If President Sadat's objective is to obtain the total evacuation of occupied territories, then he is farther from it as a result of the accord. For not since 1945 had the belligerents and their backers in the Middle

5. Kissinger, A World Restored, op.cit., p. 9.
6. Ibid., p. 20.
7. Quoted by G. Astor in Look, August 12, 1969.

East been confronted with as much incentive to reach a negotiated settlement. The Israeli need for demobilization, Egyptian concern for the Third Army, the risk of superpower confrontation, and the effects on Europe and Japan of the oil boycott disposed all parties toward a settlement. The January disengagement removed those incentives and restored the equation of occupation and war.

In explaining Egypt's acceptance of the agreement, many commentators stressed its military predicament and Sadat's need to rescue the Third Army Corps. This undoubtedly was a factor, but Cairo's predicament was less serious and one-sided than American and Israeli officials would admit. True, in a brilliant display of bold maneuver and fast movement, aided by incredibly slow and disjointed Egyptian reaction, the Israelis crossed the Suez Canal and trapped some 20,000 well-equipped Egyptian soldiers. But in the process they had also trapped themselves. Tactically, Israel enjoyed an advantage because its forces held an offensive position at the edge of Egypt's interior and to the rear of advance Egyptian columns. Strategically, however, the situation favored Egypt.

The haphazard cease-fire line, with its interlocking pattern of territorial control, rendered the Israeli enclave on the west bank extremely vulnerable to surprise attack. The mettle of Egyptian soldiers had been tested, not only in the October war but during the tug-of-war after the cease-fire, and the Israelis could not afford to underestimate the risk. To stay on the west bank they would have had to remain on alert which would have allowed, at best, only partial demobilization of its reserve units. This, Israel could not have afforded.

In the event of another outbreak of war, the 30,000 Israelis on the west side would have been subject to pounding by some 200,000 well-equipped and easily supplied First and Second Egyptian Armies to the west and north. Even if the latter had failed to improve on their past performance and fought in their usually sturdy, conventional manner, the Israelis would have needed more than ingenuity and boldness to meet them. They might have had to bring reinforcements. Reinforcing and supplying these troops would have been difficult at best, for Israel's supply lines were extended and it held only about eight miles of the bridgehead on the eastern bank. That could have been easily lost to a determined enemy willing to make sacrifices as the Arabs obviously were. The Israelis would have then found themselves in a situation worse than that of the Egyptian Third Army. Given the smallness of Israel's population and the needed skills of its reservists, the entrapment of so large a force—a setback for Egypt—would have been a disaster for Israel.

The isolation of the Third Army, while serious, was by no means as hopeless as the Western press and analysts had portrayed. It had access to sweet water and some supplies were in fact reaching it clandestinely from the mainland. Above all, the entrappers were subject to attacks from the north and west while commanding only a narrow bridgehead connecting them with their forces in the rear. In warfare, psychological factors are of crucial value. The Israelis were likely to encounter their toughest adversary in the Third Army because the latter was confronted with that rare combination of risk and hope which have historically produced heroic breakthroughs.

Most importantly, the October cease-fire line was intolerably costly for Israel. It required a state of mobilization which reduced the Israeli work force by an estimated 20 per cent. According to Itzhak Ben Aharon, former general secretary of the Histadrut (Israel's trade union confederation), the defense mobilization since October, 1973 had deprived the Israeli economy of 30 to 40 per cent of its skilled technical workers, reduced production by 30 per cent,[8] and cancelled out the equivalent of two years' economic growth.[9] These realities were beginning to be reflected in the daily lives of people. The cost of basic staples—bread, milk, and butter—were up 30 to 70 per cent; transportation by 50 per cent; and dislocations in the servicing sector—mail, phones, deliveries—were reported to be widespread.[10] The political and social costs of stalemate along the post-October line were incalculable. The mobilized men and their families were beginning to clamor for a quick end, either through war or peace.

Israel could probably have maintained the required level of mobilization if it were to have received massive amounts of economic and military aid and a large influx of skilled people from abroad. The United States is the only source of both. One doubts that Washington would have been meaningfully forthcoming. Rushing $2.5 billion in arms to save an ally from defeat is one thing; keeping it in a precarious military posture at the cost of $8 or $10 billion a year is another, especially for a Watergated president and a troubled economy. Similarly, American Zionists who live vicariously off the Jewish state were unlikely to leave the comforts of America in large numbers in order to serve in the Middle East. To the contrary, had the situation prolonged, Israel would have had to contend with growing American pressure to modify its negotiating position.

8. Comparative base of September, 1973.

9. *Le Monde*, January 19, 1974.

10. *Time*, March 4, 1974.

Israel's Options: An Appraisal

For these reasons, the Egyptian-Israeli cease-fire line of October, 1973, unlike those after the wars of 1948, 1956, and 1967 was untenable. It could not be frozen. Israel had three options: (1) start another war; (2) negotiate an agreement on separation of forces based on a commitment of withdrawal from occupied territories and a negotiating timetable toward a peace settlement;[11] (3) withdraw unilaterally from the area west of Suez to a more rational and defensible line which many Israeli and American strategists had designated, since 1968, to be the Giddi and Mitla passes.

Israel was unlikely to start a full-scale war.[12] It had no rational

---

11. At the beginning of the Kissinger rounds, this was stated to be the minimum Egyptian condition for disengagement.

12. If the resumption of full-scale war did not make sense, the threat of doing so did. Pliable Egyptian officials could use it as an argument for compromise, and a solicitous Henry Kissinger as a demonstration of concern. The ploy belongs in Dr. Kissinger's diplomatic repertoire. He believes the threat and, in appropriate circumstances, use of force to be essential to successful diplomacy. Here is a glimpse of a well-coordinated ploy just preceding the Israeli-Egyptian disengagement accord: January 3-4, General Dayan is in Washington for talks with Kissinger. The two appear before the press in an amicable mood joking with reporters. The show is designed to reassure the public, especially the supporters of Israel, of continuing U.S.-Israeli collaboration. Telecasts make a point of underlining the bonhomie. But, off-the-record, Dayan hints at differences. Later on in deep background briefings, Henry confirms the reports of differences, confiding to a select group of journalists that Israel is about to launch a military offensive. Under the ground rules the privileged journalists ascribe to an "informed source" or "official" the warning which (they state as fact) precipitated Kissinger's urgent visit to President Sadat prompting the last round of negotiations. From Kissinger's special plane, they continue to quote a 'senior official' on his progress in negotiations—70 per cent . . . 80 per cent . . . 90 per cent complete—without even hinting at the banality of these claims. (Afterall, an accord like marriage cannot be 50, 60, or 90 per cent complete.) Yet, Kissinger's hopeful statistics do not reduce Israel's brinkmanship. On January 12, the eve of his arrival in Jerusalem, tension mounts on the Egyptian front. Israel has ordered a general alert. "Sources close to its General Staff" later disclose that "preparations were made to launch offensives on Egypt in order to destroy the Second and Third Armies."(*Le Monde*, January 19, 1974).

That the reports on differences between Kissinger and Dayan and plans for Israeli offensives were planted should be obvious to those who closely follow U.S.-Israeli relations. In reality, from the beginning there was an identity of views between Kissinger and Israeli officials on the sort of disengagement they would seek. The blueprint for it was prepared early in November by Kissinger's staff in consultation with Israeli officials. It first became public at the time of the Egyptian-Israeli cease-fire agreement on kilometer 101. On November 26, 1973 *Newsweek* reported that ". . . according to informed sources, Kissinger would press for the pullback of Israeli forces from the canal to a new line just west of the Giddi and Mitla passes. Cairo would withdraw

political or military target left in Egypt. The rhetoric of Israeli generals notwithstanding, the destruction of the Egyptian army was not a practical proposition either militarily or politically. To the contrary, given Israel's position on the Egyptian front, the chances were even that in the event of full-scale war it could suffer a major setback. Secondly, without massive support from the United States, Israel could not wage such a war. It is doubtful that Washington would have sanctioned a project so fraught with risks of producing a superpower confrontation and potentially costly to U.S. interests. Thirdly, a flexible but firm Arab posture, favoring a negotiated settlement but continuing the oil boycott, would have isolated Israel and the United States and made the resumption of war difficult to justify.

The second option—a military disengagement as a first stage toward a peace settlement and withdrawal from conquered territories—represented the test of Israeli and American intentions. If Israel were at all willing to make peace with its neighboring states on the basis of complete withdrawal, it would have accepted this option. It had the obvious virtues of assuring the Arab governments of peaceable Israeli intentions, of making the accord with Egypt a model attractive to Syria and Jordan, and of linking military disengagement to the process of peacemaking. It would have permitted Israel the time to negotiate the terms of its security and freedom of navigation and to test and be assured of the intentions of the Arab states. Finally, since it was obviously attractive to the Arab governments involved, this option may have served a primary Israeli purpose: the isolation and abandonment of the Palestinian poples' demand for the restoration of their national rights.

Similarly, if Kissinger were disposed to promoting peace on the basis of complete Israeli withdrawal he would have exerted the

---

all but a token force from the Sinai and a large number of U.N. troops would be interposed between the two armies." Its correspondent in Israel cabled that "the U.S. proposal might prove acceptable to Israel." As for General Dayan's January visit to Washington, his differences with the United States, and the threat which reportedly activated Kissinger's last journeys for peace, the *Jerusalem Post* on January 15, 1974, reported that the Israeli disengagement plan which Kissinger presented to Sadat on January 14 was the one which "Dayan took with him to Washington." It added that "sources close to the Israeli government" said that Dr. Kissinger thought the Israeli plan "as constructive and generous as Israel could afford to be." This plan is the basis for the actual agreement. No one, not even President Sadat and King Faisal should nourish the illusion that the general Israeli alert on January 12 was a freak of muscle flexing or the soldier's sabotage of diplomats. Throughout his Middle East mediation the military half of Kissinger's favored duet in diplomacy was orchestrated by Israel.

considerable influence of his government in behalf of an accord which definitively linked military disengagement with a peace settlement. For someone who has consistently emphasized the necessity of linking negative military and economic pressures with positive diplomatic initiative, Dr. Kissinger performed rather strangely in the Middle East; he violated his own norms of negotiations, acting more as an adversary than a mediator. This accord, like his peace settlement in Vietnam, is distinguishable for its vulnerability to violations. Kissinger's peaceable claims and ingratiating friendliness toward the Arab leaders notwithstanding, it is intended to consecrate the division of Arab governments between pro-American and radical nationalist camps, to defuse the Arab-Israeli conflict, and to produce a stalemate by separating Egypt from the aspirations of the Palestinian and other Arab peoples.

Given their annexationist position (even the doves have declared Jerusalem, Sharm al-Sheikh, and the Golan Heights to be non-negotiable) Israeli leaders needed special inducements to admit the necessity of complete withdrawal. Because the October war shook their presumption of invincibility, underlined their isolation, and emphasized their utter dependence on the United States, they might have been more amenable to reason. In addition their national interest demanded early demobilization. Had Egypt held and Kissinger assisted with friendly advice and firm warnings, Israel may have been induced to accept complete withdrawal as a basis for disengagement and negotiations. If it refused, the third option (unilateral withdrawal from west of the Suez Canal) may have proved to be the only feasible course for Israel. Its one-sided character may have been disguised by an escalation of clashes resulting in an agreement allowing for a new cease-fire line along the Giddi and Mitla passes. The predicament of the Third Army was serious and the recovery of the Canal was important enough to make such an arrangement attractive to Egypt. But then it would have gained what it has from the present accord without the extended interposition of U.N. forces on Egyptian soil, and without the "understandings" Sadat has reportedly given Kissinger.

Sadat's Surprise

Reason and rules of diplomacy led one to assume that while maintaining a posture of moderation Egypt would reject a fourth option—disengagement from the post-October cease-fire lines to a new military frontier which Israel could indefinitely hold without full mobilization—unless it were tied to a commitment and a negotiating timetable for complete Israeli withdrawal. In the Israeli-American game-plan this option must have figured as a good counter but a bad bet. Eventually, Israel would have had to choose from the other three options. But, as Dr. Kissinger told newsmen, Anwar Sadat pulled a pleasant surprise on him. The U.S. and Israeli governments were spared the necessity of choice. In accepting the terms of the January disengagement President Sadat relinquished his strategic and political advantages in a gamble which can, at best, yield limited gains to Egypt and Egypt alone. It is more likely to accentuate the existing divisions in the Arab world, encourage Israel to seek another military confrontation as a means of recouping from the psychological and political losses of the October war, and enhance foreign involvement in the Middle East.

If Egypt were ready to accept a separate peace with Israel, Washington would pressure for the repatriation of Sinai for reasons which we discuss later in this essay. Israel may concede, although the disengagement accord did little to encourage such a concession. By establishing Israel's military line along the strategic passes (Giddi, Mitla, and Khatmia) the accord increased the temptation to turn it into a permanent frontier. Furthermore, if Egypt has recovered the Suez Canal, Israel controls the access to it. From Sharm al-Sheikh it can blockade the gulfs of Suez and Aqaba; hence General Bar Lev's recent claim that "in effect our battleships will be in a better position to close the Suez Canal."[13] Israel also retains the lucrative ($1 billion a year) Abu-Rhudeis oil fields, a prize it is unlikely to forego without substantial pressure. Unless Egypt were willing to separate itself from the aspirations of the Palestinian people and from Syria's need for the recovery of Golan, Washington is unlikely to apply the pressure.

An odd feature of the January demarcation line underscores the importance Israel attaches to these conquests: the U.N. zone of disengagement (7.4 mi. wide) is pinched to approximately half its regular width at the point where it cuts the road eastward from Ismailia leaving Israel firmly in control of the El-Tassa crossroads on the way to the Israeli military base of Bir Gufqafa in central Sinai. It is a testimony to President Sadat's faith in Washington that, while accepting severe limitations on Egypt's deployments within its own territory, he permitted this exceptional arrangement designed to facilitate Israeli military presence in Egypt.

Secret understandings, by now a recognized paraphernalia of Dr.

13. *Le Monde*, January 25, 1974.

Kissinger's magic bag, are also reported as part of the January arrangement. One is reminded that in 1969 alleged violations of similarly claimed understandings had served as the primary justification for the resumption of U.S. bombing of North Vietnam. The Vietnamese denied giving any understanding and no evidence exists to question their denials. On the other hand, the private assurances Kissinger is known to have given the Vietnamese have yet to be honored. It is worth underlining that the secret Middle East understandings so far leaked to the press from Washington and Tel Aviv are ascribed exclusively to President Sadat. These include pledges that Israeli cargo will pass freely through the reopened Suez Canal, that Egypt shall not interfere with Israeli shipping through Bab-el-Mandeb, and that Cairo will dismantle the missile launching pads (in addition to removing the missiles as stipulated in the accord) on the eastern bank of the Canal. Arab failure to conform to these or other understandings could cause a breakdown of Kissinger's peace project just as unsubstantiated allegations of Egyptian missile violations ended the Rogers Plan.

In sum, by removing the strategic and economic burdens of the October cease-fire line, the January disengagement spared Israel an urgent choice between war and negotiated peace. By fixing its military boundary along Sinai's most strategic formations, it enhanced Israeli interest in a permanent stalemate. As such, if one assumes Arab, including Egyptian, resolve to recover the occupied territories, it prepares the way for another major, probably fateful war.

The Fifth Arab-Israeli War

When the next war comes the Arab governments will find in Israel an adversary more aggressive and intensively mobilized and better equipped than in October, 1973. The advantages they enjoyed in the last war cannot be duplicated. In conventional wars, one can rarely achieve surprise more than once; in any case, the U.N. buffer zone in the Sinai guarantees against it on the Egyptian front. Moreover, Israel is likely to strike first next time, especially if the Arabs would supply a credible rationale for it as in 1967. Israeli armed forces are better prepared today than at any time before. American supplies have more than compensated for the losses suffered in the October war so that both the quality and quantity of Israeli armaments have vastly improved.

Nor would the Arabs have the advantage of wielding superior weapons unknown to the enemy as was largely the case in October, 1973 with the SAM 6 anti-aircraft missiles, the Sagger anti-tank

238 / INTERNATIONAL DIMENSIONS

missiles, and the Sukhoi 7 close support fighter planes. Since the U.S.S.R. did not make these sophisticated weapons available to the Vietnamese, the United States had no chance to crack their electronic secrets. However, during the October war the United States devised countermeasures within weeks of their capture. In addition to the countermeasures and jamming devices, Israel is now equipped with new weapons of comparable or superior quality. For example, massive U.S. supply of Maverick and Tow anti-tank missiles is designed to offset Arab possession of Saggers.[14] Only the deployment by Israel of the latest standard surface-to-air missiles developed by the U.S. Navy will make it harder for the Sukhoi 7's to support the ground forces. It can be safely predicted that Washington shall continue supplying Israel more and newer weapons. If the past (in Vietnam and the Middle East) is a guide, these supplies will be justified as a leverage, an inducement for peace.

Strategically, Egypt's position is hardly better. Its one weapon against Israeli attempts to normalize the situation had been the threat of resuming what was grandiosely described as a "war of attrition"—heat up the front lines, force a degree of mobilization on Israel, and arouse enough global concern to induce a measure of diplomatic movement toward a negotiated peace. The October war was, in effect, the last of this genre—a war of limited objectives, although in the process of succeeding beyond their own expectation the Egyptian leaders appear to have forgotten the limitation and the objective. The terms of disengagement have removed the possibility of similar Egyptian pressure in the future. Formally, 7.4 mi. of U.N. buffer zone now separate Egyptian and Israeli forces. In reality, the distance between the two armies is much greater. For Egyptian military presence in the Sinai is restricted to a token force of 7,000 men, 30 tanks, and six artillery batteries with limited range of four miles. In order to defend the east bank and to fight in the Sinai, the Egyptian army would still have to cross the canal. By contrast, the Israelis are deployed behind their restricted zone.[15]

Those who know him testify to the shrewdness of President Anwar Sadat. His conduct of diplomacy and military planning preceding the October war also suggests an astute and cautious man not prone to eccentric behavior. How then can one explain his bold, rather reckless investment of the Arab world's political and military assets

14. The Tow, especially designed against Russian T-62 tanks, was first rushed to Israel during the October war and was used in the Israeli thrust across the Suez.

15. For this reason as well, the reopened Suez Canal shall be a hostage to Israel.

on the good will of the United States? It is as unhelpful to credit it to Kissinger's manipulative genius as it is incorrect to ascribe it to the situation of the Third Army. Nor is it particularly valuable to explain it in unilinear terms of Saudi Arabia's influence, or ARAMCO's assurances, or Egypt's unremitting if unrequitted love affair with America, or everybody's ill-founded fear of Palestinians serving as a catalyst of an Arab revolution. All these are realities but only as parts of a complex mosaic of neocolonialism and counter-revolution in the Middle East. A meaningful answer to the question demands an inquiry into the nature and aspirations of the Arab ruling elites; the corrupt, colonial components of Arab nationalist ideology; the consequent degeneration of radical nationalist groupings such as the Nasserites; and the remarkable resurgence of reactionary forces in the Middle East. In considering Washington's aims, it requires an inquiry into America's global strategy, i.e., the structure for peace in which Arab governments are seeking integration.

U.S. FOREIGN POLICY IN THE 1970's: AN OUTLINE

With the defeat of American power in Vietnam, Washington has launched a new strategy designed to restore the position of global paramountcy it had enjoyed in the fifties and appears to be losing in the seventies. As such, the Kissinger-Nixon doctrine represents neither a redistribution of power nor a retreat from imperialism's forward position. Its aims are restorative, conservative, and aggressive.

The fundamental thrust of American foreign policy thus remains unchanged. With a consistency bordering on obsession, Nixon had defined the main goal of the United States as staying Number One, a superpower second to none, the guarantor of global order, the watchman of world capitalism. The decisions taken by his government, in military planning no less than in the conduct of foreign policy, confirm this preoccupation.

Since the end of World War II, the emergence and acceptance of the United States as the paramount world power had been predicated upon five factors: (1) The overwhelming superiority of the United States in strategic weaponry; (2) The decline of Western European countries and Japan as centers of power; (3) Successful U.S. military interventions against real or imaginary social revolutions in the Third World; (4) The dominance of American capital over world economy; and (5) The existence of a national consensus in behalf of a bipartisan foreign policy.

Throughout this period of American hegemony, certain ghosts have haunted Henry Kissinger as he groped for a stable international system under U.S. influence. Three of them are of long standing: the existence of a powerful U.S.S.R., national liberation movements in the Third World, and the possible loss of a domestic consensus for a forward foreign policy. Time has diminished but little of his apprehensions regarding the Soviet Union; those of the liberation movements have become accentuated; and the specter of a broken-down consensus has become a reality. To these has been added a fourth problem: that of restoring U.S. leverage over Western Europe and Japan.

In order to understand a policy, one must inquire into the assumptions of its makers. And for Henry Kissinger, as for most other makers of U.S. postwar foreign policy, power is above all a question of who controls the land. His geopolitical assumptions, so much a part of the realpolitik tradition to which Kissinger subscribes, have led him to direct his focus not on Southeast Asia but instead on the Middle East, as the most appropriate field on which to battle his ghosts.

Detente: The Politics of Antagonistic Collaboration

More than any other American strategist, Henry Kissinger has been obsessed with the challenge of the Soviet Union to the United States. The U.S.S.R., being the largest, richest, and most politically integrated land mass in Eurasia, represents the only power capable of competing successfully with the United States. As such, it is the natural enemy and permanent threat to the United States, which Kissinger views as inferior in resources and therefore in need of access to those of the Eurasian land mass.

This geopolitical view of the U.S. strategic predicament also defines Kissinger's concern with preventing the emergence of Western Europe as an independent and cohesive center of power. Given the strategic importance of the Middle East and the primacy of its resources to industrialized states, Washington gives the highest priority to preventing an expansion of Russian influence in the area, as well as to controlling the character of Europe's ties to it.

Compared with the fifties, however, the contemporary U.S. view of the U.S.S.R. is more rational and discerning. Then even Kissinger had regarded it as a threat not only in geopolitical but also in ideological terms. The Soviet Union and China were viewed by him equally as "revolutionary powers" who "do not accept the framework of the international order or the domestic structure of other states or both." Today he views both as potentially status-quo powers, i.e., those who can be induced to respect the "framework of the international order" and leave the policing of "disorder" to the United States and its clients. Hence, U.S. policy toward the Soviet Union is best described as one of antagonistic collaboration. It combines elements of co-optation and selective rewards in some areas; of confrontation and containment in others. In the Middle East, the Americans put relations with the Soviet Union squarely in the antagonistic half of the detente.

In order to fully comprehend and predict the parallelisms of antagonistic collaboration, it is necessary to remember that Kissinger attaches high value to the concept of "linkages." It defines Washington's view of the links between confrontation and collaboration, war and negotiations and above all, between show of force and retention of power. For Kissinger all international crises exist on a single continuum in that their resolution is ultimately determined by the balance of power between the United States and the Soviet Union. Hence the resolution of each issue in America's favor depends not so much on the individual merits of the case, but on the overall balance of power. A demonstration of will and strength in one area, of flexibility in another, is expected to contribute to a favorable outcome in the third. Here is how Kissinger described in 1970, the connection between the U.S. invasion of Cambodia and his objective in the Middle East:

> It is of course nonsense to say that we did what we did in Cambodia in order to impress the Russians in the Middle East. But we certainly have to keep in mind that the Russians will judge us by the general purposefulness of our performance everywhere. What they are doing in the Middle East, whatever their intentions, poses the gravest threats in the long term for Western Europe and Japan and therefore for the U.S.[16]

THE UNITED STATES AND THE THIRD WORLD: IN QUEST OF A "LEGITIMIZING PRINCIPLE OF SOCIAL REPRESSION"

A fundamental objective behind detente with the Soviet Union and China has been to isolate the revolutionary movements from the support of socialist powers. There was little or no military logic to the dramatic increase in the bombings in Indo-China (37 per cent) immediately preceding Nixon's journey to China and the mining of Hanoi and Haiphong just before his visit to the U.S.S.R. Their targets were

16. Background briefing, San Clemente, June 26, 1970.

psychological and political. The objective was to establish a link between detente (acknowledgement of the legitimacy of revolutionary power) and counterrevolution (violent denial of legitimacy to revolutionary movements). The intent was to reaffirm the presumption of paramountcy and the premises of limited war, which concede to the superpower the right to intervene with unlimited inhumanity against social revolutions.

Thus the forces for liberation in the Third World continue to be regarded in Washington as the primary and the least manageable menace to American interests. For good reasons: all revolutionary—and in some respects radical nationalist—movements seek to overthrow the existing system of power, production, and distribution. When victorious, they tend to replace the old order with new, sovereign, popular, or national institutions of power, and socialist modes of production and distribution. In other words, from start to finish they challenge the legitimacy and threaten the existence of the three basic and interlinked elements that support and perpetuate the structure of imperialism: the international corporations, the pro-Western and pro-capitalist indigenous bourgeoisie, and the state's apparatus of coercion and control. The accession of a revolutionary movement to power normally results—as it did in China, North Vietnam, and Cuba—in the severance of the ties of dependence on the dominant centers of Western industrial power.

But the requirements of public relations compel Dr. Kissinger and his colleagues to formulate the proposition somewhat differently, more abstractly and ambiguously. International stability depends, according to Kissinger, on there being a "generally accepted legitimacy," which he defines as an international consensus "about the permissible aims and methods of foreign policy . . . the acceptance of the framework of international order by all major powers . . ." Revolutionaries are not amenable to the dictates of diplomacy because, he says, "it is the essence of revolutionary power that it possesses the courage of its convictions . . ."[17] Whence comes the unsettling characteristic of revolutionary movements and leaders: unlike established socialist powers, they evince stubborn indifference to material incentives. "Revolutionaries are rarely motivated by material conditions," Kissinger says, "though the illusion that they are persists in the West. If Castro or Sukarno had been principally interested in economics,

17. Kissinger, A World Restored, op.cit., pp. 1, 3.

their talents would have guaranteed them a brilliant career in the societies they overthrew."[18]

Dr. Kissinger perceives the Third World liberation movements as threatening the "psychological balance of power," which in another of his crucial analytical distinctions he regards as being equal, if not greater, in importance to the "physical balance of power."[19] "The deepest problems of equilibrium," he has explained, "are not physical but psychological or moral. The shape of the future will depend ultimately on connections which far transcend the physical balance of power."[20]

Finally, insofar as the revolutionary forces question the justness of the present system of power, they accentuate the already critical problem of legitimacy. And, as Kissinger has rightly insisted throughout his writing, without legitimacy no stability, no orderly change is possible. Of the Third World in this context, he wrote some time before he came to power:

> The problem of political legitimacy is the key to political stability in the regions containing two-thirds of the world's population. A stable domestic system in the new countries will not automatically produce international order, but international order is impossible without it. An American agenda must include some conception of what we understand by political legitimacy.[21]

The above truism might have been worthwhile, had Kissinger attempted to offer a conception of political legitimacy; how it is gained, and why it is lost. Such an exercise might have helped him to recognize that the matter is not susceptible to political engineering; that it concerns fundamental problems—of authority, not administration; of consent, not obedience; of morality, not management—which belong in the realm of political processes rather than diplomatic or military manipulation.

The tendency to recoil from facing an admittedly fundamental problem is necessary to the search for managerial solutions. The cumulative effect of Dr. Kissinger's discoursive references is logical:

18. Henry A. Kissinger, *American Foreign Policy: Three Essays* (N.Y.: W. W. Norton, 1969), p. 39.

19. See *Ibid.*, pp. 80, 81, 84, 85.

20. *Ibid.*, p. 80.

21. *Ibid.*, p. 85.

244 / CONFLICTING SOCIETIES

if stability is the goal of policy and revolution the main threat to stability, then the latter must be contained, confronted, and destroyed. And this, he knows, requires international acquiescence to a "legitimizing principle of social repression." [22]

While searching for a new principle to replace the unilateral American doctrine of limited wars (a primary casualty of the Vietnam experience), one which will sound reasonable to the American public and the rest of the Western world, Kissinger has been building in the Third World a system whose creation he has advocated since 1955: the policy of welding regional military networks, to be supported in case of need, directly by the United States, especially by its air and naval power. In an article in the April, 1955 issue of *Foreign Affairs*, he had recommended the "creation of strategic reserves," of "nucleus defense forces in the three critical countries." [23] These countries were Iran, Pakistan, and Indo-China. Later his evaluation of the critical countries changed. But the concept held and was subsequently repeated with refinements so that in 1968, shortly before Kissinger joined Nixon's staff, it found this expression:

. . . The U.S. is no longer in a position to operate programs globally; it has to encourage them . . . we are a superpower physically, but our designs can be meaningful only if they generate willing cooperation . . . [24]

. . . Regional groupings supported by the United States will have to take over major responsibility for their immediate areas, with the United States being concerned more with the overall framework of order than with the management of every regional enterprise. [25]

Under Kissinger's Nixon Doctrine, the United States actively promoted the "development" of countries like Brazil, Iran, Israel, Greece, Portugal, Indonesia, and South Africa as primates of pax Americana. Most of the countries chosen to be the regional marshals under the

22. The phrase appears in *A World Restored, op.cit.*, p. 318. The full sentence reads: "When the unity of Europe came to pass, it was not because of the self-evidence of its necessity, as Castlereagh had imagined, but through a cynical use of the conference machinery to define a legitimizing principle of social repression, not through Castlereagh's good faith, but through Metternich's manipulation."

23. Henry A. Kissinger, "Defense of 'Grey Areas,'" *Foreign Affairs*, April, 1955.

24. *Agenda for the Nation* (Washington, D.C.: The Brookings Institution, 1969), pp. 612, 614.

25. Kissinger, *American Foreign Policy, op.cit.*, pp. 93-94, 97.

Nixon Doctrine are also the ones in which the international corporations are making massive investments. Some of them, like Brazil, Iran, Indonesia, and South Africa, have already become the major export platforms of the Third World. Others, such as Egypt, the Congo, and Nigeria, are being wooed into that role. Their attractiveness to the corporations and to the policymakers in Washington is understandable. Their strategic location and natural resources have obvious value. More to the point is the fact that Third World tyrannies seeking economic growth tend to be specially attractive and hospitable to foreign capital. The denial of distributive justice under such regimes assures a high rate of return on investments; their repressiveness secures a quiescent labor force. Their ruling classes, being antagonistic to and fearful of the masses, covet external support and make dependable allies.

U.S. Leverage over Europe and Japan

For two decades after World War II Europe and Japan were America's pliable allies because they were economically weak and burdened by a sense of insecurity. The United States enjoyed the leverage of economic dominance and of providing the umbrella of security. But, by the mid-sixties it was in the process of losing both. Detente had its beginnings in the early sixties and substantially reduced the value of America's security umbrella. Subservience to the U.S. now offers but little economic benefit to Europe or Japan. To the contrary, they are now America's competitors as sellers of finished products and as buyers of raw materials. Hence one of Kissinger's primary aims in power would be to acquire, in the short term, new leverages over the old allies, who, Kissinger has stated, are a bigger problem confronting the United States than its enemies.[26] His long-range goal is to prevent the emergence of Western Europe as a unified and independent power in world politics.

In Kissinger's strategic design NATO was destined to be depreciated from a glorified system of global alliance to a regional constellation of pro-American power. Europeans had little reason to be surprised over his declaration that "The U.S. has global interests and responsibilities. Our European allies have regional interests."[27] Bipolarity is better suited to Kissinger's balance of power approach; it also

26. He expressed this view to a group of congressmen's wives on March 11, 1974.
27. April 23, 1973.

simplifies the task of staying Number One. Hence he has been an early and consistent proponent of denying Europe a global role in world politics.

His stated reasons, however, have been varied and contradictory. At times he has invoked the threat of European ambition; at other times the lack of it, as the justification for limiting the European role in world politics. In the mid-sixties he criticized the liberals' enthusiasm for European unity and integrated Atlantic defense on the ground that "it will generate increasing demands for European participation in global decisions."[28] In 1968, just before becoming presidential advisor, he reiterated that "While there are strong arguments for Atlantic partnership and European unity, enabling Europe to play a global role is not one of them." He recommended that "cooperation between the United States and Europe must concentrate on issues within the Atlantic area rather than global partnership." In this instance, Europe—with the exception of Portugal—was disqualified from a global role because in Kissinger's opinion it had lost its imperialist ethos. He wrote:

> A nation assumes responsibilities not only because it has resources but because it has a certain view of its own destiny. Through the greater part of its history—until the Second World War—the United States possessed the resources but not the philosophy for a global role. Today the poorest Western country—Portugal—has the widest commitments outside Europe because its historic image of itself has become bound up with its overseas possessions. This condition is unlikely to be met by another European country—with the possible exception of Great Britain—no matter what its increase in power.[29]

This line of thinking was at least partially responsible for Kissinger's choice of Portugal and Greece and Israel and Iran as surrogates in a southern strategy beyond NATO.

The contradiction between Kissinger's perception of Europe as being isolationist as well as ambitious is more apparent than real. The difference is between a tactical and a geopolitical conclusion. Tactically, Kissinger views Europe as passing through a period of isolation and unlikely to make a valuable global ally of an activist power. In geopolitical terms, he can only regard the unity of Europe or the enlargement of the European Economic Community—and the conse-

28. Henry A. Kissinger, "For a New Atlantic Alliance," *The Reporter*, July 14, 1966.
29. Kissinger, *American Foreign Policy, op.cit.*, pp. 41-72.

quent emergence of another continental power—as a threat to American predominance. As stated earlier, Kissinger's estimation of America's geopolitical predicament as an "island power" does not center on the U.S.S.R. alone. "If Eurasia were to fall under the control of a single power *or group of powers,* and if this hostile power were given sufficient time to exploit its resources, we should confront an overpowering threat."[30] As geopoliticians see it, nowhere in the world is such a threat more apparent than in Europe's potential relationship to the countries south of the Mediterranean where some seventy per cent of the world's energy reserves and much of its mineral resources are to be found.

The Mediterranean as Leverage

Since the Phoenician times the Mediterranean has served as history's imperial seaway to the riches of Africa and Asia. Its hinterlands provided the human and material resources of the Roman, Byzantine, Arab, and Ottoman empires and allowed the outreach of the French and British. In recent years the actual and potential shortages of those raw materials essential to industrial economies (e.g., oil, gas, phosphates, copper) have enormously enhanced the strategic importance of the countries bounded by the Mediterranean and the Indian Ocean. Control over the production and distribution of these raw materials can only be viewed as a decisive factor by a major power straining to maintain its position of predominance. Hence in the seventies the focus of the world struggle for power has shifted from the Atlantic and Pacific to the Mediterranean and the Indian Ocean.

Three of the four ghosts we have mentioned as haunting Henry Kissinger—the U.S.S.R., national liberationist forces, and loss of leverage over Europe and Japan—converge to the south of the Mediterranean. According to his admiring biographers (Marvin and Bernard Kalb), Kissinger has an "apocalyptic vision" of a possible "change in the strategic balance of power" in that region.[31] Washington views with extreme apprehension an enhancement of Russian influence there. In June, 1970 when the presence of Russian pilots and missiles in Egypt was reported, Kissinger blew his whistle on detente and in two successive backgrounders threatened to "expel" them. He considers the existence of radical and revolutionary forces in the area as being equally reprehensible. Nixon threatened to intervene directly

30. Kissinger, "Defense of the 'Grey Areas,'" *op.cit.,* emphasis added.

31. Bernard Kalb and Marvin Kalb, *Kissinger* (Boston: Little, Brown, and Co., 1974), p. 192.

in the Middle East and put on his most elaborate arms-rattling in September, 1970 during King Husayn's war with the Palestinians. Ironically, Nixon and Kissinger committed their worst atrocities in Indochina where American power was receding. But their most dramatic displays of brinkmanship, including a worldwide nuclear alert, occurred in the region where America's strategic interest and potential military involvement was expanding.

In relation to Europe the lands bounded by the Mediterranean and Indian Ocean hold both a promise and a threat to the devotees of American paramountcy. If the United States can preserve its dominance in that region and assume the role of guardian over the production and distribution of oil and other raw materials essential to the European and Japanese economies, it would maintain an effective leverage over its allies. In addition, it would be assured of the energy supplies needed for American consumption. On the other hand, Kissinger and his colleagues can only worry over the potential association of Middle Eastern countries with the European Economic Community. For economic integration among them is likely to be at the expense of American capital. It also raises the spectre of another continental power.

Historic and economic forces favor such a development. European governments have compelling reasons to seek close ties with the producing countries of the Middle East and Africa. They fear the effects on their monetary systems of the vast outflow of cash to other regions. They cannot feel assured of stable supplies of raw materials until their economies are fully interdependent with those of the producing countries and the Arab-African elites have acquired vested interests in the European Economic Community. The proximity of the Middle Eastern and African countries to Europe and their long history of encounter with it serve as incentives to their growing association with the E.E.C. The educational, economic, and administrative structures of these countries are largely a colonial inheritance. The culture of their ruling elites is at least partially European. Hence working relations between them and Western Europeans tend to be easier than with other foreigners. Because European states like Britain and France (or Belgium and the Netherlands) have formally withdrawn from the colonies, do not possess enough military power to arouse apprehension, and appear to have lost their imperial ethos, Europe's attraction in the producer countries has increased.

The emerging Euro-Arab and Euro-African economic cooperation is probably viewed by the leaders of the "island power" as a greater long-term threat than the actual challenge posed by the U.S.S.R. In his policy-setting speech of April 23, 1973, Kissinger candidly stated: "The prospects of a closed trading system embracing the European Community and a growing number of other nations in Europe, the Mediterranean, and Africa appears to be at the expense of the United States and other nations which are excluded." The concern is understandable, for a Common Market comprising some 600 million people, Europe's advanced industrial base, a large pool of labor, and the world's richest deposits of energy and mineral resources will inevitably become a formidable locus of power. In order to stay Number One Washington must somehow maintain a controlling role in the Mediterranean and Indian Ocean regions. Kissinger seeks to achieve this through diplomatic maneuvers and maintenance of U.S. military superiority because, as his critics have invariably pointed out, he does not understand economics well, is bored by its complexities, and believes reality to be susceptible to political and military manipulation. But, most importantly, he understands enough to know that the United States has lost much of its economic leverage; hence force and diplomacy have to be his primary instruments for perpetuating American predominance.

By 1968, when Kissinger came to power, it was 'perfectly clear' that the United States was losing its economic superiority over Europe and Japan. Its rate of growth lagged behind theirs. Its balances of payments were turning unfavorable year after year. According to Max Silberschmidt, short-term dollar debts had risen to $33 billion in 1968. By 1971 they had nearly doubled to $63 billion, and in 1974 were well past $100 billion.[32] Due largely to continuing and costly U.S. intervention in Indochina, the spending on military aid, military bases, and deployments abroad, and the competition from Japan and Europe, the Nixon-Kissinger government became the first in the twentieth century to achieve for the United States a deficit on its foreign trade account—$12 billion in 1971. The dollar lost its convertibility in August of that year and was on its way to devaluation.

As one would expect, the most serious Euro-American differences have been on matters of trade, investment, and monetary relations. These divergences surfaced rather dramatically during the Arab-Israeli war when such close allies as West Germany publicly protested the use of its ports for American arms supplies to Israel and the British government barred the use of its base in Cyprus for reconnaissance.

32. Max Silberschmidt, *The United States and Europe* (N.Y.: Harcourt, Brace, 1972), p. 189. Quoted in Geoffrey Barraclough, "The End of an Era," *The New York Review of Books*, XXI, No. 2 (June 27, 1974), 18.

With the exception of fascist Portugal they all acted, Kissinger bitterly complained to a group of European parliamentarians, "as though the alliance did not exist." His policy of employing the strategic advantage of the United States to ensure European conformity had its limits. So did the invocations of Western fraternity.

Throughout its first term and in the second at least until the Arab-Israeli war of October, 1973, the Nixon Administration pursued a policy of insuring Europe's and Japan's subordination. It sought to exclude them from the rank of world powers by focusing its quest for a stable balance on the primary military powers—the United States, Russia, and the Peoples' Republic of China. The choice allowed, in the words of Professor Stanley Hoffman, a former colleague and friend and now a critic of Kissinger, "for the neo-Bismarckian *tour de force* of manipulating all relationships—a feat neither Moscow nor Peking can perform due to their own antagonism." Detente, then, serves as an instrument for perpetuating a situation of bipolarity in which the United States remains strategically ahead of the U.S.S.R.[33] In this there exists a conjunction of Soviet-American interests, for bipolarity is congenial to both. Moreover, Russia is also wary of European association with the countries south of the Mediterranean. It may be expected that while seeking to expand its own influence in that region Moscow will cooperate with Washington in frustrating an independent European role there.

Alfred Grosser of France calls Europe a "community of malaise" vis-à-vis the United States because its yearning for independence is genuine but its military dependence on the United States is fundamental.[34] Europe's security needs as perceived by its policy makers require continued military alliance with the United States. A Europe without strategic defense is unacceptable to them because they fear it will lead to dominance by Russia. Yet a European defense policy is inconceivable because it can neither exclude nor admit Germany's nuclear participation. This Kissinger knows and is determined to exploit as his carrot and stick in Europe. "Close coordination between Europe and the United States in the military sphere is dictated by self-interest," he wrote while arguing in favor of limiting the Atlantic partnership to a regional alliance "and Europe has more to gain from it than the United States."[35] Detente may have enhanced America's security leverage over Europe because, says Stanley Hoffman, "the

33. Stanley Hoffman, "Choices," *Foreign Policy*, Fall, 1973, pp. 3-42.
34. Alfred Grosser, "Europe: Community of Malaise," *Foreign Policy*, Summer, 1974.
35. Kissinger, *American Foreign Policy, op.cit.*, p. 75.

direction of the 'linkage' can now be reversed: as long as our security dilemma was as acute as our allies' we had to accept certain economic disadvantages in return for their military subordination; now we can exploit their security needs for economic redress."[36] It should be noted that Nixon, since his 1973 State-of-the-World message, and Kissinger, since his speech on a new Atlantic charter, have been unambiguous in linking the issues of security with those of economic relations with Europe.

KISSINGER'S 'SOUTHERN STRATEGY'

In a more fundamental way Kissinger's strategic design aimed not only at containing the U.S.S.R. and creating effective instruments of social repression in the Third World, but also at outflanking his European allies. One of its primary thrusts, was the creation of an informal yet cohesive military alliance in the Mediterranean and Indian Ocean regions to supercede the role in that area previously assigned to NATO and to the ill-fated Baghdad Pact (CENTO). Spain, Portugal, Turkey, Greece, Israel, Iran, and Saudi Arabia appear to have been chosen as the primates of pax Americana. The weaker clients such as Ethiopia and Jordan were to serve as secondary surrogates. It was the Mediterranean version of Nixon's "Southern strategy" which, at home, implied the realignment of the Republican party with the forces of the Right and the exclusion of Centrist elements.

The basic elements of Kissinger's design became clear by the fall of 1970 during Nixon's visit to the Mediterranean and were also discernable in the seemingly contradictory developments associated with the cease-fire along the Suez Canal. In articles written at the time I had pointed out that the Rogers Plan, which in fact was drafted by Joseph Sisco working with Kissinger's staff in the White House not by Rogers' men in the state department, was promoted to obtain some tactical gains rather than to achieve a Middle East settlement. Evidence also suggests that as Secretary of State Rogers became serious about the plan, he was sabotaged by Henry Kissinger whose intimate working relations with the Israeli government had remained, until recently, a closely guarded secret.[37] The cease-fire brought about by

36. Hoffman, *op.cit.*.

37. For examples of Israeli Ambassador Yitzhak Rabin's secret planning sessions with Kissinger see Kalb and Kalb, *op. cit.*, pp. 186–209. Rabin would "joke rather proudly that he knew more secret ways in and out of the Executive Mansion [of the White House] than the secret service."

the Rogers Plan accomplished only these tactical objectives: (1) defusing the confrontation along the Suez Canal and freezing the situation to Israel's advantage; (2) slowing down Soviet arms aid and growing influence in the Middle East at a time when Egyptian deployment of SAM anti-aircraft missiles and the arrival of Soviet flown Migs in the Middle East were viewed with apprehension in Washington; and (3) further dividing the Arabs, and isolating the Palestinians who then became a relatively easy target of King Husayn.

Nixon's 1970 visit to the Sixth Fleet underscored the importance he attached to the Mediterranean particularly as the presidential visit concentrated on the aircraft carrier Saratoga which had been poised, in a well-coordinated plan with Israel, for possible intervention in Jordan. Meanwhile, Defense Secretary Laird was the guest of the junta in Athens giving what he called "high priority" to the "modernization" of Greek forces. Subsequently U.S.-Greek military relations grew closer; and the American navy acquired home ports in Greece. Similar developments occurred in relation to Turkey and Spain. The United States reached one of its most comprehensive defense deals with Portugal in the Azores.

Sparta in the Service of Rome

If these states were being readied to act as sentinels, Israel and Iran appear to have been allotted the role of chief marshals. Israel fitted all the specifications of an ideal surrogate. Its military performance in 1967 had been a matter of unabashed envy to the Vietnam frustrated chiefs of general staff. Its air force was regarded as an effective deterrent against Syrian, Iraqi, or Libyan attacks on U.S. allies. It was the only power between France and India to enjoy the nuclear option. Its technological sophistication reassured American officials who, despite Vietnam, retained deep faith in the decisive power of machines. Above all, its economic and military dependence on the United States was viewed as being permanent; thus its durability as an ally was presumed. The image was of Sparta in the service of Rome: An irresistible opportunity.

The military buildup of Israel was also viewed at the White House as an asset in assuring the complicity of the Congress (where Israel commands virtually unanimous support) in the Indo-China war and ever-increasing defense appropriations. In relation to Israel itself the Congress gave the President, in September, 1970, the "most open-ended arms buying program in the world."[38] The Honorable John McCor-

38. *New York Times*, September 29, 1970.

mack, former speaker of the House, sounded a little amazed: "I have never seen in my forty-two years as a member of this body [Congress] language of this kind used in an authorization or an appropriation bill."[39] In its first five years the Nixon administration provided Israel with nearly twenty times as much military aid as its predecessors did in twenty years.[40] Armed with the most advanced offensive weapons in the conventional arsenal of the United States, Israel seemingly became the great power of the Middle East. The efficacy of its U.S.-backed threat to intervene in the Jordanian civil war confirmed this status and consecrated the U.S.-Israeli strategic alliance. No other country in the world enjoyed so complete a commitment from the United States. And no other state in history achieved status as a great power almost entirely on the basis of foreign support. It was only in this context that one could understand active Israeli support for the reelection of Richard Nixon in the predominantly Democratic Jewish constituency of America and Nixon's declaration that there could be no viable security for Israel without U.S. military alliance with the Greek junta.

The 'Light of the Aryans' on the Eastern Flank

Iran emerged swiftly on the eastern flank to equal Israel as a major regional power in Southwest Asia. Since the C.I.A.'s overthrow of Prime Minister Mossadeq's nationalist government in August, 1953, the Shah had been an exemplary ally. In the fifties and early sixties he used U.S. military and security assistance effectively to consolidate power. Then, while remaining hospitable to international corporations, he combined totalitarian methods for maintaining stability with what McNamara's men in the World Bank call a "successful" program of economic development. Motivated by a strong sense of 'regional responsibility' he has developed excellent relations with Israel while maintaining meaningful links with Saudi Arabia and the Gulf Emirates. He has filled the security gap allegedly created by British withdrawal from the Persian Gulf, and deploys his armed forces to suppress the liberation struggle of Arab peoples in Dhofar and Oman.

---

39. The bill gave the Executive blanket authorization to supply Israel with "ground weapons such as missiles, tanks, howitzers, armed-personnel carriers, ordinances, etc., as well as aircrafts." Its purpose, according to Mendel Rivers, chairman of the House Armed Services Committee, was to make "available to Israel the full range of U.S. weaponry."

40. See *MERIP Reports*, No. 31, October, 1974; No. 30, August, 1974; No. 8, March–April, 1972.

His armaments expenditure has soared annually from some $10 million in 1950 to $4 billion in 1973. The self-styled 'light of the Aryans' has, by a large margin, displaced West Germany as the biggest buyer of American arms. The increase, however, was not gradual. For the merchants of death the bonanza began in 1969 when, intoxicated by the dreams of duplicating Darius the Great and stimulated by Kissinger and Nixon's grand design, the 'King of Kings' (Shahinshah) doubled his purchase of weapons. The next years he went on a spree while the majority of Iranian people remained illiterate, underfed, and overexploited—$833 million in 1970; $1 billion in 1971; more than $3 billion in 1973; an expected $4 to $5 billion in 1974. With his annual oil earnings now totalling some $20 billion he is able to pay for the weapons and the American advisors who teach how to use them. For the United States it is good diplomacy and excellent business. President Nixon paid a pointed visit to the Shah in the summer of 1972 before returning to Washington from Moscow, lest he misunderstood the flexible character and limited objectives of detente. In August, 1974 the Shah became the first foreign leader to be invited to place orders for America's newest jet aircraft, the Grumman's F-14 Tomcat. He ordered eighty F-14s for $1.5 billion. This was the first time a non-NATO country was authorized to purchase a major new U.S. weapon ahead of the principal NATO countries.[41] It is also symbolic of Israel's and Iran's polar roles in the new constellation of American power that in the 1970's no three intelligence outfits worked more closely with each other than the C.I.A., the Israeli Mossad, and the dreaded Iranian Savak.

A Collapsing 'Structure for Peace.'

The design had an impressive conceptual coherence. It was an imaginative yet logical scheme based on the classical balance of power precepts. But, beneath the logic and brilliance of Kissinger's construct, there were pitfalls. An imperialist, managerial mind could not perceive these pitfalls, for such a perception, or the admission of it, would cost him his raison d'être. A conservative outlook is necessarily closed to the future. In the fall of 1970, looking objectively at the situation, I had made the following evaluation of the Nixon-Kissinger strategy in the Mediterranean and Indian Ocean regions:

It suffers from the same fundamental defects which contributed to

---

41. In 1968 Israel had its first: it was the first country outside NATO to have been supplied the Phantom jet.

American failures in Southeast Asia, and in the Middle East to the early demise of the Baghdad Pact: it runs counter to the ongoing course of history; underestimates the power of emerging social forces; seeks stability in times of change; and client states in a century of national liberation. Its future is linked to the dying status quo of injustice, which develop mainly in the direction of tyranny. Fascist Spain and Portugal, militarist Greece, monarchical Iran and Ethiopia, and Zionist Israel! In the second half of the 20th century these are falling dominoes. And the domino theory is an American product.[42]

By mid-1974, as the pro-American regimes of Portugal, Ethiopia, and Greece fell, the backbone of Kissinger's structure for peace, already strained by the October war, had broken. Its restoration would require a great deal of subversion, violence, and diplomatic manipulation. It may also mean a shift in U.S. policy toward Europe in the direction of seeking greater European participation in the Mediterranean and Indian Ocean regions.

Kissinger's design had one obvious flaw which, in the opinion of many power brokers in Washington—the oil lobby, some banking and investment establishments like the Chase Manhattan Bank, and prestigious law firms representing oil interests—needed correcting: its linkages with America's Arab allies were extremely weak. Even Saudi Arabia, the world's largest oil producer and the Arab state most intimately tied to America capitalism, was imperfectly integrated in the new regional grouping. The primary objects of this strategy were inhibited from full participation in it. This contradiction was particularly undesirable because close military ties to the rich countries of the Third World are an economic and political necessity for the United States for the following reasons:

1. Arms sales help redress the declining U.S. balance of payments. The dependence of America's domestic economic life on military spending is widely recognized and popularly expressed in phrases like the 'military-industrial complex.' The sale of armaments to the Third World is becoming a primary export item, a major factor in preventing deficits. For example, while foreign sales of most U.S. manufactured goods have declined in recent years, aerospace exports are rising and in 1972 were the only American manufactures to register a positive trade balance.[43]

2. Military ties help perpetuate the military-industrial complex in

42. Eqbal Ahmad, *Africasia.*
43. *Aviation Week and Space Technology,* May 28, 1973, p. 139.

times of domestic cutbacks in defense spending. With the decline in Vietnam-related spending, defense contracts had to be reduced and this entailed the closure of entire production lines. In cases such as Grumman Aircrafts Inc., it threatened corporate bankruptcy. In order to prevent this, production had to be geared to foreign buyers. Grumman has been saved by the Shah's purchase of 80 F-14s and Northrop's 1974 plans to sell 1,000 of its 1,500 F-5Es abroad.[44] In order to shift some of the costs of research and development upon the oil rich countries, Washington has begun lifting the restrictions on advanced foreign orders on new weapons. "R & D" can run as high as $1 billion for a single craft as in the case of the C-5A jumbo jets. By purchasing the F-14 Navy jets, the Shah has substantially reduced the Pentagon's overall development costs and helped ease its appropriation requests through Congress where opposition to their procurement was stiff.[45]

3. Arms sales to the oil-producing countries is also an ideal way to reclaim the petro-dollars without conceding the buyer any control over the American economy. To the contrary, armaments supply to technologically underdeveloped countries promotes the dependence of the recipient state on the supplier. When some congressmen expressed concern that U.S. aircrafts sold to Saudi Arabia might be used against Israel, Secretary of State William P. Rogers thought it unlikely for "it would only be a short period of time before they have problems because the planes require spare parts and maintenance that can only be done by our experts."[46] Furthermore, technologically advanced weapons are to the Third World's military elites what heroin is to the addict. They derive from their possession an artificial sense of pride, power, and security and become psychologically dependent on them and their suppliers.

EGYPT ON THE ROAD TO MODERATION

For the Nixon Doctrine to work in this region the integration of some Arab states in the Mediterranean constellation of power was a necessity. Rather, it was a part of the design which had not yet

44. The Saudis and the Shah have ordered 120 and 170, respectively.

45. *Business Week*, October 20, 1973, pp. 32-33; *New York Times*, February 22, 1973 and May 26, 1973; *Aviation Week and Space Technology*, May 28, 1973.

46. *Mutual Development 1974*, House Committee on Foreign Affairs (Congressional Hearings), p. 262.

been fully realized. "What we decided," Joseph Sisco testified in 1973, "was that we would try to stimulate and be helpful to two key countries in the area of the Persian Gulf—namely Iran and Saudi Arabia—that to the degree that we could stimulate cooperation between these two countries, they could become the major elements of stability as the British were getting out."[47] Washington's Arab friends understood this well. They repeatedly emphasized to U.S. officials that only continued Israeli occupation of Arab territories stood in the way of an uninhibited Arab-American embrace. Facts supported their contention. The Saudis, for example, while extremely generous with gifts to the Nixon family and other officials, were linking their arms buying to Washington's role in promoting a peace settlement.[48] The Zionists also opposed large-scale arms sales to Arab countries fearing that some might reach the belligerents.

The peninsular rulers played the key role in persuading President Sadat to satisfy American demands for demonstrations of good faith and moderation. "We think that Saudi Arabia has been a voice of moderation in the area," Joseph Sisco, assistant secretary of state and Kissinger's chief aide on the Middle East told a congressional subcommittee in 1973. "We believe that it is in the mutual interest of the United States and Saudi Arabia for the forces of moderation to retain the upper hand in this area."[49] Sadat did the utmost to prove his pliability and pro-western disposition. On the day of Nasser's funeral, Nixon and Kissinger, fresh from the triumph of their brinkmanship over Jordan, were provocatively flexing muscles aboard the USS Saratoga, yet Sadat assured Elliot Richardson, the official U.S. mourner, of Egypt's eagerness to resume negotiations under the Rogers Plan. To no avail! In the summer of 1971 Sadat actively aided Numeiry's bloody repression of the Left in Sudan, including the execution of the secretary general of the Sudanese Communist party. A year later, Russian military advisors were precipitously asked to leave Egypt, fulfilling the White House's wish.

"We are trying to get a Middle East settlement," Kissinger had

47. *Persian Gulf Hearings*, U.S. Congress, p. 6.

48. In 1968, U.S. arms and military sales to Saudi Arabia stood at $35.1 million—some of the orders having predated the 1967 June War. In 1969 it dropped to $4.5 million; in 1970 to $3.2 million. An upward swing followed the hopes stimulated by the Rogers Plan and by the White House's periodic assurances—$73.8 million in 1971; $307 million in 1972. Figures for 1973 were not available, but purchases for 1974 were estimated to be well over $500 million and in 1975 are expected to exceed the $1 billion mark. See *MERIP Reports*, No. 30, August, 1974, p. 13.

49. *Persian Gulf Hearings*, U.S. Congress, p. 12.

explained at the beginning of this process to his special coterie of journalists, "in such a way that the moderate regimes are strengthened and not the radical regimes. We are trying to expel the Soviet military presence."[50] In a sense he succeeded. By the end of 1972 neither the ascendancy of moderation in the Arab world nor the elimination of Russian military presence was in doubt. Yet the arming of Israel continued at an accelerated pace, and no effort was made to induce a negotiated settlement, not even after Nixon's second term had begun, and neither Jewish money nor Jewish votes (in reactionary Arab belief the determinants of U.S. foreign policy) stood in the way of his being even-handed.

In Egypt, however, "moderation" had acquired momentum. Washington noted with satisfaction the repression of the leftist student movement, the purging of radical writers and journalists from their jobs as well as the Arab Socialist Union, and the steps toward economic "liberalization"—the granting of exploration contracts to Exxon and Mobil Oil and a multimillion dollar pipeline deal with the Bechtel Corporation. Egypt, the most populous and influential of Arab states, was obviously offering itself as a pro-western export-platform country in the oil-rich region, asking in return an end to occupation.

During the three years preceding October, 1973, the White House received Egyptian entreaties through Arab emissaries. One of these was Hafez Ismail, President Sadat's special envoy who came in February, 1973 to convey Cairo's sense of desperation for a negotiated settlement, only to be followed at the White House by Golda Meir and news leaks of more Phantoms for Israel. Kissinger would call the slap a 'signal.' The Americans wanted the terms of negotiation to be more 'realistic,' i.e., more acceptable to Israel than was the Rogers Plan. In March, 1973, Sadat is reliably reported to have indicated his willingness to accept an "interim solution" involving the international control of Sharm-el-Sheikh. The White House showed interest but did not move. Six months later, the Arabs went to war essentially to get Washington moving. Its "limited objective" (Sadat's phrase) was not so much the armed liberation of occupied lands as an end to the stalemate and the start of negotiations. Under the circumstances, Kissinger's appearance at the center of the stage was hardly a feat of diplomacy.

An Ideal Stalemate

Why did the United States procrastinate for more than three years despite the entreaties of its Arab friends and President Sadat's signals

50. Background briefing, San Clemente, June 26, 1970.

of a pro-western shift in Egypt? One answer is Kissinger's faith in the stability of stalemate. In his view the cease-fire produced by the Rogers Plan, plus the ascendance of a "moderate" regime in Cairo, rendered the Israeli-Arab stalemate more durable than it was before Nasser's death. Toward the end of 1970 Kissinger viewed the Middle Eastern stalemate as a model for his genocidal policies in Vietnam. This is how he justified his build–Thieu–bomb–Vietnam tactic:

> So in a conventional war the South Vietnamese army has now become quite good. If the South Vietnamese develop and continue to develop a governmental vitality of which they are capable, then I think they have a reasonable chance. And if, in turn, Hanoi recognizes that it faces at least a protracted war, and at worst perhaps an indefinite and inclusive one, then a situation may develop very similar to the Middle East in which both parties decide that however much they dislike each other some sort of modus vivendi has to be found[51]

Kissinger and Nixon remained unimpressed despite the warnings of officials like William Rogers that, in accepting the Rogers Plan and Dr. Jarring's mediating role, Cairo had gone as far as any Arab government could in search of a modus vivendi. In effect, the Arabs were demanding as a price for peace with Israel only the return of its latest conquests, while conceding not only the legitimacy of its existence but also of its earlier conquests, i.e., of its expanded 1948 frontiers. Both Nixon and Kissinger understand power more than the human urge for intangibles such as the liberation of one's land. They were convinced of the efficacy of their *force de frappe* in the Middle East and of Israel's overwhelming superiority and its converse: Arab incompetence. They did not expect that Egypt under the pragmatic Sadat would be suicidal enough to start a war, and Syria could not do it alone. After Husayn's impressive victory in Jordan, the Palestine Liberation Organization (PLO) hardly counted in Washington except as an occasional airborne nuisance.

Nor was there much fear of loosing allies like Saudi Arabia whose rulers hate socialists and radicals with a passion few can match, even in Washington. They had not only increased their investments in the United States, but also by 1971 were ordering costly American weapons, the Zionist lobby having relaxed its opposition to U.S. arms sales in the Gulf. Kissinger obviously believed that Israel could get a generous settlement on its terms by holding out a while longer. Realism favored such a settlement, not war. In case the Arabs went

51. Background briefing, New Orleans, August 14, 1970.

to war, another Arab defeat would open an opportunity for Israel and the United States to be magnanimous (a Kissinger favorite) in victory.

ARAB EGGS, AMERICAN BASKET

The October war ended the complacency with which Washington had regarded the stalemate. It destroyed the assumptions of Arab equanimity in accepting protracted occupation, and of their incompetence in war. It demonstrated Israel's power to be too derivative to be totally dependable. The oil embargo underscored the dependence of the Japanese, European, and, to a lesser extent, American economies on Arab oil, dramatized the contradictions in Atlantic relations, and underlined the importance of the Middle East in perpetuating America's global predominance. It also confirmed the argument of Washington's Arabists that Egypt is the pivot of the Arab world. Without it no war can be sought, and no political arrangement can be stable. Under the circumstances Kissinger's bid to act as the mediator was inevitable. Given the objectives which motivated the Egyptian recourse to war and conservative Arab support for it, President Sadat's capitulation to Kissinger's blueprint for peacemaking was equally predictable.

The mutuality of perceived Arab-American interests and a common vision of the future, rather than the Arab's alleged belief in individuals—a T. E. Lawrence or a Henry Kissinger—explain the latter's remarkable rise as the magician of the Middle East. President Sadat and his advisors, like the rulers of Saudi Arabia and the sheikhs in the Gulf, believe that their interests will be best served if they can develop close ties with the United States and the international corporations. For Sadat, it is a vision of Egypt as the industrial and commercial center of the Arab world. A combination of Egyptian manpower, American corporate and technological skills, and Arab petro-dollars could yield Egypt the kind of prosperity and power its bourgeoisie has long craved. This hope has been stimulated skillfully by men like King Faisal, Richard Nixon, David Rockefeller, and Henry Kissinger. It entails a shift in Egypt's role from the vanguard of radical Arab nationalism to an alliance with conservatism. Washington believes that Egypt's defection will emaciate the radical and progressive elements in the Arab world and bring about the restoration of a neocolonial order there.

The paradoxes of post-October diplomacy underline Egyptian and Saudi obsession with the corporate neocolonial vision of the Arab future. One need mention only a few examples, some banal, others of greater importance: (1) the adoption by President Sadat as a brother and friend of the one cousin who bore the primary responsibility for overarming Israel before, during, and after the October war; (2) Kissinger's multiple visits to Riyadh, a capital where even Eric Rouleau of *Le Monde* (the most outstanding among international correspondents for the objectivity of his reporting on the Middle East and for his sympathetic understanding of Palestinian aspirations) is refused entry—for being a Jew!; (3) the acceptance of a disengagement plan which removed the immediate incentives toward a negotiated settlement; (4) the decision to apply the oil embargo in a manner that hurt countries like France, who are friendly to the Arabs, alienated potential allies (Germany in a remarkable assertion of independence refused the use of its port facilities for U.S. supplies to Israel), and aided the United States, the one country it had pretended to punish. The dollar as well as the U.S. balance of payments were strengthened in the wake of the oil embargo which severely affected the European economy. Thanks mainly to official Arab ingratiation, a major contribution of the October war was to affirm, however temporarily, the paramountcy of the United States as the world's Number One power— the 'untier of knots.'

The Arab leaders who decided to put their eggs in the American basket assumed that the energy crisis had increased their importance in Washington. This is true. They also thought that their enhanced importance had correspondingly diminished America's commitment to maintaining Israel as a regional gendarme. That is incorrect. The extent of the U.S. arms buildup in Israel since the October war (before the much publicized Soviet buildup of Syria), is a measure of U.S. commitment to maintaining Israel as a major power in the region. The setbacks which U.S. policy has suffered in Cyprus and Greece may have increased, in Kissinger's view, the importance of Israel as the guardian of the 'western flank.' Nevertheless, he would wish Saudi Arabia and Egypt to become full partners with the Shah in securing the 'eastern flank' and stabilizing the Arab world.

In the aftermath of October 1973, Washington's notion of a just peace is different from that of Israel. But not much. Israel wants to keep Sharm al-Sheikh. The U.S. is expected to advise a compromise, e.g., a formula involving Egyptian sovereignty and Israeli occupation. Israel will not withdraw from Jerusalem but is willing to concede Muslim and Christian sovereignty over their holy places. This is not much more than a euphemism for your right to pray in al-Aqsa and the Church of the Holy Sepulchre. Kissinger is likely to counsel a further concession—a thin corridor to the Harem al-Sharif so that King Faisal may arrive without treading on Jewish soil. Israel wishes to annex the pockets of Latroun and Judea. Washington may induce it to be content with demilitarization there. As for the Palestinians, the PLO's official elevation as the sole representative is unlikely to constitute a lasting hindrance to the creation of a Palestinian state in the Gaza and a truncated West Bank. Officials in Washington understand—and once its guilt-ridden hysteria is allayed Israel will realize—that mere gun-toting does not make a movement revolutionary. The British press has, unfortunately, been correct in drawing pointed analogies between the Mau Mau of Jomo Kenyatta and Al-Fatah of Arafat. The PLO commands neither a revolutionary ideology nor a mass organization. Hence, despite their rhetoric and nomenclature, its leaders are likely to be as corrupt and cooptable as the many nationalist regimes which came to power on formal decolonization.

If the belligerents can be induced to accept a settlement along these lines, a negotiated peace may be possible. Kissinger's gameplan calls for negotiations by stages. It promises Egypt the most and will prefer to deliver there first. It assumes that once Egypt's primary grievances—the closure of Suez, Israeli occupation of the Abu Rhudeis oilfields—are removed and interest in economic growth is stimulated by Saudi money and American know-how, it will shun another war. Syria will then be isolated. Negotiations over the West Bank of Jordan may be protracted and, as the ultimate arbiter, the United States will stay at the center of the stage.

It is typically a Kissingerian construct: logical and wrong; likely to crumble after an impressive opening. In seeking to manipulate realities Kissinger misinterprets, underestimates, and distorts them. His gameplan is destined to fail with possibly disastrous consequences for the Arab and Jewish peoples. He confuses peace with America's predominance and, in his eagerness to maintain the latter, ignores or distorts Middle Eastern realities. For example, since neither he nor Israel are offering much to Syria, one wonders why Damascus would let Cairo negotiate the next stage of withdrawal. Similarly, Washington's promises and the Kremlin's warnings notwithstanding, the thrust of U.S. policy in the Middle East has been provocatively anti-Russian. Kissinger has actively sought to exclude the U.S.S.R. even from the process of negotiations. Moscow is unlikely to aid Kissinger in a region where its leverages are still strong. Of the anguish and aspirations of the Palestinian people, and the moral force they represent in the Arab world, no one in Washington appears to have a clue. Above all, the U.S. government evinces little understanding of Arab nationalism. Otherwise, it would not still assume, as it did in creating the Baghdad Pact, that its efforts at isolating radicals and promoting moderates among the Arabs will yield stability. These had the contrary effect of accentuating inter-Arab differences and subjecting the moderates to mounting radical pressures. Nor would it expect, as Washington has since 1967, that Arabs will ultimately acquiesce to a peace settlement which will leave at least Jerusalem, the Golan Heights, and Sharm-al-Sheikh under Israeli occupation.

The prospects of a negotiated settlement being slim, a hardening by both sides should be expected and another war may be unavoidable. The fifth round, however, is likely to be initiated by Israel, not the Arabs. For obvious reasons: The costly and inconclusive character of the October war has put a psychological burden on Israel. A clear-cut victory over the Arabs must appear as a necessity to a leadership which sincerely believes that Israel's national security lies in keeping the Arabs permanently defeated.

Secondly, Israelis understand, if most Arabs do not, that, ultimately, American interests rather than humanitarian considerations or the Zionist lobby determine the size and quality of U.S. aid to Israel. The October war has shaken some of the U.S. faith in what used to be described as Israel's 'swift sword.' Israel may want to reassure Washington of its effectiveness as a force de frappe.

Thirdly, time does not favor Israel. Unless Arab leaders succeed in snatching failure from the jaws of success, they shall be in a very favorable position. Oil is now a primary element in defining power. If the Arabs use it wisely this decade will witness their emergence as a center of world power. Israel, on the other hand, is likely to suffer from increasing international isolation and diminishing American interest in satisfying its massive economic and military requirements. A stalemate, therefore, is not as attractive for Israel as it was prior to the 1973 war. New developments, accentuating its domestic and international difficulties and strengthening Arab interests, may tempt Israel to strike out while it still has the means to do so.

Yet Israel cannot initiate a war unless it is assured of U.S. support. Washington is unlikely to let Israel loose unless it plans to use a second oil embargo as an excuse for military intervention. Its aim will be to establish undisputed U.S. control over the production and distribution of oil—the one privilege which is expected to insure the primacy of American power. This is considered a serious option in Washington. President Ford and Dr. Kissinger have already warned of this possibility, albeit vaguely. The Pentagon's planning indicates rather clearly that the U.S. defense forces have been preparing for possible intervention in the Middle East. The Arabs will be wise to develop a strategy to discourage and, in case of necessity, defeat this kind of adventurism.

Farouk A. Sankari

WESTERN EUROPE: FROM BELLIGERENCY TO NEUTRALITY

ONE OF THE PRIMARY TARGETS of the Arab diplomatic and economic offensives launched with the outbreak of the October war was Western Europe. The Arabs believed that the Western European countries as a whole might, if united in their policies, be able to exert substantial diplomatic pressure on the United States and Israel to change their policies in the Middle East. The European response to the Arab challenge confirmed that, in the final analysis, every nation's behavior is dictated by its own national interests. The policy of neutrality declared by the nine European Economic Community (EEC) countries after the October war and their subsequent support of Arab views on Israeli withdrawal from occupied Arab territories and a solution to the Palestinian refugee problem reflected that West European foreign relations with the Arabs approached more closely than ever before the concept of a common European foreign policy.

BACKGROUND

The major Western European actors in the Middle East, France and Britain, applied force in 1956 to secure their strategic, economic, and political interests in the area.[1]

1. For details see Kenneth Love, *Suez: The Twice Fought War* (New York: McGraw-Hill, 1969), and Anthony Eden, *The Suez Crisis of 1956* (Boston: Beacon Press, 1968).

The nationalization of the Suez Canal Company by Egypt was viewed by France and Britain as an act of defiance which threatened their national interests and undermined their prestige in the Middle East and North Africa. France was feeling the pressures of the Algerian revolution, and the French government believed that Egypt was the main source of aid for the Algerian nationalists. Likewise, the British government felt the pressures created in Aden and believed that Egypt was the major source of aid for the nationalists. It was hoped both in Paris and London that by deposing Nasser, the Algerian revolution would be contained and the problems in Aden would be overcome. Israel at the time felt that her national interests with regard to Egypt were identical to those of France and Britain; the main emphasis of the Arab-Israeli conflict was shifting from the Jordanian-Israeli frontier to the Egyptian-Israeli border, where tension was high and incidents of violence were escalating. The French, the British, and the Israelis found a common goal between them which later became the basis of a united triple military attack on Egypt to depose Nasser.

The Suez episode; the subsequent establishment of arms, trade, and aid agreements between Arab nationalist leaders and the Soviet Union; the 1958 revoluton in Iraq; the 1958 civil war in Lebanon; the formation of the United Arab Republic and federation with Yemen in 1958; American support for Jordan, 1957–58, the landing of American Marines in Lebanon in 1958; and the Arab response to West German arms shipments to Israel, were significant events. They reflected the following regional and international developments which could not be ignored by Western European policymakers: (1) Challenge to Western prestige and national interests in the Arab world; (2) Force as a failing instrument in achieving Western European national interests; (3) Collaboration with Israel creating a surge of new nationalism in the Arab world which was resentful and prone to see neocolonialism in aiding Israel; (4) Emergence of neutralism in the Arab world within the context of the Bandung Conference; (5) Strong drive for Arab unity in the Arab world; (6) American desire to maintain the status quo in the Middle East; (7) Further Soviet penetration into the Middle East and the emergence of U.S.-Soviet rivalry in the Mediterranean; (8) Use of Arab oil embargo against belligerents in time of crisis.

The Western European response to the these developments remained a dual approach. Until the 1967 war, they continued their moral and material aid to Israel, while at the same time attempting to gradually normalize their political relations with the Arabs and strengthen their economic ties. France took the lead in 1967 in altering her behavior.

The arms embargo was just one of several French diplomatic moves.[2] Other Western European countries notably Britain, Italy, and West Germany counseled peace to the Arab and Israeli contestants and supported the idea of a comprehensive settlement in which both sides would make concessions.[3]

THE EVOLUTION OF NEUTRALITY

Following the October war, Western European response to Arab diplomatic and economic pressures approached the concept of a common European policy. France and Britain took the lead in initiating pro-Arab support and commitment.

The oil issue apparently outweighed unity with the United States. Key Western European countries along the arms supply route made it clear publicly and privately that U.S. aircraft bound for Israel could neither land on nor fly over their territory. The governments of France, Britain, Italy, Greece, and Spain forbade their territory to American aircraft. In the first few days of the October war U.S. air force shipments of small arms and ammunitions flew to Israel from the U.S. base at Ramstein, West Germany, and Israeli ships were loaded with U.S. weapons in Bremerhaven; but, eventually, West Germany demanded a halt to all arms shipments to Israel from their territory.[4] The West German government explained that it firmly decided not to be drawn into the Middle East conflict and that it found neutrality to be the best way to serve the interests of creating a lasting peace. Apparently the Western Europeans felt that they had no obligation to reach a common alliance position on the Middle East since their interests were different from those of the United States. Europe gets most of its oil from the Middle East, the United States does not, and the Europeans felt it was in their national interest not to alienate their suppliers.

Furthermore, Western European NATO diplomats felt that NATO is a defensive alliance aimed at protecting all of its members against an armed attack by the Soviet Union and its allies in Europe or

2. For an analysis of the impact of the arms embargo see Yair Evron, "French Arms Policy in the Middle East," *World Today*, Vol. XXVI (February, 1970).

3. For a brief survey of Western European policies on the Arab-Israeli conflict see John C. Campbell and Helen Caruso, *The West and the Middle East* (New York: Council on Foreign Relations, Inc., 1972).

4. *New York Times*, October 23, 1973, p. 18.

North America and not an instrument of U.S. foreign policy objectives. The Middle East, the Europeans argued, was never meant to be included in the alliance's design. A confrontation between NATO and the Warsaw Pact over the Middle East would be useless. The United States held a different view, feeling that the interests of the Western alliance as a whole were involved in the October war. They argued that a fine line could not be drawn when the Soviet Union was deeply involved in the Middle East.[5] The Soviets should not be allowed "to exploit the Middle East and separate the United States from its European allies."[6]

Western European policies, which were generally regarded as pro-Arab, were expressed in declarations, summit meetings, and proposals for long-term cooperation with the Arab world. The following are among the major European initiatives and commitments made since the October war.

1. A declaration supporting the Egyptian position on Israeli violation of the October 22 cease-fire and Arab views on a final settlement to the Arab-Israeli conflict was adopted by the nine EEC foreign ministers in Brussels on November 6, 1973.[7] It urged Israeli and Egyptian forces to return to the lines held on October 22—before Israeli forces surrounded the Egyptian Army's III Corps—in accordance with U.N. resolutions 339 and 340. The declaration further noted that negotiations must take place within the U.N. framework and called for a peace agreement based on:

> The inadmissibility of the acquisition of territory by force; the need for Israel to end territorial occupation it has maintained since the 1967 war; respect for the sovereignty, territorial integrity, and independence of every state in the area; and recognition that the legitimate rights of the Palestinians must be taken into account in establishing a just and a lasting peace.[8]

2. As recommended by the EEC foreign ministers in November, the first "fireside summit" was held in Copenhagen on December 14 and 15 to discuss problems of West European unity and the Middle East. The nine EEC heads of state adopted a ten-point "declaration

5. For details on American views see *New York Times*, October 26, 1973, pp. 18–19.

6. *New York Times*, November 11, 1973, p. 8.

7. "EC Ministers State Position on Mideast Conflict," *European Community*, No. 72, January, 1974, p. 4.

8. *Ibid.*

on the European identity" which included the Middle East in its definition of principles for future action. Historical links with the Mediterranean and African countries were recognized and they decided to "cooperate over the establishment and maintenance of peace, stability, and progress"[9] in the Middle East. The heads of state supported the convening of a peace conference in Geneva and called on the Arabs and Israelis to make every effort to achieve a just and early settlement. Expressing their readiness to assist in the search for peace and in the guaranteeing of a settlement, they reaffirmed their earlier position that the security of all Middle East countries can be based only on U.N. resolution 242, taking into account the legitimate rights of the Palestinians.[10]

3. In accordance with the December summit recommendation for comprehensive European cooperation with the Arab nations, the nine EEC countries made a joint proposal of long-term economic, technical and cultural cooperation with the Arab world. The following are the major elements of the proposal:

a) European-Arab cooperation should be realized by concrete actions, in numerous fields such as industry, agriculture, energy and raw materials, transportation, science and technology, financial cooperation, and the training of cadres.
b) The first objective of the Arab and European governments would be to organize contacts among themselves which would permit them to express their initial views on the character to be developed and on the efforts to be made to undertake it.
c) The nine are prepared to undertake, at the European and Arab expert level, a study of the ways and means of cooperation between them to arrive at concrete recommendations as soon as possible.
d) If the results of their work justify it, in the opinion of the two parties, a conference of the foreign ministers of the Community and of the Arab countries can be organized to take the necessary decisions.[11]

4. The first meeting of the Parliamentary Association for Euro-Arab Cooperation was held in April, 1974 and the following were included in its Policy Resolution:

a) To assist in the creation of a comprehensive and long-term coopera-

9. "First Fire Summit," *European Community*, No. 173, February, 1974, p. 6.
10. *Ibid.*
11. *New York Times*, March 5, 1974, p. 6.

tive relationship between Europe and the Arab world;
b) To promote a better understanding of the Arab peoples and their civilization among European countries;
c) To establish an association of European Parliamentarians for Euro-Arab Cooperation for the purpose of promoting cooperation between Europe and the Arab world.[12]

The primary objective of the Parliamentary Association is to inform and persuade European political leaders of the importance of establishing a Euro-Arab partnership. Their stance on the Arab-Israeli conflict is similar to the EEC position of November 6, 1973.

THE POLITICAL FACTOR: CHANGES IN THE INTERNATIONAL SYSTEM AND A NEW EUROPEAN PERSPECTIVE

What factors have contributed to the evolution of Western European policy? Is it new European perspectives on the international system? Detente? France's desire to develop a "Third Force" and a new world order? Is it economic interests and European long-term need for Arab oil? The two major determinants of Western European policy on the Middle East since the 1956 Suez crisis are new European perspectives on the international system and European economic interests, particularly interest in Arab oil.[13]

The first factor can be best illustrated by examining selected European countries' behavior, especially that of France. In order to understand French behavior toward the Middle East, it is necessary to consider the broader context of France's world strategy since the early 1960's.[14]

De Gaulle felt that detente between the two superpowers became a reality after the Cuban missile crisis, and that there was no need to view the international system as being divided into two camps. He was committed to preventing any consolidation of bipolarity in

12. Thirty-three parliamentarians from seven EEC countries attended this conference—only the Netherlands and Luxembourg were not present.

13. For details on Western European foreign policy in general see Klaus Terfloth, "Foreign Policy of the Nine-nation Community"; Sir Kenneth Younger, "Europe in the New World Power System"; and Gerhard Merzyn, "Bilateralism in a Multipolar World," *Aussen Politik*, Vol. XXIV (1st Quarter, 1973).

14. For a detailed study of French global strategy see Alfred Grosser, *French Foreign Policy Under De Gaulle* (Boston: Little, Brown, and Company, 1965).

the form of either a Soviet–U.S. confrontation or a superpower condominium, believing that bipolarity would make it very difficult for France to establish a strong position in areas considered by the two superpowers as their spheres of influence. In De Gaulle's view, there was in the early sixties an opportunity for France to reassert itself as a great power. His objective was to create a new and pluralistic world order and to develop a third force led by France and including, among others, Third World countries.[15] Such a force would restore freedom of independent decisions to France, enhance its international prestige, and enable France to become a mediator in areas of superpower confrontations including the Middle East.

Following the Evian Agreements in 1962, De Gaulle pursued an independent foreign policy on the Middle East. France's objectives were to undermine the influence of the two superpowers, isolate the Arab-Israeli conflict from the cold war, and enhance France's prestige and economic interests. From 1962 to 1967, De Gaulle succeeded in improving relations with the Arabs while at the same time continuing to be the major supplier of arms to Israel. He believed that France could best follow an independent foreign policy by exercising this kind of double approach.

De Gaulle's perspectives on a new and a pluralistic world order had influenced his Middle East policies in 1967.[16] De Gaulle believed that a war started by the Arabs or Israel would lead to either a confrontation between the two superpowers or superpower exclusiveness in settling the future of the Middle East. In either case, De Gaulle's vision of a third force influencing the behavior of the two superpowers would be shattered. This partially explains France's anti-Israeli policies during and after the 1967 war. It also explains France's deep concern over U.S.-Soviet exclusive involvement in the conflict, her deploration of U.S. support to Israel, and her consistent support to the Big Four talks, the EEC's neutral stance, and the U.N. resolutions concerning territory and refugees. There is no indication that De Gaulle's and Pompidou's legacies in the Middle East will not be carried out by the new French government. In one way

15. For Third World appeal to De Gaulle's "Third Force" see Herbert Tint, *French Foreign Policy Since the Second World War* (London: Weidenfeld and Nicolson Ltd., 1972), Chap. IV.

16. For a detailed analysis of French attitude in the 1967 Arab-Israeli conflict see Stanley Hoffman, "Franco-American Differences over the Arab-Israeli Conflict, 1967–71," *Public Policy*, Vol. XIX, No. 4 (Fall, 1971), and Edward A. Kolodziej, "French Mediterranean Policy: The Politics of Weakness," *International Affairs*, July, 1971.

the new French president could differ from his predecessors: he may attach more importance to better French-U.S. relations.

There is no evidence to show that any of the other Western European countries shared De Gaulle's vision in its entirety. Britain, like France, wanted to disengage from external commitments viewed as drains on its resources or potential sources of conflicts.[17] After 1967 Britain also shared France's desire to isolate the Arab-Israeli conflict from the cold war because she felt that deeper Soviet and U.S. involvement would lead to a polarization of forces in the area which would threaten Britain's national interests, particularly her oil interest. The British conservative government under Heath had brought British policies on the Middle East closer to those of France—a more pro-Arab position. For example, in 1970 the British government interpreted Security Council resolution 242 to mean that Israel should withdraw from all territories occupied in 1967. The closer alignment of British and French policies on the Middle East developed further after Britain joined the European Common Market. It coincided with the beginning of an attempt by the nine EEC countries to coordinate their foreign policies through regular consultations. Following the October war, Britain, like France, pressured the other seven members of the EEC to take the November 6, December 15, and March 5 initiatives to deal with the Middle East crisis. As stated earlier, these initiatives committed the nine to call for a complete Israeli withdrawal on the basis of resolution 242, recognition of Palestinian rights, and the need for long-term Euro-Arab cooperation in all areas, particularly in the economic field.

But despite the parallels in British and French policies, British leaders had no vision of a British "third force" and the establishment of a new world order. Furthermore, Britain, like West Germany, Italy, and other EEC members, has always preferred close consultations with the United States on important foreign policy issues. Two immediate examples are the February oil conference in Washington and Britain's new official position on the European-Arab summit:

1. The United States called for talks in Washington on oil supplies and oil prices between the major oil-consuming countries—the United States, Canada, Japan, and Western Europe. While Britain and other Western European countries accepted the idea, France opposed it and expressed a preference for dealing directly with the oil producers, either bilaterally or through the EEC by holding a European-Arab

17. This partially explains Britain's completed withdrawal from the Arabian Peninsula and the Gulf in 1971.

summit conference. A compromise was reached by which the EEC members agreed to attend the Washington conference but not to establish any new institutions to deal with the oil question. This division in the EEC magnified the desire of all Western European countries, except France, to conduct further consultations with the United States on energy strategy. They agreed to set up a committee for that purpose.[18]

2. The new Labor government endorsed Britain's agreement to a Euro-Arab summit conference on the condition that it should not interfere with U.S. peace efforts in the Middle East or future Washington energy conferences. At the EEC's foreign ministers meeting in Luxembourg on April 2, 1974, Britain, like the other seven members, blocked French proposals to prepare for a Euro-Arab summit conference unless the French agreed to closer consultations with the United States. Britain, like most Western European countries, is not willing to go as far as France in isolating herself from the United States. This is especially true of those countries whose vital security interests depend on the U.S. alliance.[19]

THE ECONOMIC FACTOR: TRADE AND OIL

The second major factor guiding Western European behavior toward the Middle East is economic. There has been an increase in the volume of trade between Western Europe and the Arab countries in recent years (see tables 1, 2, and 3). Western Europeans realize that their interests, particularly in the fields of banking, external trade (industrial and agricultural products), and oil, create an interdependence with the Middle East that needs to be further coordinated on a mutual basis.

The EEC countries have signed varied agreements with several Arab nations. For example, they concluded a five-year association agreement in 1969 creating a preferential system with Morocco and Tunisia, and non-preferential trade agreements with Lebanon (1965) and Egypt (1972). Within the framework of these agreements the following measures receive priority treatment: (1) Reduction of tariffs

18. For details see Emanuele Gazzo, "Conference and Crisis," *European Community*, No. 175, April, 1974.

19. For details on American-Western European relations see Wolfram Hanrieder (ed.), *The United States and Western Europe* (Cambridge: Winthrop Publishers, Inc., 1974).

in the agricultural sector of imported commodities into the EEC countries; (2) Technical cooperation intended to supplement economic cooperation in its different spheres; (3) Financial cooperation, e.g., loans, aid, to supplement needed capital for development purposes; 4) Cooperation in the field of employment to improve the conditions for taking up employment and residence, and the working conditions of the labor employed in EEC countries.[20]

The October war, the Arab oil cuts, and Arab accumulation of huge surplus capital generated by the rise in oil prices were powerful stimuli to this movement of cooperation. The March 4, 1974 proposal issued by the nine members of the EEC aimed at strengthening European-Arab cooperation in all fields, notably the economic and technical.

Europe and Arab Oil

Of all Western European interests in the Middle East, oil seems to be the one single commodity which has significantly guided Europe's behavior. The oil crisis shook Europe and threatened its economies. It was an extension of a series of events that developed in the Middle East beginning with the 1948 Arab-Israeli war. During that conflict the Arab oil-producing countries embargoed oil for those countries supporting Israel and closed the Iraq Petroleum Company pipeline between Iraq and Haifa. The boycott was ineffective, however, because Western Europe used coal for seventy-five per cent of its energy requirements and depended on oil for only ten per cent.

The fifties witnessed an unprecedented economic growth rate in Western Europe and more European dependency on oil as an energy source, accompanied by rising political and military conflicts in the Middle East. The outbreak of hostilities between Egypt and Israel, France, and Britain in 1956 marked the second event which resulted in an oil crisis in Western Europe. At that time Western European oil consumption comprised about one-fourth of Western Europe's energy consumption and seventy-two percent of oil imports came from the Middle East.[21] The shortage of oil supplies during the 1956 Suez crisis was caused by the closure of the Suez Canal and the

20. For details on these agreements see "The Relations Between the Community and the Mediterranean Countries," *Commission of the European Communities: Information Memo*, Brussels, October, 1972; and for an explanatory statement for the political rationale for the agreements see A. Rossi, "Report on the Community's Commercial Policy in the Mediterranean," *European Parliament Working Documents, 1970-71*, No. 246, Office for Official Publications of the European Communities, February 1, 1971.

21. "The Middle East Petroleum Emergency of 1967," *United States Department of Interior Office of Oil and Gas*, Vol. II, Appendix C-2 (October 1, 1969).

Iraq Petroleum Company (IPC) pipelines and the Saudi Arabian embargo against Britain and France. Oil production, however, was not affected. The most critical period of the oil crisis extended from December, 1956 until April, 1957. The closing of the Canal on October 31, 1956 and the disruption of the IPC pipelines on November 3, 1956 stopped the movement of about two million barrels per day. Western Europe's total oil needs were about three million barrels per day, of which a little over two million were imported from the Middle East.[22]

With the fullest cooperation and coordination between the United States and the Middle East Emergency Committee, on the one hand, and the Organization for European Economic Cooperation, on the other, an emergency oil program known as the Oil Lift to Europe was developed that helped overcome the oil shortage. At least three major factors contributed its success:

1. Oil supplies from the Western Hemisphere to Western Europe increased. Oil shipments from the Western Hemisphere rose from a normal twenty per cent to approximately sixty per cent of the total supplies to the area.

2. The carrying capacity of the existing tanker fleet was increased through redeployments of tanker movement and other measures. Redeployment increased supplies moving from the Persian Gulf to Europe around the Cape of Good Hope and emergency supplies moving from the Western Hemisphere to Europe.

3. Coordination between oil companies and governmental agencies achieved increased oil supplies. This was made possible by increased production in the United States and the Caribbean, heavy withdrawal of oil reserves both in the United States and the Caribbean, and the reactivation of unused terminals, nonoperating pipelines, etc., in the United States.

The 1956 oil crisis heightened Western European awareness of the economic danger of an oil shortage. The Organization for European Economic Cooperation recommended measures for joint European action to avoid a future crisis. In 1958 the organization took a major step toward establishing an alternate energy source—nuclear power—through its European Nuclear Energy Agency. Pilot plants and research facilities were soon established in partnership with the European Atomic Energy Community. But despite these and other efforts, European need for Arab oil gradually increased and by the mid-sixties oil replaced coal as Western Europe's primary source of energy (see Table 4).

22. *Ibid.*

Along with the increase in European oil consumption came the third event which triggered another oil crisis. At the outbreak of the war of 1967, Libya, Algeria, Saudi Arabia, Kuwait, and Iraq imposed an oil embargo on pro-Israeli Western users—Britain, West Germany, and the United States.

The 1967 situation was much more serious than that at the time of the 1956 Suez crisis, because not only transportation but production, too, was involved. In addition, Western European demand for oil had almost tripled. The percentage of total oil needs imported from Arab countries in 1966 were: Britain, 69; Italy, 82.2; West Germany, 73.6; France, 82.9; the Netherlands, 82.9; Belgium, 58.4; and Spain, 81.6.[23] In 1967 Western Europe depended on oil for one-half of its total energy use, whereas in 1956 oil consumption comprised one-fourth of its energy consumption.[24]

The 1967 war interrupted the normal daily flow of some ten million barrels of Arab oil to consumers in Western Europe and the Northern Hemisphere. The Suez Canal, Tapline, and the Iraq Petroleum pipeline were closed. Shortage due to closure of the Suez Canal and pipelines was 3.5 million barrels a day and 1.5 million barrels a day, respectively. Therefore, a critical supply and a transportation crisis emerged and continued Arab denial of oil and transportation facilities meant that European oil reserves would be depleted in six months. The transportation crisis meant that what had been a four-day round trip for crude oil became a seventy-day trip from the Persian Gulf to Europe and back. The cost of a charter for one round trip by a 50,000-ton tanker from the Gulf to northwest Europe rose from $125,000 via the Suez Canal in mid-May to $950,000 for the trip around Africa at the height of the crisis.[25]

Several factors contributed to the easing and ending of the crisis. The oil supply was interrupted in the summer when demand for oil was at a seasonal low. The boycotted countries had reserve stocks to be used in time of crisis, a lesson learned from the 1956 Suez crisis. Moreover, the tanker fleet was in a better position to manage a sudden increase in demand than it was in 1956 and 1957. At the outbreak of the war there were about 400 supertankers with a carrying capacity of 350,000 barrels and above. In 1956 there were no tankers of this capacity (see Table 5). There were few tankers in 1967 with

23. *Ibid.*, H-4.

24. For a graphical summary of the situation that prevailed in 1967 see *Ibid.*, pp. 18-22.

25. *Ibid.*, p. 25.

1.6 million barrels carrying capacity. The operating fleet was redeployed and expanded by speedups, reroutings, and new deliveries.

The United States played an important role in the crisis by assisting Western European countries while maintaining oil self-sufficiency. The U.S. domestic oil industry held 268.8 million barrels of crude oil in inventory as of the end of May, 1967. This readily available source was used to meet the crisis. The United States also moved to increase its oil production. The response of the producers was favorable and by August domestic production of crude oil had risen by more than one million barrels a day above the May rate. Some of the increased production was exported to Europe: twenty-six million barrels of crude oil were exported in the five months from June through October. Additional U.S. crude oil shipments were 1,954,842 in June; 6,117,397 in July; 8,220,253 in August; 4,257,004 in September; and 222,000 in October.[26]

In addition to the United States, Venezuelan and Indonesian crude oil production was increased and diverted to European markets. Soviet bloc oil exports to Western Europe increased by about 150,000 barrels a day to 900,000. Nigerian oil was of little help because ninety per cent of its sources were shut by the Nigerian civil war.

The lifting of the oil embargo in September, 1967 helped bring the crisis to an end. The importance of oil revenues to the Arabs was expressed at the September Arab Summit Conference. The boycotting countries felt that Arab oil should be used to strengthen the economies of those Arab countries which had suffered from the conflict.

OIL IN THE SEVENTIES

The seventies marked drastic changes in the world oil industry. The Arab oil-producing countries began to take charge of their oil production, marketing, and prices.[27] The oil companies which had

26. *Ibid.*, H-4.

27. For details on the changing relations between Middle East oil producers and the major oil companies and their impact on the international oil industry see "Government Partnership in the Major Concessions of the Middle East: the Nature of the Problem," *Middle East Economic Survey*, Vol. XI, No. 44 (August 30, 1968); "OPEC and the Changing Structure of the International Petroleum Industry," *Middle East Economic Survey*, Vol. XII, No. 19 (March 7, 1969); David Mitchell, "The Development of OPEC," *Middle East International*, No. 34 (April, 1974); Z. M. Mikdaski, S. Cleland, and I. Seymour (eds.), *Continuity and Change in the World Oil Industry* (Beirut: Middle East Research and Publishing Center, 1970); and Joachim Hansen,

controlled the structure of the industry and made all executive decisions found themselves taking rather than giving orders.

In the fifties and early sixties, the United States met almost all of its energy needs from domestic sources and was an exporter of oil to its allies, particularly during past crises. But a confluence of events had led to increasing U.S. dependence on imported oil. During the sixties U.S. oil imports increased six per cent annually, and since 1970 they have risen eighteen per cent annually. Domestic production in 1973 met only sixty-five per cent of U.S. needs.[28]

The emergence of the United States as a major oil importer came at a time when Western Europe and other industralized countries like Japan were also increasing their demand for energy supplies. The European Economic Community energy sources were 18 per cent non-Arab oil, 40 per cent Arab oil, 2 per cent imported coal, 4 per cent hydro-nuclear, 1 per cent domestic natural gas, 1 per cent crude oil, 11 per cent domestic natural gas, and 23 per cent domestic coal. In the same year Arab oil imports to Britain, West Germany, France, and Italy comprised 33 per cent, 37 per cent, 51 per cent, and 50 per cent, respectively, of their total energy sources.[29]

In 1973 (January–September) U.S. oil needs were met by 63 per cent domestic production, 9 per cent Arab imports, and 28 per cent non-Arab imports. Western European needs were met by 3 per cent domestic production, 69 per cent Arab imports, and 28 per cent non-Arab imports. Japan's needs were met by 43 per cent Arab imports and 57 per cent non-Arab imports.[30]

These developments indicate a substantial demand for Arab oil in 1973, brisk U.S. competition with Western Europe and Japan for energy resources, and a drastic change in the relationship between oil-exporting countries and the international oil companies. Within this framework of the oil industry—markedly different from 1956 and 1967—and in a move directly related to the Arab-Israeli conflict, the Arab oil producers embargoed oil to the United States and the Netherlands, reduced supplies to other customers, made cuts in their oil outputs up to 25 per cent, and raised oil prices. Oil prices have nearly quadrupled since then.

"A New Era in International Oil Economy," *Aussen Politik*, Vol. XXIV (2nd Quarter, 1973).

28. *International Economic Report of the President*, February, 1974, p. 44.

29. *Ibid.*, p. 45.

30. *Ibid.*, p. 47.

The October war highlighted the significance of the Arab countries in the world supply picture. Their proven oil reserves can meet the growing import needs of the United States, Western Europe, and Japan. The Middle East has 62 per cent of the world's supply, as contrasted to less than eleven per cent in the United States (including Alaska), Western Europe, and Canada.[31]

The fully coordinated Arab oil embargo and the subsequent measures taken to increase prices plunged Western Europe into disarray and political confusion. The Europeans thought hard about their economic needs and political behavior. When the EEC Commission, for example, reviewed the energy crisis and its impact on European economies, it arrived at some overall conclusions and predictions. The Commission's report, released on January 30, 1973, included the following:

During the first quarter of 1974, EC crude oil imports will probably amount to 137 million tons, compared with 141 million tons in the first quarter of 1973 and 161 million tons in the last quarter of 1973.

Average crude oil prices in 1974 are estimated at almost 180 per cent higher than in 1973.

Higher oil prices will mean a 2-3 per cent increase in the general level of prices throughout the Community.

Industries most affected by the energy crisis are chemical and plastic, building and construction, textile, cement, glass, ceramics, tourism, trade and other services, rubber, and auto and other transport construction. Other industries may be stimulated by the crisis.

Total production increases in 1974 are estimated at about 1.5 per cent.

Real economic growth in 1974 is estimated at 2-3 per cent

The impact on employment will spread unevenly over the various economic sectors. Overall, however, both an increase in the unemployment rate and a loss of employment units (number of hours worked by a person employed for one year during statutory working hours) are expected.

Solely due to the oil crisis, the EC current account vis-à-vis non-member

31. From the finds so far made and from information derived from recent drillings, it is estimated, for a probable delay of six years between the discovery of a field and its reaching peak production, that North Sea oil output may reach 15 per cent of Europe's oil needs by 1980.

countries will probably deteriorate by $17.5 billion in 1974, corresponding to approximately 1.5 per cent of EC gross product and 17 per cent of EC exports to the rest of the world.[32]

As shown earlier, the embargo made most European countries take important steps aimed at securing their oil supplies from the Arab countries and increasing their cooperation with the region.

CONCLUSION

An assessment of Western European policy toward the Middle East from co-belligerency in 1956 to neutrality since the October war shows that two determinants have played a significant role in guiding European behavior: Changes in the international system and the trade and energy situation. These factors pose a challenge of sufficient proportions to provoke what appears to be the continuation of a policy aimed at cooperating with the Arabs.

There is no reason to believe at this time that the support the Europeans have given to the Arabs since the October war will change in the near future. Europe will continue to view Arab oil as a primary national interest. Recent energy strategy for the European Community aims at a 41 per cent crude oil ratio of total energy needs in 1985 (see Table 6). European countries are no exception to the rule that, in the final analysis, every nation's behavior is dictated by its national interests. In the field of energy the EEC countries seem determined to take cooperative actions with all Middle East countries.

32. "Energy Crisis in Figures," *European Community*, No. 175, April, 1974, p. 9.

TABLE 1

Arab Trade with the European Common Market, 1966-70

(In $ U.S. Millions)

Country	Exports					Imports				
	1966	1967	1968	1969	1970	1966	1967	1968	1969	1970
Algeria	525.10	577.30	646.50	749.20	780.70	482.80	436.70	584.10	735.20	893.10
Bahrein	8.45	8.90	10.40	8.40	13.30	12.60	13.00	13.90	13.70	18.80
Egypt	69.60	66.50	67.20	90.45	157.10	207.10	129.80	167.20	181.95	307.90
Iraq	403.30	445.50	616.20	602.36	611.09	119.70	104.60	90.10	91.85	100.76
Kuwait	598.80	692.40	653.50	629.40	733.20	90.30	121.90	124.20	140.98	150.00
Lebanon	10.20	32.80	69.60	61.70	50.60	163.50	169.00	224.50	215.30	249.94
Libya	700.30	832.80	1210.70	1529.10	1622.98	189.80	230.80	286.60	281.17	273.37
Morocco	257.40	257.00	267.90	285.27	325.40	253.60	276.40	270.40	294.21	377.40
Muscat-Oman	116.60	180.10	273.50	229.80	271.20	23.80	23.00	44.50	89.50	113.10
Qator	64.18	112.30	135.30	103.90	102.70	9.30	12.40	11.50	17.80	12.20
Saudi Arabia	385.18	476.32	457.75	576.67	873.10	110.60	123.82	119.09	181.85	194.10
Sudan	74.20	80.00	87.60	80.64	81.70	41.40	37.60	49.10	54.74	43.20
Syria	26.00	26.30	25.90	37.05	84.50	75.20	77.00	78.50	96.93	82.10
Tunisia	79.10	77.90	72.80	91.00	105.15	130.40	127.30	117.40	138.77	163.84
Yemen	7.10	12.35	4.42	6.13	11.40	26.80	16.85	18.22	17.19	14.90

Source: Direction of Trade Annual 1966-1970, International Monetary Fund. International Bank for Reconstruction and Development, Washington, D.C. (adapted by the author).

TABLE 2

Western European Trade with the Middle East, 1966-70

(In $ U.S. Millions)

Country	Exports					Imports				
	1966	1967	1968	1969	1970	1966	1967	1968	1969	1970
Belgium	147.50	136.80	179.90	221.80	272.60	306.80	324.10	480.60	520.10	553.30
Britain	953.60	861.90	1076.40	1319.10	1217.90	1280.60	1394.70	1727.40	1767.00	1822.50
Denmark	50.00	57.30	61.90	70.40	80.53	80.00	142.70	145.50	149.94	175.27
France	1006.80	1019.90	1196.70	1276.10	1471.70	1634.70	1705.20	1795.90	1880.90	2055.00
Greece	35.80	38.90	34.20	40.03	43.42	68.10	72.60	77.20	92.65	95.50
Ireland	4.00	3.60	6.30	7.16	7.44	42.40	60.30	58.60	56.86	67.59
Italy	483.50	511.00	643.50	713.30	707.00	1104.30	1306.00	1411.30	1666.80	1949.50
Netherlands	172.10	183.00	203.40	234.50	259.90	498.00	541.40	670.70	770.30	1040.50
Norway	19.30	19.00	39.20	27.28	27.89	43.20	49.40	81.20	73.74	101.81
Portugal	16.30	14.50	16.20	12.47	17.24	46.50	44.20	51.20	58.15	100.11
Sweden	80.30	78.10	97.00	123.42	147.86	95.30	135.10	175.90	151.58	147.36
Switzerland	146.20	147.40	177.60	196.64	220.08	69.30	114.80	128.50	138.99	148.97

Source: Direction of Trade Annual 1966-1970, International Monetary Fund. International Bank for Reconstruction and Development, Washington, D.C. (adapted by the author).

TABLE 3
Western European Trade with the Middle East, 1973-Feb. 1974*
(In $ U.S. Millions)

Country	Exports		Imports	
	1973	1974 (Jan.-Feb.)	1973	1974 (Jan.-Feb.)
Austria	126.35	27.44	164.61	74.36
Belgium	-	457.20	850.00	-
Britain+	1675.20	-	2435.70	-
Denmark	110.89	25.03	240.34	64.95
France	1122.10	221.50	2700.50	814.60
Germany	1786.20	198.60#	2086.70	278.20#
Italy	794.40	-	2470.90	-
Portugal	11.73	1.06	111.36	1.00
Spain	178.49	29.06	876.08	229.31
Sweden	216.40	43.80	202.00	57.70
Switzerland	354.60	61.70	193.30	57.70

Source: Direction of Trade, March 1974, International Monetary Fund.
International Bank for Reconstruction and Development, Washington, D.C.
(adapted by the author).
*Excluding North Africa.
+January through November only.
#January only.

TABLE 4

Western Europe: Consumption of Energy and Dependence on Arab Oil,
Selected Years, 1955–68

Source	Thousands of Barrels Daily of Oil Equivalent				Per Cent of Total Energy Consumption			
	1955	1960	1965	1968	1955	1960	1965	1968
Nuclear energy	-	-	125	215	0	0	0.7	1.1
Hydropower	968	1,408	1,802	1,933	7.6	9.8	10.1	9.5
Coal	8,855	8,377	7,929	6,904	69.6	58.1	44.3	33.8
Natural gas	108	244	431	921	0.9	1.7	2.4	4.5
Oil	2,791	4,393	7,607	10,433	21.9	30.4	42.5	51.1
TOTAL	12,722	14,422	17,894	20,406	100.0	100.0	100.0	100.0
Arab oil	1,686	2,511	5,195	7,361	13.4	17.4	29.0	36.1
Other oil	1,105	1,882	2,412	3,072	8.5	13.0	13.5	15.0

Source: "The Middle East Petroleum Emergence of 1967," United States Department of Interior Office of Oil and Gas, Vol. II, Appendix H8 (October 1, 1969).

TABLE 5
Number of Large Tankers in World Fleet

Year	Vessels					Total	Total Capacity*
	50-60*	60-80*	80-100*	100-150*	150 and over*		
1957	-	-	1	-	-	1	86
1958	4	-	4	-	-	8	554
1959	5	1	7	-	-	13	928
1960	5	8	7	1	-	21	1,492
1961	11	13	7	2	-	33	2,236
1962	20	20	8	3	-	51	3,408
1963	42	23	15	4	-	84	5,519
1964	79	38	26	4	-	147	9,478
1965	132	77	48	5	-	262	17,160
1966	160	136	65	14	-	375	25,175
1967	176	198	86	34	2	496	35,074
1968	194	229	110	59	10	602	44,644

Source: Petroleum Press Service, September 1968.
*Thousand deadweight tons.

TABLE 6
European Primary Energy Needs in 1985

Type	1973 estimates		1985 forecasts		1985 objectives	
	Mill. toe	%	Mill. toe	%	Mill. toe	%
Solid fuels	227	22.6	175	10.0	250	16.0
Oil	617	61.4	1160	64.0	655	41.0
Natural gas	117	11.6	265	15.0	375	24.0
Hydroelectric power and others	30	3.0	40	2.0	35	2.0
Nuclear energy	14	1.4	160	9.0	260	17.0

Source: Commission of the European Community: Information Memo, Brussels, May 1974.

Barry Rubin

SOVIET POLICY AND THE MIDDLE EAST

THE OCTOBER 1973 MIDDLE EAST WAR brought new evidence of the importance of the Soviet Union's role in the Middle East and, in particular, in the Arab-Israeli conflict.

In evaluating the foreign policy of any country, one must take into account the socioeconomic structure of the state, its geopolitical position, and leadership perceptions of state interests. Factors like defense needs, ambitions, the search for product suppliers and customers, and definition of friends and enemies interrelate with political and historical realities and preferences.[1]

Political realities in the contemporary world dictate that any major regional conflict forces its participants to look outside their immediate neighborhood for powerful supporters. Ideology is secondary in this search for allies. In recent years, Egypt and Syria have tended to line up with the U.S.S.R. Israel, along with other non-Arab and some Arab states in the Middle East, has tended to ally with the United States. These alignments are generally not as irrevocable nor as rooted in history as they may seem to be. Nevertheless, they profoundly affect the direction of current events.

The Soviet alignment with some of the Arab states is based not so much on mutual economic needs—although the growing economic strength of the Arab world makes it an attractive ally—but on Soviet

1. Jean Lacouture, "The Changing Balance of Forces in the Middle East," *Journal of Palestine Studies*, Summer, 1973, pp. 28-9.

political interests combined with Arab military-political aims.[2] The U.S.S.R. has generally come out second-best to the United States on the international scene and, from this inferior position, must constantly try harder to find opportunities to gain influence, new friends, and an enhanced strategic position. While the U.S.S.R. has sought to put its Middle East position on stabler ground than merely being the provider of needed aid for Arab states involved in a conflict with Israel, it has had difficulty in transcending this role.[3] The Soviets have constantly tried to find ideologically compatible regimes and to stress their value as an ally in economic development, but recent developments in Egypt have shown the tenuousness of this kind of bond.

SOVIET-ARAB RELATIONS TO 1967

The Arab world played only a tiny part in Soviet foreign policy before 1948. Despite traditional Marxist and Soviet hostility to Zionism, the U.S.S.R. supported the U.N. partition plan and helped Israel obtain arms. The Soviet analysis was that Israel would be more likely to carry out a social revolution and oppose British influence in the region than would the semi-feudal Arab governments. The Soviets did, however, try to deal with the latter. In 1946 the U.S.S.R. demanded British withdrawal from Palestine and the granting of independence. Arab delegations were contacted, but most did not respond, either because of their ties with the British or because of their distrust of the Soviets. At the U.N. session of April, 1947 the U.S.S.R. urged Arabs and Jews to agree to establishment of a unified bi-national state and supported the Arab demand for Palestinian independence. By September, however, the Soviets had concluded that because of Jewish-Arab tension in Palestine, unification into one state was impossible. They supported partition.

On May 14, 1947, Andrei Gromyko stated what has generally remained as the Soviet position: "The population of Palestine consists of two peoples—the Arabs and the Jews. The legitimate interest of both can be duly safeguarded only through establishment of an independent, dual, democratic, homogeneous Arab-Jewish state . . . based on equality of right for the Jewish and Arab population. . . . If this plan proved impossible to implement . . . then it would be

2. M. H. Heikal, "Soviet Aims and Egypt," Al Ahram, June 30, 1972.
3. New York Times, June 5, 1974.

necessary to consider the second plan . . . which provides for partition."[4]

The U.S.S.R.'s relative disinterest in the Middle East began to change after Stalin's death and particularly after U.S. and British attempts in the early fifties to organize anti-U.S.S.R. regional alliances. Soviet involvement began in 1955 with the Czech arms sale to Egypt, the commitment to help with construction of the Aswan Dam, and the growth of Soviet relations with Syria. There were rough spots in the development of this alliance—the Soviet protests over repression against Communists in Egypt and Iraq and, conversely, Egyptian objections to early Soviet support for the Kassem dictatorship in Iraq—but mutual ties grew closer throughout the late fifties and sixties.

Several particular points on this relationship should be kept in mind. The U.S.S.R. saw economic development within the Arab states as a factor of the greatest importance, due not only to political considerations but also to the fact that fifty per cent of Soviet foreign military aid and forty per cent of its foreign economic aid was going to Arab allies.[5] This development process, they believed, required not only quantitative growth but also social changes such as land reform and nationalization of industry. Such growth was more difficult, the Soviets thought, while resources were being so heavily invested in military spending.[6]

This may have been reinforced by the fact that, as one observer wrote: "Once the U.S.S.R. in the mid-1960s began selling at high discounts and on easy-credit terms late models of planes, tanks, missiles, and other expensive equipment that it was still using in the Soviet Union and furnishing its Communist allies, the arms export policies to the Arab East grew steadily more burdensome."[7] From 1954 to 1966 the Soviets provided some \$2 billion in military aid

4. For background of this and earlier periods see Ben-Cion Pinchuk, "Soviet Penetration into the Middle East in Historical Perspective," Hans Morgenthau, "The Ideological and Political Dynamics of the Middle Eastern Policy of the Soviet Union," and Yaacov Ro'i, "Soviet-Israeli Relations, 1947-1954," in *The U.S.S.R. and the Middle East*, ed. Michael Confino and Shimon Shamir (Jerusalem: Israel Universities Press, 1973).

5. Franklyn Holzman, "Soviet Trade and Aid Policy," in *Soviet-American Rivalry in the Middle East*, ed. J. C. Hurewitz (N.Y.: Praeger, 1971), p. 111.

6. Igor Belyaev, "The Middle East in World Affairs," *Journal of Palestine Studies*, Summer, 1973, pp. 16-19, provides one example of this analysis.

7. J. C. Hurewitz, *Middle East Politics: The Military Dimension* (N.Y.: Praeger, 1970), p. 484.

to Egypt, Syria, Iraq, and Yemen.[8] Far from furnishing a profit, this aid was a drain on the Soviet economy, despite the fact that much of the economic aid was eventually paid back. The Soviet economy is centrally planned and regulated by selective subsidization rather than a profit-market system. In such a full-planning and full-employment economy, any aid tends to detract from internal development. Given the nature of the Soviet system and the long-term, low interest nature of the loans "it may be inferred that, despite the fact that most Soviet aid is extended in credit rather than as grants and requires repayment with interest, the recipient receives a substantial subsidy."[9]

During this period, the large amount of Soviet aid already being granted, coupled with their analysis of the domestic situation in the progressive Arab states, gave the Soviets an interest in avoiding an international conflict in the Middle East. This attitude reflected general Soviet international policy, their fear of a direct confrontation with the United States, and their analysis of the balance of military forces in the region as being unfavorable to the Arab states both before and after 1967. The Soviets were particularly firm in their desire not to be drawn directly into the fighting, making it clear that they would supply large amounts of aid but would not commit their own forces. Their main role, in addition to supplying arms, would be to help keep the United States out of the conflict, preventing it from direct intervention.

THE 1967 JUNE WAR

In May, 1966, the Soviets—perhaps over-eager to support their newly heightened alliance with Syria—began to warn of Israeli plans for a major attack on Syria and of Israeli troop concentrations on the Syrian border.[10] A joint communiqué issued after the visit of a Syrian delegation to Moscow a month earlier had added to the traditional formula of Soviet "full support for the lawful rights of the Arabs of Palestine" a new phrase, "in the just struggle against Zionism."[11]

8. Walter Laqueur, The Struggle for the Middle East (Baltimore: Penguin, 1972), p. 164.

9. Holzman, op. cit., p. 109.

10. Laqueur, op. cit., pp. 68-74. For an Israeli version see Avigdor Dagan, Moscow and Jerusalem (N.Y.: Abelard-Schuman, 1970), pp. 209-224. For a Soviet account see Galina Nikitina, The State of Israel (Moscow: Progress Publishers, 1973), pp. 310-28.

11. Pravda, April 26, 1966.

These warnings were the beginning of the crisis led to the 1967 June War. While the Soviets probably did not desire that war they have been known to create international crises in order to strengthen their position internationally, in this case to prove their indispensibility to the Arabs. At any rate, the U.S.S.R. bears a heavy measure of responsibility for the war although, for example, the Soviet ambassador to Cairo called President Nasser at 3:30 A.M. on May 26, 1967 and asked him not to attack Israel.[12]

Meanwhile, the Soviets had warned the United States in vigorous terms not to attempt forceful intervention in the Gulf of Aquaba, although the U.S.S.R. had apparently not been consulted over Nasser's closure of the waterway. They proposed, after consultations with Britain's Foreign Secretary George Brown in Moscow, to have a bilateral conference with the United States to calm the situation. At this point an important misunderstanding between the U.S.S.R. and Egypt developed. The Soviets reportedly explained their cautious view to Nasser's War Minister Shams Badran during his visit to Moscow on May 25. The Egyptian version of these events seems to be that, as a member of the hawkish faction, Badran distorted the Soviet position and made it seem that they had offered Egypt carte blanche. Nasser quoted these messages to Hassan Ibrahim and Abdel Boghdady who, recalling Khrushchev's attitude during the Suez Crisis—that the U.S.S.R. would offer complete political support but would not become directly embroiled in a war—asked him what the Soviet position was. Nasser supposedly replied that the Soviet Union would support Egypt to the end, even if this involved another world war.[13] Of course, it is equally possible that Nasser, wanting to win over doubters to his somewhat reckless "forward" policy, himself distorted the situation.

As for the war itself, the Soviet attitude was analogous to its policy in October, 1973: it would take no political action until it was convinced that the military tide had turned against its allies and, at that point, it would press for an immediate cease-fire. This occurred on June 7, 1967. Only a few days before Soviet Ambassador Fedorenko had argued that the crisis was being exaggerated, now he argued that the crisis was of the greatest urgency. On June 9 a meeting of Soviet bloc leaders assembled in Moscow and condemned Israel. In addition,

12. Michael Howard and Robert Hunter, "Israel and the Arab World: The Crisis of 1967," *Adelphi Paper*, No. 41 (London: Institute for Strategic Studies, 1967), p. 22.

13. Anthony Nutting, *Nasser* (N.Y.: Dutton, 1972), p. 407.

after Israel ignored the cease-fire already accepted by Syria on June 9, Kosygin used the "hot line" to warn U.S. President Lyndon Johnson that a grave catastrophe might occur involving Soviet military action if fighting did not stop immediately. This action also paralleled the events of October, 1973.[14]

The Soviets had their criticisms. Nasser, they said, had been betrayed by the military bourgeoisie because the latter thought that progressive changes in Egypt were a greater danger than that posed by Israel. The extremist slogans of Ahmad Shuqeiri although separated from the positions of the Egyptian and Syrian governments in the Soviet press, were criticized as well as those who called for a new war and rejection of the cease-fire. As for the initial Arab position on U.N. resolution 242, a leading Soviet commentator said "justified though it was, it actually played into the hands of Israel, enabling her to drag out the solution of the main issue—the withdrawal of troops."[15]

The large-scale Soviet airlift after the war tended to ease the conflict. Within a year Moscow had replaced a large proportion of the lost military supplies: 300 out of 365 jet fighters, 50 out of 65 bombers, and 450 out of 550 tanks. Ground-to-ground missiles with a range of 45 miles were provided for the first time. Economic aid, increasing dramatically within three months, provided 300,000 tons of wheat. Nasser said at that time, "We have so far paid not a penny for the arms we obtained from the Soviet Union to equip our armed forces. Actually, were it a question of payment, we have no money to buy arms. . . . "[16] Between June, 1967 and October, 1968 arms deliveries totalled an estimated $2.5 billion.[17] Another estimate placed the expense of arms aid in 1967 alone at $500 million for Egypt and $100 million for Syria.[18]

Soviet President Podgorny toured Egypt, Syria, and Iraq in June and July, 1967 to reassure Arab leaders. Boumedienne visited Moscow and was followed by Atassi of Syria, Aref of Iraq, and King Husayn. Finally, Nasser went to Moscow in July, 1968. While Podgorny was in Egypt he was asked not only for arms but also for Soviet military

14. *Ibid.*, p. 419. Some aid was sent via Algeria rather than by more direct routes, delaying it several weeks.

15. G. Mirsky in *New Times*, June 5, 1968.

16. *The Times*, April 25, 1968; *New York Times*, October 22, 1968; Walter Laqueur, *The Road to War* (London: Penguin, 1970), pp. 262-63.

17. Laqueur, *The Struggle for the Middle East, op. cit.*, p. 164.

18. Hurewitz, *Middle East Politics: The Military Dimension, op. cit.*

advisors and instructors to be attached to every brigade and, if possible, to every battalion. At first the Soviets resisted this request. Within five months, however, the advisors were supplied. Nasser told an interviewer, "Only Russia helped us after the June war with everything from wheat to fighter aircraft, while the Americans were busily helping our enemies and the occupiers of our land. What's more, the Russians have asked for nothing in return, except facilities for their warships to use Alexandria. So what should I have done? Should I have waited until the Americans would send me equal quantities of food and weapons? I'd have waited forever if I had."[19]

Actually, Nasser was not being quite candid. According to Heikal in *The Road to Ramadan*, the Soviets had only started out with demands for a command post in Alexandria. Podgorny had then asked for a repair shop there with both to be guarded by Russian Marines, then a compound including quarters for guards, then for permission to raise the Soviet flag over the whole installation. Nasser allegedly replied, "This is just imperialism. It means we shall be giving you a base."[20]

At the U.N. General Assembly meeting of June 19, 1967, Soviet Premier Kosygin was the first speaker. He demanded a condemnation of Israel, immediate withdrawal of Israeli troops from occupied areas, and payment of reparations. But the Soviet proposal did not get sufficient votes and the U.S. and African-Asian (India, Mali, and Nigeria) resolutions also failed. U.N. Resolution 242, based on the British proposal, was eventually accepted. From that time on, Soviet strategy was to be centered on support for that resolution.

SEARCH FOR A SETTLEMENT, 1968-71

There were some devastating problems facing the Soviet position in the years following the 1967 war. First, the United States and Israel were not particularly interested in a settlement along the lines of U.N. resolution 242 since their position was already so strong. Secondly, many Arabs and most Palestinians did not accept the resolution, particularly because of its ambiguity over whether all

19. Nutting, *op. cit.*, p. 446.

20. M. H. Heikal, *The Road to Ramadan* (N.Y.: Quadrangle, 1975), p. 164. Although Heikal points out that a Cairo computer study on who was benefitting from the "no peace–no war" situation gave Israel 420 points, the United States 380 points, and the U.S.S.R. 110 points, only Egypt was a loser.

occupied territories would be evacuated, its description of the Palestinian problem as a "refugee" rather than as a "national" question, and the feeling that acceptance would constitute de facto recognition of the state of Israel.

Further, the state of limbo that existed between 1967 and 1973 resulted in a turn toward the United States by a number of Arab states, symbolized by Kissinger's shuttle diplomacy successes. As Heikal had earlier put it: "All the profits made by the United States and Israel through the continuation of no peace-no war will turn into losses for the Soviet Union as long as this state of affairs continues."[21] During this five year period Soviet policy was allied to the Egyptian and Syrian military and political strategies and its losses were due more to the limitations of the situation than to any divergence.

The first stage was one of putting forward diplomatic positions. When, in a letter to U.N. envoy Gunnar Jarring in May, 1968 Egypt suggested drawing up a schedule of coordinated measures to normalize the situation, the Soviets were enthusiastic. "This is an important initiative," said the U.S.S.R.'s foreign minister, "and the Soviet government is prepared to help carry out this plan."

In December, 1968 the Soviets suggested a package plan of their own: a simultaneous declaration by Israel and the neighboring Arab states to the effect that they were prepared to terminate the state of war and achieve a peaceful settlement after withdrawal of Israeli troops from the occupied territories. This would be followed by an Israeli statement fixing a date to begin withdrawal. The plan also envisaged that the conflicting sides should coordinate, through the Jarring mission and resolution 242, provisions on security and recognition of frontiers, freedom of navigation on international waterways in the region, settlement of the Palestinian question, territorial inviolability, and political independence of each of the states in the region.[22] The plan called for withdrawal of Israeli troops in two stages: the first month to definite intermediate lines and the second month to the June 5, 1967 lines. U.N. troops would be stationed in a number of places and there might also be demilitarized zones on either side of the frontiers. It is interesting to note that this program is similar to that adopted after the October war. The objective problem which led to the failure of the inter-war period was not a lack of Soviet effort but rather that the policy of negotiations alone would not create

21. Heikal, "Soviet Aims and Egypt," op. cit.
22. Nikitina, op. cit., pp. 350-52.

a situation forcing a change in U.S. policy.[23]

Thus, the meetings of 1969-70—the April, 1969 meeting of the United States, U.S.S.R., Britain, and France; further four-power discussions over the following eighteen months; bilateral U.S.-Soviet meetings from July, 1969 to the end of 1970—had little result.[24] In February, 1970 and July, 1971 Soviet efforts were unsuccessful at accelerating the talks.[25] In the face of U.S. support for Israel and the existence of Arab positions more hard-line than their own, the Soviet's middle road was to support Egypt's approach. Nasser, they said, was "pursuing a sober and realistic approach to the problem of a political solution."[26]

What analysis of the Middle East situation lay behind this policy? "Every people has the right to establish its own independent state," Kosygin told the U.N. in June, 1967, to which a Soviet source added, "In other words, Israel has the same right to existence as any other country."[27] The problem, in the Soviet analysis, was not the state itself but Israel as: (1) an occupier of territories taken in 1967; (2) an oppressor of the Palestinian people; (3) an ally of imperialism in the Middle East; and (4) a Zionist state attempting to appeal to Soviet Jews.[28]

Strategically, to obtain these goals, a two-stage process involving negotiations would be undertaken. The rationale for this, Soviet Middle East policymakers told Syrian Communist leaders in May, 1971, was

23. Barry Rubin, "U.S. Policy, January-October, 1973," *Journal of Palestine Studies*, Winter, 1974, pp. 98-113 and "U.S. Policy and the October War," *MERIP Reports*, No. 23, pp. 3-12.

24. *Pravda*, June 5, 1969. *Kessings Contemporary Archives*, January 25-February 1, 1969, p. 23152; May 3-10, 1969, p. 23325; November 15-22, p. 23669; and January 24-31, 1970, p. 23785.

25. Nikitina, *op. cit.*, p. 349; *Pravda*, February 13, 1970 and July 21, 1971.

26. *Pravda*, June 6, 1969; *Arab Report and Record*, June 1-15, 1969, p. 251.

27. Nikitina, *op. cit.*, p. 303.

28. One additional factor in shaping Soviet policy is the fear of the U.S.S.R., with some 2.7 million Jews, of Israel's popularity within the country. Given Stalin's anti-Semitic purges and the continuing cultural oppression of Soviet Jews, the continuation of a desire among some for emigration is not surprising. Since the late fifties, 50-150 exit permits a month were issued to Jews, mostly in the course of reuniting families. In the early seventies, as internal dissent arose and U.S. pressure was exercised to broaden emigration rights, that number rose to over 2,000 a month. Soviet sources discuss at great length the calls of Israel to Soviet Jews. See Nikitina, *op, cit.*, pp. 298-308; V. Bolshakov, "Zionism: Playing International Reaction's Game," *International Affairs*, January, 1973, pp. 51-55; and V. Laderhin, "Zionism: Propaganda and Reality," *International Affairs*, February, 1973.

that there were three possibilities open to the Arab world. War was one option, but without preparation "this would lead to the liquidation of the progressive regimes—it could also lead to a confrontation between the Soviets and the Americans. We do not conceal the fact that we are not in favor of this except in the case of extreme necessity. Our opposition is not to a military solution per se, but arises only because we are realistic. This does not prevent us from working to increase the military fighting capacity of the Arab countries."[29] The second possibility was one of "no peace and no war." "Objectively," the Soviets said, "this is to Israel's advantage" since this period could be used to take measures against the Palestinian movement, weaken the Arab governments, and allow Israel to consolidate its position in the occupied territories. The third choice would be a struggle for a political solution on a just basis. "This," they said, "is the attitude of the U.S.S.R." Such a policy, the Soviet representatives noted, would strengthen the progressive regimes, bring the international climate to favor the Arabs, increase conflicts between colonialist powers (the United States and Western Europe) over questions like the opening of the Suez Canal, and make it easier to take advantage "of the conflicts between the monopolies in America itself."

This list of possibilities proved rather accurate. In practice, the United States and Israel rejected the third option, as became gradually apparent throughout 1971 and 1972. The second option, a state of "no peace and no war," with all the manifestations the Soviets had predicted, did come into existence. Thus, by October, 1973 the Arabs were left with only the first option—war. The awkwardness of both the Soviets and their allies in adjusting to this changing situation led to some friction. The problems lay around what had to be done to obtain a settlement. The Soviets held that a position of strength would bring about a gradual change in the situation, weakening the U.S. position and isolating Israel while avoiding war. Both Egypt and Syria found that they lacked the time for this technique. In Egypt the tendency was to make greater diplomatic concessions and move closer to the United States; in Syria the situation led in the opposite direction, toward a relatively more militant position and a greater opening toward a military solution.

On the question of Israel itself, the Soviets maintained their traditional position. As one Soviet policymaker stated, "Israel is a fact. . . . Israel has arisen on artificial foundations, and I do not want

29. This and following material from documents printed in the *Journal of Palestine Studies*, Autumn, 1972, pp. 187-212.

to justify it historically. But let us start from existing facts. . . . If the Arabs employ the slogan of the elimination of Israel and the liberation of their usurped homeland, they can never gain the support of world public opinion. . . . Of course, after the consequences of the (1967) aggression have been eliminated the struggle will have to continue and aim its bayonets at the Zionists."[30] The first stage, to be carried out by the Arab states and the Palestinians, would seek return of the occupied territories and a solution to the Palestinian question on the basis of the 1947–48 and later U.N. resolutions. These provided for the return of the refugees or, if they did not wish to return, for compensation. The second stage would be a struggle by the Palestinians alongside progressive Israelis, on both a class and national basis, for elimination of "the colonialist character of the State of Israel."[31]

That the Soviets would be willing to contribute to a military strategy within the context of pressuring U.S.-Israeli concessions was seen by their strong stand during the "war of attrition" along the Suez Canal. The newly provided Soviet arms and training played an important part in this war. By March, 1969, some 300 Egyptian pilots had already returned from training missions in the U.S.S.R.[32] In addition, U.S. sources reported the presence of 150 Soviet pilots and 100 advanced model interceptor MIG-21Js in 24 combat units stationed on four bases early in May, up to 15,000 advisors, and 80 Sam-3 anti-aircraft missile batteries in the country.[33] The purpose of this presence was not only for training but also to discourage Israeli air attacks against Egyptian population centers and behind the Suez fighting lines. Ahmed Khalidi writes:

> The last phase of the War of Attrition (from April to August, 1970) was marked by a reversal of the situation and the passage of the initiative once again into Egypt's hands. From April onwards its stance was once

30. *Ibid.*

31. *Ibid.* "In the estimates of our experts the two armies are incapable of defeating the Israeli army. What will happen if the Israelis decide to attack again on land and in the air? . . . Is it possible to guarantee that there will be no repetition of June, 1967. . . . That is why we are seeking a political settlement, to stem Israeli aggression and impose withdrawal from the occupied Arab territories, through political pressure by all to compel Israel and America to withdraw the Israeli army."

32. Zeev Shiff, "Wings over the Nile," cited in Ahmed Khalidi, "The War of Attrition," *Journal of Palestine Studies*, Autumn, 1973, p. 63.

33. *Aviation Week*, May 11, 1970 and May 18, 1970. See Khalidi, *op. cit.*, for an alternative estimate.

again fundamentally offensive. This was primarily due not so much to the military weight that the Soviet Union placed at Egypt's disposal, considerable though this was, but to the political pressure of the Russians in Egypt. It is clear that the U.S.S.R. had decided to take the Egyptian strategic depth under its protection, so that it was impossible for Israel to penetrate that depth without thus constituting an open challenge to the U.S.S.R.[34]

This allowed Egypt to concentrate forces at the front.

On the other hand, the military correspondent of the Israeli newspaper *Ha'aretz* wrote: "If it is true that the Russians excluded us from Egyptian air-space it is also true that at the same time they proved to the Egyptians that they were not capable of achieving even limited objectives in a war by themselves against Israel."[35] This last factor must have influenced Nasser's acceptance of the second Rogers Plan which led to a cease-fire and an attempt to resume negotiations, again through Jarring. When talks reopened, Sadat's plan was not all that different from what was accepted after the October war, but these talks—as well as more four-power and U.S.-Soviet negotiations—still resulted in no progress.

Events had shown that until the United States decided that it was in its interests to push even harder for progress little change would take place. For this to happen the Arabs would either have to offer the U.S. a positive incentive—an opening to U.S. trade and investment, a turn away from their Soviet alliance, a political turn to the right—or a negative incentive—an oil boycott, nationalization of U.S. investments and, ultimately, war. This was the genesis of the Soviet-Egyptian contradiction: to obtain U.S. backing for regaining the occupied territories, Egypt would have to turn toward war (which the U.S.S.R. opposed) or turn toward the United States (which the U.S.S.R. also opposed). Sadat was to try both options.

Prelude to the October War

Egyptian President Sadat attributes Soviet-Egyptian frictions during the two years preceding the October war to Soviet refusal to support his plan for achieving a settlement through war. Our main source for material on non-public Soviet actions is Sadat who, of course,

34. Khalidi, *op. cit.*, pp. 68-9.
35. *Ha'aretz*, September 17, 1971.

has his own motivations for supplying this version. But Sadat's account does indicate some of the problems during this period, later to be reflected in Egypt's post-October, 1973 policy.

The Soviet relationship with Sadat apparently was never as warm as that with Nasser. This was due to Egypt's increasing pressure for some kind of action and Sadat's generally more conservative positions. It is interesting to note that during this period when, according to Sadat, the U.S.S.R. was putting a brake on militancy, U.S.S.R. relations with the most militant Arab states—Syria and Iraq—were better than ever.

According to Sadat,[36] he requested Mig-23 fighter planes on a trip to Moscow in March, 1971. He said that the Soviet Union promised to send them soon and to train pilots, but that two months later, Soviet President Podgorny visited Cairo and demanded that Egypt sign a friendship treaty with the U.S.S.R. before the Migs would be delivered. The treaty was signed but no planes were given.

Between May and September, 1971 relations were tense, particularly because of a difference in position over events in Sudan. Sadat visited Moscow again in October and says he was again promised arms by the end of the year. The time element was very important, because Sadat had declared 1971 the "year of decision" in which Egypt would again confront Israel. It is also important to keep in mind, though, that Sadat was equally conscious of the diplomatic alternative and it was after his return from Moscow in October that he began to make contact with the United States. At the same time, Sadat adds, he planned to initiate a war in November or December, 1971 but postponed it because of the India-Pakistan war.

In February and April, 1972, Sadat says that he again held meetings with Soviet leaders in preparation for the U.S.-Soviet Moscow summit meeting. His position was based on three points: (1) the Soviet Union should make no agreement with the United States to restrict arms deliveries in the region; (2) the Soviet Union should push for a settlement, but; (3) they should not promise that the Arabs would make any concessions. While the U.S.S.R. did not break from Sadat's principles at the summit, predictably no progress was made on a settlement and Soviet-Egyptian relations worsened. In April, a group of ten prominent Egyptians, including Abdul-Latif Boghdady and Kamal al-Din Hussein, criticized Egypt's alliance with the U.S.S.R.[37]

36. The main source of this account is Sadat's speech of July 18 and his statement of July 24 from the *Journal of Palestine Studies*, Autumn, 1972, pp. 176-83.

37. *Al Nahar*, July 13, 1972.

In June and July, *Heikal* began a series of critical editorials on Soviet policy, which Podgorny denounced in meetings with Syrian President Hafez Assad, who attempted to mediate the split. In May, Sadat said that he sent a questionnaire to the Soviet Union on their policy toward the Middle East situation; after not receiving an answer, he moved to expel the Soviet advisors.

In a later interview, Sadat said he had found the Soviet strategy to be based on two principles:

> First, that there should not be a war again in this area, in view of their decision to avoid confrontation with the United States and secondly, that the Arabs must accept a peaceful solution. During my visit to Moscow on March 1 and 2, 1971, I said to the Russians: 'If America and Israel do not feel that we are standing on firm ground, there will be no political solution. There is no room for maneuvering on this subject. There are no longer any military secrets. Egyptian radar in Mansura is capable of disclosing the movements of Israeli planes in Haifa, and the same applies to Israeli radar. . . . This means that the Israelis are still convinced of their military superiority so that they will insist on surrender being imposed on the Arabs.'[38]

Ironically, though developments proved this analysis more or less correct, throughout the remainder of 1972 and 1973, Sadat proceeded with attempts to appeal to the United States in various ways. The October war itself was a limited offensive designed to demonstrate Egypt's feelings to the United States and Sadat's post-war policy was also in this vein. His concept of firm ground, then, was limited and mixed with positive incentives.

Even the expulsion of the Soviet advisors was a form of positive incentive for the United States. Earlier, Secretary of State William Rogers had indicated that his government would consider it "helpful" if the U.S.S.R. reduced its military presence in Egypt and U.S. consultations with Saudi Arabia had also put forward this perspective. The Saudi foreign minister apparently conveyed this to Sadat shortly before the expulsion. On the other hand, Sadat's critique of Soviet caution and of the deadend in which the U.S.S.R.'s policy found itself also seem accurate.

About two-thirds of the 16,000 Soviet advisors left Egypt and this "electric shock" helped Sadat internally after four months of demonstrations by students, workers, and refugees from the Canal area. The

38. Interview with *Al-Hawadess* (Beirut), October 6, 1972.

Soviets were apparently not too unhappy at leaving because if Sadat was indeed planning a war they would have quickly found themselves in the middle of it. There are some indications that Soviet leaders, or at least some groups within the leadership, had felt that they were too deeply involved in Egypt.

The war of words between Egypt and the U.S.S.R. was extensive. Akhbar al-Yom charged on August 19 that the Soviet Union did not supply sufficient arms to enable Egypt "to eliminate the traces of the aggression." On August 28, *Izvestia* replied that the U.S.S.R. had fulfilled its commitments and that "the only basis for peace in the Middle East is the total liberation of Arab territories from the Zionist invaders." The Soviet Union did not stand alone in its defense. Iraq had just signed a friendship treaty with the U.S.S.R. and Syria stayed neutral in the Soviet-Egyptian argument. Military equipment, including SAMs, continued to arrive in Damascus.[39] In September, Iraq's President Ahmad Hassan al-Bakr was invited to the Soviet Union for a five-day visit. The Palestinians also stated their position. *Al-Hadaf* ran a series of articles from various Arab sources supporting the Soviet position. *Filastin al-Thawra* charged that attempts were being made to "turn the conflict between us and world Zionism and American imperialism into a conflict between us and the U.S.S.R. . . . from which no one would benefit but the enemy."[40]

If Egypt and the U.S.S.R. patched up their relations, Sadat as late as February and June, 1973 said that the Soviets opposed decisive action. The latter date corresponds with the U.S.-Soviet summit when, Sadat claimed, both sides agreed to "freeze" the situation. While the Soviets had followed the path of negotiations far down the road, there seems to be ample evidence that they, too, changed their minds in mid-1973. It is hard to believe that they agreed to maintain the status quo. While both the U.S.S.R. and the United States wanted a settlement, the collapse of the Rogers Plan and the failure of U.N. resolution 242 made it seem unlikely that any progress could be made.

A break in the deadlock would have required greater concessions from either Egypt and Syria or Israel and the United States. Neither side was willing to give up very much. Only the combination of the October war, the oil boycott, and the opening of Egypt to U.S. political and economic influence accomplished even a partial Israeli withdrawal. The U.S.S.R. never had the leverage to force such a change in the inter-war period. Sadat correctly sensed that, from his frame

39. *Al Nahar*, September 24, 1972.
40. For example, *Al Hadaf*, September 2, 1972; *Filastin al-Thawra*, August 16, 1972.

of reference, pleas and threats would have to be directed at the United States. The Soviet-Arab difference was essentially one of timing—as to when the failure of the diplomatic road would lead to a switch to military means. The Soviet Union had plenty of time—it was not their land being occupied and they were intent on improving their detente with the United States. Aside from this, Egypt had its own problems in making a transition in strategy.

It is important to understand how limited Soviet influence in Egypt always remained. No true client state dependent on either the United States or the U.S.S.R. could ever have taken a single one of these actions without its government facing significant reprisals. Yet all during this period—even when tension was at its height—Soviet aid was never cut off. It is important to understand that neither Israel nor the Arab governments are puppets of outside superpowers. All these countries, although subject to pressure, operate on the basis of their own perceived interests. To view Israel as an outpost of Western imperialism or the Arab states as the spearhead of Soviet expansionism is quite misleading.

While Egypt's balance of trade with Soviet bloc states understandably went from a favorable position into a deficit in 1967 and the volume of Egypt's trade with those countries in 1969-70 was one-quarter of its total trade, this situation proved temporary. During the following years the deficit was gradually cut and Egypt's debts were being paid. Trade with Western Europe and other areas also remained at a high level.[41] At the same time, the Egyptians could not help but notice that their relationship to the Soviet Union was becoming similar to the situation vis-à-vis Britain and France in the nineteenth century. Egypt was becoming a prisoner of debt which, sooner or later, could be used as leverage by the Soviet Union. Sadat faced a clearly dangerous trend toward dependence on the U.S.S.R.

While the purge of Ali Sabry and his faction of the Arab Socialist Union (for allegedly planning a coup) was played up in the West as being the occasion for an important Egyptian-Soviet conflict, one writer unfriendly to the Russians wrote, "there is no evidence of their (the Sabry group) having informed Moscow of their intentions beforehand, and it is unlikely that the Russians would have given their blessing to such an amateurish enterprise. The Egyptian Commu-

41. Robert Hunter, "The Soviet Dilemma in the Middle East," *Adelphi Paper*, No. 59 (London: Institute for Strategic Studies, 1969), Part I, 15.

nists were certainly not involved. . . . Even the Soviet press eventually condemned the conspirators."[42]

The Soviets gained the use of repair and storage facilities in Alexandria and Port Said and several airfields for reconnaissance planes used in flights over the Mediterranean. According to several reports, there were a couple of interventions in internal affairs—requests for the removal of War Minister Sadeq and of Arab Socialist Union Secretary-General Said Marei. Although limitations did exist on arms aid, the quantity and quality of equipment furnished were quite high. From June, 1967 to June, 1972 close to $8 billion in aid, mostly military, was given. Further, the U.S.S.R. had opposed supplier restraints on arms deliveries, which the United States had favored after 1967. The Soviet delegate insisted on striking a provision out of U.N. resolution 242 which called for restricting arms exports to the Middle East.[43] The Russians consistently armed their Arab client-states with the latest equipment available to Soviet forces, sometimes even before similar equipment was made available to most satellite forces in Eastern Europe. This was the case even though much equipment that is obsolescent in Europe may still be very much usable in desert warfare in the middle East.[44]

The Soviet Union held back on only two arms categories—MIG-23s and strategic ground-to-ground missiles. While these might have been refused to prevent war in general, this seems unlikely in the light of the large amounts of other equipment given. It seems more likely that these were not given to prevent an all-out war involving civilian population centers—the kind most likely to trigger what the U.S.S.R. saw as a potential world conflagration. The defensive limitations of Soviet weaponry are closely related to the general defensive orientation of the Soviet military itself.[45] At any rate, both Egypt and Syria had missiles by the time of the October war and MIG-23s were delivered to Syria afterwards.[46]

While Soviet-Egyptian relations eroded, Soviet-PLO ties improved. After the 1967 war the Soviet Union was negative toward the Palestinian

42. Walter Laqueur, "On the Soviet Departure from Egypt," *Commentary*, LIV, Part I, No. 6, 63.

43. Jon Kimche, *There Could Have Been Peace* (N.Y.: Dial, 1973), p. 318.

44. Hurewitz, *Soviet-American Rivalry in the Middle East, op. cit.*, p. 3.

45. Hunter, *op. cit.*, p. 12.

46. Riad Ashkar, "The Syrian and Egyptian Campaigns," *Journal of Palestine Studies*, Winter, 1974, pp. 16-17.

groups because it perceived them as an adventurist threat to their strategy of diplomacy. Beginning in 1970, with the leftist shift away from the Shuqeiri leadership, relations began to improve. They were critical of Ahmad Jibril, leader of the PFLP-General Command, who they cited as saying that Israeli Jews "from European Countries . . . we shall send away." "Of course," a Soviet specialist commented, "this is a step forward in comparison with Shuqeiri's attitude." But Arafat and another Palestinian leaders were favorably quoted, the latter arguing, "We must contact the democrats in Israel with a view to common struggle against the Zionist leadership."[47] The respect gained by Palestinian groups in the battle of Karameh, Yasir Arafat's first visit to Moscow, the debate within the PLO over admission of the Communist "partisan" guerrilla group in mid-1970, and the events of September, 1970 in Jordan were decisive to Soviet-PLO relations. They led to a Soviet understanding of the popular support the Palestinians had in the Arab world.

In the months immediately preceding the October war, Soviet-Palestinian ties made some important gains. During the Communist-sponsored World Youth Festival held in East Berlin during the summer of 1973, Arafat was one of the two main speakers and, for the first time, the Palestinian flag was flown at such an event. Fund-raising campaigns for the PLO were started in Eastern Europe and the PLO opened offices in East Berlin and Prague. Communiqués during Arafat's trip indicated heightened official recognition of the national rights of the Palestinians. *Filastin al-Thawra*, official organ of the PLO, commented, "The Palestinians regard this as a victory for their struggle, and an important step along the road to the recognition of our people's full right to continue their struggle to liberate their homeland."[48]

THE OCTOBER WAR

At approximately the same time Sadat was making his decision to launch the war (February, 1973), the Soviet Union was changing its policy toward approval of a military option. A March 4 Radio Moscow broadcast stated that "the promotion of Soviet-Arab cooperation in the military field assumes special importance in the light of Israel's open refusal to give up relying on the force of arms as

47. *Washington Post,* June 11, 1974.
48. *Filastin al-Thawra,* August 15, 1973.

a method to settle the present Middle East dispute in its interest." In an April 5 speech, Kosygin said, "We believe that Egypt has a right to possess a powerful army now in order to defend itself against the aggressor and to liberate its own lands." Sadat, in an April interview in *Newsweek*, said the Soviets "are providing us now with everything that's possible for them to supply. I am now quite satisfied."[49]

Perhaps the first sign of this change of policy was the Radio Moscow broadcast of January 16: "The Arab countries are preparing to repel new attacks by Israeli militants. They feel forced now to look even further, to prepare for the complete liberation of the Arab lands seized by Israel." Similar statements continued over the next nine months. The Soviet media also made a number of false charges of impending Israeli attacks on neighboring states; they made similar charges before the 1967 June War.[50] Finally, the Soviet Union indicated its new attitude toward the U.S. negotiating position. "As for the various American 'peace initiatives,'" said Soviet Middle East expert Igor Beliayev in March, "like the Rogers Plan, their main objective has been to achieve a cease-fire on the dividing line—that is, in practice, their aim has been to postpone the reaching of a political settlement."[51]

When war broke out on October 6, the Soviet Union immediately declared its full support of the Arab allies. Military supplies began arriving in Egypt and Syria almost immediately. Some 300 transport planes were involved in the airlift, carrying between 200,000 and 225,000 tons of military equipment during the war.[52] U.S. Deputy Defense Secretary William Clements said that the Soviet sealift arrived simultaneously with the beginning of the war and that it would normally take ten to fourteen days for Soviet ships to reach Egypt and Syria, indicating a close coordination of the military effort.[53] These supplies given at a time when both countries' armies were on the offensive, despite the U.S. government's offer to suspend supplies to Israel in exchange for similar Soviet action toward its Arab allies.

At the beginning of the war, as in the 1967 war, the U.S.S.R. opposed outside intervention. On October 7, the United States called for an

49. *Noyoye Vremia*, No. 5, April, 1973, p. 8. For more evidence see F. Kohler, L. Goure, and M. Harvey, *The Soviet Union and the October Middle East War* (Washington: Center for Advanced International Studies, University of Miami, 1974).

50. See Kohler *et al.*, *op. cit.*, pp. 47-51.

51. Belyaev, *op. cit.*, p. 19.

52. *Aviation Week*, October 15, 1973; *New York Times*, November 28, 1973.

53. *Washington Post*, November 6, 1973.

immediate U.N. Security Council session to arrange a cease-fire. Soviet and Arab representatives opposed this plan. Soviet U.N. Ambassador Malik argued that what was needed was "not any new resolution of the U.N." but rather implementation of resolution 242. Malik warned that "the adoption of any new resolution in circumvention of this principal key issue will be exploited by the aggressors again only to distract attention from this key issue and to continue to occupy and annex other peoples' lands." The ambassador continued this line of argument for several days although Washington was still going easy on the Soviet Union in the interest of detente. On October 10 the U.S. cease-fire proposal failed to gain Soviet support.

Kissinger commented, "This first attempt failed, on Saturday, October 13, for a variety of reasons—including perhaps, a mis-assessment of the military situation by some of the participants."[54] Events proved him correct. As the military tide turned, Soviet policy changed but for the moment it did all possible to ensure that the tide would not turn. The U.S.S.R. called for full international support for Egypt and Syria, messages were sent to Algeria and other countries calling for Arab unity and the use of the oil weapon was urged.[55]

The Egyptian and Syrian advances were stopped and the Israeli army began to make gains on the ground. Kosygin's visit to Cairo on October 16 coincided with the Israeli crossing of the Canal. Egypt's limited war had gained its objectives and they now called for an immediate cease-fire. When Kosygin returned to Moscow on October 19, the Soviet position had also changed. Serious talks with the United States started that evening and two days later the United States and the U.S.S.R. presented their cease-fire resolution to the United Nations.

As in 1967 this was not enough to end the fighting. After the October 22 passing of U.N. resolution 338, the Israeli military continued its advance on the west side of the Canal. On October 23 the Soviet Union condemned these cease-fire violations and warned of the "gravest consequences " if fighting continued. The next day, Sadat, probably at Soviet urging, appealed for Soviet and American troops to police the agreement. This seemed to be an essentially political move to pressure the United States to gain Israeli compliance with the October 22 cease-fire lines, but it also involved the mobilization of large numbers of Soviet troops. The United States did not back down and President Nixon called for a worldwide troop alert the following morning. Husayn Fahmi, chief editor of *al-Akhbar*, praised

54. Press conference of October 25, 1973.

55. *FBIS—Middle East and Africa*, October 16, 1973, pp. 1-2; *New York Times*, October 10, 1973.

the Soviet action by saying, "the stern Soviet warning to Israel, and the alerting of the Soviet forces to go to the Middle East to establish peace and stop the aggression changed the situation completely."[56]

The October war, more than any other war in recent times, illustrates that warfare is simply the carrying on of politics by military means. With the cease-fire in force, the Soviet Union advanced a negotiating strategy within which the war figured as a powerful argument for the undoing of the events of June, 1967. Within the context of its interests and aims, the Soviet Union wanted an integrated process which would strengthen its influence and that of its allies—the anti-imperialist bloc in the Arab world. They were quite aware of the numerous cards held by the United States and the continued undermining of the Soviet position in Egypt by Sadat's turn to the West.

The Soviets tried to hold together an alliance with Egypt, Syria, Algeria, and the majority of the PLO. They also sought to maintain good relations with Iraq and Libya. As part of maintaining the unity of this bloc, a strong negotiating position, and enhancing Soviet influence at the expense of the U.S. position, the Soviet Union favored maintenance of the oil embargo. A March 28, 1974 Radio Moscow broadcast to the Middle East asserted that "U.S. efforts are not aimed at compelling Israel to recognize the legitimate rights of the Arabs and to implement the U.N. resolution, but at proving U.S. goodwill towards the Arabs and compelling them to lift the oil embargo." When the negotiation process started, the U.S.S.R. downgraded the disengagement accords and played down Kissinger's role while trying to take credit for any progress made. Gromyko's visits paralleled Kissinger's in the Middle East. They urged an advance of the negotiation process but, in the case of Syria, a minimum of concessions. The other main aim of Soviet policy was to funnel any diplomatic progress through the Geneva conference framework in which they, as co-sponsor, would have a position equal to that of the United States.

These themes were coupled in Brezhnev's January 30, 1974 speech in Havana. "The Geneva conference must carry out its main mission," the Soviet leader said, "achieve a fundamental political settlement and establish lasting peace in the Middle East. But this aim can be achieved only provided Israeli troops are withdrawn from all the Arab territories that were occupied in 1967 and the legitimate rights of the Arab people of Palestine are respected."[57] In the Soviet-Cuban

56. Radio Moscow, February 16, 1974.
57. *Pravda*, January 31, 1974.

communiqué signed during that trip, the two countries called for a "radical settlement" in the Middle East. Brezhnev reiterated this at an April 11, 1974 dinner honoring Assad's visit to Moscow: "The danger lies in the fact that against the background of a certain decrease of tensions, the aggressor and its patrons may try again to avoid a radical all-encompassing solution of the problem."[58]

The U.S.S.R. feared not only a return to the 1967-73 situation but the more dangerous possibility of a situation in which the United States held both Arabs and Israelis dependent on it as an "honest broker." Since the United States maintained good relations with both Israel and the majority of the Arab states and was the only country that could pressure Israel for withdrawal, it is not surprising that the United States played this role in the aftermath of the war. This new power was symbolized by the shuttle diplomacy of Kissinger, something the U.S.S.R. tried to publicly ignore. Privately, though, the U.S.S.R. was most conscious of the erosion of its position in the Arab world.

Kissinger was smart enough to avoid rubbing in the U.S. advantage. "Obviously," he told Congress in June, 1974, "the Soviet Union is a major power with global interests; obviously the Middle East is an area of great concern to the Soviet Union. Therefore we have no intention—indeed we have no capability—of expelling Soviet influence from the Middle East."[59]

As we have already seen, the Soviet Union considered the domestic situation of its allies to be of great importance, not only affecting their ability to wage the struggle with Israel but as the very basis of their alliance with the U.S.S.R. as well. The United States was trying, the February 19, 1974 Radio Moscow broadcast said, "to force the Arab countries to abandon social, economic, and political gains" and was prepared to "pay" for this "by returning a certain part of the territories which lawfully belong to the Arabs."

Soviet relations were particularly strained with Egypt. Although Sadat stated several times that he wished to maintain good relations with the U.S.S.R., it was quite a different thing from the alliance of the sixties. Radio Moscow warned on March 6, 1974: "There is another aim behind the talk about Western participation in the rebuilding of Egypt. It is to distract the world's attention from the fact that the United States is continuing to assist Israel. . . . U.S. assistance to Egypt for reconstruction projects is first and last aimed

58. *Soviet News*, April 23, 1974, p. 140.
59. *New York Times*, June 7, 1974.

at safeguarding the interests of the American monopolies and infiltrating the Egyptian economy."

There is no reason to believe that the Soviet Union can stop the U.S. advance as long as Kissinger's strategic shift in U.S. policy holds sway. It is also important to keep in mind that the traditional opposition to Soviet influence in the Arab world—both Islamic-cultural as well as political—is as strong as ever. Saudi Arabia, Kuwait, and other such states are more powerful not only because of their oil revenues, but also due to their alliance with a more popular United States.

Still, it would be wrong to underestimate the power of the Soviet's appeal. Within the context of the Arab-Israeli conflict, the skill of Soviet diplomacy has been seen in its ability to maintain good ties even with those who tended to oppose moves toward a settlement. Praise for the Soviet role has continued, for example, from the Popular Front for the Liberation of Palestine and from Iraq.[60] The success of the United States has also encouraged a tightening of the Soviet alliance with Syria, Algeria, and Libya, although on an economic level they are carrying out detente policies similar to those of the U.S.S.R.

Soviet relations with the PLO have become more important than ever. All factions within the PLO are as interested as is the Soviet Union in preventing an only partial or fragmented settlement. Consequently, the Soviet Union encouraged the Palestinians, to put forward a program after the October war. The U.S.S.R.'s policy supports establishment of a West Bank-Gaza state along with the right of return for Palestinians into Israel or compensation. Given the historic Soviet policy this probably means the recognition of the right of return in principle—as embodied in the resolution passed by the United Nations in November, 1974—but in practice the coexistence of two separate states, Israel within its 1967 borders and Palestine in the West Bank and Gaza Strip. The U.S.S.R. would probably then reestablish relations with Israel and try to build strong ties with the Palestinian state.

The options for the U.S.S.R. in its Middle East policy were outlined by Henry Kissinger in his December 27, 1973 press conference. The Soviet Union could seek to maintain tension in the Middle East "because this will guarantee permanent Arab hostility to the United States and enhance the possibilities of Soviet influence." The other option is that after three Middle East wars and the realization that these "costly and inconclusive" conflicts could bring on an international confrontation, the Soviet Union "now has an interest" in

60. *PFLP Bulletin*, No. 8, December, 1973, pp. 4-5.

cooperating with the United States in achieving a "stabilization of the situation."

The latter option seems to be the most likely choice of the Soviet Union. Still, the question of the nature of that settlement or stabilization remains quite important. The Soviet Union has always favored a settlement of the Arab-Israeli conflict and in recent years the detente policy has increased Soviet concern that the Middle East is a "hot bed" of wars that threatens to set off a worldwide conflagration. They have also understood that there simply cannot be peace without justice for the Palestinians. In addition, they have been most suspicious of a settlement based on Arab–American accord, because of the threat it poses to their own interests.

CONCLUSION

Clearly, peace in the Middle East can be achieved only through concessions by both sides—guarantees for Israel accompanied by the return of the occupied territories and establishment of a Palestinian state. This is not that far from current Soviet policy. Indeed, such a settlement would have a number of advantages for the U.S.S.R., including use of the Suez Canal, savings on military aid, increased emphasis on economic relations with the Arab world, establishing relations with Israel so that it (like the United States) could have contacts on both sides of the conflict, and a position as one of the most important friends of the new Palestinian state. Consequently, the Soviet role in the Middle East should be an important factor in the region for a long time to come.

The new strength of the United States in the Middle East only accelerates Soviet support for social change in the Arab world, the Arab struggle against Israeli occupation of their lands, and the Palestinian movement. The Soviets will not endorse a settlement which puts the United States and its allies on top. On this point, its position coincides in general with that of its Arab allies.

It is this struggle over the definition of a settlement which has been brought to the forefront by the October war. As Boris Ponomarev, a candidate member of the Soviet Politburo, explained the U.S.S.R.'s policy: "The Soviet Union will continue in the future to do everything necessary to defend the legitimate interests of the Arab countries, to make its contribution to the liquidation of the Near East crisis, and not to permit a 'settlement' which would in practice encourage the aggressor. That would damage both the cause of peace and the interests of the national liberation struggle. But it should not be so, and it will not be so."[61]

61. Kohler, *op. cit.*, p. x.

M. S. Agwani

ASIA AND THE ARABS

THE ATTITUDES AND POLICIES of the Asian nations toward the continuing
Arab-Israeli and Palestinian-Zionist conflicts have been largely condi-
tioned by two sets of factors: practical considerations and political
principles. In the past, the widest measure of Asian consensus on
principles governing the Palestine question was recorded in the
communiqué issued at the conclusion of the Bandung Conference
in April, 1955:

> In view of the existing tension in the Middle East caused by the
> situation in Palestine and the danger of that tension to world peace,
> the Asian-African Conference declared its support of the rights of the
> Arab people of Palestine and called for the implementation of the United
> Nations resolutions on Palestine and for peaceful settlement of the
> Palestine question.[1]

The outcome of the 1967 June War lent a far more serious dimension
to the Palestine question than the one recorded above. From its
seemingly innocuous beginnings in the nineteenth century, Zionism
had now graduated into an exclusivist-expansionist doctrine whose
field of operation now extended far beyond the geographical boundaries of Palestine to occupied Egyptian and Syrian territories. Israel's

---

1. Text of the communiqué in G. H. Jansen, *Afro-Asia and Non-Alignment* (London,
1966), pp. 412–14.

intentions regarding the future disposition of these territories and the rightful owners thereof were reflected as much in its occupation policy as in its sustained clamor for "secure and agreed frontiers."

Shortly before the outbreak of the June war Levi Eshkol, the Israeli prime minister, had proclaimed that his government had no territorial ambitions; but no sooner had the war ended than his defence minister, Moshe Dayan, made a public pronouncement in the captured Old City of Jerusalem: "We have returned to this most sacred of shrines, never to part with Jerusalem again." The Old City was soon annexed. About the same time, Moshe Dayan was reported by *Ha'olam Hazeh,* Israel's mass circulation weekly, to have observed:

> Our fathers had reached the frontiers which were recognized in the partition plan. Our generation reached the frontiers of 1949. Now the Six-Day generation have managed to reach Suez, Jordan, and the Golan Heights. This is not the end. After the present cease-fire lines there will be new ones. They would extend beyond the Jordan—perhaps to Lebanon and perhaps to central Syria as well.[2]

Dayan's pronouncement was not repudiated by the Israeli government. On the contrary, the latter adopted the bizarre procedure of permitting its ministers to float their respective private plans for the disposition of occupied territories.

The Israeli government left no one in doubt that it would not return to the pre-June war frontiers and that the new cease-fire lines would not be exchanged except for secure and agreed frontiers. On March 13, 1971 the London *Times* published an interview with Prime Minister Golda Meir in which she gave the official Israeli interpretation of the terms *secure* and *agreed:* the first implied that Israel would retain its hold on the Jordan Valley, Jerusalem, the Golan Heights, and Sharm al-Shaykh (together with territorial contiguity of access between Sharm al-Shaykh and Israel); and the second meant that what remained after the above annexations would be disposed of by negotiations between Israel and the Arab states concerned.

The other indicator of Israel's intentions was its occupation policy. On the face of it, Israeli opinion on occupation policy remained sharply divided between the advocates of total absorption of the occupied territories and their peoples and those who favored minimum absorption consistent with secure frontiers. In actual practice, however, Israeli

2. Quoted in Ian Gilmour, "Zionist Doctrine and Israeli Expansionism," *The Times* (London), June 25, 1969.

occupation policy seemed to be directed towards the wider goal of liquidation of the Palestine question. It was partly reflected in the systematic expulsion of Palestinians from the West Bank and Gaza. Impartial observers placed the number of these new expellees from the West Bank alone at 165,000. For many of them it was a second expulsion, the first one having occurred in 1948. Israeli policy was also implicit in the semicolonial relationship that Tel Aviv established with the occupied West Bank, which now forms an important source of unskilled labor for Israeli industry and agriculture. The West Bank also serves as a captive market for Israeli-manufactured goods and its crop pattern has been suitably adjusted to meet the requirements of Israeli consumers.

The Asian response to the Arab-Israeli and Palestinian-Zionist conflicts in the post-June, 1967 phase was largely influenced by these ominous developments. This is not to suggest that the Asian nations reacted to these conflicts in an identical fashion. On the contrary, their reactions formed a wide spectrum reflecting the varying political, economic, and ideological interests and needs of the nations concerned. This interplay of interests and principles is underscored in the Middle Eastern policies of states as diverse in outlook and orientation as China, Pakistan, and India.

CHINA AND THE MIDDLE EAST

China's response to the 1967 June War and its aftermath must be seen in the context of that country's ideology and interests. The two factors are in fact too closely interrelated to permit of any examination of them in isolation from each other. The basic element in China's ideology is Mao Tse-tung's theory of revolution, a theory rooted in the Chinese experience of the thirties. Revolution, according to this theory, can be accomplished only through a protracted war to be fought by a united front headed by a Communist party.[3] In Mao's model for nation-building, protracted war is "the highest form of struggle." It generates national strength and unity and is a kind of antitoxin "capable of transforming many things." Secondly, a revolutionary war must be conducted by united front tactics involving mass participation rather than collaboration among established regimes. Hence the distinction between a "united front from above" and a

3. See W. A. C. Adie, "Peking's Revised Line," *Problems of Communism* (Washington, D.C.), September–October, 1972, pp. 57–58.

"united front from below." The Communist party must of course play the key role in the revolutionary struggle. And to accomplish this, it must strike up an alliance with a portion of its foes against the common enemy.

The relevance of Mao's theory of revolution to the Middle East lies in the Chinese conviction that Palestine and Yemen are two of the twelve areas where "excellent revolutionary situations" exist.[4] On the practical plane, the Chinese link the Arab struggle against U.S.-backed Israel to their own struggle against U.S.-backed Taiwan and against the designs of the superpowers to divide and dominate the world. This is not to suggest that Chinese policy is exclusively geared to support protracted armed struggle in Palestine or elsewhere in the Middle East. On the contrary, the diversity of Peking's interests in the area has favored a flexible and pragmatic policy. Since its recognition by Cairo in 1956, Peking has made considerable headway in establishing diplomatic ties with several Middle Eastern states ranging from radical republics to conservative monarchies. The arrival of Chinese diplomatic missions in Arab capitals marked the beginning of flourishing economic and trade exchanges. China's exports to the Arab world zoomed from £17 million in 1962 to over £60 million in 1969. Another indicator of Peking's stake in the Arab world is its economic assistance to selected Arab countries, particularly to Syria, Egypt, Yemen, and the People's Democratic Republic of Yemen. Chinese economic assistance to the Arabs since the mid-fifties totaled $312 million or about 28 per cent of Peking's total aid to foreign countries. An important point to note is that China has not permitted ideological considerations to inhibit its foreign political and economic relations. A classic example of this is China's sustained economic and technical assistance to Yemen both under the Imamate and the Republic. Likewise, China's strident criticism of Moscow's Middle East policy is at least partly due to its anxiety about the adverse consequences of Soviet ascendancy in that area for Peking's economic and long-term security interests.

China's Middle East policy thus reflects a ceaseless interaction between ideology and interest; but this does not preclude the dominance of one factor over the other in its detailed application to individual cases. The emphasis varies from trade in Kuwait and Bahrain

---

4. See John K. Cooley, "China and the Palestinians," *Palestine Studies* (Beirut), I, No. 2, (winter, 1972), 33-34. The other ten areas as identified on a map published in *Peking Review* in 1968 are Angola, India, Burma, Vietnam, Laos, Thailand, Malaya, the Philippines, Indonesia, and Latin America.

to armed revolution in Palestine and Oman. The radical Arab republics with which Peking has developed both political and trade and economic relations fall into the middle category. These are also the countries where Chinese diplomacy is engaged in an abrasive competition with its vastly more resourceful rival, the Soviet Union. This is the broad framework of China's Middle East policy.

At the time of the 1967 June War China was being rocked by the internal convulsions that marked the Cultural Revolution. Its diplomatic activity in the Middle East, as elsewhere, had come to a virtual standstill following withdrawal of Chinese ambassadors from all Arab capitals except Cairo. Prime Minister Chou En-lai was nevertheless prompt in sending messages of support to Syria, Egypt, and the Palestine Liberation Organization (PLO). Peking also took the opportunity to stress the need for a protracted struggle and to articulate its own assessment of the Soviet role in the conflict.

On the eve of the 1967 war Peking accused the Soviet Union of "peddling the sinister ware of Tashkent spirit"[5] and pledged resolute support to the Arabs. After the cease-fire, the Chinese blamed Arab reverses on U.S. support for Israel, Soviet "treachery" and, in the final analysis, "collusion" between Moscow and Washington. As the Soviet Union stepped up its efforts for political settlement in the United Nations, Chou En-lai wrote to Ahmad Shuqeiri, chairman of the PLO, expressing the hope that "having taken up arms, the revolutionary people of Palestine and the entire Arab people" would not "lay down their arms . . . [but] like the heroic Vietnamese people fight on unflinchingly, resolutely, and stubbornly, until final victory."[6] The exhortation to fight on was accompanied by offers of interest-free loans of $10 million and 150,000 tons of wheat to Egypt.

The twin themes of protracted struggle and suspicion of Soviet motives continued to dominate Chinese actions and attitudes in regard to the two major issues that dominated the Middle Eastern scene in subsequent years, namely the Arab-Israeli impasse and the Palestinians' militant struggle for their national rights.

Chinese Support for the PLO

China was the first country outside the Arab world to lend official support to the PLO. In March, 1965, when a PLO delegation headed

5. This refers to the Indo-Pakistani disengagement agreement reached through Soviet mediation shortly after the 1965 conflict.

6. Quoted in R. Medzini, "China and the Palestinians: A Developing Relationship?," *New Middle East* (London), No. 32, May, 1971, p. 36.

by Ahmad Shuqeiri arrived in Peking on the invitation of the Chinese government, it was accorded a tumultuous welcome. Shuqeiri was treated like a visiting head of state and was received by top-ranking Chinese leaders. Addressing the delegation, Mao Tse-tung observed:

> Imperialism is afraid of China and of the Arabs. Israel and Formosa are bases of imperialism in Asia. You are the front gate of the great continent, and we are the rear. Our goal is the same. . . . Asia is the biggest continent in the world, and the West wants to continue exploiting it. The West does not like us, and we must understand this fact. The Arab battle against the West is the battle against Israel. So boycott Europe and America, O Arabs![7]

The occasion marked the conclusion of the first military and diplomatic agreement between China and the PLO. Under the agreement, the PLO was accorded diplomatic status and was promised undisclosed quantities of Chinese arms as well as facilities for military training in China. A PLO office was soon opened in Peking.

Evidently the Chinese looked upon the PLO as a movement with tremendous potentialities. If sustained, it could give a revolutionary dimension to the Palestinian movement which it had hitherto lacked. By 1966 batches of PLO guerrillas trained in China returned to Arab territory. Peking is also believed to have supplied them with arms. In any event, a section of the Palestinian activists began to speak of Mao's thesis of people's war as the only way to liberate Palestine. Shortly after the outbreak of the 1967 June War the *People's Daily* commented that "in the few days and nights of war the political consciousness of the Arab people rose more than in any normal year" and that they would emerge victorious should they "undertake a protracted, heroic struggle."[8]

With the intensification of the Palestinian struggle against Zionism, the PLO emerged as an autonomous force committed to a meaningful objective of its own. It did not talk any more of "throwing the Jews into the sea"; rather it emphasized the need for a popular armed struggle against Israel leading eventually to the establishment of a secular, democratic, and multi-racial state in Palestine. Peking was quick to see in this development an incontestable vindication of its revolutionary thesis. And it was perhaps on this ground that China

7. Cooley, *op.cit.*, p. 21.

8. Quoted in W. A. C. Adie, "China's Middle East Strategy," *The World Today* (London), XXIII, No. 8 (August, 1967), 324.

thenceforth bestowed more attention on the smaller, Marxist-oriented groups inside the PLO such as George Habash's Popular Front for the Liberation of Palestine (PFLP) or Nayef Hawatemah's Popular Democratic Front for the Liberation of Palestine (PDFLP) than on the more numerous and more moderate Al-Fatah. For the same reason, the Chinese attitude towards Yasir Arafat, the new PLO chief, was one of reserved acceptance. This was evident from the moderate reception accorded to Arafat during the latter's visit to Peking in March, 1970.

Despite the shift in Chinese support, Chinese theories about "people's war" and "luring the enemy into the hinterland"—which Moscow decried as outmoded, irrelevant, and self-defeating[9]—had an irresistible appeal to the PLO rank-and-file. The appeal grew stronger in the wake of the gruesome massacre of the Palestinian commandos at the hands of the Jordanian army in September, 1970. Abu Iyad, a top-ranking Al-Fatah leader, declared in January, 1971 that China was the "principal international friend" of the commandos and that in the future Al-Fatah would be leaning more and more on Peking for support and help.[10] This coincided with a corresponding shift in Chinese policy toward the commandos emphasizing unity among the various groups within the PLO. An official statement issued in Peking on September 21, 1970 accused the United States of setting the scene for the liquidation of the Palestinian "revolutionary armed forces." It also assured the commandos of China's "firm support" for their struggle and exhorted them to fight "a long war" which, it declared, they were bound to win.[11]

Peking's policy in regard to the various efforts made at the U.N., superpower, or four-power levels in search of a political solution of the Arab-Israeli question is a corollary of its thesis on people's war. It consistently rejected "imposed," "compromise," or "superpower" solutions of the Arab-Israeli problem, arguing that a political settlement would not only scuttle the Palestinian people's struggle for their national rights but also entail surrender of some Arab territory in Sinai, the West Bank, and the Golan Heights. It said that rights or territories lost in war, could be regained only through war. It explained its rejection of the Security Council resolution of November 22, 1967 in these terms, and also on the grounds that

9. Medzini, op.cit., p. 36.

10. See Arab World Weekly (Beirut), February 13, 1971, pp. 6–13.

11. Robert Guillain, "China in the Middle East," Survival (London), XIII (January, 1971), 22–24.

it was the outcome of "U.S.-Soviet collaboration in speeding up the creation of a Middle East Munich." The point was reiterated by Chiao Kuan-hua, the head of the Chinese delegation, in his maiden speech before the United Nations General Assembly in November, 1971: "No one has the right to seek to conclude political deals behind the backs of the Palestinians and other Arabs so as to injure their right to existence and their other national rights." [12] Peking also accused the United States and the Soviet Union of promoting a "no war, no peace" situation in the Middle East. According to this thesis, Moscow and Washington were on the one hand struggling against each other over the Middle East and on the other conspiring together. [13]

China's criticism of the superpower moves toward a cease-fire and a negotiated settlement following the 1973 October War was even more scathing. In Peking's view, Israel had been encouraged by the "support and connivance of the superpowers" to launch a premeditated attack on the Arabs. The "American imperialists" were as much responsible for the Israeli adventure as the "Soviet revisionists and social imperialists." The former gave massive arms aid to Israel, the latter gave it manpower support by permitting emigration of Soviet Jews. The Soviet arms aid to the Arabs was intended not to help the Arabs win the war but to "bind the limbs of the Arab countries and people." [14] On October 23, Chiao Kuan-hua told the Security Council that the draft resolution produced by the superpowers on the previous day was "even more ambiguous than resolution 242." He denounced it as "a scrap of paper, a fraud, which can solve no problems" and added that "the broad masses of the Arab people will never allow themselves to be confronted by the two superpowers perpetually." [15] The Chinese, however, did not veto the cease-fire resolution. Instead, they abstained from the vote in deference, according to Chiao Kuan-hua, to "the desire of certain countries concerned." [16]

In sum, Chinese policy favored a military solution through protracted struggle. To achieve this goal, the Chinese recommended the course

---

12. Quoted in Cooley, *op.cit.*, p. 19.

13. Chou En-lai's statement at a banquet in honor of Husain al-Shafei, the Egyptian vice-president, on September 21, 1973. *Indian Express* (New Delhi), September 22, 1973.

14. See the article by "Commentator" in the *People's Daily*, October 8, 1973. Reproduced in *Peking Review*, No. 41, October 12, 1973, p. 4.

15. Text of Chiao Kuan-hua's speech in *Peking Review*, No. 44, November 2, 1973, pp. 5-7.

16. *Ibid.*

of self-reliance and vigilance against the designs of the superpowers. It is needless to add that Peking's policy did not fully accord with Arab appraisal of the realities of the situation. The Arabs no doubt attached considerable value to China's general political support; but they were not convinced of the practicability of the Chinese thesis of people's war. Nor were they eager to take sides in Peking's ongoing ideological feud with Moscow.

PAKISTANI AND INDIAN POLICY IN THE MIDDLE EAST

Shortly after the outbreak of the 1967 June War Pakistan's President Mohammad Ayub Khan declared that it was his country's "bounden duty and fixed policy to support all just causes of the Muslims."[17] In October, 1973, Prime Minister Zulfiqar Ali Bhutto observed:

> The way we look at the Middle East conflict is that the whole of the Muslim world is on trial. This is a test not only for the Arabs but for the Islamic world . . . this is as much our struggle, this is as much a part of our destiny as it is of the Arabs. We cannot draw a distinction.[18]

These two statements underline the pronounced emphasis in Pakistan's Middle East policy on the bond of Islamic unity. It can be traced to the "two-nation theory," first propounded by Mohammed Ali Jinnah, the founder of Pakistan, which regarded the Hindus and Muslims of India as constituting two distinct nations, the latter having a special bond with the Muslim world. Shortly after its creation, Pakistan was designated an Islamic republic, and, one of the directive principles laid down by its first constitution stipulated that "the State shall endeavour to strengthen the bonds of unity among Muslim countries."

In its early phase, Pakistan's Middle East policy was directed toward the establishment of "a Commonwealth of Muslim nations." On a wider plane, however, there was keen interest in close relations with the Western powers, evidently with a view to obtaining foreign economic and military aid. In April, 1954, Pakistan and Turkey concluded an agreement for friendly cooperation, which Pakistan projected as the first major step towards Islamic solidarity. About 1955, however, this agreement was consummated into the Baghdad

17. *Dawn* (Karachi), June 8, 1967.
18. *Motherland* (New Delhi), October 31, 1973.

Pact and its Islamicity became suspect. The pact envisaged cooperation between the signatory states "for security and defence" within the larger framework of "maintenance of peace and security in the Middle East region"—a proposition which inevitably aroused the suspicion of nonaligned Arab nations. The broad Arab consensus was that the pact was designed to contain the soaring upsurge of Arab nationalism and to perpetuate Western presence in the Middle East under the facade of a security alliance. The pact also enjoyed the official blessings of the United States—a country whose solicitude for Israel was well known—and thus gave rise to speculation about its possible implications for the Arab-Israeli problem. Even conservative Saudi Arabia was astonished to find that an "Islamic state as that of Pakistan should accede to those who have joined hands with the Zionist Jews." [19]

The inherent contradiction between Pakistan's commitment to pan-Islamism and its enthusiastic membership in a Western-sponsored military alliance surfaced during the 1956 Suez crisis. The Anglo-French-Israeli invasion of Egypt in October aroused deep public indignation in Pakistan toward that country's pro-Western policy. Although Prime Minister Suharwardy conceded that the invasion was a threat to the Muslim world, he added that the threat came not from the United Kingdom but from elsewhere. After the Baghdad Pact council meeting in November, 1956 (from which the United Kingdom was excluded), the Pakistani prime minister blamed Egypt for "blocking" the Suez Canal. [20] President Nasser countered by objecting to the inclusion of a Pakistani contingent in the United Nations Emergency Force. Pakistan's Middle East policy then began to shift from pan-Islamism to "pak-Islamism," on the supposition that every Muslim country must first become strong and then think of Islamic unity.

The Iraqi Revolution of July, 1958 was a serious setback to the Baghdad Pact and caused Pakistan to realize the importance of Arab nationalism. During his visit to Egypt in November, 1960, President Ayub Khan observed that Islam was no longer a solid tie between peoples and that nationalism was the dominant force, though he also added that "no territorial or political consideration will separate Muslims from Muslims." [21] In his political autobiography Ayub Khan frankly decries the pan-Islamists as being "no more than a bunch of busybodies dabbling and interfering in the affairs of others on

19. Arif Hussain, *Pakistan: Its Ideology and Foreign Policy* (London, 1966), p. 142.
20. *Ibid.*, p. 144.
21. *Ibid.*, pp. 150–51.

the pretext of universal Muslim brotherhood."[22] In actual practice, however, Pakistan's Middle East policy continued to be articulated in Islamic rather than secular terms. For example, Islamabad gave unreserved support to the Arabs on the issue of restoration of Jerusalem to Arab sovereignty, but was reticent about the commandos' liberation struggle.

Another constricting factor in Pakistani policy is its tie with the Western powers, particularly the United States. Although the CENTO link is a relic of the Cold War era with little or no practical current relevance, the tie with Iran and Turkey has been sustained under the Istanbul Pact on Regional Cooperation for Development (July, 1964). The link with the United States is exemplified by the U.S.-Pakistani bilateral agreement on cooperation for security and defence of March, 1959. Pakistan's close relations with pro-Western monarchies are partly an extension of its pro-American policy. Both in 1967 and in 1973, however, Pakistan gave full-throated support to the Arab cause. Its permanent representative to the United Nations moved the two resolutions on Jerusalem adopted by the General Assembly in July, 1967. At the same time, Pakistan supported the Jordanian monarchy in its confrontation with the commandos in September, 1970. The presence of Pakistani military personnel in Amman was confirmed by an official announcement that thirteen Pakistanis had been killed and seventeen injured. This lent substance to the charge levelled by commando organizations—notwithstanding strong denials by the Pakistani ambassador in Amman—that Pakistani troops had actively participated in the military operations against the Palestinians.[23]

India's policy toward the Arab-Zionist conflict has been influenced by a mixture of moral and practical considerations. The moral factor springs from the ethos generated by India's struggle for freedom. The Indian National Congress opposed the imposition of a "Jewish National Home" on the reluctant Palestinians beginning in the twenties when the Palestine question first emerged on the international scene. Gandhi, the unrivalled colossus of the Indian political scene during the three decades before independence, questioned the moral and political postulates of the Zionist claim. Nehru, on the other hand,

22. Field Marshal Mohammad Ayub Khan, *Friends Not Masters: An Autobiography* (London, 1967), p. 201.

23. See Najib E. Saliba, "Impact of the Indo-Pakistani War on the Middle East," *World Affairs* (Washington, D.C.), CXXXV, No. 2 (Fall, 1972), 131; and *Tribune* (Ambala), October 21, 1970.

saw the Palestine problem as a manifestation of the wider phenomenon of colonialism, as an attempt by the British to play off Jewish religious nationalism against Arab nationalism in order to protect their own imperial interests. India voted against the partition of Palestine and against Israel's subsequent admission to the United Nations on this ground.

In the post-independence period India developed manifold contacts with the Arab world. These contacts spanned an extensive field encompassing trade, joint industrial ventures, and mutual consultations on such major international issues as colonialism, racialism, and world peace. India also felt the Arab apprehension about the deleterious effects of global polarization on the security and independence of the developing nations. This found expression in the doctrine of nonalignment or positive neutralism and in the periodic conferences of nonaligned nations. More importantly, developments in the Middle East had a direct bearing on India's national needs and interests. About three-fourths of its exports and imports passed through the Suez Canal before its closure in June, 1967. More than two-thirds of India's oil requirements are met by imports, mostly from Arab producers. Above all, India was alarmed by recurrent Pakistani attempts to give a religious color to political issues confronting the Middle Eastern nations.

India's policy reflected the interplay of these factors and rested on three tenets: (1) rejection of the doctrine of religio-racial exclusiveness; (2) inadmissibility of territorial acquisitions by conquest; and (3) the desirability of a just and equitable political settlement. The first two principles were underlined by Prime Minister Indira Gandhi in an *Al Ahram* interview: "We oppose Israel not only because of our friendship with the Arabs, but also because we are opposed to the creation of states on a religious basis. Nor can we recognize territorial gains made through aggression."[24] India's concern about a just and equitable solution was exemplified by initiatives in various international forums regarding the legitimate rights of the Palestinians and the dispute over the waters of the Jordan River.

New Delhi's response to the 1967 June War was in keeping with its established policy on the Arab-Israeli problem. A fortnight before the war Indira Gandhi made the cautious statement that "India would not say or do anything which would have the effect of aggravating the situation" and that India's interests required peace in the area.[25]

24. Quoted in the *National Herald* (New Delhi), May 15, 1967.
25. *Hindustan Times* (New Delhi), May 22, 1967.

Peace was shattered by Israel's premeditated attack on Egypt, Syria, and Jordan and consequent occupation of Arab lands beyond the old armistice lines. Foreign Minister M. C. Chagla outlined India's stand in his address before the U.N. General Assembly on July 22, 1967. Chagla argued that the closing of the Straits of Tiran did not warrant the subsequent Israeli action because there was no universally established rule of international law on freedom of navigation applicable to the Gulf of Aqaba and also because, even under the Geneva convention, innocent passage of foreign ships through the territorial waters of another state was not an absolute right. Enunciating the cardinal principles by which a lasting peace could be established in the Middle East region, Chagla said that a country could not go to war merely because it felt that a threat to its security existed. Secondly, no aggressor could be permitted to retain the fruits of aggression. Thirdly, it was not permissible for a country to acquire the territory of another state in order to be able to bargain from a position of strength. And, finally, rights could not be established, territorial disputes could not be settled, and boundaries could not be adjusted, through an armed conflict.[26]

Early in July, India and Yugoslavia, on behalf of eighteen nonaligned nations, moved a draft resolution in the General Assembly calling for unconditional Israeli withdrawal from the occupied lands. Explaining India's stand G. Parthasarathi, India's permanent representative to the U.N., told the assembly that Israeli withdrawal should precede consideration of other issues. The problem, he emphasized, could be dealt with only on the basis of the "first thing coming first." Speaking of the Latin American draft, which India did not support, Parthasarathi observed:

> It couples withdrawals with a settlement of complicated issues and thus it becomes a formula for bargaining from a position of strength by Israel. . . . it does not give primacy to the central issue of immediate withdrawals. No state member of the U.N., particularly no small state, could ever

---

26. On the following day, Gerald Ford, minority leader of the U.S. House of Representatives, criticized India for siding with Egypt as "it [India] may now be losing badly needed grain because of action of the U.A.R. government." (This referred to the closure of the Suez Canal which affected food shipments to India.) Ford continued: "It is the crudest of ironies that India should be deprived of 27,000 tons of American surplus grain by a nation whose side it has taken in an international dispute. I would suggest the Indians reconsider their attitude towards the disputants in the Middle East." *Times of India* (New Delhi) and *Indian Express*, June 24, 1967.

agree to negotiate so long as alien forces remain on its soil and it is subjected to duress.[27]

Neither of the two draft resolutions could muster the required two-thirds majority. New Delhi then sounded Belgrade and Cairo with a view to evolving a new draft which would combine mutually reconcilable elements of the nonaligned and Latin American draft resolutions. Early in November, 1967, together with Mali and Nigeria, India moved a draft resolution in the Security Council which, while calling upon Israel to vacate the territories it had occupied, stipulated that "every state has the right to live in peace and complete security free from threats or acts of war and, consequently, all states in the area should terminate the state or claim of belligerency and settle their international disputes by peaceful means." It also called for "a just settlement of the question of Palestine refugees" and for "guarantees of freedom of navigation in accordance with international law through international waterways in the area."[28] Even though the draft was acceptable to several member states, it did not find favor with the U.S. government, which emphasized the need to formulate what it called "conceptual guidelines" rather than a specific determination of the principles of settlement. Abba Eban, the Israeli foreign minister, took exception to the exclusion of the Straits of Tiran from the three-nation draft and wildly branded it an "irrational draft" and even an "Arab draft."[29] The Israeli prime minister, on the other hand, found the draft unacceptable because it called for unconditional withdrawal, and he alleged that the Soviet Union was the moving spirit behind the three-nation initiative.[30] The British draft eventually adopted by the Security Council on November 22, 1967 was deliberately ambiguous on the vital question of Israeli withdrawal from all the occupied lands.

India's pro-Arab policy was subsequently severely tried by India's unfortunate exclusion from the Rabat Islamic summit. The summit was occasioned by the burning of the Al-Aqsa Mosque in Jerusalem in August, 1969, a sacrilege promptly condemned by India. "The shocking incident," said India's minister for external affairs in a

27. *Times of India,* July 6, 1967.
28. *Times of India,* November 9, 1967.
29. *Hindustan Times,* November 10, 1967.
30. *Times of India,* November 14, 1967.

statement before Parliament, "makes it imperative that the Security Council resolution on Jerusalem be implemented without delay." "Israel," he added, "could not be absolved of responsibility for this outrage."[31] Samar Sen, India's permanent representative to the U.N., told the Security Council on September 11, that "this incident represents a much wider malaise and is a direct consequence of the illegal occupation by Israel of the holy city of Jerusalem and many other Arab areas." He also warned against attempts to turn it into a "religious issue" which would only complicate further the difficult Arab-Israeli problem. Some Arab monarchies, nevertheless, issued a call for *jehad* against Israel and later, under Pakistani instigation, rescinded India's invitation to the summit. In India the incident led to a barrage of indignant criticism of India's pro-Arab policy and the recall of envoys from Morocco and Jordan. The storm soon blew over as the commonalty of Indo-Arab interests healed the rift.

India's response to the 1973 October War reemphasized New Delhi's policy on the Arab-Israeli problem. Shortly after the outbreak of war an official spokesman stated that Israel's aggression and its refusal to vacate the occupied territories was the cause of tension in the Middle East. This intransigence on the part of Israel was also "the basic cause leading to the present outbreak of hostilities." He further added that if an escalation of the conflict was to be averted it was essential that the Security Council resolution of November 22, 1967 be implemented forthwith by Israel.[32] On October 20, Indira Gandhi declared that India's "total sympathies" were with the Arabs, whose lands had been occupied following the Israeli aggression.[33] Earlier, Samar Sen had outlined the Indian stand on the cease-fire proposal in his statement before the U.N. Security Council:

> Israel must withdraw from the territories occupied by its forces as a result of the June, 1967 war. Unless this basic principle is accepted by the Council as a whole it will be both unfair and unjust for the Council to ask for a cease-fire which will leave vast territories of Egypt, Jordan, and Syria in the illegal occupation of Israel. . . . We, like all other delegations, would like to see the present hostilities cease, but they can cease only when withdrawal of Israeli forces has been accepted by Israel and in practice begun.

31. *Patriot* (New Delhi), August 27, 1969.
32. *National Herald*, October 8, 1973.
33. *Hindustan Times*, October 21, 1973.

In a pointed reference to the U.S. representative's suggestion that the parties concerned should return to the "position before the hostilities broke out," Sen remarked: "We agree with the statement, but since the hostilities broke out on June 5, 1967, the parties concerned should return to the line that separated them on that date."[34]

The Indian press and public opinion were, however, less than unanimous in their response to the October war. While the government's policy enjoyed wide public support, the opposition parties, excluding the Communists, criticized it in varying degrees mainly on the ground that the Arab countries had supported Pakistan during the Indo-Pakistani conflict over Bangladesh in December, 1971. This criticism was also mirrored in the national press. Representative of the temperate reaction was an editorial comment in the *Hindustan Times:*

> Even though Egypt and Syria may have taken the initiative in the latest round of fighting, their action cannot be termed as aggression in so far as they are fighting in their own territories lost to Israel in 1967. The war is being fought on Arab soil, and, in a larger sense, Israel has provoked the war by not adopting a more flexible attitude in negotiating a peace settlement, especially after the overtures and substantial concessions made by President Sadat.[35]

CONCLUSION

The attitudes and policies of India, Pakistan, and China towards the Arab-Zionist conflict signify both consensus and divergence. While China articulates its policy in ideological terms, the Indian approach stresses the need for just and equitable settlement consistent with the twin principles of national self-determination and the inadmissibility of making territorial gains through aggression. Pakistan gives primacy to the religious factor. The resultant nuances of style and accent reflect the respective interests and concerns of the three nations. At the same time, their policies indicate a measure of positive consensus on the merits of the Arab case—a consensus broadly shared by most of the Asian nations.

34. *The Hindu* (Madras), October 11, 1973.
35. October 8, 1973.

Ragaei el Mallakh

ARAB OIL AND THE WORLD ECONOMY

THE YEAR 1973 HAS PROVEN PIVOTAL in the place of the Arab nations within the world economy. The October war precipitated the first effective imposition by the Arab oil producers of an embargo shored up by production cutbacks. Aside from the political leverage exerted on the consuming countries, this move helped set the stage for a long sought increase and rectification of crude oil prices. The rise in prices has enabled the members of the Organization of the Petroleum Exporting Countries (OPEC), Arab and non-Arab alike, to accumulate massive capital surplus funds estimated as high as $60 billion by the end of 1974. Such a surplus, employed efficiently and judiciously, could assist the still underdeveloped Arab world to meet its developmental efforts in industry, agriculture, and the upgrading of human resources. It might be important here for those who begrudge this surplus to the oil producers to recall that the average per capita income in the Arab world is still very low, about $700 annually as compared to over $4,500 for the United States. The regional potential of the Arab economy remains basically untouched.

THE EMBARGO AND "PROJECT INDEPENDENCE"

The impact of the Arab embargo on the American economy has been considerable. By January, 1974, oil imports were down by 2.7 million barrels per day, lowering overall petroleum supply by some

14 per cent below expected consumption, this according to the Federal Energy Administration's *Project Independence: A Summary* issued in November, 1974. The report finally admitted that, in addition to the inconvenience caused by gasoline shortages, the gross national product (GNP) of the United States dropped by $10 to $20 billion during the embargo and unemployment caused by the embargo amounted to 500,000 workers. It went on to note:

> It is true that a few years earlier, an embargo would have had no appreciable domestic effect. On the other hand, if the embargo had been delayed until several years in the future, when petroleum imports would have amounted to 50 percent of domestic consumption, there would have been no effective means of cushioning the domestic economy from the impact.[1]

Admitting this reality was a slow and reluctant process. The constant revision upwards of statistics regarding U.S. dependence on Arab oil served to confuse and decrease the public's credibility vis-a-vis governmental pronouncements and furthered the image of governmental mismanagement, poor planning, and even lack of basic knowledge in the realm of energy requirements.

The first element in the painful acknowledgement of the embargo's actual economic impact on the United States has been the reticence of government officials to link security of supply of Arab oil with the Arab-Israeli problem and, more specifically, American foreign policy. In March, 1973, Assistant Secretary of State Joseph Sisco was still insisting that the mutuality of economic interest between Arab petroleum countries and the United States would most likely not be "jeopardized" by the Arab-Israeli dispute.[2] President Nixon's first energy message in April of that year made no connection with the Middle East in the section on oil imports, particularly in failing to mention the source for the expected increases in imports. The degree of dependence on Arab oil was estimated only with an eye to Europe, not to the United States.[3] In September, responding to a Saudi Arabian initiative urging a more evenhanded American stance in the Middle East, Nixon for the first time linked U.S. oil requirements to foreign policy. The misconceptions he reiterated at that press conference

1. Federal Energy Administration, *Project Independence: A Summary* (Washington: U.S. Government Printing Office, November, 1974), p. 18.
2. *Platt's Oilgram*, March 30, 1973, p. 1.
3. *Petroleum Intelligence Weekly*, April 23, 1973, Supplement, p. 19.

330 / INTERNATIONAL DIMENSIONS

included: (1) an implied low level of American dependence on Arab oil, by contrasting U.S. reliance with that of Europe and (2) that the Arab producing countries needed the United States as a market quite as much as the United States needed them as a source of petroleum.[4] Indeed, the October war scuttled the long-cherished U.S. government hopes that talk of a cutoff was bruited only by the so-called radical Arab states—that oil and politics need not mix—although why such an idea was attached to Middle Eastern oil is surprising when there is abundant evidence that oil and politics mix domestically in the United States in Texas, Alaska, Colorado, and Louisiana to cite but a few examples.

The failure to clearly explain the degree of American need for Arab oil has proven self-deluding. Some oil experts have belittled the American dependence on Middle Eastern petroleum—Morris Adelman placed the share of U.S. imports from the Arab world and specifically Saudi Arabia as insignificant, under 5 per cent.[5] U.S. government estimates, and those of Senator Henry Jackson, were also on the order of 5 per cent, this just prior to the embargo. In early October, 1973, the government placed the expected shortage at about 10 per cent. But faced with the cold reality of an Arab oil cutoff, Nixon contended in his energy message of November 7 that the United States was confronted by "the most acute shortages of energy since World War II," at least a 10 to 17 per cent gap between demand and supply during that winter.

Admission of the actual dependence on Arab oil slowly edged nearer reality. A reputable trade publication, *Petroleum Intelligence Weekly,* placed the level of oil imports (crude and product combined) from Arab sources until the end of November, 1973 at a staggering three million barrels per day or 17 per cent of total U.S. demand.[6] Rationing, conservation, and increased domestic production could raise supply by as much as 1.5 million barrels per day or half the 1973 level of Middle East imports—at best eight per cent of that level of consumption.

Without subjecting the reader to an inundation of supportive details, it suffices to point out that for at least the next decade, like it or not, the United States will have ever closer and most extensive energy ties with the Arab world. For several reasons: (1) in order to have

4. *Ibid.,* September 10, 1973, pp. 7-9.

5. Letters to the Editor, *The New York Times,* September 10, 1973.

6. *Petroleum Intelligence Weekly,* October 29, 1973, pp. 1-2. Product imports refer to refined petroleum products.

avoided a shortage in 1973, the United States expected not only no cutoff, but an estimated 30 per cent annual increase from Saudi Arabian production alone (the world's largest single exporter and possessor of petroleum); (2) raising domestic production cannot be effected immediately or at low cost. New offshore production has a lead-time of approximately five years with spiraling costs. Opening Alaska's North Slope oil fields depends on the pipeline, expected now to cost almost $6 billion and to reach maximum delivery capacity by about 1980.

The much-touted shale oil development, apart from serious environmental drawbacks and problems of water scarcity for processing, cannot be commercially available much before 1981. The use of nuclear technology to release natural gas through underground detonations was dealt a sharp reversal through the passage of a referendum in the state of Colorado in the November 1974 general elections; the public voted that no future nuclear blasting of this type could take place without allowing a state-wide vote on each such undertaking. The nuclear energy goal in "Project Independence" is to reduce the lead-time from ten to six years in bringing nuclear power plants onstream. Speeding up the process may mean lower safety and pollution standards as well as higher costs. Expanded coal production also faces obstacles such as mine safety standards, the lowering of pollution control levels to allow burning of higher sulfur content coal, capitalization requirements, and logistics to get the fuel to major consumption centers. Moreover, coal prices for the high grade of this fossil fuel have quadrupled since the 1973 oil embargo. Being realistic, petroleum's share in total energy consumption cannot be drastically reduced without cataclysmic repercussions in the transportation and industrial sectors.

Given the energy consumption patterns which indicate the continued leadership of oil and natural gas, where will the United States get the required amounts? Canada and Venezuela, the so-called secure Western hemisphere sources, cannot and will not take up the slack. Both have national conservation policies and the latter has decreasing oil reserves. In November, 1974 Canada announced a curb on oil exports to the United States. This stunned the American government, which has had a habit of viewing Canadian natural resources as something of an extension of its own domestic supply. Canadian supplies are scheduled to drop to 800,000 barrels per day by January 1, 1975, 650,000 barrels per day by mid-1975, and zero by 1983.[7]

7. *Oil and Gas Journal*, December 2, 1974, p. 23.

Nearly one-fourth of U.S. crude oil imports normally has originated from Canada. Furthermore, with natural gas production declining in the United States by about 3 per cent in 1974 as compared with the previous year, severe shortages for the 1974-75 winter months are anticipated. The shortfall between supply and demand of natural gas was complicated by the recent Canadian decision to almost double the price of natural gas exported to the United States by January, 1975. Additionally, the United States was given the option of accepting the price increase or paying the current (1974) price with termination of Canadian imports after two years.[8] Nearly all American imports of natural gas are from Canada.

The fervor with which some in the United States greeted recent oil discoveries in Mexico was immediately dampened by the Mexican government avowal to price its oil in line with prevailing international costs and to peg its future production (still a matter of conjecture depending upon the extent of reserves) to achieve maximum governmental income with no preferential arrangements for the United States. As for other possible sources of petroleum imports, Nigeria and Indonesia, compared to the Middle East, are still relatively small producers with much lower reserves. By 1980, about 40 per cent of U.S. petroleum consumption will come from imports of Middle Eastern and North African oil.

OIL PRICES AND U.S. SCAPEGOATISM

In the months since the embargo, a coalescence has evolved in the United States incorporating a doomsday mentality on inflation and oil prices, scapegoatism in explaining American economic woes, and opportunism by a few politicians. In speaking before a New York audience on September 21, 1974, Senator Henry Jackson stated: "I think the entire industrialized world faces a clear and present danger of economic destruction by the Arab oil cartel."[9] If an oil cartel exists, and many question that it strictly falls into the cartel category, then it is OPEC. Seven Arab nations belong to OPEC, along with Ecuador, Gabon, Indonesia, Iran, Nigeria, and Venezuela—all non-Arab states.

In excess of two-thirds of U.S. oil imports come from Venezuela, Canada, and other non-Arab sources. As noted earlier, both Venezuela

8. *Monthly Energy Review* (Federal Energy Administration), October, 1974, p. 4.
9. *Denver Post*, September 22, 1974.

and Canada have supported higher petroleum prices as well as production cuts and/or limiting exports to the United States. Yet how often does one see a cartoon showing the oil spigot held by a business-suited Canadian or a sombrero-wearing Latin American instead of the stereotyped Arab in flowing robes and headdress? In this vein, much of the mass media in the United States has fallen into the habit of using the terms OPEC and Arab interchangably with the result that, by plan or merely chance, the Arabs almost solely bear the onus for the energy crisis and the price levels for petroleum.

In tracing recent events, a key date is October 16, 1973, when OPEC announced that the price of crude oil produced by its members would be doubled. Although this move was given its leading impetus by the Shah of Iran, the trend toward higher posted prices was discernable in negotiations between the producing nations and the oil companies over the preceding two years. Since 1970 the producing countries had felt the negative impact of two dollar devaluations and rising inflation in industrial imports as well as in certain imported agricultural products. Not only was the increase substantial, but OPEC had moved unilaterally for the first time. The outbreak of the October war and the Arab embargo and production cutbacks coincided to reinforce the price hike by throwing supply and demand out of balance.[10] A rush to buy up the oil left on the market led to a further doubling of the price announced December 23 by the Shah of Iran. In less than three months, from October 16 until January 1, 1974, oil prices had quadrupled over the level formerly established.

Since the opening of 1974, the only initiative to reduce oil prices has emanated from Arab producers such as the November 11, 1974 decision by Saudi Arabia, United Arab Emirates, and Qatar. Regardless of the actualities in oil pricing, Senator Jackson advanced his scapegoat theme by suggesting that economic countermeasures in food be applied by the United States: "I'm not talking about the non-Arab world. I'm talking about the Arab world."[11] Despite the OPEC increases, the alternates to Middle Eastern oil are as expensive if not more so. For example, North Sea oil, always expensive to produce, is even more costly due to runaway inflation. A concrete platform ordered

10. The sustained OPEC negotiations and an examination of the functioning of that body as a cartel is examined in Shukri Ghanem, "OPEC: A Cartel or a Group of Competing Nations?" in Ragaei El Mallakh and Carl McGuire (eds.), *Energy and Development* (Boulder, Colorado: International Research Center for Energy and Economic Development, 1974), pp. 175–190.

11. *Denver Post*, September 22, 1974.

in December, 1973 is expected to cost about $88.8 million installed, while another of the same design ordered only six months later is estimated to cost $129.6 million.[12] Synthetic fuels are still above the current OPEC price levels. Liquefied coal or shale oil produced in quantity in the 1980's would be approximately $15 per barrel without taking into consideration inflation in the intervening years.[13]

The oversimplification often evident in discussions of Middle East oil and international energy problems can lead to dangerous miscalculations; it can raise the American public's expectations that a single item (that is, higher oil prices due to Arab "greed") is to blame for galloping inflation and the U.S. energy crunch. Yet the American inflationary spiral "took off," so to speak, much before the energy crisis. The Vietnam war was a key factor which did not end with the withdrawal of troops; the more than $130 billion spent there had no positive effect on the U.S. economy. The United States continues sizable expenditures for armaments and military assistance to a few selected countries; this is inflationary in itself and negatively affects the U.S. balance of payments. Instead of facing up to their own responsibility for inflation, some would prefer to blame the problems on an outside sinister force. One high ranking government official recently even linked the energy crisis and high oil prices to "our [United States] liberty that in the end is at stake."

The excessive fears, as voiced by Arthur Burns of the Federal Reserve Board, that the petro-dollar accumulations will actually ruin the economic system of the United States and the industrialized West are clearly unfounded when analyzed. In the first nine months of 1974, the oil-producing nations have invested about $10.5 billion in the United States of which $5 billion went into U.S. government securities. A number of economists question the decisions of Arthur Burns which followed an excessively loose monetary policy allowing for an eight per cent annual increase in the supply of money. The abrupt reversal of that inflationary policy, cutting back to a 2 per cent increase, no doubt is contributing to the economic straits of the United States.

A good case can be made that the oil producers deserve the prices they are getting. The cost of petroleum is tied directly to the cost of industrial products, and commodity prices have risen faster than oil prices. In real terms, the price of petroleum was lower in 1973

12. *Oil and Gas Journal*, November 25, 1974, p. 56.

13. Estimate by Robert Baldwin, president of Gulf Energy and Minerals Company, in El Mallakh and McGuire, *op. cit.*, p. 197.

than in 1959. Certain oil countries have only fifteen to twenty years of remaining reserves at their current production rate. These states cannot be expected to sacrifice their futures, including their industrial development and attempts to build more self-sustaining balanced economies, simply to meet consumer requirements without some sort of trade-off. The blustering of some American politicians is not especially conducive, considering that these same spokesmen now want to ignore, at least in relation to oil prices, the functioning of the very market system they claim to cherish.

In equating food and oil, as is frequently done, a very crucial distinction is thrust aside—agricultural products are renewable while petroleum is a wasting asset. If the current oil price is contrived and artifically high as has been suggested, then that price would not have lasted. Actually, the posted price in 1973 and 1974 has, at times, fallen below the realized price per barrel. Those who begrudge the oil nations $8 to $9 per barrel should look to the consumer nations where per barrel taxes on gasoline alone are estimated at $5 in the United States, $14 in Japan, and $28 in Western Europe. Recently other raw material prices have skyrocketed: bauxite rose almost 500 per cent, phosphates tripled, and tin increased 42 per cent.

Suddenly there is hand wringing over the plight of the poorer nations. Senator Jackson insisted: "I think we have to seriously consider how far we're going to let them (the Arabs) injure the poor in our country and the poor in other countries of the world."[14] The developing world sees such concern largely as lip service for three reasons:

1. U.S. economic aid to this bloc has been declining in both absolute and relative terms. It was noted in the Rome food conference concluded in autumn 1974 that the United States is extending but one-fifth its level in grains of a decade ago.

2. The OPEC nations themselves fall into the developing category. As cited earlier, the Arab world's average per capita annual income remains at about $700.

3. The OPEC countries give massive amounts of aid. Kuwait's foreign assistance accounts for almost 8 per cent of its GNP, a proportion over 15 times greater than the U.S. half of 1 per cent. Saudi Arabia is the world's largest donor to developing countries, exceeding $3 billion a year as compared to the U.S. total of $2.5 billion annually.[15] It is helpful to recall the relative economic bases of the U.S. and Saudi economies: the former has a population of

14. *Denver Post*, September 22, 1974.

15. *Christian Science Monitor*, October 15, 1974 (Western edition).

210 million, while the latter has no more than six million.

Instead of orchestrating for confrontation or even war, it might be wiser to press for cooperation and coordination.[16] The United States should move forward in energy conservation and simultaneously push the rational development of alternative energy in conjunction with the oil nations themselves. Petroleum is becoming too valuable and limited to be burned simply as fuel—the traditional usage pattern to date. The world is clearly interdependent in natural resources as seen in present American imports: at least eighty per cent of U.S. consumption of bauxite, nickel, tin, manganese, chromium, and one-third of its iron needs. Aside from raw materials supply, there are economic ties to be forged and strengthened in investment, trade, and resources mobility. Scapegoatism could make global economic interdependence more difficult but it cannot alter the reality of that interdependence.

ARAB ABSORPTIVE CAPACITY: A REGIONAL PERSPECTIVE

A spinoff effect of the October war has been a substantial upsurge of interest and study of the impact of the rapidly accumulating capital surplus funds in the Arab oil countries and the absorptive capacity of their economies. Institutions such as the International Bank for Reconstruction and Development (World Bank), the International Monetary Fund, and the Organization for Economic Cooperation and Development (OECD), as well as non–Arab governments, private corporations, and banks are actively pursuing such investigations. The Arab world itself is lagging far behind in this research. This interest has been motivated not only by the energy crisis but also by the desire (and actual need) to attract Arab funds to Western countries and international agencies as well as to lessen the impact of the growing Arab financial influence within the world monetary system. Understandably, the impetus behind the non–Arab world's attention is geared more to its protection and economic interests than toward the economic

16. The possibility of military action in the Middle East to secure petroleum has been explored and mentioned by politicians, some U.S. government officials, and journalists. Examples include "Will U.S. Seize Mideast Oil?" and "Odds Are Still Against a Depression," *U.S. News and World Report*, December 2, 1974, pp. 18-20 and 57. In an ad by the Zionist Organization of America, it is suggested that Israel could, in the event of another Middle East conflict, move to take over "the active sources of revenue for the Arab war chest [the Arab oil countries]," *The New York Times*, November 20, 1974.

development of the region—that should be the target of the Arab states themselves. And the most efficient approach to this latter goal would be a regional perspective.

The surplus funds currently accumulated have initiated a new international balance of wealth. Nonetheless, the entire Arab world requires the channeling of this newly acquired financial wealth into developmental economic power. As of 1974, the Arab surplus funds totaled some $40 billion, a substantial amount of which could be absorbed on the regional level. The Arab countries as a group would have a higher absorptive capacity than if the individual states' capacities were merely totaled. This result could be attributed to (1) regional projects, particularly in transport, communication, regulation of shared rivers, and complimentarities in industries and agriculture, and (2) economies of scale to be derived from massive economic enterprises. Perhaps the most crucial characteristic of oil exploitation is that petroleum is a nonrenewable asset; direct oil revenue has, therefore, a limited life span and accordingly investment in diversified and renewable growth is absolutely critical.

A perspective on regional absorptive potential can bé gleaned from a brief résumé of the agricultural and industrial bases. For example, although the total area of the Arab world is about 3 billion acres, with 350 million acres cultivable, only 50 million are under cultivation of which only 15 million are under irrigation. Potentially the cultivable land, rainfed or irrigated, could be raised to over 300 million acres. The Arab world's population could reach approximately 150 million by 1985 and the density would then be two agricultural acres per person, a ratio close to that prevailing in the United States by that date. Development of Arab agriculture ultimately will depend on expanding output through mechanization (a costly process requiring capital which is a scarce factor in Arab capital deficit nations), coordination and specialization among the states of the region, and the development of agro-business complexes. If such development is attained, income from agriculture in the Arab Middle East could be increased from $3.5 billion to about $9.5 billion (at 1972 prices). Obviously agriculture, on a regional basis, is capable of absorbing large amounts of capital.[17]

17. Ragaei El Mallakh, "The Absorptive Capacity of the Arab World and Investment Policies," a paper given to the Conference on Investment Policies of Surplus Funds of Arab Oil Producing Countries sponsored by the Arab Planning Institute (a United Nations affiliate) and the Kuwait Economic Society, February 18-21, 1974, Kuwait, Kuwait, pp. 5-6.

Turning to industrialization, one can distinguish between the oil and non-oil based economies. The apparent line of industrialization in the petroleum states is petrochemicals, a capital intensive industry with considerable potential. To date, industry has played an extremely modest role in the oil-producing countries. In 1971, the total value of Saudi industrial production, excluding oil refining, represented only 1.7 per cent of the GNP. Out of approximately nine thousand industrial enterprises, only four employed two hundred or more persons. Industry in Libya faces certain constraints including the limited population of only two million, making the domestic market extremely small. Moreover, inadequate skills have led to a relatively low absorptive capacity. This is seen in the rapid growth of financial reserves and the fact that only half of the development allocations from 1970 to 1972 have actually been spent. As for the capital surplus Gulf oil producers, primarily Kuwait, Bahrain, Qatar, and the United Arab Emirates, they share certain characteristics: small populations, usually small geographical territories, relatively scanty agricultural sectors, if any, and a paucity of non-oil physical resources and water. Quite clearly, given these limitations and the need to develop more self-sustaining, balanced economies, industrialization in oil-based undertakings is the major, if not only, effective avenue currently available to them. Hence, conservation of their petroleum resource is a valid and long-term concern.

The non-oil producing Arab countries have a much greater potential for diversified growth. These nations have an abundance of more skilled labor and a more balanced sectoral mix. Industrialization can still be expanded substantially. The share of industrial production to GNP has reached the highest level in Egypt (23 per cent), followed by Tunisia and Syria (17 per cent each), Lebanon (13 per cent), and Jordan (11 per cent). A regional approach in the Arab world could circumvent the consequences of size and narrowness of the individual domestic markets. It could facilitate the movement of labor, managerial ability, and capital, as well as other production factors. In the past, mobility of capital has not been adequate.

There are three areas in which the absorptive capacity of the region and better utilization of funds could be expanded and improved:

1. The various Arab aid extending agencies and funds which have proliferated in recent years can be consolidated and/or coordinated. These include the Kuwait Fund for Arab Economic Development, the Abu Dhabi Fund for Arab Economic Development, the Arab Fund for Economic and Social Development, the Arab-African Bank, the Arab Bank for Industrial and Agricultural Development in Africa,

the newly created Iraqi and Saudi Arabian funds for external aid and financing, and the Islamic Development Bank.

2. Arab surplus funds could be used in payment of the outstanding foreign debts of non-oil Arab states such as Egypt, Jordan, and Syria. This would lessen the political and economic pressure on these states from non-regional powers, giving them greater freedom in economic and political matters.

3. Investment of Arab funds abroad might remain a valid option; however, this money should be invested not only where it is needed or the returns are secure or high, but where the atmosphere is appreciative if not welcoming. For example, the inflow of Arab dollars to the United States has been greeted by some public officials (e.g., former Senator Howard Metzenbaum) with insinuations of sinister motives along with excessive fears of foreign control. For years, American investments in foreign economies totaling some $90 billion have played important, sometimes dominant, roles. That the United States is now on the receiving end as well may take some getting used to. The fact that Arab investment in the United States is reducing the U.S. balance of payments deficit is overlooked. It also partially offsets the U.S. oil import bill owed to its major petroleum suppliers—Canada, Venezuela, and Nigeria—all non-Arab.

It took the military action of the 1973 October War to precipitate U.S. recognition and acknowledgement of the economic significance and validity of the Arab world. It also has opened up numerous avenues for extensive cooperation to the betterment of the entire international community given an acceptable political atmosphere and establishment of the concept of economic reciprocity.

Joe Stork

THE OIL WEAPON

THE CLOSE AFFINITY of politics and oil and politics and war have made it almost inevitable that war and oil in the Middle East should be closely intertwined. Conscious of this fact since at least 1948, U.S. political and military strategists have long attempted to formulate a policy toward the Zionist-Palestinian conflict. Since that time more than one Arab leader has publicly raised the threat to cut off oil exports to those countries supporting Israel. But the level of political collaboration and technical competence in and between the Arab states has been very slight; and the dependence of the industrialized countries on Arab oil has been limited. The Saudis refused to entertain such notions from the beginning, and the threat remained dim and distant.

Although limited embargoes were implemented in 1956 and 1967, they had little effect. In 1956 the United States was able to make up deliveries to Britain and France from domestic production. In 1967 the small percentage of U.S. imports from the Arab states and the ability of the major companies to re-route supplies rendered the embargo a farce. Arab radicals blamed this failure on the perfidy of reactionary oil producers like Saudi Arabia, who reciprocated by pinning the failure on the incompetence of the radicals.

The oil weapon was the implementation of production cutbacks and destination embargoes by the Arab producer states in order to pressure the United States and its allies to force Israel to withdraw from Arab territories seized in 1967 and 1973. The 1973 October War and the implementation of the oil weapon acquired a momentum and decisive influence. These two events effected qualitative changes in the structure of the world oil industry and altered the present alignment of political power in the Middle East. They accentuated the competitive economic and political relationship of the United States with the other industrial capitalist countries of Europe and Japan. Thus it is in an international context that the background, the course, and the consequences of the oil weapon must be explicated.

SAUDI MOVES BEFORE THE OCTOBER WAR

There has never been a unanimous consensus in the Arab world on the effectiveness of the oil embargo. While oil revenues can make the Arab soldier more effective, money, in the final analysis, has never been an effective substitute for direct military force. In other words, the strategic values of oil and petrodollars were not as military weapons: an economic boycott could never be of direct use to the Arab soldier facing Israeli gunners. The much touted power of the purse never meant much when the purse was used against a gun. So, with these notions in mind, the Arabs were never very much enchanted with the idea of an embargo. The rich oil–producing states wrapped a cloak of virtue around ever expanding production by declaring that oil had to be used as a "positive weapon." Oil would be a source of ever-growing revenues and it might then be discreetly dispensed to build up the military and economic strength of those Arab states that behaved themselves politically.

Debate about the potential of the oil weapon continued nonetheless. Given the conditions of surplus production and capacity that prevailed through 1970, it appeared axiomatic that no embargo could be effected without the support and participation of at least one of the two major producers, Saudi Arabia and Iran. They accounted for about two-thirds of Middle East production. Besides being non-Arab, Iran had a tacit strategic alliance with Israel, which was facilitated by the United States. In 1967, Iranian production was increased and used to supplement the Arab cutbacks. Iran, in short, could be counted on to sabotage and neutralize any Arab oil offensive. Saudi Arabia, for her part, had to maintain a modicum of solidarity with the rest of the Arab states in the struggle with Israel; oil–financed subsidies to Egypt and Jordan followed the Khartoum Conference in 1967. The oil weapon was, for Saudi Arabia, a lever for modifying and controlling the political behavior of the radical Arab states, notably Egypt. To those who called for a more direct use of Saudi oil production to pressure the

United States into a less pro-Israeli position, the constant Saudi refrain was that "oil and politics don't mix." Oil Minister Yamani offered a unique interpretation of the oil weapon in November, 1972:

> I must say that we do not believe in the use of oil as a political weapon in a negative manner. We believe that the best way for the Arabs to employ their oil is as a basis for true cooperation with the West, notably with the United States. In this way very strong economic ties are established which will ultimately reflect on our political relations.[1]

The changes in the structure of the oil industry which accelerated after 1970, notably the disappearance of surplus production and the increasing government control over production levels, renewed the momentum for a more militant stance. Imports of low-sulfur crude to the U.S. east coast were rising. Though still a small proportion of U.S. supplies, these imports accentuated the slowly growing reliance of the United States on Eastern Hemisphere sources. Studies by the oil industry lobby in the United States, such as the National Petroleum Council, stressed the growing shortage of domestic energy supplies and the accelerating dependence on foreign supplies. The Middle East, in particular Saudi Arabia, were stressed as the most likely if not the only sources for the coming decade. While much of this was self-serving propaganda in the drive for higher prices, profits, and subsidies, the general thrust of the argument was assailed by very few: the voracious appetite of Americans for energy resources could only be met over the next decade by Middle East imports.

This realization focused a good deal of attention on the stability and potential disruption of that source. The Saudis had managed after the 1967 war to isolate their oil policies from the contagious political emotions connected with the conflict with Israel. The new role of Saudi Arabia as the one country with the capacity and the willingness to expand production to meet growing American oil needs signalled the end of that isolation. In 1972, the Economic Council of the Arab League commissioned a study concerning the strategic use of Arab economic power in the fight with Israel.[2] The report took the view that while Arab interests in the long run would be best served by developing independent and autonomous industrially-based economies, in the short term a more restrictive policy towards

1. *Middle East Economic Survey (MEES)*, November 3, 1972.

2. The report, in Arabic, is reviewed in *Journal of Palestine Studies*, No. 9, Autumn, 1973.

oil production would both conserve wasting resources for future use and bring a significant degree of pressure to bear on the industrial consuming countries regarding their support for Israel. The report did not call for an embargo or cutback in oil production, but a slower rate of expansion than that desired by the consuming countries.[3] This tactic would allow maximum flexibility for escalation and de-escalation. The tactic of a freeze or constraint on production expansion was endorsed by a top Arab oil economist and former OPEC secretary general, Nadim Pachachi, in June, 1973, when he predicted it would be "quite sufficient to cause a world-wide supply crisis in a fairly short period of time."[4]

At this time Saudi Arabia was coming under considerable and increasing pressure to limit its rate of expansion, as its isolation from the Arab-Israeli confrontation was ending. Another factor in this process was the Egyptian shift to the right under Sadat. In order to consolidate the power of the new and old bourgeoisie represented by the Sadat regime, some concession to the patriotic sentiments of the Egyptian masses was necessary. Some means of restoring Egyptian sovereignty over the occupied Sinai was essential to undercut the insurgent political movement of students and workers that regularly had brought Egypt to the edge of political crisis since the 1967 war and especially since Nasser's death. With the changing balance in the oil markets, and the growing testimony from the United States about the importance of Middle East oil in that balance, politically conscious Arabs saw the irrefutable need for an oil policy that would match the rhetorical militance of the politicians. For Egypt the logical partner by geography and political temperament appeared to be Libya, and this was matched by Qaddafi's stress on the need for some specific form of Arab political union or federation. Qaddafi's staunch Islamic fundamentalist and anti-imperialist politics, though, forced Sadat to look to Saudi Arabia as an alternative. Faisal's regime, looking for a role that would give it pan-Arab legitimacy and limit the influence of radicals like Qaddafi, was inclined to cautious cooperation.

Qaddafi's inclination to confrontation and popular mobilization was countered by Faisal's emphasis on close ties to the United States. Faisal apparently had some role in Sadat's decision to expel the Russian military advisors in 1972 as a way of inviting the United States to use leverage with Israel to secure some territorial concession. There was no perceptible change in U.S. policy. Sadat went ahead with

3. *MEES*, June 15, 1974; *Washington Post*, April 19, 1973, and June 17, 1973.
4. *MEES*, June 1, 1973.

plans for an Arab federation comprised of Egypt, Libya, and Syria. In early 1973, after renewed clashes in Egyptian cities between militant students and workers and security forces, Sadat dispatched his national security advisor, Hafez Ismail, to Washington to sound out any possibile shifts in U.S. policy. Ismail's visit coincided with that of Golda Meir, and Washington's response was to leak word of a new shipment of Phantom jets to Israel. It appears that the Egyptian decision to go to war was made in the aftermath of these events.

The Saudis had some stake in the outcome, having argued to Sadat that a diminished Russian role would lead to a change in U.S. policy. In April Oil Minister Yamani paid one of his frequent visits to Washington, where he publicly linked oil and Israel for the first time. He reportedly told U.S. officials that Saudi Arabia would not expand production at the desired rate in the absence of a change in U.S. policy toward Israel. In a story accompanying an interview with Yamani, the *Washington Post* wrote:

> The Saudis are known to feel under increasing pressure from the radical Arab states and the Palestinian guerrillas to use their oil as a political weapon for pressuring Washington into forcing Israel into a compromise settlement with the Arabs.

It was later reported that King Faisal then called in the president of Aramco to stress that Saudi Arabia was "not able to stand alone much longer" in the Middle East as an American ally. Aramco cabled the details of Faisal's remarks to the American parent companies, who began taking out newspaper ads and appearing at Congressional hearings to warn of the need for an evenhanded American policy in the Arab-Israeli dispute. On the May 15, 1973 anniversary of the establishment of Israel, four oil-producing states engaged in a minor but symbolic stoppage of crude-oil production: Algeria, Kuwait, and Iraq for one hour and Libya for a full day. In June Libya nationalized the small American independent Bunker Hunt, invoking U.S. imperialism and support for Israel as a primary reason. Washington responded to the Saudi initiatives by offering to provide a squadron of Phantom jets. Saudi Arabia indicated the offer was not acceptable as a substitute for changing U.S. policy toward Israel. In July, the Palestine Liberation Organization endorsed the tactic of freezing oil production at present levels. Faisal let it be known that the debate inside Saudi ruling circles was between those who wanted to limit production increases and those who wanted to freeze them. Saudi Foreign Minister Saqqaf predicted that Arab oil would be denied to "those who help our enemy," but indicated any decision might not come for as long as a year.[5]

The Saudi campaign to use oil as a weapon was consistently restricted to the arena of communiqués and press interviews. Production for the first seven months of 1973 increased thirty-seven per cent over the previous year; July production was up an incredible sixty-two per cent, to 8.4 million barrels per day, with production scheduled to hit a whopping 10 million barrels per day by the beginning of 1974. The campaign aimed to secure an equally public and superficial indication of change in U.S. policy that would validate the Saudi-U.S. relationship and preclude the need to implement the "weapon." Above all, it was designed to neutralize mounting public pressure throughout the Arab world for some move, especially after the U.S. veto of a U.N. resolution condemning continued Israeli occupation of Arab territories captured in 1967. In August, Prince Abdullah, Faisal's brother and head of internal security forces, was in Britain and France shopping for arms and advisors, where he urged:

> All the Arab countries, whether oil producers or not, should act to prevent the debate on the use of oil from being transferred to the street . . . I deem it imperative for the Arabs to draw up a higher Arab oil policy whose aim should be to consolidate relations between friends and to isolate enemies. . . . We must differentiate between the uncompromising enemy and the potential friend. Only reason and a historical sense of responsibility can provide the right answers to these questions.[6]

This finely balanced public maneuvering continued through August and into early September when, at the conference of nonaligned nations in Algiers, it was predicted that some joint Arab oil stand would emerge. Standard Oil of California, one of Aramco's parents, sent a letter to its stockholders stressing the need for U.S. policy to understand "the aspirations of the Arab people and more positive support of their efforts toward peace in the Middle East." This aroused a predictable flurry of protest from some American Jewish organizations. The Libyan takeover of majority interest in Occidental and Oasis in mid-August and its nationalization decree of September 1, 1973, heightened the sense of brewing confrontation. Nixon's subsequent press statement involving the spectre of Mossadeq, along with well-

5. *Ibid.*, September 14, 1973.
6. *Ibid.*, August 17, 1973.

publicized desert warfare training operations of the U.S. Marines, did nothing to de-escalate the politics of oil.

A meeting of Arab oil ministers in Kuwait on September 4 was expected to produce policy suggestions for the Arab heads of state meeting in Algiers, but the traditional politics of the participants showed that nothing had really changed in the Saudi approach. There were no recommendations from the conference. It reportedly split between those states advocating seizure of controlling interest in U.S. oil operations, led by Libya and Iraq, and "those urging that oil shouldn't be used as a political weapon." Saudi Arabia reportedly stressed the need for a wait-and-see approach. Nixon reciprocated the next day with a statement that "both sides are at fault" in the Arab-Israeli conflict, prompting the *Wall Street Journal* headline: "Nixon Mutes Support for Israel as Arabs Appear to Get Results With Oil Threats."[7] The day after Nixon's press conference, the Saudis were delivering messages in various Western capitals playing down the widespread press reports of possible output restrictions directed against the United States.[8] Later in September there were reports of two new Kissinger initiatives: one was a secret peace plan which would have settled most of the particular territorial claims between Israel and the Arab states in Israel's favor; the other was an equally secret decision to pursue the special relationship with Saudi Arabia proposed a year earlier by Yamani. The policy under the new secretary of state was to be one of "compatability rather than confrontation."[9]

THE OIL WEAPON AND THE OCTOBER WAR

On October 6, 1973, Egypt and Syria launched full-scale military attacks against Israeli occupation forces. There were immediate calls from several quarters for the use of oil as a political weapon, including the Palestine Liberation Organization and the radical nationalists in the Kuwait National Assembly. Only Iraq, among the oil-producing Arab states, moved to action by nationalizing the U.S. (Exxon and

---

7. *Wall Street Journal*, September 5 and 6, 1973.

8. *Platt's Oilgram News Service*, September 7, 1973.

9. The Arab-Israeli plan was divulged by the *Times* (London) on September 26, 1973. The Saudi approach is discussed in *Platt's Oilgram News Service*, September 27, 1973. *Platt's* notes that this approach was decided after consideration of military options to secure oil supplies presented in a Joint Chiefs of Staff "security seminar" in early August.

Mobil) interest in the Basra Petroleum Company. Although the amount of oil lost to the companies was not more than several hundred thousand barrels per day, it was a serious long term blow because it cut them off from a relatively cheap and expanding source of crude. In addition, the Iraqi action set a militant tone to the prevalent debate about the oil weapon. But it was more than a week before any further steps were taken.

When war broke out, the Gulf states via OPEC were preparing to enter negotiations to raise the price of crude. For almost a year the more militant producing countries had been pressing inside OPEC for a revised price schedule that would take account of the galloping rate of inflation, currency revaluations, and rising market prices for crude oil and its products. Saudi Arabia and Iran stood resolutely against these pressures. In September Algeria and Libya had unilaterally raised their posted prices to the $5 range. Even Yamani had to admit that "the Teheran Agreement is either dead or dying and is in need of extensive revision." [10]

The negotiations opened on schedule on October 8 and were apparently conducted in an unreal isolation from the war. Press reports suggested that the producers were asking for a posted price hike of thirty-five to fifty per cent. Negotiations, formal and private, stretched over five days before they were broken off on October 12. The oil companies asked for a two-week recess; the countries refused, and scheduled a meeting among themselves for October 16 in Kuwait. There they approved what the radicals had been advocating for several years: a unilateral determination of crude oil prices by the countries. The posted price for Gulf crudes was hiked about seventy per cent— from $3.01 to $5.12 for Arabian Light. This meant a boost in government revenue per barrel from $1.77 to $3.05.

In the war zones, full-scale fighting continued uninterruptedly, bringing more and more calls for the oil producers, and particularly Saudi Arabia, to use the oil weapon. On October 10 President Sadat sent a special emissary to Saudi Arabia and the other Gulf oil-producing states, who urged them to put pressure on the United States to refrain from resupplying Israel with arms. Apparently Faisal had assured Sadat in August, on Sadat's visit to Riyadh, that Saudi Arabia would support an Egyptian war effort with its oil. When, after four days of fighting, there was no movement by the oil producers (except Iraq's nationalization), Sadat felt the need to increase public pressure on Faisal. By the end of the first week, the only interference with Middle

10. *MEES*, September 7, 1973.

East oil supplies had been the disruption of about a million barrels per day of Iraqi oil from Syria, due to heavy Israeli bombings of port and refinery installations.

OAPEC Policy During the War

The Arab oil ministers, following their OPEC price meeting, stayed on in Kuwait as OAPEC to formulate an oil policy for the war. The earlier divisions persisted as Saudi Arabia still urged a cautious policy that did not include an embargo. Faisal had reportedly sent a message to Nixon via his foreign minister that "if the United States becomes too obvious a resupply agent for Israel in the present war, it would be almost impossible for him to withstand pressure to halt oil shipments."[11] At the October 17 meeting, Saudi Arabia successfully resisted embargo attempts, although U.S. resupply efforts to Israel had just begun. It was decided to implement a general five per cent cutback in production plus five per cent reduction per month until occupied lands were liberated and Palestinian rights restored. The reaction in industry and government circles was one of relief and a sense that the oil producers could not have done much less. "The effects thus far appear to be more psychological than actual" summed up initial reaction.[12] The next day, when evidence of massive U.S. military support for Israel increased, Saudi Arabia announced an immediate ten per cent cutback. Abu Dhabi announced an embargo on all shipments to the United States. On October 19, following Nixon's request for Congressional authorization of $2.2 billion in military aid to Israel, Saudi Arabia also declared an embargo against the United States. By October 22, all the producers had embargoed shipments to the United States; some had added Holland to the list; and Iraq nationalized the Dutch holdings (through Shell) in the Basra Petroleum Company. Kuwait declared an overall production cut of twenty-five per cent, including amounts embargoed to the United States. Saudi Arabia added its embargoed amounts to the planned cutback, bringing the total cutback to more than twenty-five per cent. In addition, each state had its own list of friendly, neutral and "aiding the enemy" states.

In order to standardize the embargo and the production cuts, another meeting of oil ministers was held on November 4, where the overall cutback was set at twenty-five per cent. This meant further reduction for the North African states. It actually allowed for a slight increase

11. *Washington Star-News*, October 12, 1973.
12. *New York Times*, October 18, 1973.

in production for Saudi Arabia. Although it did not sharply further reduce the amount of oil available, the meeting did take measures to prevent oil from reaching embargoed destinations by indirect means. This applied mainly to European and Caribbean refineries which ship products to the United States. A special supervisory committee composed of the oil ministers of Saudi Arabia, Algeria, Kuwait, and Libya was set up to enforce the embargo, and a meeting of foreign ministers was set to divide consuming countries into "friendly, neutral, or aiding the enemy" categories. Ministers Yamani of Saudi Arabia and Abdessalam of Algeria were designated as emissaries to tour the industrialized countries and explain the details and purpose of the cutbacks and embargo and to press for diplomatic endorsement of Arab aims vis-à-vis Israel.[13]

Iraq followed its own policy of expropriation of Western oil interests and embargoed shipments to the United States, Holland, and, eventually, Portugal, South Africa, and Rhodesia, but dissociated itself from the OAPEC production cutbacks. In a formal statement in December, Sadam Hussain, vice president of the Revolutionary Command Council, condemned the cutbacks as having been devised by "reactionary ruling circles well-known for their links with America." The embargo is sound, he said, but not enough; nationalization is necessary. As for production cutbacks, they "generally harmed other countries more than America" and "led to results which run counter to its stated purpose." It is a "serious political mistake," he warned, to implement policies which tend to hurt allies and potential allies (Europe and Japan) more than avowed enemies (the United States). "The occurrence of a suffocating economic crisis in Western Europe and Japan may drive them to issue relatively good statements now, but these countries will find themselves forced in the next phase to abandon their independent policies and rely more and more on America." Hussain also cited the recent price hikes as being "conducted in a hysterical manner" and helping the profits of the international companies as much as anyone else, making them stronger than the independent European and Japanese companies. Hussain did not mention that Iraq had just begun expanding oil production after a dozen years of stagnation. More than any other country, Iraq was dependent on those revenues and had the most to lose under the OAPEC policy. When criticism of the Iraqi policy came, it was not from the reactionaries but from Algeria, which pointed out that the effectiveness of

13. *MEES*, November 2 and 16, 1973.

the embargo in turn depended on the tightness of oil supplies in general.[14]

The production cutbacks initially had the desired effect: in November both Japan and the European Economic Community (EEC) issued formal statements referring to Israeli occupation of 1967 territory as illegal. The European countries, mainly Britain and France, moved individually and quickly to set up special deals with Saudi Arabia, Libya, Iraq, and other producers, exchanging crude oil for arms or capital goods. A total break in diplomatic and economic relations with Israel was desired from Japan. Europe was partially rewarded when OAPEC announced that the expected five per cent reduction for December would not be applied to European supplies. At the end of November an Arab summit, boycotted by Iraq and Libya, endorsed the Saudi-led oil program, saying that reductions would continue to the point where the cut in oil revenues would equal twenty-five per cent of 1972 revenues. Given the price hikes, this allowed production cuts of up to seventy-five per cent.

At a December 9 meeting, the Arab oil ministers (again Iraq excepted) decreed a further five per cent cutback for January, which would amount to a loss of some 750,000 barrels per day and a total reduction, on paper at least, of more than five million barrels per day. Although the oil moves by the Arab states did produce some favorable diplomatic statements by the consuming countries, there were real questions being raised about the actual shortage effected by the cutback and embargo. Forecasts of world-wide economic recession were moderated as a distinct lack of shortage appeared. In late December tanker unloadings in European ports were higher than ever. Rotterdam, for example, a boycotted port, took in 5.6 million tons of crude one week in mid-December, just under the normal figure of 6 million tons. After a meeting of the oil committee of the Organization for Economic Cooperation and Development (OECD), officials said oil would not be scarce in the coming weeks and months, but that consumers would have to pay dearly for it.[15] In December Yamani met with Kissinger and indicated that the embargo and cutbacks would be modified when Israel began its withdrawal. This represented a significant shift from the original demand for total and unconditional withdrawal. Yamani also indicated how far he was prepared to look beyond the embargo by reiterating earlier predictions that Saudi production could reach 20 million barrels per day, with much of that geared to U.S. markets.

14. *Ibid.*, December 28, 1973.
15. *New York Times*, December 22, 1973.

Yamani also met with oil company executives in New York, one of whom later predicted that even if the embargo were kept for its symbolic value, production and shipments of Arab oil to the United States would increase by February.[16]

The Arab stand on the cutbacks softened by the end of December. At a December 25 meeting in Kuwait, OAPEC announced a ten percent hike in output in place of the scheduled five percent cut, bringing the total cut from the September production level to fifteen percent. "We only intended to attract world attention to the injustice that befell the Arabs," said Yamani.[17] Kissinger's early success in negotiating a cease-fire agreement between Egypt and Israel on terms that left Egyptian forces on the east side of the Suez Canal was considered to be a major factor, and the OAPEC communiqué "noted with satisfaction the gradual change in the trends of American public opinion which has begun to show a tangible understanding of the Arab problem and the expansionist policy of Israel."[18] There were reports that Faisal was seeking a formal American declaration supporting the principle of Israeli withdrawal in order to lift the embargo. The Americans, meanwhile, were counting on Sadat to persuade Faisal and the other Gulf oil producers to lift it on the basis of the revolution in U.S. policy in the Middle East as demonstrated by Kissinger's shuttle diplomacy.

The Oil Price Hike of December, 1973

The world of oil was being affected from another direction in these months, related to but separate from the embargo. The spiralling market prices which led to the October 16 price hike by OPEC continued to mount, accelerated by the cutback-induced shortages, and, for the United States, the premium on non-embargoed oil from non-Arab sources. European and Japanese independents bid up the price on all available royalty and participation crude. Those governments made particular efforts to line up sizeable exchanges of crude for arms and industrial goods. A Nigerian auction of crude in November brought reported high offers of more than $16 a barrel. At the end of November Iran announced an auction of 109 million barrels, and the *Wall Street Journal* commented that bidding was likely to be "spirited." Spirited it certainly was: Iranian officials announced later that bids of more than $17 a barrel were received, and that virtually all of the high

16. *Ibid.*, January 19, 1973.
17. *Ibid.*, December 26, 1973.
18. *Ibid.*, December 27, 1973.

bids had come from American independents. The usual "villains," the Japanese and Europeans, had dropped out once quotations had left the $10 range. OPEC, meanwhile, had asked the majors to submit proposals for setting a new schedule of prices based on the market and indicated after a meeting in late November that none of the company proposals had been "constructive." A meeting to decide on prices was set for December 22 in Teheran. The auction in Iran 10 days earlier had tested the water.

The OPEC decision in Teheran was to increase the price of crude oil by 128 per cent, raising the posted price to $11.65 and the government take to $7. The Shah announced the price hike with a declaration that "The industrial world will have to realize that the end of the era of their terrific progress and even more terrific income and wealth based on cheap oil is finished." To which a British official commented: "The last chicken of colonialism is coming home to roost."[19] The new price, scheduled to take effect on January 1, was 470 per cent higher than the price a year earlier. OPEC officials described the new price as moderate based on comparison with the costs of alternative energy sources and with the actual auction prices received by Iran and other countries. The Shah of Iran and others had reportedly pressed for a price closer to that received at auction. Saudi resistance was reported to be the main factor in the compromise figure.

As 1974 began, government officials were somewhat in a state of shock as they tried to plot out the implications of the price rise for balances-of-payments and the transfer of financial wealth and power to the oil producers. Major oil company spokesmen dutifully expressed surprise for the record, but it was quickly apparent that the companies stood to gain as much as the producing countries by the new price plateau. They were not paying $17 a barrel in Iran to sell it for any less in New York, where prices as high as $27 were reported. The average profit per barrel for the major companies was nowhere near $10, but it was well over $1 a barrel, or more than triple the rate of the previous few years. Oil stocks, at an all time high, were revalued upwards, as were domestic reserves in the ground, resulting in vast paper profits on inventory. Domestic price levels were hiked to more than $5 a barrel for old oil and $10 for new oil, even though the actual costs of production had not risen.[20] In addition, the higher

19. *Ibid.*, December 26, 1973.

20. The distinction is based on rate of production in 1972. Any oil produced above the 1972 rate, or from a well not in production in 1972, is considered new oil. As old wells are shut down and new ones opened, or as more prolific wells are stepped

prices tended to make other projects like oil shale and coal gasification economical, a factor which was strengthened by the vast subsidies promised under Nixon's Project Independence. In the Middle East, Sadat had already brought pressure on the oil producers to relax the cutback, and an end to the embargo was in sight with the completion of the Egyptian-Israeli disengagement accord. The companies' enthusiasm for the price hikes was not matched by government officials, but the United States could get some satisfaction in that its economy would be hurt least.

THE EMBARGO AND THE U.S. OIL GIANTS

It was clear at the beginning of 1974 that, barring another outbreak of war between Israel and the Arab states, the worst effects of the oil weapon had already been felt. Europe had suffered little, because of a mild winter and because the actual reductions were apparently not as great as claimed. The same could be said for the United States, although in this case the continuing embargo restricted imports below demand levels. A study by the International Longshoreman's Association (ILA) calculated that in December, the month of the deepest cutbacks, oil shipments from the Persian Gulf were only 7.4 per cent below the September, or pre-war level.[21] Japan, which had not yet been accorded the status of a "friendly" country by OAPEC, seemed to be the country worst hit by the oil measures, but even there the main crisis was caused by the sharp increase in prices, fueling an already severe rate of inflation, rather than shortages per se. The ILA study determined that production increases by non-Arab producers like Indonesia, Nigeria, and Iran had kept the over-all global shortfall to around five per cent in December. With the nominal reduction now reduced to fifteen per cent, the situation was expected to ease enough to bring about a rough equilibrium of supply and demand, albeit at sharply higher prices for the consumers.

Semi-official (American Petroleum Institute) figures showed a declining rate of imports in the last weeks of December and the first weeks of January, coinciding with the arrivals of the last tankers loaded before the embargo. Gasoline stocks were down but heating

---

up, a greater proportion of oil becomes new and thus not subject to price control. The present proportion of new to old oil is between 30 and 40 per cent.

21. *New York Times*, February 6, 1974.

oil stocks up from levels of a year earlier. Attempts to check and verify this information with actual refinery runs of crude oil into specific products met a familiar refusal by the companies to divulge such information. The *New York Times* wrote: "The energy crisis is a dramatic paradox: crude oil flows in huge quantities, but information about it has been cut to a murky trickle."[22] Rather than harm the economies of the United States and Europe, the Arab oil embargo seemed to provide a short-term crisis during which long-term policies were set. These policies shared the common feature of higher prices for energy resources. As noted by the industry-financed Conference Board Energy Information Center report, these effects were hardest felt domestically by low-income groups and internationally by the non-oil producing countries of Asia, Africa, and Latin America.[23]

Most of the published figures purporting to demonstrate the effectiveness of the oil embargo were contradictory and self-serving. Before the embargo, when the Nixon Administration was interested in minimizing the potential threat in the face of the decision to resupply Israel, they pointed out that Arab producers supplied only six per cent of U.S. crude imports. A month later, when the effectiveness of the embargo had to be asserted in order to deflect criticism of the companies for shortages and dislocations, the percentage was upped to account for imports of refined products from Caribbean and European refineries dependent on Arab crude. Between early October and late November various statements by Department of the Interior and State Department spokesmen assessed U.S. imports from the Middle East as ranging from 1.2 to 3 million barrels per day. These wild and ever-growing estimates certainly helped create the panic buying and price hikes in the weeks to follow.[24] Reliable statistics include the following:[25] U.S. crude and refined imports for 1973 were averaging 6.2 million barrels per day just before the embargo, of which 1.6 million were from Arab countries. Half of the daily Arab supply came from Saudi Arabia. Arab supplies accounted for twenty-six per cent of total imports and nine per cent of total consumption, then running under 17 million barrels per day. In addition, the embargo included

22. *Ibid.*, January 7, 1974; *Wall Street Journal*, January 7, 1974.

23. *Journal of Commerce*, January 31, 1974.

24. See the articles in the *Philadelphia Inquirer*, reprinted in *Congressional Record*, January 30, 1974, pp. S774–88.

25. Legislative Reference Service of the Library of Congress, "The Arab Oil Embargo and the U.S. Oil Shortages: October 1973 to March 1974," prepared at the request of Rep. Dante Fascell, p. 5.

U.S. military purchases and resulted in a 325,000 barrels per day drain on domestic reserves to supply the U.S. armed forces and client regimes in South Viet Nam and Cambodia.[26] Assuming a totally effective embargo, U.S. supplies would have been reduced by about 10 per cent.[27] The embargo, of course, was far from totally effective.

The effects of the embargo and cutback were partially offset by increased production in non-Arab countries. U.S. imports increased by some 200,000 barrels per day from Iran and at least 100,000 barrels per day from Indonesia. According to American Petroleum Institute (API) figures, the 6.2 million barrels per day import average dropped to 5.5 million in December and a low of 4.5 million in mid-February. Interestingly, the API figures show a decline in domestic production from 9.3 million to 9.1 million barrels per day which coincides with the embargo period—an unexplainable phenomenon in light of skyrocketing prices designed to increase supply. At the worst point in mid-February, total daily supplies were less than 14 million.[28] A warm winter and conservation measures reduced daily demand to around 16 million. No more than 1 million of the shortfall could be attributed to the embargo.

When the Shah of Iran suggested in a CBS interview in late February that more oil than ever was getting into the United States, energy czar William Simon accused him of "inexcusable and reckless remarks." Actually, the Shah had said much the same thing almost two months earlier, while relaxing in St. Moritz. Simon's response then was to have the Commerce Department quietly classify all information regarding the origin of crude imports and to publicly assert that the embargo was fully effective.[29] After this first tiff in memory between a Shah and a "czar," the American Petroleum Institute told the *Journal of Commerce* that the "Shah's remarks may have had some validity a few weeks ago, when there was substantial leakage. Lately, though, we've seen a dramatic drop in our imports which indicates that the embargo has become very tight."[30]

According to a Sunoco executive, leakage at that time was running

26. *Washington Post*, November 16, 1973; *New York Times*, December 1 and 13, 1973 and February 3, 1974.

27. Other projections, including one by the Library of Congress (not cited above), assumed an exceptionally cold winter. There was no indication of where the outlandish demand figures were obtained.

28. Library of Congress, "The Arab Oil Embargo . . .," *op.cit.*, pp. 7–8.

29. *Platt's Oilgram News Service*, January 2 and 7, 1974.

30. *Journal of Commerce*, February 26, 1974.

as high as two million barrels per day.[31] While that estimate seems grossly exaggerated, it is clear that the "dramatic drop in our imports" was related to a shared policy of the major companies to stop importing crude oil which they would have had to share with crude-short (mainly small independent) refiners under the allocation system mandated by Congress. While Simon was proclaiming the effectiveness of the embargo, the companies were openly suggesting that as much as one million barrels per day were available if the allocation rules were revised.[32] Crude oil imports over the embargo period were up eleven per cent from the previous winter, and U.S. stocks of crude and refined products on March 1, 1974 were nearly eight per cent higher than the previous year.[33] Gasoline shortages suddenly evaporated in March, although the embargo was still officially on. Perhaps some explanation lies in the fact that companies like Chevron (Standard of California) were raking in an extra $500,000 per day thanks to the price hikes of thirty to fifty-five per cent.[34]

More exact figures on leakage became available in April when the Commerce Department declassified the crude import data for the embargo period. Libya, which was blamed in the media for most of the leakage, did export 4.8 million barrels in November and 1.2 million barrels in December to the United States, but none after that. Imports from Saudi Arabia, however, were much higher, amounting to 18 million barrels in November and 7 million barrels in December. Moreover, Saudi oil continued to arrive, albeit at a sharply reduced rate, in January (257,187 barrels) and February (552,212 barrels). Tunisia, Algeria, Kuwait, and the United Arab Emirates were responsible for small shipments during the embargo. Although the figures do not specify, it is fair to presume that most of the oil imported from Europe during that period was actually Arab oil.[35]

It is not too surprising that in the face of the facts the giant companies like Exxon and Chevron continue to assert that they were not responsible for any leakage, and that the embargo was responsible for the shortages of products that existed in the United States over this period. More astounding is the virtuoso performance by Simon, now promoted to treasury secretary, in assuring the public that "not one drop" of crude was leaked from Saudi Arabia, even though imports from that

31. *New York Times,* February 22, 1974.
32. *Ibid.; Journal of Commerce,* February 22, 1974.
33. *New York Times,* March 27, 1974.
34. *Ibid.,* April 12, 1974.
35. *Wall Street Journal,* April 9, 1974.

country averaged half the normal rate during the embargo. Using the conjurer's tricks he learned while becoming a multimillionaire Wall Street investment banker, Simon insisted that it took up to four months for Saudi oil to reach U.S. ports, a trip that normally takes four to six weeks. Small wonder that Simon's assistant Eric Zausner, when pressed by the *Journal of Commerce* for a clarification, admitted that "I've had a rough time sorting out these numbers myself."[36]

The political and economic chicanery of the major oil companies and the Nixon Administration in conjunction with the Arab oil embargo makes it virtually impossible to measure with precision the actual impact of the embargo on the American economy. Alternative fuels like coal more than doubled in price. Electric utility rates reflected these fuel costs. The Federal Power Commission has used the crisis to grant large price increases to natural gas producers and the industry is pressing on with its bid for complete deregulation of prices.[37] As treasury secretary, Simon pushed for greater tax incentives such as very rapid depreciation write-offs for the energy industry, while opposing individual tax reductions as inflationary.[38] As for Congressional capacity to effect even moderate reforms in the operation and regulation of the energy industry, the first half of 1974 certainly bore out the prediction of top industry lobbyist Charles Walker last January: "When it all shakes out, I think we'll see a lot of rhetoric and some action but not that much in terms of radical change affecting the industry."[39] Oil company profits are described in the financial press as "embarrassing." The friendly Federal Energy Office characterizes them as "whoppers," and even these reported increases have been criticized as understatements.[40] Walter Heller, former chairman of the Council of Economic Advisers, calculated that the "siphoning off of consumers' dollars away from other goods and services" represents "an effective reduction in real income" of some $20 billion in 1974. This rise in sales proceeds will be realized on a lower sales volume, representing a savings for the oil companies of about $4 billion. Of the $24 billion differential, $8 billion will go to foreign governments, while $3 billion will go to the U.S. government if a windfall profits tax is enacted. This leaves a minimum of $13 billion as increased earnings, and Heller assumes that "petroleum accountants

36. *Journal of Commerce,* April 10, 1974.
37. *New York Times,* May 31 and June 22, 1974.
38. *Ibid.,* June 10, 1974; *Journal of Commerce,* June 17, 1974.
39. *Wall Street Journal,* January 25, 1974.
40. *Ibid.,* January 21 and April 4, 1974; *New York Times,* April 8 and 27, 1974.

will likely be inventive enough to keep a considerable part of this windfall from showing on the bottom line."[41] The overall effect of the oil weapon in the U.S. economy was to enhance, at least temporarily, the capacity of the giant oil and energy companies to gouge the consuming public and consolidate their monopoly position not only in the energy sector but within the economy as a whole.

POLITICAL AND STRATEGIC DIMENSIONS

The political and strategic implications of the oil weapon must be evaluated from two directions: its role in the struggle for political hegemony among various national and class forces in the Middle East, and its role in the competitive struggle between the industrialized capitalist countries of Europe, Japan, and the United States. The strategy and diplomatic tactics of the United States under the direction of Henry Kissinger are important in both of these areas.

Kissinger's Policy in the Middle East

Kissinger's fundamental approach has been to reestablish strong American political and economic influence throughout the Middle East by encouraging and promoting the alliance between Faisal in Saudi Arabia and Sadat in Egypt. It is doubtful that Kissinger ever believed that American interests in the Middle East could be assured by a militarily dominant Israel.[42] Nevertheless, this had been the prevailing view among U.S. policymakers. During the visits of Israeli and Arab leaders to Washington in February and March of 1973, unnamed Middle East experts were stressing that "there seems to be no cause for urgency and that a strong case could be made for preserving the status quo."[43] In Kissinger's view, stability had to rest on the viability of moderate regimes with firm political bases. One condition for that, as demonstrated by the continued political turbulence in Egypt following the 1967 war, was a solution to the Arab-Israeli impasse on terms that gave those moderate regimes a stake, economically and politically, and a defense against more radical

41. *Wall Street Journal*, January 8, 1974.

42. During the October war Sen. Henry Jackson wrote a short piece in the *New York Times* in which he concluded that U.S. interests demanded that Israel win the war "decisively." For a view of Kissinger's prewar attitude toward Israel's occupation of Arab territories, see *Jerusalem Post Weekly*, December 18, 1973.

43. *New York Times*, February 7, 1973.

elements internally and elsewhere in the Arab world. The key moderate in this scenario is Sadat, who moved after 1971 to transform Egypt into a private-enterprise economy open to Saudi and other capital investments and allied with the United States rather than the Soviet Union. The October war provoked the crisis that could be used to justify an appropriate shift in U.S. strategy. For Kissinger it provided a "golden opportunity."[44]

During the war Kissinger used all available means—mainly Israeli dependence on the U.S. arms—to help bring about a military cease-fire which left neither party in a clearly superior position. The United States could then provide the necessary mediation. The shift in the U.S. stance vis-à-vis Arab war aims was immediately apparent in Kissinger's October 25 remark that "the conditions that produced this war were clearly intolerable to the Arab nations and that in a process of negotiations it will be necessary to make substantial concessions. . . ."[45] Subsequent reports noted that U.S. pressure had forced Israel to permit resupply of the Egyptian Third Army trapped on the east bank of the Suez Canal. This new policy achieved the quick restoration of diplomatic ties with Egypt in early November after Kissinger's first trip to the Middle East.

Faisal was the second key to renewed U.S. influence in the Arab world as he controlled the largest single source of crude oil. Before the war, it was sufficient for Faisal merely to talk about not raising production. Once the war broke out, Faisal had to act. While Faisal certainly wanted to pressure the United States into a more pro-Arab stand, he was also compelled to participate in the embargo or face a loss of influence in the Arab world, and perhaps even his throne. At the end of October, Yamani told a visiting delegation of U.S. Congressmen that "King Faisal has done his best in the last two weeks to represent American interests. . . . We did not want the embargo. We hope that we can do something, but there must be something that we can show as change. . . ."[46]

44. *Ibid.*, November 8, 1973.

45. *Ibid.*, October 26, 1973. Although other administration spokesmen, notably the president, Defense Secretary Schlesinger, and former Defense Secretary Laird made more conventional hardline statements, subsequent events show that Kissinger was in charge. For example, Nixon stated on October 15 that U.S. policy would be like that in 1958 in Lebanon and in 1970 in Jordan, i.e., real or threatened military intervention.

46. "United States Oil Shortage and the Arab-Israeli Conflict," Report of a Study Mission by the House Foreign Affairs Committee, December 20, 1973, p. 51.

Kissinger evidently thought that the Egyptian-Israeli cease-fire and POW exchange might be change enough. He asserted at a press conference on November 21 that "economic pressures" against the United States, while understandable in the course of the war, were "inappropriate" during peace negotiations, that U.S. policy would not be influenced by such pressures, and that unspecified "counter-measures" might be necessary.[47] The result was a temporary escalation of rhetoric, as Yamani responded that countermeasures would be met by an eighty per cent cut in production and that the oil facilities would be sabotaged in the event of any military moves.[48] A week later Defense Secretary Schlesinger announced that U.S. naval forces in the Indian Ocean would be beefed up because of the "enhanced interest" of the United States in the Persian Gulf area growing out of the oil embargo.[49] Kissinger, meanwhile, was busy lobbying among members of Congress that the October war and the embargo precluded any settlement resembling the pre-war balance of forces, that Israel's international isolation was increasing and even public support in the United States was contingent on Israeli flexibility, and that this might be the last chance for Israel to secure a peace not totally imposed on it.[50]

This pattern of tough talk and conciliatory diplomacy continued over the next two months. During that time the Israeli-Egyptian disengagement was worked out and production cuts were eased for Europe and Japan. Kissinger initiated an American campaign to take the lead in developing new relationships between oil producing and consuming countries. Numerous hints were dropped from Arab and American "informed sources" that the days of the embargo were numbered. On January 22, Kissinger suggested that he had gotten pledges from certain Arab leaders that the Israeli-Egyptian disengage-ment warranted an early end to the embargo:

> We have had every reason to believe that success in the negotiations would mark a major step toward ending the oil embargo. We would therefore think that failure to end the embargo in a reasonable time would be highly inappropriate and would raise serious questions of confidence in our minds with respect to the Arab nations with whom we have dealt on this issue.[51]

47. *New York Times,* November 22, 1973.
48. *Ibid.,* November 23, 1973.
49. *Ibid.,* December 1, 1973.
50. See James Reston's column in *Ibid.,* December 9, 1973.
51. *Ibid.,* January 23, 1974.

Meanwhile Sadat was in the midst of a six-day trip to Arab capitals to explain the disengagement accord and argue for an end to the embargo.[52] Faisal was understood to be disposed to lifting the embargo, but there was sharp opposition from Syria and Algeria, as well as Libya and Iraq. Syria was openly critical of Sadat's willingness to disengage the Suez front without any negotiations on the Golan, permitting the Israelis to concentrate their forces there. Any proposal to weaken or end the embargo would have had small chance of acceptance by a good number of Arab states without Syrian concurrence. It is possible that Saudi Arabia told the United States that it would try to have the embargo softened at an upcoming meeting of OAPEC scheduled for February 14 in Tripoli. This possibility was immediately sabotaged by President Nixon when he announced, in his State of the Union address on January 30, that on the basis of his contact with unnamed "friendly Arab leaders" he could announce that "an urgent meeting will be called in the immediate future to discuss the lifting of the oil embargo."[53]

Besides being a misrepresentation of the facts (the meeting had long been scheduled), Nixon's statement amounted to a virtual challenge to the "friendly Arab leaders" to produce an end to the embargo, a challenge certain to fail in the face of a majority consensus among the Arab leaders that their demands had not nearly been met and that progress on the Syrian front was essential. Any slim chance that Sadat and Faisal could have carried the February 14 meeting was thus eliminated.

Nixon's move is difficult to explain. Possibly he was trying to build up his tattered political image with the idea that he was in control of the energy crisis and in fact indispensible to its solution. His characterization of the meeting as a new development of which only he and certain Arab leaders had knowledge would support this interpretation. On the other hand, Kissinger told a Congressional committee the next day that Faisal and others had indeed indicated that they would recommend lifting the embargo at the February 14 meeting. Following the reports of Nixon's statement, Syria's President Assad flew to Riyadh and received "firm pledges" from Faisal and Kuwait's ruler, Sheikh al-Sabah, that the embargo would be maintained until a disengagement accord for Golan had been worked out on Syrian terms, meaning "part of a plan for a total Israeli withdrawal" and "an assurance of Palestinian rights." On February 6, Kissinger repeated his expectation that the embargo would be lifted and said

52. *Ibid.,* January 30, 1974.
53. *Ibid.,* February 1, 1974.

that failure to do so would be "a form of blackmail." The result of all this bluster was predictable: the Arab oil ministers' meeting was "postponed indefinitely at the request of Saudi Arabia and Egypt," reportedly because they needed more time to persuade other leaders to lift the embargo. An Algiers meeting between presidents Sadat, Assad, and Boumediene and King Faisal produced no public decisions but was followed by an announcement in Washington that Kissinger would soon be back on the diplomatic beat between Tel Aviv and Damascus.[54]

It seems likely that Saudi Arabia and Egypt called off the Tripoli meeting at the last minute out of fear that a majority of the countries would vote to maintain the embargo, perhaps with specific conditions regarding a Syrian settlement that would have delayed any end for months. The chances of this happening had surely been enhanced by Nixon's State of the Union statement. Given the fact that this whole episode is precisely contrary to Kissinger's style of secret diplomacy, the events suggest that this mini-confrontation may have been staged in order to help bolster Faisal's image and influence in the Arab world, giving him a chance to stand up to U.S. blandishments. In any case, the "confrontation" between Kissinger and Faisal came and went. At the beginning of March, Saudi officials in Washington said that an end to the embargo would be announced shortly after Kissinger returned from his current visit to the Middle East. Egypt then proposed that the Arab oil ministers meet on March 10 in Cairo, indicating that enough apparent progress had been made in the Syrian-Israeli disengagement talks to justify renewed consideration of the embargo. This time U.S. officials refused to comment on the probability that the embargo would, in fact, be lifted.[55]

As the date for the Cairo meeting neared, the splits within the Arab world over the embargo question became sharper and more public. Saudi Arabia made an official statement supporting the end of the embargo. Syria, Algeria, and Libya were opposed, and insisted that the meeting be held in Tripoli, as originally scheduled. Sadat evidently hoped that the more pro-American environment of Cairo would help carry the swing votes. The Cairo meeting failed to get off the ground when the Syrian, Libyan, and Algerian representatives refused to attend. Algeria was to chair the meeting, and in the view of Yamani and others, Algerian presence at the meeting was necessary in order

54. *Ibid.*, February 5, 7, and 14, 1974; *Wall Street Journal*, February 20, 1974.

55. *Journal of Commerce*, March 1, 1974; *New York Times*, March 4 and 6, 1974; *Wall Street Journal*, March 6, 1974.

to neutralize radical nationalist and leftist opposition to the decision. The meeting was rescheduled for March 13 in Tripoli. In the interim, Egypt and Saudi Arabia held strategy meetings with the other Gulf producers and announced "full agreement on the oil situation" the day before the Tripoli meeting. There the producers reportedly agreed to lift the embargo, but postponed any official announcement for an upcoming OPEC meeting in Vienna, presumably so as not to antagonize Libya, which continued to oppose the decision.[56]

When the Vienna meeting opened on Sunday, March 17, Syria made a formal proposal to lift the embargo provisionally until June, stipulating the need for a formal decision at that time in order to keep the embargo lifted. Egypt and Saudi Arabia rejected this proposal, insisting that the embargo be lifted without conditions. This resolution carried. Algeria's last-minute addendum that the decision be subject to review was allowed by Egypt and Saudi Arabia with the clear understanding that they would prevent any reimposition of the embargo. On this basis Kissinger quickly noted that "we do not believe it is probable that the embargo would be reimposed," and indicated that he based that assumption on Saudi and Egyptian assurances that they would stand fast against such a move. The official announcement finally came on March 18, with unofficial predictions that production levels would be restored to pre-war levels. Saudi Arabia pledged an increase in production of 1 million barrels per day for the U.S. market. Syria and Libya maintained their opposition to the decision. The embargo on Holland, Portugal, South Africa, and Rhodesia was not lifted.

The embargo meeting coincided with an OPEC meeting on prices, in which Algeria, Indonesia, and Iran reportedly proposed a further fifteen per cent hike in posted prices, a move favored by a clear majority of OPEC countries. Saudi Arabia's Yamani reiterated his view that prices were already too high and should be reduced so as not to jeopardize the economic and political stability of the industrialized capitalist countries. In what was described as a "stormy session," Kuwait and Abu Dhabi placed in the conference record a censure of Saudi Arabia, accusing it of discouraging buyers from paying high auction prices. This coincided with separate reports from international oil brokers that the Aramco parent companies were offering large volumes of crude in Europe at prices well below current market levels. In the meeting, Yamani threatened to break from OPEC and set lower

56. *New York Times*, March 10-14, 1974.

prices if the proposed increase was voted. According to the *New York Times* account:

> On the major issues of the embargo and the oil prices decided here, Saudi Arabia virtually imposed conditions that were closely in line with American desires, with considerable risk to the unity of the Arab countries and the world's major oil-producing nations.[57]

Since the embargo was lifted, Saudi-American interests have been further cemented by official agreements to expand economic, political, and military ties "in ways that will enhance the stability of the Middle East." The initial focus of the agreements was on internal security. Prince Fahd, Faisal's brother and heir-apparent, headed the delegation to Washington in June. Minister of interior, Fahd is in charge of internal security and heads the Saudi Economic Affairs Committee. One agreement involves a U.S. commitment to reequip and train the National Guard, which is responsible for the security of Faisal, the Royal House, and oil production facilities. At least five thousand guardsmen have been guarding Aramco installations since 1967. Two large fires at Aramco's Ras Tanura refinery in 1973 were caused by Palestinian sabotage. Only by beefing up his security forces will Faisal feel confident of refusing to participate in any future embargo. This agreement also provided for expansion of the National Guard by at least two battalions. In earlier agreements the United States promised $750 million in naval equipment and training and allowed for the Saudi purchase of some two hundred jet fighters. U.S. military personnel number more than two hundred, in addition to an undetermined number of former military men working on contract to U.S. arms firms like Northrop, Raytheon, Bendix, and Lockheed. The head of a British consulting firm who was awarded a contract to recruit four hundred key personnel for the Saudi airforce described his job as "setting up a quasi-military operation."[58]

Just months after the embargo U.S.–Saudi ties were stronger than ever. Special efforts were being made to involve American corporations in Saudi economic development and to channel Saudi oil revenues into U.S. securities and markets. Both countries seemed to be gearing up for the time when the contradictions will prevent Faisal from

57. *Ibid.*, March 17, 20, and 26, 1974.

58. *Washington Post*, April 6, 1974; *Middle East Economic Digest* (London), June 21, 1974.

playing both sides of the fence. The dimensions of these developments aroused more than a little suspicion of the motives of both parties. Following the general accord on economic and military cooperation,

> . . . some Saudi and Arab circles concerned are now asking themselves whether this move towards strengthening economic and defense cooperation with Saudi Arabia is evidence of a sincere long term intention on the part of the United States to assist in the industrialization and economic development of Saudi Arabia . . . or whether, on the contrary, it represents no more than a transitory tactical maneuver designed to outflank and torpedo European and Japanese efforts to secure bilateral oil deals of their own, with a view to promoting what may be the fundamental U.S. objective of securing a global approach to energy questions under American hegemony.[59]

Economic Competition Between the Industrialized Countries

Over the last decade the relationship between the United States and its erstwhile allies in the industrialized capitalist world has been one of increasing tension and competition in the economic and political spheres. This was nowhere more pronounced than in the politics of oil and the Middle East. The attempts of some European states, notably France and Italy, to achieve some measure of autonomy with regard to energy supplies and to reduce their dependence on the major international companies led to some of the most profound changes in the industry to date, beginning with the famous ENI joint venture with Iran back in 1957. After the 1967 June War, France took a markedly detached position toward Israel and repaired its damaged relations with a number of Arab countries. Because of this stance France received special treatment in Iraq during the phase of oil nationalization. Japan also strove mightily to develop some independence via-à-vis the major oil companies. This effort was concentrated in Indonesia and to a significant extent in the Persian Gulf.

The vehicle for implementing independence from the major companies generally took the form of a national oil company or strong state financial backing of private national firms. The growing role of national oil companies in the producing states, through nationalization, participation, joint ventures, and marketing of royalty crude, made an increasing number of commercial and barter deals possible.

59. *MEES*, April 5, 1974.

As a result a growing share of world oil trade was moving outside the channels dominated by the major companies. The move on the part of the OPEC countries to focus on industrialization as the cornerstone of their oil policies is bound to accelerate the trend. ENI of Italy articulated some of the strategy from a European perspective in its 1971 Annual Review, calling for a "basic European policy" in which national oil companies would "assume positions of increasing commitment and responsibility with regard to energy imports." According to ENI Vice-President Francesco Forte, writing in *The Times* (London):

> These agreements should be concluded between the national company of each supplying country and national companies of the EEC countries acting jointly. . . . They would be agreements at the national company level to ensure flexibility and economic efficiency, but they would be fitted into national government plans and the terms of EEC directives.
>
> The agreements have to cover the supply of large quantities of crude oil in predetermined terms, exploration financed by the companies of the purchasing countries under ancillary contracts, and the provision by the purchasing country of goods and services in exchange for oil purchased, contributing to local economic development as part of general collaboration with the EEC.
>
> These agreements should be ample in scope and number. Clearly they could not cover all needs, but they would replace the existing machinery, under which the supplying countries and the great international groups confront one another, while the European countries, which are the really interested parties, take no part in the decisions but have to put up with the consequences.[60]

While some of the specifics of this European analysis would be debated by the oil producers, the trend was much the same on their side. The Eighth Arab Petroleum Congress (Algiers—June, 1972) resolved that "the oil-producing Arab countries should practice direct and effective control over their oil industry . . . establish direct contact with markets importing Arab oil" and "should conclude agreements for the sale of oil through their national companies and the importing companies in these markets."[61] In a presentation to the XXXII (Extraordinary) Conference of OPEC in March, 1973, Iraqi Oil Minister

60. *MEES*, July 7, 1972.
61. *Middle East Economic Digest*, June 16, 1972.

Hamadi discussed the future direction of oil relationships in terms of guaranteed export markets and industrial projects as part of any future oil deals. These deals would be new types of arrangements like service contracts and joint ventures. As for marketing of crude oil, he continued:

> National oil companies . . . have at their disposal increasing volumes of crude oil to sell in the world market. . . . Instead of being marketed in conventional ways, these volumes of crude oil could be disposed of in package deals of five years' duration specifying not only the terms of normal free market sales like price, payment, etc., but also the implementation of a number of development projects in the seller country on terms to be agreed upon. In this way, the marketing of crude oil would evolve into a relationship between national oil companies and groupings of project implementing firms from the oil–consuming countries over periods of time longer than one year and involving more than one spot deals—thereby bringing about a more stable relationship.[62]

One reflection of this evolving relationship between the oil producers and the consuming countries was a growing European unhappiness with U.S. policy. They viewed the U.S.-Israeli alliance as myopic, due perhaps to the fact that the United States was not as threatened as they by the potential cutoff of Arab oil.[63] This divergence became apparent with the outbreak of the October war. Among the NATO members only Portugal allowed the United States to use its territory for resupplying Israel. West Germany demanded that U.S. arms stocked at German NATO bases not be sent to the war zone. In a series of secret NATO meetings during the war, U.S. attempts to have the allies "take steps to chill their trade and political relations with the Soviet Union" were rebuffed. The failure of the allies to wholeheartedly support the U.S. "alert" confrontation on October 24 caused Kissinger to remark that he was disgusted with NATO.[64] A joint November 5 statement by the European Economic Community supported Arab demands for total Israeli withdrawal. Japan later made a similar statement. Britain and France, in particular, initiated a series of high level contacts with the individual oil producers (including Iran) in

62. *MEES*, May 18, 1973.

63. See the General Accounting Office report to the House Foreign Affairs Committee, "A Summary of European Views on Dependency of the Free World on Middle East Oil," August, 1973.

64. *New York Times*, October 31, 1973.

order to secure crude supplies. The United States regarded this as irresponsible and divisive, arguing that a joint response through a consuming nations organization or through the OECD was the only way to deal with the oil producers on questions of supply or prices. Kissinger opened a public campaign in this direction in a December speech in London in which he proposed that:

> the nations of Europe, North America, and Japan establish an energy action group of senior and prestigious individuals, with a mandate to develop within three months an initial action program for collaboration in all areas of the energy problem. . . . The energy crisis of 1973 should become the economic equivalent of the Sputnik challenge of 1957.[65]

Neither a group as broad as the one Kissinger proposed nor even a joint European position was forthcoming. The OECD and EEC energy committees were busy drawing up plans and forecasts, but the individual countries went much their own way in practice. France was in the forefront of those wanting to establish a special relationship between Europe and the Arab world, while West Germany and Holland pressed for a common European stand that would share supplies and shortages even in the face of Arab opposition. Bilateral dealings and the threat of competitive devaluations and export subsidies by the industrial countries in order to cope with the higher costs of oil led the United States to propose a meeting of "major oil-consuming nations" in Washington on February 11. The American delegation, as senior and prestigious as they come, would be headed by Kissinger, Simon, and Treasury Secretary George Schultz. The Common Market countries, plus Canada, Japan, and Norway were invited. The reservations of the French and others towards U.S. leadership in formulating joint energy policies made the meeting's prospects very limited. The oil producers warned against the formation of any kind of "counter cartel." In an interview in *Le Monde,* Algerian President Boumedienne called the Washington conference a "plan designed to prevent contacts between the oil-producing and consuming countries." He continued:

> The Europeans at the present moment have the possibility of laying the basis for a long-term cooperation which would guarantee their oil supplies for 25 years in exchange for their participation in the development of an area in which they are vitally interested. The Washington Conference aims to slow down the new policy of direct links between producers

65. *Ibid.,* December 13, 1973.

and consumers. This is the policy of the future and may well mark the beginning of the end of the system imposed by the cartel, which made everyone quake but which has been broken by the oil weapon. In addition, the real policy of the U.S. is not to lower prices but to control the sources of energy and thus ensure its political power. This is the truth. If the Europeans yield before the American 'big stick' they will once again return to the sidelines of history. It is a question of choice.[66]

The conference, which the French continued to regard as simply "an exchange of views," produced nothing immediately notable. The final communiqué, "dotted with French demurrers," spoke of "a comprehensive action program to deal with all facets of the world energy situation," including emergency allocations, research, and monetary measures to avoid competitive devaluations.[67] Special working committees, as well as the existing OECD apparatus, were to prepare detailed plans along these lines for future meetings. In early March, the EEC announced plans for a high-level conference on long-term economic cooperation between Europe and the Arab world, following suggestions to that end from Arab representatives at an earlier EEC meeting. Kissinger interpreted this as a French–inspired move directed at wrecking any chance for his goal of coordination among all the industrial consuming countries. The State Department officially objected to the EEC plan, complaining that there had been no consultations with the United States, a line that was rejected even by the Germans. *Agence France Presse* quoted a "very high American official" as saying "off the record":

> We want to avoid a confrontation between the Europeans and ourselves, but this confrontation has become inevitable. The Europeans cannot compete with the U.S. in the Middle East, and if we fight them there we will eventually win. The Arab countries need the U.S. more than they need Europe.[68]

A month later a joint announcement from Washington and Riyadh said that the two governments would hold negotiations "to expand and give more concrete expression" to their relations. When the full

66. *MEES*, February 8, 1974.
67. *New York Times*, February 12-14, 1974.
68. *MEES*, March 8, 1974.

series of bilateral agreements was signed in early June, the State Department had to go through some verbal gymnastics to suggest that they were somehow different from the European and Japanese deals they had been criticizing.[69] This agreement, plus those signed with Egypt during Nixon's quick June trip and Simon's July visit, reflect renewed U.S. determination to be the paramount power in the Middle East, and, if possible, in the whole international energy sector.

The summer of 1974 was marked by two OPEC conferences: one in Quito, Ecuador in late June and the other in Vienna in mid-September. Both meetings showed evidence of a general resolve on the part of the oil-exporting states to consolidate crude oil prices at the high level set in the aftermath of the October war. The June meeting was characterized by most observers as a rather rancorous affair, with Yamani alone arguing that the existing level of crude prices was ruining the global capitalist economy and, among other things, giving unfair advantage to the socialist bloc, with its relative self sufficiency in energy. Yamani's analysis, which sounds remarkably like that of Kissinger, led him to dissociate Saudi Arabia from the OPEC decision to raise the royalty on that crude oil still belonging to the companies (equity crude, or about forty per cent of current production). Following the meeting Algeria's Abdessalam defended the existing price level, saying that the October war "at the most played the role of a catalyst in taking a decision which was already well-prepared and well-justified on the economic level." He warned that attempts to use Saudi Arabia's capacity for increased production to drive down prices would amount to "a dangerous game" which would lead to a coordinated reduction of output by the other OPEC producers.[70] Average crude prices going into the summer were about $9 a barrel in the Gulf and $13 a barrel at Mediterranean ports.

The September OPEC meeting featured an instant replay of the June meeting. All the producers except Saudi Arabia levyed an increase in royalty and income tax rates to net them an average increased take of $.33 per barrel, which was calculated to be equivalent to the rise in world inflation over the preceding three months. This represented a compromise itself, with some producers arguing that the inflation rate should be calculated at the annual rate, which was more like fourteen per cent. Saudi Arabia finally aligned itself with the other OPEC countries on the price issue in mid-November, 1974.

69. *Journal of Commerce*, June 11, 1974.
70. *MEES*, July 5, 1974.

Behind these complicated and confusing manuevers lies a continuing struggle for power and influence in the world of Middle East oil —a struggle between the United States, allied with Saudi Arabia and the other Gulf states, and Europe, allied with Algeria, Libya, and Iraq. Of course, the lines are not quite that neatly drawn, but there is some pattern in these developments which show an attempt by the more progressive oil-producing states to offset the post-October war alliance between the United States and Saudi Arabia and Egypt by promoting trade and aid deals with European countries and Japan. The moves by OPEC to trim the profits of the major companies as well as their access to crude oil seemed designed to benefit the smaller independent and state-owned companies and develop new channels for the flow of resources not controlled by the seven giant companies.

OIL PRICES AND THE INTERNATIONAL CAPITALIST ECONOMY

Even before the embargo and the spectacular price hikes of late 1973, the industry and the media fostered the notion that even if "they" do not cut off "our" oil, the increasing amounts of money accruing to the "Arabs" (as all the oil-producing countries are invidiously lumped together) will result in the subversion and destruction of the international monetary system. Typical of the racist distortions presented as analysis was the comment of oil industry guru Walter Levy:

> Not the least of the dangers posed by this extreme concentration of oil power and 'unearned' money power is the pervasive and corruptive influence which this will inevitably have on political, economic, and commercial actions in both the relatively primitive and unsophisticated societies of the producing countries and the advanced societies of the dependent industrialized nations.[71]

Levey's remarks fly in the face of the evidence that currency fluctuations and disturbances over the last several years were the work of speculation and hedging by the treasurers of multinational U.S. corporations and banks. By the end of 1971, according to the U.S. Tariff Commission, U.S. corporations and banks held $268 billion in short-term liquid assets.[72] With few exceptions, Arab and other

71. *Foreign Policy* Summer, 1973, p. 166.
72. *Business Week*, February 17, 1973.

oil country revenues were barely adequate to meet import needs at that time. Moreover, most oil country revenues are simply paid into country accounts at a few large banks in New York and London.[73] Oil country revenues had little effect on the instability of the monetary system and the decline of the dollar as the basic reserve currency. The global inflation fueled by chronic U.S. balance-of-payments deficits over the fifties and sixties had already forced the devaluation of the dollar and the suspension of convertibility in August, 1971. Another devaluation occurred in February, 1973. This process of disarray and disintegration was pronounced and well developed when the energy crisis emerged.

The OPEC Currency Surplus

There is no doubt that the price hikes after October, 1973 substantially accelerated this process, but speculative and self-serving calculations of the surpluses and deficits have escalated even more. A confidential World Bank study predicts that OPEC currency reserves may rise to more than $1.2 trillion by 1985.[74] Estimates are more commonly half that amount, but without much more substantiation.[75] A more concrete assessment is presented by the Organization for Economic Cooperation and Development (OECD), an official grouping of the Western industrial countries and Japan. OECD economists calculated that its member countries would spend an additional $55 billion on oil imports in 1974.[76] The oil bill for underdeveloped countries was expected to rise by approximately $10 billion. Calculations by the London-based Middle East Economic Digest estimated 1974 Middle East oil earnings of about $58 billion, with cumulative earnings for the 1973–83 decade of around $635 billion.[77] Of course such projections are highly tenuous and include assumptions about price and consumption levels that cannot be pinpointed at this time. It is useful to consider the OECD assumptions that prices for oil will remain more or less constant at 1974 levels, that oil country imports from the industrialized countries will increase helping to

73. The Economist, May 5, 1973.

74. Washington Post, July 28, 1974.

75. At the International Bankers Conference in June, 1974, David Rockefeller estimated oil country surpluses would amount to $70 billion in 1974 and $200 billion by 1976. New York Times, June 7, 1974.

76. OECD, Economic Outlook, No. 15, July, 1974 p. 109.

77. Middle East Economic Digest, March 15, 1974.

offset the deficit, and that the effect of the higher oil prices will tend to reduce industrial country imports of oil to 1973 levels by 1980. All of these assumptions, OECD admits, are optimistic, but they are not unrealistic. Under these conditions the OPEC surplus balance of nearly $60 billion in 1974 could decline to $15 billion in 1980, with the cumulative surplus by that year coming to $300 billion. An increase in expected demand in the industrial countries, or a lower level of imports by OPEC countries, could increase this by as much as another $100 billion. Whatever the exact figures, the OECD analysts conclude that "the OPEC current surplus is likely to decline significantly during the second half of this decade."[78]

The oil producers' monetary surplus, even if it is likely to be closer to $300 billion than $1 trillion in the next decade, still poses a serious challenge to the capitalist monetary system already ravaged by inflation, uneven distribution, and exploitation by the United States as "an instrument of imperial taxation."[79] This prospective shift of monetary wealth is taking place against the background of increased international liquidity of nearly $110 billion, more than doubling the total of world reserves. Most of this new money, created over a four-year period (1970–73), was a function of the continuing U.S. balance-of-payments deficit.[80] This has taken place mainly in the international Eurodollar market, not subject to the monetary controls of any single national authority. One of the largest New York investment banks, Morgan Guaranty, which incidentally manages a large portion of the Saudi reserves and even has a representative on the board of the Saudi Arabian Monetary Authority,[81] reports that this Eurodollar market grew from $105 billion in 1972 to $150 billion in 1973. It increased a further $10 billion in the first three months of 1974.[82] The increase in oil prices is related to these developments, but the forces at work are more substantial and more pervasive, a fact that is recognized by the international bankers even if they join in the popular pastime of blaming it on the oil producers. As Otmar Emminger, deputy governor of the Deutsche Bundesbank and German representative on the Economic Policy Committee of the OECD, commented in June, 1973:

78. OECD, *op.cit.*, p. 96.

79. David Calleo and Benjamin Rowland, *America and the World Political Economy* (Bloomington, 1973), p. 116.

80. OECD, *op.cit.*, p. 57.

81. *The Economist*, May 5, 1973.

82. *Wall Street Journal*, June 28, 1974.

The structural adjustment between the major economies and currencies of the world to the new realities of the 1970s—a normalization process after the previous period of absolute predominance of American industrial power—has been a once-for-all process of historic dimensions. It has strained the system of fixed parities [i.e., the post-war Bretton Woods monetary system] beyond the breaking point.[83]

One can only ponder what the direction of Dr. Emminger's "normalization process" may be, considering that the period preceding the decades of American hegemony were punctuated by fierce competitive struggles among the capitalist industrial countries, twice leading to world wars. The solution to recurring crises in recent years, Emminger notes, has been "a further turn in the inflationary spiral in the world economy." He said that:

Thus we have here a close parallel to what has evolved in domestic economic policies: here, too, there is a growing tendency to resolve economic or social conflicts of all kinds by papering them over with inflationary settlements. Inflation as a general instrument for pacification, for resolving conflicts in the domestic as well as in the international field![84]

Currency Imbalances in the Industrialized Nations

The increased oil bill for the importing industrial countries has increased the pressures on a system already breaking apart under the expansionary strains of post-war boom policies. The problem, however, is less rooted in the gross size of the overall deficit than in the specific distribution of surpluses and deficits among the industrial countries. As the OECD study describes it, "for the area as a whole there should be no financing problem, but, until satisfactory recycling arrangements have been worked out, this may seem a somewhat academic point to an individual country with a large current deficit."[85] Of the total OECD area reserves of $137 billion, Germany alone holds $33 billion.[86] Germany, the United States, Canada, and the Benelux countries, with sixty per cent of OECD's gross national

83. Otmar Emminger, "Inflation and the International Monetary System," Proceedings of the 10th meeting of the Per Jacobson Foundation at the University of Basle, June 16, 1973, p. 15.

84. Ibid., p. 16.

85. OECD, op.cit., p. 46.

86. Ibid., p. 94.

products (GNP) are in positions of surplus or balance. Germany and Benelux have strong export positions in industrial and capital goods. Canada is a net exporter of energy and other resources. The U.S. position has been shored up by the need of importing countries for U.S. financial services, the profits of the U.S.-based international energy companies, and U.S. dominance of high technology export markets. The remaining OECD countries, chiefly Britain, France, Italy, and Japan, with forty per cent of the total GNP for the OECD countries, had to share among themselves the estimated total deficit for 1974 of around $45 billion.[87]

The customary mercantilist solution to this problem of imbalance has been for the country in deficit to reduce internal demand (usually meaning a reduction in worker's incomes) and stimulate exports in order to earn the foreign exchange necessary for achieving a balanced or surplus position. This motivated the successive dollar devaluations of the Nixon Administration, and similar moves by other countries. In late 1972, then Commerce Secretary Peter Peterson (now head of the New York investment banking house of Lehman Brothers) warned of the trade implications of an "energy deficit":

> One result could be that all the major deficit countries would find themselves forced to engage in a wild and cannibalistic scramble for external earnings to pay their bills. This could create an extremely rigorous competition for manufacturing exports and the sorts of export subsidies which would be deleterious to the interest of all parties in the long run.[88]

The response of intergovernmental organizations like OECD and the International Monetary Fund has been to stress the need to work cooperatively to head off any cannibalistic scramble. In May, 1974 an OECD ministerial meeting produced a draft agreement under which the members pledged for a period of one year "to avoid having recourse to unilateral measures . . . to restrict imports" and "to avoid measures to stimulate exports . . . artificially."[89] But the pledge carried no sanctions, only a moral committment. Italy, the industrial country in the most dire financial straits, had already initiated restrictive import measures even against its Common Market partners. Italy's trade

87. *Ibid.*, p. 47.
88. *Platt's Oilgram News Service,* November 15, 1972.
89. *New York Times,* May 30, 1974.

position for the first half of 1974 indicated a deficit "superior to the pessimistic forecasts" of the beginning of the year.[90] Britain based its eventual salvation on North Sea oil production, while France and Japan intensified efforts to secure long-term bilateral trade agreements with major oil producers. France's $4.5 billion deal with Iran, swapping nuclear reactors and other industrial projects for oil and cash, and Japan's similar $1 billion arrangement with Iraq indicated a probable future pattern. France openly embarked on a course designed to make it "the key commercial intermediary between Europe and the developing countries of Africa and the Middle East," based on its "historic ties with former colonies that are now major producers of raw materials, and, more significantly, because its coastlines, harbors, and river systems provide easy access to Europe's industrial heartland."[91] Morgan Guaranty analysts concluded in June, 1974 that no major country appeared to be willing to "accept the implications of its own balance-of-payments policies," as France, Italy, and Britain moved to eliminate their deficits, and Germany acted to preserve its surplus.[92]

The U.S. approach was to consolidate its trading positions particularly in the Middle East. Even the proposed sale of nuclear reactors to Egypt and Israel during Nixon's tour was motivated primarily by the fear of losing that market to European competition. In June, 1974, according to Wall Street's *Journal of Commerce*, "U.S. businessmen have booked all of the hotel rooms in Cairo, Kuwait, and Riyadh for months in advance."[93] The government pushed the business community to move faster and further. The Commerce Department set up a special Commerce Action Group for the Near East to take advantage of what Secretary Dent described as a "staggering proliferation of marketing opportunities, for everything from consumer goods to whole industrial systems and massive infrastructure projects." Nixon's tour of the area, according to Dent, "has already opened the door to these markets and has created the most receptive possible climate for American goods."[94] U.S. exports to the Persian Gulf area increased about thirty-five per cent each year since 1970, "greater than for any major world geographic area except Eastern Europe."[95]

90. *Journal of Commerce*, August 8, 1974.

91. *Ibid.*, July 1, 1974.

92. *Ibid.*, June 20, 1974.

93. *Ibid.*, June 20, 1974.

94. *Ibid.*, July 17, 1974.

95. Statement of Francois Dickman, State Department Bureau of Near East and South Asian Affairs, in "New Perspectives on the Persian Gulf," hearings before the House Foreign Affairs Committee, Washington, 1973, p. 175.

Competition with other industrial countries, though, was heated. In 1972, the Persian Gulf countries imported forty-four per cent of their import requirements from Europe, thirteen per cent from Japan, and only nineteen per cent from the United States. The desire to improve this position led to increased diplomatic presence in the area, including new embassies and commercial officers. The State Department appealed to Congress for funds to "top off" salaries of American experts who could serve as advisors to countries in the area "in order to encourage development of natural resources of interest to the United States, to encourage a favorable climate for trade, and to stimulate markets for U.S. exports."[96] The most important component of the drive for new markets was in the military sector. In fiscal year 1974 the United States sold $8.5 billion worth of arms, $7 billion of that to the Middle East area and $4 billion to Iran alone.[97]

Response of the International Monetary System
Countries facing severe short-term deficit problems are forced to rely on conventional financial markets, notably the international banking system dominated by New York and London banks, or loans from other governments. Italy and Britian have approached oil-producing countries for loans. The flow of monetary reserves from the importing countries to the producers remains in the system for the most part, but is much more concentrated in the hands of the very largest banks and on short-term deposits. The consumers, needing large and long-term loans, are facing an increasingly constricted capital market. The banks with the funds have grown extremely cautious in their lending policies, resulting in an informal blacklist of under-developed countries and Italy as well. Italian central banker Carli was forced to declare that in the developing situation the United States would be the "lender of last resort."[98] West Germany stepped in with credits worth several billion dollars, but this was a very temporary solution. Following Nixon's decision to lift restrictions on

96. Figures and quote from former Deputy Assistant Secretary of State Rodger Davies in *Ibid.*, pp. 154–5. Davies was killed in August, 1974 while serving as ambassador to Cyprus.

97. *New York Times*, July 10, 1974. The figures do not include $1.5 billion in arms granted to Israel and several million more granted to Jordan and Lebanon. For a full analysis of the role of arms exports in the U.S. economy, see Chris Paine, "The Political Economy of Arms Transfers to the Middle East," *MERIP Reports*, No. 30, August, 1974.

98. *New York Times*, June 27, 1974. By April, Italy, Britian, and France had borrowed $25 billion from the Federal Reserve and other central banks. *Journal of Commerce*, April 22, 1974.

exports of capital, the largest component of capital export was not direct investment but loans by U.S. banks to foreign borrowers, including governments.[99] The United States competed for oil country funds, notably by pressuring Saudi Arabia to purchase several billion dollars worth of special nonnegotiable Treasury notes.

One aspect of the uncertainties and crisis of the international monetary system reflected the lack of any national political authority which could make comprehensive decisions on an international level comparable to the role of central banks in individual countries. According to top private bankers like David Rockefeller of Chase Manhattan, the international banking system could not extend further loans to cover national deficits. Commenting on developments at the Conference of International Bankers in June, 1974, the *New York Times* financial analyst wrote that "In the coming tug-of-war between the prudence of bankers and the desperate need of national governments to borrow money to pay for the higher cost of imported oil, the prudence of bankers is likely to prevail." [100] The closest approximation to such an international financial authority is not the International Monetary Fund (IMF), with its nearly global membership, but the Bank of International Settlements (BIS), whose directors are the central bankers of the dominant industrial powers. BIS met frequently in 1974 under its usual shroud of secrecy.

The crisis atmosphere in international financial circles was curiously lacking among some important U.S. policymakers. At the IMF and World Bank meeting in Washington in October, 1974, discussion focused on the need to recycle oil revenues from the producers to the consumers. The general consensus on the need for the expansion of a special lending facility under the auspices of the IMF was met cooly by Treasury Secretary Simon, who said that private financial markets were adequately handling the problem. This view was repeated by Treasury Undersecretary for Monetary Affairs Jack Bennett at a news conference following the IMF meeting. Bennett, a former Exxon official, took the view that "there is no proof yet" of the need for more official or multilateral assistance to oil importers. West Germany and the United States, the two industrialized countries with balance-of-payments surpluses, declined to respond to the IMF invitation to contribute to the special oil facility.[101]

99. OECD, *op.cit.*, pp. 103-4. According to former Federal Reserve governor Arthur Brimmer, such loans were up by more than one-third to $8.5 billion. *New York Times*, July 18, 1974.

100. *New York Times*, June 10, 1974.

101. *Ibid.*, October 2 and 5, 1974.

This approach, while seemingly out of step with the doomsday warnings of President Ford and Kissinger, was consistent with the fact that the private financial markets performing the recycling tasks were the large New York banks and their London branches. This laissez-faire approach reflected the profits of the banker friends of Simon and Bennett and was endorsed on more than one occasion by the *Wall Street Journal.* In an editorial called "IMF Petrojitters" on October 3, 1974, the paper noted that "a year ago, before the increase in oil prices, officials were flitting about the world worrying about how to recycle $100 billion in petrodollars by 1980. Since that time we have already recycled $100 billion in a year." The editorial concluded that "so long as the world's governments don't panic and throw up a bunch of restrictions, the petrodollars will be handled by the most efficient recyclers around, which are the capital markets in London and New York."

On October 10, the *Journal* ran an article by William Cates, former deputy assistant secretary of the treasury for industrial nations finance. Arguing that the U.S. balance of trade deficit owing to crude oil prices had been more than compensated for by the inflow of capital from the oil producers, Cates urged the United States to take advantage of the structural shift occurring in the world economy, "Willy-nilly we are moving from trader to banker, and we must learn to understand and accept our role." He concluded: "Either we step up, when and if required, to the novel role of superbanker, with all its current and future problems, or we risk collapse of the present system, with all the misery and upheaval that such a collapse would entail."

The International Inflationary Spiral

The sanguine approach of the Treasury Department and the *Wall Street Journal* might have been appropriate if the economic crisis had been rooted in the OPEC price hikes. Most observers, especially the top private and official bankers in the Western countries, recognized that any attempt to deal with the underlying inflationary crisis posed a virtually unprecedented problem: the whole OECD area was in the middle of "a substantial reduction in aggregate demand in relation to supply capacity, both for internationally traded commodities and within countries."[102] This classic dilemma of capitalism, forestalled for several decades by inflationary panaceas on domestic and international levels, was brought to a head by the oil price increases. According to the OECD analysts:

102. OECD, *op.cit.*, p. 6.

As a corollary to the large deterioration on current account for most countries the financial savings of the various domestic sectors—households, enterprises, and governments—must, in total, change by the same amount. . . . Equilibrium occurs when the deterioration in financial positions is willingly undertaken by households, companies, or the public sector.

"The major doubt," the analysts conclude, "is whether wage earners will acquiesce to such a situation in 1974."[103] They predicted that "inflation based on oil and commodity prices may ease but there is a danger, however, that high rates of inflation will be kept going by a wage/price spiral, as different groups within the community struggle to offset the large changes in relative prices that have occurred and to maintain their real incomes."[104]

This analysis was shared by the Joint Economic Committee of the U.S. Congress. In an interim report prepared for Ford's economic summit in September, 1974, they observed that "large wage increases certainly threaten to become an inflationary factor in the months ahead as the workers struggle to recover lost ground." The inflation already experienced, according to the committee report, could be substantially attributed to the monopoly structure of the American economy. They explained that high world prices for oil and other raw materials:

do not explain why wholesale industrial prices have risen at an annual rate of 35% in the past three months; why iron and steel prices are up 44% in the past year, nonferrous metals 45%, industrial chemicals 62%; why at a time of reduced demand and production cutbacks, automobile prices are up by $700-800 and more within a single year. . . . Increasingly, a significant part of the current inflation can be understood only in the context of administered prices in concentrated industries which typically increase despite falling demand . . . [and are] unexplainable except in terms of the ability of concentrated industries to resist competitive forces and to achieve a target return on investment in good times and bad.[105]

The primary beneficiaries of the commodity price increases over the last few years have been the developed primary producers (the United States, Australia, Canada, South Africa) rather than the Third

103. *Ibid.*, p. 17.
104. *Ibid.*, p. 5.
105. Interim report of the Joint Economic Committee, September 21, 1974, p. 3.

World countries. Commodity prices for the products of the developed countries increased eighty-five per cent by the first quarter of 1973 over 1968–70 averages, while the index for the products of the less developed countries increased only thirty per cent. Only after the first quarter of 1973 was this situation reversed, with increases of twenty-eight per cent and seventy-seven per cent respectively.[106] Strong commodity prices boosted reserves of underdeveloped countries by some $15 billion in the following two years, but, as in the industrial countries, the economic benefits were not shared equally. The Indian subcontinent, Sahelian Africa, and the Caribbean were economically devastated by oil and other price increases. After noting that Third World exporters would have to improve their trade balances with the industrial countries in order to pay their oil bills, OECD analysts predicted that:

> the terms of trade of primary products relative to manufactures have probably reached a cyclical peak, and may well decline considerably. The cooling off period in the OECD area will, therefore, adversely affect both the price and volume of developing countries' exports.[107]

It took until 1970 for most commodity prices to reach their 1951 peaks of the Korean war boom. Reserves of most minerals are plentiful and present shortages are due to limited production capacity and sudden increases in demand, based in the uncertainty and disarray within the world capitalist economy.

The OECD analysis may be off the mark in one respect: while the inflationary demand for primary commodities may decline with the deceleration of the advanced capitalist economies and the deflationary impact of the huge commodity inventories that have been built up, present high prices for oil and some other materials will likely be consolidated, through increased wages in the producing countries and the concerted political actions of OPEC and similar organizations. The disarray among the leading industrial countries, coinciding with a relatively high degree of unity among the raw materials producers, may lead to an outcome different from that of the fifties. The chances of curtailment of production and price hikes in other commodities are not very great, but a steady if uneven push on the prices of various commodities by producers acting singly and together seems more likely. As before, the impetus may not always

106. OECD, *op.cit.*, p. 36.
107. OECD, *op.cit.*, p. 39.

come from the Third World. In August, 1974 leading Australian mining companies, backed by their government, initiated demands for higher prices from Japanese steel companies. One Japanese executive commented that "we have been concerned for some time now about the obvious rise of nationalism in those countries supplying resources to the Japanese economy." Initial talks were held in "utmost secrecy" in order to "keep news of developments from reaching suppliers in India, Brazil, and South Africa. But this is clearly an impossibility and accounts for the gloom in Japanese steel circles."[108] This uncoordinated but unrelenting pressure on mineral resource prices accounted for the concern of U.S. strategists like Fred Bergsten that prices would rise "with sufficient subtlety that tough U.S. responses would be difficult to mobilize."[109]

The relatively strong U.S. position vis-à-vis the other capitalist countries is based on several, probably temporary, factors: (1) the large flow of petrodollars into U.S. capital markets, aiding the balance of payments and strengthening the dollar against other currencies; (2) the surge in U.S. commodity export prices which have probably peaked. Industrial exports like steel did well in the last few years, but competition from Japan, Germany, and other countries began to cut into U.S. markets at home and abroad. Even the higher prices that those competitors had to pay for raw materials did not offset this trend.

While the roots of the energy crisis in the demand of oil–producing countries for a greater share in the world product (as inadequately reflected in money payments) have indeed produced fundamental changes in the structure and direction of the world capitalist economy, previous trends will not be entirely displaced. These certainly must include the declining competitiveness of U.S. exports due to the slower growth of U.S. productivity. The resurgent strength of the dollar has been due precisely to the need of consuming countries to pay for oil imports in dollars and, to a lesser extent, in sterling. Thus the reserves previously held by France and Japan, for example, are being transferred to the accounts of the oil producers. There is little reason to believe that either the new holders or the old will be indefinitely content with monetary relationships based on previous privilege rather than a materially more productive economy.

108. *Journal of Commerce*, August 22, 1974.

109. Emma Rothschild, "The Next Crisis," *New York Review of Books*, April 4, 1974, p. 31.

CONCLUSION

The oil weapon was an integral feature of the October war. The same popular pressures that forced the Sadat regime to undertake a limited military campaign also forced Faisal to implement an embargo of oil to the allies of Israel, particularly the United States. Its success or failure is largely bound up with an assessment of the success or failure of the October war to achieve its stated and unstated goals. The war certainly broke down the balance of "no war—no peace" forces in the region and was enough of a political and military success to give the Arab states a much stronger hand in negotiations with Israel. The oil weapon was specifically instrumental in cutting into Israel's diplomatic and political support among the Western countries. It prompted the United States to limit its support for Israel and to initiate Kissinger's mediation in creating a settlement that would return most of the land seized in 1967. Just as the war itself was limited in its scope and purpose, the oil weapon's effectiveness was important but limited.

The unstated goals of the October war included the consolidation of political power and legitimacy by rightist or moderate forces in the front-line countries and in the Arab world as a whole. In this sense the oil weapon should be appreciated as a class weapon, an instrument for providing the Sadat regime with a political victory over Israel and a means of expanding the political and economic role of Saudi Arabia, Iran, and other conservative forces throughout the Arab world. It thus furthered the political trend set in motion by the defeat of the radical nationalist Arab regimes in Egypt and Syria in 1967.

The success of the oil embargo as a class weapon has been limited at best. None of the contradictions in the Middle East which led to the war have been more than partially defused or deflected. Even the question of the occupied Egyptian and Syrian territories has not been successfully resolved, not to speak of the much more intractable question of Palestinian demands. The Sadat regime's honeymoon with the Egyptian people soon showed signs of strain. The uncertain state of Saudi hegemony was attested to by Kissinger himself in his famous *Business Week* interview:

The Saudi government has performed the enormously skillful act of surviving in a leadership position in an increasingly radical Arab world. It is doing that by carefully balancing itself among the various factions and acting as a resultant of a relation of forces, and never getting too far out ahead.[110]

In discussing oil prices and the inadvisability of military intervention, Kissinger clarified well the extent to which the United States identifies itself with the current ruling classes in the Middle East against the popular and revolutionary forces in the area:

> The only chance to bring oil prices down immediately would be massive political warfare against countries like Saudi Arabia and Iran to make them risk their political stability and maybe their security if they did not cooperate. That is too high a price to pay even for an immediate reduction in oil prices.

> If you bring about an overthrow of the existing system in Saudi Arabia and a Khadaffi takes over, or if you break Iran's image of being capable of resisting outside pressures, you're going to open up political trends that could defeat your economic objectives.[111]

The oil weapon has had the paradoxical result of strengthening the role of the United States and the friendly ruling classes in the Middle East, while disrupting the international political and economic hierarchies that prevailed for almost two centuries. The occasion of the war and the oil weapon was seized by the oil-producing states to take control unilaterally of pricing and production of crude oil. Popular pressures for this seizure had been building for decades. The war was the political tremor that unleashed this capacity. The consequent transfer of wealth to a few countries previously outside the temples of power will exacerbate international and local class conflicts. These conflicts extend into the industrial countries themselves to a degree not witnessed since the Great Depression of the 1930's. These longer-term dimensions of the energy crisis, certainly not intended by the likes of Faisal and Sadat, are the consequence of new contradictions emerging from the extension of the global contradiction between abundance and scarcity, wealth and destitution, to the countries of the industrialized West. As the authors of the *Strategic Survey* for 1973 stated: "The interaction between the energy crisis and social tensions in the advanced industrial economies could

110. *Business Week*, January 13, 1975, p. 68.
111. *Ibid.*, p. 67.

well prove the most powerful of all shaping forces for the future."[112] The oil weapon, implemented at a time of growing crisis and contradiction within the international capitalist economy, is not so much an effective cause of these potential developments as a milestone in the ongoing struggle for a fundamental redistribution of the world's wealth and control of its resources.

112. International Institute for Strategic Studies, *Strategic Survey, 1973*, (London, 1974) p. 2.

PART 3: THEORETICAL ANALYSIS

Anouar Abdel-Malek

THE CIVILIZATIONAL SIGNIFICANCE OF THE ARAB NATIONAL LIBERATION WAR

> For to win one hundred victories in one
> hundred battles is not the acme of skill. To
> subdue the enemy without fighting is the acme
> of skill.
> Thus, what is of supreme importance in war is
> to attack the enemy's strategy.
>
> Sun Tzu, *The Art of War*

ONE YEAR AFTER THE 1973 OCTOBER WAR, a wide range of disagreements and a whole panoply of ambiguities continued to cloud the long-term assessment of these fateful eighteen days and nights. Specialists and public opinion alike are conversant with the reductionist assessment of the conflict which is deemed to have been but a carefully planned vigorous American counteroffensive, aimed at recuperating imperialist influence in the Arab world behind a glittering smokescreen of heroic and basically well-conducted military action. On the other side of the river, the consensus of the Arab masses echoes the assessment of the major political class in each country, as well as the wide range

The author dedicates this essay to the living memory of Ibrahîm al-Rifâ'î, colonel commandant of the 'Asifah commando brigade, who fell for the fatherland on October 17, 1974.

of opinion in the Arab national movement. The latter maintains a highly positive political assessment of the October war for the Arabs.

In between these two ranges of analyses, there lies a varigated spectrum of middle-range, courteous, sedate or ambiguous assessments, which constitute really an expression of the structural ambiguities in the national-cultural identity of a meaningful group of political leaderships. Thus, answering a question about his party's views of the array of political crises in the world, a member of a progressive revolutionary party in a Northern European country, replied: "As we see it, there are Vietnam, Cambodia, Laos, Chile, and the energy crisis." Four conflicts signalled by the names of the countries involved, and a fifth one designated as an economic phenomenon. Would it not have been better to use a more coherent listing: either Vietnam, Cambodia, Laos, the Arab world, and Chili; or rice, bamboo, soya, oil, and copper? Was it only a slip of the tongue? Or is it not indicative of the general tone of comments on the sequence of processes unleashed by the October war? One can clearly perceive here the fundamental identity between left wing reductionism (the center and periphery approach, interpreting any Arab initiative as a reflection of the intentions of imperialist or anti-imperialist superpowers) and the traditional Western view. Be it liberal, conservative, or reactionary-imperialist, Western opinion sees the Arab national liberation war as a political initiative made possible only by the vast oil reserves in the OPEC countries: economism as a prop to politics and warfare.

The historic significance of the Arab national liberation war in general and the October war in particular could be postulated in such terms. Discussions would then concentrate on two classic levels:

1. The tactical level: How did the growing energy crisis relate to the planning and launching of the October war? How do the relative interests of Western Europe and Japan compare via-à-vis the oil-producing countries? Other tactical items would include: the volume and profile of military equipment supplied by both the United States and the Soviet Union; the efficiency of the arms embargoes imposed by France and Great Britain on the confrontation states; the success of inter-Arab military planning; Arab initiatives and the evolution of minds in Asia, Africa, and Latin America; combat techniques, efficiency of operations, and planning skills of staff officers and headquarters; and the depth and type of popular support in both camps.

2. The strategic level: Did the October war advance the process of Arab unity? Other key items would include: the October war and anti-imperialist strategy; the problem of politics and military

alliances with the U.S.S.R., and China; the effects of the war on the relations between the Arab world and Mediterranean Europe; and the evolution of the interrelations between social systems and the availability of cadres. A strategic study would also compare Arab potential with the subsequent performance.

Yet, despite the apparent thoroughness of the classic lines of study, something seems to have been left out. Somehow, in many ways, vital problems of this epoch seem to have been strangely brought to light with the October war. These concerns include population, food, and energy. The impasse of productivity and conspicuous consumption has become evident in the post-industrial societies. There has been an accompanying deterioration of the quality of human life in both urban and rural areas, notably through environmental pollution. The value contents of the different civilizational patterns which encompass all human and societal activities in our planet are under scrutiny.

Realization of these problems began gradually after 1945, and accelerated in the last decade, notably around the Vietnam conflict. Yet the 1973 October War seems to have played a highly dynamizing role, triggering a whole network of dialectically convergent crises, or better, it has acted as a *révélateur* and catalyst to the present.

THE CIVILIZATIONAL FRAME OF REFERENCES

The Arab national liberation war, like all major phenomena in world history, can only be understood from the civilizational perspective.[1] Secondly, the proper assessment of the Arab national liberation war in general and the October war in particular should be approached from the viewpoint of its interaction with, specific relevance to, and influence upon the dialectics of civilizations and cultures in our world nearing the end of the twentieth century of the Christian era.

Three major interwoven circles constitute the frame of comparatist analyses of major societal processes. This frame of references is directly inspired by the towering and seminal thought and work of Joseph

1. This essay is based upon theses I have presented in previous publications, notably *La Dialectique Sociale* (Paris, 1972); *Al-Fikr al-'Arabî fî Ma'rakat al Nahdah* [Arab Thought in the Struggle for Renaissance] (Beirut, 1974); "Min ajl Strâtijiyyah Hadâriyyah!" [For a Civilizational Strategy], *Al-Thaqâfah al-'Arabiyyah* (Beirut), April, 1973, pp. 116-31; "Al-Nahdah al-Hadâriyyah" [The Civilizational Renaissance], *Qadâyâ 'Arabiyyah*, No. 1, April, 1974, p. 10; and "Al-Wihdah wa'l-Nahdah," *Al-Ma'rifah*.

Needham, with due attention to other major contributors to the philosophy of history, notably Arnold Toynbee.

1. "Civilizations" is the outer, more general circle. As defined along the lines of Needham's approach, it specifies: (a) the circle of Indo-Aryan (or Indo-European) civilization; and (b) the circle of Chinese civilization.

2. "Cultural areas" is the mediating circle, sometimes confused with the larger civilizational circle, as in Arnold Toynbee's work. In the Indo-Aryan civilization circle the following cultural areas can be circumscribed: (a) Egyptian, Persian, Mesopotamian antiquities; (b) Greco-Roman antiquity; (c) the European cultural area; (d) the North American cultural area; (e) the Indo-European cultural area in Latin America; (f) the sub-Saharan African cultural area; and (g) the Arab-Islamic and Persian-Islamic cultural areas. Cultural areas in the Chinese civilizational circle include: (a) China proper; (b) Japan; (c) Mongolia-Central Asia; (d) Vietnam and South-East Asia; (e) the Indian subcontinent; (f) Oceania (with the exception of Australia-New-Zeland); and (g) the Asian-Islamic cultural area.

3. "Nations" represents the third circle of reference. They are the basic units for evolution of macro-societal processes and can be defined in the following categories: (a) the fundamental renascent nations (Egypt, China, Persia, Turkey, Vietnam, Mexico, and Morocco); (b) the European, then Occidental, nation-state; (c) the new nation-states heading towards unification (Ethiopia, Ghana, Mali, Burma, Thailand, etc.) and the national formations within the framework of multinational ensembles (Armenia, Georgia, Ouzbekistan, etc.); (d) the new states with a national vocation (mainly in parts of sub-Saharan Africa and a minor portion of central and south Latin America).

Civilizational areas are defined by the interrelation between cultures, nations, and societal formations on the one hand, and the time-dimension on the other hand. More than a strict vision of the world, it is this philosophic relation to time, and its consequences, which can be said to distinguish East from West. Cultural areas can then be seen as societal ensembles sharing a common *weltanschauung*, more in terms of historical-geographical determinism through history than in terms of philosophy proper. Nations are easier to delimit, once agreement is reached on the indispensable structuring typology.[2]

Having posited the three major interwoven types of circles, we

2. Anouar Abdel-Malek, "Meaningful Social Theory: the Cross-civilizational Perspective," a paper presented to the I.S.S.C. conference on "Priorities in Comparative Sociology" held in Cologne, May 20-23, 1973.

have a topographical description or anatomy for comparatism. The different units within each of the three circles can be related dialectically to the two surrounding wider and narrower circles. This is the purpose of introducing the concept of specificity.[3]

The two major outer circles can also be interpreted through the historically fundamental difference between the two worlds of mankind: East and West. The West is composed of the major portions of Indo-Aryan civilization. "East" can be viewed as constituting the following: (1) the circle of Chinese civilization; (2) the circle of Islam; (3) parts of the Indo-European cultural area of Latin America directly linked with Africa, i.e., Brazil and the Caribbeans; and (4) the sub-Saharan Africa cultural area.

In pondering the general map of interrelations between these interwoven circles, the exceptional position of the Islamic cultural area is quite apparent. It constitutes the one major link between the two major civilizational molds, ranging from Morocco to the Philippines. The Arab world has been the privileged area of mediation between East and West, because of its geopolitical situation around the Mediterranean. It was the "sea of decision" long before it was so labelled by Admiral Fetcheler in his 1949 paper—in fact since Ramses, the Phoenicians, and Alexander the Great.

Therefore, a major persistent process of power or decadence, of expansion or subjugation of the Islamic cultural area, could not be isolated. Rather it would be a vital part of the ebb and flow of the dialectics of civilizations, the structuration and dismantling of major centers of power, the systems of socioeconomic functioning, and the philosophic conceptions of man. This factor is the hidden part of the iceberg which helps to formulate a clear orientative interpretation of the Arab national liberation war, particularly the October war.

It is clear that the October war gave the Arab world, via its unique position of mediation in both civilizational and geopolitical terms, what seems to be a more dynamizing role in contemporary and prospective world processes. Comprehension of its significance can

3. This concept has been developed in a number of my works. Starting with *Egypte, Société Militaire* (1962), now published under the original title of *Al-Mougtama'al-Miçrî wal-Gaysh* (Beirut, 1974). It continued through *Idéologie et Renaissance Nationale: l'Egypte Moderne* (Paris, 1969) and *La Pensée Politique Arabe Contemporaine* (Paris, 1970). It was formalized in *La Dialectique Sociale*, and "The Concept of Specificity," a paper presented to the VIIIth World Congress of Sociology held in Toronto, August 1974. Also see "Al-Khouçoûçiyyah wa'l-Açâlah" [Specificity and Authenticity], a preliminary outline paper presented to the Kuwait Symposium of April, 1974, *Al-Âdâb*, May, 1974, pp. 41–3.

be furthered by a series of concentric approaches—ranging from the world balance of power to the philosophy of civilizations.

THE WORLD BALANCE OF POWER

The West rose to its position of undisputed hegemony after the fifteenth century. Immense sources of raw materials in distant continents were discovered and dominated. Maritime, mercantile, and manufacturing bourgeoisies arose in the European nation-states. There were bourgeois revolutions around the French Revolution. Centuries of intra-European warfare culminated in the two major conflicts— 1914-18, 1939-45. The consolidation of monopolist capital and the making of classical imperialism came after centuries of colonialism. Modern nationalism became the ideology of the rising bourgeoisies and its industrial revolution. The West consolidated control of the oceans, inner seas, travel, communications, and transports. These elements, as well as electricity and advanced modern technologies, made it feasible, for the first time in the history of mankind, to bring the whole world under the control and domination of industrially and scientifically advanced Western Europe and, then, North America.

The rise of the West was accomplished through a growing concentration of violence, first against the dispossessed ruling classes, and then, and immensely more so, against the nations and peoples of the non-Western world—from the Crusades to Vietnam. This history is the story of both the destruction, dismantling, and domination of hitherto leading sectors in the world (essentially, the Arab-Islamic world, followed by the Indian subcontinent; and then China and Japan) and the sheer destruction of the human potential of the African continent, coupled with the marginalisation of Latin America. It was natural, therefore, that this downward curve would seek ways and means to overcome dependency and decadence, both within itself and in the world around.

The nineteenth century, noted as the golden era of capitalism and imperialism, was also a magnificent period in the upsurge of the East. The two major instances are the Egyptian Renaissance, led by Mohamed Ali and the transformation of Japan around Meiji. It also included a century of wars of independence and liberation in Morocco, Algeria, Syria, Palestine, Iraq, and the Sudan; the potent Indian national movement; the Opium Wars in China; and the Turkish war of independence after 1919.

Should the history of the modern and contemporary world ever be written in political and civilizational terms—instead of present Western-centered handbooks or international cultural histories—an immensely more balanced view of the interaction of East and West would emerge. By the first quarter of the twentieth century, the domination of the non-Western sectors of the world by classical imperialism, as analyzed by V. I. Lenin, was beginning to face radical and irreversible challenges. The first wave of formal independence occurred between 1919-47 and 1947-56. Radical independence came after the break-up of the classical colonial empires, between the world economic depression of 1929-32 and World War II. The Arab world took a major role in this process. It was, therefore, not unnatural to find its key-component parts playing an enhanced role in the great wave of national liberation movements, ranging from the classical national revolution to the socialist transformation of several Oriental societies.

The first major wave of struggle between classical imperialism and the national movements of the East was powerfully influenced by a second factor: the October 1917 Socialist Revolution in Russia. It divided the hegemonic West into two systems: the capitalist and imperialist system, whose axis of power rapidly shifted from Western Europe to the United States; and the socialist system, first limited to the vastly diminished territory of the Soviet Union, later extended to the Socialist states in Eastern and Central Europe, under U.S.S.R. leadership. This process was immensely magnified by the rise of socialism in China, as well as Mongolia, parts of Korea, and Vietnam. Thus, in spite of the fact that the Western system still retains a leading position under the new superpower imperialism of the United States, it is a fact of contemporary history that the world balance of power is now rapidly changing. The two other major centers of power are the Western socialist system of states and revolutionary Asia. Such was the image at the end of the Vietnam war in 1971-72. But even then no one wholly dismissed the emergence of new powers, mainly Japan and a unified Western Europe. Other names were mentioned occasionally, but always in the guise of sub-powers, e.g., Brazil as a sub-imperialism of the United States.

Very few among the political elites could look beyond these dimensions. The vast majority of these political elites, both in the West and in the East, were acting to the best of their knowledge. While several felt that the process of restructuration could not be stopped, few, in truth, visualized the immense changes which were then literally at hand. A majority consensus of the political class in the West and East alike seemed to accept as inevitable the idea that the hitherto dominated countries of the world would follow and imitate the economic, social, and value patterns of the industrialized, Western capitalistic countries. This was the central idea in the panoply of pseudo-concepts of social and political theory—"modernization," "acculturation," the sacrosanct "development," et alia. And one cannot easily dismiss the effects of the proclaimed policy of the socialist states of Europe to reach and then bypass the level of economic achievements of the advanced capitalist systems. It has powerfully enhanced the credibility of this one-way process of evolution which, in fact, constitutes a global attempt at reductionism, i.e., the conception of the future of any given society as unable to be anything but another instance of what the advanced industrial capitalistic West had achieved.

The masterminds of the new hegemonic imperialism furnished the theoretical tools. For security or hegemony to be maintained, it was necessary to control the whole range of patterns of development, whatever the ideological or political labels. Control would come through highly sophisticated utilization of scientific and technological advances and also through the potentials accumulated by the United States. Success in this global conception would result in world hegemony.[4]

Yet, there were signs of a global dialectical process which ought to have attracted the attention of scholars and politicians alike: The general ideological, philosophical, and political feud between the U.S.S.R. and China, for instance, centering around basically different conceptions of man in a socialist society. The meaning of Vietnam went much beyond its incredible heroism. Several key links of imperialism were shattered by national radical and populist movements, notably those in Egypt, Algeria, Cuba, Palestine, Indonesia, Syria, Iraq, Peru, Chile, and Panama. The Catholic Church struggled toward aggiornamento as ecumenism rose, and there were attempts at constructive dialogue between meaningful ideologies (Christianity and Marxism; Islam and Christianity). These signs, however, were not perceived as part of a dialectical world process.

THE TIMING OF THE OCTOBER WAR

As time goes by, the historical moment of the war itself appears to have provoked literally unsuspected consequences, both in the

4. As presented, inter alia, in Robert S. McNamara, *The Essence of Security* (New York, 1968). Compare with my conception in "Pour une Sociologie de l'Impérialisme,"

regional scene and upon the new balance of world power slowly emerging after Vietnam.

Between 1945 and 1973—from Yalta, to Vietnam and the 1973 October War—powerful and oft-hidden forces and influences were at work to remodel world patterns. Two major factors were brought together in 1973:

1. Awareness of the irrational character and deeply structured menaces of the industrial capitalistic patterns of development which have molded the West since the late 16th century was growing. Arnold Toynbee stated:

> We are unique in one respect only—in science and technology, and this unprecedented technological development is producing some unintended effects which bring out certain enduring features of human nature: pollution, war, greed, and aggressiveness. . . . The present distinctive feature of the West is wealth produced by the systematic application of science and technology in the service of greed, which is a universal human characteristic. But people are beginning to see that this scientifically gratified greed is going to be self-defeating. It is going to produce, short of atomic war—pollution and the exhaustion of resources.[5]

Because of the immense strains of the war of national liberation, coupled with the relentless exhaustion of natural resources by the non-awareness of major industrial states in the West, the perception of the new menacing factors culminated in 1973. These factors, however, were seldom related to the historical formation of modern Western civilization itself.

2. A sense of shame, public disaffection, and lack of certainty surfaced, notably in the United States, but also in Western Europe. There was doubt that the West could shoulder its ethical responsibilities with credit and optimal recognition. This enhanced the inner perception by the Western political class of the threats at large. It would suffice to recall several instances: the 1968 student movement, the revival of millenarianism and parapsychic practices, the return to a "greening" adolescence, the crisis in family and state loyalties, and

---

L'Homme et la Société (1971), No. 20, pp. 37-54; No. 21, pp. 279-98; and *Sociologie de l'Impérialisme* (Paris, 1971). The notion of "hegemonic imperialism" is there posited and developed, and is not to be confused with the cosmopolitan-reductionist conception of "center-and-periphery."

5. Arnold J. Toynbee and G. R. Urban, *Toynbee on Toynbee* (New York, 1974), pp. 50, 59-60.

the growing manifestations of negativism in all fields of culture, especially the arts and mass media.

These two major factors served as an exceptionally powerful influence to magnify the impact of a major historical decision by the Arabs to take central political initiatives into their hands. Additionally, this decision occurred in the one region in the world where geopolitics and the dialectics of civilizations and culture operate at maximal efficiency level. The result was that the military offensive, launched by Egypt and Syria on Saturday, October 6, 1973, far surpassed its decisive regional impact, and set in motion a whole series of consequences. It signalized the beginning of a new historical era, both in the world balance of power, and in the interrelations between major civilizations and cultures.

By comparison the most heroic war ever fought in the history of the world, i.e., the liberation war of the people of Vietnam, inflicted an historic blow to the feeling of irreversible superiority which appears to be the unescapable characteristic of hegemonic imperialism. But the Vietnam conflict had its greatest impact in Asia, specifically in Southeast and East Asia, while its global role as a catalyst was greatly more limited than the twenty days of war in 1973. In the case of Vietnam, both geopolitics and the cross-civilizational factors were of a much lesser relevance than in the Arab East.

It might be argued that this was a chance effect: How could the Arabs be capable of computing such a timing? Yet, when all is said and done, they did. And a close scrutiny of significant writing between the tragedy of June, 1967 and the October war clearly indicates that minds were at work with renewed sophistication, seeking ways and means to break the iron blockade forced upon the renaissance of the Arab world.

The key to understanding the Arab initiative lies, as it always does, in the realm of political power of decision. Political decision, especially in Egypt, burdened itself with several controversial measures, notably the crisis in Egypto-Soviet military relations in 1972. The crisis led wide circles of opinion, including leading military circles as well as the traditional left, to believe that no military action could be taken, as long as the rift was not healed. This was a central mistake which resulted from the contemptuous reductionist approaches prevailing in Western political thought and elites. It held that no major initiative could ever be taken in a totally unfavorable context: a sequence of four lost wars, a country of the East, the need to unite national will, popular action and support, and the national state and its army. If such an initiative could be visualized, what of the sacrosanct division of the world between two superpowers at Yalta? What of the irreversibly minor role of medium and small nations?

In assessing the influence of the political decision to launch war on October 6, 1973, it is necessary to realize that the stakes were very high and unpredictable. The rise and fall of Mohamed Ali stood as a constant reminder to the Egyptian political leadership that the hegemonic West would never tolerate a powerful Arab state united around Egypt and controlling the southern and eastern flanks of the Mediterranean. The 1967 June War showed how a complex of internal and external factors and initiatives could explode from the upsurge of Egypt's national liberation under Gamal Abdel Nasser and lead to his death.

Yet three years after Nasser's death, the October war was possible, feasible, and accomplished. In turning the tides of history, the Egyptian and Arab political leadership relied upon the deep and broad national radical feelings of the masses and the army cadres. They made up for the uneven character of organized political mobilization in the Arab countries, especially Egypt. Only by using the full dynamizing factor of national feeling and action could the centers of political decision remold the armed forces, while counting on an unbounded wave of popular support. As in Vietnam, yet in totally different terms and context, the October war was a landmark in the history of the national factor in politics, a vindication of its decisive role with regard to wars of national liberation and confrontation with imperialism.

The October war was literally the "negation of the negation," the defeat of defeat. It advanced the process of the Arab national liberation war. Before October, 1973, the road seemed devastated, despite the powerful wave of national movements toward the twentieth century renaissance: the Egyptian revolution led by Nasser, the heroic Algerian national liberation war, the Arab unity movement initiated by Syria and the Arab East, and the Palestinian resistance. After October the doors of progress reopened. While progress was to remain a lengthy, arduous process, this process is now seen as irreversible. No tactical defeat or retreat could put the clock back. For the first time since the end of the fourteenth century, the Arab and Islamic worlds felt that the gates towards a revival in contemporary terms of what was best in their great history were decisively open. Thus, the October war was not the fourth Arab-Israeli war, but the turning point between decadence and renaissance in the Arab world and political Islam.

It would be relevant here to ponder the relation between renaissance and power. Recent discussions have centered around the relative importance of rationality and aesthetics, or more generally, culture, in the renaissance process. This sidesteps the question. Never has history witnessed a major cultural buildup, let alone a civilizational renaissance, separated from and alien to the world of power. The Greece of Pericles was founded upon that which made the empire of Alexander possible. The Italian Renaissance was based upon the great maritime discoveries, coupled with the emergence of powerful bourgeois establishments around the harbors of central and northern Italy. The French Revolution was built upon the wealth and conquests of the great kings and Napoleon. Victorianism started from the Industrial Revolution and the control of the oceans. Socialist culture without the network of socialist states would be a mere ideology. Neither could the Cultural Revolution and the thought of Mao Tse-tung be divorced from the Long March.

It has been argued that theories advancing the close relationship between power and cultural renaissance denigrate the role of the popular masses and enhance the role of the army as the axis of power.[6] This is a rearguard approach, totally divorced from the broad feeling of unity between the popular masses and the armies of their states. A denial of this alliance is alien to the whole range of historical experiences. On the other hand, this does not automatically imply that "power" is "renaissance," but only one of the vital component elements in cultural renaissance. The role of critical thought and revolutionary action remains ample.

THE PRIMACY OF POLITICS

The primacy of politics is the first and non-dispensable precondition for any meaningful historical process. In the growth of the Arab renaissance it means, first and foremost: to discard resolutely the culturalist approach to renaissance. Formative members of the political class in Arab countries, as well as the broad consensus of intellectuals and public opinion, fully realize the cultural lag of their societies, as compared with the advanced West. The very process of Arab renaissance acquired its pace through the confrontation with recurring

---

6. "L'Armée dans la nation: Contribution à une Théorie sociologique du Pouvoir," in *La Dialectique Sociale*, pp. 339-63; *Al-Gaysh wa'l-Harakah al-Wataniyyah* (Beirut, 1974), I; "La Perception Nouvelle des Menaces," a paper presented to a UNESCO symposium held in Paris, Nov.-Dec., 1973; *Le Monde Diplomatique*, March, 1974; and the forthcoming *L'Armée dans la Nation*.

waves of Western colonial and imperialist penetration from the late eighteenth century.

This fact becomes the very foundation for the imitative attitude of that section of the Arab intelligentsia, which seeks to reproduce the very patterns of the advanced West. In culture the imitation centers around the attitudes of the "traditional" intellectual, as pictured by Gramsci. In politics it aims at political pluralism, as if political parties had been the one and only instrument for political struggles and activity in the whole range of political history; in fact they are but late products, dating from the rise of the bourgeoisie. In economics the servile attitude aims at the conspicuous consumption patterns of the advanced industrialized societies, now visibly caught in the impasse of their ruthless expansionist logic. The stubborn refusal to accept one's self as one possibility, to listen humbly to the lessons of history, to study the pioneering paths opened by the Eastern world, and above all, the deep reluctance to accept one's self as one of the major actors in world history contribute to the "cultural mirage." Accepting these realities would mean abandonment of the tactical benefits of subservience: the possibilities of ever-growing facilities, themselves provided for by the exploitation of Eastern nations and societies for centuries.

As long as the Arabs remain away from the advanced mainstream of culture and civilization, they will meet only defeat and cannot possibly hope for better than reaching for, or being offered, "honorable" terms for their self-inflicted and fully-deserved backwardness. Hence, the contemptuous assessments of the October war, the reluctance to acknowledge its seminal historical role in world politics, and the building of doubt, ambiguity, and self-castigation as the basic attitudinal frame toward the Arab national liberation war. It is a logic of contempt, internalized and accepted by a minority sector of those entrusted with the task of comprehending the historical perspective of their own peoples and societies.

How can this cultural lag be overcome? By waiting and renouncing action in the struggle for national liberation, the cultural lag can be overcome only through imitation of the West. Such a posture means the burying of self-reliance in the name of the cultural lag. Hope is abandoned because of the ever-present threats that accompany meaningful action. The promise of the Arab renaissance is dismissed for the privileges of the culturally-advanced hegemonic West and its appendix, the Zionist state. Thus the tenants of "culturalism" objectively undermine the united national front.

Against this context, the Arab national movement, from its inception to its more elaborate contemporary forms, has taken a resolutely activist stand. Its leaders and organizations always understood the primacy of the political and the urgency to take action so as to change the course of history. They have been prepared to join battle before thinking of fully readying one's armor and to bear the brunt of much higher sacrifices and risks, owing to the accumulated cultural and material lags of the era of decadence, if the natural order of things is ever to be reversed and the historical initiative finally seized. Such is the lesson of Mohamed Ali and Abd al Krim, of Ahmad Arabi and the Algerian F.L.N., of Nasser and the Palestinian resistance, of South Yemen and oil politics. Such is the lesson of the October war. For here, as ever, the profound truth is verified of that ancient verse from the Jâhiliyyah (pre-Islamic times): "Time is a sword. If you do not cut it, it cuts you." The world and its cutting edge has been blunted by the activist voluntarism of the Arab world. The way forward can only be forged through the utilization of political decision to literally compel a profound transformation of Arab societies and culture.

The necessity to couple national liberation with social revolution is well-known, and broadly accepted, albeit in vastly different fashions, by the different social forces making up the national front. It is only too apparent that the stagnation of the front's leadership in the hands of the traditional bourgeoisie, diffident of the masses of the rural and urban working population, can only act as a brake on the consolidation of the national movement, and as a stumbling block in the path of the achievement of its liberation goals. Such was the significance of the June, 1967 catastrophe, in both political and military terms.

Politics and the Uses of Power

The primacy of politics directly leads to formulating the problem of the organic interrelations between power and culture. The central question of the uses of power, can only be answered in the positive mode in the whole gamut of societies that make up the Arab world now surging towards its renaissance.

Power can be used to achieve those historic aims defined by the broad front of the Arab Long March. In the Arab case, socioeconomic aims include displacement of the national conservative or center-right social groups and classes. Linked to the predominantly commercial and agrarian capitalism of the colonialists, these groups sometimes act as the compradores of the imperial metropolis and represent a combination of conservative ideology coupled with Western-oriented liberal ideas. The subsequent rise to power of the national radical or center-left social groups and classes would result in the dismantling of colonial and imperialist penetration and the restructuration of the national economy in the direction of industrialization and agrarian reform. State capitalism and cooperativism would become the leading sectors in an economy developed under a plan of economic and social development and oriented toward socialism. This process would be coupled with a front of converging ideologies, from the radical fundamentalist or "political Islam" to the national progressive.

Such a socioeconomic and political vision belongs to the realm of political strategy, deployed at the tactical and organizational level through the unceasing ebb and flow of the national movement. A redistribution of socioeconomic power does not, however, exhaust the range of historic aims. Arab society, as the key mediating civilizational-cultural circle in the world, was once the major power and cultural area of the world. Until the fifteenth century, it was the seat of a magnificent empire, stretching from the Atlantic to the China seas, where philosophy, science, art, and literature suggested a great and lasting national-cultural ensemble. It was accomplished through a fusion of the oldest nations and civilizations of the world within the wider national-cultural framework of Islam and Eastern christianity. It is therefore not a slip of the tongue if the major figures of the Arab national movement choose the term *Nahdah* to define what they visualize as the true historic aim of their action. And it is no accident to see this aim—the renaissance of the Arab world—as the specific historic aim of the Arab national movement in all Arab lands.

Civilizational Strategy

Because of this larger aim of the Arab movement, it is necessary to conceive, develop, and implement a civilizational strategy—as distinguished from a mere political strategy. This civilizational strategy aims at mobilizing all energies toward the revival of the Arab ensemble in terms of contemporaneity. The masses of the population, rural and urban, will come to play the major role in this process, at the center of the broad united national front. The historic process of vanquishing decadence and promoting a renewal of an independent, national, contemporaneous life will be accomplished through, and coupled or identified with, the remolding of the power elite, from the traditional elites to the national radical vanguards.

The elaboration of the Arab civilizational strategy must address itself to several component elements:

1. The primacy of the political must be asserted. The organic relationship between national liberation and social revolution should be viewed both from the specificity of the Arab world as a whole and each of its major national units and from the geopolitical standpoint, particularly the changing patterns of world power and medium range perspective.

2. At the cultural level a philosophy of contemporaneity must evolve which is capable of inspiring the broad spectrum of societal formations, political trends, and intellectual schools within the national front. A general philosophic framework will weld the broad Arab masses with a clear vision of their contemporary identity as it relates to specific contribution to the future of mankind. Such a philosophy of culture, which can also be labelled a philosophy of civilization, ought to be concerned with the fundamental problems of philosophy: a system of values, man's self-image, and the meaning and quality of contemporary life. It will put an end to the absurd and pernicious drive towards economism. It will reassert the concern of man as "zoon politikon," the civic man. This process will be conducted both in a direct, national-cultural way, and in a comparatist way, i.e., studying the nature of other national-cultural projects within the network of the dialectics of civilizations.

It would never be feasible to restrict the process of the Arab renaissance to the mere politist level because major political processes appear to be immensely more loaded with culture than was visualized in the ideologies of Europe's industrial revolution. The future will depend on comprehension of the dialectics of civilizations and national cultures. That understanding will chart a new historic course enabling Arab nations to become major actors in the molding of the destinies of mankind.

The dialectics of civilizations and cultures necessitate a discussion of the following dimensions:

1. The specific philosophy of culture or civilization prevailing in the relevant area can provide a key to a complex set of problems. These often include: the image of man; the range of variable patterns of acceptable social organization; the range of outside challenges; and the type of reaction mounted to face such challenges, e.g., economic autarcy, racial-imperial invasions.

2. The historic phase during which such cultural philosophies are deploying is significant because of the relative and varying stresses on themes, ideas, policies, and confrontations. For example, Europe launched the Crusades against the Arabs during the Middle Ages; while the West is now trying to control the manifold processes of

economic, social, and cultural development by using the energy crisis in a global counteroffensive.

This method would lead to elaborating the interactions of specific courses of vision and action, each emanating from different civilizational and national-cultural circles and units, in a select series of variable patterns ranging from dialogue to global confrontation. Yet they would be complementary. The key to the study of the dialectics of civilizations and cultures seems to be the Maoist theory "On Contradiction," especially the distinction between the principal, antagonistic contradiction and secondary nonantagonistic contradictions, each category to be determined by the respective political leaderships.

Thus, the primacy of the political—via the negation of the culturalist approach—leads directly to the need to raise culture to the level of politics and develop a vision of civilizational renaissance.

THE CHALLENGE OF CONTEMPORARY ARAB HISTORY

Wave after wave of converging analysis shape critical understanding of the civilizational significance of the Arab national liberation war. One question remains paramount: Is the Arab world or its present political leaderships prepared to meet the challenges of contemporary history, as a vital part of the rising East now seizing upon the keys of historical initiative?

The Arab world has shown itself capable of taking action, of breaking the "logic of contempt," of imposing its own political decision in matters relating to its own national identity and future history. Yet, inadequacies, contradictions, divisions, regressive ideas, and patterns of behaviour, are hindering the surge forward in a powerful manner. Discouraging, scornful, and contemptuous evaluations tend to dismiss the whole process, and particularly its most visible element, the October war.

One difficulty in approaching the civilizational renaissance resides in the very texture of the Arab world. Egypt has been, is, and shall remain, the major unit of Arab thought and action during modern times. The first stage of the Arab renaissance started with the rise of the new state formation in Egypt under Mohamed Ali, Ibrahim, Tahtâwi, and their companions. It took all the combined power of Europe to break what was then the first modern state in the Orient, two generations before Meiji, a century before Ataturk and the Long March. The destruction of the navy and armed forces of Egypt between 1836 and 1847 and the dismantling of its economic autarky were aimed at blocking the road to Istanbul in front of Mohamed Ali. Otherwise, a renewed center of power, led by Egypt, would have been able to deploy and develop as the major Mediterranean power. It, therefore, had to be, and was, broken, from the London Treaty of 1840 until the British occupation in 1882.

The process began anew after the rise of the Arab national movement around Egypt in the second phase of the renaissance, from the Wafd to Nasser. It was no coincidence that Egypt had to bear the brunt of four wars, particularly the June, 1967 disaster, and find itself in the distressing economic condition which its population now has to endure. It was Egypt's decision to go to war, on October 6, 1973, that unleashed the "oil war"—and not vice-versa. It was, and still is, the political and cultural potential of Egypt that has given momentum to the Arab march towards liberation and unity, the Palestine resistance movement, and the waves of liberation and radical transformation which unfolded in several Arab lands, particularly during Nasser's rule.

The difficulty resides in the ways and means to develop a viable, forward-looking, positive pattern of integrated interaction between all parts and elements of the Arab national movement, around Egypt, keeping both a sense of coordinated direction and optimal flexibility. It is, in other words, the basic problematic of Arab unity, a historic process now vastly magnified by the October war. Most of the political leaderships now entrusted with the responsibility of charting the Arab renaissance clearly belong to the traditional conservative bourgeois pattern, attuned to either the liberal capitalistic Western model, or a contemporary version of Islamic fundamentalism. There are also important sectors of a genuinely national-radical type, at work to shape the unity between national liberation and social revolution, as the first requisite towards the renaissance process.

The major part of these political leaderships should be capable of visualizing the complexity of the historic tasks ahead. But there are objective reasons why such groups cannot shoulder, or shoulder alone, the massive and highly difficult array of tasks ahead: class interests, habits of thought and behaviour, the incapacity to imagine a different structuration of the national front, a reluctance to rely on the popular masses, and a profoundly inadequate comprehension of the meaning and necessities of an Arab civilizational strategy oriented towards a national-populist renaissance. The combination of vested interests and lack of cultural vision magnifies these tendencies.

Several factors show that the role of the rural and urban masses in the long process of national liberation and social revolution in the Arab world has been immensely more important and creative than official history admits. Official history speaks of Omar Makram, but not the "mob" of Cairo and Alexandria; Tahtawi, but not the workers of the Bulaq printing press and school teachers; Ibrahim pasha, but little about his fellahin-soldiers; Arabi and his companions, but nearly nothing about the peasant insurrections; the Wafd, but, till recently, nothing about its secret organization for armed struggle; the "Free Officers" around Nasser but nothing about the privates and noncommissioned officers that constituted the bulk of the radical movement in the royalist army; socialism, but not the ideas and actions of the communists and progressives.

It remains, however, to prove the capacity of the popular masses to better conceive and direct civilizational strategy. The proof is perforce orientative, not assertive: there is immense talent, imagination, intelligence, and human potential available amidst the people, especially at times of rapid and radical national liberation movements. The correct answer would not be in another bout of Manichean choice, but, rather, in the following formulation: the tasks of the Arab renaissance can better be approached and achieved through the restructuration of Arab united national fronts to include all social groups and classes not linked with imperialism and all national schools of thought and action involved in the renaissance process. The leadership of these fronts should be in the hands of the popular sectors, profoundly inclined to engineer, or support, that combination of protracted national liberation struggle with radical populist policies in depth that is required by a meaningful advance of the Arab peoples through the renaissance of their world.

Such appears to be the contemporary challenge in historical terms. By deploying the great potentials and opportunities opened by the October war, a united national front should learn how to bring together—in a non-antagonistic contradictory confrontation through action—both the level of all social classes and groups devoted to independence and liberation, and the different schools of thought and action rooted in the national culture, now decisively oriented toward its future.

Edward W. Said

SHATTERED MYTHS

There is therefore one language, which is not
mythical, it is the language of man the
producer: whenever man speaks in order to
transform reality and no longer to preserve it
as an image, whenever he links his language
to the making of things . . . myth is
impossible.

Roland Barthes

MYTHS ARE A LANGUAGE: organized, systematic, bearers of a code they
articulate but do not either question or fully reveal. There are no
innocent, no unideological myths, just as there are no "natural" myths.
Every myth is a made object, and it is the essential bad faith of
a myth to seem, or rather to pretend, that it is a fact and a "natural"
presence without origin or source. Yet in discussing myths generally
one must avoid the trap by which myths endanger their investigator.
For a myth to be decoded it must first be specified; no myth should
be referred to as merely existing, otherwise its "naturalness" would
thereby be endorsed and the whole point of investigating and de-
mythifying lost. A myth's first and greatest enemy is analysis and
specification, by which its seemingly durable presence—like that of
a natural object—is shown to have been made in a specific way,
out of specific materials, and for specific reasons. Most important,
the locale of the myth must be identified. Every myth takes place,

but where and how are the crucial questions, especially since myths are neither stable nor made up of simple elements.

The aftermath of so complex an event as the 1973 Arab-Israeli war includes the breakup of myths. I use the word *breakup* advisedly, since a common mistake made about myths is that they disappear once they have been shattered. For what usually happens is that a myth is decomposed into the fragments that make it up; a decisive event is most often necessary for such a change, which makes the myth less useful than formerly. Later, however, a new myth will emerge, just as during historical periods of marked individuality (the Age of Modernism, the Jazz Age) new idioms and expressions emerge, often from out of the wreckage of old systems of signification. Myths are more like plastic than wood, which wears out and away.

We cannot yet tell what new myths will be born, but we can now examine the systems of myth that obtained before the war, which the war jarred, and which are even now gathering again to be reborn. But first we must ask ourselves, where are (or, where were) the myths? what were they? where did they come from? what did they do? what supported them?

Perhaps one should say at the very outset that myths can, and indeed must, be discussed scientifically. Since a myth is nothing if not a belief (or at least a strongly recommended imperative toward belief) it seems to take a position putting it beyond question. The divine right of kings, for example, uses a typical mytho-logic: Kings are divinely ordained, therefore to question a king's right is to set oneself against God, which (given the theological premises of the argument) is either blasphemous or impossible, or both. Myths are no respecters of what they mythify—a myth merely uses a subject (kings, for instance) to preserve a point of view. In this sense, therefore Barthes is correct in saying that "statistically, myth is on the right. There, it is essential; well-fed, sleek, expansive, garrulous, it invents itself ceaselessly. It takes hold of everything, all aspects of the law, of morality, of aesthetics, of diplomacy, of household equipment, of literature, of entertainment."[1] Calling a myth a myth is to intervene between the myth and what it has appropriated. It is to replace mytho-logic with history, nature with the struggles of culture, man the victimized with man the producer, facts with the organized structures of an oppressing language. To discuss myths scientifically

1. Roland Barthes, *Mythologies,* trans. Annette Lavers (New York: Hill and Wang, 1972), p. 148. Much of my discussion of myth is generally indebted to Barthes's book, especially its final section "Myth Today," pp. 109–159.

is at once to de-mythify and to make evident what previously had been hidden and taken for granted. "Let the myths appear" should be the first rule.

The myths of Arab society under discussion here are those preserved in the discourse of Orientalism, a school of thought and a discipline of study whose focus includes "the Arabs," Arabism, Islam, the Semites, and "the Arab mind." It should be immediately evident that Arab society *in fact* cannot be discussed, because the Arabs all told number over a hundred million people and at least a dozen different societies, and there is no truly effective intellectual method for discussing all of them together as a single monolith. Any reduction of this whole immense mass of history, societies, individuals, and realities to "Arab society" is therefore a mythification. But what it is possible to do is to analyze the structure of thought for which such a phrase as "Arab society" is a kind of reality—and this structure, as we shall soon see, is a myth, with its codes, discourse, and tropes. This structure has a history (albeit a far simpler one than the subject it purportedly treats) and is upheld by a set of institutions that give it whatever power and validity it seems to have. For this myth the October war was a surprise, but not because "the Arabs" fought well; rather because the Arabs, according to the myth, were not supposed to fight at all, and because the war seemed therefore to be a deviation out of context, a violation of a well-established logic. This is a chorus found in many places; it is worth examining in some detail because today the myths of Orientalism surface there most readily.[2]

Myths Unleashed by the October War

One of the commonest motifs to appear in discussions of the October war was not that the war took place, but rather that it took place

2. My strategy in this essay will be in three parts. First I shall analyze the myths and their structures of Orientalism summoned by the war. What I can discuss will be a few cases that clearly are reasons why Orientalism found the war, specially the fact that the Arabs went to war, a surprise. I shall generalize of course, leaving it to be understood that I will discuss the discourse as a systematic whole, and not every instance of it. Space dictates such a procedure, as well as a conviction that exceptions to the rules of Orientalism as a discourse prove the rules. Secondly, the present institutions that sustain Orientalism are analyzed as the result of the modern history of Western scholarship of the Orient. And finally my concern is with ways of dealing methodologically and practically with Orientalism as a myth system and as a type of thought.

in the form of a Western and Israeli intelligence failure. This is as inventive as saying that the American use of napalm in Vietnam was really the natives' failure to use suntan oil. On October 31, 1973 the *New York Times* quoted Henry Kissinger as follows: "the gravest danger of intelligence assessments" is in trying "to fit the facts into existing preconceptions and to make them consistent with what is anticipated." The *Times* went on by itself: "This is a judgement widely shared in the intelligence community." True, and what is interesting is that such a community can exist because it speaks a common language of myths for which "intelligence" is possible with regard to the Middle East because of a hoard of practical knowledge, historical lore, and unshakable conviction ultimately derived from Orientalism. According to Orientalism, Orientals can be observed as possessing certain habits of mind, traits of character, and idiosyncrasies of history and temperament; the sum total of these characteristics inclines Orientals towards certain types of action. Kissinger objected to the rigidity of these inclinations, not as unreal objects, but as mistakenly formulated. In other words what mattered here was the sophistication and flexibility of a formula for predicting human behavior (and congruently, the bases in social scientific attitudes of the formula) not the notion that any formula for prediction will necessarily be inadequate, so long as it relies on such schools of thought as Orientalism.

A startling piece of Orientalism clarifies the problem with which Kissinger was trying (hopelessly, I think) to deal. In its February, 1974 issue *Commentary,* the leading Jewish intellectual journal in the United States, gave its readers an article by Professor Gil Carl Alroy entitled "Do the Arabs Want Peace?" Alroy teaches political science at Hunter, and is the author of two works, *Attitudes Towards Jewish Statehood in the Arab World,* and *Images of Middle East Conflict,* so he is a man who professes to know the Arabs, and he is obviously some sort of expert on image–making. His argument is quite predictable: that Arabs want to destroy Israel, that Arabs really say what they mean (and Alroy makes ostentatious use of his ability to cite evidence from Egyptian newspapers, evidence which he everywhere identifies with "Arabs" as if the two, Arabs and Egyptian newspapers, are but one), and so on and on, with unflagging, one-eyed zeal. Quite the center of his article, as it is the center of previous work by other "Arabists" (synonymous with "Orientalists") like General Y. Harkabi whose province is something called the "Arab mind," is a working hypothesis on what Arabs, if one peels off all the outer nonsense, are really like. In other words Alroy must prove that because Arabs are first of all as one in their bent for bloody vengence, second, psychologically incapable of peace, and third, congenitally tied to a concept of justice that means the opposite of that, because of these then they are not to be trusted and must be fought interminably as one fights any other fatal disease. For evidence Alroy's principle exhibit is a quotation taken from an essay modestly entitled "The Arab World" and written by Harold W. Glidden for the February, 1972 issue of the *American Journal of Psychiatry*. Alroy finds that Glidden "captured the cultural differences between the Western and the Arab view" of things "very well." Alroy's argument is clinched therefore, the Arabs are unregenerate savages, and thus an authority on the Arab mind has told a wide audience of presumably concerned Jews that they must continue to watch out. And he has done it academically, dispassionately, fairly, using evidence taken from the Arabs themselves—who, he says with Olympian assurance, have "emphatically ruled out . . . real peace"—and from psychoanalysis.

Harold Glidden turns out to be a retired member of the Bureau of Intelligence and Research, U.S. Department of State, a Ph.D. graduate of Princeton, Department of Oriental Languages, and no doubt he is an instance of those legendary Arabists of whom one has always heard so much. What his work is doing in a reputable psychiatric journal is beyond me, and Alroy—or any other social scientist for that matter—would never dare to quote such trash about any other nationality. It is not only naked racism; it is also the poorest sort of scholarship, even though it is essentially a repetition of canonical Orientalist myths. Glidden's article is nothing less than a four page, double-columned psychological portrait of over one hundred million people, considered for a period of 1300 years, and he cites exactly four sources for his views: a recent book on Tripoli, one issue of *Al-Ahram, Oriente Moderno*, and a book by Majid Khadduri. The article itself, purports to uncover "the inner workings of Arab behavior" which from Glidden's or the Western point of view is "aberrant" but for Arabs is "normal." This is an auspicious start, for thereafter we are told that Arabs stress conformity and that the Arabs inhabit a shame culture whose "prestige system" involves the ability to attract followers and clients. (As an aside we are told that "Arab society is and always has been based on a system of client-patron relationships.") The analysis further states that Arabs can function only in conflict situations, that prestige is based solely on the ability to dominate others, and that a shame culture—and Islam itself—makes of revenge a virtue. (Here Glidden triumphantly cites the June 29, 1970 *Ahram* to show that "in 1969 (in Egypt) in 1070 cases of murder where the perpetrators were apprehended, it was found that 20 per cent of the murders were based on a 'desire to wipe out shame,' 30 per cent on a desire to satisfy real or imaginary wrongs, and 31 per cent on a desire for blood revenge.") We are told that if from a Western point of view "the only rational thing for the Arabs to do is to make peace . . . for the Arabs the situation is not governed by this kind of logic, for objectivity is not a value in the Arab system."

Glidden continues now, heady with the power of his analysis: "it is a notable fact that while the Arab value system demands absolute solidarity within the group, it at the same time encourages among its members a kind of rivalry that is destructive of that very solidarity"; in Arab society only "success counts" and "the end justifies the means"; Arabs live "naturally" in a world "characterized by anxiety expressed in generalized suspicion and distrust, which has been labelled free-floating hostility"; "the art of subterfuge is highly developed in Arab life, as well as in Islam itself"; the Arab need for vengence overrides everything, otherwise the Arab would feel "ego-destroying" shame. Therefore if "Westerners consider peace to be high on the scale of values" and if "we have a highly developed consciousness of the value of time," this is not true of Arabs. "In fact," we are told, "in Arab tribal society (where Arab values originated), strife, not peace, was the normal state of affairs because raiding was one of the two main supports of the economy." The purpose of this learned disquisition is merely to show how on the Western and Arab scale of values "the relative position of the elements is quite different."

When Alroy was challenged for his use of this shabby stuff he replied with the supreme innocence of a man confident in the tradition of his learning that "what is said [in his article and in Glidden's] is about as controversial amongst Orientalists as the multiplication table."[3]

Alroy is altogether too trivial an intelligence to bother with for long. He is, however, useful as a symptom. Anyone who refers blithely to a humanistic tradition whose uncontroversial tenets are as irrefutable as multiplication tables can only be expected mindlessly to repeat their underlying code. Neither Glidden nor Alroy disappoints. As with all mythologies theirs is a structure built around a set of simple oppositions, which initiate the distinction between Orientalism and every other form of human knowledge. This then is the key reduction. On the one hand there are Westerners and on the other there are

3. This statement was made by Alroy in a response following a letter of mine to *Commentary*, LVII, No. 5 (May, 1974).

Orientals; the former are (in no particular order) rational, peaceful, liberal, logical, capable of holding real values, without natural suspicion and distrust, and so forth. Orientals are none of these things. These are explicit distinctions. Less explicit is the difference between *us* (Europeans, whites, Aryans) and *them* (non-Europeans, blacks or browns, Semites). The great irony of course is that in many cases non-Europeans—Arabs or Jews—may be Orientalists who consider themselves part of the European, non-Oriental camp; the political meaning of such a confusion will be alluded to from time to time in this essay. The point here is how the myths of Orientalism rely upon a set of differences that may even scant the really real, or empirical, distinction between a European and a non–European Orientalist.

The Oriental as Seen by the Orientalist

A still more implicit and powerful difference posed by the Orientalist as against the Oriental is that the former writes about, whereas the Oriental is written about. For the latter passivity is the presumed role, for the former, the power to observe, study, and so forth. As Barthes said, a myth (and its perpetuators) can invent itself (themselves) ceaselessly. The Oriental is given as fixed, stable, in need of investigation, and in need even of knowledge about himself. There is no dialectic either desired or allowed. There is a source of information (the Oriental) and a source of knowledge (the Orientalist): in short, a writer and a subject matter otherwise inert. The relationship between the two is radically a matter of power, for which there are of course numerous images. Here is an instance taken from Raphael Patai's *Golden River to Golden Road: Society, Culture, and Change in the Middle East:*

> In order properly to evaluate what Middle Eastern culture will *willingly accept* from the embarrassingly rich storehouses of Western civilization, a better and sounder understanding of Middle Eastern culture *must first be acquired.* The same prerequisite is necessary in order to gauge the probable effects *of newly introduced traits on* the cultural context of tradition directed peoples. Also, the ways and means *in which new cultural offerings can be made palatable* must be studied much more thoroughly than was hitherto the case. In brief the only way in which *the Gordian knot of resistance* to Westernization in the Middle East *can be unraveled* is that of studying the Middle East, *of obtaining a fuller picture* of its traditional culture, a better understanding of *the processes of change taking place* in it at present, and *a deeper insight* into the psychology of human groups brought up in Middle Eastern culture. *The task is taxing, but the prize, harmony between the West*

and a neighboring world area of crucial importance, is well worth it. (italics added)⁴

The metaphorical figures running through this passage (indicated by italics) come from a variety of human activities, some commercial, some horticultural, some religious, some veterinary, some historical. Yet in each case the relation between the Middle East and the West is really defined as sexual. The Middle East is resistant, as any virgin would be, but the male-scholar wins the prize by bursting open, penetrating through the Gordian knot (the hymen, clearly), despite the taxing task (energetic foreplay?). "Harmony" is the result of the conquest of maidenly coyness; it is not by any means the coexistence of equals. The underlying power relation between scholar and subject-matter is never once altered: it is uniformly favorable to the Orientalist. Study, understanding, knowledge, and evaluation, masked as blandishments to harmony, are instruments of conquest.

The verbal operations in such writing as Patai's (who has outstripped even his previous work in his more recent *The Arab Mind*)⁵ aim at a very particular sort of compression and reduction. Much of his paraphernalia is anthropological—he describes the Middle East as a culture area—but the result is to eradicate the plurality of differences among the Arabs (whoever they may be in fact) in the interest of one difference, that one setting Arabs off from everyone else. As a subject matter for study and analysis they can be controlled more readily. Moreover, thus reduced they can be made to permit, legitimate, and valorize such general nonsense as that found in Sania Hamady's *Temperament and Character of the Arabs:*

> The Arabs so far have demonstrated an incapacity for disciplined and abiding unity. They experience collective outbursts of enthusiasm but do not pursue patiently collective endeavors, which are usually embraced half-heartedly. They show lack of coordination and harmony in organization and function, nor have they revealed an ability for cooperation. Any collective action for common benefit or mutual profit is alien to them.⁶

4. Raphael Patai, *Golden River to Golden Road: Society, Culture and Change in the Middle East* (3rd ed.; Philadelphia: University of Pennsylvania Press, 1969), p. 406.

5. Raphael Patai, *The Arab Mind* (New York: Scribner's, 1973).

6. Sania Hamady, *Temperament and Character of the Arabs* (New York: Twayne

The style of this prose tells more perhaps than Hamady intends. Verbs like *demonstrate, reveal,* and *show* are used without an object: to whom are the Arabs revealing, demonstrating, showing? To no one in particular, obviously, but to everyone in general. This is another way of saying that these truths are self-evident only to a priviledged or initiated observer, since nowhere does Hamady cite generally available evidence for her observations. Besides, given the inanity of the observations what sort of evidence could there be? As her prose moves along her tone increases in confidence, e.g., "any collective action . . . is alien to them." The categories harden, the assertions are more unyielding, and the Arabs have been totally transformed from people into no more than the putative subject of Hamady's style. The Arabs exist only as an occasion for the tyrannical observer.

And so it is throughout the work of the contemporary Orientalist— assertions of the most bizarre sort dot his pages, whether it is a Halpern arguing that even though all human thought processes can be reduced to eight, the Islamic mind is capable of only four,[7] or a Berger assuming that since the Arabic language is much given to rhetoric Arabs are consequently incapable of true thought.[8] These assertions

---

Publishers, 1960), p. 100. Hamady's book is a favorite among Israelis and Israeli apologists; Alroy cites her approvingly, and so too does Amos Elon in *The Israelis: Founders and Sons* (New York: Rinehart and Winston, 1971). Monroe Berger (see note 8) also cites her frequently. Her model is a book like Edward William Lane's *Account of the Manners and the Customs of the Modern Egyptians* (1833-35), but she has none of Lane's literacy, wit, or general learning.

7. Halpern's thesis is presented in "Four Contrasting Repertories of Human Relations in Islam: Two Pre-Modern and Two Modern Ways of Dealing with Continuity and Change, Collaboration and Conflict and the Achieving of Justice," a paper presented to the 22nd Near East Conference at Princeton University on Psychology and Near Eastern Studies, May 8, 1973. This treatise was prepared for by Halpern's "A Redefinition of the Revolutionary Situation," *Journal of International Affairs,* XXIII, No. 1 (1969), 54-75.

8. Monroe Berger, *The Arab World Today* (New York: Anchor Books, 1964), p. 140. Much the same sort of implication underlines the clumsy work of quasi-Arabists like Joel Carmichael and Daniel Lerner; it is there more subtly in political and historical scholars who include Theodore Draper, Walter Laquer, Elie Kedourie. It is strongly in evidence in such highly-regarded works as Gabriel Baer, *Population and Society in the Arab East,* trans. Hanna Szoke (New York: Frederick A. Praeger, 1964) and Alfred Bonne, *State and Economics in the Middle East: A Society in Transition* (London: Routedge and Kegan Paul Ltd., 1955). The rule seems by consensus to be that if they think at all Arabs think differently, i.e. not necessarily with reason, and often without it. See also Adel Daher's RAND study, *Current Trends in Arab Intellectual Thought* (RM-5979-FF, December, 1969) and its typical conclusion that "the concrete

are myth in their function and structure, and yet one must try to understand what other imperatives govern their use. Here one speculates of course. Orientalist generalizations about the Arabs are very detailed when it comes to critically itemizing Arab characteristics, far less so when it comes to analyzing Arab strengths. The Arab family, Arab rhetoric, the Arab character, etc., despite copious descriptions by the Orientalist, appear denatured, that is, without human potency, even as these same descriptions possess a fullness and depth in their sweeping power over the subject matter. Hamady again:

> Thus, the Arab lives in a hard and frustrating environment. He has little chance to develop his potentialities and define his position in society, holds little belief in progress and change, and finds salvation only in the hereafter.[9]

What the Arab cannot achieve himself is to be found in the writing about him. The Orientalist is supremely certain of his potential, is not a pessimist, and is able to define not only his own position, but the Arab's as well. The picture of the Arab-Oriental that emerges is determinedly negative; yet why this endless series of works on him? What grips the Orientalist, if it is not—as it certainly is not—love of Arab science, mind, society, and achievement?

Orientalist Fascination with the Arab

Two factors attract the Orientalist: number and generative power. Both qualities are reducible to each other ultimately, but are separated for the purposes of analysis. Almost without exception, every contemporary work of Orientalist scholarship (especially in the social sciences)

---

problem-solving approach is conspicuously absent from Arab thought," p. 29. In a review–essay for the *Journal of Interdisciplinary History,* IV, No. 2 (Autumn, 1973), 287-298, Roger Owen attacks the very notion of "Islam" as a concept for the study of history. His focus is *The Cambridge History of Islam* which, he finds, in certain ways perpetuates an idea of Islam (to be found in such writers as C. H. Becker and Max Weber) "defined essentially as a religious, feudal, and antirational system, [that] lacked the necessary characteristics which had made European progress possible." For a sustained proof of Weber's total inacurracy see Maxim Rodinson's *Islam and Capitalism,* trans. Brian Pearce (New York: Pantheon Books, 1974), pp. 76-117. There is a useful short account of Orientalist myths militarily in operation before and during the October war by Yassin el-Ayouti, "Al-jabha al-ma 'anawiya fi harb October," *Siyassa Dowaliya,* No. 35, January, 1974, pp. 66-72.

9. Hamady, *op. cit.,* p. 197.

has a great deal to say about the family, its male-dominated structure, its all-pervasive influence in the society. Patai's work is a typical example. A silent paradox immediately presents itself, for if the family is an institution for whose general failures the only remedy is the placebo of modernization, it must be acknowledged that the family continues to produce itself, it is fertile, and it is the source of Arab existence, such as it is, in the world. What Berger refers to as "the great value men place upon their own sexual prowess"[10] suggests the lurking power behind Arab presence in the world. If on the one hand Arab society is represented in almost completely negative and generally passive terms—to be ravished and won by the Orientalist hero—we can assume on the other that such a representation is a way of dealing with the great variety and potency of Arab diversity, whose source is if not intellectual and social then sexual and biological. Yet the absolutely inviolable taboo in Orientalist discourse is that that very sexuality must never be taken seriously. It can never be explicitly blamed for the absence of achievement and "real" rational sophistication the Orientalist everywhere discovers among the Arabs. And yet this is the missing link in arguments whose main project is criticism of "traditional" Arab society, such as Hamady's, Berger's, Lerner's, and others. They recognize the power of the family, note the weaknesses of the Arab mind, remark on the importance of the Oriental world to the West, but never say what their discourse implies, that what is really left to the Arab after all is said and done is an undifferentiated sexual drive. On rare occasions—as in the work of Leon Mugniery—the explicit is made clear: that there is a "powerful sexual appetite . . . characteristic of those hot-blooded southerners."[11] Most of the time, however, the belittlement of Arab society and its reduction to platitudes inconceiveable for any except the racially inferior is carried on over an undercurrent of sexual exaggeration: the Arab produces himself, endlessly, sexually, and little else. The Orientalist says nothing about this, although his argument depends on it. "But cooperation in the Near East is still largely a family affair and little of it is found outside the blood group or village."[12] Which is to say that the only way in which Arabs count is sexually; institutionally, politically, and culturally they are nil, or next to nil. Numerically and sexually Arabs are actual.

10. Berger, *op. cit.*, p. 102.

11. Quoted by Irene Gendzier, *Frantz Fanon: A Critical Study* (New York: Pantheon Books, 1973), p. 94.

12. Berger, *op. cit.*, p. 151.

The difficulty with this view is that it complicates the passivity among Arabs assumed by Orientalists like Patai, and even Hamady, and the others. But it is in the logic of myths, like dreams, exactly to welcome radical antitheses. For a myth does not analyze or solve problems. It represents them as already analyzed and solved; that is, it presents them as already assembled images, in the way a scarecrow is assembled from bric-a-brac and then made to stand for a man. Since the image uses all material to its own end, and since by definition the myth displaces life, the antithesis between an over-sexed Arab and a passive doll is not functional. The discourse papers the antithesis over. An Arab is that impossible creature whose sexual energy drives him to paroxysms of overstimulation, and yet, he is as a puppet in the eyes of the world, staring vacantly out at a modern landscape he can neither understand nor cope with.

Just preceding the October war such an image of the Arab seemed to be notably relevant, and it was often occasioned by scholarly discussion of those two recent favorites of Orientalist expertise: revolution and modernization. Under the auspices of the School of Oriental and African Studies there appeared in 1972 a volume entitled *Revolution in the Middle East and Other Case Studies* edited by Professor P. J. Vatikiotis. The title is overtly medical, for we are expected to think of Orientals as finally being given the benefit of what traditional Orientalism had usually avoided: psychosexual attention. In this imposing compilation of studies by noted scholars the argument is obviously vulnerable as knowledge and as reading of the modern Arab world. At this point it is not of interest to examine the book's failures: the distortions, the willful slanting of scholarly evidence, the unbending desire to discredit and debunk the Arabs as a people and as a society. What is interesting is how close to the surface defensive fear of Arab sexuality has come. Having exhausted his timeworn arsenal of racial criticism made with scholarly detachment, the Orientalist now sheds his disguise, and attacks the very thing he fears most.

Professor Vatikiotis sets the tone of the collection with a quasi-medical definition of revolution, but since Arab revolution is in his mind and in his readers', the naked hostility of the definition seems acceptable. There is a very clever irony here about which I shall speak later. Vatikiotis's theoretical support is Camus, whose colonial mentality was no friend of revolution or of the Arabs, as Conor Cruise O'Brien has recently shown, but the phrase "revolution destroys both men and principles" is accepted from Camus as having "fundamental sense." Vatikiotis continues:

. . . all revolutionary ideology is in direct conflict with (actually, is a head-on attack upon) man's rational, biological and psychological makeup.

Committed as it is to a methodical metastasis, revolutionary ideology demands fanaticism from its adherents. Politics for the revolutionary is not only a question of belief, or a substitute for religious belief. It must stop being what it has always been namely, an adaptive activity in time for survival. Metastatic, soteriological politics abhors adaptiveness, for how else can it eschew the difficulties, ignore and bypass the obstacles of the complex biological-psychological dimension of man, or mesmerize his subtle though limited and vulnerable rationality. It fears and shuns the concrete and discrete nature of human problems and the preoccupations of political life: it thrives on the abstract and the Promethean. It subordinates all tangible values to the one supreme value: the harnessing of man and history in a grand design of human liberation. It is not satisfied with human politics which has so many irritating limitations. It wishes instead to create a new world not adaptively, precariously, delicately, that is, humanly, but by a terrifying act of Olympian pseudo-divine creation. Politics in the service of man is a formula that is unacceptable to the revolutionary ideologue. Rather man exists to serve a politically contrived and brutally decreed order.[13]

Whatever else this passage is—purple writing of the most extreme sort, counterrevolutionary zealotry—it is nothing less than fascism proclaimed in the name of the human, and a brutal identification of sexuality (pseudo-divine act of creation) with cancerous disease. Whatever is done by the "human" according to Vatikiotis is rational, right, subtle, discrete, concrete; whatever the revolutionary proclaims is brutal, irrational, mesmeric, cancerous. Procreation, change, and continuity are identified with sexuality and madness; not only with that but, wonder of wonders, with abstraction.

Vatikiotis's terms then are weighted and colored emotionally (from the right) by appeals to humanity and decency, and (against the left) by appeals to safeguard humanity from sexuality, cancer, madness, irrational violence, and revolution. Since it is Arab revolution that is in question the passage is to be read as follows: this is what revolution is, and if the Arabs or the Middle East want it, then that's a fairly telling comment on them, on what kind of inferior race they are. They are capable only of sexual incitement not Olympian (and Western

13. P. J. Vatikiotis (ed.), *Revolution in the Middle East, and Other Case Studies; proceedings of a seminar* (London: Allen and Urwin, 1972) pp. 8-9.

or modern) reason. The irony of which I spoke earlier now comes
into play. For a few pages later we find that the Arabs are so inept
that they cannot even aspire to, let alone consummate, the ambitions
of revolution. By implication, too, Arab sexuality need not be feared
for itself, but for its failure. In short we are asked to believe with
Vatikiotis, who has an almost Wildean skill with delicate paradoxes,
that revolution in the Middle East is a threat precisely because
revolution cannot be attained.

> The major source of political conflict and potential revolution in many
> countries of the Middle East, as well as Africa and Asia today, is the
> inability of so-called radical nationalist regimes and movements to
> manage, let alone resolve, the social, economic, and political problems
> of independence. [14]

> Until the states in the Middle East can control their economic activity
> and create or produce their own technology, their access to revolutionary
> experience will remain limited. The very political categories essential
> to a revolution will be lacking. [15]

Damned if you do, and damned if you don't. In this masterful, sneering
series of dissolving definitions revolutions emerge as figments of
sexually crazed minds which on closer analysis turn out not to be
capable even of the craziness Vatikiotis truly respects—which is human
not Arab, concrete not abstract, asexual not sexual.

Myth and the Arabic Language

The scholarly centerpiece of Vatikiotis's collection is Bernard Lewis's
essay, "Islamic Concepts of Revolution." The strategy here is extremely
refined. Most readers will know that for Arabic-speakers today the
work *thawra* and its immediate cognates means revolution; they will
know this also from Vatikiotis's introduction. Yet Lewis does not
describe the meaning of *thawra* until the very end of his article,
after he has discussed concepts such as *dawla*, *fitna* and *bughat* in
their historical and mostly religious context. The point there is mainly
that "the Western doctrine of the right to resist bad government is
alien to Islamic thought" [16] which led to "defeatism" and "quietism"
as political attitudes. At no point in the essay is one sure where

14. *Ibid.*, p. 12.
15. *Ibid.*, p. 13.
16. *Ibid.*, p. 33.

all these terms are supposed to be taking place except somewhere in the history of words. Then near the end of the essay:

> In the Arabic-speaking countries a different word was used for [revolution] *thawra*. The root th-w-r in classical Arabic meant to rise up (e.g., of a camel), to be stirred or excited, and hence, especially in Maghribi usage, to rebel. It is often used in the context of establishing a petty, independent sovereignty; thus, for example, the so-called party kings who ruled in eleventh century Spain after the breakup of the Caliphate of Cordova, are called *thuwwar* (sing. *tha'ir*). The noun *thawra* at first means excitement, as in the phrase, cited in the Sihah, a standard medieval Arabic dictionary, *intazir hatta taskun hadhihi 'lthawra*—wait till this excitement dies down—a very apt recommendation. The verb is used by al-Iji, in the form of *thawaran* or *itharat fitna*, stirring up sedition, as one of the dangers which should discourage a man from practising the duty of resistance to bad government. *Thawra* is the term used by Arabic writers in the nineteenth century for the French Revolution, and by their successors for the approved revolutions, domestic and foreign, of our own time.[17]

The entire passage reeks of condescension and bad faith. Why introduce the idea of a camel rising as an etymological root for modern Arab revolution except as a clever way of discrediting the modern? One can tolerate this sort of ploy when it is used by Vico in the *New Science* (1744) as he tries to show the etymological relations between the word for father and a shriek of fear; Vico's interest is in polemically attacking Cartesian rationalism. Yet Lewis's reason is patently to bring down revolution from its contemporary valorization to nothing more noble (or ugly) than a camel about to raise himself from the ground. Revolution is excitement, sedition, setting up a petty sovereignty and nothing more. One's best counsel (presumably only a Western scholar and gentleman can give it) is "wait till the excitement dies down." One wouldn't know from this slighting account of *thawra* that innumerable people have an active commitment to it, in ways too complex even for Lewis's pseudo-Gibbonian sarcasm and scholarship. But it is this kind of essentialized description that is canonical for students and policymakers concerned with the Middle East: that the upheavals and the energies among "the Arabs" are as consequential

---

17. *Ibid.*, pp. 38-9. Lewis's study *Race and Color in Islam* (New York: Harper and Row, 1971) expresses similar disaffection with an air of great learning; more explicitly political—but no less acid—is his *Islam in History: Ideas, Men and Events in the Middle East* (London: Alcove Press, 1973).

as a camel rising, as worth attention as the babblings of yokels. When Lewis's wisdom about *thawra* suddenly appears in a *New York Times* article on modern Libya (by Eric Pace, January 30, 1974) in the throes of revolutionary agitation, we are comforted to know that *thawra* originally—how contemptible is the adverb here—means a camel getting up, and so all the fuss about Libya and Qaddafi is pretty funny.

Lewis's association of *thawra* with a camel rising, and generally with excitement, hints much more broadly than is usual for him that the Arab is scarcely more than a neurotic sexual being. Each of the words he uses to describe revolution is tinged with sexuality: stirred, excited, rising up. But for the most part it is a bad sexuality he ascribes to the Arab. In the end, since Arabs are really not equipped for serious action, their sexual excitement (an erection) is no more noble than a camel's rising up. Instead of revolution there is sedition, setting up a petty sovereignty, excitement, which is as much as saying that instead of copulation the Arab can only achieve foreplay, masturbation, coitus interruptus. These are Lewis's implications, no matter how innocent his air of learning or parlor-like his language. Since he is so sensitive to the nuances of words he must be aware that his words have nuances as well.

Lewis's quasi-philology links him to a fairly widespread method among contemporary Orientalists, especially those specialists in Arab affairs whose work is connected to government intelligence agencies (Harkabi with Israeli intelligence)[18] or government propaganda machines (Alroy with the Zionist movement). For such specialists Arabic indicates the nature of the Arab mentality. Words are unmediated indices of irreducible character traits, regardless of culture, history, or social and economic circumstances. Arabic words reveal the Arab's obsession with oral functions (note the sexual motif creeping in again, ascribing sexuality to the Arab, then showing it to be an impaired, or immature sexuality) and the words' meanings are instances of either a malicious hidden significance (proving that Arabs are innately dishonest) or a fundamental inability to be like the "normal" Westerner.

The contemporary *locus classicus* for these views of Arabic is E. Shouby's "The Influence of the Arabic Language on the Psychology of the Arabs."[19] The author is described as "a psychologist with training

18. General Yehoshafat Harkabi, *Arab Attitudes Toward Israel,* trans. Misha Louvish (New York, 1972). Harkabi is the former chief of Israeli intelligence.

19. Originally published in the *Middle East Journal,* V (1951). Collected in *Readings in Arab Middle Eastern Societies and Cultures,* eds. Abdulla Lutfiyya and Charles

in both clinical and social psychology." His views have wide currency, probably because he is an Arab (a self-incriminating one at that) himself. The argument Shouby proposes is lamentably simpleminded, perhaps because he has no notion of what language is and how it operates. Nevertheless the subheadings of his essay tell a good deal of his story; accordingly Arabic is "General Vagueness of Thought," "Overemphasis on Linguistic Signs," "Overassertion and Exaggeration." Shouby is frequently quoted as an authority because he speaks like one and because what he hypostatizes is a sort of mute Arab who, at the same time, is a great word–master playing games without much seriousness or purpose. Muteness is an important part of what Shouby is talking about, since during his entire paper he never once quotes from the literature of which the Arab is so inordinately proud. Where then does Arabic influence the Arab mind? Exclusively within the mythological world created for the Arab by Orientalism. The Arab is a sign for dumbness combined with hopeless over-articulateness, impotence with hypersexuality, poverty with excess. That such a result can be attained by philological means testifies to the sad end of a once noble learned tradition, exemplified today only in individuals like M. M. Bravmann.[20] Today's Orientalist by and large is the last infirmity of a once-great scholarly discipline.

Language plays the dominant role in all the myths under discussion. It brings opposites together as "natural"; it presents human types in scholarly idioms and methodologies; it ascribes reality and reference to objects (other words) of its own making. Mythic language is discourse, that is, it cannot be anything but systematic; one does not really make discourse at will, nor statements in it, without first belonging—in some cases unconsciously, but at any rate involuntarily—to the ideology and the institutions that guarantee its existence. These latter are always the institutions of an advanced society dealing with a less-advanced society. The principal feature of mythical discourse is that it conceals its own origins as well as those of what it describes. Arabs are presented in the imagery of static, almost ideal types, neither as creatures with a potential in the process of being realized nor as a history being made. The exaggerated value heaped upon Arabic as a language permits the Orientalist to make the language equal to mind, society, history, and nature. Undoubtedly the absence

---

W. Churchill (The Hague: Mouton and Company, 1970), pp. 688–703.

20. See in particular his *The Spiritual Background of Early Islam: Studies Ancient Arab Concepts* (Leiden: E. J. Brill, 1972).

in Arabic of a full-fledged tradition of reported informal personal experience (autobiography, novel, etc.) makes it easier for the Orientalist to let the language as a whole have such uncontrolled significance; thus for the Orientalist the language speaks the Arab, not vice versa. There are historical and cultural reasons for this distortion.

MYTH-SUSTAINING INSTITUTIONS OF THE WEST

Most universities and institutes in the West have confined Orientalism since World War II to the culturally decadent thesis of the regional studies program. The reasons for this confinement are obvious, as all combinations of political expediency with unimaginative intellectual bureaucracy are obvious. The particularity of literary tradition, which is the way cultures survive, are transmitted, and exist (for the purposes of a scholar), was completely violated. Instead quite stupid bulks of knowledge began to appear masquerading as information about The Middle East, The Communist World, The Latin American countries, and Southeast Asia. New identities, quite without ontological validity, were created, each laced with fraudulent descriptions. One striking result is that nowhere in the West today is there a flourishing school of traditional Oriental philology or a serious attention paid to literary-humanistic Arab literature since the classical period. Near East institutes, Middle East area programs, Oriental studies or Oriental languages and civilization programs hash and rehash the same sociopolitical cliches about the Arab-Israeli conflict, Arab nationalism, the Arab mind, and Islamic institutions. Very few programs include a study of the traditions of Orientalism, let alone critiques of Orientalist methodology, or rational examination of what in fact is the material of Orientalism; it is only the occasional scholar who seriously asks himself why things are this way. Whole generations of Arab and Jewish students, whose stake in Orientalist theory and practise is very large, are educated into this corrupt racism, believing themselves to be gaining the "objective" methods of analysis their teachers have urged upon them. The result is Jews talking about "the Arab mind" and Arabs talking about "the Jewish mind": in the long run, both are equally bad.

We are very far from knowing today what true expense the people of the Middle East have paid for this kind of knowledge and for the kind of political action it has prompted. Nevertheless certain assessments can be made. To say that Orientalism is simply an academic school of thought and that it has no political, social, and even economic significance is unacceptable. For one thing is sure: the study of the Middle East in the West has not been disinterested. The oil and strategic wealth of the region as well as its historic importance have made scholarship an act of acquisition in the grossest way. Conversely to say that Orientalism is near the root of the Middle East problem is as great an exaggeration. As a thesis the cultural imperialism of the West (a form of which is Orientalism) is attractive, yet analytically and methodologically it is still a very gross, even crude notion. Since the modern history of the Middle East is very tightly linked to the history of Orientalism, two systems of knowledge supporting each other, it is difficult to detach them from each other and proclaim one the unilateral bloodsucker and the other the blood. What must not be forgotten, but rather investigated, is that the Orient was available as a subject matter; if Orientals were not informants to Orientalism in the traitorous way such a noun implies, they were nevertheless participants in a process they helped create. Moreover because Orientalists themselves have not often bothered with the matter of their work, its origins, its purposes, they cannot be excused for adhering to the traditions of their caste. Recent attempts to streamline Orientalism with contemporary techniques (like psychoanalysis) merely increase complicity in the mythology of the Oriental, his mind, race, and character. An accurate assessment would have to recognize the dialectic between Orientalist and Oriental. And also the restorative dialectic by which the Oriental asserts his actuality. As Fanon put it in describing a parallel situation: "It is the white man who creates the Negro. But it is the Negro who creates negritude. To the colonialist offensive against the veil, the colonized opposes the cult of the veil."[21]

The value of such events as the October war is that they highlight the prevailing system of ideas with which these events form a radical discontinuity. The mythology, in its detail as much as in its global structure, denied the Arabs a possibility for any sort of action. Vatikiotis visited Egypt in early 1973 and saw what he wanted to see: a sort of emblem of Oriental despondency. The army, he said, was "in a state of high combat readiness, I would suggest for military inaction"; the regime was dependent "on the condition of no war no peace."[22]

21. Fanon, A Dying Colonialism, trans. Haakon Chevalier (New York: Grove Press, 1967), p. 47. For a more recent analysis of the relationship between Arab and Westerner in common myths see Sadek G. al-Azm, Nagd al-thaty ba'd al-hazima (Beirut, 1969).

22. P. J. Vatikiotis, "Egypt Adrift: A Study in Disillusion," New Middle East, No. 54, March, 1973, p. 10. See also his hostility to Jacques Berque—stated on the basis of Berque's "ideological" approach, Vatikiotis being of course beyond ideology—in "The Modern History of Egypt Alla Franca," Middle Eastern Studies, X, No. 1 (January, 1974), 80–92.

No matter how much or how little one thinks of Anwar Sadat's political tactics since the war there can be no gain-saying the fact that his people moved from inaction to action, and it is precisely this rupture of continuity which Vatikiotis, Orientalism, and their joint myths, cannot account for. Not only does the rupture present insuperable epistemological problems for a discourse made up of legends of a supine and impotent Oriental, but it also casts many doubts upon the whole notion of political stagnation between 1967 and 1973. What in the history of Orientalism produced the myths so disturbed by the October war? Why were those myths so acceptable culturally and politically to the schools of thought for whom the October war was a shock?

Linguistic Concepts

Until the last third of the eighteenth century it was uniformly believed that the origin of language and culture was the Middle East. Proofs for this among Christian scholars and thinkers were linguistic for the most part—an important fact. The argument was that since the Bible was the word of God, and since the Bible originated in the Middle East, then Hebrew was the first language, and Adam, Abraham, and Christ the direct genealogical parents of modern man. The human community, barring primitive tribes in Africa and America, was a dynastic result of a first word, a first place, and a first man. Many of the people who believed these ideas had no knowledge of Hebrew, nor of Arabic; the two languages, along with other Semitic dialects, were connected to each other and with a vague place and time signifying the origin of knowledge and man.[23] Orientalists were antiquarians and/or Biblical scholars like Richard Simon. In short the Orient (or at least the Near Orient) until the late eighteenth century was a religious domain.

A great change in European knowledge, linguistic, philosophic and historical, took place roughly between 1780 and 1830. A very large part of this change had to do with the discrediting of such notions as that of the first language spoken by men and the discovery of much older, and more sophisticated languages than Hebrew. Sanskrit, in particular, caused an extraordinary shift in the conception of history and language. Prior to William Jones's descriptions of Persian and Sanskrit, such writers as Vico, Herder, and Rousseau had argued against

23. This is true of Dante in *De vulgari eloquentia* which sets forth the canonical view. For the situation in the 16th and 17th centuries see D. C. Allen, "Some Theories of the Growth and Origin of Language in Milton's Age," *Philological Quarterly*, XXVIII, No. 1 (January, 1949), 5-16.

the thesis of a particular original, divine language, preferring instead a sort of Ur-Speech theory linking man to his language in an irreducibly human way. But the concreteness of the work done by Jones, Wilkins, Colebrooke, de Sacy, and others solidly placed the study of language and cultures on an entirely new basis. During the first twenty years of the nineteenth century comparative philology was born as a discipline. Through the work of Bopp, the two Schlegels, Wilhelm von Humboldt, Grimm, and their disciples, the discovery of the Orient, especially Hindu thought and culture, created a revolution in European knowledge.

This is an enormously complicated change to describe, and no one has done it better and in greater detail than Raymond Schwab in his *La Renaissance Orientale*.[24] The change can be described briefly as the replacing of a dynastic idea of human language, culture, and knowledge with a communal, comparative, pluralistic view. Whereas formerly a line could be traced from the language given by God to Adam in Eden, through such events as the building of the Tower of Babel, down to Latin, and the European vernaculars, the new philologists of the early nineteenth century instead distinguished families of languages, whose univocal origin they admitted could never be discovered. Bopp says this explicitly on the first page of his *Comparative Grammar* (1836). Etymologies of words leading back to Hebrew, for example, now seemed like fanciful, unscientific exercises. The New Philologist was interested in the structure of a language, not in the derivation of all words from one word. Formerly a religious issue, language became a linguistic issue properly speaking, and thereafter a political and philosophic issue.[25]

The new science of comparative grammar viewed languages grouped into families with very distinct identities. Sanskrit taught linguists that no necessary connection could be assumed between a very old language and a simple language; compared to Hebrew or Greek, for instance, Sanskrit was not only older but had a more highly developed grammar and grammatical tradition. Therefore within the linguistic, and hence the cultural, families the new philologist postulated a skeletal beginning language—a kind of ideal type—whose structural, phonological, and syntactic features were shared by individual languages in the group. During the space of about thirty years in the early

24. Schwab, *La Renaissance orientale* (Paris: Payot, 1950).

25. See my "The World, the Text, the Critic," in *The Legacy of Structuralism: Polymorphic Criticism*, ed. Carl A. Rubino and Josué Harari (Baltimore: The Johns Hopkins Press, 1976).

nineteenth century European philology had identified and described the Indo-European, Semitic, Slavic, and Germanic language families. The Indo-European attracted the most attention, obviously, since for the first time it was possible to see the connection between the farther, older Orient and Europe.

Racism and the New Philology

Most accounts of these linguistic discoveries have paid little attention to the accompanying changes in political and philosophic views. For the German romantics the Orient was attractive because of its novelty, because it superseded the classics of Greece and Rome, because of its distance, and because of its indefinable reach into "spirit" and "time." The intimate relation between the Orient and German romanticism is conveyed in Friedich von Schlegel's assertion "Im Orient müssen wir das höchste Romantische suchen." Such an attitude carried itself into even the most austere philological studies, as well as into the poetry and philosophy of most of Western Europe. Just as during the seventeenth century French and English writers outdid each other trying to prove that their respective countries were the true descendants of Aneas or Brutus, now European scholars vied for the honor of showing how their languages carried the Indo-European spirit most faithfully.

What seems today like an obscure terminological quarrel between scholars had a crucial importance at the time: was *Indo-European* the correct name for that family of languages, or was *Indo-Germanic* more suitable? Clearly if the divine origin of language and history was no longer a very debatable issue, the burning question of the day, intellectually and politically, was the hierarchy of languages and cultures within and without the great linguistic-cultural groupings. Not only does this question coincide in time with the growing interest in definitions of cultural and national genius, it also corresponds to a moment when the enthusiasm for linguistic discovery allowed such brilliant men as von Humboldt to identify linguistic structure with mental structure. Thereafter the debate about language included such problems as the comparative study of levels of intellect and culture attainable by any given national group, the priority and value accorded one culture and language over another, and the attempt to provide typologies of mind based on general characteristics of linguistic structure. If the religious problem presented by the historical development of peoples and cultures had been superseded by the middle of the nineteenth century it was because theories of comparative cultural and linguistic value had taken center stage. Value was now defined: Which language most approaches perfection and, conversely, which culture and national character has achieved or may achieve the highest development, given the universal laws binding together all human societies and cultures and languages?

Inevitably such questions led to fully-fledged racism. This too is a little-remarked episode in the history of modern regional studies, but it is of major importance. Both before and during the discovery of the Orient the basic anthropological attitude of European writers was staunchly ethnocentric. Even in works like Montesquieu's *Lettres Persanes* and Goldsmith's *The Citizen of the World* where the Orient is used to criticise Europe, there is little doubt that Europe is the center of the world, and consequently one finds no sensitivity to the uniqueness of a foreign culture. This ethnocentric feeling intensified during the Oriental renaissance. This is not to say that learned men did not appreciate the particular quality of a distant culture, but that the prevailing feeling took the Orient as a region for Europe to discover, cherish, and speculate. The single most impressive work produced as a more or less direct result of the Oriental discoveries of this period, von Humboldt's *Uber die Verschiedenheit des Menschlichen Sprachbaues und ihren Einfluss auf die geistige Entwicklung des Menschen-geschlechts* (1836),[26] exudes an expansive pluralistic air when it comes to mankind and what Goethe had called the concert of nations and civilization. Humboldt asserts repeatedly that all languages and civilizations have intrinsic value, since each contributes something to the general good of mankind as a whole. Nevertheless, he draws an evaluative distinction between inferior and superior kinds of languages and minds. The more impressive are synthetic languages which have organic form (Sanskrit, Indo-European generally), whereas the less impressive are agglutinative, they merely add and subtract letters (Semitic mainly). The distinction had been made more insistently by Friedrich von Schlegel in his *Philosophie der Sprache und des Wortes* (1828-9), [27] and the view rapidly gained currency.

Von Humboldt's generous humanism had muted the severity of his judgement that certain languages were superior to others. He knew perfectly well, one feels, that according to his extraordinarily sophisticated, even epoch-making linguistics, language and mind were inter-

---

26. I have used the Prussian Academy edition of Wilhelm von Humboldt's *Gesammelte Schriften* (Berlin: Behr, 1903—1936), in this case Vol. VII, Part I, ed. Albert Leitzmann (1907).

27. See the *Kritische Friedrich-Schlegel-Ausgabe*, X, ed. Ernest Behler (Munich: Verlag Ferdinand Schöningh, 1969).

changeable, and that consequently a judgement in favor of one language was also an esteeming of that language's nation and race over others. One gets the impression in reading Humboldt's text that that was a conclusion he could logically see, but humanistically wished to mute and even deny as much as possible. That avoidance of the inevitable is to Humboldt's individual credit; it does not in any way cancel out the implications definitely present in the new philology that he, and a whole generation of European thinkers, espoused.

From the point of view of Orientalism the crucial text is Ernest Renan's major philological work, *Histoire générale et système comparé des langues semitiques,* which he published in 1847 near the beginning of his career. He states in the 1855 Preface that he projected the study as doing for the Semitic languages what Bopp had done for the Indo-European languages. It was to have been a philological treatise in the grandest possible style, not just a narrow grammatical survey of a linguistic grouping. Renan's models were Bopp, of course, and all those German *philologen* whose ranks included and were to include Wolf, August Boekh, Schleirmacher, Strauss, and Nietzsche. That is men for whom philology was the study of a language as the synthetic, sympathetic, historic total of an entire culture. Renan correctly stated that the Semitic languages had since 1800 been less in the center of European linguistic science (even though he seems to have forgotten Fabre D'Olivet's important *La Langue hebraique restituée*)[28] and, as if in justification, his writing is dominated by statements insisting on the comparative poverty of the Semitic languages. These languages, he says, are useful to modern linguistics because they are "incomparably less fecund" than Indo-European studies, therefore the philological investigator can be more "assured" in dealing with them, less subject to deceptions.[29]

Renan's opinions in the very first chapter, were they to have come from almost any other writer of the century, would have been dismissed as the rankest prejudice. Semites, he begins his long series of qualifications, are strangers to science or philosophy; in comparison with the Indo-European race, Semites "represente une combinaison inferieure de la nature humaine"; Semites have neither the high spiritu-

---

28. Antoine Fabre D'Olivet, *La Langue hebraique restituée* (Paris: Editions de la Tete de Feuille, 1971); Fabre was an important influence on Benjamin Lee Whorf. See the latter's *Language, Thought, and Reality,* ed. John B. Carroll (Cambridge, The MIT Press, 1969), pp. 74-76.

29. Ernest Renan, *Histoire generale et systeme comparé des langues semitiques* (3rd ed.; Paris: Michel Levy Frerès, 1863), p. xiii.

alism of the Indians or the Germans, nor the sense of perfect measure and beauty willed by Greece to the neo-Latin nations, nor the delicate and profound sensibility of the Celtic peoples; Semites have a clear consciousness but it is not a wide one, and they are incapable of a sense of multiplicity; the Semites never produced a mythology, nor an epic literature; they are a fundamentally monotheistic people, and hence fanatically intolerant; they do not have a creative imagination; Semites never produced sculpture or painting; the Semitic genius is incapable of either discipline or subordination; and morally speaking, the Semite acknowledges duties only toward himself. The climax of these descriptions comes when Renan avers that the Semites never produced a civilization as "we" understand that word: incapable of organizing empires, possessing no commerce, no public spirit, the Semitic peoples produced one sort of society only, that of the tent and of the tribe. And what is more, Semitic civilization is so limited as always to repeat itself, always to remain exactly the same.[30] Lastly:

> One sees that in all things the Semitic race appears to us to be an incomplete race, by virtue of its simplicity. This race—if I dare use the analogy—is to the Indo-European family what a pencil sketch is to painting; it lacks that variety, that amplitude, that abundance of life which is the condition of perfectibility. Like those individuals who possess so little fecundity that, after a gracious childhood they attain only the most mediocre virility, the Semitic nations experienced their fullest flowering in their first age and have never been able to achieve true maturity.[31]

We read similar structures with more strident racialist expression in the work of Gobineau. A contemporary of Renan and a scholar whom Renan cites in later editions of his Semitic philology, Gobineau does not coat the "truths" he expresses: the white race is superior, and if there is any virtue to be seen among the brown or mixed races it is because they have had white mixed in. In the *Essai sur l'inegalité des races humaines* Gobineau treats the Semites with a little more respect than Renan;[32] but that is because he sees whites

30. *Ibid.*, pp. 13-17.

31. *Ibid.*, p. 17 (the translation here, as in all the quotations from Renan, is mine). Renan's view is softened somewhat in his "Mahomet et les origines de l'islamisme," *La Revue des Deux Mondes*, December 15, 1851.

32. Comte de Gobineau, *Essai sur l'inegalité des races humaines*, I (Paris: Firmin-Didot, 1940), pp. 225-365.

and Semites as closer together than Renan saw them. Both Renan and Gobineau, as well as later Orientalists, treat the Semites as perpetually determined by their simple origins. Linguistically such a treatment makes some slight sense since Semitic is built around an omnipresent triliteral root and since after their early flourishing, Semitic languages never underwent radical change or development. But to judge the race unvaryingly as a repetition of one simple fact amounts to an unconscionable intellectual failure.

It scarcely needs mention that what Renan and Gobineau say about the Semites is practically identical with what one finds in works by the contemporary Orientalists. There is some economy here. For if the Semites (Arabs and Jews) are characterized as incapable of anything but simplicity (whatever that is), then simple, irrefragably uncomplex truths about them need never change. This is a perfect instance of how myths form and re-form themselves. Before the discovery of the connection between Sanskrit and the other Indo-European languages, Hebrew was believed to be the first, that is, the original, simple, and irreducible language from which all the others grew. After the linguistic revolution the Semitic languages as a family retain their quality of simplicity if not their special religious privilege. One reason for this combination of change and permanence is that so far as the West is concerned there is a direct, extralinguistic relation between the Near Orient and Europe. The Bible effectively antedates the Greek and Roman classics in the dynasty of Western civilization; hence even if it can be scientifically demonstrated that Sanskrit is more closely connected say to Greek or French, the Semitic languages and their civilization played the role of originators (through the sacred texts) of a major portion of European culture. The Orient therefore is held captive in its simple origin from which the higher Western ethos originated, departed, and flourished.

The Myth of Semitic Simplicity

This central distinction has been carried forward by generation after generation of Orientalists. If we add to this notion the very real sociopolitical dominance exerted by Europe over the Orient we see that the distinction became institutionalized. It accomodates equally the scholarly enterprise of the learned investigator, the political and economic organization of the colonizer or multinational corporation, and the racial bias of the anthropologist. Semitic simplicity, by which both Renan and the contemporary Orientalist mean that it is possible to reduce the inconceivable variety of all (and especially Semitic) existence to a univocal set of features, is not only a canonical belief; it is also a practice, just as saying that blacks have a natural sense of rhythm is a belief and a practice, in other words a myth. You treat the words as if they were true, and you convert your words into a method for giving reality your sovereign imprint. One reduces all instances of behavior to an endlessly recurrent feature, as when Henry Ford said of all history that it was bunk.

The Moroccan scholar, Abdullah Laroui, recently did a brilliant retrospective analysis of Gustave von Grunebaum's Orientalism using precisely the motif of reductive repetition as a practical tool of critical anti-Orientalist study. Laroui's case on the whole is impressively managed. He asks himself what it is that causes von Grunebaum's work, certainly one of the most learned and detailed among contemporary Arabists, to remain reductive. Laroui says "the adjectives that von Grunebaum affixes to the word *Islam* (medieval, classical, modern) are neutral or even superfluous: there is no difference between classical Islam and medieval Islam or Islam plain and simple. . . . There is therefore [for von Grunebaum] only one Islam that changes within itself." [33] Modern Islam according to von Grunebaum has turned away from the West because it remains faithful to its original sense of itself; and yet Islam can only modernize itself by a self-reinterpretation from a Western point of view. In describing von Grunebaum's conclusions—which add up to a portrait of Islam as a culture incapable of innovation—Laroui does not mention that the need for Islam to use Western methods to improve itself has become almost a truism in Middle Eastern studies. (David Gordon's *Self-Determination and History in the Third World*,[34] urges "maturity" on Arabs, Africans, and Asians; he argues that this can only be gained by learning from Western objectivity).

Laroui's analysis shows how von Grunebaum employed A. L. Kroeber's culturalist theory to understand Islam, and how this tool necessarily entails a series of reductions and eliminations by which Islam is represented as a closed system of exclusions. Each of the many diverse aspects of Islamic culture could be seen by von Grunebaum as a direct reflection of an unvarying matrix, a particular theory of God, that compelled them all into meaning and order. Development, history, tradition, and reality in Islam are interchangeable. Laroui rightly maintains that history as a complex order of events, temporali-

33. Laroui, "Pour une méthodologie des études islamiques: L'Islam au miroir de G. von Grunebaum," *Diogene*, No. 83, July-September, 1973, p. 30.

34. David Gordon, *Self-Determination and History in the Third World* (Princeton: Princeton University Press, 1971).

ties, and meanings cannot be reduced backward to such a notion of culture, in the same way that culture cannot be reduced to ideology, nor ideology to theology. Von Grunebaum has fallen prey to a particular feature of Islam, that there is to be found in it a highly articulated theory of religion and yet very few accounts of religious experience, a highly articulate political theory and few precise political documents, a theory of social structure and very few individualized actions, a theory of history and very few dated events, an articulated theory of economics and very few quantified series, and so on.[35] The net result, except for von Grunebaum's extraordinarily brilliant accounts of Islamic theories of articulation (poetry, grammar, etc.) is a historical vision of Islam entirely hobbled by a theory of the culture incapable of doing justice to, or examining, its existential reality in the experience of its adherents.

So deeply entrenched is the theory and practice of Semitic simplicity that it operates with little differentiation in well-known anti-Semitic European writings (*The Protocols of the Elders of Zion,* for example) as well as in remarks such as these by Chaim Weizmann to Arthur Balfour on May 30, 1918:

> The Arabs who are superficially clever and quick witted, worship one thing, and one thing only—power and success. . . . The British authorities . . . knowing as they do the treacherous nature of the Arabs . . . have to watch carefully and constantly. . . . The fairer the English regime tries to be, the more arrogant the Arab becomes. . . . The present state of affairs would necessarily tend toward the creation of an Arab Palestine, if there were an Arab people in Palestine. It will not in fact produce that result because the fellah is at least four centuries behind the times, and the effendi . . . is dishonest, uneducated, greedy, and as unpatriotic as he is inefficient.[36]

The common denominator between Weizmann and the European anti-Semite is the Orientalist perspective, seeing Semites, or subdivisions thereof, as by nature lacking the desireable qualities of Occidentals. Yet the difference between Renan and Weizmann is that the latter had gathered behind his rhetoric the solidity of institutions. Is there not in twentieth century Orientalism that same unageing "gracious childhood"—heedlessly allied now with scholarship, now

35. Laroui, *op. cit.,* p. 41.

36. Doreen Ingrams, *Palestine Papers,* 1917–1922 (London: John Murray, 1972), pp. 31–32.

with a state and all its institutions—that Renan saw as the Semites' unchanging mode of being?

Yet with what greater harm has the twentieth century version of the myth been maintained. It produced a picture of the Arab as seen by an "advanced" quasi-Occidental society. The Palestinian was either a stupid savage, or a negligible quantity, morally and even existentially. According to Israeli law only a Jew has full civic rights and unqualified immigration privileges, but Arabs are given less, more simple rights: they cannot immigrate and if they seem not to have the same rights, it is because they are less developed. Orientalism governs Israeli policy towards the Arabs throughout. There are good Arabs (the ones who do as they are told) and bad Arabs (terrorists, who fit the picture the nineteenth century anthropologists had of black savages in Africa to whom merciless punishment was paternal admonishment). Most of all, as the months before the October war testify, there are all those Arabs who, once defeated, can be expected to sit obediently behind an infallibly fortified line, manned by the smallest possible number of men, on the theory that Arabs have had to accept the myth of Israeli superiority and will never dare attack. One need only glance through the pages of Harkabi's *magnus opus,* that artificially large collection of bias and racism dressed up as scholarship, to see how—as Robert Alter put it admiringly in *Commentary*[37]—the Arab mind, depraved, anti-Semitic to the core, violent, and unbalanced, could only produce rhetoric and little more. One myth supports and produces another. They answer each other, tending towards symmetries and patterns of the sort that as Orientals the Arabs themselves can be expected to produce, but as a man no Arab can afford: Israelis and Jews are superior, Watergate was a Zionist conspiracy, the CIA runs the Middle East.

Of itself, in itself, as a set of beliefs, as a method of analysis, Orientalism cannot develop. Indeed it is the doctrinal antithesis of development. Its central argument is the myth of the arrested development of the Semites. From this matrix other myths pour forward, each of them showing the Semite to be in opposition to a Westerner, and irremediably the victim of his own weaknesses. By a concatenation of events and circumstances known to most Arabs the Semitic myth bifurcated in the Zionist movement; one Semite went the way of Orientalism, the other, the Arab, was forced the way of the Oriental. Each time tent and tribe are solicited, the myth is being employed;

37. Robert Alter, "Rhetoric and the Arab Mind," *Commentary,* XLVI, No. 4 (October, 1968), 61-65.

each time the concept of Arab national character is evoked, the myth is being employed. The hold these instruments have on the mind is increased by the institutions built around them. For every Orientalist, quite literally, there is a support system of staggering power, considering the ephemerality of the myths. In order to write the kind of thing turned out by Middle East experts you need universities, institutes, teachers, other students, dozens of periodicals, an enormous clientele, armies, air forces, and police. The myth is no mere chance effusion: it is there to be used when Orientals demand the justice and equality to which all men are entitled, to beat back Orientals to a tent or an "endogamous family," to drum out the chorus of Oriental depravity, rhetoric, vindictiveness, and underdevelopment.

All signifying systems (myths or discourse) have what some linguists call a zero degree. The zero degree is that element in the system that sets off the system from meaninglessness; it is the first element in the system, without which the system would be incoherent gibberish. For Orientalism the zero degree is a being without qualities, the Oriental, who acquires significance by the addition of negatives (e.g., he is not an Occidental, he is not capable of coordinated action, etc.) and of reductive positives (e.g., Semites are of the tribe and of the tent). His history is always assumed to be history *about* him (Orientalism) and not a history he has himself made. When his problems are described (e.g. the Arab-Israeli conflict) they are represented as *sui generis* irrational, or more exactly, as resolvable into rationality by Occidental insight. Always the myth system is symmetrical: for the Arab there is the Jew, for the U.S.S.R. the U.S., for autocracy and war there is freedom and peace, and so forth. The only asymmetry allowed is by direct Western intervention or, indirectly, by the imitation of Western schemes. Thus from its zero degree to its highest articulation the Orientalist myth system signifies power compelling weakness.

COUNTERING THE ORIENTALIST MYTH SYSTEM

It is no use opposing facts to myths, since as Dwight McDonald once showed, facts can be myths too. The October war did not disprove the old myths by proving that Arabs can be good fighters, can develop, etc. Such a simple solution is impossible since "factual" challenges to myths cause their breakup in order for a new, more adequate set to re-form. Myths resemble syrup; they yield to the pressure of a sharp object introduced into them, but they ooze back around it in a new configuration. This is an important truth. Otherwise Orientals are put in the position of having to demonstrate their prowess every so often, not so much for their satisfaction, but so that Orientalists can take note of their humanity. This is scarcely a better situation than the one now obtaining.

Nor is a mad rush to "develop" any better. One of the themes running through Arab and even Western writing since the October war is that the Arabs now have the capacity and the resources to develop. In and of themselves oil and money are not particularly reassuring; they seem to guarantee at least the appearance of modernity and advancement, but the world is not a vacuum, and history is hardly an inert substance ready for the wealthiest customer. An evident danger is that the enthusiasm for development together with the immense material power to implement schemes will license illusions of development, especially if the value system into which this development is introduced is as myth-ridden as ever. The development of a people, of a nation, of as complex a grouping as "the Arabs" is not a linear drive forward. Yet development can appear to be a simple matter, and an immediate one, something like "the oil weapon" which is a sort of Aladdin's lamp at "Arab" disposal.

Here we encounter the first dilemma seriously provoked by the War: what are the claims of the global thesis of Arab unity (what is Arab unity? how is it to be conceived both theoretically and practically?) and what are the claims of the particular Arab community, the nation-state like Egypt or Syria, or the people like the Arab Palestinians? A second dilemma is the need to devise a set of analytic instruments capable of responding first to the old and then to the re-formed myths. If we oppose "reality" to myths then the burden of formulating reality falls very heavily upon us as demythifiers. In any case, there is no such thing as plain, or unadorned, or brute, or naive reality. Every reality is a potential item of meaning, and since human perception is the act of making meaning, then *how* meaning is made—since it is made, never merely given—becomes the crucial question. Orientalism has been the chief producer of meaning, intellectually speaking, with regard at least to the relation between the Arabs and the rest of the world. If that set of myths is to be changed, how and with what instruments can it be done? The third and final dilemma asks for a decision on the terms and the perspective by which Arab development, in all its complex many-dimensional richness, can be envisaged, understood, and implemented. Obviously the three dilemmas are so intertwined that separating them is only an analytic device. Coming as an interruption in the carpet of Orientalism's everweaving discourse of myths, the 1973

October War compels either acquiescence in the re-formed myths already beseeching acceptance (e.g. development, Arab oil, and money) or, alternatively, a critical theory of Arab reality. In other words Arabs face the difference between unconsciousness or self-consciousness.

Critical Theory
In considering the problems in greater detail, I shall be speaking of polarities although absolute differences are impossible. Rather the polarities indicate the extreme choice facing the Arabs since the war, from which certain mixtures will necessarily be chosen. One pitfall is vulgar analogy; that is, the theory and practice of using analogies drawn from geometry (all development is linear and good), from other histories (Arabs must do as the Vietnamese did), from other theories (pragmatism, technological expertise, unaltered vulgar Marxism— *Marxismus* in the pejorative sense of that word). Clearly there is such a thing as an Arab experience, not as simple as "tent and tribe" but not so complex that only a hedgehog-like scheme drawn from elsewhere can make sense of it. Nor is this experience so ineffably private that authenticity becomes a search for transcendence right out of the world. Neither analogy nor total mysticism will do. And cynicism is no useful attitude either. Wilde says of the cynic that he knows the price of everything, and the value of nothing: that is more clever perhaps than completely true, but it suggests good reasons for not adopting uncritically the model of the marketplace. More important is the trap of positivism, which includes every variety of quantification, blind fact-gathering, optimistic anti-theorizing technocracy. The standard objection to theory is that it is only abstract, hence the virtue of hard facts and figures. Yet one objection, correct or not, does not automatically license computers and illiterate engineers to determine the future. Theory can be abstract, and there is much to be said in favor of abstractness, but it is not abstraction *tout court*. As I understand it critical theory is a way of producing reality and meaning, not as an engineer produces a blueprint, but rather the way a fully conscious intelligence creatively perceives that combination of phenomenon, historical and moral dimension, affect, and self we call actuality.

Sobering statistics or catalogues have a role to play at this point in the discussion. In the Arab world today there is not a single institution devoted exclusively either to the critical study of Arab contemporaneity, nor to the study of the West, the chief foreign participant, politically and economically, in modern Arab history. There are numerous technical, social, and pure scientific institutes;

there are institutes for the study of particular problems; there are groups for strategic, corporate, industrial, economic, and management research. But there is no institution devoted to the study of either foreign or local values and value-systems, nor to the critical theory of Arab or Western society, nor to the various processes by which historical actuality is produced. There is no shortage of time devoted to solving problems; as for how the problems are put—given that the way a problem is formulated determines its solution, and determines its very reality—they are supposed to be articulated on an *ad hoc* basis, either as the result of market demand or as a Western expert believes they should be. What is worse there are droves of Arab Westerners—the equivalent of black skins in white masks—trained for many generations in skills suitable for the Western market economy, and able to repeat the old formulas with neither awareness nor imagination. They absorb the expertise into a moral and evaluative vacuum, and it is their society, impoverished in the long run, that will pay an exhorbitant price for them. Of what use is knowledge of gas turbines, computer languages, or the latest in food technology, if their social context is never defined? Both communal and individual traditions wither under the onslaught of these new professional demands placed on the individual. He gains highly specialized skills that crowd out older loyalties to family, clan, or religion; the traditional principally literary (as opposed to scientific) Arab culture erodes, and what takes its place is a new illiteracy, in which all mental and moral assets are either subordinated to or chaotically redistributed by the all-consuming need to do a job and be paid. That both the job and the payment appear to be largely value-free—in the sense that since all jobs and all money are good in themselves, therefore all values are equal, and nil—enhances their attractiveness.

The answer to this problematic vulnerability is not to be found mainly in either religion or occult new creeds and methods. On the other hand religion's role cannot be overlooked in any survey of social and cultural fields of play and force. The notion of context or the field of play in which things take place must be explored. The discourse of Orientalism, to which the myths of Arab society belong, inhabits a particular circuit of institutions and power, historically and in the present. By reading this discourse for the codes it concealed and the meanings it produced, I prevented Orientalism from being taken for the natural reality of the Arab world, character, or society. Orientalism read the Arabs and wrote about them distortingly. I am not saying that there is a way of apprehending the social and cultural processes of a given society without either reading or writing; there is no unmediated vision of things like that.

Moreover, all reading and writing is distortion, or at least de-forma-tion. The difference between mythological reading and writing and demythification, or what I have been calling critical theory, is that the former pretends to having no theory, to being natural, scientific, factual reporting, whereas the latter openly admits its theoretical and even interested methods, for its premise is that society is process, and that the role of critical theory is participation in the process, not its reification into stable characteristics (like "tent and tribe," for example). Myths never go away of their own accord. They must be disassembled into the interests they serve but whose presence they always hide. Conversely we must be able to show that a myth displaces something as well as producing a particular meaning of its own. The immediate task then is to understand generally how meaning is produced—for it is a process taking place in a particular context or field of play—and precisely what the myth has displaced.

The Orientalist myth displaces what it has reduced to the concept of "tent and tribe." Instead of seeing a whole web of Arab societies, cultures, and realities, the myth volunteers one key to all mysteries and says "this is all the Arab really is; do not be misled by his apparent modernity; it all comes down to tent and tribe. His tempera-ment and character, now and always, are as follows." What enables us to deal with a myth such as this is not merely a gesturing at humanism or appeals to the rich traditions of the Islamic world, or anything of that sort at all. It is knowledge of how in fact Orientalism works; and the way we know that is by studying it in the context of other systems like it. Mythological thought is impertinent; it pretends that certain statements, images, descriptions are natural, when in fact they are made up; it pretends that words are not merely words but the real thing. Critical theory, on the other hand, argues that all meaning and value-systems are man-made; they have a provenance; they are cultural; nature is not a maker of sense, men in society and history are. Moreover, it argues that all meaning has an intention, or what I have been calling a theory.

There is no meaning plain and simple; all meaning from the beginning is intended by whom and whatever makes it.[38] Thus if I say that the "Arabs must develop," I must also realize that I cannot intend very much when I say that, unless I also specify for what they must develop, how they develop, and indeed what "develop"

38. I have discussed this as a theoretical problem in my *Beginnings: Intention and Method* (New York: Basic Books, 1975).

itself means. If I refuse to do that and content myself with repetitions of "development" then I stop the word from intending anything (and stopping it is an intention all its own, rather like the Orientalist myth). To stop the word is to deny that development is a process of a very specifiable sort, that it does take place in a multitude of possible ways, that it has a whole range of effects (all ascertainable) and a whole range of dialectical consequences (e.g., if I develop a market economy then the government must be of a certain type).

All this is not very difficult. The truly important and difficult part is a method for describing the units of meaning and their relations with each other. The universality of intention needs first to be recognized; one cannot do that unselfconsciously, nor can it be left to chance. Thus everything making up contemporaneity must be envisaged as conveying, indeed embodying a definite man-made intention or perspective. Clearly the Orientalist who saw the immediate pre-October period and concluded that the Arabs were preparing for inaction saw only his own perspective, that of the observer to whom all Arabs are an endless confirmation of one or two terminal features like laziness or abstraction. If the perspective were not that of the mythologist he might perhaps have read Naguib Mahfouz's 1973 novel *Hub Taht al Mattar* and recognized the kinds of processes taking place that only a novelist can intend and which may not perhaps have predicted a war but only confirmed a more dynamic social actuality.[39] That is, he would have realized for any assessment to be worthy of the name it would have to adumbrate the field in which the Arab lived, and that that field included a whole range of movement which was the opposite of retrograde Arab laziness or irrationality.

Since a people is at least as complex a thing as a literary text we may say that to understand contemporaneity we must at least be able to read it. Reading is decoding, or decipherment; even in one's own language what one reads is in fact a new foreign language being made, an idiolect.

The mental gymnastics imposed on any deciphering of a foreign language text, ancient or modern, is healthy training in the understanding

39. It is the great virtue of some scholars to have attempted analyses based precisely upon those humanistic and literary elements that make up the more intimate, actual part of contemporary Arab culture. As instances there are H. A. R. Gibb's studies, especially those collected in his *Studies on the Civilization of Islam* (London: Routledge and Kegan Paul, 1962), Jacques Berque's *Les Arabes d'hier a demain* (Paris: Seuil, 1960), and Albert Hourani's *Arabic Thought in the Liberal Age 1789–1932* (Oxford: Oxford University Press, 1962).

of any *human context,* in that *understanding* characteristic of the humanities. This effort is of a particular kind, quite different from the procedure in mathematics in which one deduces consequences from a few, very simple axioms which have been isolated from the whole of reality. In any deciphering one is faced with a whole network of difficulties which present themselves in a lump at the same time: words, word-meanings, constructions, in themselves perhaps known to us, must be fitted together into that unique mosaic which alone makes sense—and, in addition (and this is again quite different from mathematics, which, once it has left the realm of outward reality, need not return to it), the particular outward situation described in the text may be unknown to us: the meaning of the text may become clear not by the *Sprachgefühl* for the particular language alone, but only by the additional application of our general experience which may tell us which word-meaning and which constructions might fit the outward situation described in the text.[40]

It seems to me apt to take this paragraph as a guide for decoding not only the verbal language of a society but also its people and objects; all of them are produced, but it is the sensitive attitude that sees them as producing themselves that principally delivers the decoder, or reader, from the tyranny of myths. Myths after all seem never to have been produced, still less can a mythological object like "the Arabs" appear to be more than a product of univocal traits and an undifferentiated sexual urge. If we take Arab contemporaneity as being produced then everything in it has meaning, has intention, has theory whose sense and direction one can decode. But only if it is conceded that every meaning inhabits a context and does not take place in a vacuum, can we maintain the dynamical perspective to keep myths at bay.

A context, as I understand it, is not an inert envelope. For every phenomenon to acquire identity it must move (since, as we have said, the only stationary phenomenon is the myth) within a space which is particular to it, and which in part it creates like an aura around it. As an instance of what I mean take the novel in Arabic. Unlike the European novel it has a very short history, it undertook various national and cultural tasks, and it derives from wholly different narrative sources than its European counterpart. In short, its context is different, which is not to say that it can be confined back into

40. Leo Spitzer, "Language—The Basis of Science, Philosophy and Poetry," in *Studies in Intellectual History* (Baltimore: Johns Hopkins University, History of Ideas Club, 1953), p. 82.

the pigeon-hole of "tent and tribe." Rather it can be examined for the kind of meaning it produces, for the kind of activity it is, for the historical role it has played.[41] All these together in a sense form around the novel a space which, although very much its own, has connections with other spaces. Its context is a field of force which, again unlike the European novel, is on the whole a nationalist-progressive one. The same is doubtless true of the drama or the film in Arabic, or any of the artforms produced by contemporary society. They fulfill uses, just as they create aesthetic realities that correspond with the social and political realities around them. Art is "a kind of code language for processes taking place within society which must be deciphered by means of critical analysis."[42] Such analysis does not aim to show how "content" reflects a particular historical moment passively; "content" thereby becomes a fetishized object, instead of an integral undetachable part of the work of art.[43] Critical analysis translates the artwork into the wholly concrete processes of work (artistic, social, or political) of which it is one aspect. Mahfouz's novels and stories since 1967, for example, are part of the narrative prose aspect of the effects of the June war, a meditation on and analysis of the psychology of uncertainty and fear, and a reality created for dealing with another reality. Important events such as those of 1948 and 1967 become something more than happenings; they are elucidations of existing, constantly being-produced activities by and within the society, and in this respect a prose work and the condition of the army are carriers of the same codes generally though in different languages. Consequently it is useless to study the October war as the result by simple addition of a finite series of events. An event of that scale obviously has dialectical connections with numerous forces, but only if they are grasped as organized into fields can one begin to see how a group of men crosses an armed barrier, how a nation forges the will to fight, and so forth.

Even the smallest objects inhabit a field, and create their context.

---

41. See my Introduction to Halim Barakat, *Days of Dust,* trans. Trevor LeGassick (Wilmette, Illinois: Medina University Press, 1974).

42. Cited by Martin Jay, *The Dialectical Imagination: A History of the Frankfurt School and the Institute of Social Research,* 1923-1950 (Boston: Little, Brown and Company, 1973), p. 177.

43. As examples of content analyses there are Z. Gabay, "Nizar Qabbani, the Poet and his Poetry," *Middle Eastern Studies,* IX, No. 2 (May, 1973), 207-222, and Menahem Milson, "An Allegory on the Social and Cultural Crisis in Egypt: 'Walid al-'Ana' by Najib Mahfuz," *International Journal of Middle East Studies,* III, No. 3 (July, 1972), 324-347.

If what I have been saying about the novel is true, it is no less true of—to take a few banal examples—the role of sunglasses or prayer beads, of newspapers, of the word *Allah,* and so on. They are all signs whose use is circumscribed by fields of use they create and which dialectically contribute to their creation. What makes the format of Arabic newspapers have a particular style and not another? When does the word *Allah* pertain and when not? Statistics will never tell the story since languages operate quite differently than numbers, and reading, as Spitzer says quite correctly, is not mathematics. What I am advocating as a replacement for the mythical, reified discourse of Orientalism is the collaborative articulation of a theory for investigating (reading) the native forces giving Arab society (or societies) their specific identity (identities). No one person can do this alone. But the common attitude shared by critics must be that the tendency of myths is to reduce, stop, make everything monochromatic, whereas theory reveals the plurality of forces, their fields, their dialectic connections. And only by acknowledging the undisputable conviction that men can act consciously, intentionally, with a theoretical grasp of their world, will the work be done.[44]

In large measure as I have been using the word *theory,* I have also been implying *hypothesis.* For it is impossible for any person or persons to hope to grasp every particular of any given situation; this hope is the positivist pretence. When one has a healthy respect for the vast range of detail conveyed by a written text, how much more will his respect increase for the sheer wealth of detail expressed by a society. Yet the irrationalist attitude that says "we can never know" is no answer either. Theory proposes a possible general framework for the tendencies that can be verified by the research I have been describing. As the results develop, the framework alters. But the very proposal of a theoretical framework is an act of will asserted against myths saying that "this, and only this, is Arab society."

CONCLUSION

The October war itself now seems like an act of theoretical will. To the extent that armies were ordered out of inaction there must have been a general theoretical possibility that successful action might prove actual. The limited military gains of the war need not be the

44. This is the thesis proposed by Georg Lukacs in *History and Class Consciousness,* trans. Rodney Livingstone (London: Merlin Press, 1971), pp. 83–222.

only gains: we can match the war's strictly material gains with an intellectual hostility to the myths (like the Bar-Lev line) supposedly confining Arabs to "tent and tribe." The effort although different in kind must be no less great, and it must be far more successful. Two safeguards against mere theory-spinning are:

1. An exhaustive attention at the beginning paid to determining the material for study. Too many recent studies passing themselves off as emanating from the social sciences avoid the problems presented by the absence in Islamic tradition of a developed reportorial or confessional or autobiographical literature. Thus anyone seeking to study child-rearing practises say in northern Syria must reckon that his informants (if he is not to rely exclusively upon what he can directly observe, which cannot be very much) can answer questions, but they probably cannot formulate answers of the sort that would get at the essence of what in fact they do or think about child-rearing. Their answers are answers for the questions; they are made for those questions, which in turn necessarily impose the investigator's own training upon the material. This is a problem faced constantly by ethnographers. In the Arab context it has been the case that the very muteness in the tradition vis-à-vis personal experience licenses the kind of impositions I associated with Orientalist discourse. Therefore critical theory must devote itself initially to this problem, and to articulating a nuanced praxis for the definition of problems and materials from within, or in some way out of, the cultural field itself.[45]

2. A concentration upon those activities in Arab society by which knowledge is transmitted, institutionalized, acted upon, preserved, reactivated, and discarded.[46] Every society has a systematically organized, although not necessarily fully conscious, way of dealing with knowledge—of itself, of the world, of the past, of the future and present. At certain moments one can notice, for example, that certain figures and their teachings from the past are reactivated, certain others discarded, certain others altered in a particular way. The fame of a given poet or statesman is a social reality which, in political discourse for instance, is drawn upon and fashioned for a particular use. Similarly in any culture believing itself different from another (e.g. Egypt as different from England, or from Syria) there is a tendency to make those differences by absorbing certain kinds of knowledge and rejecting

---

45. I have discussed this in my "Al-tamanu' wal-tajanub wal-ta'aruf," *Mawaqif*, No. 19-20 (March, 1972).

46. For an elucidation see Michel Foucault, "Response à une question," *Esprit*, No. 5 (May, 1968), pp. 850-874.

certain others. How does this happen, and in what ways, in what circumstances, by what peculiar concert of forces does this become possible? Why is a certain type of expression considered more appropriate than another? The investigation would have to specify the place from which answers are sought, the kind (not just the number) of frequency and recurrence with which that knowledge turns up, and so on. In other words what needs examination is the value system by which something—say a name, or a slogan—appears correct, and another incorrect. Or even more interesting, how does a culture at any given moment identify itself with sanity, and by implication, how does it formulate its notion of what is insane, or irrational?

These are some of the methods that can challenge the mythical discourse that has been for so long a blight upon Arab self-knowledge and self-making. The great lesson of the October war is that one can take one's fate in one's own hands; this alone, as Vico and Marx were among the first to realize, restores men to their history, and puts a distance between them and those myths about them that have closed off their historical actuality. Every myth today speaks as if what it says cannot be contradicted, and again, it speaks as if there is nothing more to be said. Yet once men know that no reality in history need be final—and this is not the same as saying pejoratively that Arabs cannot face reality—their consciousness is transformed from that of an object into that of the producing subject. The October war is but one among many perhaps less dramatic opportunities for changing Arab status from that of object to that of subject. A war finally determines nothing; at bottom it is only violence. What is most needed is the intellectual equivalent of the war, which is sustained anti-mythological, self-conscious thought.[47]

47. See Foucault, *Folie et deraison: Histoire de la folie à l'âge classique* (Paris: Plon, 1961) and *Les Mots et les choses: Une archéologie des sciences humaines* (Paris: Gallimard, 1966).

CHRONOLOGY
1969–1975

1969

June   Beginning of the war of attrition along the Suez Canal.

1970

January 7   Israeli bombing of the Egyptian interior began.

January 22   Nasser flew to Moscow to seek military assistance.

February 12   Israeli aircrafts bombed an Egyptian factory at Abu Za'bal, killing eighty-eight workers.

April 8   Bahr El-Baqar, a village school in the Nile delta, was bombed by Israeli aircraft, killing forty-six children.

August 7   A cease-fire came into force as part of the Rogers Plan.

1972

January 13   Sadat explained that only the international preoccupation with the Indo-Pakistani war had prevented Egypt from going to war against Israel at the end of the "year of decision."

April 28   An Israeli plane destroyed the crops of the West Bank village of Akraba by spraying them with defoliant.

September 9   Israel raided sixteen Lebanese villages. An Israeli tank drove over a taxi squashing to death a Lebanese family of seven.

September 16   An Israeli battalion of 15,000 crossed the Lebanese border into the villages of Bint Jubeil, Anyata, Kan, Juwaya, and Nabatiya.

October   Sadat named Ahmed Ismail to replace Mohamed Sadek as minister of war.

1973

January 1   The secretary-general of Egypt's Arab Socialist Union said that the Arabs should put economic pressure on the U.S. and that a survey of American economic interests in the Arab world had been prepared on orders of President Sadat.

January 3   Egypt's five universities and twenty colleges were closed following clashes between students demonstrating against Sadat's policies and the police.

January 5   The U.N. Security Council condemned Israel for its April 10 raid on Beirut in which three PLO leaders were assassinated.

January 8   The massive outpourings of student protest led Sadat to close the universities.

Israeli planes raided Syria killing at least 150 civilians and wounding 70, according to Damascus reports and U.N. observers.

Sadat said in an *Al Bairaq* (Beirut) interview that he had abandoned all hope of seeing the U.S. return to an impartial position and had lost all his illusions about American friendship for Egypt.

Israel said it shot down six Syrian Migs in air battles and destroyed six tanks in artillery duels in the Golan region. Syria said it lost three Migs and destroyed four Israeli planes and fifteen tanks.

January 8–10   Sadat and Qaddafi reached agreement on measures to strengthen the proposed political merger between Egypt and Libya.

January 10   The Egyptian information minister, replying to Syria's criticism of Egypt's failing to go to war, said that a courageous leader does not allow himself to go to war prematurely.

Syria reported that five hundred persons were killed by Israeli raids on January 8.

January 11   Sadat said he had no choice but to fight to regain the lands occupied by Israel.

January 28   Egypt's War Minister Ismail was appointed commander-in-chief of the Syrian, Jordanian, and Egyptian fronts by the Arab Joint Defense Council.

February 10   Following a visit to Moscow by Egyptian envoy Hafiz Isma'il an Egyptian communiqué said Isma'il told Moscow that Egypt would reject any "partial solution" to the conflict with Israel and that the U.S.S.R. expressed understanding of this position.

February 19   Iraq's official al-Thawrah said a peaceful settlement in the Middle East could not satisfy all parties concerned and that Iraq regarded U.N. resolution 242 as a "surrender to the enemy."

February 21   A Libyan civilian airliner was shot down by Israeli fighters over the Sinai killing 106 passengers and the crew.

The northernmost corner of Lebanon was invaded by air and seaborne Israeli soldiers, killing forty civilians.

February 24   Libyan Information Minister Abu Zayil Umar Durdah said the downing of the Libyan jet was "premeditated mass murder."

February 26   Israeli Premier Golda Meir arrived in Washington for talks on the Middle East situation with Nixon. She later received a commitment for a shipment of forty-eight Phantom jets and thirty-six Skyhawks.

February   Sadat dispatched special emissary Hafez Isma'il on a tour of European capitals and then to the U.S. to meet with Nixon.

March 3   Black September killed two American diplomats and one Belgian, who had been kidnapped the day before in Khartoum, Sudan.

A Black September statement, issued through *al-Muharir* of Beirut, said that the Khartoum operation would "teach the world to take us seriously and to respect our word."

March 13   Beirut's *al-Bayraq* quoted Kuwait's ruler Shaykh Sabah al-Salim al-Sabah as saying that support for the Palestinian commandos was "continuing and unlimited and that Kuwait would use oil as an effective weapon."

April 10   Israeli commandos raided Sidon and Beirut killing three Palestinian guerrilla leaders (Muhammed Yusuf Najar, Kamal Adwan, and Kamal Nasir) and blew up the offices of al-Fatah.

April 15   U.S. Senate Foreign Relations Committee Chairman J. W. Fulbright said the U.S. was unable to exert pressure on Israel because "Israel controlled the Senate."

April 18   Saudi Minister of Oil Shaykh Ahmad Zaki Yamani told the *Washington Post* that Saudi Arabia would not expand its oil production to meet U.S. demands unless the U.S. altered its pro-Israel stance.

April 21   The U.N. Security Council resolution condemned all acts of violence threatening innocent lives and Israel's "repeated military attacks" against Lebanon. The U.S., U.S.S.R., and China abstained from voting.

May 1   Sadat said that the cease-fire in the Middle East was benefiting Israel and it was up to Egypt "to begin to move" to break the stalemate.

May 15   In protest against Israel's 25th anniversary, Algeria, Kuwait, and Iraq halted the flow of oil exports for one hour and Libya halted the flow for one day.

May 16   Soviet Ambassador to Lebanon Sardar Azimov met with PLO Chairman Yasir Arafat and warned of possible large-scale Israeli attacks on Palestinian commandos in Lebanon and Jordan.

May 19   Sadat made a lightning visit to Damascus.

May 28   Egyptian Foreign Minister Zayyat told the Security

Council that there would be no stability in the region until the Palestinians have an independent state, whose boundaries the Palestinians must help to determine.

Saudi Foreign Minister Umar al-Saqqaf warned that Arab countries would deny their oil to Western Countries that "help our enemy."

The OAU meeting in Ethiopia pledged "to effectively and actively support the Arab Republic of Egypt and other Arab countries until the total liberation of the occupied territories resulting from the Israeli aggression in June, 1967."

June 6	A Syrian military delegation arrived in Cairo.
June 12	Sadat returned to Damascus with his chief of staff.

Beirut's *L'Orient-Le Jour* reported that Egypt, Syria, Jordan, Algeria, and Saudi Arabia were studying the possibility of establishing a Palestinian state on the West Bank.

June 13   Israel's U.N. Ambassador Tekoah told the Security Council, "The allegations that the Palestinians have not yet vindicated their inalienable rights to self-determination and statehood are without foundation. The Arabs of Palestine exercise these rights in the Palestinian state of Jordan."

Palestinian guerillas attacked Shamir and an Israeli kibbutz near the Lebanese border.

June 20   Tunisian President Habib Bourgiba told the International Labor Organization in Geneva that the Arabs and Israel should hold talks to establish a "just and lasting peace" based on Israel's right "not to be exterminated" and on the need for a Palestinian homeland.

Golda Meir disclosed that Israel had asked a neutral state to try to set up a meeting between Israel and Tunisia.

July 6   King Faisal warned that it was difficult for Saudi Arabia to cooperate with the U.S. in the petroleum field unless the U.S. moved toward a more balanced policy in the Middle East.

July 22   Cairo's *Rose al-Yusuf* quoted PLO Chairman Arafat as saying that the PLO supported the freezing of Arab oil production levels as a means of pressuring Israel.

July 29   Beirut's *al-Nahar* reported that Algeria and Saudi Arabia arrived at a joint plan for using oil as a political weapon in the Arab-Israeli conflict.

August 1   The Palestine National Front (PNF) was set up in the West Bank as a union of varied indigenous and progressive underground groups under the leadership of the PLO.

August 1   Assistant Secretary of State Joseph Sisco told an Israeli audience that American energy needs were "a factor" in the Middle East situation.

August 10   Israeli jets over Lebanon diverted an Arab airliner bound to Baghdad from Beirut and forced it to land in Israel where a check of the passengers was conducted. The plane returned to Beirut.

August 15   Israeli Chief of Staff David Eleazar, commenting on the Lebanese airliner operation, said that more such "operations may be expected."

The U.N. Security Council unanimously condemned Israel "for violating Lebanon's sovereignty" and for "the forcible diversion and seizure by the Israeli airforce of a Lebanese airliner from Lebanon's air space."

August 18   The Syrian government reopened the border with Lebanon which had been closed in May.

August 23   King Faisal held secret talks with Sadat.

The U.S. said it was opposed to changes in the status of occupied territories.

August 27   U.N. Secretary-General Kurt Waldheim arrived in Syria at the beginning of a Middle East tour that would take him to Lebanon, Israel, Egypt, Jordan, and Algeria.

September 3   The Israeli Labor Party Secretariat approved a plan providing for public and private purchase of land in the territories occupied by Israel.

September 4   King Faisal said on U.S. television that U.S. support for Zionism "makes it extremely difficult for us to continue to supply U.S. petroleum needs and even to maintain our friendly relations."

September 5   President Nixon said the U.S. was giving "highest priority" to a Middle East settlement and would use its influence with both sides to get the situation "off dead center."

September 10   Cuba informed the Israeli government that it was severing diplomatic relations.

September 11   President Sadat met with Syrian President Hafez al-Assad and King Husayn to discuss ending Jordan's isolation in the Arab world and reviving the "eastern front" against Israel.

September 12   Egypt announced that diplomatic relations were restored with Jordan after talks were concluded between Sadat, Assad, and Husayn.

September 13   Israel said it shot down thirteen Syrian jets and lost one during an air battle over the Mediterranean near Latakeya. Syria said it lost eight while shooting down five Israeli jets.

September 16   The *New York Times* reported Jordanian officials as saying that Jordan, Egypt, and Syria had agreed to take a common stand on "political issues" in the Middle East.

September 19   More than seven hundred political prisoners were released from captivity in Jordan following an amnesty declaration by King Husayn.

September 21   Togo broke diplomatic relations with Israel in protest over the occupation of Arab territories.

September 23   The *Washington Post* reported that Syria told Waldheim on August 28 that Syria would not object to a settlement based on U.N. resolution 242.

September 24	The U.S. said it offered to sell Lebanon a squadron of 18 A-4 Skyhawk jets.
September 26	The C.I.A. reported that the Egyptian army had been placed in a state of alert and that reserves were being mobilized.
September 28	Sadat announced clemency measures for two hundred journalists and students who had been arrested or lost their jobs because of political activities.

Al-Hayat (Beirut) reported that Syrian troops formerly stationed on the Jordanian border were moved to the Golan cease-fire line facing Israel.

October 2	The *Washington Post* reported that the U.S.S.R. sent Iraq twelve TU-22 jet bombers with a range of 2250 km.

After a Vienna meeting with Golda Meir, Austrian Chancellor Kreisky said that the Jewish transit facility at Schonau Castle would "be no longer available," but that individual Soviet Jews would be allowed through Austria "by the shortest route and with the shortest possible stop." The action came in response to the seizure of three Jews and an Austrian official by a Palestinian group, "The eagles of the Palestinian Revolution."

October 3	The *Jerusalem Post* reported Syrian and Egyptian troop buildups on the cease-fire lines as "probably routine movements."
October 4	Syria announced the resumption of diplomatic relations with Jordan.
October 5	*Al-Muharir* (Beirut) reported that due to increasing tension on the Golan cease-fire line, the Palestinian commando organizations were put on full alert.
October 6	1:50 P.M. Egyptian tanks and infantry attacked across the Suez Canal at five points.

2:00 P.M. Syrian forces launched a two-pronged attack against Israeli positions along the Golan cease-fire line.

U.N. observers reported that Arabs initiated the attacks on both fronts.

Fifty ships of the U.S. 6th Fleet were placed on alert.

Egypt declared Red Sea waters above the 23rd parallel to be war zone and warned that ships entering would do so at their own risk.

Syria announced that it had occupied Mt. Hermon for the first time since 1967.

Both Egypt and Syria sent notes to the U.N. accusing Israel of starting the fighting.

4:40 P.M. Israel reported that an emergency meeting of the cabinet had warned of the Egyptian and Syrian military buildup for offensive purposes and had taken measures to urge "political quarters" to act to prevent an Arab attack.

The Israeli defense minister said that Israel's goals were to inflict "very heavy casualties" and to return to the cease-fire lines.

October 7   Israel claimed it had counterattacked on the ground and had control of the air, and that four hundred Egyptian tanks were isolated east of the canal. Syria claimed it halted an Israeli offensive and made further gains in the Golan region. Egypt said it drove back a counterattack.

2:30 A.M. Syria reported a midnight naval engagement near Latakeya and claimed four Israeli boats were sunk. Israel claimed to have sunk five Syrian ships.

Iraq nationalized the interest of two American oil companies, Exxon and Mobil, and said that a squadron of planes was on its way to the Suez front. Algeria said planes were being sent to aid Egypt.

Nixon instructed Kissinger to call for a U.N. Security Council meeting.

A U.S. 6th Fleet tank force left Athens for waters off Crete.

Italy called for consultations by the E.E.C. to make

a "positive commitment" to restoring the armistice.

India blamed the renewal of hostilities on "Israeli intransigence."

Pakistan expressed support for the Arabs and accused Israel of aggression.

Tunisia said that it would send troops to the front.

7:30 P.M. Israeli military spokesman Hertzog said that Egypt had four hundred tanks on the east side of the canal and that Syria had eight hundred tanks on the front. He said Israel's big success of the day was to nearly destroy the Syrian anti-aircraft missile network and the bridges across the Canal.

Evening: Nixon and Brezhnev exchanged messages on the war situation.

October 8   Morning: Iraq announced a unilateral resumption of diplomatic ties with Iran and asked Iran to accept the gesture so Iraqi troops would be free to fight against Israel. Iran welcomed the announcement.

11:15 A.M. Hertzog said that the armored reserves had been mobilized, the initiative was now in Israeli hands, and Israel was still facing a "difficult and fateful battle."

Saudi forces were placed on alert.

Egyptian commandos engaged Israeli troops at Sharm al-Shaykh.

Eban told the U.N. that if Israel had been back on the borders which existed before the 1967 war, the present Arab attack might have destroyed Israel.

Jordan said it shot down two Israeli jets in Jordanian airspace.

The U.S. Senate passed a resolution deploring "the outbreak of the tragic hostilities" and urged the U.S. to seek a cease-fire and restoration of the lines of October 6.

Evening: Egypt announced that its troops raided

oilfields in the occupied Sinai at Birlayim and that Israeli planes attacked Port Said on the Mediterranean.

Israeli Chief of Staff Eleazar said the Golan region was nearly cleaned of Syrian troops and that the counterattack was making good headway with Israeli troops reaching the Canal at some points.

Syria said the advance of its forces was continuing.

The U.S. asked the U.N. Security Council to bring a halt to the fighting and restore the cease-fire lines that existed on the morning of October 6. China called the U.S. proposal "preposterous," and the U.S.S.R. expressed support for Egypt and Syria.

Sudan announced that armed units were on their way to the battlefield.

The Palestinian press agency in Damascus said Iraqi troops had arrived at the battlefield.

October 9   10:00 A.M. Israel reported that Syria had launched twenty Soviet-built Frog rockets against civilian settlements in Israel.

Israeli jets raided Damascus and bombed the Soviet Cultural Center reportedly killing six Soviets. An oil refinery in Homs was damaged and a radar station in Lebanon was destroyed.

Israel claimed its target in Damascus was the Syrian Defense Ministry located near the Soviet Cultural Center. Reporters in Damascus said the ministry was not hit.

Egyptian Presidential Advisor Ashraf Ghurbal said Egypt's goals were the recovery of the Sinai and recognition by Israel of the rights of the Palestinians.

The U.N. Security Council convened for the second day. Soviet Ambassador Yakov Malik walked out as Israeli Ambassador Yosef Tekoah expressed condolences for the death of Soviets in Damascus.

The U.S.S.R. sent messages to all Arab governments.

The note to Algeria stated in part: "Syria and Egypt must not be alone in their struggle."

Evening: Eleazar said that Israel had begun to "break and destroy" the Egyptian and Syrian armies. The Israeli spokesman said Israel had "no territorial ambitions whatsoever" but would seek to destroy enemy forces whenever they could be found.

Israel said it had abandoned the Bar-Lev line and formed a new defense line three to six kilometers from the canal.

October 10

Israeli armor pushed beyond the cease-fire line in Syria.

Iraq reported that Iraqi jets flew eighty sorties on the Syrian front and that Iraqi forces were in action on the Suez front as well. Israeli jets attacked Damascus and industrial targets in Homs.

Security Council President Lawrence McIntyre said there was little point to holding another "fractious" council meeting while neither combatant wanted a cease-fire. No meeting was held.

The U.S. said that the U.S.S.R. was resupplying Syria and Egypt thus putting a "new face" on the conflict. The Soviets refused comment.

Britian announced an embargo of arms sales to the Middle East combatants.

Iraq said Sudanese troops had joined the fighting on the Suez front.

Evening: Israel said the Syrian army was completely driven out of the Golan sector, but that Egypt still had five divisions and six hundred tanks on the east bank of the Suez.

October 11

Israeli forces penetrated six miles beyond the 1967 line into Syria and Israeli planes bombed eight airfields in Syria.

In response to Israeli requests the U.S. said that it was supplying ammunition and missiles to Tel Aviv in rush deliveries on orders placed before October 6.

The U.S. said it was sending a second helicopter carrier to the Mediterranean.

Arab diplomats in Washington said the Arab aim was a "limited war" to establish a new equilibrium by retaking at least part of the territory occupied in 1967.

Israeli jets attacked the ports of Latakeya, Tartus, and Baniyas and destroyed the oil depot at Homs and a large power plant. Heavy ground fighting was reported as Israeli forces advanced in Syria.

Egypt said it won a major tank battle in the Sinai and repulsed Israeli air attacks on airfields in Egypt.

October 12   11:00 A.M. Kissinger warned that a prolonged war would create "a high possibility of great power involvement." He said that the Soviet airlift to the Arabs was "fairly substantial, but moderate" and did threaten detente. The U.S. objective, he said, was "to end hostilities on terms that are just to all."

Heavy fighting was reported in Syria and Israeli troops encountered Iraqi forces. The Israeli attack toward Damascus slowed down.

Egypt called the shipment of U.S. arms to Israel "outright provocation of the Arabs" and warned of "consequences."

Evening: The U.S.S.R. said a Soviet ship was sunk by Israel in a Syrian port with a loss of civilian lives and warned that "the continuation of criminal acts by Israel will lead to grave consequences for Israel itself."

October 13   Heavy tank battles were reported in the Sinai as Egyptian forces tried to break through the Israeli defensive line, but advances were not made by either side.

Israel said its forces were approaching Sa'sa, twenty miles from Damascus, and were broadening and consolidating their position in Syria.

Israel claimed it destroyed an Iraqi division including seventy tanks in Syria. Meir denounced the Soviet "aerial railway" of military supplies to the Arabs.

U.S. officials said the U.S. was preparing to send jet fighters to Israel to replace some losses.

Algeria restored diplomatic relations with Jordan.

Jordan announced that it sent a "detachment of its best military formations" to Syria. *Al-Nahar* (Beirut) reported that one thousand Saudi troops which had been in Jordan had also crossed to Syria.

Syria said it contained the Israeli advance from the Golan region.

Israel reported that its artillery shelled targets on the outskirts of Damascus.

U.S. military sources said that the Soviet airlift to Egypt and Syria amounted to more than one hundred flights since October 9. A White House spokesman said it would create "serious difficulties" between the U.S. and U.S.S.R. if it continued.

October 14   Egypt launched a major offensive in the Sinai and claimed to have reached new objectives and forced Israeli forces to retreat.

Kuwait announced that OAPEC (Organization of Arab Petroleum Exporting Countries) would meet in Kuwait on October 16 to discuss using the oil weapon in the war.

The secretary general of NATO said an oil cutoff by the Arab states would "come very close to a hostile act."

Israel reported for the first time that 2 French-built Mirage jets were downed over the Sinai front.

Iraqi President Baker said Iraq had put its "entire military potential" into the battle.

Meir said Israel would respond quickly to any cease-fire proposal.

Evening: Israel said it repulsed heavy armored assults

by Egypt, destroying 220 Egyptian tanks and suffering only light casualties.

Syria said it had repulsed an Israeli attack. Moshe Dayan said the Syrian army was "badly beaten and defeated . . . and is now licking its wounds." Dayan added that he would oppose any cease-fire based on the current military positions.

October 15   Israel said it had destroyed the remnants of an Iraqi division but had not advanced towards Damascus beyond the village of Sa'sa; Syria reported fighting all along the front and said Israeli troops were as close as twenty miles from Damascus.

Egypt said it repulsed Israeli counterattacks and was consolidating its position on the east bank of the Canal.

Syrian officials were quoted as saying that Syria would not accept a cease-fire in place, but that a cease-fire would only be reached by Israeli withdrawal from territory occupied in 1967 and recognition of the rights of the Palestinians.

Following talks between Russian leaders and Algerian President Boumedienne, a joint communiqué said that the U.S.S.R. declared "determination to assist in every way."

October 16   An Israeli spokesman said that a "fairly large" task force had crossed the Suez Canal and was attacking Egyptian artillery and missile positions. Egypt said that of the seven Israeli tanks that had crossed the Canal, three were destroyed and four were being pursued.

Syrian and Iraqi forces counterattacked Israeli forces south of Damascus.

Sadat proposed a cease-fire to be followed by Israeli withdrawal from land occupied in 1967 and a peace conference at the U.N. He said that Egypt had a missile capable of hitting any part of Israel but added that the Arabs do not call for the "annihilation" of Israel "as has been claimed."

Sadat told his National Assembly that he issued orders to begin clearing the Suez Canal as soon as the liberation of the east bank was complete.

Meir said that no cease-fire proposal had been made to Israel and that the fighting would end when the enemy had been beaten.

Kuwait decided to contribute $350 million to the Arab war effort.

U.S. officials said that twenty-five F-4 Phantoms and fifty A-Skyhawks were being rushed to Israel.

October 17   Eban characterized Sadat's peace proposal as "totally unacceptable" and said that there could be no political preconditions for a cease-fire. He added that Israel would make "substantial compromises" for a final settlement provided that basic security is not affected.

Israel reported that hundreds of tanks battled on the Suez front and that the Israeli task force on the west bank was still operating against Egyptian positions.

Headed by Saudi Foreign Minister Umar al-Saqqaf, four Arab diplomats met in Washington with Nixon to propose a peace plan and urge the U.S. to participate directly in mediating the conflict.

Artillery and tank duels continued in Syria but no advances were reported.

Eleven Arab oil-producing countries meeting in Kuwait announced that oil exports to countries "unfriendly" to the Arab cause would be reduced by 5 per cent each month until the land occupied by Israel in 1967 was evacuated and Arab rights respected.

October 18   A huge tank battle involving an estimated one thousand tanks was being waged in the central sector of the Suez front.

Evening: Israel said its task force on the west bank of the Suez had been substantially reinforced and was engaged in heavy fighting.

Abu Dhabi announced a halt to all oil exports to

the U.S. and Saudi Arabia announced a 10 percent cut in oil production and warned that all oil exports to the U.S. would be halted if the U.S. continued to aid Israel.

Egypt reported that a second Israeli force had "infiltrated" across the Canal and were under seige on the west bank.

Egypt announced that Kosygin had met three times with Sadat in Cairo, before leaving for Moscow in the evening.

Kuwait announced its $48 million annual subsidy to Jordan.

October 19   Nixon asked the U.S. Congress for $2 billion in emergency aid for Israel.

Evening: Egyptian officials said the Israel forces on the west side of the Suez were no longer a threat.

Libya ordered a cutoff of all oil exports to the U.S. and raised the price of oil from $4.90 to $8.92 per barrel.

Israeli forces estimated at 10,000 men and 200 tanks drove into Egypt fifteen miles beyond the Suez Canal.

October 20   Morning: Kissinger flew to Moscow to discuss "means to end hostilities" and met for two hours with Brezhnev.

Saudi Arabia announced a halt to all oil exports to the U.S.

Malagasy broke diplomatic relations with Israel.

October 21   Kuwait, Qatar, Bahrayn, and Dubai announced a total embargo of oil shipments to the U.S.

Israel said that Palestinian guerrillas had shelled forty-two northern settlements, injuring sixteen and killing one, since October 6.

Iraq nationalized holdings of Royal Dutch Shell in the Basrah Petroleum Co.

Egypt said that the Israelis had established two

positions on the west bank and accused the U.S. of flying supplies directly into Sinai.

Evening: Israel said that it controlled twenty-four miles of the west bank of the Suez and that the Syrian front was relatively quiet and static.

October 22   12:49 A.M. (Eastern) The U.N. Security Council passed U.S.-Soviet sponsored resolution 338 (dated October 21) calling for a cease-fire in place to begin no later than twelve hours after the adoption of the resolution. The vote was 14-0, with China abstaining.

7:00 A.M. Israel announced acceptance of the cease-fire.

Kissinger arrived in Israel from Moscow for talks with Israeli leaders.

Israeli General Shlomo Gazit said that Israel was holding an area 20 miles deep toward Cairo and 33 miles along the canal from the outskirts of Ismailia to 7 miles north of Suez.

2:30 P.M. Sadat announced that Egypt would accept the cease-fire on the condition that Israel simultaneously adhere to the resolution calling for withdrawal.

The cease-fire went into effect on the Egyptian front at 6:52 P.M., but fighting continued in Syria. Syria said that it was considering the proposal. Jordan announced acceptance in the evening, but added that its troops in Syria were under Syrian command.

The Palestinian Resistance Movement rejected U.N. resolution 338.

October 23   Morning: Heavy fighting resumed on the Egyptian front. Both sides accused the other of violating the cease-fire.

Israeli troops on the west bank of the Suez pushed south, surrounding the city of Suez and cutting off the Egyptian 3rd Army.

Syria reported Israeli attacks in the strategic Mt. Hermon region.

4:00 P.M. Dayan proposed a new cease-fire to Egypt, through U.N. observers.

Evening: The U.S.S.R. accused Israel of violating the cease-fire and warned of "gravest consequences" if fighting continued.

Syria informed the U.N. that it accepted the cease-fire conditional upon Israel's complete withdrawal from territory occupied in 1967 and recognition of the "rights of the Palestinians."

The U.N. Security Council passed resolution 339 confirming its call for a cease-fire and calling for assignment of U.N. observers to supervise the cease-fire lines.

October 24   Morning: Israel announced agreement with Egypt, arranged through the U.N., on a new cease-fire to take effect at 7:00 A.M. on the front.

Eban said the cease-fire was still in effect despite repeated violations and added that Israel would enter negotiations with the position that "everything is negotiable."

9:00 P.M. Sadat appealed to the U.S. and U.S.S.R. to send troops to police the cease-fire. The U.S. rejected the appeal and expressed "hope that other outside powers will not send troops to the Middle East."

October 25   3:00 A.M. The U.S. placed all military forces on a worldwide alert as a "precautionary" measure in reaction to an assumption that the U.S.S.R. was planning to send troops to the Middle East.

12 noon: Kissinger said that the U.S. opposed the "unilateral introduction by any great power . . . of forces into the Middle East, in whatever guise." He said that U.S. policy was to assist a U.N. observer force and to seek a political solution.

Afternoon: The Security Council voted 14 to 0 to establish an emergency peace force to insure the cease-fire.

Egypt accused Israel of continuing to violate the cease-fire and said that Israel cut the road from Cairo to Suez City during the day.

Nigeria severed diplomatic relations with Israel.

October 26   Israel said that the Egyptian 3rd Army tried unsuccessfully during the day to break out of its encirclement by Israeli troops.

October 27   Israeli sources confirmed that the straits of Bab al-Mandab were blockaded by Egyptian warships assisted by South Yemen.

Zambia broke off diplomatic relations with Israel.

The first contingent of U.N. observers reached Suez City.

Israel proposed through the U.S. that a meeting be held between Israeli and Egyptian military leaders on the Suez front to discuss the problem of Egypt's 3rd Army. The U.S. relayed the proposal to Egypt and the U.S.S.R. Egypt agreed at 12:30 A.M.

October 28   1:30 A.M. Israeli General Aharon Yariv met with an Egyptian general and arranged for a convoy of Egyptian trucks to take food and water to the trapped Egyptian 3rd Army. The Israelis said they agreed to the resupply only at American insistence.

Ghana and Senegal broke diplomatic relations with Israel.

October 29   Assad said that Syria accepted the cease-fire after the U.S.S.R. offered guarantees that Israel would withdraw from all occupied territory and recognize the rights of the Palestinians.

Iraq said it would withdraw its troops from the front.

Al-Nahar (Beirut) reported that the PLO agreed to suspend its military operations against Israel from southern Lebanon.

A U.N. officer said that the peacekeeping forces did not have the means of determining what the Egyptian-Israeli lines were on October 22 when the cease-fire was supposed to have begun.

October 30   Egypt said that it would not release Israeli prisoners until Israel returned to the lines of October 22.

October 31   Palestinian leaders in Beirut said that the Palestinians would be willing to join peace talks with the Arab states and Israel.

Egyptian Foreign Minister Fahmy met with Nixon who proposed that a corridor to the 3rd Army from Cairo be created under the control of U.N. personnel.

The U.S. ended its worldwide military alert.

November 1   Golda Meir arrived in the U.S., met with Nixon, and said later that she was "reassured" of continued U.S. support for Israel.

Sadat and Assad flew to Kuwait for "strategy talks."

November 2   Egypt reported that Sadat flew to Saudi Arabia for talks with King Faisal.

Kissinger held separate meetings in Washington with Meir and Fahmy.

November 3   Soviet Deputy Foreign Minister Vasily Kuznetsov concluded four days of talks in Cairo and flew to Syria.

November 4   OAPEC decided to raise the production curb to 25 percent and to send the oil ministers of Saudi Arabia and Algeria on a tour of Western states to explain the measures.

November 5   U.S. Deputy Secretary of State Kenneth Rush said that the Nixon Administration's request for $2.2 billion in military aid for Israel would replace military losses and make Israel stronger than before.

November 6   The EEC called on Israel and Egypt to return to the cease-fire lines of October 22.

Israel said that 1,854 Israelis were killed in the October fighting and about 1,800 wounded.

November 7   Kissinger met with Sadat in Cairo for three hours and it was announced that the U.S. and Egypt would resume diplomatic relations.

The U.S. Department of Defense said that the Soviet airlift of supplies to Egypt and Syria had halted for two days and then resumed.

November 8   The Ivory Coast broke diplomatic relations with Israel.

Kissinger flew to Jordan where he met with King Husayn and then flew on to Saudi Arabia where he was joined by Sisco.

A Japanese foreign ministry spokesman said that the Arab states tried to persuade Japan to break diplomatic relations with Israel and impose a trade embargo.

November 9   The U.S. delivered the text of an agreement to Waldheim which both Israel and Egypt told Kissinger they were prepared to sign. It included six points: (1) both sides would observe a cease-fire; (2) both sides would agree to hold immediate discussions to settle the question of return to the October 22 lines; (3) Suez City would receive food, water, and medicine and wounded civilians would be evacuated; (4) nonmilitary supplies would not be impeded from crossing to the east bank of the Canal; (5) Israeli checkpoints on the Cairo-Suez road would be replaced by U.N. checkpoints, but Israeli officers could join the U.N. officers at Suez in inspection of supplies; and (6) after the U.N. checkpoints had been established, all prisoners of war would be exchanged.

American and Saudi sources said that Kissinger was told by King Faisal that Saudi oil production limits would not be lifted until Israel withdrew from territory occupied in 1967.

November 11   At 3:00 P.M. in the no-man's land of the Cairo-Suez road, Israeli General Aharon Yariv and Egyptian General Muhammed Abd al-Ghani Gamasi signed the cease-fire accord.

November 12   Kissinger said that the U.S. was considering a mutual security treaty with Israel as a means of guaranteeing its borders and that the Arab oil embargo would not force the U.S. to drop its support of Israel.

November 14   The U.S. Pentagon said that it had ended its airlift to Israel, but that supplies would continue by sea.

November 28   The Algiers summit conference of heads of Arab states adjourned with a recognition of the PLO as the sole legitimate representative of the Palestinian people.

November 29   The U.S. and U.S.S.R. delivered an invitation to Egypt, Syria, Jordan, Israel, and the U.N. secretary-general to attend a conference in Geneva.

December 6   Kissinger told intellectual leaders in the American Jewish community that he had "deliberately stalled" on getting a cease-fire during the October war to "gain time" for Israel.

               The U.S. Congress voted $2.2 billion in military and economic aid to Israel.

December 31   General elections were held in Israel.

1974

February   Jordanian troops who had fought in Syria during the October war mutinied taking over barracks at Zarqa.

March   The Lahore Islamic conference recognized the PLO as sole representative of the Palestinian people.

May 15   Guerilla units from the Democratic Popular Front for the Liberation of Palestine attacked an Israeli school in Maalot, killing twenty-four Israelis.

May 16   Thirty-six Israeli aircraft attacked Nabatiyeh and several other Palestinian refugee camps in Lebanon, killing 25 Arabs and wounding 134.

June   Nixon visited Egypt, Syria, Saudi Arabia, Jordan, and Israel.

June 8   The Palestinian National Council endorsed the concept of a Palestine National Authority to be established in liberated Palestinian territories in the West Bank and Gaza.

June 17–20   Israeli planes attacked Palestinian refugee camps at

Ein Al Hilwah, Mieh Mieh, Al-Rashidya, Burj Al-Shemali, and Ras Al-Ein in southern Lebanon, killing scores of civilians.

July   Sadat and Husayn issued the "Alexandria Communiqué" which stated that the PLO was the representative of the Palestinians "outside" Jordan. The PLO was recognized as "legal but not sole" representative of the Palestinian people.

July 8   Israeli naval boats raided three Lebanese ports sinking about thirty-nine vessels.

August 15   The Israeli Parliament rejected a call for a national referendum on the future of the West Bank.

September 17 Belgium closed the last commonly used route for former Soviet Jews who, after emigrating to Israel, chose to move to North America.

September 21 Egypt, Syria, and the PLO reaffirmed the Algiers summit position on the PLO.

September 23 The Popular Front for the Liberation of Palestine withdrew from the PLO Executive Committee and Central Committee.

December 3   Israel's scientist President Ephraim Katzir declared that, if Israel needs atomic weapons, "it will have them."

1975

January 2   Kissinger said in an interview that the U.S. would not rule out the use of force to secure Middle East oil resources in a situation of "gravest emergency."

January 12   A joint French-Soviet communiqué called for the implementation of U.N. resolutions on the Middle East and pressed for the continuation of the Jarring mission, for complete Israeli withdrawal, and the respect of the rights of the Palestinian people.

January 23   The U.S. administration informed Congress that it would sell Israel about two hundred of the advanced Lance ballistic missiles.

January 29   U.S. Senator Charles Percy said that Israel would have to become more flexible and realistic in its negotiating position if it hoped to retain its traditional congressional backing.

February 10   Kissinger embarked on a Middle East trip hoping to achieve a second Egyptian–Israeli disengagement accord.

March 22   Kissinger suspended his mission declaring that a "reassessment" was needed due to "irreconcilable" differences between the protagonists.

March 25   King Faisal was assassinated.

May 23   The *New York Times* reported that the Soviet Union agreed to sell Libya $800 million worth of military equipment.

June 1   Presidents Ford and Sadat met in Salzburg.

June 5   Egypt opened the Suez Canal.

September 1   An interim Sinai accord was reached by Egypt and Israel under Kissinger's auspices.

BIBLIOGRAPHY

Abboushi, W. F. *The Angry Arabs.* Westminster, 1974.

Abu-Lughod, Ibrahim, ed. *The Arab-Israeli Confrontation of June 1967: An Arab Perspective.* Evanston, Ill: Northwestern University Press, 1970.

Allen, Richard. *Imperialism and Nationalism in the Fertile Crescent: Sources and Prospects of the Arab-Israeli Conflict.* Fair Lawn, N.J., 1974.

American Friends Service Committee. *Search for Peace in the Middle East.* Philadelphia: AFSC, 1970.

Arab-Israeli Research and Relations Project. *Controversy in the Middle East: The October War.* N.Y.: International Publishers Service, 1974.

Arora, J. S. *West Asia War 1973: The October Arab-Israeli War* (Illus.). N.Y.: International Publishers Service, 1974.

Aruri, Naseer, ed. *The Palestinian Resistance to Israeli Occupation.* Wilmette, Ill: Medina University Press, 1970.

Askkar, Riad and Khalidi, Ahmed. *Weapons and Equipment of the Israeli Armed Forces.* Beirut: Institute for Palestine Studies, 1973.

Associated Press. *Lightning out of Israel: The Six Day War in the Middle East.* Englewood Cliffs, N.J.: Prentice-Hall, 1967.

Avineri, S., ed. *Israel and the Palestinians.* N.Y.: St. Martin, 1971.

Avnery, Uri. *Israel Without Zionism: A Plan for Peace in the Middle East.* Riverside, N.J.: MacMillan, 1971.

Barker, A. G. *The Six-Day War.* New York: Ballantine, 1974.

Beling, W. A., ed. *The Middle East: Quest for an American Foreign Policy.* Albany, N.Y.: Suny Press, 1973.

Ben-Gurion, David. *My Talks with Arab Leaders.* New York: Third Press, 1973.

Bentwich, Norman. *Israel: Two Fateful Years, 1967–1969.* New York: Drake Publications, 1972.

Bober, Arie. *The Other Israel: The Radical Case against Zionism.* Garden City, N.Y.: Doubleday, 1972.

Brown, George. *In My Way.* London: Gallancy, 1971.

Burdett, Winston. *Encounter with the Middle East: An Intimate Report on What Lies Behind the Arab-Israeli Conflict.* New York: Atheneum, 1969.

Carmichael, Joel. *Open Letter to Moses and Muhammad.* (Open Letter Series) New York: Heineman, 1968.

Cattan, Henry. *Palestine: The Arabs and Israel: The Search for Justice.* London: Longmans, 1969.

Chaliand, Gerard. *The Palestinian Resistance.* Middlesex, England: Penguin Books, 1972.

Chomsky, Noam. *Peace in the Middle East? Reflections on Justice and Nationhood.* Westminster, Maryland: Random, 1974.

Christman, Henry M. *The State Papers of Levi Eshkol.* New York: Funk and Wagnalls, 1969.

Cooley, John K. *Green March, Black September: The Story of the Palestinian Arabs.*

Portland, Oregon: International Scholars Book Service, 1974.

Davis, Moshe, ed. *The Yom Kippur War: Israel and the Jewish People.* New York: Arno Press, 1974.

Draper, Theodore. *Israel and World Politics: Roots of the Third Arab-Israeli War.* New York: Viking, 1968.

Elkordy, Abdul Hafez M. *Crisis of Diplomacy: The Three Wars and After.* San Antonio, Texas: Naylor, 1971.

Ellis, Harry B. *Israel: One Land, Two Peoples.* New York: T. Y. Crowell, 1972.

Elon, Amos and Hassan, Sana. *Between Enemies: A Compassionate Dialogue Between an Israeli and an Arab.* Westminster, Maryland: Random, 1974.

Evron, Yair. *The Middle East: Nations, Superpowers, and Wars.* New York: Praeger, 1973.

Ferguson, Pamela. *The Palestine Problem.* London: Martin, Brian, and O'Keefe, 1974.

Fisher, Roger. *Dear Israelis, Dear Arabs: A Working Approach to Peace.* New York: Harper and Row, 1972.

Freedman, Robert O. *Soviet Policy Toward the Middle East Since 1970.* New York: Praeger, 1975.

Gendzier, Irene L., ed. *Middle East Reader.* Indianapolis, Indiana: Pegasus, 1970.

Geyer, Georgie Anne. *The New 100 Years War.* New York: Doubleday, 1972.

Gilbert, Martin. *Atlas of the Arab-Israeli Conflict.* Riverside, N.J.: Macmillan, 1975.

Habeychi, Gen. Abdallah. *The Palestine Problem.* Damascus: Al-Tawjih Press, 1971.

Handel, Michael I. *Israel's Political-Military Doctrine.* Cambridge, Mass.: Center for International Affairs, Harvard University, 1973.

Harkabi, Y. *Arab Attitudes Towards Israel.* New York: Halstead Press, 1974.

Hart, Harold H. *Yom Kippur plus 100 Days: The Human Side and its Aftermath as Shown in Columns of the Jerusalem Post.* New York: Hart, 1974.

Hatem, M. Abdel Kader. *Information and the Arab Cause.* London: Longman, 1974.

Hauer, Christine E. *Crisis and Confidence in the Middle East.* New York: Quadrangle, 1970.

Heikal, M. H. *The Cairo Documents.* New York: Doubleday, 1973.

――――. *The Road to Ramadan.* London: Collins, 1975.

Heradsveit, Daniel. *Arab and Israeli Elite Perceptions.* New York: Humanities Press, 1974.

――――. *Jews and Arabs: Conflict Perceptions and Conflict Strategies.* Oslo: Norsk Utenrikspolitik Institutt, 1972.

Husayn, H. M. King. *My War with Israel.* Translated by June P. Wilson and Walter B. Michaels. New York: William Morrow, 1969.

International Institute for Strategic Studies. *The Military Balance 1973/1974.* London, 1973.

Jabber, Fuad. *Israel and Nuclear Weapons: Present Options and Future Strategies.* London: Chatto and Windus, 1971.

Jansen, G. H. *Whose Suez? Aspects of Collusion, 1967.* Beirut: Institute for Palestine Studies, 1968.

Jansen, Michael E. *The U.S. and the Palestinian People.* Beirut: Institute for Palestine Studies.

Jewish Liberation Project and Committee to Support Middle East Liberation. *Arab-Israeli Debate: Toward a Socialist Solution.* New York: Times Change, 1971.

Kalb, Marvin and Bernard. *Kissinger.* Boston, Mass.: Little, Brown, 1974.

Kenan, Amos. *Israel: A Wasted Victory.* Tel Aviv: Amikan Publishers, 1970.

Kerr, Malcolm H. *The Arab Cold War, 1958-1970: A Study of Ideology in Politics.* Fair Lawn, N.J.: Oxford University Press, 1971.

———. *The Middle East Conflict.* New York: Foreign Policy Association, 1968.

———. *Regional Arab Politics and the Conflict with Israel.* Santa Monica, Calif.: Rand Corporation, 1969.

Khalid, Leila. *My People Shall Live.* London: Hodder and Stoughton, 1973.

Khouri, Fred J. *Arab-Israeli Dilemma.* Syracuse, New York: Syracuse University Press, 1969.

Kimche, David, and Bowly, Don. *The Six-Day War: Prologue and Aftermath.* New York: Stein and Day, 1971.

Koch, Jr., Howard. *Six Hundred Days.* New York: Arab Information Center, 1969.

Kodsy, Ahmad E. and Lobel, Eli. *The Arab World and Israel.* New York: Monthly Review Press, 1970.

Kohler, F. D., Goure, L., and Harvey, M. L. *The Soviet Union and the October, 1973 Middle East War: The Implications for Detente.* Miami, Florida: Center for Advanced International Studies, University of Miami, 1974.

Kosut, Hal. *Israel and The Arabs: The Six-Day War.* New York: Facts on File, 1974.

Laffin, John. *Fedayeen: The Arab-Israeli Dilemma.* London: Cassell, 1973.

Lacquer, Walter Z. *Israel-Arab Reader.* New York: Bantam Books, 1970.

———. *Road to Jerusalem.* Riverside, N.J.: Macmillan, 1968.

———. *Operation Spark: The Yom Kippur War.* New York: Quadrangle, 1974.

Mason, Herbert, ed. *Reflections on the Middle East Crisis.* Atlantic Highlands, N.J.: Humanities Press, 1970.

McLane, Charles B. *Soviet-Middle East Relations.* London: Central Asian Research Centre, 1973.

McLeigh, Roderick. *The Sun Stood Still: Perspectives on the Arab-Israeli Conflict.* London: MacDonald, 1968.

Monroe, Elizabeth. *The Arab-Israeli War, October 1973: Background and Events.* London: Farrar-Huckley, 1975.

Moore, John N. *The Arab-Israeli Conflict.* Princeton, N.J.: Princeton University Press, 1974.

O'Ballance, Edgar. *The Third Arab-Israeli War.* Hampden, Conn.: Shoe String, 1972.

———. *Arab Guerrila Power.* Hampden, Conn.: Shoe String, 1974.

O'Neill, Bard E. *Revolutionary Warfare in the Middle East: The Israelis vs. The Fedayeen.* Boulder, Colo.: Paladin Press, 1974.

Pennar, Jan. *The USSR and the Arabs: The Ideological Dimension.* New York: Crane-Russak, 1973.

Peretz, Don. *The Palestinian Arab Refugee Problem.* Santa Monica, Calif.: The Rand Corporation, 1969.

Pfaff, Richard H. *Jerusalem: Keystone to an Arab-Israeli Settlement.* Washington: American Enterprise, 1969.

Polit, D. K. *Return to Sinai: The Arab Offensive, 1973.* Columbia, Mo.: South Asia Books, 1974.

Pryce-Jones, David. *The Face of Defeat: Palestinian Refugees and Guerrillas.* New York: HR & W, 1973.

Quandt, William. *Palestinian Nationalism: Its Political and Military Dimension.* Santa Monica, Cal.: The Rand Corporation, 1971.

Rodinson, Maxime. *Israel: A Colonial Settler State?* New York: Monad Press, 1973.

———. *Israel and the Arabs.* Translated by Michael Pere. Westminster, Maryland: Pantheon, 1969.

Rostov, R. *The US and its Role in the Middle East Conflict.* Moscow: Novosti Press, 1973.

Shiff, Zeev, and Rathstein, Raphael. *Fedayeen.* New York: McKay, 1972.

Schliefer, Abdullah. *The Fall of Jerusalem.* New York: Monthly Review Press, 1972.

Schmidt, Dana A. *Armageddon in the Middle East.* (NYT Survey Series) New York: John Day, 1974.

Segal, Ronald. *Whose Jerusalem? The Conflicts of Israel.* New York: Bantam Books, 1974.

Shahak, Israel. *Civil Rights in Israel Today.* London: Committee for Justice in the Middle East, 1972.

Sharabi, Hisham. *Palestine and Israel: The Lethal Dilemma.* Indianapolis, Indiana: Pegasus, 1969.

Sobel, Lester A., ed. *Israel and the Arabs: The October, 1973 War.* New York: Facts on File, 1974.

A Special Kind of State: Israel and the London Times. Beirut: Hermon Books, 1970.

Stetler, Russell, ed. *The Arab-Israeli Conflict.* Palo Alto, Calif.: Ramparts Press, 1972.

Sunday Times. *Insight on the Middle East War.* London, 1974.

Tahtinen, Dale R. *The Arab-Israeli Military Balance Today.* Washington: American Enterprise, 1973.

————. *The Arab-Israeli Military Balance since 1973.* Washington: American Enterprise, 1974.

Talmon, J. L. *Israel Among the Nations.* (Mandel, To, eds.) Riverside, N.J.: Macmillan, 1971.

Taylor, Alan R. and Tetlie, Richard N. *Palestine: A Search For Truth.* Washington: Public Affairs Press, 1970.

Tuma, Elias H. *Peacemaking and the Immoral War: Arabs and Jews in the Middle East.* New York: Harper-Row, 1972.

Tuma, Emil. *American Policy in the Middle East.* (Arabic) Haifa, 1973.

U.S. Congress. House of Representatives. *The Impact of the October Middle East War.* Hearings before the Subcommittee on the Near East and South Asia of the Committee on Foreign Affairs, 93rd Congress, Washington, 1973.

————. Committee on Foreign Affairs. *Jerusalem: The Future of the Holy City for Three Monotheisms.* 92nd Congress, Washington, 1971.

————. Committee on Foreign Affairs. *The Near East Conflict.* 91st Congress, Washington, 1971.

————. Committee on Foreign Affairs. *Problems of Protecting Civilians Under International Law in the Middle East Conflict.* 93rd Congress, Washington, 1974.

U.S. Congressional Quarterly. *The Middle East: US Policy, Israel and the Arabs.* Washington, 1974.

Vatikiotis, P. J. *Conflict in the Middle East.* Totowa, N.J.: Rowman, 1971.

Vicker, Ray. *The Kingdom of Oil: The Middle East; its People and its Power.* New York: Scribners, 1974.

Waines, David. *The Unholy War: Struggle for Palestine.* Wilmette, Illinois: Medina University Press, 1970.

Waskow, Arthur. *Bush is Burning.* Riverside, N.J.: Macmillan, 1971.

Yodfat, A. *Arab Politics in the Soviet Mirror.* New York: Halstead Press, 1973.

Young, Peter. *The Israeli Campaign 1967.* London: Kimber, 1969.

The Contributors

ANOUAR ABDEL-MALEK is Maître de Recherche, Centre National de la Rechérche Scientifique and Chargé de Conferences à l'Ecole des Hautes Etudes en Sciences Sociales, Paris. He is Vice-President of the International Sociological Association and a member of the Editorial Board of *Qadâriyâ 'Arabiyyah* (Beirut) and the *International Journal of Critical Sociology* (Jaipur). His published works include: *Egypte Société Militaire* (1962), *Dirassat Fi'l Thaqâfah Al-Watan-iyyah* (Studies on National Culture, 1967), *Idéologie et Renaissance Nationale: l'Egypte Moderne* (1969), *La Dialectique Sociale* (1972), and *Al-Fikr Al-'Arabi Fi Ma'rakat Al-Nahdah* (Arabic Thought in the Struggle of Renaissance, 1974).

AS'AD ABDUL RAHMAN is Assistant Professor of Political Science at Kuwait University. He is the author of *Al-Tasalul Al-Israeli Fi Asia* [Israeli Penetration of Asia], (1967); *Al-Munathama Al-Sahiouniya Al-Alamiya* [The World Zionist Organization], (1968); and editor of *Al-Harb Al-Arabiya Al-Israeliya Al-Rabi'a* [The Fourth Arab-Israeli War], (1975).

IBRAHIM ABU-LUGHOD is Professor of Political Science at Northwestern University. He is the author/editor of numerous studies on the Middle East including *Arab Rediscovery of Europe* (1963), *The Arab-Israeli Confrontation of June 1967* (1969), and *The Transformation of Palestine* (1972).

M. S. AGWANI is Professor of West Asian Studies and Dean, School of International Studies, Jawaharlal Nehru University, New Delhi. He is editor of the quarterly journal *International Studies* (New Delhi) and author of *Communism in the Arab East* (1969) and *The Lebanese Crisis: 1958* (1965).

EQBAL AHMAD is Director of the Transnational Institute at the Hague and fellow of the Institute of Policy Studies in Washington, D.C. He is the author of several studies on national liberation movements and the forthcoming *Time Bomb: Citizen's Guide to U.S. Foreign Policy in the 1970's*.

LT. COLONEL AL-HAYTHAM AL-AYOUBI is a former officer in the Syrian army and is currently Director of the Arab Center for Strategic Studies in Beirut and the military correspondent of the Beirut weekly *Al-Usbu Al-Arabi*. He is the author of *Korean National Liberation War* (1973), *Lessons of the Fourth War* (1974), *Studies on the October War* (1975), and *The Strategic Balance in the Middle East, 1974* (1974).

HALIM BARAKAT is affiliated with the Center for Education Research and Development in Beirut and the Department of Sociology at Lebanese University. He is the author of *Days of Dust* (1974) and the forthcoming *Commitment to Change: A Sociological Study of the Student Movement in Lebanon* as well as numerous articles on refugees, alienation, and education.

HANI A. FARIS is Assistant Professor of Political Science at Kuwait University. He is the author of *Al-Tamtheel Al-Arabi Al-Diplomacy* [Arab Diplomatic Representation], (1969); *One In Three Millions: The Life of a Palestinian* (1971); and the forthcoming *Conflict Resolution In A Multi-religious Society: Lebanon.*

ELAINE HAGOPIAN is Professor of Sociology, Simmons College, Boston. She was Visiting Professor of Sociology at the American University of Beirut during the 1973–74 academic year. The author of numerous articles on politics and development in the Middle East, she is also co-editor of *The Arab-Americans: Studies in Assimilation* (1969).

AHMED S. KHALIDI is affiliated with the Department of War Studies at Kings College, Oxford. He has contributed to the *United Services Institute* Journal (India), the *Journal of Palestine Studies,* and other publications. He also served as correspondent for the Beirut daily *Al-Nahar* on the Syrian front during the October war.

RAGAEI EL MALLAKH is Professor of Economics at the University of Colorado in Boulder. He is the author of *Kuwait: Economic Development and Regional Cooperation* (1968) and the co-editor of *Energy and Development* (1974).

KHALIL NAKHLEH is Assistant Professor of Anthropology, St. John's University, Collegeville, Minnesota. He has conducted extensive field research in Israel, the results of which have been reported in various scholarly journals and in a forthcoming book.

BARRY RUBIN is a free-lance journalist specializing in the Middle East. He has written for the *Progressive, The Nation, Journal of Palestine Studies, New Times,* and other publications.

EDWARD W. SAID is Professor of English and Comparative Literature at Columbia University and a Fellow of the Center for Advanced Study in the Behavioral Sciences (1975–76). He is the author of numerous literary and political studies including *Beginnings: Intention and Method* (1975).

FAROUK A. SANKARI is Associate Professor of International Politics and Middle Eastern Studies, University of Wisconsin-Oshkosh. He has published "The Middle East in International Perspective," in Al-Marayati, *The Middle East: Its Government and Politics* (1972); "Plato and Al-Farabi: A Comparison of Some Aspects of their

Political Philosophies," *The Muslim World,* July, 1970; and "The Cost and Gains of Israel: Pursuit of Influence in Africa," *Africa Quarterly,* 1975.

ELIAS SHOUFANI is associated with the Institute for Palestine Studies in Beirut and was formerly a Professor of History at the University of Maryland. He is a specialist in Palestinian-Israeli affairs and has published numerous studies in English, Arabic, and Hebrew.

JOE STORK is a founder and staff member of the Middle East Research and Information Project and an editor of its monthly journal, *MERIP Reports.* He is the author of *Middle East Oil and the Energy Crisis* (1975). His articles and reviews have also appeared in *The Journal of Palestine Studies, Middle East Journal,* and *Ramparts.* He writes a regular column for *Elements,* a resource economics journal published in Washington, D.C.

JANICE J. TERRY is Associate Professor of Middle East History at Eastern Michigan University. She is co-editor of *The Arab World From Nationalism to Revolution* and has published articles on U.S. press coverage of the Arab-Israeli conflict, U.S. Congressional attitudes, and Egyptian political history.